INSIDE NEW YORK
2009

AN
Inside New York
GUIDEBOOK

Inside New York

PUBLISHER	Jared Hecht
EDITOR-IN-CHIEF	Joseph Meyers
DINING EDITOR	Katie Han
NIGHTLIFE EDITOR	Allison Davis
NEIGHBORHOODS EDITOR	John Klopfer
FEATURES EDITOR	Jordan Fraade
ASSOCIATE EDITORS	Grace Chan
	Sam Reisman
LAYOUT EDITORS	Grace Chan
	Yipeng Huang
GRAPHIC DESIGNER	Madeleine Lopeman
MAP DESIGNER	Jed Dore
SENIOR STAFF EDITOR	Billy Goldstein
STAFF EDITORS	Cedric Cheung-Lau
	Miranda Elliot
	Joy Guo
	Ariel Hudes
PHOTO EDITOR	Hazel Balaban

STAFF WRITERS
W.M. Akers, Chris Allison, Sarah Case, Winston Christie-Blick, Lindsey Cornum, Lisa Dorfman, Alessandra Gotbaum, Sophia Guy-White, Jennie Halperin, Sarah Hsu, Aarti Iyer, Kathleen Kan, Chris Kelly, Tim Lam, Chris Leyton, JD Stettin, John Vullo, Meredith Wing

CONTRIBUTORS
Elizabeth Burke, Samantha Carlin, Rachel Cox, Jessie De Luca, David Fishman, Matt Herzfield, Adrian Haimovich, Hillary Juster, Dustin Newman, Carly Pifer, Laura Reposo, Sahasra Sambamoorthi, Sarah Shore, Alana Sivin, David Zhu

CONTRIBUTING PHOTOGRAPHERS
Helena Anrather, Lindsey Cornum, Sophie Finkelstein, Meena Hasan, Lily McKeage, Mbali Ndlovu, Emily Schenkein, Jane Waterfall, Daniel Yeow, Daniella Zalcman

ASSOCIATE DIRECTORS OF ADVERTISING SALES
Dustin Newman, Alana Sivin

www.insidenewyork.com
2960 Broadway MC 5727 • New York, NY • 10027
Phone: 212-854-2804 • Fax: 212-663-9398

Printed by: Ripon Printers
656 S. Douglas St.
Ripon, WI 54971-0006

Inside New York copyright © 2008. All rights reserved. No part of this book may be used or reproduced in any manner without the written permission of the publisher, except in short quotations embodied in critical articles or reviews, provided that sources are accurately cited. The opinions expressed herein are those of the authors exclusively, and are not necessarily endorsed by the publication staff, its advertisers, or any university. Information in this book is, to the best of our knowledge, factually correct as of August 1, 2008.

Inside New York® and the Inside New York logo are trademarks of Inside New York, Inc. and Columbia University.

Advertising Disclaimer: Advertisements do not imply endorsements of products or services by Inside New York and Inside New York does not vouch for the accuracy of information provided in advertisements.

If you are interested in purchasing advertising space in Inside New York, contact Inside New York • 2960 Broadway MC 5727 • New York, NY 10027 • 212-854-2804 • adsales@insidenewyork.com.

For bulk sales, university sales, corporate sales, or customized editions, please call 212-854-2804 or email info@insidenewyork.com.

If your bookstore would like to carry Inside New York, please contact CU Press at 1-800-944-8648.

This is a publication of the Student Enterprises Division of Columbia University.

WELCOME TO NEW YORK

Long before they step onto the JFK tarmac for the first time, most people have already fallen in love with their own New York. These visions of the city are culled from images both cinematic and literary: sweeping panoramas of a sparkling skyline, grim portraits of crime and urban decay, and epic sagas of dissipation and redemption. All of these swirl about in a whirlwind of trope from which we craft the New York that most appeals to us.

A city of immigrants both foreign and domestic, New York has long been whatever its newcomers have needed it to be. For centuries a symbol of liberty to millions, today it is usually something decidedly more than that.

Now that you are here, you will need something more specific than vague impressions and tall tales to help you make New York your own. Whether you are visiting for a week, studying for a degree, or moving in and laying down roots, our goal is to give you a true map to the city. Not a wide-angle aerial shot, but a block by block guide to the best, cheapest, and most memorable spots in this jam packed metropolis, where more restaurants and bars close in a week than you could visit in a year.

New York is not a collection of destinations, but of neighborhoods, each a world unto itself with its own cultural climate. We've organized our guide so that you can get a feel for each of these different worlds, rather than a shotgun blast of stereotype.

Go ahead, dive in. We can't make you a New Yorker, but we can damn well show you how to act like one.

Jared Hecht, Publisher
Joseph Meyers, Editor-in-Chief

TABLE OF CONTENTS

CITY LIFE
Transportation	10
Settling In	14
Money Matters	18
Government & Safety	20
Dining & Food	26
Nightlife	30
Museums	34
Arts	38
Shopping	42
Outdoor NY	44
Central Park	48
Day Trips	50
LGBT	52
Media	54
Hostels	56
Classes	58
Religion	60
Cheap NYC	62
Events Calendar	68

WALKING TOURS
Architecture	74
Film	76
Public Art	78
Famous Deaths	80
Music History	82
Radical History	84

MANHATTAN
Financial District	89
SoHo & Tribeca	99
Chinatown	109
Lower East Side	119
East Village	133
Greenwich Village	145
Chelsea	159
Gramercy	169
Midtown East	179
Midtown West	187
Upper East Side	205
Upper West Side	217
Morningside Heights	231
Central Harlem	261
Spanish Harlem	269
Upper Manhattan	277

BROOKLYN
Greenpoint	283
Williamsburg	291
Brooklyn Heights & Dumbo	301
Fort Greene	307
Carroll Gardens	313
Park Slope	319

QUEENS
Long Island City & Astoria	329
Flushing	339
Jackson Heights	349

South Bronx	355
Staten Island	363

Best of the Best

DINING

MOST ROMANTIC
Antica Venezia 147
Grotto 122
La Luncheonette 163

GROUP FRIENDLY
Landmarc 103
Jing Fong 113
BLT Burger 148

WEIRD BUT GOOD
Kyotofu 192
Matilda 136
Gahm mi Oak 173

BEST DESSERTS
Bar Boulud 219
Dessert Truck 150
Payard Patisserie 210

BEST BURGERS
Burger Joint 193
Lucky's Famous 194
BLT Burger 148

BEST SANDWICHES
Saigon Bahn Mi 112
Panino Sportivo 237
Peanut Butter Co. 150

SPECIAL OCCASION
Kittichai 102
Picholine 220
Tocqueville 172

ROOM WITH A VIEW
Metrazur 183
The River Room 280
Sequoia 95

DRUNK MUNCHIES
Belgian Fries 138
Momofuku Ssam Bar 137
Forte Baden Baden NY 173

SUPER CHEAP
Prosperity Dumpling 113
Taco Mix 275
Super Taste 114

AMERICAN
Good 148
Penelope 174
Bridge Café 95

BBQ
Hill Country 163
Oklahoma Smoke 264
Rack & Soul 235

CHINESE
Grand Sichuan 112
Pig Heaven 212
Nice Green Bo 111

COMFORT FOOD
Market Table 150
Little Giant 122
Max SoHa 237

FRENCH
Ouest 220
L'École 103
Sel & Poivre 212
Bar Boulud 219

INDIAN
Dèvi 172
Saravana 175
Roti Roll 237

ITALIAN
Pisticci 235
Giorgione 307
Gusto 149

JAPANESE
15 East 171
Tea Box Café 184
Izayaka Ten 163

KOREAN
Unidentified Flying Chicken 353
Gahm Mi Oak 173
Hyo Dong Gak 173

LATIN
Empanada Mama 192
La Fonda Boricua 274
El Cocotero 163

MEDITERRANEAN
Fig & Olive 211
Knife & Fork 136
Nanoosh 223

MEXICAN
Rosa Mexicano 174
Mercadito 136
Super Tacos 223

MIDDLE EASTERN
Bread & Olive 193
Alfanoose 96
Halal Chicken & Gyro 194

NEW AMERICAN
The Little Owl 149
Casellula Cheese & Wine Café 192
Dressler 293

PIZZA
Artichoke 138
Fascati 303
Adrienne's Pizza Bar 96

SOUTHERN
Madaleine Mae 222
Amy Ruth's 264
Miss Mamie's Spoonbread Too 234

SPANISH
Mercat 122
Islero 183
809 Sangria Bar & Grill 280

THAI
Kittichai 102
Eat-pisode 121
Rice Avenue 352

VEGAN
Jill's 315
Wild Ginger 111
Urban Spring 310

VIETNAMESE
Saigon Banh Mi 112
Bao Noodles 173
Doyer's Vietnamese 112

NIGHTLIFE

BEST BEERS
Beer Table *325*
Blind Tiger Ale House *151*
Burp Castle *140*
Cafe Katja *114*

BEST LGBT
Bar 13-Snapshot *142*
Duplex *152*
Cattyshack *325*

BEST LADIES NIGHT
Dove Parlour *152*
The Box *124*
Planet Rose *142*
Socialista *154*

BEST SINGLES SCENE
Moe's *310*
The Dark Room *124*
Marquee *166*

BEST DATE BARS
Auction House *213*
Barcibo *224*
Vol de Nuit *154*

BEST MUSIC
St. Nicks *281*
Joe's Pub *140*
Studio B *287*
Le Royale *153*

CHUG LIKE A FRAT BOY
Turtle Bay *185*
Dorrians *214*
Bourbon Street *224*

BEST DATE BARS
Auction House *213*
Barcibo *224*
Vol de Nuit *154*

DRINK AWAY YOUR WOES
Biddy's *213*
Death and Co. *140*
Holland Bar *195*

BEST DIVES
Jeremey's Ale House *97*
Welcome to the Johnson's *126*
Rudy's Bar and Grill *195*

BEST AFTER WORK SCENE
Rink Bar *184*
Mé Bar *195*
Mason Dixon *124*

BEST COCKTAIL
Sweet Ups *297*
Milk and Honey *124*
En Shochu *152*

DRINKS WITH A VIEW
Rare View *176*
Martini Bar at the Met *214*
The Stanton Public *126*

DRINK AND EAT
Pop Burger *153*
The Den *266*
Jake Walk *316*

BEST DANCE FLOORS
Lit Lounge *141*
Mansion *165*
Santos' Party House *105*

ATTRACTIONS

SHOPPING
Maxilla and Mandible *225*
Toy Qube *347*
Enchantments Inc. *143*
Brooklyn Superhero Supply *327*

BEST BOOK STORES
The Strand *155*
Book Culture *239*
Partners & Crime *154*

FILM
Angelika *146*
Eagle Theatre *351*
Film Forum *146*

GALLERIES
Wooster Project *101*
Graffiti Hall of Fame *271*
Pierogi Gallery *293*
5Pointz *330*

FOOD SHOPS
New Beef King *116*
Pickle Guys *127*
Moscow on the Hudson *281*
Zabar's *225*

CLOTHES
Exquisite Costume *116*
French Sole *215*
Harlem's Heaven Hat Boutique *267*
Armacord Fashion *298*

OFF THE MILE
PS1 *331*
Rubin Museum of Art *161*
Bronx Museum *358*

MINOR MILE
The Frick *208*
The Whitney *209*
Neue Gallerie *209*

INSIDE NEW YORK 9

TRANSPORTATION

Thanks to the pedestrian-friendly street grid, one of the largest subway systems in the world, ubiquitous yellow taxicabs, and an interconnected network of buses and trains, you don't need a car to get around in New York City—many natives don't even have a driver's license.

WALKING

Weather and distance permitting, the best way to get from Point A to Point B is on foot, which is made easier by New York's straightforward **grid system**. North of Houston Street, most of Manhattan is divided into sequentially numbered and lettered north-south **avenues** that run the length of the island, and numbered **streets** that run east-west across the island. Streets begin north of Houston with 1st Street, and count up. Avenues count down as you move east from 11th Ave on the West Side, but after Bowery move up alphabetically from Avenue A. Madison Ave, Park Ave, and Lexington Ave are squeezed between 5th Ave and 3rd Ave. North of 59th Street, 8th Ave through 11th Ave change their names to Central Park West, Columbus, Amsterdam, and West End, respectively. **Broadway**, once a Native American foot path, cuts across Manhattan at an angle from northwest to southeast. Navigating the streets of New York can get tougher south of Houston Street, where the city is no longer on the grid system (the West Village, between 14th St and Houston and west of 6th Avenue, is also famously labyrinthine). In general, 20 north-south blocks or seven crosstown blocks are a mile.

SUBWAYS AND BUSES

The **New York City subway system** provides the quickest and most efficient way to get around; in the eyes of many New Yorkers it is the city's great equalizer— *4.5 million* people ride it every day, including everyone from hourly workers to Mayor Bloomberg. The system serves Manhattan, Queens, Brooklyn, the Bronx, and Staten Island via the Staten Island Railway. There are 26 interconnected subway routes, grouped by color and then divided into letters (**A**-**Z**) or numbers (**1**-**7**), and 468 subway stations—just 35 fewer subway stations than exist in the rest of the nation combined. Subway fare cards, called MetroCards, are $2 one-way, and can be bought at vending machines in the stations. You can also purchase 11 rides for the price of 10 or unlimited-ride passes for one day, one week, or one month. **Local trains** generally stop at every station along a route, while **express trains** stop only at select stops. Check the name before you get on the train: local and express lines often run along the same track and are marked with the same color, making them easy to confuse. The subway runs 24-hours a day throughout the year, though after midnight and on weekends service slows down. Since the subway never sleeps, construction and repairs can alter your route—trains will often skip certain stations on the weekend or late at night to free up track space, and express trains often run on the local track by night. Signs detailing these changes can usually be found posted near the subway platform.

Renovations over the past 20 years have made the subway relatively safe. The color of the lighted lampposts outside subway stations indicate whether that particular entrance is open at night or has a token booth. Green means the token booth is open 24 hours, while red means the station is closed at night. The initiative was introduced in the 1990s to prevent riders from wandering into empty stations and falling victim to muggers.

MetroCards can also be used to ride buses, though you can also pay with exact change (no bills). The $2 fare allows you to make one free transfer between buses or subways within two hours of fare payment. Buses stop at street corners designated by a tall blue sign with its route number. There are approximately 200 local and 40 express routes, covering all five boroughs. Like the subway, the bus is generally a safe way to travel. As a part of the Request-a-Stop bus service, when riding a bus between 10pm and 5am, you have the option of getting off at a safe location that is not a normal bus stop. Learn to love crosstown buses above 59th St, where subway lines don't go from the West to East Side. A series of crosstown buses go through Central Park, and are generally safe and efficient. Keep in mind, though, that the bus system is not 24/7. After midnight, service tapers off noticeably, save for late-night buses that come once an hour on certain routes.

TAXIS

There are over 10,000 taxis in New York City. Though costlier than subways, they are often faster and more convenient. Available taxis have lit-up numbered signs on the roof of their car—dimmed signs mean the taxi is taken. Lights on the side of the numbered sign mean the cab is off-duty. After spotting an available taxi, hail it by sticking your arm out. Taxi fares are metered, and start out at $2.50. Some surcharges may apply, like the $1 during peak times between 4pm and 8pm Monday through Friday, and the 50-cent night surcharge from 8pm to 6am. Any tolls incurred are also added to your fare. Each one-fifth of a mile, or about every four blocks, the meter adds 40 cents. The meter also adds 40 cents for every

TRANSPORTATION 11

minute spent idle. Trips between JFK and Manhattan are a flat fare of $45 plus tolls, while rides between Newark International Airport and New York City include a $15 surcharge plus tolls (usually coming out to around $90). All other rides to and from the airport are metered.

Avoid using gypsy cabs, non-licensed cars (often black Lincoln Towncars) which will often overcharge you and can be unsafe. Licensed cabs are all yellow and have a New York Ciy Taxi and Limosine Commision medallion bolted to the hood. All cabs accept cash, though many now also accept credit cards via Taxi TV, an otherwise annoying in-cab television program consisting of news features, reviews, and advertisements. When paying, include a 10-15% tip.

From purses, strollers, and umbrellas to Yo-Yo Ma's $2.5 million cello, people leave their things in taxis all the time. If it happens to you, call the **Taxi and Limosine Commission** (*212-692-8294*). Be sure to take your receipt every time you leave your taxi: they have the taxi's number on them, which you'll need to recover your lost luggage. If you don't have the taxi number, give them a call anyway–sometimes miracles happen.

COMMUTER RAIL AND BUS

Traveling out of New York is about as easy as moving within it: no car required. Trains are a popular mode of transportation— tracks criss-cross the eastern seaboard, from Boston to Atlanta, and it's usually cheaper than catching a plane. National train service **Amtrak** (*amtrak.com*) departs from Penn Station (33rd St between 7th & 8th Aves, underneath Madison Square Garden), as do commuter services **New Jersey Transit** (*njtransit.com*) and **Long Island Rail Road** (*mta.info*). **Metro-North** trains (mta.info), which go to northern locations in upstate New York and Connecticut, leave from the stunning **Grand Central Terminal** (*42nd St at Park Ave*) and the Harlem-125th St Station (*E 125th St and Park Ave*), a continual sore point for Long Islanders and Jerseyites who are forced to put up with the busier, but hideous, Penn Station.

Luckily, Penn Station and Grand Central both serve as subway stops—just follow the signs. Penn Station is conveniently located on the 🅐🅒🅔 and 🔴①②③ lines, while Grand Central is located on the 🟢④⑤⑥ and 🟣⑦ lines. A convenient shuttle also runs one-stop service to Times Square.

NATIONAL BUS LINES

Most buses depart from **Port Authority** (42nd St at 8th Ave), the biggest bus station in the U.S., conveniently located a block away from Times Square (panynj.gov). The most popular carrier for national service is **Greyhound** (*greyhound.com*), which features a number of special prices on fares to and from New York, and local bus lines to New Jersey also leave from the terminal.

College students on a budget can check out one of the several **Chinatown Bus** companies that operate cheap service from Chinatown to Boston and Philadelphia. Fare is dirt-cheap—usually about $10-15 one-way—although safety problems on the buses are not unheard of. Sometimes overworked drivers plus underkept buses equal major accidents and passenger fatalities, so count your pennies carefully. The most popular companies are **Fung Wah Bus** (*fungwahbus.com*) and **Lucky Star** (*luckystarbus.com*). They depart every hour on the hour at the intersection of Bowery Ave and Canal St.

AIRPORTS

The New York area is served by three major airports: John F. Kennedy Airport (JFK), LaGuardia (LGA), and Newark (EWR).

John F. Kennedy (JFK) primarily handles international flights. Located 15 miles from midtown Manhattan in Queens, JFK is deceptively close. The overcongested highway, especially during rush hour, can make the trip more than an hour long. If you're in Manhattan, taking the LIRR to Jamaica station is a faster way to get there. That said, JFK services all major airlines and, if you're flying overseas, chances are you'll be using it. The airport itself is disorganized and difficult to get around, though recent improvements, especially the AirTrain system, have made a positive difference. AirTrain makes getting from terminal to terminal relatively simple, and for $5, it also connects flyers to the **A E J** and **Z** lines of the subway system as well as the LIRR.

LaGuardia (LGA) handles domestic flights. The smallest New York airport, LaGuardia is also the closest. Its small size makes getting around it relatively easy, but still budget time for the normal congestion. Getting to and from LaGuardia is cheap, as various buses connect LGA directly to Manhattan and the subway system, but unfortunately, the airport has no subway stop of its own, so many travelers use a taxi or car service. Cabs directly to Manhattan take about 30 minutes, and cost about $25 depending on where you want to be dropped off (unlike JFK, it's not a flat fare).

Newark International Airport (EWR) handles both international and domestic flights. Newark is typically less congested than both LGA and JFK, and is located 15 miles southwest of Midtown in New Jersey. Newark is a hassle to get to, though travelers sometimes excuse the distance for the modern facilities and cheaper fares Newark affords. An express bus to Grand Central or Port Authority will cost you about $15. Passengers can also connect to Amtrak or NJ Transit trains through Newark's AirTrain system, which provides an indirect though cheap trip to Penn Station.

TOP FIVE FUN WAYS TO GET AROUND

CARRIAGE IN CENTRAL PARK
Touristy, yes, but worth doing with someone special at least once. Carriages depart from Grand Army Plaza (*59th St & 5th Ave*).

RICKSHAW IN TIMES SQUARE
Soak in the bright lights while weaving in and out of New York traffic.

STATEN ISLAND FERRY
This 25-minute ride across the harbor is free, and boasts great views of the Downtown skyline and Statue of Liberty.
siferry.com. **1** *to South Ferry.*

CHINATOWN BUS
The cheapest way to get out of New York.
fungwahbus.com or luckystarbus.com.
Fung Wah: **N R W J M Z 6** *to Canal.*
Lucky Star: **B D** *to Grand.*

ZIPCAR
For those who need a car for a day, this service is easier than using a traditional rental agency, and available to those older than 21.
zipcar.com.

TRANSPORTATION 13

Real estate in New York is blood sport, and looking for a place to call home can become a painstaking process if you don't know the process well. Don't expect to find many secret bargains, because there are very few—be ready to pay a lot of money for a very small living space, and above all, be flexible. With a little research, patience, and determination, you can come out on top.

FINDING AN APARTMENT

Setting Your Priorities

Before you start looking, it's important to set clear guidelines regarding what you're looking for. Whether you're a student, a bachelor, or a couple looking to start a family, New York has something to offer everyone. There are generally decent deals for students around educational institutions, the outer boroughs offer safe suburban neighborhoods for families, and developing areas in Manhattan provide perfect hip and modern pads. Regardless, it is important to consider the lifestyle you want, your income, safety, space needs, and—if you have children— the educational system. Taking these factors into consideration will help eliminate some areas immediately, making your search more streamlined and efficient, and much less daunting.

Timing

People are constantly flowing in and out of New York, so it's imperative that you begin your search well in advance of your arrival. Deals do not last long; when they pop up, it's essential that you jump on them. While not a decision to be made hastily, finding a place you like will be difficult, and hesitating in hopes of finding something better may cost you. Chances are that if you think it's a deal, others will too, and they will snatch it. During the hot and humid summers many people opt for vacation homes outside the city, and apartments are available for sublet. In this academic city, professors on sabbatical may make the same offer. So start early, and with a little luck and persistence, a deal can land in your lap.

Renting

If you're looking to rent in the city, the most extensive list of available spaces will probably be on **Craigslist.com**. Other popular websites include **RDNY.com**, **bestaptsnyc.com**, and **manhattanapts.com**. While this may take hours of looking at a screen and clicking refresh, it's also the best way to find the unbeatable deal. Though the internet may prove invaluable, there are also plenty of listings in local papers. For recent grads or hires, the best time to rent seems to be in May, when prices consistently take a light dip before rising again for peak rental season. If you're on a tight budget, it's a good idea to look into parts of Brooklyn, Queens, or the Bronx. Young people, chased out of Manhattan by rising rents, have been moving to these boroughs in droves in recent years (although some Brooklyn neighborhoods, such as Williamsburg, aren't much cheaper than Manhattan anymore). Living far uptown, in Washington Heights or Inwood, is also a newly popular option. Remember, however, that there will be utilities to pay on top of the housing—cable, telephone, internet, electricity, water, heating, and air conditioning add a considerable amount to the monthly cost, so keep these in mind when figuring your budget.

Buying

New York has one of the highest average incomes in the nation, which makes the money-saver's search considerably more difficult. With the average price for apartments in Manhattan reaching $1.4 million— don't be too scared, this is largely due to high-end apartments costing over $10 million—it's important to know which neighborhoods are developing or where the market is flatter. While Manhattan's market is still rising, some areas in Queens and Brooklyn have dropped a little and become relatively stable, with median prices around $500,00-600,000.

Visiting the Apartments
When you begin to visit apartments, take notes on the neighborhood and details such as distance from the nearest subway or bus lines, the supermarket, and other conveniences. Try to gauge the safety of the area and the state of the buildings. Of course, you can ask the landlord these questions, but remember to take what he or she says with a grain of salt. Given the competitive state of housing, the landlord will also be judging you, so be on your best behavior. In general, following your instinct about the neighborhood is a good choice—if you don't feel safe, look elsewhere and do some further research by talking to people in the area.

Brokers
If you can afford a broker—someone with extensive knowledge of the housing market and often information on apartments that aren't available to the general public—your search will undoubtedly be more pleasurable. Their knowledge of the market will help guide your search according to your budget, and they can expedite the paperwork at the end. For all the convenience, though, it may be better to do your own research if you're on a budget. In Manhattan, they generally charge about 12-15% of the year's rent. In the outer boroughs, brokers can charge between a month's rent and 12% of the year's rent. These fees are only paid at the time of the signing of the lease. There are however, flat-fee agencies where you pay a cheaper fee up front, and there are also plenty of no-fee apartments where the buildings pay for the brokers, saving you the considerable cost.

AMENITIES
In a city moving this quickly, one can hardly survive without the internet and a cell phone. In terms of high-speed internet at home, the giants—Time Warner, Comcast, and Verizon—dominate the market, but Time

SETTLING IN 15

Warner's **Roadrunner** service is the most widespread. Its appeal lies in both its reliability and speed, as well as the packages the company offers, which can also include cable television and home phone service. To get international phone calls, a flat rate of $20 is put on top of its packages, the most expensive of which is $130 a month.

Establishing a home internet connection can be tricky and often expensive, but wireless is becoming more and more prevalent in the city. It's easy to find free access points for WiFi in outdoor spaces such as Lincoln Square and Union Square, public libraries and hotels throughout the five boroughs, and the campus areas of universities like Columbia, Fordham, and NYU. However, certain airports and hotels may try to charge for access. There are still many places without wireless internet, but a movement pushing for citywide wireless can be found at **nycwireless.net**. This group has valuable information, including a map of the city that indicates some of the many free hotspots.

You'll have a tough time finding an area in New York where you can't make a call on your cell phone. The most reliable servers have proved to be AT&T and Verizon Wireless. T-mobile and Sprint users seem to experience service problems at certain times and certain buildings may further inhibit cell phone service, but generally service should be reliable. Most service providers have several locations throughout the city, so if you have any problems with your service you should be able to have it fixed quickly. Prices vary according to the plan you choose, but services generally range from $40 to $140 a month.

CLIMATES AND SEASONS

Like the rest of the Northeast, New York "enjoys" all four seasons, and generally experiences a fair amount of rainfall, so bring a sturdy raincoat, umbrella, and a good pair of boots for rain and snow. The city has two uncomfortable seasons and two pleasant ones. **Winter** usually lasts from mid-November to late March, with temperatures averaging in the 30s. Grey skies are common, and snowfall occurs but is usually not excessive due to the city's coastal location. Nonetheless, a heavy winter coat will be necessary. **Summer**, which usually begins in late May and lasts through early September, is oppressively hot and humid, and the lightest clothing will come in handy, although most buildings are now air-conditioned. It's at this time that many New Yorkers leave town for vacation homes—the city becomes a ghost town in August. **Autumn**, which lasts roughly from September through November, is perhaps New York's most glorious season, with mild temperatures, sunny days, and low humidity. **Spring**, from late March through May, is similarly lovely although prone to frequent rainstorms and altogether too brief. For either of these seasons, a light sweatshirt or jacket will be invaluable.

PETS

Many of New York's citizens are pet owners, and despite the metropolitan landscape, New York is extremely pet-friendly. While dogs are not allowed in areas such as playgrounds, swimming pools, or ball courts and fields, many parks contain fenced dog exercise areas as well as unfenced areas where dogs can roam off-leash. It's not uncommon to see dog owners bring their dogs to these parks on early mornings and congregate with each other.

If you don't have time to walk your dog, **dogwalkers** are available (a ubiquitous sight on city streets, walking up to four or five dogs at a time), and for supplies, pet stores such at **Petco** (*petco.com*) are common throughout the city. While there is more than one option for dog **obedience schools**, the most popular is **Biscuits and Bath** (*biscuitsandbath.com*)— with six locations throughout the city, it also offers pet supplies and adoptions.

If you are looking to **adopt a pet**, the **ASPCA** (*aspca.org*) has a great website with valuable information about adoption centers and information on taking care of your pets. In addition, the ASPCA does monthly outreach programs that help pet owners get the necessary immunization shots for their pets. There is also a branch of **Animal Control and Care** (*nycacc.org*) in every borough, where you can adopt. Animal hospitals are available in every neighborhood, but among the most respected are **Park East Animal Hospital** (*52 E 64th St, 212-832-8417*) and **New York Veterinary Hospital** (*150 E 74th St*). **Urban Vets**, in the East Village, makes 24-hour house calls in critical situations (*212-674-6200*).

SETTLING IN 17

BANKING

Choosing a bank is an essential part of living in New York. It's best to choose one of New York's major banks, which tend to have better security and more perks. The banks with the most ATMs are Bank of America, Chase, Citibank, Commerce Bank, Wachovia, and Washington Mutual. Most major banks have special packages designed for students; do some research to find which benefits best suit your spending style. For example, if you tend to use credit more, compare the interest rates of several banks before signing up. If you rely more on checking or savings accounts, take a look at hidden costs, like the minimum amount you need to keep in the bank to avoid penalties.

Take note of what's in your area—don't pick a bank that is nowhere near your job or apartment, or one that's closed whenever you're free. Most banks charge fees for using competitors' ATMs, which can add up quickly. While you may not be able to find a branch of your bank in every corner of the city, there will always be at least one ATM handy; they are available 24 hours a day in most banks, and can also be found in many convenience stores, drugstores, bars, and restaurants. Most stores, restaurants, and even taxis accept credit cards now, but it is still important to keep some cash on hand for those that don't. Be wary of unaffiliated ATMs in seedy locations—instances of identity theft are rare but do occur. Always withdraw money from a major bank if you have the option.

BUSINESS HOURS

New York is famous for its 24/7 culture, but not everything is open around the clock. Most **banks** are open from 9am to 3:30 or 4pm during the week, although some stay open later on Fridays and many have Saturday service. Most **post offices** are only open during the week, from around 8am to 5pm, but those that are open on Saturday usually close by 1pm. **Museums** tend to open between 9 and 11am and close by 5:30pm, and most are closed at least one day per week (usually a Monday or Tuesday). Some museums will stay open later on certain days of the week, such as Fridays or Saturdays. **Public libraries** open around 10am and close by 6 or 8pm (earlier on Saturdays), and most are closed on Sundays. **City parks** are usually closed after dusk, although some stay open until midnight.

Many expensive **restaurants** only serve dinner, opening at around 5pm and closing by midnight. Restaurants that serve lunch are open from around 11:30am to 3pm and may close briefly before dinner. More moderately priced restaurants tend to serve continuously throughout the day and evening. **Bars** tend to open at around 5pm for happy hour and close by 4am. **Clubs** open between 8 and 10pm and close anytime from 4 to 7am, depending on the night of the week.

For most **offices**, 9-6 has replaced the 9-5 routine, but this being New York, it's not uncommon to see office buildings still lit up at 9pm. **Shops and department stores** operate all week, opening at around 10am and closing by 8pm. **Service-oriented stores**, like dry cleaners and salons, tend to open early (around 7am) and close late (around 9pm) to catch customers on their way to and from work.

Night owls needn't fear inconvenience, however. Many **drugstores** and some

grocery stores stay open all night, and there are many **delis and diners** that serve at any hour. **Public transportation** also runs nonstop, a hallmark of New York living (and a true rarity in other major cities), but is noticeably slower between midnight and 5am.

TIPPING

Like it or not, tipping is a New York custom that is rarely optional. Unless your service was truly horrendous, you are always expected to tip. Keep in mind that many service jobs pay lower than minimum wage and that workers rely on tips to make up the difference.

At a **restaurant**, tip around 15-20% of the pretax bill. Many people double the tax (8.375%) and add a dollar or two. Some restaurants include gratuity in the bill, especially for large groups. **Sommeliers** should also be tipped 15-20% of the wine bill. **Bartenders** receive $1-2 per drink or 15-20% of the total bill on a tab. Be careful if planning to leave a tip at the end of the night—a bartender may overlook you if he or she sees you aren't tipping. **Coat check attendants** are tipped $1-2 per item or visit. Tip **deliverymen** 10-15% of your bill, but add a few dollars if the weather is stormy.

At a hotel, tip **porters** $1-2 per bag and more if the bags are heavy or fragile. Tip the **valet** $1-2. **Concierges** receive $1-2 for hailing a cab and around $5 if they help carry luggage. **Room service waiters** are tipped 15% of the bill (although this will often be automatically included). **Taxi drivers** should be tipped 10-15% of the fare, but never less than $1. If your ride was short, round to the nearest dollar and then add one. Most other personal care and service providers, like **salon and spa employees**, should be tipped 15-20% of the cost.

TAXES

Taxes are another unavoidable cost in New York City. The state and city each impose a sales tax of four%, and there is also a surcharge of 0.375% that goes towards the Metropolitan Transportation Authority, amounting to a total sales and use tax of 8.375%.

Most **tangible personal property** (furniture, electronics, motor vehicles, etc.) is taxed. Most **services** are also taxed, including the servicing of automobiles or appliances, storage, safe deposit boxes, and parking in a garage. In addition, most **utilities** in the home are taxed—gas, electricity, refrigeration, steam, and telephone. **Hotel or motel rooms** are also taxed.

There are a number of **services uniquely taxed in New York City**, including credit reporting, barbering or beautician services, tanning, manicures and pedicures, electrolysis, massage services, weight control or health salons, and gymnasiums. **Services exempt from taxes** include visits to a doctor, laundering, dry cleaning, shoe repair, and veterinary services.

Food and drink that is prepared by a restaurant is taxed. However, food at a grocery store is tax-free. Generally, items considered luxuries (alcohol, tobacco, candy, soda, and cosmetics) are taxed whereas other beverages, drugs and medicine, prosthetic devices, and eyeglasses are not. **Newspapers and magazines** are also exempt.

Clothing and footwear are also completely exempt of taxes as of September 2007 (items over $110 were subjcct to taxes before this date). This exemption includes all clothing, hats and neckwear, formalwear, and diapers. However, jewelry, handbags, watches, umbrellas, pet or doll clothes, and other accessories are still taxed.

MONEY MATTERS 19

City government in New York is not taken lightly. Confronted with a population larger than those of 39 states and with some of the wiliest citizens in the world, public officials are tough and professional. Navigating the system is usually a headache, but understanding it can be extremely useful and rewarding to anyone who wants to exert influence and get what they want.

GOVERNMENT
CITY OFFICIALS

The **Mayor** of New York City is a strong executive with sweeping powers of enforcement and appointment. "Hizzoner" Michael Bloomberg (I) has used this post since his 2001 election to reshape the bureaucracy, further centralizing the administration and bringing it under the direction of experienced private-sector managers. Bloomberg delegates a great deal of responsibility to his commissioners, though the agenda is ultimately set by City Hall.

Second in power to the mayor is the **Public Advocate**, a citywide ombudsman and investigator in matters of administrative policy and conduct. The **Comptroller**, currently William C. Thompson, Jr. (D), audits city finances and contracts, reports on the economy, and manages our debt.

There was a time when **Borough Presidents** held greater power than City Council members, but now their role is largely ceremonial. Able to influence zoning policies—and, via zoning, businesses—by making appointments to **Community Boards**, BPs are generally seen as advocates for their boroughs and aspirants to higher office.

The New York **City Council** consists of 51 members elected to represent districts of approximately 155,000 constituents each. Speaker Christine Quinn (D) is the majority leader of this body, which approves budgets, monitors agencies, holds public hearings, and votes on local legislation. Council members are elected locally, and are typically responsive to constituent concerns.

In 1993 New Yorkers imposed a limit of two consecutive terms on all citywide elected officials, in a referendum proposed by the son of Estée Lauder, philanthropist and former mayoral candidate Ronald Lauder. Public opinion has recently favored this law, which will generate heavy turnover at all levels of city government in the 2009 elections—many city officials began their first four-year terms in 2002.

A dominant Democratic party ensures that most city elections are fought in the primaries over vacant seats. Fundraising and media relations are the keys to success, and there are few better ways to get involved and understand city government than to volunteer for a local campaign.

STATE & NATIONAL ELECTED OFFICIALS

Although the government of New York state has limited influence over the daily affairs of New Yorkers, Albany does affect jobs, markets, and transportation.

The **Governor** of New York state, David Paterson (D), was sworn in on March 17, 2008, after former Governor Eliot Spitzer resigned. Paterson has used his post to push for upstate economic development, increased school funding, and gay rights.

The New York State Legislature consists of a 50-member **Senate** led by Majority Leader Dean Skelos (R) and a 150-member **Assembly** led by Speaker Sheldon Silver (D). All legislators serve two-year terms with no term limits. Assemblymen represent districts of roughly 127,000 constituents, whereas Senators represent counties in pairs, leading to a divide between a Democratic majority in the Assembly (representing more populous urban counties) and a Republican majority in the Senate. Consequently, Albany is infamous for not passing city initiatives due to legislative gridlock.

New York's delegation to **Congress** includes Senators Charles Schumer (D) and Hillary Clinton (D) and senior Representative Charles Rangel (D). This delegation, like the City Council, is largely Democratic. Gaining access to their constituent services is hard though not impossible, and can be useful in federal matters such as the expedited reissue of a passport.

BUREAUCRACY

Mayor Bloomberg's mayoralty hinges so crucially on **311**—the city's customer-service number—that a huge monitor in his main office counts incoming calls to the number on any given day. Live operators answer residents' calls at all hours and direct them to the city's various services. 311 provides callers with tracking numbers that can be used to ensure that cases are handled in a timely manner, although the number is not the best way to pressure an unbending agency.

When a call to the mayor does not get results, your best option may be to call agencies yourself using the city's directory (**Green Book**), or alternatively, to seek the help of your district councilman, who can be found at the City Council website. Constituent caseworkers can raise issues with officials who outrank 311 contacts, and often have working relationships with key actors in government and the press.

The best-known branches of the city bureaucracy are the **Police** and the **Fire Department**. They are divided into autonomous precincts, and engines or ladders. Precincts issue permits for outdoor amplification and street activity, and make official records of concerns from theft to bar noise. FDNY ladders and engines investigate hazardous working practices and fire code violations.

Complaints about general noise or about flooding from sewerage go to the **Department of Environmental Protection**.

The **Department of Buildings** is large, overburdened, and slow, though it can be useful where neighbors and landlords put up scaffolding or renovate apartments without the right permits. Information on permits can be found on the DOB's Building Information System, online. This is also a useful tool for judging whether a landlord will be helpful. If tenants have filed complaints in the past year, lease elsewhere.

Problems with trash and recycling, though rare, can be referred to the **Department of Sanitation**.

The **Department of Health and Mental Hygiene** is known for handing out NYC Condoms and obtaining a ban on trans fats in restaurants, but it also operates free clinics, inspects eateries, reports on beach restrictions and closings, and offers a crisis intervention hotline.

Subway and rail services in New York are operated by the **Metropolitan Transportation Authority**, a state agency, the Port Authority, and New Jersey Transit; the **Department of Transportation**, which manages city roads, is charged with replacing broken signs and streetlights, renaming streets, and running a citywide bike program. Call to restore light to your block, to memorialize a family member, or to re-

GOVERNMENT 21

HELPFUL SITES

LAWS AND ADMINISTRATIVE CODE
24.97.137.100/nyc

GREEN BOOK (TO ORDER)
nyc.gov/html/dcas/html/features/
greenbook.shtml

CITY COUNCIL
council.nyc.gov

LOCAL SERVICES
gis.nyc.gov/doitt/mp/Portal.do

BUILDING INFORMATION
nyc.gov/html/dob/html/bis/bis.shtml

HEALTH
nyc.gov/html/doh/html/home/home.shtml

BLOCK PARTY NYC
blockpartynyc.org

ceive a free map of bike paths.

The **Department of Consumer Affairs** enforces consumer protection laws and may be able to help in cases of false advertising or pricing, undelivered products and services, or delayed billing, in addition to lease and loan disputes.

Community Boards, local advisory boards whose members are appointed by borough presidents, control one critical service: permits to throw block parties. Plan well in advance for this kind of event and fill in the appropriate paperwork with the board and the local police precinct. **Block Party NYC**, an NGO, offers free advice on how to do this, and lists other area events.

GETTING YOUR WAY

Knowing who is responsible for your concerns is half the battle in getting things from the government. Getting your way takes persistence and attention to detail.

Contacts: Except when writing letters, speak to agency officials positioned low on the ladder—lieutenants with the NYPD and FDNY, inspectors with the departments, and constituent-affairs staff with legislators. This is counterintuitive, but you can appeal to a higher level if things don't go your way.

Demands should be couched in terms that appeal to common sense or to the duties of the relevant agency. To have a car removed from your street, refer to "danger to drivers" or to "illegal parking." Make your concerns the agency's concerns by showing that any reasonable neighbor would agree.

Paper trails should always be kept when making a case. Hanlon's Razor gives good advice: "Never attribute to malice what can be adequately explained by stupidity." If your case is mishandled, it is always good to have a record that can be presented to supervisors or elected officials. Take down names, numbers, and case numbers. Save letters.

Support will be necessary to push through less popular requests, or ones not addressed in the law. When you cannot share your concerns with an agency, an aggressive tack—any stance opposed to the agency's—should be taken only with the support of a legislator or accompanied by a campaign of letter writing and press releases.

SAFETY
COUNSELING SERVICES

New York is famous for its shrinks and their clients, who range from madmen in the streets to multimillionaires. The city and many local groups provide services for everything from addictions and eating disorders to anxiety and depression; it's not necessary to go to a professional directly, though if you have a health plan, there are many options.

The first stop for mental health services is the Department of Health and Mental Hygiene's toll-free line, operated in partnership with the **Mental Health Organization of New York City**. This line can be reached 24/7 by calling 800-543-3638, and offers free assessments and referrals on all mental-health and substance-abuse issues.

If you are on a student insurance program, you likely have access to university psychiatrists through your school's health services center. If you are on a corporate plan, contact your primary care doctor for a referral in order to work with a therapist accepted by your plan—professional therapy can cost $100-300 per hour in the city, and is rarely covered in full by insurance.

Cheap options include the **National Institute for the Psychotherapies Training Institute**, which offers counseling by trainees and new therapists for $20-50 per hour, and either the **Depressive and Manic-Depressive Group** (917-445-2399) or the **Mood Disorders Support Group** (212-533-6374), which offer free meetings to those suffering from depression.

The **Renfrew Center** offers inpatient and outpatient services for eating disorders at 11 E 36th St, and the **NYU Medical Center** (917-544-0735) offers information on the city's free and confidential health clinics. The **New York State Office of Mental Health** (212-330-1650) offers an extensive list of resources as well.

In addition to all of these resources, suicide hotlines are available through both the **US Department of Health and Human Services** (800-273-8255) and the **Samaritans of New York** (212-673-3000).

STREET SMARTS

Traffic safety in the city applies to personal safety as well: the best advice you'll hear is a shouted, "**Watch where you're going!**" No matter whether you are jaywalking, hailing a cab, or walking home late at night, the same basic rules apply. Keep your head up and be aware of your surroundings, both by looking and by listening.

From the 1970s through the 90s, New York City was among the most dangerous places to live in the country. The bad news is that you won't be able to flaunt your daring ways anymore—the city was as safe as Provo, Utah by 2002. The good news is that violent and property crime has been drastically reduced so that even rough areas like the South Bronx, North Central Harlem, and central Brooklyn are safer than in the past.

Even in a safe city, criminals prey on those who are vulnerable, unaware of their surroundings, and unable to get help. The best way to avoid becoming the victim of a crime is to project alert confidence. **Know where you are going** and if you do not, act as though you do, walk briskly, and watch for street signs. **Travel in company** and don't loiter at night. **Acknowledge other pedestrians** and don't hesitate to look behind you or cross the street. **Do not wear headphones or earpieces**, which indicate that you are not paying attention, in addition to offering an attractive target for theft. **Walk on crowded and well-lit streets** wherever possible. If you are uncomfortable with being approached, **demand space**, and, should you have to call for help, **single out another pedestrian**.

Purse snatchings are rare in the city these days, but pickpockets are not. To avoid losing your wallet, your phone, or your camera, **keep important items in front pockets** while in crowded areas, **hold bags in front of you**, and don't sling them over your shoulder. Muggings are relatively uncommon, but it's not a bad idea to **avoid carrying lots of cash** on your person—abundant ATMs ensure that this is a minor inconvenience.

If you are uncomfortable in a neighborhood, **consider taking a cab** instead of a bus or the subway. If you do take the subway, **stay in sight of the station attendant** until a train arrives, and **board near the conductor**. If you take a cab, **take a yellow cab**; take gypsy cabs only when necessary, and **negotiate the price up front**. In gypsy cabs, it is important to remain alert and **be a backseat driver when possible**, asking to be let off in an area with good lighting if necessary.

A history of crime aside, most New Yorkers are friendly, honest people—a Columbia University professor of sociology did a study on lost wallets that showed more than 90% were returned, nearly half of them still stuffed with bills. If you find a wallet, you may have it sent back to the owner anonymously and for free by dropping it into a USPS mailbox, as long as it contains identifying information.

PANHANDLERS & SCAMMERS

The quickest way to get fleeced in the city is to walk into Bergdorf Goodman. After that comes scamming. Not everyone who asks you for money is a scammer though; rising housing prices and scarce jobs contribute to a growing population of chronically homeless residents.

Some 35,000 people are living in homeless shelters today, although crime and abuse in many shelters have led thousands to live on the street. Only 17% of the homeless are employed, due to mental illness, addiction, and the difficulty of obtaining and holding down a regular job without equally regular access to shelter and other basic necessities. Consequently, panhandling is common throughout the city.

If you choose to give, **keep cash apart** from your wallet for this purpose: beggars are rarely dangerous, but may be pushy if they are experienced. **"No, I can't help you,"** is usually the best answer to aggressive panhandling. Instead of giving money, many New Yorkers **offer food** to the homeless or **give to charities** like Coalition for the Homeless and the Doe Fund. The advantage of donations is that they do not support drug addiction, alcoholism, and other behavior that may reinforce the cycle of homelessness.

Scammers, like beggars, are comfortable approaching strangers for money. What sets them apart is a talent for deception that can be betrayed by common traits. Look for **skill in public speaking or storytelling**, accompanied by the **flawless delivery** of a well-practiced professional. Scam artists may **ask for money before you make eye contact**, and will try to play strangers off against each other. Common scams involve requests for cab fares and demands to make good on broken glasses or dropped food. Because most scammers are hoping to prolong their careers by staying out of jail, they tend to avoid aggression—to discourage them, ask probing questions, offer to file a police report and insurance claim, or laugh at their stories. Keep moving, though—some may be working to distract you while a friend picks your pockets.

EMERGENCY NUMBERS

911
Emergency Services

311
Government Information and Services

POLICE SWITCHBOARD
646-610-5000

POLICE TIP LINE
800-577-8477

SUICIDE HOTLINE
800-273-8255 or 212-673-3000

CRIME VICTIMS HOTLINE
212-577-7777

SEX CRIMES REPORT LINE
212-267-7273

DOMESTIC VIOLENCE REPORT LINE
800-621-4673

CRISIS INTERVENTION
800-543-3638

GAS LEAK REPORT LINE
212-683-8830

POISON CONTROL
800-222-1222

DINING & FOOD

New York's smorgasbord of restaurant choices is both a blessing and a curse. While the city is guaranteed to harbor delights for every eater, the sheer number of offerings can be overwhelming. Naturally inquisitive explorers might forgo guided information, but for others, knowing where to go, what to order, and how to stay in the loop makes all the difference.

GOING OUT

Reservations

Most New York restaurants accept reservations—popular ones often require them. Even at more casual restaurants, it's a good idea to make a reservation in advance, since New Yorkers dine out frequently on both weekends and weekdays. Most restaurants take reservations up to 30 days in advance, and making reservations is best done as early as possible, since by Thursday or Friday, a popular place will often be fully booked for the weekend. All but the most popular restaurants accept walk-ins as well, so arrive before peak hours (7-9pm) to score a table. If you have trouble getting a reservation, be sure to call the restaurant during the afternoon of the day you want to go—there may be cancellations. **OpenTable.com** allows users to set up a free account to browse availabilities and make reservations at participating restaurants. Whether you make the reservation by phone or online, always call a day or two in advance to confirm. Do *not* arrive late and expect the table to still be waiting; there is usually a 15-minute grace period before the table is released to walk-ins. Do call the restaurant if you are delayed, since chances are they can hold it for you. Can't score a reservation at the busiest restaurants? If you're willing to shell out some cash, **PrimeTimeTables.com** holds reservations for the most popular restaurants during prime dinner hours.

Dress

Dress codes, even at fancy restaurants, have relaxed in recent decades. Men can't go wrong with a jacket and tie at nicer establishments, but these days, neat jeans and an Oxford have become standard fare at many restaurants. Restaurants that require jackets for men will almost always say so on their website, so check before you go. In general, however, it's better to dress up a bit—it's easier to start fancy and take it down a notch than the other way around, and dressing up means keeping it clean and neat—no baggy shirts, holey jeans, too-tight skirts, or rubber flip-flops.

Paying

In general, 15 to 20% of the meal's cost *before* tax is the recommended amount for adequate service—competent but nothing special. Tip below this number if someone was outright rude, you had to wait forever for a reserved table, or the dishes were wrong. Tip at the high end for a helpful sommelier and waiters who are friendly yet tactful. Parties larger than five or six will often automatically be subject to an 18% gratuity—if this is added to your bill, take note since you won't want to tip again. When in doubt (restaurants will often try to make this charge look like a tax), ask your server. Finally, remember that some restaurants don't accept plastic—always know whether you should have enough cash on hand to pay for your meal.

TOP 5 FOOD CARTS

53RD AND 6TH HALAL CART
Follow the lines for sizzling halal chicken or gyro meat over rice, salad, and white and red sauces. A legend that serves businessmen and clubgoers alike.
53rd Street and 6th Ave. E V to 5th Ave-53rd St.

THE AREPA LADY
In a heavily Colombian neighborhood, this cart serves two types of arepas, made with corn batter and grilled until crispy.
Roosevelt Ave near 78th St, Jackson Heights. 7 to 74th St-Broadway, E F R V to Jackson Heights-Roosevelt Ave.

TREATS TRUCK
The cookies, brownies, and other sweets at this truck may not be meals, but with prices this low and food this good, who cares?
Various locations. TreatsTruck.com.

NY DOSAS
This Washington Square legend serves crepe-like South Indian dosas that are fully vegetarian and attract NYU students and expats alike.
W 4th St at Sullivan St. A C E B D F V to W 4th St.

THE JAMAICAN DUTCHY
A rotating menu accompanies classics like jerk chicken and fried plantains at this Midtown favorite.
51st St between 6th and 7th Ave. E B D to 7th Ave.

Helpful Hints

Peering in windows, or looking for a line, is generally a good rule of thumb—busy restaurants are so for a reason. Likewise, especially in ethnic neighborhoods, go where the locals go—don't be daunted if the menu is in a foreign language and the staff barely speaks English. You'll often end up with an authentically prepared meal at a bargain. Avoiding overly touristy places is imperative to making sure you get your money's worth as well. Of course, there are always exceptions; doing some research can you help you learn to distinguish between the wheat and the chaff. In fact, staying informed is the single best way to hear about hot restaurants, special promotions, hole-in-the-wall dives, and get others' opinions as well. *Time Out New York*, *New York* magazine, and *The New York Times*' Wednesday Dining section are a few major news outlets, but the numerous blogs and online resources compete by providing diners' reviews, insider information, and more. Popular sources include **Eater.com** and **Chow.com**.

STAYING IN

Greenmarkets
The freshest produce in New York usually comes from the farmers themselves, at one of many farmers markets. The Union Square Greenmarket is by far the city's largest open-air market, offering hundreds of local farmers space to sell fresh produce, fish, and meats on Monday, Wednesday, Friday, and Saturday for most of the year. As the Greenmarket is usually swarmed on the weekends and chefs usually scoop up the best of the

TOP 5 MARKETS

UNION SQUARE GREENMARKET
Get the city's freshest produce—if these local farmers are good enough for New York's most famous chefs, they'll be good enough for you.
Union Square West at 16th St.
❶❷❸ ❹❺❻ ❼ to 14th St-Union Sq.

TRADER JOE'S
This national chain draws in locals with its emphasis on environmentally friendly and organic foods. The "Two Buck Chuck" wine is actually three bucks, but no one's counting.
142 E 14th St at Irving Place.
❶❷❸❹ ❺❻❼ ❽ to 14th St-Union Sq.

FAIRWAY MARKET
The single best supermarket in the city, with huge locations, unbelievable variety, and wholesale prices.
Broadway at 74th St, ❶❷❸ to 72nd St.
12th Ave at 132nd St (under the West Side Highway), ❶ to 125th St.

WHOLE FOODS
It's expensive, trendy, and filled with yuppies and tourists—so keep your wits about you as you navigate the organic and specialty food at these mammoth stores.
Time Warner Center at Columbus Circle;
❶ⒶⒷⒸⒹ to 59th St-Columbus Circle.
4 Union Square South, ❶❷❸❹ ❺❻❼
to 14th St-Union Sq.

MANHATTAN FRUIT EXCHANGE
A huge selection of fruits and vegetables at great prices awaits at this emporium within chichi Chelsea Market. Cash only.
75 9th Ave between 15th & 16th St. ⒶⒸⒺ
to 14th St, Ⓛ to 8th Ave.

produce in the early morning, be on the lookout for the dozens of smaller Greenmarkets in different neighborhoods. Consult the Council on the Environment of New York City's website (*CENYC.org*) to locate the nearest one.

Ordering

It certainly is healthier and more cost-efficient to shop at a local supermarket, pack lunches, and cook dinner, but if you're busy (or just lazy), ordering take-out is the easiest solution. Chances are your apartment building lobby is littered with piles of takeout menus, but if you want to find adventurous dining from the comfort of your couch, **MenuPages.com** will have a list of restaurants that deliver to your neighborhood, sorted by cuisine and price. Chinese takeout and pizza are definitely not the only options. At lunchtime, **SeamlessWeb.com** lets you order from nearby restaurants without ever having to get on the phone. Orders are placed online and delivered right to your desk.

Dietary Restrictions

Vegetarians and vegans need not fear—almost every grocery store in the city stocks plenty of options. To serve the many vegetarians and vegans in the city, there are also several notable restaurants that keep raw, vegetarian, or vegan. The most comprehensive lists include the yellow pages and listings at **CitySearch.com**, which allow you to search restaurants by cuisine.

Due to the city's large Jewish community, kosher food is widely available, although you may have to travel to get it. The Upper West Side has a number of kosher restaurants, covering everything from steak to Moroccan, and Brooklyn neighborhoods such as Flatbush and

Borough Park will have plenty of small grocery stores that cater to the local community. The website **Kosher-NY.com** keeps tabs on restaurants, but for grocery shopping, **Fairway Market** (*FairwayMarket.com*) is a good bet—its cold room is famous for its huge selection of kosher meats. **Zabar's** (*Zabars.com*) is also stocked with a wide variety of kosher foods. Halal food is somewhat harder to find in grocery stores, although Muslim communities in Brooklyn will have stores with more options. **Zabihah.com** has an extensive list of halal restaurants throughout the city, including the halal chicken-and-rice carts that dot the city.

SAVING MONEY

During **Restaurant Week** (*NYCVisit.com/RestaurantWeek*), a two-week-long biannual event, prix-fixe lunches and dinners are available for $24 and $35, respectively, at many of the city's finer restaurants. The price does not include tax, tip, or beverages, all of which rapidly raise seemingly low prices. Scope out Midtown as well; dozens of food carts (some of which are legendary in their own right) set up shop during lunch and early dinner hours to cater to the corporate crowd. Most offer huge portions at cheap prices.

DINING & FOOD 29

NIGHTLIFE

For decades Manhattan nightlife has delivered the innovative, trendsetting, and über-exclusive, from Prohibition-era speakeasies, to the glitz and glamour of Studio 54, to the velvet rope circus of today's clubs. The smorgasbord of offerings ensures that everyone can find a good time out on the town.

WHERE TO GO

Midtown East and West
These areas are best suited for grabbing drinks after work, before or after the theater, or after sightseeing. Midtown West is a blend of tourists and older office patrons looking to unwind. Midtown East attracts a younger crowd of the recently employed, and the numerous bars, pubs, and lounges keep their doors open late.

Chelsea/Meatpacking District
The trendiest "hotspots" are clustered around here. Clubs notorious for their door policy are the main draw for socialites and their hangers on. Native New Yorkers know these nightclubs are best during the weeknights and less desirable on weekends when long lines, steep cover charges, and bridge-and-tunnelers make it difficult to get in. The best way to bypass the velvet rope? Find a promoter to get you on the guest list and comped for a night, or make very good friends with the over-muscled bouncers that hold the keys to the castle.

West Village
Its close proximity to the Clubland of Chelsea and the Meatpacking District means that the bars and lounges in this area absorb some of the pretension, but the West Village is noted for its cozy, sophisticated bars filled with neighborhood locals, trendy lounges, booming LGBT scene, and relatively low-key nightlife scene.

SoHo
Sleek lounges and bars full of beautiful people—drinking outrageously expensive cocktails—keep up the highbrow element of SoHo nightlife, while neighborhood bars and the occasional dive cater to all kinds of nocturnal preferences.

East Village
The city's most distinguished dive bars can be dug up here. The neighborhood attracts an interesting blend of starving artists looking for a cheap drink, NYU students looking for cheap drink and easy ass, local residents, and adventurous Uptowners.

Lower East Side
A little older than its nearby East Village cohorts, the LES still attracts a blend of starving artists, recent college grads, and scenesters looking for a fun, late night—and with more bars down here than there are Starbucks uptown, there is a spot for every brand of tight jeans and horn-rimmed glasses.

Upper East Side
Full of sports bars, the Upper East Side attracts those fluent in frat and finance. The scene is beer-guzzling, Jager-loving, no-frills, sweaty fun.

Upper West Side
A mix of wine bars, dive bars, and neighborhood spots, the UWS caters to a wide range of ages and backgrounds. Many bars are geared toward college kids, while quieter bars bring in a calmer, older crowd. The neighborhood's various wine bars offer places for a quiet drink after taking in a show or an intimate date where you can show off your knowledge of wine.

Williamsburg
Home to old Hipsters and new Scruffles, Williamsburg offers a budding social scene. With friendly patrons in their twenties and thirties, it's a perfect place to let loose with an non-judgmental crowd.
Plenty of dive bars and cheap drinkeries make this a hot spot for Brooklyn residents and Manhattan travelers alike.

WHAT TO DO

The best part of New York nightlife is its potential for the unexpected—the bars and clubs in the city offer up tons of surprises. Bars offer the most low-key option, lounges are more upscale places to sit and drink and occasionally dance, while clubs are all about getting down on the dance floor. New York also offers random parties that pop up throughout the five boroughs and offer some of the best nightlife options. Parties like **Mondo** (*Mondo-NYC.com*), a bimonthly indie dance party, or the crazy **Toshi Parties** (*ToshiParties.com*) are popular choices. **Turntables on The Hudson** (*TurntablesOnTheHudson.com*), a traveling dance party, and Sunday evening dance parties at **The Yard** (*TheYard.ws*) in Carroll Gardens showcase both new and established DJs. Check InsideNY.com for upcoming events.

WHAT TO DRINK

When standing in front of an impatient bartender at a crowded bar, a panic can set in—the panic that causes patrons to order things like "Cranberry Vodka," "Coors Light," or the dreaded "Cosmo". If you're at your local dive bar, order away. But if you find yourself further afield, be adventurous and try a few of these locally brewed beers or classic cocktails.

Beers

New York's local beer, **Brooklyn Lager**, is a tap staple at most bars in the city. It's brewed right at Brooklyn Breweries in Williamsburg (*BrooklynBrewery.com*, see *page 285*), which offers a happy hour every Friday and factory tours every Saturday. Check out their seasonal offerings, such as their popular Summer Ale. Sixpoint Sweet Action is sweet, creamy American blonde ale that's brewed with Hudson water. To discover more local or rare beers, visit any of the several specialty beer bars in the city, such as Beer Table (*page 325*), Blind Tiger Ale House (*page 151*), or Burp Castle (*page 140*).

Cocktails

New York City has given birth to some truly fantastic cocktails that will make the ubiquitous vodka tonic obsolete. **The Old Fashioned**, the first concoction to receive this title, was supposedly the brainchild of one Colonel James E. Pepper and popularized at the famed Waldorf-Astoria Hotel. It's a potent mix of bourbon, Angostura bitters, soda water, and sugar. Given its namesake, the origins of the **Manhattan** are obvious. Introduced at a banquet for Samuel J. Tilden, the mix of whiskey, vermouth, Angostura bitters, and a maraschino cherry has remained a fashionable cocktail with a big punch. When all else fails, ordering a classic **Martini**—a mix of gin and vermouth, garnished with an olive—makes you look like you know what you're doing.

Mixology

There are now several bars that specialize in the art of mixology, where bartenders invent freshly made cocktails out of surprising flavors. For the real cocktail connoisseur, these bars are a godsend; for the novice boozer, these bars can be a welcome diversion from

the typical bar scene. Try Milk and Honey (20 7th Ave South, 212-929-4360, page 124) for a mean Dark and Stormy, Pegu Club (77 W Houston St, 212-473-7348) for a Pisco sour, or Death & Company (433 E. 6th St, 212-388-0882, page 140) for a personalized cocktail.

If you'd like to learn to pick up the shaker yourself, give the **Columbia Bartending Agency** a call. In business since 1965, they offer the cheapest courses in mixological studies in the city. For $195, you get five classes taught by experienced Columbia bartenders, each of which ends with an hour long practical session when you can practice making the drinks you just learned from a fully stocked open bar. They also provide bartending and catering services for private parties at a discount rate of $28/hr. (212-854-4537 to enroll in classes or hire a bartender).

HOW TO DRINK

Bar Etiquette
The number-one rule to being a good bar patron is: don't be an ass. When at a bar, do not heckle the bartender, sigh impatiently when your drink takes a long time, sexually harass anyone, push other bar patrons, or ask for your drink to have more mixer.

Tipping
Remember to tip—and to tip fairly well. The standard rule is $1 per drink; however, if you are at a more upscale venue, the typical 20% is proper. Well-treated bartenders will make you better drinks and won't keep you waiting.

Dress Codes
Some clubs have explicit dress codes, but most have unwritten yet exactingly partic-

ular rules about what is acceptable. These rules govern who gets in, so be sure to look sharp.

Smoking Laws
The Bloomberg administration has outlawed smoking in all clubs, bars, and restaurants, but most establishments have outdoor smoking sections. If freezing your ass off in the winter to enjoy a cigarette doesn't sound appetizing, serious smokers can check out the few smoking lounges in the city, such as Circa Tabac in SoHo (see page 105).

HOW TO STAY OUT OF PRISON

Bostonians and Washingtonians rejoice— you've come to the state with the most lenient alcohol laws in the Northeast. You can purchase beer in supermarkets or drugstores, but everything else—wine or liquor—can only be found in liquor stores. Beer can be sold 24 hours a day while liquor cannot be sold after midnight or before 9am on weekdays and Saturdays, or after 9pm on Sundays. Alcohol cannot be served from 4am to 8am, hence last call at 3:45am.

Liquor Laws and Fake IDs
If you want to drink alcohol, buy alcohol, or sit in an establishment that serves alcohol, you legally have to be 21. This has, of course, proved problematic for most college students who want to take advantage of New York's nightlife scene. Luckily for some, a large cottage industry has sprung up to supply fake IDs to thirsty undergrads. Purchasing these is illegal, and undercover cops have been cracking down on their sale recently. Getting one is far from impossible, but it will run you at least $100. Just don't get caught–purchasing or possessing a fake ID is a felony that sometimes carries jail time.

Bars have become stricter on fake ID use in recent years. New scanning technology made for spotting fakes, often used by large bars and clubs, has made many fakes unreliable. If you're unlucky enough to be in a bar that gets raided by the cops, show them your real ID. If you deny that you got into the bar using a fake, the bar will generally get fined, but you'll suffer few repercussions. If a bouncer rejects your ID upon entry, don't hang around—the longer you loiter, the more likely they are to call the cops.

SAFETY

Common sense is usually long gone when you stumble out of a bar at 4am, but while you're partying, it will serve you well to keep these obvious things in mind:

Watch your drinks. Roofies may not have the same popularity they did 10 years ago, but they're still used.

Travel in groups–especially on the subway. If you are in a larger group, splitting a cab is often economical. However, don't puke in the cab or you'll be paying a hefty cleanup fee.

Never leave a fellow reveler behind. Your friend may look like she really wants to go home with that 45-year-old man who says he's a lawyer. She may even seem angry when you pull her away and get her home safely. Just take comfort in knowing you wont have to file a missing persons' report the next day.

NIGHTLIFE 33

MUSEUMS

New York's more famous museums are must-sees on every tourist's list—and with good reason—but there's far more to the city's offerings than the big names. Museums range from gargantuan to closet-sized, and whether art lover, history nerd, coin collector, or celebrity worshiper, there's something for you here.

TAKING ADVANTAGE

Many museums pride themselves on being cultural institutions, which means the exhibitions are just the first stop—a lot of the more in-depth and interesting cultural education is in the events and programs. When you go to any museum, make sure to spend more than a passing moment at the information desk; most will have a calendar of events and information about ongoing programs.

Paying for Museums

Make sure to be on the lookout for two magical words: "suggested donation." For instance, at the Met, adult admission is listed as $20. Don't be fooled. That is a suggested price. You can give as little as a penny and still get in (expect a few dirty looks if you opt for the cheap rout). A lot of museums around the city have a similar deal, so keep your eyes peeled.

Most museums require a valid student ID for student admissions prices; be sure to take yours with you.

ART

The Metropolitan Museum of Art

The largest art museum in the Western Hemisphere, the Met is known as a "collection of collections", with unparalleled diversity and something for every art lover. Famous exhibits range from the Greek and Roman galleries to the Costume Institute on the bottom floor.
1000 5th Ave (at 82nd St). 212-535-7710. Tues–Thurs 9:30am–5:30pm, Fri-Sat 9:30am–9:00pm, Sun 9:30am–5:30pm. MetMuseum.org. ❹❺❻ *to 86th St. Suggested donation: $20 adults, $15 seniors, $10 students. Page 209.*

The Cloisters

This uptown extension of the Met holds its collection of medieval art, including the famous unicorn tapestries. Located in Fort Tryon Park, this museum's ambiance is quiet, reflective, and, because of its isolation, almost otherworldly.
99 Margaret Corbin Dr. Tues–Sun 9:30am–4:45pm (November–February), Tues-Sun 9:30am–5:15pm (March–October). 212-570-3828. ❶ *to 190th St. Suggested donation: $20 adults, $15 seniors, $10 students. Page 278.*

The Brooklyn Museum

Brooklyn's largest museum is known for its collection of worldwide art ranging from ancient to modern times—with a focus on the non-Western world—and historical artifacts. One of the city's most impressive cultural institutions, it is housed in a beautiful Beaux-Arts building on Prospect Park.
200 Eastern Parkway. 718-638-5000. Mon-Tues closed, Wed-Fri 10am-5pm, Sat-Sun 11am-6pm. BrooklynMuseum.org. ❷❸ *to Eastern Parkway-Brooklyn Museum. Suggested donation: $8 adults, $4 seniors and students. Children under 12 free. Page 321.*

The Museum of Modern Art

A trip to the MoMA is sure to excite, inspire, baffle, and educate. The art collection includes pieces by well-known modern masters such as Picasso, Pollock, Warhol, and some sculptures, video installments, and multimedia pieces by people you may have never heard of.
11 West 53rd St (between 5th Ave and 6th Ave). 212-708-9400. Sat-Mon 10:30am–5:30pm, Tues closed, Wed-Thurs 10:30am-5:30pm, Fri 10:30am-8pm. MoMA.org. ❸ⓥ *to 5th Avenue-53rd Street;* ❸ⒹⒻ *to 47th-50th St-Rockefeller Center. Adults $20, seniors $16, students $12. Children under 16 free. Page 181.*

PS1 Contemporary Art Center

An affiliate of the MoMA, this nonprofit center is devoted entirely to bleeding-edge contemporary art. This museum stands out from others for its dedication to bridging the artist/audience divide and is known for its unique

34 MUSEUMS

exhibits.
22-25 Jackson Ave (at 46th Ave). Thurs-Mon 12pm-6pm. 718-784-2084. PS1.org. ❼ to 45th Rd-Courthouse Sq. Suggested donation; $5 adults, $2 seniors and students. Page 331.

Solomon R. Guggenheim Museum
The spiral-shaped building that houses this museum is a masterpiece in itself. The permanent collection has notable pieces from modern art regulars, but the temporary exhibitions are what really draw the crowds.
1071 5th Ave (at 89th St). 212-423-3500. Sat–Wed 10am–5:45pm, Fri 10am–7:45pm, Thurs closed. Guggenheim.org. ❹❺❻ to 86th St. Adults $20, students and seniors $15. Children under 12 free. Page 209.

Neue Galerie
This museum features early 20th century German and Austrian art and design. Featuring paintings from Gustav Klimt and Otto Dix and encompassing movements from Bauhaus to Expressionism, the Neue also exhibits one of the most expensive paintings ever sold: Klimt's *Portrait of Adele Bloch-Bauer I*.
1048 5th Avenue (at 86th St). 212-628-6200. Thurs-Mon, 11am-6pm, Fri 11am-9pm, Tues-Wed closed. NeueGalerie.org. ❹❺❻ to 86th St. Adults $15, seniors and students $10. Page 209.

Cooper-Hewitt National Design Museum
Located in the Carnegie mansion, this museum is dedicated exclusively to the history of design. Organized into Applied Arts, Industrial Design, Prints and Textiles, and Wall-coverings, it includes everything from mass-produced articles to one-of-a-kind works of art.
2 E. 91st St (at 5th Ave). 212-849-8400. Mon–Thurs 10am–5pm, Fri 10am–9pm, Sat 10am–6pm, Sun 12pm–6pm. CooperHewitt.org. ❹❺❻ to 86th Adults $15, senior and students $10. Children under 12 free. Page 207.

Whitney Museum of American Art
The Whitney made its name here by buying pieces from living artists who were not necessarily big stars in the art world. It continues this legacy today by buying pieces for the famed annual and biennial exhibitions, which are a must for any NYC art lover.
945 Madison Ave (at 75th St). 212-570-3600. Mon–Tues closed, Wed–Thurs 11 am–6 pm, Fri 1pm–9 pm, Sat-Sun 11am-6pm. Whitney.org. ❻ to 77th St. Adults $15, seniors and students $10. Page 209.

The New Museum of Contemporary Art
The recently built structure that houses this museum is just as controversial as the art it houses. Inside, the collection focuses on underrepresented modern artists as well as new media. "New Art, New Ideas" is the mission statement, and the New Museum stays true to its word.
235 Bowery (near Prince St). 212-219-1222. Mon-Tues closed, Wed 12pm-6pm, Thurs-Fri 12pm-10pm, Sat-Sun 12pm-6pm. NewMuseum.org. Ⓕ Ⓥ to 2nd Ave-Lower East Side; Ⓙ Ⓜ Ⓩ to Bowery; 6 to Spring St; Ⓡ Ⓦ to Prince St. Adults $12, seniors $8, students $6. 18 and under free. Page 121.

The Drawing Center
One of the smaller museums in the city, the Drawing Center has worked hard to make a name for itself as a respected purveyor of historical and contemporary drawing exhibits. Through the center's Viewing Program, emerging artists can arrange one-on-one portfolio reviews with a curator.
35 Wooster St (near Grand St). 212-219-2166. Tues-Fri 10am – 6pm, Sat 11am–6pm. DrawingCenter.org. ❶Ⓐ ❻Ⓔ to Canal St. Free admission.

Museo Del Barrio
As New York's only museum dedicated exclusively to the art of Latin America and the Caribbean, the majority of art here is of Puerto Rican origin, but frequent revolving exhibits and education programs promote awareness of Latino culture at large.
1230 5th Ave (at 104th St). 212-831-7272. Wed-Sun 11am-5pm. ElMuseo.org. ❻ to 103rd St, ❷❸ to 110th St. Suggested donation: $6 adults, $4 students and seniors. Page 271.

MUSEUMS 35

American Folk Art Museum
On the same street as the MoMA, this is a fun museum to check out for a completely different type of art. There are more than 5,000 pieces of folk art at the museum, including quilts, portraits, paintings, and weather-vanes.
45 W. 53rd St (near 5th Ave). 212-265-1040. Mon closed, Tues-Thurs 10:30am-5:30am, Fri 10:30am-7::30pm, Sat-Sun 10:30am-5:30pm. FolkArtMuseum.org. B D F V *to 47th-50th St-Rockefeller Center. $9 adults, $7 seniors and students. Children under 12 free.*

Bronx Museum
Known for featuring up-and-coming artists regardless of their fame, this gem is unique in New York for its visitor-friendly gallery attendants and laid-back attitude. Interaction with the exhibits is encouraged, and the high-concept exhibitions are updated frequently.
1040 Grand Concourse (at 165th St). 718-681-6000. Mon 12pm-6pm, Tues-Wed closed, Thurs 12pm-6pm, Fri 12pm-8pm, Sat-Sun 12pm-6pm. BronxMuseum.org. 4 B D *to 167thSt. Suggested donation: $5 adults, $3 seniors and students. Children under 12 free. Free admission on Fridays. Page 356.*

The Frick Collection
Everything here—including the building—is antique. Located in the former mansion of steel tycoon Henry Clay Frick, this small museum's collection consists of minor works by the old European masters, as well as sculptures and furniture primarily from the 18th century. Children under the age of 10 are respectfully denied admission.
1 E. 70th St (near 5th Ave). 212-288-0700. Tues-Sat 10am-6pm, Sun 11am-5pm. Frick.org. 6 *to 68th St-Hunter College. $15 adults, $10 Seniors, $5 students. Pay what you wish Sundays 11am-1pm. Page 208.*

Rubin Museum of Art
The premier Himalayan art museum in the Western hemisphere, this elegant gallery displays the paintings, sculptures, and textiles of a somewhat obscure artistic tradition. On Friday nights, the museum turns into a bar and lounge which serves cocktails to a sophisticated crowd.
150 W. 17th St (near 7th Ave). 212-620-5000. Mon 11am-5pm, Tues closed, Wed 11am-7pm, Thurs 11am-5pm, Fri 11am-10pm, Sat-Sun 11am-6pm. RMAnyc.org. 1 *to 18th St. Adults $10, seniors students and artists $7, neighbors (zip codes 10011 and 10001) $7. Children under 12 free. Free admission Fridays 7-10pm. Page 161.*

CULTURAL

The Hispanic Society of America
Dedicated to the study of the art and cultures of Spain, Portugal, and South America, this museum includes galleries of paintings by the Spanish masters, and a comprehensive research library. Best of all, admission, tours, and gallery talks are all free.
613 W. 155th St (near Broadway). 212-926-2234. Sun 1pm-4pm, Mon closed, Tues-Sat 10am-4:30pm. HispanicSociety.org. 1 *to 157th St. Free admission. Page 278.*

The Jewish Museum
The Jewish Museum prides itself on providing artifacts of Jewish culture and art from past to present. The collection of paintings, drawings, ceremonial pieces, and antiquities is impressive for its sheer breadth and the passion with which it is presented.
1109 5th Ave (at 92nd St). 212-423-3200. Sat-Wed 11am-4:30pm, Thurs 11am-8pm, Fri closed. TheJewishMuseum.org. 6 *to 96th St. $12 adults, $10 seniors, $7.50 students. Children under 12 free. Free admission Sat 11am-5:45pm. Page 209.*

Museum of Chinese in America
This museum is unique for its concentration on both Chinese culture and how that culture has changed and flourished in America. The collections preserve cultural relics, such as photographs, oral histories, artifacts, and more. The museum also holds festivals, conferences, and workshops.
70 Mulberry St, 2nd Floor (near Bayard St). 212-619-4785. Will open again Fall 2008. MOCA-NYC.org. 6 N O R W J M Z *to Canal St. Adults $3, seniors and students $1.*

National Museum of the American Indian

Located in the beautiful Hamilton U.S. Customs building, this museum houses not only pieces of artistic and historical value, but also rare religious artifacts of great spiritual significance.
1 Bowling Green (near Broadway). 212-514-3700. Daily 10am-5pm. AmericanIndian.si.edu. 4 5 to Bowling Green, 1 to South Ferry; R W to Whitehall St. Free admission. Page 94.

HISTORY AND SCIENCE

Museum of Natural History

The young and young-at-heart come in droves to see this museum's amazing exhibits of natural life on this earth. The famous T-Rex model, giant blue whale model complete with ocean sounds and lighting, and Rose Center for Earth and Space are all must-sees.
Central Park West at 79th St. 212-769-5100. Daily 10am-5:45pm. AMNH.org. B C to 81st St-Museum of Natural History. Adults $15, seniors and students $11, children $8.50. Page 218.

The New York Historical Society

It seems the masterminds behind this museum just decided to collect as much stuff as they could. Spoons, statues, sunglasses, teapots, and hats dating from the 1800s to the present are all on display. Keep an eye out for periodic exhibits featuring a variety of fascinating artifacts.
170 Central Park West (near 76th St). 212-873-3400. Mon closed, Tues-Sat 10am-6pm, Sun 11am-5:45pm. NYHistory.org. B C to 81st St-Museum of Natural History. $10 adults, $7 senior citizens and educators, $6 students. Children under 12 free. Free admissions Fridays 6-8pm. Page 218.

Lower East Side Tenement Museum

This guided-tour-only museum offers a fascinating look into the lives of the thousands of immigrants who passed through its halls. Visitors are taken on a journey through old urban living and able to witness the first place many immigrants called home in America.
108 Orchard St (near Delancey St). 212-431-0233. Daily 11am-4:30pm. Tenement.org. F to Delancey St; J M Z to Essex St; B D to Grand St. Adults $17, seniors and students $13.

Morgan Library

Little is missed by this library and museum. Beyond books, there are huge collections of art and musical works covering the medieval, Renaissance, and modern times.
225 Madison Ave (at 36th St). 212-590-0300. Tues-Thurs 10:30am-5pm, Fri 10:30am-9pm, Sat 10am-6pm, Sun 11am-6pm. MorganLibrary.org. 6 to 33rd St. Adults $12, students and seniors $8, children under 16 $8. Children under 12 free.

SPECIAL INTEREST

Museum of Sex

While the name is surely meant to shock, this museum is actually quite proper. Not so much kinky as scholarly, the collection includes works of art, photography, costumes, and "technological inventions."
233 5th Ave (at 27th St). 212-689-6337. Sun-Fri 11am-6:30pm, Sat 11am-8pm. MuseumofSex.org. N R W to 28th St. Adults $14.50, seniors and students $13.50. Page 171.

American Museum of the Moving Image

Although currently closed for renovation until winter 2009-10, exhibits in this museum are multimedia experiences that cover almost every aspect of film, television, and digital media. Visitors can make their own flip-books, animations, and sound effects. Both educational and exhilarating, this museum is a unique institution.
35th Ave at 36th St. 718-784-4520. Tues-Fri 12pm-5pm, Sat-Sun 11am-6pm. MovingImage.us. G R V to Steinway, N W to Broadway. Adults $10, seniors and students $7.50, children 5-18 $5. Free admission on Fridays 4-8pm.

MUSEUMS 37

ARTS

Tourists, performers, groupies, and artists alike flock to New York City every year to experience a part of the city's endless art scene. Whatever your passion, be it books, music, theater, or visual art, the city's culture of people and places, discounts and splurges, holes-in-the-wall and upscale venues will suit any art lover.

MUSIC

Lincoln Center (*Columbus Ave at Broadway and 64th St, lincolncenter.org*) is the premier performing arts venue in the city. Avery Fisher Hall, home to the New York Philharmonic, sells tickets that easily run into triple digits. Student tickets are available online or at the box office. Most of the other programs at Lincoln Center, including the Metropolitan Opera, Jazz at Lincoln Center, and the New York City Opera, offer similarly discounted student tickets, which can be found in the student guide on Lincoln Center's website.

The equivalent name for more modern music is **Madison Square Garden** (*7th Ave between 31st and 33rd St, thegarden.com*), a 20,000 seat venue. Tickets are priced high and often sell out quickly, and because MSG is a commercial operation, the concept of "student tickets" doesn't really exist.

Seeing up-and-coming and under-the-radar names is often the best way to get a great value, and the city abounds with smaller clubs and venues. **The Village Voice** (*VillageVoice.com*) lists all the performances happening in town each week, and **NY.com/clubs/jazz** is a great resource for the upcoming performances in the jazz world. **Smalls** (*183 W 10th St. 212-252-5091.*) and **St. Nick's Pub** (*773 St Nicholas Ave. 212-283-9728.*) are both known for consistently having solid jazz performances at low covers. Those in search of New York's legendary jazz clubs can spend an evening at **The Village Vanguard** (*178 7th Ave. 212-255-4037.*), **Blue Note** (*131 W 3rd St. 212-475-8592.*), or **Birdland** (*315 W 44th St. 212-581-3080.*), although they'll fork over a lot of cash in the process. For rock fans, **Joe's Pub** (*425 Lafayette. 212-967-7555.*) is a performance space/lounge/restaurant that has multiple different shows each night of the week, featuring both stars and newcomers. Tickets are a reasonable $15-20, and the 2-drink minimum can be mitigated by substituting for $12 of food— an easy way to get dinner and a show on a student budget. Many rock venues are increasingly moving away from the gentrification of Manhattan—**Music Hall of Williamsburg** (*66 N 6th St. 718–486–5400.*) and **Warsaw** (*261 Driggs Ave. 718-387-0505.*), both located in Brooklyn, are well-known small places with a lot going on. The scene hasn't entirely left Manhattan, though—the **Highline Ballroom**, **Bowery Ballroom** (*6 Delancy St. 212-260-4700.*), and newly opened **Terminal 5** (*610 W 56th St. 212–582–6600.*) are all relatively smaller venues that host a variety of shows throughout the year. **Studio B** (*259 Banker St. 718-389-1880.*) consistently offers the best electronic music shows and DJ sets in the city.

DANCE

From the world's most well known names like American Ballet Theater to companies rooted in New York culture, dance is everywhere in the city. The big names perform at **Lincoln Center** (*Columbus Ave at Broadway and 64th St, lincolncenter.org*), home to the New York City Ballet and ABT. Regular tickets are expensive, but both companies offer student discounts. Smaller companies can be found in their in-house theaters around the city or at venues like

Dance Theatre Workshop (*219 West 19th Street. 212-691-6500.*)—a performance space used by different dance companies through the year—where students always get a 33% discount. **Alvin Ailey** (*405 W 55th St. 212-405-9000.*) and **Martha Graham** (*316 E 63rd St. 212-838-5886.*) are two of the most well known studios in the city—each has its own company that performs at venues around the city. Tickets to these and other under-the-radar shows can be found at **The New York City Center** (*130 W 56th St. 212-247-0430.*), which offers $10 tickets for college students.

VISUAL ART

New York's museum culture is legendary; from the Metropolitan Museum of Art, the Western Hemisphere's largest art museum, to smaller, special-interest galleries scattered here and there, the city's museums serve as cultural institutions that often feature talks, films, and special events in addition to their regular collections.

Galleries are great for checking out emerging artists and scoring glasses of free wine. Unlike museums, galleries usually operate on limited schedules, so use a site like ***TheNewYorkArtWorld.com*** for a complete list of venues and hours.

Chelsea

New York's most famous gallery neighborhood. Between 20th and 27th Streets from 9th to 10th Avenue, sidewalks are lined with galleries and showrooms which house everything from paintings to ceramics and installation art. Most galleries are open weekdays from 11am to 6pm, but the best time to check them out are Thursdays between 6pm and 8pm, when many galleries have free public openings. Experienced gallery owners immediately spot gallery-hoppers, but for those able to shrug off disgruntled glares, this is a great way to load up on free food and early-evening booze.

Williamsburg
Galleries are a part of the culture in this famously artistic neighborhood. Showrooms span all of Williamsburg, from Kent to Havemeyer between S. 5th Street and N. 10th, but the largest cluster is on Grand Street just east of Bedford. It's the perfect place for an afternoon stroll past cutting-edge art.

DUMBO
The wide-open studios and spaces in this Brooklyn neighborhood make it the ideal place for art-lovers to browse. On the first Thursday of every month there is a Gallery Walk from 5:30pm to 8:30pm in which all the galleries open their doors to fellow artists, buyers, and appreciators alike.

THEATER

A Broadway show is an essential NYC experience, but this prestige comes with a downside. Times Square, once a haven for hookers and hustlers, is now packed to bursting with chain restaurants and tourists. Many Broadway shows have also gone the way of cheap profits: rehashed jukebox musicals or Disney movies are just as common as groundbreaking theater on Broadway. Luckily, those in search of more worthwhile performances have plenty of options in Off-Broadway theaters.

Broadway tickets bought the old-fashioned way can run up to $450, and orchestra-level tickets for almost any major show will cost $100 at minimum. A great way to get low-price tickets to a Broadway show (by definition, one in a theater with over 499 seats) is by "rushing" the show. Rush tickets are available the day of the performance for about $20, and are often in the first few rows of the orchestra sections. Some shows have general rushes, which operate on a first-come, first-serve basis—meaning you may need to show up pretty early to secure your spot in line. Other shows have lottery-rushes in which anyone at the theater at a specific time can put their name into a lottery for the prime, cheap seats. For a complete (constantly changing) list of Broadway rush policies as well as information about standing-room-only tickets, visit **Playbill.com**.

The **TKTS** booth in Times Square (*Marriott Marquis, W. 46th St between Broadway and 8th Ave, tdf.org/TKTS*) is a beloved New York institution that sells cheap day-of-show tickets to many Broadway shows. Again, expect to wait in line. Tickets are rarely as well priced or placed as the ones you can score from a rush, but they will save you 25 to 75% of the regular ticket price.

Bigger doesn't always mean better, and for a lot less money, Off-Broadway shows often offer all, if not more, of the excitement, and creativity of Broadway shows. The theaters where these shows take place are generally more aware of student budgets than their larger neighbors, and almost all of them offer student tickets ranging from about $10 to $20. The most well known names in Off-Broadway theater include **Playwrights Horizons** (*416 W 42nd St. 212-564-1235.*), **New York Theatre Workshop** (*79 E 4th St. 212-780-9037.*)**, The Public Theater** (*425 Lafayette St. 212-539-8500.*), and **Manhattan Theatre Club** (*Various locations. 212-399-3000.*). Look at individual websites for student policies. Sometimes tickets to the best of the best can be completely free. Tickets to **Shakespeare in the Park** (*Delacorte Theater in Central Park, PublicTheater.org*) and shows at **Juilliard** (*Lincoln Center, Juilliard.edu*) will only cost you the time of waiting in line.

FILM

Going to a movie theater in the city can be a trip—ticket lines stretch out the door even at the most irregular times, theaters are often stacked up many flights of escalators, and rowdy crowds overfilling the cinemas make watching a movie an interactive experience. **AMC/Lowes** (*AMCTheatres.com*) is the biggest, most expensive name for blockbuster films—they have theaters around the city and throughout the boroughs.

For art and independent films, the options are endless. Film festivals are constantly held around the city and are a great way to score cheap tickets to the newest, hippest flicks, as well as to experience genuine cinema culture. The most well known festivals are the **New York Film Festival** (*Filmlinc.com/nyff/nyff.html*), the **Tribeca Film Festival** (*TriBeCaFilmFestival.org*), and the **Rooftop Films** festival (*RooftopFilms.com*), which takes place during the summer at outdoor venues throughout the boroughs.

The **Walter Reade Theater** (*at Lincoln Center, FilmLinc.com*) has a regular schedule of indie films and interesting film-related events like receptions and classes. The Museum of Modern Art also regularly shows art films (*53rd St between 5th and 6th Ave, MoMA.org*). **The Angelika** (*18 W. Houston St, AngelikaFilmCenter.com*) and **Film Forum** (*209 W. Houston St, FilmForum.org*) are the city's most well known art-houses—they play the blockbusters and big names of the art-film world with schedules as regular and convenient as big-name movie theaters. Unfortunately, at 12 bucks a pop, ticket prices aren't any better than at regular theaters.

TOP 5 INDEPENDENT BOOKSTORES

SPOONBILL AND SUGARTOWN BOOKSELLERS

fter you sell your books, nestle up on antique rugs with the housecat and read from the extensive selection of rare art books at this cozy Williamsburg spot.
218 Bedford Ave between N. 4th and 5th Streets. (718) 387-7322. SpoonbillBooks.com

SHAKESPEARE AND CO BOOKSELLERS

This self-described "independent alternative" has several locations throughout Manhattan and Brooklyn at which you can buy and sell books and attend frequent readings.
To find a location: .ShakeandCo.com

DRAMA BOOKSHOP

This favorite of actors and writers often serves as more of a no-borrow library where artists come to peruse, read, and study the most current scripts.
250 W. 40th St. between 7th and 8th Avenues. (212) 544-0595. DramaBookshop.com

BOOK CULTURE

Columbia students and professors use this packed, academic bookstore rather than more commercial options for the best names in university presses and used textbooks.
536 W. 112th St. between Broadway and Amsterdam. (212)-865-1588. BookCulture.com

THE STRAND

The store's motto says it all: "Over 18 Miles of Books." Used, new, and rare in every subject you can imagine.
828 Broadway (at 12th St.) 212-473-1452. StrandBooks.com

SHOPPING

It is no surprise that shoppers love New York City—prices run the gamut from dirt-cheap to mortgage-sized. Whether you're looking for something utilitarian or truly quirky, you can find everything you ever wanted and never knew you needed. There are nearly as many boutiques, department stores, and specialty shops as there are restaurants and delis to refuel for more shopping. So patience, comfortable shoes, and the ability to take in a lot at once are musts.

HIGH-END ATTIRE

Greenwich Village boutiques arguably represent the best of New York shopping. Barely the size of large walk-in closets, the area's boutiques boast off-beat jewelry and funky clothing by burgeoning young designers. Many are brand-name powerhouses that have capitalized upon the Greenwich Village name, such as Comme des Garcons (*520 W. 22nd St, 212-604-5900*), Chanel (*139 Spring St, 212-334-0055*) and Anna Sui (*113 Greene St, 212-941-8406*). Yet others like Sorelle Firenze (*139 1/2 Reade St, 212-571-2720*) carry girly knickers and dresses you will not find anywhere else. Numerous other hole-in-the-wall boutiques, unique for their ability to bridge the gap between art gallery and mere clothing shop, dot the neighborhood.

Diverging from the bohemian aesthetic of the Village boutiques are the **Fifth Avenue flagship stores** that one typically associates with Manhattan: Louis Vuitton (*1 E. 57th St, 212-759-5195*), Gucci (*685 5th Ave, 212-826-2600*), Saks Fifth Avenue (*611 5th Ave, 212-753-4000*), Bergdorf Goodman (*754 5th Ave, 212-872-2700*), and every other store and designer listed in *Vogue*. Though for most of us, a thousand-dollar dress is not quite worth sleeping on the sidewalk for a month, window-shopping in this neighborhood is downright fun.

CLOTHING ON THE CHEAP

For those who want the designer pieces while still being able to feed themselves on a daily basis, fear not. Only blocks from Fifth Avenue shopping you may be able to find that same designer belt or bouclé jacket at one of the many **Upper East Side thrift shops** like Designer Resale (*324 E. 81st St, 212-734-3639*), where last season's pieces have been tossed away for the rest of us to pick. Because designer clothing gets snapped up not only by Manhattan fashionistas, but also due to the infinite photo shoots, design houses, and entertainment projects happening at any given moment, the city is a goldmine for couture at bargain prices. The second-hand shop INA (*208 E. 73rd St, 212-249-0014*), for instance, recently sold off the wardrobe of the 2008 blockbuster *Sex and the City*. Other department stores specialize in bargain-priced, brand-new designer clothing that has found its way to the store because it is overstock, a slightly odd make, or simply last season.

Many of the city's **bargain department stores** will be helpful. Century 21 (*22 Cortlandt St, 212-227-9092*) in the Financial District has been known to carry Pucci bikinis for $80, Costume National dresses for under $50, and other rare finds worth the digging. Stores like Daffy's (*3 E. 18th St, 212-529-4477*) typically have less to offer, but may still offer a Theory dress for $50. The "Vault" section of Filene's Basement (*620 6th Ave, 212-620-3100*) may look dismal at first, but after calculating the deductions and untangling the hangers, you might come up with a Chloe dress at one-fifth the price. When shopping at these stores, be forewarned that they do not offer the same leisurely atmosphere of a SoHo boutique. A good two hours is needed to dig through bins and sort through racks of discounted goods.

Other **downtown thrift stores** have developed a cult following for their funky pieces and designer labels which, unlike many designer resale stores in the city, are actually sold for thrift-store prices. At Tokio 7 (*64 E. 7th St, 212-353-8443*), for instance, a Vivienne Westwood vest may be snatched up for a tenth of the original price. Screaming Mimi's (*382 Lafayette St, 212-677-6464*) offers boldly patterned, retro dresses that would make your mother proud. Best of all, one can even turn the hunt into a philanthropy event: Housing Works Thrift Shops sells designer duds and housewares gems, and its proceeds benefit people living with HIV/AIDS. The store has several locations around the city, including Chelsea (*143 W. 17th St, 212-366-0820*), Gramercy (*157 E. 23rd St, 212-529-5955*), and the Upper West Side (*306 Columbus Ave, 212-579-7566*).

Yet the more practical shopper, who is in the market for perhaps a warm winter jacket and not a pair of patent leather stilettos, should not fret. For every flower pin and cashmere shrug that can be found, more typical, everyday items can also be found. Go to Macy's (*151 W. 34th St, 212-594-0018*), the hallmark of Herald Square, or Lord & Taylor (*424 5th Ave, 212-391-3344*) in Midtown East to find basics like Perry Ellis oxfords and Calvin Klein boxer-briefs. The ambiance may remind you of the suburban mall of your childhood, but while these big stores carry the same labels as their other branches, many of them also show designer lines to cater to the New York clientele.

SHOES AND ACCESSORIES

The shoes, bags, and other accessories one needs to complete a look can be found in these mega-stores as well as their intimate boutique counterparts. Major sales and discounts at stores like Century 21 mean that one can snatch up a pair of Pucci heels for about half of the original price tag, or a Betsey Johnson belt for $40. Other stores that have become favorites of accessory addicts on a budget include Forever 21 (*50 W. 34th St, 212-564-2346*) and H&M (*640 5th Ave, 212-489-0390*), where a trendy vinyl clutch can be bought for the price of lunch.

For women seeking to decorate themselves with accessories that no one else has, the jewelry shops in the **Garment District** promise an overwhelming selection. Beginning at Times Square, a walk down Broadway or 6th Avenue towards Herald Square holds enough beads and baubles to distract even the most focused passerby. Loads of semi-precious to not-so-precious stones and beads can be bought for wholesale prices, allowing one to string together a necklace that would sell in Bloomingdale's for 10 times as much.

If this all sounds like too much effort, head to the **weekend flea markets** where you can combine your accessory shopping with eating. Vendors at the SoHo Antiques Fair (*Grand St and Broadway, 212-682-2000*), held every Saturday and Sunday from 9-5, arrive bearing collections of jackets, vintage purses, antiques, and other creations. You can look forward to people-watching while you shop for those funky, one-of-a-kind pieces. The Hell's Kitchen flea market (*125 W. 18th St, 212-243-5343*) also promises vintage jewelry finds, among an eclectic assortment of other treasures, and is open 6:30am-5pm every Saturday and Sunday.

OUTDOOR NY

Living in a city of skyscrapers is no excuse for staying indoors all the time. In New York life is just as good in the great outdoors as it is in the great indoors, with a variety of options for all seasons and tastes.

PARKS

Even the least adventurous city dwellers have no excuse not to take advantage of New York's many beautiful parks—almost every neighborhood is bound to have one within walking distance. Parks are generally open from sunrise until 1am unless otherwise noted.

Central Park
New York's biggest and most famous park, stretching 50 blocks and spanning 3 avenues. See pages 48-49.

Riverside Park
Stretching four miles along the Hudson River, from 72nd to 158th Street, this park is perhaps the most pleasant of New York's waterfront parks. Not only does the serpentine riverside path provide a scenic route for joggers, bikers, and strollers, the park also includes a skate park, playgrounds, sports courts and fields, as well as shady areas perfect for picnicking. Also contained within the park's sprawling property is a big chunk of the Manhattan Waterfront Greenway and the 110-slip public marina, an important part of the New York Water Trail.
72nd-158th St along the Hudson River. ❶❷❸ *to 72nd or 96th.*

Hudson River Park
Picking up near where Riverside Park ends, the Hudson River Park reaches from 59th Street to Battery Park and provides the most access to boating activities on the Hudson. Kayak trips, lessons, and launchings are available at piers 96, 66, and 40; a kayak and canoeing permit is required, but can be acquired on-site. Fishing is also an option, and although no permit is required, there are regulations as to how many and what kinds of fish can be caught. Back on land is the Habitat Garden adjacent to Pier 66, in Chelsea, where a wide array of butterflies and moths make their home.
Battery Park-59th St along the Hudson River. ❶ *to Christopher St.*

East River Park
Along FDR Drive and the East River from Montgomery to E. 12th Street is the East River Park, another project of former NYC Parks Commissioner, Robert Moses. The largest open green space in the Lower East Side, the park includes a recently renovated amphitheatre, football, soccer and baseball fields, tennis and basketball courts, running and cycling paths, a river promenade, and great views of the Manhattan and Brooklyn Bridges. This is a park to be active in; there are not many places to simply sit and relax.
Montgomery St to 12th St along the East River. ❻❿⓯⓴ *to Delancey St-Essex St.*

Prospect Park
Brooklyn's largest and most popular park is a 586-acre world unto itself, and a great place to spend a day of recreation and relaxation. Attractions, amenities, and activities are many, including the Long Meadow, the largest meadow in any US park, kayaking, canoeing, or paddleboating in the park's waterways, athletic fields of every kind, picnic and barbecue areas, birdwatching locales, and fishing spots.
Prospect Park West to Ocean Ave between Parkside Ave and Eastern Parkway. ❽❾ *to Prospect Park.* ❷❸ *to Grand Army Plaza.* ❻ *to 15th St-Prospect Park.*

Flushing Meadows Corona Park
The largest park in Queens was the sight of two 20th century World's Fairs and can still dazzle visitors today with its state-of-the-art recreation center and other attractions. Not only does the park include the regular assortment of playing fields (with a rare treat in the cricket field), playgrounds, and promenades, it also boasts a zoo, an art museum, a botanical garden, a science

museum, and a baseball stadium.
Between Grand Central Parkway and Van Wyck Expressway north of Jackie Robinson Parkway. 7 *to Willets Point-Shea Stadium.*

Van Cortlandt Park
This park located in the Bronx occupies more than 1,000 acres. Playgrounds and playing fields are scattered around the outer edges of the park, circling a heartland of richly forested grounds where visitors can play golf, ride a horse, stroll by the borough's largest freshwater lake, or simply enjoy the shade of a lofty oak.
Between Broadway and Jerome Ave north of West Gun Hill Rd. 1 *to 242nd or* 4 *to Woodlawn.*

SUMMER

Summers in New York aren't extraordinarily hot, but the humidity can be unbearable. Fortunately, the city is an archipelago, so a day at the beach, an afternoon boat ride, or a short dip in the pool is always within reach.

Beaches
The city's urban beaches are surprisingly clean and only a subway ride away. Day-trippers can check out the many suburban beaches within reach of the city.

Rockaway Beach
Wryly referred to as the Irish Riviera, Queens' Rockaway Beach is a friendly, well-maintained place, despite being the country's largest urban beach. Sports courts are available; for some more risqué fun, head to the clothing-optional Federal Beach.
718-318-4000. A *to Beach 25-116.*

Coney Island
There may be no better place to spend a summer day than the world-famous Coney Island. Everyone should come to this landmark location at least once, and quickly, before it is changed beyond recognition by a multi-million-dollar reconstruction project. Hot dogs, cheese fries, and cotton candy provide the bulk of the food here. Fun is provided by Astroland, the endangered amusement park, with rides that range from the kid-friendly to the stomach-churning. The Cyclone, the park's famous wooden roller coaster, leaves even longtime veterans screaming on the first drop. The beach itself has been cleaned up considerably in past years and provides a beautiful backdrop for a walk along the boardwalk or a good place to take a refreshing dip (just remember to wait a half an hour after that chili-cheese dog.)
ConeyIsland.com. N Q F *to Coney Island-Stillwell Ave.*

Jones Beach
The closest Long Island beach is also the most popular for city residents, meaning it is sure to be crowded. Still, the two-mile boardwalk, two public pools and six-mile stretch of beach should be enough to ensure a good time, and the short distance from the city makes it perfect for a one-day vacation.
516-785-1600. JonesBeach.com. LIRR to Wantagh, $3 shuttle to Jones Beach.

Jacob Riis
Noted for its clean sands and clear water, this Queens beach in Gateway National Recreation Center also boasts a topless/clothing-optional area. Come for the diverse mix of people, as typical family groups flock elsewhere. The more isolated East End is a famous spot for gay New Yorkers.
718-318-4300. 2 *to Flatbush, Q35 bus to Riis Beach.*

Boating
At many waterside city parks, there are places to launch a kayak and canoe or rent a paddleboat. For those who don't want to row their own boats, there are also companies that provide commercial boating services.

NYC Water Trail
The NYC Water Trail winds around all five boroughs and connects 160 square miles of rivers,

bays, creeks, inlets, and ocean for kayaking, canoeing, and open-water rowing crafts. The scenery ranges from city skylines to natural wonders such as bird sanctuaries and marshlands.

Maps and permits required for kayaking and canoeing are available online at the NYC Parks site.
NYCGovParks.org/Sub_Things_To_Do/Facilities/Kayak

The Chelsea Screamer
The fastest high-speed commercial boat in New York is available June through October on a charter basis. Parties of up to 54 people can enjoy a rollicking ride that goes by the Brooklyn Bridge, Ellis Island, the New York Harbor, and the Statue of Liberty.
Chelsea Piers (W 23rd Street at the Hudson River). 212-924-6262. ❶ to 23rd. ChelseaScreamer.com

Circle Line
A more relaxing boating journey is provided by Circle Line, which advertises itself as a mini-vacation. It certainly does seem that way on its cruise ships, which all have food, beverages, beer, and wine on board. There are several cruise options to choose from, including the 3-hour full-island cruise and the 75-minute Liberty cruise, not to mention special live music and holiday cruises.
Pier 83 (W 42nd St at the Hudson River). 212-563-3200. ❶❷❸❺❻❼❽❼ to 42nd St-Times Square, ❹❻❺ to 42nd.

Exercise
New York has no shortage of opportunities for exercise. Biking, running, horseback riding—the city is a great place to do it all.

Greenways and Bicycling
NYC Greenways are paths and trails linking parks and communities throughout the city and providing space for biking, jogging, walking, and in-line skating. Most Greenways are waterside or next to flourishing green spaces.
NYCGovParks.org

Mountain Biking
Because the Greenway system does not allow off-trail riding, the New York City Mountain Bike association partnered with the Department of Parks and Recreation to open mountain biking trails in Highbridge Park in Manhattan and Cunningham Park in Queens.
NYCGovParks.org/Parks/HighbridgePark, NYCGovParks.org/Parks/CunninghamPark. Highbridge Park: ❶ to 168th, Cunningham Park: LIRR to Hollis Station.

Horseback Riding
For equestrian fun, a select number of New York parks provide horse rentals and bridle paths. At Pelham Bay Park, horseback riders can visit the Bronx Equestrian Center and rent a horse for $30/person for a one-hour trail ride or take a 30-minute private lesson for $40. Another center is the Riverdale Equestrian Centre in Van Cortlandt Park. The center has four outdoor riding rings and an indoor arena, and provides lessons throughout the year.
Bronx Equestrian Center: 718-885-0551. Riverdale Equestrian Centre: 718-548-4848.

WINTER
Winter in New York can be both brutal and beautiful. The snow-draped city may be a peaceful sight from a heated room, but for those willing to bundle up and put on some long johns, the great white outdoors can be a fabulous time.

Sledding
The most popular locales for sledding enthusiasts are Central Park, particularly Pilgrim's Hill right past the 74th St boat pond, and Riverside Park, which has long slopes at nearly every entrance. For a true daylong sledding expedition, head out to Brooklyn's Fort Greene Park, where countless hills offer straight-down drops, slower slopes, and even obstacles.
FortGreenePark.org. ❷❹❺❻ to DeKalb Ave, ❷❸❹❺ to Nevins.

Skiing
For some, winter means the beginning of cross-

country skiing season. This can be a great form of exercise and can be done nearly anywhere from parks to even the streets—just be careful of cars. For those who prefer faster speeds and downhill thrills, there are many ski resorts in the Hudson Valley, some just an hour's bus ride away.

Hunter Mountain
This three-mountain resort is the largest in the area and is suited for skiers and snowboarders of all abilities and inclinations, whether they prefer bunny slopes or steep speed rides.
800-486-8376.

Holiday Mountain
Located in Monticello, NY, this resort is a favorite of city residents who want to take a day trip. There are fifteen slopes and trails and seven lifts. Not just a ski resort, Holiday Mountain also provides such activities as go-karts, bumper cars, rock-climbing walls, and a potato-sack slide.
845-796-3161.

Ice Skating
It may be tempting to go ice skating in Rockefeller Center, what with the iconic Christmas tree looming above and the hundreds of lights all around. Leave this spot for the tourists—it is more of a photo-op than a quality skating experience. Wollman Rink in Central Park is the largest skating locale in the city, but it is not ideal for a quiet evening. Probably the best place to spend a night on ice is Bryant Park at what is simply called The Pond, which offers free skating admission.
Wollman Rink: East Side at 62nd St. 212-439-6900..
N R W *to 5th Ave.*
Bryant Park: 42nd St at 5th Ave. 212-661-6640..
B D F V *to 42nd St-Bryant Park.*

CLUB ATHLETICS
Compete in games, venture out on trips, and party at social events with other young professionals in their 20s and 30s at **Zog Sports** (*ZogSports.org*). Zog donates part of its proceeds to charity, allowing you to "play for your cause"—the winning team gets to select which charitable organization to sponsor. **New York City Social Sports Club** (*NYCSSC.com*) takes a more casual approach ("Playing the game is good, but going to the bar with your team afterwards is better!"), encouraging members to play "casually competitive," co-ed alternative sports like broomball, dodgeball, kickball, or wiffleball. Soccer fanatics should check out **Urban Soccer** (*UrbanSoccer.com*), which features men's, women's, and co-ed soccer—5, 6, 7 and 8-a-side—with multiple leagues for different abilities. The state-of-the-art turf, league referees, and trophies for the winners allow Urban Soccer to provide the right environment for a devoted recreational or competitive player. A nonprofit alternative to other pricey leagues in the city, **New York Fast Pitch Softball League** (*NewYorkFastPitch.com*) is a primarily male 14-team league, though women are allowed to join as well. **Out of Bounds** (*OOBNYC.org*) is a nonprofit organization that supports and promotes sports and recreation for the LGBT community of the greater New York City area, though everyone is invited to play.

RUNNING
New York's many parks and riverside paths make it an ideal city for running. Join a competitive or recreational, track or "road runner" club for athletic motivation, or to contribute points for your team at races. With over 40,000 members, **New York Road Runners** (*NYRR.org*) is an umbrella organization that contains many local running clubs. Membership is not required to join local, affiliated clubs, but many encourage it. Benefits include eligibility for guaranteed entry to the New York City Marathon, reduced fees for NYRR races, fitness classes, clinics, and lectures. Membership fees start at $40/year. **Gotham Knights Track Club** (*GKTC.blogspot.com*) is a more competitive group that runs a variety of races around the city. An affiliate of New York Road Runners, they offer coaching and group runs in addition to races with other clubs. Membeship is free.

OUTDOOR NY 47

CENTRAL PARK

Despite the fact that much of New York's oldest and most iconic park is sculpted to look natural, the park is, in fact, a triumph of urban landscaping. When friends and relatives come to town and want to see "real New Yorkers," take them to visit Manhattan's massive backyard.

Designed by Frederick Law Olmsted and Calvert Vaux and built between 1858 and 1872, 843-acre Central Park stretches from 59th to 110th Street between 5th and 8th Avenue. Construction was a monumental task—to compensate for the swampy terrain, topsoil had to be carted in from New Jersey. For much of the 20th century, the park was in disrepair, but starting in 1980, the **Central Park Conservancy** (*CentralParkNYC.org*) led efforts to revitalize the park. The Conservancy continues to play a huge role in the park's upkeep by organizing programs year-round.

BELOW 86th STREET

It's hard to find a spot in Central Park that isn't great for wandering, but those looking for something to *do* will find more options in the park's southern half. **The Dairy** (*Mid-park at 65th St, 212-794-6564*) is the park's main visitor center; it stocks maps and information on the park, as well as a collection of tchotchkes for tourists. Nearby, **Wollman Rink** (*East Side at 62nd St*) is many natives' pick for the city's best skating rink; unlike the tourist trap at Rockefeller Center, the skaters here tend to be a mix of New Yorkers and out-of-towners. During the holiday season, the mood is especially festive despite the blaring Top-40 hits.

Above the 65th Street Transverse are some of the park's loveliest grounds. The **Sheep Meadow** (*West Side between 66th and 69th St*) provides a huge open space for sunbathers, frisbee players, and readers that's usually packed during the summer. **The Mall** (*Mid-park from 66th to 72nd St*) serves as Central Park's great promenade. Flanked by enormous elm trees, this part of the park leans toward the formal, and leads to the spectacular **Bethesda Terrace and Fountain** (*Mid-park at 72nd St*), which provides a lookout towards the Lake and is often packed with musicians, dancers, and families. To the west is **Strawberry Fields** (*West Side at 72nd St*), a quiet garden dedicated to the memory of adopted New Yorker John Lennon; its famous "Imagine" mosaic is usually cluttered with candles and rose petals. Those with children will face the unavoidable—a trip to either the landmark **Carousel** (*Mid-park at 64th St*) or the **Central Park Zoo** (*East Side at 65th St, 212-435-6900*), which, despite its tiny size, manages to be pretty fun.

North of 72nd Street, the crowds thin out a bit. The **Lake** (*Mid-park between 79th and 72nd St*) has some of the park's most picturesque views. It's hard to pass cast-iron **Bow Bridge** (*74th St*) without interrupting someone's wedding photos. **Loeb Boathouse** (*East Side between 74th and 75th St, 212-517-2233*) has rowboat rentals for fairly inexpensive prices. Across the lake is **The Ramble** (*Mid-park between 73rd and 79th St*), which has proven the bane of many hurried New Yorkers; its flowing streams, meandering paths, and thick web of trees make it a popular spot for wandering, and bird enthusiasts enjoy the superb bird-watching opportunities the area affords.

Belvedere Castle (*Mid-park at 79th St*), constructed atop the second-highest natural hill in the park, is home to a nature center, but the real attraction is the lookout tower, which has some of the best views of the surrounding area. Immediately north is the **Great Lawn** (*Mid-park between 79th and 85th St*), the geographical heart of the park and the site of many of Central Park's famous outdoor concerts. **Summerstage**, on the East Side near 72nd St, hosts a recurring summer concert series that's also popular (*Summerstage.org*). It's the **Delacorte Theater** (*Mid-park at 80th St*), though, that may be nearest and dearest to New Yorkers—the summer Shakespeare in the Park series, sponsored by the Public Theater (*PublicTheater.org*), provides Shakespeare plays, often featuring big-name actors, free of charge. Waiting in line for tickets, usually for several hours, is a New York tradition and a true endurance trial–lines usually form by 6am.

ABOVE 86th STREET

The space between 86th and 96th Streets is dominated by the **Jacqueline Kennedy Onassis Reservoir**, which is surrounded by the city's most popular running path. A complete loop is 1.58 miles, and it's not uncommon to see the rich and famous on their daily runs.

Above 96th Street, the park is filled almost entirely with locals. The **North Meadow Recreation Center** (*East Side at 97th St, 212-348-4867*) has a collection of sporting equipment for the nearby North Meadow, another one of the park's great open spaces. The equipment is rented out for free, and the center also has a number of indoor sporting facilities, including basketball courts and a rock-climbing wall. The **North Woods** (*Mid-park between 102nd and 110th St*), though, is the main attraction this far north; designed by Olmstead and Vaux to mirror an Adirondack ecosystem, this dense patch of woods is a protected preserve guaranteed to make visitors forget they're in New York—the babbling streams and birdsong drown out all traffic noise.

In the northeast corner of the park are two of the park's most stately landscapes. The **Conservatory Garden** (*East Side at 104th Street*) is one of the few parts of Central Park that resembles a French garden; the neat rows of shrubs, fountains, and statues seem a world removed from the rest of the park. The **Harlem Meer** (*East Side between 106th and 110th St*) is surrounded by open lawn space that's perfect for local families; catch-and-release fishing is permitted as well. The Meer sits next to the **Charles A. Dana Discovery Center** (*East Side at 110th Street, 212-860-1370*). The park's newest visitor center, the Dana Center is geared toward family programs, which include walking tours and youth education, and also sponsors a number of holiday events. The summertime **Harlem Meer Performance Festival** is one of the most popular, now celebrating its 15th year of bringing jazz, blues, gospel, and world artists to the northern edge of the park.

CENTRAL PARK 49

DAY TRIPS

Even the most devoted New Yorker will admit that sometimes you just need a break from the city. Luckily, there are plenty of quick and easy ways to escape, if only for a day. Rediscover nature, explore history, wander through fairs and amusement parks, or simply enjoy the change in scenery. It's all only a short bus or train ride away.

On the easternmost tip of Long Island about 120 miles away from the city, lies the small coastal town of **Montauk**. It was bought and developed by entrepreneur Carl Fisher in the 1920s, who envisioned it as "the Miami Beach of the north." The stock market crash of 1929, however, halted tourism and shattered Fisher's dream. Montauk then served as a Navy Base during World War II, and housed Air Force radar stations during the Cold War. Today, Montauk, more casual than the Hamptons, is once again a popular tourist destination, which appeals to sunbathers, adventurers, and history buffs alike. Authorized by President George Washington and built in 1797, the **Montauk Point Lighthouse** (*631-668-2544, MontaukLighthouse.com*) is the oldest lighthouse in the state. Brave the 137-step climb to the top for great views and visit the museum for exhibits on Montauk's history.

Spend the rest of the day relaxing on Montauk's famous beaches. Learn how to surf at **Eastend Surfing School** (*917-613-2662, EastEndSurf.com*) and take on the waves at **Ditch Plains beach.** If you prefer, sail away, take a fishing trip or cruise on one of the many boats dotting the marina. Have dinner watching the sunset at the **Sea Grille at Gurney's Inn** (*631-668-2345, Gurneys-Inn.com*) before heading back to New York City. The Long Island Railroad makes regular trips to Montauk from Penn Station (*MTA.info*, $30 round trip), while the Hampton Jitney offers bus service to Montauk from various stops in Manhattan and Brooklyn (*HamptonJitney.com*, $53 round trip).

The **New York Renaissance Faire** (*RenFair.com/NY*) runs from early August to late September in Tuxedo, N.Y., about 35 miles northwest of the city. Buses leave from Port Authority directly to the fair and back. Leave your inhibitions at home and dress up if the mood strikes you, for a genuinely good time exploring the sights, sounds, and tastes of a recreated medieval village. There's jousting and knife throwing, minstrels and troubadours, spectacular shows and performances, and of course, roasted turkey legs. Don't miss the production of Shakespeare's, *A Midsummer Night's Dream*, a NY Renaissance Faire tradition.

For even more history, hop on a Port Authority bus or train departing from Penn Station for **Philadelphia**. William Penn, an early proponent of religious freedom, founded the city in 1682, and it rose to eminence as the largest city in the American colonies. Of course, Philadelphia's history is linked to the American Revolution; the city hosted the first meetings between colonies in response to the taxes imposed by the British, saw the signing of the Declaration of Independence, and served as the nation's first capital. Start your day off in the city's historic district. Make lots of time for **Independence National Historic Park**—it's dubbed "the most historic square mile in America" for a reason. In this small area, you'll find Independence Hall, where delegates signed the Declaration of Independence and adopted the Constitution. There's also Liberty Bell and Congress Hall, where the nation's first senators and representatives convened. In the surrounding area, visitors can also find Benjamin Franklin's grave at Christ's Church, Betsy Ross' house, the City Tavern, and the Edgar Allen Poe National Historic Site. The Independence National

Historic Park **Visitors Center** *(800-537-7676, IndependenceVisitorCenter.com)* offers walking tours, just in case all the sights get a little overwhelming. Once you've had your fill of history, stop by the **Reading Terminal Market** *(215-922-2317, ReadingTerminalMarket.org)* and meander through the stalls of produce, flowers, cheese, and handmade soap. Philadelphia is also home to many great museums: You can find Rodin's famous statue, *The Thinker*, at the **Rodin Museum** *(215-568-6026, RodinMuseum.org)*, or see the handwritten manuscript of James Joyce's *Ulysses*, a first-edition copy of *Pilgrim's Progress*, and other cultural artifacts at the **Rosenbach Museum** *(215-732-1600, Rosenbach.org)*.

At the turn of the century, **Atlantic City** was a real-estate hot spot and the playground of the rich and famous. Large, ritzy hotels lined the city's boardwalk, each more glamorous than the one before. After World War II, however, the opulence and grandeur of Atlantic City's gold-capped landmarks died away as the city was ravaged by divestment, poverty, and crime. Casino gambling was legalized in Atlantic City in 1978 in an attempt to revitalize its failing economy, giving rise to the first casino on the east cost, Resorts International. Atlantic City may lack the splendor it held in its heyday, but it retains its own slightly self-conscious charm. Atlantic City invented the amusement pier in 1882, and the legacy lives on boardwalks like Central Pier and Steel Pier, which feature amusement park favorites like roller coasters, ferris wheels, kitschy shops, and street food. While casino gambling is Atlantic City's main draw, the casino resorts, like Donald Trump's **Taj Mahal** *(609-449-1000, TrumpTaj.com)* are worth a visit on their own merit. There's also a **Ripley's Believe It or Not Museum** *(609-347-2001 RipleysAtlanticCity.com)* and an Atlantic City Historical Museum. New Jersey Transit *(NJTransit.com)* and Greyhound *(Greyhound.com)* offer bus service to Atlantic City departing from Port Authority; the ride takes about 2 ½ hours.

If you're looking to escape the urban confines of the city, the laid back arts-centered town of **Beacon** is little more than an hour's train ride away on than Metro-North railroad. The ride takes you up along the Hudson, providing breathtaking views of the river as well as the Palisades.

Over the past years, the town has been developing a name as the next big thing in the art world. The main arts attraction in the town is the prestigious **Dia:Beacon** *(845-440-0100)*. The foundation has transformed an abandoned Nabisco box-making warehouse along the Hudson into a feat of modern architecture and landscaping, forcing comparisons to the likes of Renzo Piano. Inside, one sees slivers of the gorgeous hills outside juxtaposed with large scale art projects from 1960 to the present, including works by Andy Warhol, Sol LeWitt, Louise Bourgeois, and Richard Serra. Allow several hours to meander the huge rooms and bask in the great works or take a walk through their sculpture garden.

The little town however, also provides a number of alternative activities. With Chelsea type galleries lining Beacon's **Main Street** beside antique stores, there are a plethora of shopping and browsing choices. If you're not in the mood for art or shopping, the town offers a number of small parks as well as the **Hudson Highlands State Park** *(845-225-7207)* just south of the town. Whether you want to go for a hike or a pleasant stroll, the town offers it all. Of course, there are also a number of dining options and leisurely cafes where locals will come to chat, read, or relax. Without a doubt, the town's easy-going attitude and friendly locale makes this the ultimate day trip for the city escapist.

DAY TRIPS 51

LGBT

Meeting people in New York can be hard, even more so if you're gay. The sometimes overwhelming options from fast-paced club scenes to rowdy Pride celebrations to laid-back discussion groups can leave the newly relocated wondering where to find a niche. But LGBT life in New York offers a little something for everyone—you just need to know where to look.

COMMUNITY

Many people seek a community upon first arriving in the city, wanting low-key environments in which to meet other LGBT New Yorkers. **The LGBT Community Center** *(208 W. 13th St, 212-620-7310)* is a great place to start, hosting various drop-in groups, film screenings, political discussions, and much more. Volunteering or interning for organizations such as **Lambda Legal, GLAAD,** and the **LGBT Project of the ACLU** not only supply opportunities to meet others in the LGBT community, but also help create social change. Gay men can make friends and meet future lovers participating in cultural, athletic, nightlife, and travel excursions through **Urban Outings** *(UrbanOutings.com)*. Pop into **The Oscar Wilde Bookshop** *(15 Christopher St at Gay St, 212-255-8097)*, the oldest LGBT bookshop in the world, for a great selection of gay-themed books, DVDs, and gift items. For more of an LGBT art fix, head to New York's Annual LGBT Film Festival **NewFest** *(IFC Center, 323 6th Ave at W. 3rd St, 212-571-2170)*, presenting film, video, and other media addressing LGBT themes from all over the world.

Those in need of queer-friendly, low-cost medical services need look no further than **Callen Lorde Community Health Center** *(356 W. 18th St, 212-271-7200)*, devoted to the health concerns of the LGBT communities regardless of ability to pay. Most commonly known within the transgender community for the low-cost, cross-gender hormones prescriptions they provide, Callen Lorde also offers services for lesbian health, sexual health, and senior health, among other services.

NEIGHBORHOODS

Gay pride flags abound throughout **Chelsea**, where muscle shirt-clad gay men strut the streets. For a break from all the glitter, **Hell's Kitchen** has become the latest destination for gay men to see and be seen. Gay women can find a home among the tree-lined streets of **Park Slope**. These days, Park Slope has become overrun with yuppies pushing twin strollers, leading many queer women to find homes in other locations throughout Brooklyn, Queens and the Bronx.

PRIDE EVENTS

For the entire month of June, gay pride takes center stage in New York, inspiring countless Pride parties at gay bars and clubs, as well as many festivals. The largest are Manhattan's huge **Pridefest** and **Pride Parade** *(NYCPride.org)*, when painted drag queens don sequined gowns, lesbians sport bikini tops, and straight allies hold signs proclaiming their love for gay family members and friends.

Each borough hosts its own Pride festival each weekend of June. The month kicks off the first weekend with **Queens Pride**, beginning with a parade and ending with a rally. Staten Island locals gather together the second weekend for the **Staten Island LGBT Pride Parade & Festival**. **Brooklyn Pride** follows, taking over Prospect Park for a daytime Pride festival leading into a night parade. Baretto Point Park gets a little bit gayer during the **Bronx Pride Festival** the third weekend of the month.

In response to male-dominated, corporate-sponsored Pride events, the **Dyke March** (*NYCDykeMarch.org*) is a protest rather than a parade, held the day before the Manhattan Pride Parade. Participants bring drums, hula hoops, and signs in a fun, socially conscious rally for change.

NIGHTLIFE

A gay night on the town can run the gamut from strobe-light-filled gay boy bars to trendy lesbian dance parties to casual mixed bars. Take your pick from the varied clubs, parties, and lounges, providing a place for all looking for a fierce, fabulous night out. Queer women dance the night away at **Cattyshack** (*249 4th Ave at Carroll St, Brooklyn, 718-230-5740*), where hip hop hits blast downstairs, '80s favorites play upstairs, smokers hang out on the outdoor deck, and pool players can grab a game. Those seeking a friendly neighborhood bar atmosphere can walk a few blocks over to **Ginger's Bar** (*363 5th Ave near 5th St, Brooklyn, 718-788-0924*). For more casual conversation and jukebox music, lesbians head over to Greenwich Village's **Cubbyhole** (*281 W 12th St at W 4th, 212-243-9041*). A few blocks over, young New Jerseyites, tourists, and New Yorkers alike come together on the dance floor of **Henrietta Hudson "Bar and Girl"** (*438 Hudson St at Morton St, 212-924-3347*). If you're in the mood for thumping bass beats and more racially diverse crowds, **Chueca** (*65-04 Woodside Ave, Astoria, Queens, 718- 424-1171*) is the place to be for a wild time of dancing, hookah smoking, and throwing back shots served by hotshot girls.

Gay men looking for a raunchy night should look no further than Chelsea's **Splash** (*50 W. 17th St, between 5th and 6th Ave, 212-691-0073*). If the go-go boys are too hot to handle, head up to Hell's Kitchen to **The Ritz** (*269 W. 46th St, 212-333-2554*) for a slightly tamer, yet still raucous party. While in the neighborhood, **Therapy** (*348 W 52nd St near 8th Ave, 212-397-1700*) provides a hip setting to sip well-mixed specialty cocktails and even catch a comedy or variety show. Around the corner, **Vlada** (*331 W 51st St, 212-974-8030*) also provides a chic locale in which to catch a show and savor 15 infused vodkas, where refreshingly chilled vodka shots are nestled in a bed of ice. Even sports lovers can find a place of their own and join fellow athletic enthusiasts at **Gym Sports Bar** (*167 8th Ave near 18th St, 212-337-2439*), the only gay sports bar in New York City.

Don't miss out on regular queer parties, which can sometimes be harder to hear about. The most established and most diverse party, ***snapshot*** (*Tuesdays at Bar 13, 35 E 13th St, 212-979-6677*), welcomes all regardless of sexuality, gender identity, or race. Touting itself as "New York's Best Kept Underground Secret," **LoverGirlNYC** (*Saturdays at Club Cache, 221 W. 46th St, 212-252-3397*) provides a welcome alternative to the overwhelmingly white nature of many of the popular gay and lesbian clubs. Other parties to check out include **GirlNation** (*Saturdays at Nation, 12 W 45th St, 212-391-8053*), and monthly parties **Choice Cu*ts** (*at Sultana, 160 N. 4th St near Bedford Ave, Brooklyn, 212-228-7678*), mixed **Sexy Bitch** (*at Sugarland, 221 N. 9th St near Roebling St, Brooklyn*), and mixed **Pantyhos** (*Traveling Fridays; check MySpace.com/PantyHos for location*).

The only group for whom myriad options do not exist is the 18-21 set. 18+ options for gay clubs include mostly male, twinky fun at **Rush** (*formerly known as Heaven, 579 6th Ave, 212-243-6100*) or the recently-revived 18+ "Campus Thursdays" at **Splash** (*50 W 17th St, 212-691-0073*). The best bet for the 18+ female and trans crowd is to check out occasional 18+ queer concerts and dance parties immediately after, held at venues like **Southpaw** (*125 Fifth Ave, Brooklyn, 718-230-0236*) or **Studio B** (*259 Banker St, between Meserole Ave and Calyer St, Brooklyn, 718-389-1880*).

LGBT 53

MEDIA

Trying to navigate the cultural world of New York can be a discouragingly Byzantine undertaking. Transplants looking for guidance may find that the overwhelming volume and variety of media outlets constitutes a puzzle in its own right. Here is a brief sketch of the major newspapers, magazines, radio & television stations, and websites that keep New York informed.

NEWSPAPERS

As the national "paper of record," the **New York Times** *(nytimes.com)* is the gold standard for investigative journalism and features comprehensive coverage and a reliably left-wing editorial page. Its Metro section covers all things New York (and Tri-State); minute-by-minute updates can be found in the section's blog, **City Room** *(CityRoom.Blogs.NYTimes.com)* . The prestige of the *Times* among New York papers is rivaled only by that of the **Wall Street Journal** *(WSJ.com)*, a worldwide powerhouse for business and financial news with a more conservative slant. Though now owned by Rupert Murdoch's News Corp, the *Journal* maintains its high standards and does not (yet) in any way resemble the **New York Post** *(NYPost.com)*, a paper respected for its Sports section but infamous for its emphasis on sensationalism and scandal. The *Post*'s chief competitor in the tabloid market, the **New York Daily News** *(NYDailynews.com)* is sometimes prone to similar theatrics, but it enjoys a reputation for impressive, higher quality photos. Founded as an alternative to the *Times*, the **New York Sun** *(NYSun.com)* places New York news front and center, slants right, and is known for erudite arts coverage. The oldest Spanish-language daily in the US, **El Diario La Prensa** *(ElDiariony.com)* covers local and world affairs, with special attention paid to Latin America. Coming on the scene only recently, the tabloid-format free dailies **AM New York** *(AM.NY.com)* and **Metro New York** *(NY.Metro.us)* are distributed by paid hawkers in areas of high pedestrian traffic. With its left-leaning analysis of culture and current affairs, the **Village Voice** *(VillageVoice.com)* is New York's leading alternative weekly. The **New York Observer** *(Observer.com)* is a weekly paper by and for the rich and powerful, with a focus on culture, real estate, and local politics. The **New York Amsterdam News** *(AmsterdamNews.org)* focuses on issues relevant to the African-American community. The only daily in the city concerned solely with Brooklyn, the **Brooklyn Daily Eagle** *(BrooklynEagle.com)*, is a descendant of the paper Walt Whitman once edited. Perhaps the city's most essential newspaper, **The Onion** *(TheOnion.com)* is a free satirical weekly (with a non-satirical entertainment section, the *A.V. Club*) whose incisive headlines and deadpan style can make it every bit as informative as the *Times*.

MAGAZINES

A dominant force in America, **The New Yorker** *(NewYorker.com)* has been a home for work by J.D. Salinger, Philip Roth, John Updike, and Vladimir Nabokov. Besides being among the most prestigious venues for literary fiction, *The New Yorker* is the quintessential magazine of urban sophistication, featuring scholarly criticism and commentary, reportage, essays on singularly eccentric topics. Also included: "Goings on About Town," a section of reviews and event listings that encompasses a vast portion of New York City's cultural life, as well as "The Talk of the Town," a collection on letters for the better part of its 80+ year existence, of vignettes about life in the city. Required reading for aspiring sophisticates.

Founded in 1968 as a competitor to *The New Yorker*, **New York Magazine** *(NYMag.com)* generally hews a little closer to home. Among the first of the so-called "lifestyle" magazines, *New York* trains a microscopic eye on the food, drink, culture, politics, and gossip of the city. The magazine's website is notable for its exhaustive database of restaurants and bars, as well as its armada of blogs covering the same.

One of the jewels of Tony Elliott's magazine empire, **Time Out New York** (*TimeOut.com/NewYork*) is, like all the other *Time Out*s, published weekly and chock-full of event listings for theater, film, literature, dating, fashion, and art, along with dining and drinking guides. *TONY* is a little showier and has a little less personality than its unbranded cousin, *New York*.

RADIO

New York is the largest media market in the nation, and as such is home to the largest radio audiences. WNYC (*WNYC.com*, 93.9 FM or 820 AM) is the local home of National Public Radio and boasts the largest radio audience in Manhattan and the largest public radio audience in the country. It carries nationally-syndicated programming as well as homegrown shows. In 2006 it spun off WNYC2 (93.9-2 FM), an all-classical channel available over HD radio or the internet. Owned by Columbia University and staffed largely by undergrads, WKCR (*Columbia.edu/cu/wkcr*, 89.9 FM) is a popular noncommercial station committed to alternative, arts-friendly programming and noteworthy for its heavy jazz rotation. Fordham's radio station, WFUV (*WFUV.org*, 90.7 FM), is also a noncommercial station, notable for its adult alternative album format, as well as its affiliation with Public Radio International. Rounding out the independent stations is the listener-supported WFMU (*WFMU.org* 91.1 FM), a national leader among open-format, indie stations.

New York is the birthplace of America's first 24/7 sports talk station, WFAN (*WFAN.com*, 660 AM), formerly the employer of shock jockey Don Imus, as well as home to many prominent commercial stations: WXRK, or K-Rock (*923KRock.com*, 92.3 FM), for modern rock, Hot 97 WQHT (*Hot97.com*, 97.1 FM) for hip-hop, the *Times* owned classical station WQXR (*WQXR.com*, 96.3 FM), and the Spanish-language WSKQ, La Mega 97.9 (*LaMega.LaMusica.com*)—"con la Mega no se juega."

TV

In addition to housing the major American television networks and many cable channels, New York supports many local and public-access channels, including the oldest in the country: the **Manhattan Neighborhood Network** (*MNN.org*), beloved for its offbeat and diverse programming. Owned by the **NYC Media Group** (a city agency), **WNYE-TV** broadcasts **nyctv** (*NYCTV25.com*), which airs "hip," locally-themed shows aimed at a youthful, urbane audience. Channel 13 or **WNET** (*Thirteen.org*) is the local PBS affiliate. On cable, there is **NY1** (*NY1.com*),which is dedicated to 24-hour news and is esteemed for its outer-borough and City Hall coverage.

INTERNET RESOURCES

Traditional media too slow? Try the net. **Gothamist.com** keeps a watchful eye on New York minutiae, which it divides into standard categories like "News," "Arts and Events," and "Food." **Gawker.com** is a snarky gossip and media blog with a fondness for celebrity sightings, while **Curbed.com** covers the vagaries of New York real estate. For indie rockers there is **OhMyRockness.com**, a carefully edited show list with band profiles and features. **NYCBloggers.com** is an aggregate of neighborhood-themed blogs. And finally, should you ever leave your computer, there is **HopStop.com**, a map and directions site which, unlike most of its competitors, provides updated information on subway and bus closures and delays.

HOSTELS

If you want to stay in New York City for cheap, you're going to make some sacrifices in comfort. The most important rule: Be flexible.

Hotels are usually very expensive, especially in Manhattan. For students, a better bet is to stay in a hostel, where you'll get a bed to sleep on and little else, but where you'll rarely spend more than $20 a night. Know your priorities: In general, the cheapest beds come in barracks-style rooms of 10 or more beds, and you run the risk of having your belongings stolen. If you're traveling with a group or need your privacy, you can sometimes get group suites or even single rooms for a bit more.

If you'll be staying in the city for a longer period of time, check **CraigsList.com** for apartment sublets—many residents will sublet their apartments for periods as short as a week at bargain prices. New York real estate offers are snatched up fast, so diligent searching and a fast mouse-finger are the keys to landing a good place.

Jazz Hostels

This chain runs five hostels throughout Manhattan, and its commitment to hospitality and cleanliness makes it a popular choice. Four of the hostels are located in the area between the Upper West Side and Harlem, including the original one, Jazz on the Park, located at 106th Street right next to Central Park. The fifth location, Jazz on the Town, is at Union Square, another prime location offering easy access to all the popular destinations in New York. While prices rise as the number of beds per room decreases, the cheapest beds cost just under $20. The Union Square location is the most popular, despite being the only one without WiFi and an included breakfast. Most people sacrifice these amenities for the location and price. As with most hostels, the rooms are quite small, but the staff's friendliness and knowledge of the city cannot be beat. Good locations and prices make the Jazz hostels a great place to start looking for living accommodations in the city.

Jazz on the Park Hostel. 36 West 106th St **A C E 1 2 3** *to 103rd St. 212-932-1600.*
Jazz on the Town Hostel. 307 E. 14th St **L N Q R W** *to Union Square. (212) 228-2780.*

Continental Hostel

Located on the Upper West Side, this hostel is very popular with student travelers. While rates differ depending on the season, prices generally fall between $15 and $23 for a six-person mixed room and around $40 for a two-person private room. It even offers a single room for $75; while that may seem pricey, not many hostels even offer the security and privacy of your own room. The interior is sleek and modern, and its cleanliness is comparable to its Hotel cousin. Cheap prices coupled with clean rooms and a number of amenities, including WiFi, a lounge filled with popular bar games, and bike and kite rentals make this hostel a prime spot for anybody interested in staying in New York on the cheap.

330 West 95th St **1 2 3** *to 96th St (888) 646-7835.*

Chelsea International Hostel

Once you start moving downtown, prices begin to rise quickly. At this location in Chelsea, prices are generally around $28 a bed and do not come with nearly as many services as the cheaper uptown ones. In one of the safest neighborhoods in New York

and a stone's throw away from the most popular tourist destinations, perhaps the money you save in subway fare will make up the difference.
251 W. 20th St ①②ⒶⒸⒺ *to 23rd St (212) 647-0010.*

Village Inn Hostel
This may be one of the few hostels that doesn't have internet available, but geography and cleanliness again make it extremely sought after. It offers free continental breakfast and one of the most exciting locations in the city, and its proximity to NYU makes for a bustling nightlife scene. Prices rise into the $30s per bed, but with so much to do, you won't find yourself regretting the extra money you spent.
27 E. 7th St ⓃⓇⓌ *to 8th St,* ④⑤ *to Astor Place. (212) 228-0828.*

Lafayette International Hostel
This sparsely furnished hostel is perfect for the traveler seeking only a place to sleep. It is considerably roomier than Manhattan hostels and it offers many of the same amenities, but it is also a little more expensive—rising to $25 for a 6-person mixed room. Located in the heart of Fort Greene, it is a short walk away from world-famous Brooklyn Academy of Music, as well as a number of galleries in nearby Brooklyn Heights.
484 Lafayette Ave, Brooklyn. Ⓖ *to Classon Ave.*

Crown Brownstone
Also in Brooklyn, the size and price make for one of the best deals in the city. At $25 a bed or $125 for a 4-5 person suite, it is perfect for a small group. Four blocks from the nearest subway, the ride to Manhattan may be a little long, but the hostel's proximity to Prospect Park will give you the chance to acquaint yourself with New York's other great green space.
958 St. Mark's Ave, Brooklyn. ②③④⑤ *to Kingston Ave. (347) 240-6593.*

HOSTELS 57

CLASSES

Whether you're a beginning dancer or a published author, creative and professional classes cater to every skill set and proficiency level. Many famous dance studios, culinary institutes, and other institutions host classes taught by accomplished instructors open to the public for a small fee. The classes can serve as stepping stones toward future accomplishment in the field or simply a fun way to spend a Saturday afternoon.

COOKING

Budding chefs can learn basic knife skills while the more experienced study specialized food preparation techniques. From pizza to Thai to Southern, **The Institute of Culinary Education** (*50 W. 23rd St, ICECulinary.com*) has it all. Costs may be steep for cooks on a budget, but the skills learned from these experts make it well worth the price. For instruction in French cuisine, head over to **The French Culinary Institute** (*462 Broadway, FrenchCulinary.com*). Become skilled with a knife in Knife Skills, Deboning, and Filleting and then wow your friends with 25 recipes learned in Essentials of Fine Cooking. Such butter-heavy French cooking may overwhelm calorie counters, who can learn to whip up nutritious meals that actually taste good at the **Natural Gourmet Institute for Food and Health** (*48 W 21st St, NaturalGourmetSchool.com*). Health-minded food lovers can learn gluten-free recipes, explore cooking with seitan or tempeh, or discover the role that organic and grass-fed meat and poultry products play in a healthy diet.

DANCE

Alvin Ailey Extension Classes (*405 W 55th St, AlvinAiley.org*) put Ailey's philosophy—that dance is created by and for the people—into practice. These open-to-the-public classes cover a wide range of styles, from traditional ballet to less traditional pop and lock. For more drop-in dance options, check out the **Broadway Dance Center** (*322 W 45th St, BWYDance.com*). Students can learn traditional ballet, jazz or tap, or variations on those, such as street jazz. Those not already familiar with capoeira, the Brazilian blend of martial arts and dance, can find a friendly introduction at **The Arte Capoeira Center** (*1 E. 28th St at 5th Ave, ArteCapoeira.com*). Capoeira enthusiasts can not only learn techniques and skills, but can also catch Brazilian cultural events including film screenings and parties.

LANGUAGE

Always wanted to learn Japanese? Need to brush up on your French? At **ABC Language Exchange** (*135 W. 29th St, ABCLang.com*), students can choose from over 20 languages, or request instruction in any language desired, taught in one-on-one or group settings. Elevate your American Sign Language finger-spelling skills to conversational signing fluency at the **Sign Language Center** (*39 E. 30th St, SignLanguageCenter.com*).

WRITING

For top-tier writing instruction, **The New School for General Studies** (*NewSchool.edu/GeneralStudies/cont_ed.aspx*) offers poetry, fiction, and nonfiction courses as well as classes on writing fundamentals. Prices here can be steep, so those looking for a more affordable (or free) but still high-quality option should look into the **Gotham Writer's Workshop** (*Various locations, WritingClasses.com*). Writers can not only develop their fiction and poetry abilities, but also their travel writing and stand-up comedy skills.

ACTING

Actors trying to break into the New York theater scene, as well as those looking for a fun experience in their spare time, should check out the huge number of film and theater acting classes. Learn more about acting techniques for TV and movies from established actors, commercial agents, and casting directors at **TVI Actors Studio** (*165 W. 46th St, TVIStudios.com*). Many classes require an audition, but can be taken in the evenings after school or work, like those at **The Acting Studio, Inc.** (*244 W. 54th St, ActingStudio.com*), which offers four levels of instruction. For a more serious conservatory-style experience, actors can audition for the two-year program or the summer workshops of the **Neighborhood Playhouse School of the Theatre** (*340 E. 54th St, NeighborhoodPlayhouse.org*). **Upright Citizens Brigade** offers a variety of improv classes, from Improv 101 to advanced workshops and comedy writing seminars (*307 W. 26th St, UCBTheatre.com*)

YOGA

With so many different yoga studios and types of classes, it can be difficult to know which one to choose. The city's largest yoga center, Jivamukti (841 Broadway near 13th St and 853 Lexington Ave between 64th and 65th St, JivamuktiYoga.com), offers multiple classes per day welcoming yoga newcomers, as well as early-morning meditation classes. Get ready to sweat at Bikram Yoga NYC (*Various locations, BikramYogaNYC.com*), which includes an hour of standing exercise and an hour of floor work. Yoga Works (*Various locations, YogaWorks.com*) offers a wide selection of styles and difficulty levels.

CLASSES 59

RELIGION

New York may be a world away from the Bible Belt, but every conceivable religion and denomination is represented here. Newcomers looking for the faith they were raised with will have plenty of options, and those curious about a more unusual worship experience with have plenty of options.

HOUSES OF WORSHIP

Catholic

Irish, Italian, and Latin American immigrants have historically fed New York's large Catholic community. **St. Patrick's Cathedral** (*5th Ave at 50th St, SaintPatricksCathedral.org*) is the city's largest Catholic church. **St. Ignatius Loyola Parish** on the Upper East Side (*980 Park Ave at 84th St, StIgnatiusLoyola.org*) is a Jesuit church with a Baroque interior and a variety of community events, including extensive sacred-music programming. On the West Side, the **Church of the Blessed Sacrament** (*152 W. 71st St between Broadway and Columbus Ave, BlessedSacramentNYC.org*) is known for its beautiful tapestries. Greenpoint's **St. Anthony-St. Alphonsus Church** (*862 Manhattan Ave at Milton St, gscomm.net/SaintAnthony*) features a prominent steeple that can be seen throughout the neighborhood, as well as a massive Columbus organ.

Episcopalian

The Episcopal Church administers many of New York's most beautiful and historic churches. In the Financial District, **Trinity Church** (*89 Broadway at Wall St, TrinityWallStreet.org*) is one of the most well known. The awe-inspiring **Cathedral Church of St. John the Divine** (*1047 Amsterdam Ave at 112th St, StJohnDivine.org*) is the city's flagship Episcopalian church, and in the East Village**, St. Mark's Church in the Bowery** (*131 E. 10th St, StMarksChurch-in-the-Bowery.com*) provides a calm contrast to the bustle of nearby St. Mark's Place. **St. Bartholomew's Church** (*Park Ave at 51st St, 6 to 51st St, StBarts.org*) is one of the city's largest churches, housed in a landmarked Romanesque/Byzantine-style building. The congregation is famous for extensive lay participation in services and outreach programs.

Baptist

Harlem is the epicenter of New York's Baptist community, and the **Abyssinian Baptist Church** (*132 W. 138th St, Abyssinian.org*) is by far the neighborhood's most famous. **Canaan Baptist Church** (*132 W. 116th St*), like Abyssinian, is known for its gospel choir and lively Sunday services. Further downtown, **Calvary Baptist Church** (*123 W. 57th St between 6th and 7th Ave, CBCNYC.org*) holds a variety of traditional and contemporary services, in addition to special programs for young singles and 20-somethings, and bills itself as "the voice of evangelism in New York City."

Jewish

Jews comprise 12% of New York's population, and the city is home to synagogues of every variety. Reform synagogue **Temple Emanu-El** (*1 E. 65th St at 5th Ave, EmanuelNYC.org*) is the largest synagogue in the world. Across town, Orthodox **Congregation Shearith Israel** (*8 W. 70th St at Central Park West, ShearithIsrael.org*) is the oldest Jewish congregation in the United States, founded in 1654. Frequently called "The Spanish and Portuguese Synagogue," it is located inside a Moorish-style building that it has inhabited since 1897. The **Park Avenue Synagogue** (*50 E. 87th St at Madison Ave, PASyn.org*) is the city's largest Conservative synagogue, but those in search of smaller, local synagogues can find choices throughout the Upper West Side or Borough Park in Brooklyn, home to the city's largest Orthodox population.

Muslim

The majority of New York's Muslim community resides in Brooklyn and Queens, but **The Mosque of New York** (*1711 3rd Ave between 96th and 97th St*), housed inside the Islamic Cultural Center of New York, is by far the city's largest, with beautiful, ornate architecture and scheduled prayer five times a day. Classes are also available for children and adults.

Buddhist
The Buddhist temples of Chinatown may qualify as tourist attractions, but those looking for a more peaceful house of worship can find it at **New York Buddhist Church** *(332 Riverside Dr at 105th St, NewYorkBuddhistChurch. org)*, where Dharma services are complemented by introductory programming for those interested in learning more about the religion. **Soka-Gakkai International USA** *(7 E. 15th St, SGI-USA.org)* is based on the teachings of Nichiren Daishonin, a 13th-century Japanese monk, which focus on the inherent dignity of each individual.

Hindu
The Vedanta Society of New York (34 W. 71st St, Vedanta-NewYork.org) was founded in the late 1800s as the first society in New York to affiliate itself with the Ramakrishna movement. Its services focus on Vedanta Hinduism, with a mix of lectures, meditation, and discussion.

NEW EXPERIENCES

Traditional services abound throughout New York, but people looking to broaden their cultural horizons, or try a new version of their childhood faith, also have a wealth of options. In Morningside Heights, **Riverside Church** *(490 Riverside Dr at 120th St, TheRiversideChurch.NY.org)* is one of the city's most progressive. Upper West Side **Congregation B'nai Jeshurun** *(257 W. 88th St between Broadway and West End Ave, BJ.org)*, affectionately called "BJ," is famous for its young membership and intellectual, activist approach to Judaism. BJ's Friday night services are some of the city's liveliest, replete with music, dancing, and community spirit.

Facing Washington Square Park, **Judson Memorial Church** *(55 Washington Square South, Judson.org)* is an interdenominational congregation that defines itself as "a sanctuary for progressive activism and artistic expression." With a focus on social-justice issues, the church is unabashedly liberal, supporting gay and immigrant rights and calling for an end to the war in Iraq. For those with more secular sympathies, the **New York Society for Ethical Culture** *(2 W. 64th St at Central Park West, NYSEC.org)* is dedicated to the promotion of a humane society irrespective of religious creed; the society has a storied history of attracting freethinkers, nontheists, and activists. In place of worship services, Sunday mornings are devoted to lectures, music, and discussions aimed at stimulating the intellect.

LGBT RELIGIOUS LIFE

Religious life in New York has always gone hand-in-hand with social justice and community activism, so it's no surprise that there are plenty of religious institutions in the city that cater to the LGBT community. **Congregation Beth Simchat Torah** *(57 Bethune St, CBST.org)* is the most well known LGBT synagogue in the city, founded in 1973. In addition to its custom-made prayerbooks and egalitarian services, the congregation is known for its work with a variety of social causes and HIV/AIDS relief.

The **Metropolitan Community Church of New York** *(446 W. 36th St between 9th and 10th Ave, MCCNY.org)* is a popular church among members of the LGBT community; its programming is dedicated to counteracting the view that homosexuality is incompatible with Christianity, and the church sponsors a number of social-justice initiatives including hunger relief and marriage-equality advocacy. The Methodist **Church of St. Paul and St. Andrew** *(263 W. 86th St between Broadway and West End Ave, SPSANYC.org)* also features LGBT-friendly services every Sunday at 11am, and frequently holds services in St. Paul's Chapel at Columbia University in addition to its Upper West Side location.

RELIGION 61

CHEAP NYC

New York may be the country's most expensive city, but students and young people in the know can take advantage of a multitude of opportunities to save on day-to-day necessities. Almost everything in the city, from sandwiches to Gucci purses, can be found at a reduced price, and those who make the extra effort to find the deals will find that living in New York doesn't mean you have to live in debt as well.

CLOTHING

There's discounted and then there's *cheap*. For the latter, you'll want a consignment shop or, if you don't mind looking slightly ratty, a thrift store. In the way of consignment shops, you might try **Beacon's Closet** (*88 N. 11th St, Brooklyn, 718-486-0816*), which specializes in reasonably priced hipster-wear. Label-junkies flock to **Buffalo Exchange** (*504 Driggs Avenue, Brooklyn, 718-384-6901*) to buy, sell, and trade an eclectic selection of clothing. Thrift stores are everywhere, like the plague—most neighborhoods will have an infection, or two, or three. For the lowest of the low, head to a **Salvation Army Thrift Store** (*112 4th Ave, 212-873-2741, SATruck.com for more locations*).

SEASONAL SALES

Almost every month, some major designer or popular New York store has a major sale meant to allure the masses with huge discounts. Some of the best deals are at the after-Christmas sales, which occur at the big department stores such as **Macy's** (*151 W. 34th St, 212-695-4400*) and **Saks 5th Avenue** (*12 E. 49th St, 212-644-1704*). At stores such as **Barneys** (*660 Madison Ave, 212-826-8900*), known for its annual summer sale that kicks off in the first week of June, the mad rush for discount clothes can be overwhelming. Some of the best cutbacks are at the showroom and sample shows put on by labels such as Dolce and **Gabbana** (*825 Madison Ave, 212-249-4100*) in May and individual designers such as **Yeohlee** (*225 W. 35th St, 16th floor, 212-631-8099*) in March. Some snobbier designers such as **Manolo Blahnik** (*31 W. 54th St between 5th and 6th Ave, 212-582-3007*) and **Sigerson Morrison** (*28 Prince St at Mott St, 212-625-1641*) hold private sample sales open only to fashion editors, but insiders know that the Blahnik sale opens to the public right after the press leaves, and some swear that a confident swagger with an "I belong here" look can often get you into the door at the more exclusive Sigerson. The half-off discounts at showroom and sample sales often come with unsettling drawbacks though—such as an absent dressing room. Check **TheBudgetFashionista.com** for hints on upcoming sales.

HAIRCUTS

If you're looking for a $100-quality haircut at a fraction of the price, the best place to find it is at various beauty schools, many of which offer severely discounted haircuts for students to hone their skills. While some do walk-ins, many require an appointment, and remember: your barber may be a fashion maestro-in training, but right now they're just a student. Accidents can happen. **Carsten Institute of Hair & Beauty** (*41 Union Square West, 2nd floor, 212-675-4884*) offers $17 trims by Institute students on weekday mornings, extra for coloring. Call ahead for an appointment. **Rumor Salon** (*15 E. 12th St, 212-414-0195*) has *free* model cuts on Tuesday mornings between 9am and noon. **Bumble and Bumble** (*415 W. 13th St, 212-521-6500*) offers free cuts by appointment every

Monday night between 5:30 and 6:30pm. A haircut at the **Atlas Barber School** (*34 3rd Ave, 212-475-1360*) will set you back a five-dollar bill and the **Empire Beauty School** (*22 W. 34th St, 866-232-2771*) will do a wash, cut, and blow-out for $8.32.

To maintain frugality even while being coiffured, there are also several options at professional barbershops. **Astor Place Hair** (*2 Astor Pl, 212-475-9854*) has been chopping locks at reasonable prices for 50 years. A short haircut begins at $14, while the standard wash/blow dry/cut combo starts at $25 and goes up, depending on hair length. For an old-school barbershop experience, **Neighborhood Barber** (*439 E. 9th St, 212-777-0798*) offers $14 haircuts (and $15 back/chest shaves); walk-ins only. With nine locations throughout Manhattan, **Dramatics NYC** (*DramaticsNYC.com*) is a big step up from *Supercuts* in everything but price: A shampoo and cut starts at $20 and tops out at $45.

TAILORS

AVA Kerolos & William Taylor (*7 Dey St. Suite 203, 212-267-8762*) offers quick and quality service for great prices, such as $10 for shirt alterations and $12 for jacket adjustments. **Nelson Tailor Shop** (*176 Rivington St, 212-253-7071*) is a reliable fixture in the Lower East Side, boasting the ability to hem a pair of jeans while you wait for only $8. **Victor & Tailors** (*205 Mott St, 212-941-0348*), purportedly the best tailoring service in New York City, feature convenient hours, unbelievable deals (two pairs of jeans hemmed for only $10), and even custom-made curtains. No credit cards accepted.

COBBLERS

Although **Cobbler Express** (*222 E. 41st St, 212-867-7156*) may lean towards the expensive side for some services, such as a starting fee of $49.95 for trimming leather soles and heels, you'll be comforted by the thorough quality of repairs and the same-day service. Frequent coupon deals should also take some of the sting off. The dilemma behind buying stunning shoes that refuse to fit has been permanently solved by **Hector's Shoe Repair** (*11 Greenwich Ave, 212-727-1237*), which re-heels, resoles, shines, tightens, and loosens even the most ravaged shoes at reasonable prices. At **Arty's Shoe Service** (*243 8th Ave, 212-255-1451*) both newly bought Christian Louboutins and worn sneakers are given the same treatment—each pair of shoes that comes through Arty's door is guaranteed to fit perfectly after he's finished.

MANICURES

There are probably more than a hundred places in the city to get cheap manicures and pedicures. The problem is that with a cheap price sometimes comes the pain of infections due to unsanitary tools. Fortunately, there are a few places in the city that offer low prices but don't compromise hygiene. The most popular place for cheap, dependable manicures is **Bloomie Nails** (*44 W 55th St, 212-664-1662*) which offers a fast, yet meticulous, manicure for $12. There are several locations throughout the city. **Athena's Nails** (*3111 30th Ave, Astoria, Queens, 718-278-4597*) is a neighborhood favorite in Astoria. Manicures are only $6 and pedicures $12. The fashionista on a budget will love **SoHo Nails** (*458 W Broadway, 3rd Fl, 212-475-6368*), which offers high quality mani-pedis for the low price of $23.

HEALTH SERVICES

As if you needed any more assurances that you're in the greatest city in the world, New York City produces its own brand of condom and distributes more than three million a month for *free*. Check out **NYC.gov/Health/Condoms** for an exhaustive list of NYC bars, restaurants, and other locations where you can pick up your free pack.

If you've got morning-after worries, there are eleven city-run clinics offering free STD testing and emergency contraception spread across all five boroughs. All are open Monday through Friday and some on Saturday mornings. Services offered and operating hours vary from clinic to clinic, so check **NYC.gov/Health** or call 311 for complete listings.

The **NYC Department of Health and Mental Hygiene** maintains a Bureau of Immunization that oversees five health centers which offer free walk-in immunizations against influenza and, for women, HPV.

The **New York City Health and Hospitals Corporation** provides health care, regardless of a patient's financial situation, through hospitals, nursing and treatment centers, and over 80 community health clinics. Check **NYC.gov/hhc** for a location appropriate to your means and needs, should you require it.

FOOD

Dumpster diving isn't for everyone, but for those without qualms over days-old food cast away in plastic bags, there are many locations, recommended by the anti-capitalist environmental group **Freegans** (*freegan.info*), whose dumpsters or sidewalks are loaded with food for the taking. The uptown supermarket **Garden of Eden** (*2780 Broadway, 212-222-7300*) is heralded as one of the best diving locations in the city: not only are there loads of fruits, vegetables and bread, but also yummy leftovers from the store's buffet. For some good diving in Brooklyn, Freegans recommend **The Bagel Store** (*754 Metropolitan, 718-782-5856; 247 Bedford Ave, 718-218-7244*), which throws out bags of bagels every night

64 CHEAP NYC

after closing at 10pm. Many bagel stores and bakeries also offer discounts right at closing or hold onto food and sell it cheaply the next day.

Brooklyn offers more cheap food at the **Park Slope Food Coop** (*782 Union St, 718-622-0560*) and **Costco** (*976 3rd Ave, Brooklyn, 718-965-7603*), which both require memberships. For cheap produce, the **Greenmarkets** (*CENYC.org*) are great for fresh and local food that can be found for better prices than that at Whole Foods. The biggest one is at Union Square, and is so well-regarded that it's also a popular spot for restaurant chefs. More cheap produce and seafood is available in the markets of Chinatown, which are the best at the hotspot streets **Canal Street, Mott Street,** and **Grand Street**. Finally, the cavernous **Fairway Market** (*2328 12th Ave, 212-234-3883*) is perhaps the city's most popular location for cheap food; its spacious digs under the West Side Highway give it enough room for a dizzying selection and wholesale prices.

WINE AND BEER

For great selections at reasonable prices, the prudent wine connoisseur, casual boozer, or party-thrower can get her fix and not break the bank. **Trader Joe's Wine Store** (*138 E 14th St, 212-529-6326*) made its name with Two Buck Chuck (which is actually $3 in New York), a smattering of varietals from the Charles Shaw label, and probably the cheapest vino in the city. The two NYC locations for the East Coast chain **Best Cellars** (*1291 Lexington Ave, 212-426-4200, 2246 Broadway, 212-362-8730*) are ideal spots to find unparalleled prices and finally become the oenophile you've always wanted to be. The wide selection is divided into eight categories—fizzy, fresh, soft, luscious, juicy, smooth, big, and sweet—and each location offers free walk-in tastings every night. Beer drinkers might want to check out **New Beer Distributors** (*167 Chrystie St, 212-473-8757*), a warehouse stocked with 800 varieties from over 30 countries (the Belgian selection boggles the mind).

BIKES

Bikes are one of the best ways to get around the city for those who don't have a lot of money for MetroCards. While many people may run to Craigslist to find their wheels, there are more dependable places around the city that offer high-quality used bikes that won't require you to pay another hundred dollars in tune ups. **Recycle-a-Bicycle** (*RecycleaBicycle.org*) takes donated bicycles and bicycle parts and makes new bikes for sale. They have two retail locations in the city, one in DUMBO (*35 Pearl St, 718-858-2972*) and another on the Lower East Side (*75 Ave C, 212-475-1655*). Get $5 off a bike lock with the purchase of a bike. **Eddie's Bicycle Shop** (*490 Amsterdam Ave, 212-580-2011*) has gently used bikes at reasonable prices, but call ahead to see what is in the shop and for how much, as the selection is small and constantly changing. Even a quality bike sometimes needs a repair. The **Time's Up! Bike Co-op** (*73 Morton St, 212-802-8222*) holds free workshops that teach bike owners valuable repair lessons.

BOOKS AND MUSIC

For cheap books it's hard to beat the famous **Strand Bookstore** (*828 Broadway, 212-473-1452*), home to 18 miles of used, new, rare, and out-of-print books. To buy new, inexpensive books *and* stick it to the man all at once, head to **Unoppressive Non-Imperialist Bargain Books** (*34 Carmine St, 212-229-0079*) and fight the power! The tremendous row of $1 books at **BOOKOFF** (*12 E 41st St, 212-685-1410*) is filled not with rundown salacious romance tripe (or the genre equivalent), but recent hardcovers and paperbacks—not to mention classics. For a more outdoorsy purchasing experience, head to **Broadway** between about **110th & 116th St**—during the day used-book vendors line the sidewalk with their battered tables and bargain books.

There are several major reasons to not steal music digitally: ethics, sloth, technophobia, and the desire to interact with fleshy humans. Should you claim any of these reasons as your own, you'll need somewhere to buy music. A few suggestions: **Etherea Records** (*66 Ave A, 212-358-1126*) has a classically judgmental staff, as well as a large selection of new, used, rare, and independent CDs. **Future Legend** (*796 9th Ave, 212-707-8180*) has an affordable cross-section of CDs in many genres. The electronics mega-store **J & R** (*23 Park Row, 212-238-9000*) has an extensive assortment of new and used CDs.

KITCHEN EQUIPMENT

At the slightly cramped **Bowery Kitchen Supply Equipment** (*460 W. 16th St, 212-219-1457*), you can find everything from stuff you'll use once or twice (corn zippers, cheesecloths) to items that you just can't live without (pasta rollers, custom-made sheet pans). After gorging on kitchen gear, make sure to check out the sandwich deli also tucked inside the block-long Chelsea Market. You really don't need that Wusthof: the **Bowery Restaurant Supply** (*183 Bowery, 212-254-9720*) offers quality knives starting at $3 and $6 whetstones to keep them cutting. Dig a little deeper into the store and you'll find thermometers, tongs, bowls, sheet pans, graters, and grinders, all for under $15. Restaurant owners and individual decorators alike flock to the cavernous **Leader Restaurant Equipment & Supplies, Inc** (*191 Bowery, 212-677-1982*), which offers deals on chinaware, chopsticks, and glasses. Lazy aficionados of kitchen utensils, rejoice! Customers of the **Sang Kung Company** can order online (*110 Bowery, 212-226-4527, SangKung.com*).

LIGHT APPLIANCES

Hunting for that elusive lamp to complement your room? Try searching through the multitude of choices at **Lighting & Beyond** (*35 W 14th St, 212-929-2738*), where lighting fixtures are neatly sorted into traditional, contemporary, and modern categories. True to its title, **Surprise! Surprise!** (*91 3rd Ave, 212-777-0990*) provides plenty of kitschy goods that will add an astonishing and unique gleam to the dowdiest dorm room, including a $17 Double Happiness Chinese Takeout Lamp, $20 Animal Accent Lamps, and a variety of string lights for less than $20. Breeze past the ornately carved Victorian sconces, priced at $500 per pair, at **City Knickerbocker, Inc**. (*665 11th Ave, 212-586-3939*) and head on over to the huge selection of lamps found within the store's Lighting Fixture Showroom where you can choose from $9 antique shades.

FURNITURE

It will take you around a day to sort through **Bobby's Department Store** (*1628 Church Ave, Brooklyn, 718-856-7600*), which has an overwhelming selection of discount furniture, from bric-a-bracs to bookshelves. **Downtown Furniture, Inc.** (*165 Grand St, 800-966-7088*) provides free delivery and assembly for a purchase of $150 and up. The problem of buying a rug that satisfies your taste in the store and then looks horrendous at home, is solved. Murat, the owner of **Double Knot Rug Gallery** (*13 White St, 212-966-9113*), recommends that customers take two rugs home, compare, and then buy. At **The Antiques Garage** (*112 W. 25th St, 212-243-5343*), you can browse furniture from several eras, such as Victorian tables, Deco shelves, and 80s disco balls. The **Salvation Army** (*546 W 46th St, 212-757-2311*) is known as the best location for furniture, and in between street scrounging and store shopping is the **Annex Antique Fair and Flea Market** (*6th Ave from 24th to 26th St*), which, although frequented by celebs, has incredible deals on unique antiques.

MOVING SERVICES

Moving in the city without the aid of a car is torturous. Fortunately, there are independent moving companies around the city that will pick up, transport, and unload for reasonable prices. The most prominent is **Man With a Van** (*888-482-1083*), which not only loads and transports but also offers other services such as packing/unpacking and removing doors and AC units from windows. Another popular choice is **Moving Man** (*212-662-4000*), which drops off free moving boxes and cheap packaging supplies before pick-up day. If your new place is feeling cramped and you need extra storage space, **Manhattan Mini-Storage** (*800-786-7243*) is a cheap, convenient option that many people choose for its 24-hour access and many locations.

CHEAP NYC 67

JANUARY

New York Times Art and Leisure Weekend
Early January
Actors, musicians, writers, and other celebrities assemble to discuss their work at this festival sponsored by one of New York's most venerable institutions.
TimesCenter (41st St between 7th and 8th Ave). 888-698-1870. ArtsAndLeisureWeekend.com. Ticket prices vary.

New York National Boat Show
Mid-January
Shop or browse the most exquisite yachts, boats, and sailing gear at this convention of boating enthusiasts from around the country.
Jacob Javits Center (11th Ave at 35th St). 212-984-7016. NYBoatShow.com. Tickets $15.

Winter Antiques Show
Late January
This festival features all kinds of antiques from furniture to jewelry spanning from ancient times to the 20th century.
Park Avenue Armory (Park Ave at 67th St). 718-292-7392. WinterAntiquesShow.com. Tickets $20.

Martin Luther King Jr. Parade
Third Monday in January
A parade and onlookers celebrate the life and legacy of America's greatest civil rights leader.
5th Ave from 61st to 86th St.

Chinese New Year Celebration
Late January or Early February
Lighted lanterns, snapping firecrackers, and a dragon parade on Canal Street ring in the Chinese New Year, on a date determined by the lunar calendar.

Winter Restaurant Week
Late January or Early February
The city's finest restaurants reduce prices drastically and provide three-course meals to the other half. A wonderfully democratic dining experience.
NYCVisit.com. Lunch $24, Dinner $35 (not including beverage, tax, or tip).

FEBRUARY

Empire State Building Run-up
Early February
Over 100 runners race up 1,576 steps to the 86th floor of New York's most famous skyscraper.
Empire State Building (5th Ave at 34th St). ESBnyc.com.

Mercedes Benz Fashion Week
Second week of February
Designers, models, journalists, and enthusiasts flock to Bryant Park to see the most cutting-edge fashions for next fall from designers worldwide.
Bryant Park (42nd St at 5th Ave). MBFashionWeek.com.

Westminster Kennel Club Dog Show
Mid-February
Hundreds of the world's most pampered dogs meet and mingle, competing for the coveted Best in Show crown. The people-watching is equally exciting.
Madison Square Garden (34th St between 7th and 8th Ave). 800-455-3647. WestminsterKennelClub.org. Tickets: One-Day $40; Two-Day $75; Reserved $125.

International Art Expo
Late February-Early March
Paintings, prints, sculpture, and jewelry bring artists, dealers, and enthusiasts to the Javits Center.
Jacob Javits Center (11th Ave at 35th St). 800-827-7170. ArtExpos.com.

MARCH

St Patrick's Day Parade
March 17th
Beer flows freely and Fifth Avenue becomes a sea of green (but please, no orange) as the city celebrates its Irish heritage.
5th Ave from 44th to 86th St. 212-465-6741. SaintPatricksDayParade.com.

Annual Urban Pillow Fight
March 22nd
Feathers blot out the sky over Union Square as hundreds of New Yorkers grab their pillows and let out a year's worth of pent-up aggression in one of the year's most unorthodox events.
Union Square (14th Street at Broadway). NewMindSpace.com.

Greek Independence Day Parade
March 25th
The streets fill with all things Greek to celebrate their Declaration of Independence and the birthplace of democracy.
5th Ave from 49th to 59th St. GreekParade.org.

Blades Over Broadway
Late March
Figure skaters hit the ice to Broadway showtunes.
Riverbank State Park (Riverside Dr at 145th St). 646-698-3440. FigureSkatinginHarlem.org. Suggested donation $5.

APRIL

Major League Baseball
Early April
The coming of spring brings baseball season, so go root for the Mets or the Yankees—but not the Red Sox. *MLB.com.*

Macy's Easter Flower Show
Week before Easter
Macy's comes into bloom with fresh flowers in ornate display, all over the store and in the front windows.
151 W. 34th St at Broadway and 6th Ave. 212-695-4400.

Easter Parade
Easter Sunday
The city shows off its Sunday best—extravagant hats and flowery floats are the accessories of choice in this informal parade open to the public.
5th Ave from 44th to 59th St.

New York International Auto Show
April 10-19
This weeklong party for car fanatics features everything from concept cars to consumer models.
Jacob Javits Center (11th Ave at 35th St). 800-282-3336. AutoShowNY.com. Tickets $14.

Tribeca Fim Festival
Late April-Early May
Robert De Niro's brainchild focuses on new and indie flicks; the stars come out in droves. Venues are throughout lower Manhattan.
212-941-2400. TribecaFilmFestival.org. Ticket prices vary, special passes $64-$1100.

MAY

Great Five Boro Bike Tour
Early May
30,000 competitors bike through New York City's boroughs on a 42-mile course.
Start at Battery Park. 212-932-0778. BikeNewYork.org.

9th Ave International Food Festival
Weekend after Mother's Day
This 20-block street fair boasts foods from around the world and carts from around the city—come gorge yourself, and then watch the live dancing and music.
9th Ave from 37th to 57th St. 212-581-7217.

EVENTS CALENDAR 69

Fleet Week
Late May
Thousands of sailors, coast guardsmen, and marines disembark for a week, interacting with New Yorkers and displaying the newest in military technology aboard their ships.
FleetWeek.navy.mil.

Washington Square Outdoor Art Exhibit
Late May to early June
Some 250 artists gather in Washington Square for an annual exhibit started by Jackson Pollock and Willem de Kooning.
Washington Square Park (W 4th St at MacDougal St). 212-982-6255. WashingtonSquareOutdoorArtExhibit.org.

Rooftop Films Summer Festival
Late May to mid-September
Around 200 feature length and short underground films are shown on various rooftops throughout the city in this summer long film event.
RoofTopFilms.com. Tickets $6-9.

JUNE

River to River Festival
Early June through mid-September
Founded in order to revitalize downtown post-9/11, this festival utilizes mostly outdoor venues for a free performing arts festival covering all genres and tastes. Events continue throughout the summer, on both weekdays and weekends.
Venues throughout Lower Manhattan. RiverToRiverNYC.com.

Puerto Rican Day Parade
Second Sunday in June
The world's largest one-day celebration of Puerto Rican history and culture is open to the public and consistently draws millions of people. It's not just a New York affair—Puerto Rican groups from all over the country attend.
5th Ave from 44th to 86th St. 718-401-0404. NationalPuertoRicanDayParade.org.

Museum Mile Festival
Second Tuesday in June
5th Avenue is closed to traffic as all the museums on Museum Mile open their doors for free, and the streets are filled with food, music, dance, and other activities.
5th Ave from 82nd to 105th St.. 212-606-2296. MuseumMileFestival.org.

Brooklyn Pride
Mid-June
This nighttime parade through Park Slope offers a decidedly more low-key atmosphere than Manhattan's Pride parade and is the culmination of a weekend of festivities.
15th St and Prospect Park West to 7th Ave and Lincoln Pl. 718-928-3320. BrooklynPride.org.

Central Park Summerstage
Mid-June through Late August
Free outdoor concerts in Central Park have become some of the city's best-loved summer events due to this festival, which brings a dizzying array of artists and genres to Rumsey Playfield.
Central Park (East Side at 71st St). 212-360-2756. Summerstage.org.

Shakespeare in the Park
June through September
Sponsored by the Public Theater, these free performances, frequently starring big-name actors, have become a New York institution—be prepared to wait in an extremely long line for tickets.
Delacorte Theater, Central Park (West Side at 80th St). 212-539-8750. PublicTheater.org.

Celebrate Brooklyn!
Late June through August
The Prospect Park Bandshell plays host to music, dance, theater, and film throughout the summer, bringing New Yorkers from all boroughs into the heart of Brooklyn. Aside from a few benefit shows each summer, almost all performances are free.
Prospect Park West and 9th St, Brooklyn. 718-855-7882. BricOnline.org/Celebrate.

NY Philharmonic Concerts in the Parks
Late June to mid-July
The city's most famous orchestra performs free in parks across the city. Bring family, friends, and a picnic dinner.
NYPhil.org.

Mermaid Parade
Late June
Held at Coney Island, this colorful parade pays homage to the area's past and features handmade aquatic costumes. Celebrities often appear as King Neptune and Queen Mermaid, the parade's leaders.
Coney Island Boardwalk at W. 10th Street. ConeyIsland.com/Mermaid.shtml.

Lesbian and Gay Pride Parade
Last Sunday in June
Commemorating the anniversary of the Stonewall Riots, this parade is one of the city's most entertaining—come to cheer in solidarity, or just to see the costumes.
5th Ave and 52nd St to Christopher St and Greenwich Ave. 212-807-7433. NYCPride.org.

JULY

Festa Del Giglio
First Weekend after Independence Day
Celebrating the altruism of San Paolino, the Italian community of Williamsburg comes together for a weekend of feasting and parading.
www.OLMCFeast.com.

Lincoln Center Festival
Throughout July
The performing-arts hub hosts performers and troupes from around the world in this month-long festival.
Lincoln Center (Columbus Ave at 64th St). LincolnCenter.org.

Macy's Fireworks Display
July 4th
The nation's largest fireworks display lights up the Manhattan skyline, with plentiful viewing space along both banks of the East River.
East River between Battery Park and 42nd St. Macys.com.

Siren Music Festival
Mid-July
Music fiends flock to Coney Island for a free Saturday of indie bands, sponsored by the *Village Voice* and featuring a new lineup every year.
Surf Ave between W 10th St and Stillwell Ave. VillageVoice.com/Siren.

Summer Restaurant Week
Late July or Early August
The city's finest restaurants reduce prices drastically and provide three-course meals to the other half. Still a wonderfully democratic dining experience.
NYCVisit.com. Lunch $25, Dinner $35 (not including beverage, tax, or tip).

AUGUST

Lincoln Center Out of Doors
Throughout August
Free performances are given in the outdoor spaces of Lincoln Center. Programming is heavily geared towards families.
Damrosch Park Bandshell (62nd St at Amsterdam Ave). LincolnCenter.org.

Harlem Week
Mid-August
Live music, poetry readings, children's activities, and more celebrate Harlem's history and culture.
212-862-7200. HarlemWeek.HarlemDiscover.com.

New York International Fringe Festival
Mid-August
An exciting 16-day event featuring an array of performing art gems.
212-279-4488. FringeNYC.org.

U.S. Open
Late August to Early September
The biggest U.S. tennis event of the year is held at Arthur Ashe Stadium in Queens.
USTA Billie Jean King National Tennis Center (Flushing Meadows Corona Park), Queens. 800-go-tennis. USOpen.org.

SEPTEMBER

Richmond County Fair
Labor Day
A traditional county fair with staples such as cotton candy and pie-eating contests takes over historic Richmond town.
Historic Richmond Town, Staten Island. 718-351-1611. HistoricRichmondTown.org.

West Indian Carnival Parade
Labor Day weekend
Brooklyn's West Indian community celebrates its heritage with a parade and entertainment at the Brooklyn Museum.
Eastern Parkway, Brooklyn. 718-467-1797. wiadca.com.

Feast of San Gennaro
Second Thursday to the third Sunday of September.
Though reportedly freed from the mob, this street festival of two weeks has not been freed from the mass of tourists and locals who cram Mulberry Street seeking sausages, zeppole, and a glimpse of the statue of San Gennaro paraded down through Little Italy by the congregation of the Church of the Most Precious Blood.
Mulberry Street and surrounding streets. LittleItaly.NYC.com (N)(Q)(R)(W)(5)(6)(J)(M)(Z) *to Canal.*

Brazilian Festival
Early September
Brazilians from across the city (and often the country) come to this yearly festival featuring food, art, and live performers.
E. 46th St between Times Square and Madison Ave. BrazilianDay.com.

New York Is Book Country
Mid-September
This festival, sponsored by publishers and bookstores around the city, brings New Yorkers out to celebrate the joys of reading. A portion of the proceeds is donated to literacy programs.
Central Park. NewYorkIsBookCountry.com.

New York Film Festival
Late September through mid-October
Sponsored by Lincoln Center, one of the city's most high-profile film festivals features flicks from around the globe and, usually, entries from well-established filmmakers.
212-875-5050. FilmLinc.com.

Mercedes-Benz Fashion Week
Mid-September
Got spring fever already? Preview designs for the coming spring in the counterpart to February's Fashion Week.
Bryant Park (42nd St at 5th Ave). MBFashionWeek.com.

Fall for Dance Festival
Late September
Each year New York City Center brings together the best dance troupes in the world, from a myriad of dance styles, to perform for ten straight nights. Tickets are only $10, so be sure to get yours before they sell out.
New York City Center, 130 W 56th St (between 5th Ave and 6th Ave). NYCityCenter.org.
(A)(C)(B)(D)(1) *to Columbus Circle,* (N)(Q)(R) *to 57th.*

OCTOBER

Harlem Open Artist Studio Tour
First Weekend in October
Over 150 artists and galleries in Harlem open their doors to exhibit and sell their art for the weekend. Maps available in participating galleries.
www.HOAST.org. (1)(2)(3)(A)(B)(C)(D)(4)(5) (6) *to 125th St.*

72 EVENTS CALENDAR

Columbus Day Parade
Second Monday in October
This parade celebrates New York's Italian-American heritage and culture.
5th Ave from 44th to 86th St. 212-249-2360. ColumbusCitizensFD.org

International Vintage Poster Fair
Mid-October
Vendors sell thousands of original posters from the 1890s to 1980s.
Metropolitan Pavilion (123 W 18th St). 800-856-8069. PosterFair.com.

Greenwich Village Halloween Parade
Oct 31
For over-the-top costumes, huge crowds, and a parade open to anyone and everyone, there's no better place to be. This Village tradition is the nation's largest Halloween parade and its only major nighttime one—anyone in costume can march.
6th Ave from Spring to 23rd St. Halloween-NYC.com.

NOVEMBER

New York City Marathon
Early November
Open to everyone from professional athletes to running enthusiasts, this 26.2-mile race snakes its way through all five boroughs.
Fort Wadsworth, Staten Island to Central Park. 212-423-2249. NYCMarathon.org.

New York Comedy Festival
Early November
Stand-up comedians descend upon the city for five days and perform throughout the city.
NYComedyFestival.com.

Chocolate Show
Mid-November
Who needs therapy when you've got this? A weekend of creativity and innovation with nature's most perfect substance.
Pier 94 (12th Ave and 55th St). ChocolateShow.com. Adults $28 per day.

Tree Lighting at Rockefeller Center
Late November
The crowds pour in to be serenaded by popular singers and watch the famous tree light up.
Rockefeller Center (5th Ave at 50th St). 212-632-3975.

Macy's Thanksgiving Day Parade
Fourth Thursday in November
The city's most iconic parade attracts gaggles of children with massive floats, celebrities, and Jose Feliciano.
From Central Park West and W. 79th St to Broadway and 34th St. Macys.com.

Radio City Christmas Spectacular
Mid-November through December
After decades, families still flock to Midtown to see this show starring the famous Rockettes.
Radio City Music Hall (6th Ave at 50th St). 212-307-7171. RadioCity.com. Tickets $40-150.

DECEMBER

Menorah Lighting Ceremony
"They tried to kill us, we won—let's eat!" Celebrate Judaism's most artery-clogging holiday with the lighting of a huge menorah during each of the eight nights of Hanukkah.
Grand Army Plaza (5th Ave at 59th St).

Kwanzaa Fest
The city's largest celebration of the African-American cultural holiday features food, arts, and live performances.
Jacob Javits Center (11th Ave at 35th St). 212-216-2000.

New Year's Eve
December 31st
Crowds? Claustrophobia? Freezing cold? The legends are all true—join millions of revelers to watch the ball drop in Times Square to ring in the new year.
Times Square (42nd St at Broadway and 7th Ave). 212-768-1560. TimesSquareNYC.org.

TOUR: ARCHITECTURE

The popularity of window-shopping notwithstanding, some of New York's greatest eye candies are its buildings. The architectural styles that have graced the streets of New York range from the utilitarian to the exuberant, and while architecture buffs will find plenty to gawk at, you don't have to be a connoisseur to enjoy this tour of New York's greatest architecture. Start by heading downtown to the Financial District.

Wall Street

Take the ④,❺ to Wall Street, where some of the most beautiful skyscrapers ever designed preside over the cobblestone remains of 18th century New York. Start at the intersection of Broadway and Wall St and head east down Wall Street to **Federal Hall** (*26 Wall St at Broad St*), a vestige of Revolutionary War-era architecture which once served as our nation's capitol. While there are several other gems in the area—the New York Stock Exchange, the Chamber of Commerce—the best architecture resides several hundred feet above your head, where the grand dames of Wall Street—**Trump Building** (*40 Wall St near William St*), **20 Exchange Place, One Wall Street,** and **American International Building** (*70 Pine St near Pearl St*)—are the real stars of the show. These pre-World War II treasures testify to an era when skyscrapers weren't just office buildings, but were true works of art. Highlights include: the graceful spires of the Trump Building, the soaring windows of 20 Exchange Place, and the ornate architectural embellishments that go all the way up the American International Building.

Victorian Architecture in Greenwich Village

Get on an uptown ④❻ at Broadway-Nassau and take it to West 4th St, where you can take a step back into the 19th century and explore Greenwich Village, home to the bulk of New York's remaining Victorian architecture. The natural starting point is **Washington Square Park** (*W 4th St at MacDougal St*), the north side of which is lined with stately mid-19th century brick townhouses, the likes of which—due to New York's penchant for bulldozing its treasures—are found nowhere else in New York. Travel a few blocks east to see the magnificent **Jefferson Market Courthouse** (*425 6th Ave at 10th St*), a massive, whimsical hulk of a building whose total disregard for right angles predates (and outperforms) Frank Gehry by many years. Rushing from site to site in Greenwich Village is not the way to do it. Pick a street between 8th and 13th, take a leisurely stroll, and marvel at street after street of impeccably preserved townhouses.

The Peaks of 42nd St

Hop on the ④, ❻, or ❺ again and take it uptown to 42nd St, home to four of New York's five tallest buildings. Start at Renzo Piano's recently-completed **NY Times Tower** (*42nd St at 8th Ave*), whose first-in-New York, unclad high-rise steel frame gives the building a sleek, mechanical look. Head east on 42nd Street, and between Broadway and 6th Avenue, you'll find neighbors **Condé Nast Building** (*4 Times Square at Broadway and 42nd St*) and the newly completed **Bank of America Building** (*1 Bryant Park at 42nd St and 6th Ave*). The former is notable for its electronic billboard and is home to the city's main TV antenna; the latter can only be described as a deconstructionist glass marvel, and is billed as the most eco-friendly skyscraper in the world. Keep heading east towards Lexington Avenue where you'll find the crown jewel of 42nd Street: the **Chrysler Building** (*405 Lexington Ave at 42nd St*). William Van Allen's Art Deco masterpiece and one-time tallest building in the world needs to be seen up close and personal to appreciate the level of detail invested in the building, which even today regularly tops architects' lists of the finest buildings in New York.

Modern Architecture

For the first time since the booming 1950s, New York is once again an epicenter of urban architecture. This revolution is not confined to office buildings, either. Take the **LVMH Tower** (*21 E 57th St between 5th and Madison Ave*), home to the otherwise demure Christian Dior brand, whose fantastical, fractured glass façade not only stands as a landmark of design, but also a revolution in retail architecture. The nearby **Museum of Modern Art** (*53rd St between 5th and 6th Ave*) and the recently revamped **Museum of Art and Design** (*2 Columbus Circle at 8th Ave*) demonstrate how modern architecture has found a home in New York's museums. Both recently unveiled masterpieces are, unlike the LVMH Tower, open to the public. Great modern architecture is also not limited to Midtown. Take the ❶ train from Columbus Circle to Christopher Street, and head west to see modern masterpieces such as Richard Meier's dynamic **Perry Street Towers** along the Hudson River Park (*173/176 Perry St at West St*) or Frank Gehry's ghostly, undulating **IAC Tower** (*West St between 18th and 19th St*), which even Gehry detractors will love.

Mansions of the Upper West Side

Finish up by taking a ❶❷❸❶❸ train to the Upper West Side—if you're a fan of residential architecture, there is no better place in all of New York City to visit. Dwellers settled on the Upper West Side in the last few decades of the 19th century, and is therefore graced with the remains of that era's extravagant architecture. Central Park West is home to the city's finest apartment buildings, including the **Beresford** (*81st Street at Central Park West*) and its four handsome cupolas, the soaring Art Deco glamour of the **San Remo Towers** (*74th St at Central Park West*), and one of the world's most famous apartment buildings, **The Dakota** (*72nd St at Central Park West*). The Upper West Side is also home to New York's grandest townhouses; stroll down Riverside Drive to see the best of them, most of which were originally built as single-family homes. The most beautiful of these include the white marble **Schinasi mansion** (*Riverside Dr at 107th St*), which is the only private, stand-alone house left in New York City, the gargantuan red-brick **Rice Mansion** (*Riverside Dr at 89th St*) which is now a yeshiva, and the massive **1 Riverside Drive** (*Riverside Dr at 72nd St*). For a look at smaller-scale residences, a stroll down most of the neighborhood's streets in the 70s or 80s reveals more discreet—but equally beautiful—19th century brownstones, some of which have been painted in bright colors since their construction.

TOUR: ARCHITECTURE

TOUR: FILM SPOTS

To shoot a film in New York is to create an enduring image of a time and place that may never exist again or may never have existed at all. The cinematic Midtown of Martin Scorsese's Taxi Driver (1976), with its flesh shops and porno theaters, resembles today's New York about as closely as it does the Land of Oz. The New York subway has little in common—thankfully—with the gangland battleground featured in The Warriors (1979). These and countless other films have created a cinematic New York that no tour can map out. But for the visiting film buff, a trip to these cinematic hotspots can be well worth the effort, if only to see how they compare with the reel version. Grab a Metrocard all-day pass—you'll need it—take the ❶ train to 145th St... and Action!

From Amsterdam Ave, turn west onto 144th St and enter a hidden corner of the city: a timeless and picturesque street, lined with historic redbrick houses, that feels worlds removed from the hectic neighborhood of Hamilton Heights just a block away. It was here that director Wes Anderson found the ideal location for **Tenenbaum House** (*Convent Ave at W 144th St*) in *The Royal Tenenbaums* (2001). In his bizarrely romantic spin on New York, the distinctive and majestic building, built in 1890, was located at the fictional "Archer Avenue."

Hop on the M100 bus for a straight shot down **125th St**—the main thoroughfare of Harlem. Spike Lee used the street, exhaustively redressed for various historical periods down to the last street sign and trashcan, to provide authenticity and energy for *Malcolm X* (1992). The film opens with a spectacular crane shot that descends from the elevated ❶ train—looming over Broadway—down to a street-level view of a gorgeously realized 1940s Harlem. Lee's film also featured a recreation of a 1960s political rally in the exact location where the original event took place—in front of the **Apollo Theater** (*253 W 125th St between Frederick Douglass and Adam Clayton Powell Blvd*).

Get off the bus at Lexington Ave and take the ❹❺❻ train down to the East 80s, and step into a different New York. The parks, cafés, and stately apartments of the Upper East Side have served as the romantic backdrop for nearly all of Woody Allen's films. Alvy Singer (Allen) and Annie Hall (Diane Keaton) had their first awkwardly flirtatious conversation in Oscar-winner *Annie Hall* (1977) on **E 68th St at Park Ave** in front of the white bricks of a 1909 building, preserved today as an historical landmark—for reasons unrelated to the movie—exactly how it appears in the film. And Annie Hall's apartment still exists on **E 70th St between Lexington and Park,** which Allen admits is his "favorite block in the city." If you find yourself in the Financial District around twilight, you might want to stop off at **Pier 11** (*Wall St at East River*), where Alvy declared his love for Annie Hall with a fading sun and the Brooklyn and Manhattan Bridges in the background. Perhaps the most memorable image in the entire Allen oeuvre is the iconic shot from *Manhattan* (1979) of Allen and Keaton sitting on a park bench at dawn, gazing at the East River and the Queensboro Bridge. Fans seeking to find the original bench may be disappointed, as New York City's parks have undergone extensive renovation since Allen shot his black-and-white masterpiece, but **Sutton Place Park** (*E 58th St at Sutton Pl*) offers a serene courtyard and benches that offer the same riverside view.

As the Upper East Side gives way to Midtown, be sure to stop at the **United Na-**

76 TOUR: FILM SPOTS

tions Building (*1st Ave at E 42nd St*), which was sealed from visiting movie crews for five decades until director Sydney Pollack was allowed to film *The Interpreter* (2005) within its walls. In 1959, however, Alfred Hitchcock used a hidden camera to steal an unauthorized shot of Cary Grant walking up the steps at **1st Ave and 45th St** for *North by Northwest* (1959). Just a few blocks away, overlooking the breadth of 42nd St and offering a spectacular view of Midtown, is **Tudor City** (*42nd St between 1st and 2nd Ave*), where Jason Bourne (Matt Damon) evaded a cadre of CIA agents on a wild goose chase in *The Bourne Ultimatum* (2007).

Take a downtown ❻ train to the Lower East Side and have a bite at **Katz's Delicatessen** (*205 E Houston St at Ludlow St*), where Meg Ryan's orgasmic moaning in *When Harry Met Sally* (1989) prompted a nearby patron to "have what she's having." Just a few blocks uptown—at **6th St and Ave A**—Francis Ford Coppola recreated an entire block of 1920s Little Italy for *The Godfather Part II* (1974). And if you have the time to scale the entire island, head down to Battery Park—at at the corner of **Greenwich St and Battery Pl**, there's an unassuming little edifice that supposedly maintains the exhaust from the Brooklyn Battery Tunnel. Barry Sonnenfeld transformed the nondescript gray building into the nerve center of a government conspiracy when he made it the Men In Black Headquarters (1997).

Catch the uptown ❶ at South Ferry and get off at 59th St-Columbus Circle, where you'll emerge at the southwest tip of **Central Park** (*59th St at Central Park West*). The Oscar-nominated song "That's How You Know" from *Enchanted* (2007) was memorably staged on some of the park's myriad paths and bridges, and the 1967 Central Park Be-In was recreated for the film version of *Hair* (1979). The **Bethesda Fountain** (*mid-park at 72nd St*) brought a transcendent quality to crucial scenes in *Angels in America* (2003) and the new musical version of *The Producers* (2005).

On the Upper West Side, you'll find the haunted apartment building from *Ghostbusters* (1984) on the corner of **66th St and Central Park West.** And just six blocks uptown is the historic **Dakota** (1 W 72nd St at Central Park West), built in 1884 as one of the city's first apartment buildings. Its most famous current tenants include Lauren Bacall and Yoko Ono, but for horror buffs, the building itself is the star. The building portrayed the fictional "Bramford" in Roman Polanski's *Rosemary's Baby* (1968), where it acted as a haven for urbanite Satanists. Walking up to the **American Museum of Natural History** (*Central Park West at 81st St*), visitors can find the ocean-life exhibit featured in *The Squid and the Whale* (2006), which turned the *Clash of the Titans* diorama into a metaphor for childhood fears.

Finish by taking the uptown ❶ to 116th St, where a number of films have taken advantage of the historic architecture and collegiate energy at **Columbia University** (*116th St between Broadway and Amsterdam Ave*), including *Marathon Man* (1976), the *Spider Man* films (2002-7), and *Across the Universe* (2007). A few blocks downtown from the University's gates is **Tom's Restaurant** (*2880 Broadway at 112th St)*, the exterior of which stood in for the outside of Monk's Café, from the long-running television show *Seinfeld*.

TOUR: FILM SPOTS 77

TOUR: PUBLIC ART

A strict definition of "public art" implies something temporary and site-specific that puts the idea of the public under analysis—a form of culture that is not meant to be limited to the cognoscenti. But public art also exists in everyday ways. "Art" is frequently associated with Museum Mile or Chelsea galleries, so it surprises many New Yorkers that Midtown is home to a lot of art within skyscrapers or along 42nd St and 5th Avenue. Crowds, canvassers, and slow pedestrians are unavoidable—it is Midtown, after all—so grab comfy shoes and 20 bucks (but please, not a fanny-pack) and be prepared to swim with the masses.

Start by taking the subway to Times Square-42nd St. Walk east and you'll see the southwestern corner of **Bryant Park** (*42nd St and 6th Ave*). Parks are usually venues for public art, not artworks in and of themselves, but Bryant Park has a unique European feel to it that will please your inner classicist. Fuel yourself for the day by heading to the **wichcraft** kiosk (the sandwich chain by Tom Colicchio of *Top Chef* fame) for a grilled-cheese or slow-roasted pork sandwich—sublime alternatives to a street-cart pretzel.

After lunch, head towards the entrance of the **New York Public Library** (*498 5th Ave at 42nd St*). Occupying the lot that was once the Croton Reservoir, construction for the Beaux-Arts building began in 1902 and was completed in 1911. These palatial digs feature a vaulted entrance with white marble finishes and Romanesque arches. The jewel in this landmark's crown, however, is the Rose Reading Room, featuring 52-foot ceilings, chandeliers, and ceiling murals.

For a look at another impressive ceiling, stop by **Grand Central Terminal** (*E 42nd St at Park Ave*). The façade facing 42nd is crowned with the largest original Tiffany glasswork in the world—a 13-foot clock—and a sculpture of Hermes, the Greek god of voyages. The station's cavernous main concourse has a majestic, Old-World quality that conveys the glamour once associated with railroad travel. Ignore the hurried commuters and look up; the ceiling mural, once covered with a century's worth of soot, has been remarkably restored. Painted by French artist Paul César Helleu, the mural is of a flattened celestial sphere. Careful observers will see that it is, however, a backwards depiction. Helleu based the painting on a Medieval manuscript that showed a reflection of night sky, though other rumored explanations say that it was God's view of the sky, or a mere accident.

After a tour around the station, take a walk north up Park Ave to the **Lever House** building (*390 Park Ave at E 53rd St*). Not only is the building an architectural landmark, it also houses the Lever House Art Collection in its lobby and a sculpture garden in the outdoor plaza. The art collection shows rotating exhibitions of modern art, with tinges of the avant-garde—past exhibits have featured media ranging from light installations to Hello Kitty sculptures.

Walk west along 53rd St past Madison Ave, and as you near 5th Ave on the north side of the street you'll find a graffiti-covered piece of the **Berlin Wall**, one of four pieces in New York City.

Continue along 53rd and come to **Paley Park** (*E 53rd St between Madison and 5th Ave*), a beloved and oft-used urban space named for its benefactor, former CBS Chairman William Paley. The waterfall in the rear of the pocket park is lit at night and runs year-round, blocking out urban hoots and hollers. The park also has movable furniture and shady honey locust trees.

Head towards 5th Avenue and walk two blocks south to the northern entrance of **Rockefeller Center** (*5th Ave between W 49th and 50th St*) across from St. Patrick's Cathedral. If the sight of Bermuda-short-clad sightseeing hordes induces nausea, rest easy

78 TOUR: PUBLIC ART

and skip away through **Channel Gardens**, so named for its location between the British Empire and La Maison Francaise buildings. The entrance to the promenade is flanked with panels, one for each country. The British panel, called "Industries of the British Empire," features nine gilded figures that reference industries found throughout the former British Empire. The French panel symbolizes the friendship between France and America with figures named Poetry, Beauty, and Elegance.

The buildings and artwork in the plaza are all in 1930s Art Deco fashion. Lee Lawrie's "Wisdom, Light, and Sound" sculptures mark the entrance to 30 Rockefeller, the tallest building in the plaza. Lawrie also designed the Atlas statue facing 5th Ave. Inside 30 Rockefeller are **murals by Jose Maria Sert**. The entrance murals were originally supposed to be painted by Diego Rivera, who did, in fact, paint a mural titled *Man at the Crossroads Looking With Uncertainty but With Hope and High Vision to the Choosing of a Course Heading to a New and Better Future*. But before it debuted, the Rockefellers dismissed Rivera for the mural's Marxist undertones. Unfortunately, the original mural has been destroyed, and Sert's mural of giant, muscular men toiling away, titled *American Progress: the Triumph of Man's Accomplishments Through Physical and Mental Labor*, replaced Rivera's incendiary painting.

Continue along through the plaza and exit at 51st St, heading west towards 6th Ave. The **AXA Equitable building** (*1290 6th Ave at W 51st St*) displays a set of murals by Thomas Hart Benton in the lobby, painted during the mid 1930s under the commission of the Works Progress Administration. The murals depict the Jazz age of the United States with images of booming industry and cabaret culture. Of the 10 separate pieces, only one, *Outreaching Hands*, hints at the Great Depression. Snap your pictures surreptitiously, lest the bored and officious security guards ask you to leave.

Across the street is the **UBS Art Gallery** (*1285 6th Ave at W 51st St*), which offers space to nonprofit arts groups and holds four exhibitions per year. After walking the length of the gallery, continue down the corridor to the **7th Avenue Galleria** (*7th Ave between W 51st and 52nd St*). A pedestrian-only atrium, the Galleria connects the UBS building with another AXA building. In the atrium outside hangs Sol Lewitt's *Bands of Lines in Four Colors and Four Directions, Separated by Gray Bands*. As a Minimalist, Lewitt's title is also a description of his work. Some say boring, some say bold.

If it's before 6pm, head through the other set of doors down the corridor to the atrium of the **AXA Equitable Center** (*787 7th Ave at W 51st St*). AXA created this public space in exchange for more building stories, although the developers seem to have tried to prevent the space from being useful to the public; there are rules prohibiting eating, and the only furniture gracing the giant space is cold and uncomfortable. Roy Lichtenstein's *Mural with Blue Brushstroke* was commissioned by AXA, a French bank, and executed on-site in 1985. Even if you don't "get" Pop Art, the giant painting easily impresses.

Head back out towards the Galleria for one final stop. The Italian restaurant in the Galleria, **Piano Due** (*151 W 51st St between 6th and 7th Ave*), has a restaurant upstairs and a bar right off the atrium. Artist Sandro Chia painted four murals for the walls of the bar, and vibrant hues of red and orange warm the space. Grab an advantageous barstool, peep at the walls, and unwind with a glass of red wine and a bowl of pasta.

For other public artworks, PublicArtFund.org lists upcoming projects sponsored by the Public Art Fund of New York, a nonprofit organization that has been organizing installations and exhibits in public spaces for over 30 years.

TOUR: FAMOUS DEATHS

Death. What is it good for? Today, death (not yours, thankfully) is a way for you to connect with the gloomier history of New York. Many of the locales in this tour are not glamorous, and only a few of them bear traces of their past as sites of tragedy. This makes them all the more suitable for morbid meditations: What does it mean for all vestiges of a great calamity to wash away? Will I myself be so forgotten? With any luck, you'll find yourself perceiving the city with fresh eyes.

Start things off by grabbing an uptown ❶ train to 168th. Three blocks south is the **Audubon Ballroom** (*3940 Broadway at 165th St*), where Malcolm X was assassinated on February 21st, 1965 during a weekly meeting of the Organization of Afro-American Unity. Columbia University demolished most of the building to build a biotechnology research facility, but community protests led to a partial restoration of the façade and the creation of a museum, the **Malcolm X and Dr. Betty Shabazz Memorial and Educational Center**.

Take a downtown ⓒ train from 163rd and Amsterdam to 72nd Street and Central Park West. You'll find yourself directly in front of the **Dakota** (*1 W 72nd St at Central Park West*), outside of which John Lennon was shot on December 8th, 1980. Just inside the park is **Strawberry Fields**, a memorial named for the famous Beatles song "Strawberry Fields Forever"; at the locus of the memorial is a mosaic whose center reads "IMAGINE," the title of Lennon's famous Utopian songvision. Typically, the mosaic is covered with roses and surrounded by tourists. On some days—the anniversary of his death, his birthday (October 9th), any summer afternoon—people gather to sing songs and remember.

If you're a sports fan, hop on the M72 crosstown bus and get off at York Ave. The **Belaire Apartments** (*524 E 72nd St at York Ave*) are where Yankees pitcher Cory Lidle died in an airline crash on October 11th, 2006. Lidle was flying with his flight instructor—it's not known who was piloting. Lidle is the *third* Yankee to die in a crash of his own plane.

From either the Dakota or the Belaire, you'll need to hoof it into Midtown. From the east, make your way to the **Hotel Elysee** (*60 E 54th St between Madison and Park Ave*), where playwright Tennessee Williams choked to death on an eyedrop bottle cap in 1983. Williams would, bizarrely, keep the cap under his tongue while administering the drops. It has been suggested that his large drug and alcohol intake was a factor in his failure to simply cough it up. Nearby is the Park Central Hotel, formerly the **Park Sheraton Hotel** (*870 7th Ave between W 55th and 56th St*), in the barbershop of which Murder, Incorporated hitman and Mangano crime family boss Albert Anastasia was whacked by agents of Vito Genovese on October 25th, 1957. After having one round unloaded on him, Anastasia lunged at a mirror containing his assailants' reflections. The second round killed him. The barbershop is long gone; in its place is the imaginatively named Café New York.

From the Park Central Hotel, get on the ⓝⓡⓠⓦ trains at 57th and 7th and ride it to Canal St. Walk two blocks north on Broadway and hang a right. You'll come to **421 Broome St** (*between Crosby and*

Lafayettte St), the site of Heath Ledger's accidental overdose. Since there's really nothing to see, try to imagine the quiet street as it must have been the night of January 22, 2008: swarming with gawkers hoping to catch sight of a corpse.

Walking north on Lafayette Street will get you to Great Jones Street. Near the end of the block is a building once owned by Andy Warhol, **57 Great Jones St** (*between Lafayette St and Bowery*), where on August 12th, 1988, graffiti artist turned Neo-Expressionist Jean-Michel Basquiat overdosed on coke and heroin speed-balls in the loft gifted him by Warhol.

Up Broadway and west on 11th Street is **St. Vincent's Hospital** (*7th Ave at W 11th St*), where "Do Not Go Gentle" poet Dylan Thomas roared his last words. Just west of St. Vincent's is **63 Bank Street** (*between W 4th and Bleecker St*), where Sex Pistols bassist Sid Vicious overdosed on heroin at the home of new girlfriend Michelle Robinson. Released from Riker's Island on February 2nd, 1979, Vicious was celebrating making bail ($50,000 put up by his mother) after spending 55 days in the can. At the end of the block is **Abingdon Square** (*Bleecker St, Hudson St, and 8th Ave*), the site of actor/director Adrienne Shelly's November 1st, 2006 hanging. Briefly thought to be a suicide, six days later a construction worker was arrested and charged with murder. He entered a guilty plea on February 14th, 2008 and is now serving a 25-year sentence. Back down Hudson is the **White Horse Tavern** (*567 Hudson St at W 11th St*), the bar Dylan Thomas gave himself alcohol poisoning in; after a night out, he fell ill and slipped into a coma on November 5th, 1953, dying four days later at St. Vincent's.

Head up 8th Avenue and turn right on 23rd Street—you'll see a seedy looking sign for the **Hotel Chelsea** (*222 W 23rd St between 7th and 8th Ave*). In addition to being the residence of Thomas at the time of his death (hanging in the lobby is a haunting portrait of a white horse), the Chelsea was home to Sid Vicious and girlfriend Nancy Spungen when the latter was found stabbed in the gut on October 12, 1978. She bled to death, a mere four months before her lover's death. The murder weapon was traced to Vicious, who in all likelihood was too far gone to have committed the crime. Some theories hold that Spungen was murdered by one of the two drug dealers who visited the suite that night, Rockets Redglare and Neon Leon. *The Lost Weekend* author Charles R. Jackson committed suicide in his room on September 21st, 1968. Painter Alphaeus Philemon Cole lived at the Chelsea for 35 years before passing away November 25th 1988, aged 112, at that time the world's oldest living man. Last but not least, New York School poet and Pulitzer Prize winner James Schuyler died there following a stroke on April 12th, 1991.

With that, the Manhattan portion of our tour comes to an untimely end. For the Thanatotic, head out to **90-10 Merrick Blvd** (*between Hillside and Jamaica Ave, Queens*), where Run-DMC founder Jam Master Jay was gunned down in his recording studio. Or leave New York City altogether and play the ponies at **Belmont Park** (*Hempstead Tpke at Cross Island Pkwy*) in Elmont, where jockey Frank Hayes died of a heart attack in the middle of a race. He and his horse Sweet Kiss finished first, despite his handicap.

TOUR: FAMOUS DEATHS 81

TOUR: MUSIC HISTORY

For over a century, New York City has been home to a diverse, thriving, and ever-changing music scene. Whatever your musical tastes, there is almost certainly something to pique your interests.

Start your tour in Harlem, where on November 21st, 1934, an unknown 17-year-old named Ella Fitzgerald made her singing debut at the **Apollo Theater** (*253 W 125th St between Adam Clayton Powell and Frederick Douglass Blvd*), quickly making a name for herself and the venue. Before long, the theater was known as "Where Stars are Born and Legends are Made," and the famed "Amateur Night"—where stars such as Billie Holiday, James Brown, Ben E. King, Michael Jackson, and Lauryn Hill have all performed—still happens every Wednesday at 7:30pm. Hour long tours are also available by appointment every day of the week.

From Harlem, it's only a short ride on the Ⓒ or Ⓑ train to get to **Strawberry Fields** (*W 72nd St at Central Park West, inside Central Park*), a memorial to late Beatle, writer, and activist John Lennon. The center of Strawberry Fields contains the iconic "Imagine" mosaic, around which fans keep near-constant vigil. Across the street are the Dakota Apartments, Lennon's home for the last seven years of his life, and the site of his tragic assassination. The Dakota has also been home to Leonard Bernstein, Judy Garland, and Paul Simon.

Moving from rock to classical music, walk downtown to 57th Street to see two monuments to New York's classical heritage. A performance at **Carnegie Hall** (*881 7th Ave between 56th and 57th St*), arguably the most prestigious concert hall in the world, has been the defining moment in the lives of countless musicians since the hall's opening in 1891. Across the street is **Steinway Hall** (*109 W 57th St between 6th and 7th Ave*), which houses many of Steinway's most significant designs and the "piano bank," which holds an elite collection of concert grand pianos. Many of the greatest concert pianists in the world hand-picked their instrument here before their performance, and the collection contains "fan mail" from Paderewski and Rachmaninoff.

It's a six-block walk to the **Iridium Jazz Club** (*1650 Broadway at W 51st St*), where on Monday nights you can see a living monument of musical history. Les Paul, the father of the electric guitar, invented reverb and multi-track recordings, essential components of modern recording, and co-designed the Gibson Les Paul, perhaps the most iconic guitar of all time. Les usually hosts a "surprise" guest, and over the years Paul McCartney, Keith Richards, Tony Bennett, Slash, Jeff Beck, Steve Miller, Brian Setzer, Al Dimeola, and George Benson have come to pay their respects and jam. Les may be 93, but he puts on a great show, and always takes the time to meet fans and sign autographs after the 10pm show.

A few blocks south of the Iridium, between 6th and 7th Avenues is "Music Row," a stretch of music shops on 48th Street known for famous clients and huge selections. The most famous is **Manny's** (*156 W 48th St between 6th and 7th Ave*), whose legendary "Wall of Fame" is adorned with the photos, signatures, and receipts of the legends who shopped there, including Benny Goodman, Charlie Parker, Buddy Holly, The Beatles, Jimi Hendrix, Eric Clapton, and Nirvana. Unlike many high-end music shops, beginners and pros alike can try out equipment, and musicians can jam and trade tips.

New York City is also the birthplace of hip-hop. It's a quick ride on the 6 train to **Hush Tours** (*292 5th Ave between 30th and 31st St, Suite 608*), which has special tours that take participants to a variety of spots in the genre's history. Visitors can pick from a menu of tours based on their particular interests, but some of the sites include the Graffiti Hall of Fame (*106th Street and Park Avenue*) and record store Bobby's Happy House. The guides at Hush Tours encourage audience participation. There's even a "Show your Skills Freestyle" portion in which tourists can battle hip-hop legends.

From hip-hop to Bohemia, it's only a short walk from Midtown to the **Chelsea Hotel** (*222 W 23rd St, between 7th and 8th Ave*). Famous residents and visitors in the hotel have been artists of all kinds, but it's the musicians who stayed there that colored it with their antics and immortalized it in song. In the 1960s, Leonard Cohen, Janis Joplin, Joni Mitchell, Bob Dylan, the Grateful Dead, Jimi Hendrix, and The Velvet Underground all frequented the hotel. In the 70s, it hosted the Stooges, Television, The Ramones, Tom Waits, and Patti Smith. The hotel is the setting or subject of dozens of popular songs, including "Sara" by Bob Dylan, "Chelsea Morning" by Joni Mitchell, "Chelsea Hotel #2" by Leonard Cohen, and "Chelsea Girls" by Nico. But the hotel is most famous for being the site where Sid Vicious allegedly murdered girlfriend Nancy Spungen in 1978.

A few stops downtown on the 1 train is the **Village Vanguard** (*178 7th Ave at W 11th St*). Since its opening, the Vanguard has become one of the most vital institutions in jazz music. It's been suggested that the unusual shape of its basement room accounts for its remarkable acoustics. Whatever the reason, the Village Vanguard owns a piece of music history as almost 150 live albums have been recorded here, including the legendary LPs of Sonny Rollins in 1957, Bill Evans and John Coltrane in 1961, and Dexter Gordon's 1976 *Homecoming*. More recently, Paul Motian, Wynton Marsalis, Fred Hersch, and Chris Potter have continued the "Live at the Village Vanguard" tradition.

Of course, these sites can only scratch the surface of New York's immense music history. The city has played a role in the development of almost every major American genre, and whether explorers come looking for the echoes of the past or a taste of New York's thriving music scene, they're sure to find something fascinating.

TOUR: MUSIC HISTORY 83

TOUR: RADICAL HISTORY

The cafés where Emma Goldman, Eugene O'Neill, Alexander Berkman, and other turn-of-the-century agitators once sat may be long gone, but their legacy lives on in the squats, collectives, and co-ops that dot this tiny island. If you're feeling like an anti-Christ, an anarchist, or want to take a stand against The Man, take a tour of some of Manhattan's most radical spots. But please—don't destroy the passersby.

This tour, while possible on foot or by subway, is best done on a bicycle. Susan B. Anthony once said that the bicycle "has done more to emancipate women than anything else in the world," so hop on your revolution-making-mobile and head down to the first location.

Head all the way downtown to Wall Street and start at the site of the country's first revolution, the **Fraunces Tavern** *(54 Pearl St at Broad St)*. Built in 1719, it is one of Manhattan's oldest buildings. George Washington bade farewell to his troops here at the end of the American Revolution. Earlier, the daughter of the building's African-American owner had prevented a bodyguard's assassination attempt on Washington.

Head uptown to the Lower East Side, for a less historic, but no less revolutionary, adventure at **ABC No Rio** *(156 Rivington St between Suffolk and Clinton St)*. ABC No Rio is a legendary anarchist art space that houses a zine collection, darkroom, computer lab, backyard garden, and is the kitchen for New York's Food Not Bombs. Founded in 1980 as a squat, the space has nurtured hundreds of artists. Murals cover the long hallways and the large event room has cheap beer, vegan cupcakes, and handmade T-shirts or patches for sale at every event. Saturdays feature a hardcore/punk matinee. But punk rock bikers beware: bike space is limited; the best bet is to lock up on a Rivington parking meter. After screaming out pent-up aggression at the matinee, catch your breath at **Bluestockings Bookstore** *(172 Allen St at Stanton St)*, a collectively owned radical bookstore, café, and activist space selling over 6,000 progressive texts, zines, and magazines. The airy space, fun staff, and easygoing atmosphere is the perfect spot to sip a cup of coffee, grab a copy of *Bitch* or *$pread* magazine, and settle in for a bit. Throw back something a little stronger amid self-proclaimed freaks, artists and renegades over at the **Marz Bar** *(21 E 1st St at 2nd Ave)*, referred to as the "last dive in Manhattan." Sidle up to the filthy graffiti-covered bar and order an incredibly strong drink served by mostly drunk, belligerent bartenders.

Peddle over to **Tompkins Square Park** *(E 7th St at Ave B)* for a history lesson. This park's radical history dates back to the 1850s, when striking immigrants used the recently built park for demonstrations against unfair working and living conditions. From the 1850s through the 1980s, this was considered one of the most ethnically diverse and least desirable areas of the city. The park was a refuge for the ethnic community that surrounded it, and in the mid-1960s, hippies took over, using the park for an anti-Vietnam War march in 1966. During the city's economic degradation in the 1970s and 1980s, landlords began to set fire to the buildings surrounding the park, increasing the rent 400% due to the availability and relative safety of the area. By the late 1980s, the park acted as a homeless shelter, and in this volatile environment, the infamous Tompkins Square

sexuality. However, a few blocks over at the **Christopher St. Pier** *(Pier 54 at Hudson River)*, a battle rages between residents of this area supporting development projects along the Hudson River and queer homeless of youth of color, who may lose access to this area that they have historically used as a safe gathering place.

The last Friday of every month, politically minded bikers gather at Union Square *(14th St at Broadway)* for the **Critical Mass Bicycle Ride** *(Critical-Mass.info)*. A fun way to meet fellow bicyclers and engage in peaceful, nonviolent environmental protesting, the ride has no clear leader and no direction. The **Lower East Side Ecology Center** *(LESEcologyCenter.org)* provides a way to help the environment by bringing compost to their tent at the Union Square Greenmarket on a Monday, Wednesday, Thursday, Friday, or Saturday.

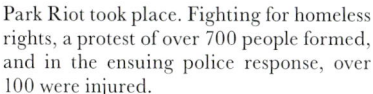

Park Riot took place. Fighting for homeless rights, a protest of over 700 people formed, and in the ensuing police response, over 100 were injured.

After a long day of biking and rioting, grab a bite at **Kate's Diner** *(58 Ave B at E 4th St)*, which offers delicious vegan selections, or the **Sidewalk Café** *(94 Ave A at E 6th St)*, the home of the anti-folk movement.

Moving west, head over to the **Stonewall Inn** *(53 Christopher St between W 4th St and Waverly Pl)*, the site of the Stonewall Riots. This is the place where a police raid turned into a violent protest that paved the way for the gay rights movement. Today, LGBT New Yorkers often consider this area a haven where they can openly express their

On the way home, stop by the new but temporary **Time's Up! space at the Hub** *(73 Morton St between Hudson and Greenwich St)* to pump your tires and sit down for a rest. Time's Up! is an environmental direct action organization that helps organize Critical Mass and also provides free bike-repair workshops.

Whether you're a communist or a capitalist, working class or bourgeoisie, New York's radical spaces provide a different kind of history—one that takes into account the struggle against injustice in all its forms that New York's forgotten citizens have waged throughout the years.

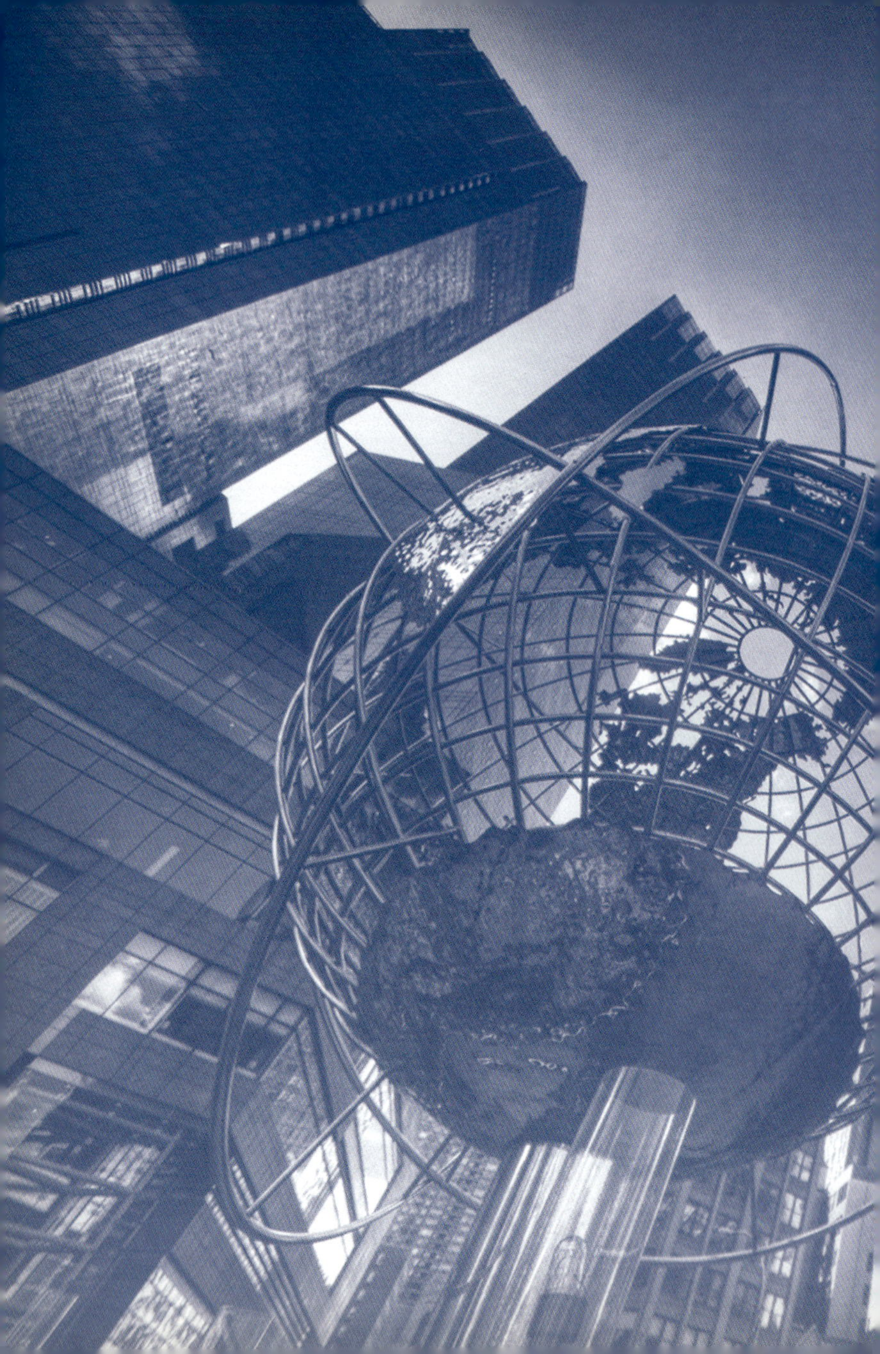

MANHATTAN
BROOKLYN
QUEENS
THE BRONX
STATEN ISLAND

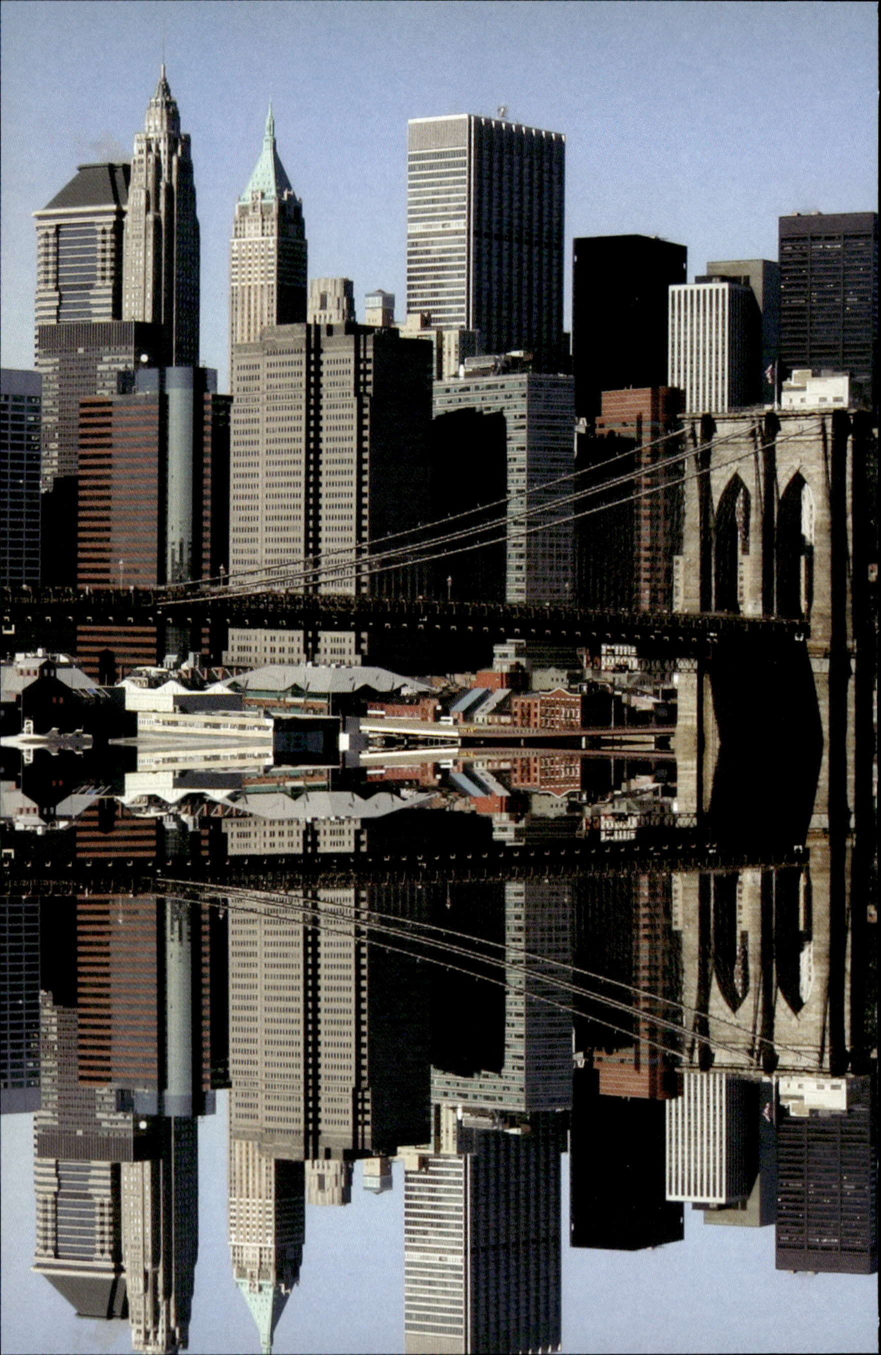

FINANCIAL DISTRICT

Of all the neighborhoods of New York City, the Financial District most encapsulates its historic evolution, from the very first Dutch trade settlements to the commercial center of the world that it is now. Wall St, now synonymous with the expansive economic power of the United States, is so named because it was once the walled northern boundary of the New Amsterdam colony.

Cold gleaming glass-and-steel skyscrapers tower alongside the first national capitol and some of the oldest buildings and churches in America. Bowling Green Park, a small patch of green, is reputedly the site where Manhattan was purchased from the Native Americans for mere dollars. Further south, the New York Harbor, a strategic military site in the 17th and 18th centuries, then the welcoming gate to millions of immigrants in the 19th and 20th centuries, is now the site of the family-friendly Battery Park. From the cobblestoned South Street Seaport historic district to the east to the luxury high rises of Battery Park City to the west, the Financial District's past and present create an interesting juxtaposition indeed.

Today, the neighborhood rouses and retires with the opening and closing bells, after which the frenetic bustle of Wall Street suits gives way to a ghost town and even the local Starbucks shuts down for the weekend. The impact of the World Trade Center attacks reverberate to this day, as Lower Manhattan continues to remain the focus of numerous development projects. Ground Zero, still a gaping hole four blocks square, serves as a constant reminder both of past tragedy and the city's failure to rally around the reconstruction of the site.

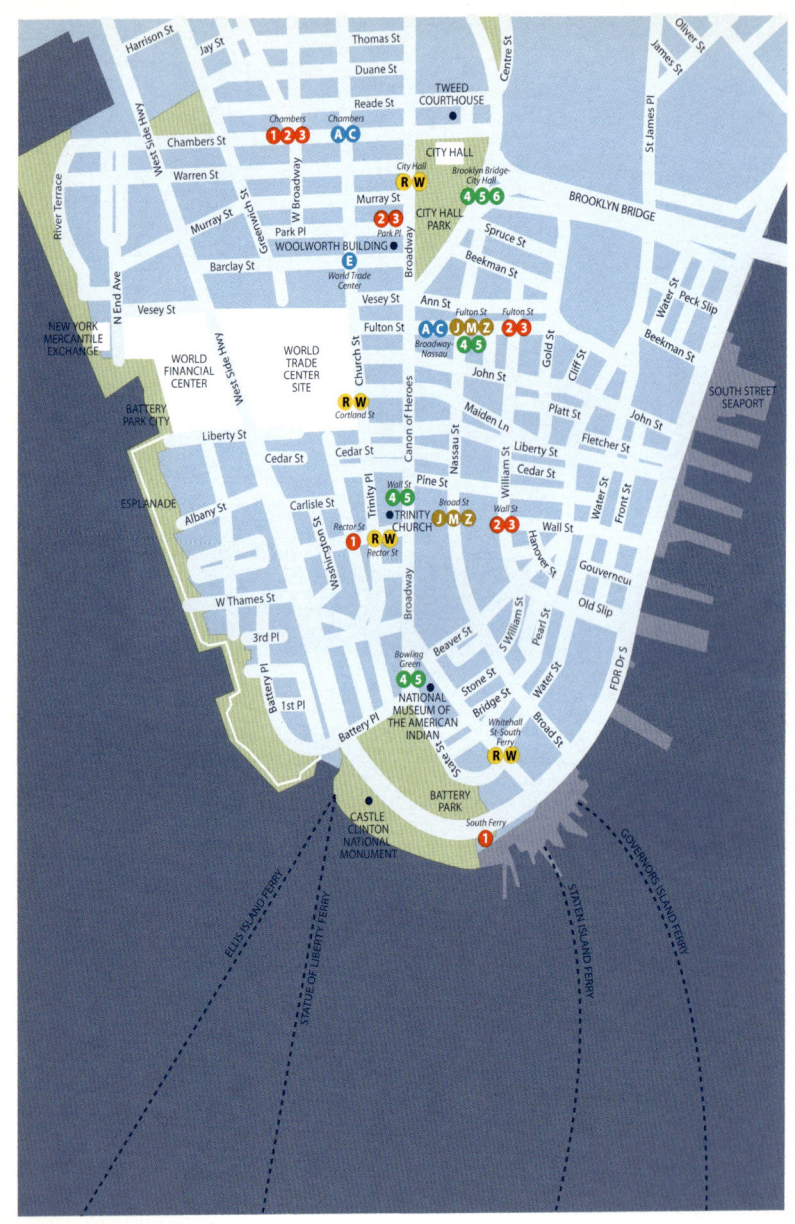

90 FINANCIAL DISTRICT

ATTRACTIONS

Battery Park
Occupying the southernmost tip of Manhattan, the Battery once served as an artillery outpost overlooking the harbor. It is now home to over two dozen monuments, statues, and public art installations. Its various memorials include the Sphere, once located between the World Trade Center towers, its accompanying Eternal Flame commemorating the victims of 9/11, the WWII memorial, and the Korean War memorial. The park offers year-round cultural programming, most notably the summer River to River Festival, but with its unhindered views of the Statue of Liberty and Ellis Island, Battery Park is always worth a stroll.
Battery Pl. (at State St). ❹❺ *to Bowling Green,* ❶ *to South Ferry, or* ❻Ⓦ *to Whitehall.*

Bowling Green
This small public park once faced the water, evidenced by the presence of the former Cunard Lines and U.S. Custom House buildings on its borders. After the creation of Battery Park by landfill, however, the only water visitors will see today is in a pool under the park's large fountain. As the oldest public park in the city, Bowling Green still draws many visitors from nearby offices. Some come to eat lunch in the shade, some patronize the local hawkers, and others join the tourists at Arturo di Modica's *Charging Bull*, where they rub its horns for luck and its testicles for courage—and, no doubt, a measure of hubris.
Between Whitehall and State Sts. ❹❺ *to Bowling Green.*

Brooklyn Bridge
The majestic gothic towers, sweeping arches, and winding steel wires of Brooklyn Bridge, while beautiful from a distance, are most impressive when admired from underneath. After 13 years and two dozen work-related deaths (including that of the original designer-architect), the Brooklyn Bridge opened to the public on May 23, 1883 as the world's longest suspension bridge. In recent years, the Brooklyn Bridge has seen several notable mass pedestrian crossings—following the 9/11 attacks, the 2003 blackout, and the 2005 transit workers strike. However, every New Yorker should take the leisurely half-hour stroll (or bike ride) across the Brooklyn Bridge at least once to enjoy spectacular views of the New York skyline and to gain new appreciation for one of the great engineering landmarks of the U.S.
❹❺❻ *to Brooklyn Bridge/City Hall,* ❷❸ *to Park, or* ❻Ⓦ *to City Hall.*

Canyon of Heroes
The ticker-tape parade that originates here before moving up Broadway to City Hall is one of New York City's oldest traditions and highest honors. Noted heroes include Amelia Earheart, Senator John F. Kennedy, and, recently, the New York Giants, winners of Super Bowl XLII. More than 200 plaques, installed by the Downtown Alliance, mark the Canyon of Heroes and remembers the parades that have taken place there since the first in 1886, for the dedication of the Statue of Liberty. Because many of the earliest dignitaries to parade up Broadway would have disembarked at the Battery, Bowling Green became the starting point for all honorees down to the present.
Bowling Green to 250 Broadway. ❹❺ *to Bowling Green.*

New York City Hall
Completed in 1816, this Beaux-Arts building is the oldest city hall in the country still serving its original governmental function. Over the years, it has seen its share of historic events—the landmark rotunda has housed the coffins of Ulysses Grant and Abraham Lincoln—while accumulating historical artifacts including Washington's desk in the Governor's Room. Free tours of the building are offered on weekdays with an online reservation. Outside, the quaint and quiet park furnished with 19th century gas lamps and a central fountain provides a refuge from the bureaucratic bustle of the surrounding buildings. Hang around the area long enough and you just might catch a glimpse of the mayor or a horde of protesters making their regular rounds.
260 Broadway (at Murray St.). 212-639-9675. ❹❺❻ *to Brooklyn Bridge-City Hall,* ❷❸ *to Park, or* ❻Ⓦ *to City Hall.*

Ellis Island
Between 1892 and 1954 Ellis Island processed more than 12 million immigrants. A typical immigrant spent 3-5 hours at the island; you should expect to spend at least that much time there, if not more. The museum features three

FINANCIAL DISTRICT 91

FOLEY SQUARE

It is hard to imagine that this symbol of NYC government was once a) part of the notorious Five Points district, and b) a polluted pond which, before being drained, supplied NYC citizens with water — and cholera. Today, this patch of green space is surrounded by the **New York County Supreme Court**, the **Thurgood Marshall Federal Courthouse**, and the **United States Courthouse**, all sporting impressive columns in the neo-Classical style. To the east is the looming **New York County Municipal Building** which is topped by *Civic Fame*, a golden statue of a Greek woman holding a crown with five turrets that symbolize the five boroughs of the city. At the center of Foley Square a monument pays tribute to the **African Burial Ground** site, unearthed at the time of the park's construction, which contains the remains of 400 Africans buried during the 17th and 18th centuries. **Tweed Courthouse**, its construction funded by Boss Tweed, lies just around the corner, and offers free tours on Fridays at 2pm. The Foley Square Greenmarket operates year-round on Fridays on the corner of Centre Street between Worth and Pearl Streets.

Intersection of Duane St, Lafayette St, Centre St and Pearl St. ❹❺❻ to Brooklyn Bridge-City Hall, or ❻❼ to City Hall.

floors of exhibits, which recreate the immigration inspection experience. Beginning in the baggage room, visitors can tour medical facilities, hearing rooms (where individual cases were considered), and a fully-restored dormitory, amongst other relics. If you happen to be one of the 40% of Americans who can trace their ancestry back through Ellis Island, pay a visit to the American Family Immigration Center, which allows the public to browse the records of all immigrants who passed through the island.
212-363-3200. Labor Day-Memorial Day: daily, 9am-5pm. Memorial Day-Labor Day: daily, 7:30am-7pm. ❹❺ to Bowling Green, ❶ to South Ferry, or ❻❼ to Whitehall St. Take ferry from Castle Clinton, Battery Park. Adults $12.

Federal Hall National Memorial
Before there were DC and Philadelphia there was Federal Hall, the first capitol of the United States. A bronze statue of George Washington stands on the front steps, marking the original site of his inauguration in 1789. In September 2002, approximately 300 members of Congress convened in Federal Hall to show support for New York City, the first time Congress had met in the city since 1790. Although the original structure was razed in 1812, the current building, erected in 1842 as the country's first Customs House, is one of the best examples of Greek revival architecture in New York. The rotunda houses exhibits on the site's history, including Washington's inauguration (the Bible on which he took his oath is on display) and New York's ratification of the Bill of Rights. Visit Federal Hall on April 30th for the annual reenactment of Washington's inauguration, courtesy of the New York Freemasons.
26 Wall St (at Broad St). 212-825-6888. Mon-Fri 9am-5pm. ❹❺ to Wall, ❶❷❸ to Broad, or ❶❷❸ to Rector.

Federal Reserve Bank
In 1932, the young author Céline wrote, "It was the precious place, as someone explained to me later, the place for gold: Manhattan." Four years earlier, the New York branch of the Federal Reserve Bank had built the world's largest gold storage vault eighty feet under the streets of lower Manhattan, and today this vault holds over 25% of the world's monetary gold supply. With few concerns for security, the Fed allows visitors the opportunity to ogle its clients' massive stock of gold in person—just be sure to reserve several weeks in advance, and to bring identification. For those who haven't made reservations, skip the Fed's exhibit about itself and take an hour to admire its gallery on the history of money, which rivals the British Museum's in quality. The American Numismatic Society's coins include those that George Washington removed from circulation, calling the use of his portrait 'tyrannical,' and the last 1933 Double Eagle—the world's most valuable coin.
33 Liberty St (near Nassau St). 212-720-5200. Mon-Fri 10am-4:30pm; call ahead and bring identification. Tours 1:30pm and 3:30pm; advance reservation required. Free admission. ❷❸❹❺❻❼ to Fulton or ❹❺ to Broadway-Nassau.

St. Paul's Chapel

Completed in 1766, the churchyard and cemetery of St. Paul's sit across from the east side of the World Trade Center site, to which the church's present and future are now inextricably tied. The chapel, which itself withstood the attacks, offered refuge for rescue workers for the eight months following and continues to house ongoing exhibits on the disaster. Offering a more intimate feel than its awe-inspiring sister church, Trinity, St. Paul's is also Manhattan's oldest public building in continuous use. Among its earliest parishioners was George Washington, who attended services there on his Inauguration Day and whose original pew is still preserved today.

209 Broadway (at Fulton St). 212-233-4164. Mon-Sat 10am-6pm, Sun 8am-4pm. Free concerts every Mon 1pm-2pm. ❷❸❹❺❿❾❷ to Fulton, or ❹❼ to Broadway-Nassau.

South Street Seaport

Perhaps more than anyplace else in the city, the South Street Seaport represents a fusion of old and new New York. A commercial hub of the 19th century and the former site of the Fulton Fish Market, its streets are lined with former warehouses and counting houses, evoking a particularly historic feel. Wander its cobblestone streets on any given evening and encounter street performers at every step: magicians, jugglers, living statues, and sometimes even odder sights. The piers offer clear views of the Brooklyn Bridge and the Brooklyn skyline, and on summer nights, a variety of dancing and live music engage the heavy crowds of families and tourists. The museum gives tours of the old ships docked at the port, including the Peking, Wavertree, and Ambrose. Those seeking a more modern spectacle can check out the acclaimed Bodies exhibit.

Fulton and South Sts. 212-732-8257. ❷❸❹❺❿ ❿❷ to Fulton, or ❹❼ to Broadway-Nassau.

Statue of Liberty

Standing 305 feet tall from toe to torch and seen by millions of immigrants arriving in the U.S. in the 19th and 20th centuries, the Statue of Liberty remains one of the most iconic statues in the world. Although the statue, a gift from France in 1886, drew inspiration from the Colossus of Rhodes, Emma Lazarus' famous poem, inscribed on a plaque inside the pedestal, reminds: "Not like the brazen giant of Greek fame with conquering limbs astride from land to land… from her beacon-hand glows world-wide welcome." The statue has been closed to the public since the 9/11 attacks, so you'll have to settle for the view from the pedestal observatory. The museum in the pedestal, which includes the original torch, historical background, and a variety of firsthand accounts from immigrants, is also worth a look.

Entry to the monument pedestal is by Monument Pass only. Call 877-523-9849. For tours, reserve time-stamped tickets by calling 866-782-8834. Daily, 9am-5pm. ❹❺ to Bowling Green, ❶ to South Ferry, ❼❾ to Whitehall. Take ferry from Castle Clinton, Battery Park. Adults $12.

Trinity Church

When Trinity Church was consecrated in 1846, its 25-story Neo-Gothic spire dominated the lower Manhattan skyline. Though today the church is overshadowed by the surrounding skyscrapers, its massive bronze doors and stained glass windows—among the country's oldest—remain a sight to behold. To the left of the entrance lies the "Trinity Root," a

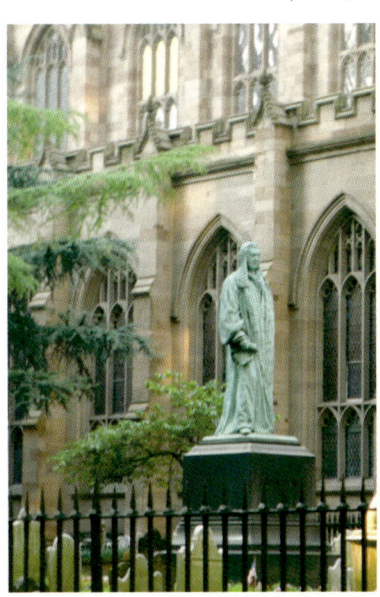

FINANCIAL DISTRICT 93

WORLD TRADE CENTER

The media has mocked our generation for delaying construction on Ground Zero for nearly five years, in the city where the Greatest Generation designed the Empire State Building in two weeks and built it in 410 days. Visit the **World Trade Center Site** between Liberty and Vesey Streets at Church Street to see what all the fuss is about, and to watch construction on the foundations of five of six new towers that will be built there, one of them being the 1,776 foot tall Freedom Tower, along with the first steel beams of the Reflecting Absence memorial and related projects. Also under construction is the World Trade Center Transportation Hub, designed by Santiago Calatrava to resemble a bird being released from a child's hand.

The greatest memorials to the catastrophe of 9/11 are more ephemeral than these, however – the Tribute **WTC Visitor Center** at 12 Liberty Street offers walking tours ($10) guided by those who lived and worked in Lower Manhattan on the day of the attacks, which benefit the September 11th Family Association. Lucky passerbys may also meet Harry Roland, who quit his job as a security guard a block away in order to show pictures and tell the stories of 9/11 for free.

The best view of the Twin Towers' site is from the **Winter Garden** at 2 World Financial Center, from which the Survivor's Stairway is still visible by Vesey St. Another poignant memorial is the **World Trade Center Cross** formed from two fallen beams moved to St. Peter's Church at 22 Barclay Street. Every New Yorker has seen the Tribute in Light, two parallel beams that will pierce the sky every year on September 11th until the completed Freedom Tower directs its single beam upwards.

E to World Trade Center Site, **2 3** to Park, or **4 5** to Fulton.

bronze sculpture made from the roots of the century-old sycamore of St. Paul's Chapel that was felled by World Trade Center attacks. The adjoining graveyard houses tombstones that date back to the 1700s, including those of Robert Fulton and Alexander Hamilton. Trinity Church is particularly known for its organ concerts—check the website for programming schedules.
74 Trinity Place (Broadway and Wall St). 212-602-0800. www.trinitywallstreet.org. Daily 7am-6pm. Tours daily at 2pm. **4 5** *to Wall,* **1 R W** *to Rector, or* **J M Z** *to Broad.*

CULTURE & ARTS

Museum of the American Indian
It might seem strange at first that the National Museum of the American Indian is housed inside the former U.S. Customs House, a stately work of Western Beaux Arts architecture: the murals lining the skylight in the beautiful second-floor rotunda depict the early explorers of the Americas, while the four imposing sculptures outside symbolize the conquest of four continents. Nevertheless, this relatively small (and free) branch of the Smithsonian, occupying only two floors of the building, is a stunning tribute to Native American culture. The first floor's Diker Pavilion, lined with exhibits of Native American garb and other artifacts, doubles as performance space and hosts regular traditional dance and musical performances, as well as workshops and lectures. The second floor houses the main exhibits of the museum, with two impressive exhibition galleries dedicated to the art, culture, and artifacts of different regional and specific tribes, as well as one gallery featuring contemporary Native American art.
1 Bowling Green. 212-514-3700. www.americanindian.si.edu. Sun-Wed and Fri-Sat 10am-5pm, Thurs 10am-8pm. **4 5** *to Bowling Green.*

Sports Museum of America
It's not surprising that New Yorkers consider their city the center of the nation, but it is surprising when the nation grudgingly agrees. On this principle, the Sports Museum of America has convinced more than 50 halls of fame and athletic governing bodies, along with hundreds of athletes and collectors, to share the nation's greatest sports artifacts with the city. These include runner Jesse Owen's Olympic diary,

soccer player Brandi Chastain's famed sports bra, and astronaut Alan Shepard's Wilson six iron, swung on the moon. For those not awed by memorabilia, engaging interactive exhibits that showcase the role of sports in social change and American culture are reason to visit.
26 Broadway on Beaver St. 212-747-0900. Mon-Fri 9am-7pm, Sat-Sun 9am-9pm. ❹ ❺ to Bowling Green, ❶ ❼ Ⓦ to Rector. Adults $27.

DINING

UPSCALE

EDITOR'S PICK

Bridge Café *American*
Continuously in operation since 1794, this tavern has calmed down a bit since its heady days as a brothel and speakeasy, but it remains connected to its past with chummy service, a grown-up menu of classic drinks, and an impressive collection of scotch, bourbon, and whiskey. The menu is appetizer-heavy, since many guests come early and drink with friends into the night. Fresh, thumb-sized oysters are perfectly fried, their light and crispy breading complementing rather than masking the bivalve's briny flavor. Crab dishes are on par with the best, especially the crab, spinach, and artichoke fondue. Entrées consistently please, even if their accompanying sides occasionally underwhelm. Atlantic soft-shelled crab is fried to perfection, and the spicy rack of lamb is well paired with a sweet adobo sauce. By day the bar is filled with City Hall and Wall Street types, but when night falls the crowd can turn unpredictable, as hipsters and tourists bump shoulders with Blackberry-toting regulars. Don't leave without trying the carrot cake.
279 Water St (at Dover St). 212-227-3344. Sun-Mon 11:45am-10pm, Tues-Fri 11:45am-11pm, Sat 5pm-12am. ❹ ❺ ❻ to City Hall, ❶ Ⓙ Ⓩ to Chambers. Average entrée $27.

MID-RANGE

Waterstone Grill *American*
This underwater-themed restaurant thrives because it does not aspire to be upscale, choosing instead to offer a wide range of seafood, steaks and burgers served in typical fashion. While not wildly original, the food is very well prepared. To start, it's hard to beat the seafood risotto—creamy, smooth sauce dresses an abundance of fruit de mare while mushrooms and asparagus provide textural variety. Follow this with the flaky and buttery lemongrass-crusted Chilean sea bass or the Po-Boy sandwich, both of which the Waterstone is deservedly proud of. Key lime pie and the banana foster make great finishers. The laidback atmosphere is sometimes blemished by partying Wall Street types freshly freed from work.
79 Pearl St (at Coenties Alley). 212-943-1602. Mon-Fri 11am-10pm, Sat 12pm-9pm. Ⓡ Ⓦ to Whitehall, ❹ ❺ to Bowling Green, ❷ ❸ to Wall, or Ⓙ Ⓜ Ⓩ to Broad. Average entrée $20.

Sequoia *American*
Gorgeous views of the Brooklyn Bridge, a young and lively crowd, and quality fish make Sequoia a truly transporting dining experience. Head straight for the seafood, the menu's best offerings. The Prince Edward Island Mussels—cooked with white wine, green peppers, parsley and lemon zest–will attract even shellfish skeptics. It's a splurge, but the grilled Maine lobster really shouldn't be missed if it's in season—it bursts with unbelievable coconut-butter flavor and is well worth whatever the market price may be.

FINANCIAL DISTRICT 95

A variety of frozen margaritas, mischievously potent, are great for a hazy summer night. During warmer months, outer deck tables are booked weeks in advance, but the breathtaking views make the wait a worthy sacrifice.
89 Fulton St (between William and Gold St). 212-732-9090. Hours are seasonal, call for details. ❷❸❹❺🅙🅜🅩 *to Fulton,* 🅐🅒 *to Broadway-Nassau. Average entrée $23.*

CHEAP
Adrienne's Pizza Bar *Italian*
A Wall Street after-hours hotspot, Adrienne's Pizza Bar offers quality and authentic Italian food in a sleek, hip setting. Appetizers include a seasonal selection of antipasti and fresh salads. Though they are known for their "Old Fashioned Pizza," a classic square and thin-crust pie, their equally impressive "Piatti Al Forno" (plates baked in the pizza oven) selection includes a range of Italian pastas and fish preparations. Inventor of the Nutella-tini, which is just what it sounds like, the bar serves other inventive cocktails as well. A wine pairing is also offered, unusual for a pizza joint. Midday patrons should expect a fast-paced scene, crowded with Wall Street workers on their lunch break.
54 Stone St. (between Hanover Square and Coenties Alley). 212-248-3838. Mon-Sat, 11:30am-11pm; Sun, *11:30am-10pm.* 🅡🅦 *to Whitehall,* ❹❺ *to Bowling Green,* ❷❸ *to Wall, or* 🅙🅜🅩 *to Broad. Average entrée $16.*

Alfanoose *Middle Eastern*
Widely regarded as the best falafel in New York, Alfranoose continues to live up to its reputation. The hummus and baba ghanoush, both of which are creamy and tangy with garlic and lemon, are easily on par with the falafel. Shish tawook, a heavily spiced and char-grilled chicken, can be enjoyed freshly baked in a pita sandwich or as an entrée. Everything is made to order, and the restaurant offers a clean and spacious dining room for lunch and dinner. The meat and vegetarian platters, served with pita, a side salad, and a generous pile of hummus, baba ghanoush, or tabouli, are reliable, filling deals.
8 Maiden Ln (between Broadway and Nassau). 212-528-4669. Mon-Sat 11:00am-9:00pm. ❷❸❹❺🅙🅜🅩 *to Fulton,* 🅐🅒 *to Broadway-Nassau. Average entrée $10.*

L and L Hawaiian Barbecue *BBQ*
L and L Hawaiian Barbecue's New York outpost does for chicken katsu and spam teriyaki what McDonald's does for the hamburger, but certain touches betray differences between New York and Honolulu. It's not just the surfboards and posters of hula queens hung on the walls. All dishes are made to order with fresh ingredients, and the menu is much broader than those at many fast food joints, with room for teriyaki, tempura, short ribs, and roast pork. For the person who has tried everything on the menu, there is even a sushi bar at the entrance. Touches like hand-cut cucumbers and drink options including Aloha Maid Pass-o-Guava juice set L and L apart from cookie-cutter fast food franchises.
64 Fulton St. (at Gold St.). 212-577-8888. Mon-Sun 11am-11pm. ❷❸❹❺🅙🅜🅩 *to Fulton,* 🅐🅒 *to Broadway-Nassau. Average entrée $7.*

NIGHTLIFE

Bin No. 220 *Bar*
This warmly lit little wine bar offers a sophisticated space in which to relax, enjoy a glass of wine, and nibble on tapas against a beautiful brick wall or at the gleaming wooden

bar. In the early evening hours, the bar remains quiet save for financiers and the occasional tourists looking to enjoy a calm drink or standard Italian tapas before heading to their next destination. Later into the night, the place is abuzz with conversation while patrons select wine from the mainly Italian selection of 60 wines by the bottle and 20 by the glass.

220 Front St (between Beekman St & Peck Slip). 212-374-9463. Daily 4pm-12am. ⒶⒸ to Broadway–Nassau, ❷❸❹❺ⒿⓂ❼ to Fulton. Average drink $10.

Jeremy's Ale House *Bar, Dive*

If the weekday "breakfast special"— 32 oz buckets of Original Coors for $1.75 between 8am and 10am—doesn't draw you in, at least come back for dinner: these ice cold Styrofoam monstrosities available all day for only $4. The bar, a cavernous space with nautical tchotchkes (and bras) hanging from the ceiling, brings in an odd mix of salty dockworkers, vaguely dipsomaniacal businessmen making use of the free Wi-fi, and the same 20-something crowd that pops up every bar where the floor is dirty and the booze is cheap. Jeremy's boasts a large beer selection in addition to the cheap stuff. Gentlemen, don't expect to pick up anything other than a plate of perfectly fried clams and an enormous cold beer.

228 Front St (between Beekman St and Peck Slip). 212-964-3537. Mon-Sat 8am-midnight; Sun 12pm–10pm. ❷❸❹❺ⒿⓂ❼ to Fulton, ⒶⒸ to Broadway-Nassau. Average drink $5.

SHOPPING

Century 21

With prices from 40 to 70% off retail, Century 21 is the place to go for designer discounts. The store has 15 departments which provide the illusion of organization—household and electronics in the basement, men's on the mezzanine level, women's on the second and third floors, etc—but don't come here if you must find some specific item. Rather, Century 21 is a store where finding those perfect designer duds on the cheap means browsing endless racks. On weekends and in the evening, the store can get busy, so the best time to go is when everyone else is at work.

22 Cortlandt St (between Church and Broadway).

DAY TO DAY

Community Board 1: *49-51 Chambers St, Rm 715. 212-442-5050.*

Groceries: Zeytuna Market: *59 Maiden Ln Basement, 212-742-2436.* Jubilee Marketplace: *99 John St (between Cliff St & Gold St), 212-233-0808.* Gristedes: *90 Maiden Ln (between Gold St & Liberty St), 212-651-8255.*

Average Rent: Studio: $2,000; One-bedroom: $2,400.

Hospitals. New York Downtown Hospital: *170 William Street. 212-312-5000.* Saint Margaret's House Medical Center: *49 Fulton Street. 212-608-3980.*

Dog Runs: Fishbridge Park: *Dover Street (between Pearl & Water St).* River Terrace Run: *River Terrace (at Murray St).*

Movie Theater: Regal Cinemas Battery Park Stadium 11. *102 North End Avenue.*

Best Happy Hour: Dakota Roadhouse *43 Park Pl. 212-962-9800. Daily, 11am-4pm. Happy Hour Mon-Wed 5pm-7pm.*

212-227-9092. Mon-Wed 7:45am-8pm, Thurs-Fri 7:45am-10pm, Sat 10am-8pm, Sun 11am-7pm. ⒶⒸⒺ to Chambers, ⓃⓇ to Cortlandt.

Mariposa: The Butterfly Gallery

Stepping into Mariposa feels like stepping into a glass case, where the customer himself is being put on display. Resembling a museum more that it does a shop, Mariposa showcases hundreds of pinned butterflies in beautiful arrangements in the glass cases on the walls. Although on the pricier side, the place makes for a breathtaking browse, and some of its more affordable offerings would make great unique gifts.

Pier 17 Pavillion. Fulton and South Sts. 212-233-3221. ❷❸❹❺ⒿⓂ❼ to Fulton, ⒶⒸ to Broadway-Nassau.

FINANCIAL DISTRICT 97

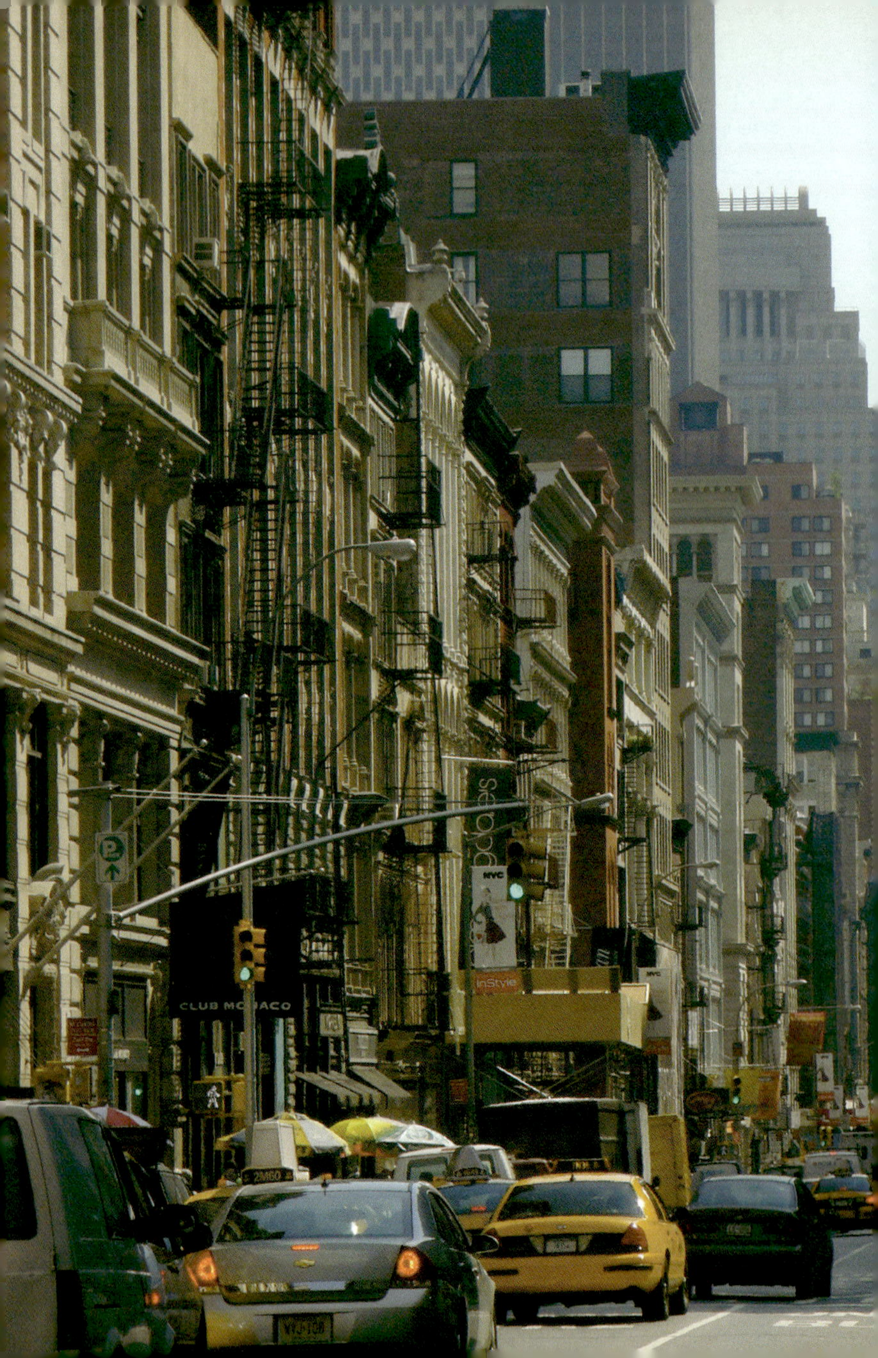
NYC
InStyle

SOHO & TRIBECA

SoHo ("South of Houston," but never, ever call it that) has consistently thought of itself as one of the hippest neighborhoods in the city. Once a flagship arts district, the area has seen its artist and gallery populations dwindle as rising rents have made everyone's favorite dwelling—the loft—largely unaffordable for creative types. In their stead have appeared denizens of the fashion world, more capable of affording the high prices. With boutique stores lining the cobblestone streets, a mixture of American Apparel clad hipsters and Prada adorned models make for a self-consciously pretty mix.

While the North end of SoHo has been infiltrated by the wealthy and fashionable, the South still retains much of its character (and artsy, loft-dwelling population) from the old days. Crowds thin out and suddenly one can see the neighborhood's original cast-iron architecture. Even some of the old factories remain, though their days are numbered; the real-estate boom continues unabated, and Donald Trump has been rumored to be snatching up property.

South of SoHo lies TriBeCa ("Triangle Below Canal," see above for usage notes) which, like SoHo, was once dominated by warehouses that have now been turned into loft apartments. After September 11th the area suffered financially, but rebounded with some help from the government. It has since become the trendiest of residential neighborhoods, listed as the 12th most expensive zip code in the US. Between this newly acquired glitz and the annual TriBeCa Film Festival in May, don't be surprised to see a star or two on the street; Gisele Bündchen, Jay-Z, and Jon Stewart all call the neighborhood home.

100 SOHO & TRIBECA

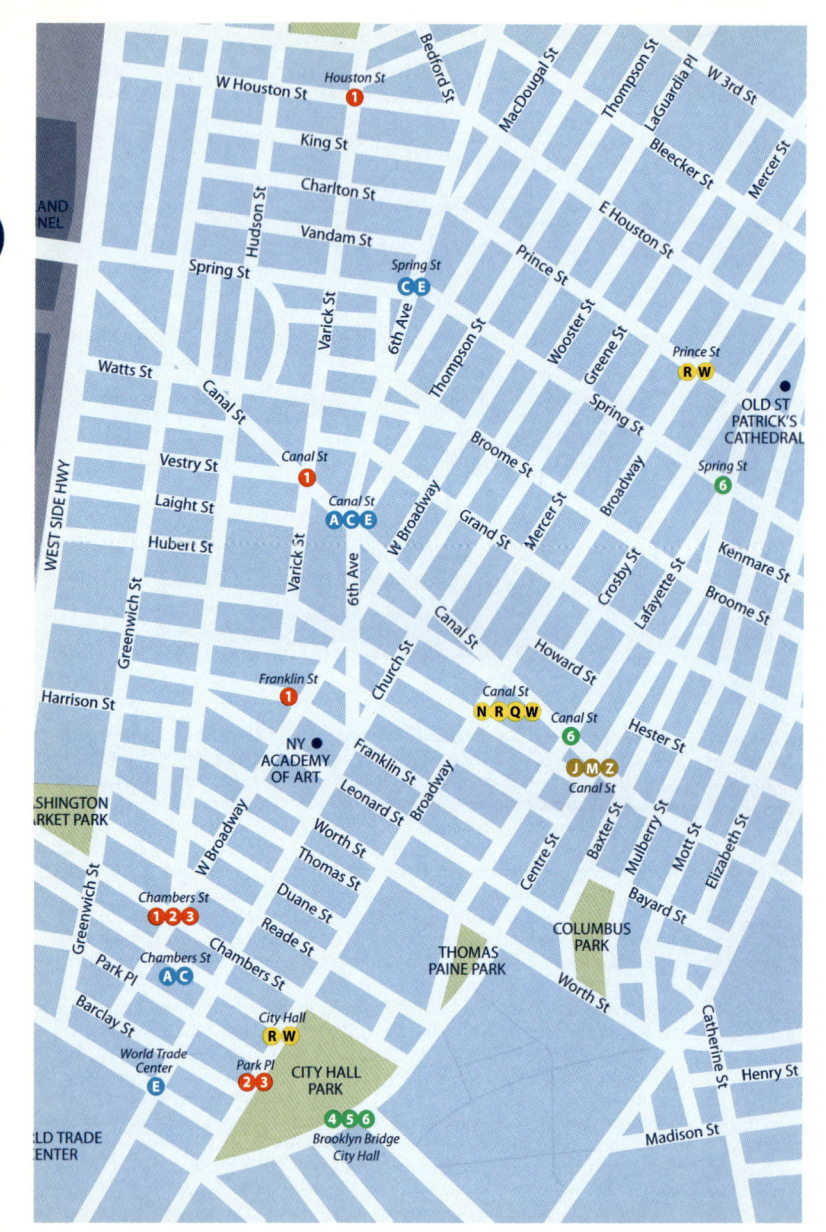

ATTRACTIONS

NYC Fire Museum
Located in a 1904 firehouse, this museum displays collections of FDNY artifacts and memorabilia dating as far back as the 1700s, while the most recent exhibition honors the heroic efforts of the firefighters who died in action on 9/11. This unique museum illustrates the evolution of firefighting techniques and equipment, including old fire engines, fire helmets, coats, and an assortment of tools. The museum also holds a fire-safety education program, teaching fire prevention and escape. Visiting the 9/11 memorial area is very emotional for some, to say the least.
278 Spring St (between Hudson & Varick St). 212-691-1303. Tues-Sat 10am-5pm, Sun 10am-4pm. ❶ *to Houston,* ❸ *to Spring. Admission $4*

Saint Patrick's Old Cathedral
Built in 1809 by the same architect behind City Hall, this cathedral has weathered many historic events and a constantly changing community. Although this church is dwarfed by its newer brother parish, its value is measured not in size but in time, as well as design. The simple and modest façade gives way to a majestic and intricate interior. From the old cemetery to the organ, history permeates the walls of this building, which have managed to stand the test of time. Its parish is extremely diverse: Sunday masses are held in English, Spanish, and Chinese, allowing for just about all of the local Catholics to participate.
264 Mulberry St (at Prince & Mott St). 212-226-8075. Daily- 9am. ❻ *to Bleecker or* ❶❻ *to Prince.*

CULTURE & ARTS

Storefront for Art and Architecture
Located on a triangular corner, the façade of this gallery is composed of twelve panels that pivot open vertically and horizontally. Designed by artist Vito Acconci and architect Steven Holl, the building's exterior can be morphed at will—it is as much an artwork as anything on exhibition inside, much of which is site-specific and incorporates the building's structure in novel ways. Exhibitions focus primarily on architecture and the lived environment, with a secondary emphasis on art and design.
97 Kenmare St. (between Mulberry & Lafayette St). 212-431-5795. Tue-Sat 11am-6pm, Closed Sun-Mon. ❶❻ *to Prince,* ❸❶❻❻ *to Lafayette.*

Swiss Institute of Contemporary Art
Originally devoted to delivering Swiss art to a Swiss audience, this gallery has grown to become venue for international art and cultural dialogue between Switzerland, Europe, and the US. Despite having expanded their stable of artists beyond Swiss borders, the loft's museum-quality space still frequently features shows with only Swiss artists. They deal in all mediums and also offer screenings of recent Swiss films as well as dance performances and concerts.
495 Broadway 3rd Floor (between Spring & Broome St). 212-925-2035. Tue-Sat 11am-6pm. ❶❻ *to Prince,* ❻ *to Spring.*

The Wooster Group
For three decades the Wooster Group has been developing theatre techniques old and new at The Performing Garage—their home in SoHo. Under the direction of Elizabeth LeCompte, the group works as an ensemble to juxtapose theatrical elements like video, movement, and script-reinterpretation to create theatre pieces which engage with modern theatre. Past pieces have included a reinterpretation of *Hamlet* based on Richard Burton's 1964 movie and a postmodern, multimedia interpretation of Eugene O'Neill's *The Hairy Ape*.
33 Wooster St (near Grand St). 212-966-9796. ❶❷❸❻❻❻ *to Canal.*

DINING

UPSCALE
Aquagrill *Seafood*
Though the cheesy "upscale" twist on nautical decor may not impress diners, don't despair; the menu is plenty grand. The restaurant itself is a comfortable, cheerful setting where families and trendy urbanites gather to enjoy some of the best seafood in Manhattan. If the selection of over 50 oysters at the raw bar doesn't impress, the rest of the menu certainly will. The Crabcake Napoleon is full of fresh, spicy, crab meat, without an ounce of filler. Entrée-wise, seared diver scallops over

SOHO & TRIBECA 101

peekytoe crab risotto is a perfect combination of flavors. Skip sides such as the potato hash for the rich truffle polenta. The kitchen pays special attention to dessert, offering complimentary petit fours as well as a selection of other treasures, including a special "Saturday Night Soufflé."
210 Spring St (at 6th Ave). 212-274-0505. Mon-Thurs 12pm-3pm, 6pm-10:30pm, Fri 12pm-3pm, 6pm-11:30pm, Sat 12pm-3:30pm, 6-11:30pm, Sun 12pm-3:30pm, 6pm-10:15pm. ⒸⒺ to Spring, ❶❷ to Houston. Average entrée $25.

Fiamma *Italian*
Fiamma offers another colorful, esoteric take on Italian cuisine. The duo of wagyu beef and ravioli filled with sheep's milk ricotta are excellent choices for appetizers. Smoked fingerling potato gnocchi provides an interesting twist on the rather trademark Italian dish and the spicy calabrese chiles and chervil combine to produce a strong, marked flavor. For the carnivores, the Emerald Farms baby lamb is exquisite. Perhaps the most impressive element of this establishment, however, is its elegant décor. With three lavishly appointed floors and a glass elevator, Fiamma is aesthetically stimulating on every level.
206 Spring St (near 6th Ave) 212-653-0100. Mon-Thurs 12pm-2:30pm, 5:30pm-11pm, Fri 12pm-2:30pm, 5:30pm-12am, Sat 5:30pm-12am, Sun 5pm-10pm. ⒸⒺ to Spring. Prix fixe $85-$125.

Giorgione 307 *Italian*
Fresh and simple are the buzzwords for this chic SoHo spot. From the industrial metal tables set against gray leather banquettes to the sleek, glass-topped bar, the sophisticated décor exudes a modern elegance also found in the cuisine. High quality ingredients are the key to this restaurant's success, and the dishes that excel the most are the straightforward compositions that allow the naked flavor of the food to shine through. Grilled baby octopus, always a favorite, is perfectly tender and complemented accordingly with crisp celery, grape tomatoes, and just a hint of bitterness from black olives. Branzino and sautéed broccoli rabe with a hint of lemon and olive oil is a lighter option, while ribeye steak with roasted shallot and nebbiolo reduction is a generous indulgence. If you still have room for dessert, cheesecake is a wonderfully creamy treat.
307 Spring St (between Hudson St and Greenwich St). 212-352-2269. Sun-Thurs 6pm-12am, Fri-Sat 6pm-1am. ⒶⒸⒺ to Spring. Average entrée $30.

EDITOR'S PICK
Kittichai *Thai*
It is easy to feel cynical about nouveau Asian cuisine, but this remarkable restaurant gets right what so many others get wrong. While innovative, the food stays true to its traditional roots even in the midst of its most playful conceits. The pineapple braised short rib, resting in a pool of green curry sauce dotted with Thai eggplant, is a flawless synthesis of heavy protein and delicate spice. As is the duck breast, which is gently glazed with a spicy tamarind sauce. When it comes to the details, Kittichai doesn't miss a step. Appetizers such as the banana blossom and artichoke salad with cashews and chili jam are exceptional, as are the side dishes. The bar offers stellar house cocktails which effectively blend complex ingredients and, though many feature tropical fruit, none are saccharine sweet. Richly colored drapery on the walls, gentle lighting, and a calmly gurgling pond in the middle of the dining room create an atmosphere simultaneously serene and sexy while well spaced tables provide ample privacy.
60 Thompson St (between Spring & Broome St) 212-219-2000. Breakfast 7am-11am, Brunch Sat-Sun 11am-2:45pm, Lunch Mon-Fri 12pm-2:45pm, Dinner Sun-Wed 5:30pm-11pm Thurs-Sat 5:30-12am. ⒸⒺ to Spring, ❶ to Canal, ⓇⓌ to Prince. Average entrée $25.

MID-RANGE
Duane Park *American, Southern*
Duane Park offers a consistently solid, novel dinner, from the first piece of bread and white bean sauce to the classic American desserts. When in season, don't miss their delicious grilled figs, stuffed with Gorgonzola cheese and served with prosciutto, which demand a slow, thoughtful chew in order to savor each layer of flavor. For the main event, the fluffy-on-the-inside, crispy-on-the-outside scallops are their pride and joy. The steak, too, has a wonderful texture, but is perhaps overshadowed by the heavenly grilled Yukon gold potatoes that accompany it. A charming interior resembling the state room of a mansion—complete with chandelier, white columns, and white wallpaper with ornate etchings—creates a cozy and intimate ambiance for diners.
157 Duane St (near West Broadway). 212-732-5555. Lunch Mon-Fri 12pm-3pm. Afternoon Tea Mon-Fri 3pm-4pm. Dinner Mon-Sun 5:30pm-11pm. Brunch Sun 11:30am-3pm. Average entrée $23. ❶❷❸ⒶⒸ to Chambers.

Landmarc *New American*
A mix of French, Italian, and Steakhouse fare, Landmarc defies categorization. Appetizers range from the familiar, like fried calamari, or smoked mozzarella and ricotta fritters, to the more refined—it's not every day you have a chance to order roasted marrow bones with onion marmalade. Entrée selections are just as diverse; they include daily pasta specials, mussels with a choice of sauce, steaks, and savory offal preparations like sweetbreads, braised tongue, and calf's liver—all executed well. Landmarc is equally known for its wine selection; the globe-spanning list is extensive and affordable. Landmarc does away with high mark-ups and charges a pittance more than the bottle's retail price. Most plates, including the dessert sampler, are easily shared and make for a group-friendly dining experience.
179 West Broadway (near Leonard St). 212-343-3883. Mon-Fri 11am-2am, Sat-Sun 9am-2am. ❶ *to Franklin. Average entrée $22.*

L'Ecole *French*
Senior students from the French Culinary Institute showcase their skills at L'École ("The School"), one of New York's better and more unconventional French restaurants. The bargain priced prix fixe menu changes quarterly, offering varied and inventive selections like cold avocado soup or the creatively prepared seared duck. Accompanying the delicious fare are clever cocktails, an excellent wine selection, and a cheese plate to rival the most decadent dessert. The crème brulée has a delicately burned top with a smooth finish that pairs well with a glass of Muscat.
462 Broadway (at Grand St) 212-219-3300. Lunch Mon-Fri 12:30pm-2pm, 4-Course Prix Fixe Dinner Mon-Sat 5:30pm-7pm, 5-Course Prix Fixe Dinner: Mon-Sat 8:00pm-9:00pm. ❶❻❽❾ *to Canal. Average dinner $42.*

Turks and Frogs *Mediterranean*
From Turks and Frogs Bar in the West Village has sprung a full-fledged restaurant that shares both its name and its romantic, vintage atmosphere. Upholstered in red velvet, dotted with peeling oil paintings, and lit by brass chandeliers, Turks and Frogs is as visually pleasing as it is delicious. A menu of Mediterranean-inspired cold and hot appetizers, including homemade eggplant hummus and zucchini pancakes with yogurt sauce, are a vegetarian dream. The menu is always interesting with unique dishes such as salmon wrapped in grape leaves, a pistachio pudding dessert, and artful cocktails (ask resident bartender Cosme to whip you up

the cocktail du jour).
458 Greenwich St (between Watts St and Debrosses St) 212-966-4774. Sun-Thurs 11am-11pm, Fri-Sat 11am-1am. ❶ *to Canal. Average entrée $18.*

CHEAP
Bonbon Chicken *Korean*
When lunch hour rolls around, FiDi commuters hit this takeout location that's boldly trying to bring integrity back to the chain-dominated fried chicken market. The small menu has some Asian-inspired twists, like kimchi coleslaw, fish and rice bowls, and fries with wasabi mayo, but people come for the chicken. Deep fried to an impeccable crispiness and glazed in sweet or sour sauces, the chicken comes served with rice, on buns, in salads and sandwiches, or à la carte. It's all made-to-order, so be prepared to wait up to 20 minutes during rush hours–Bonbon cheerfully stretches the definition of fast food to produce a higher quality drumstick.

98 Chambers St (at Church St) 212-227-2375. Mon-Sat 11am-10pm, Sun 12pm-9pm. ❶❷❸Ⓐ❻ *to Chambers. Average entrée $8.*

Rice to Riches *Dessert*
Looking for a healthy, light dessert? Then move on, because Rice to Riches spares no calories in its quest to create the perfect rice pudding, especially since it's the only thing they sell around here, in 20 glorious flavors. This is rice pudding at its richest and best, topped with fresh seasonal fruit. The whipped cream-smothered Chocolate Chip Flirt and the Rest in Peach, topped with roasted fruits, are particularly excellent.

37A Spring St (near Mulberry St). 212-274-0008. Sun-Wed 11am-11 pm, Thu-Sat 11am-12am, ❹❻ *to Spring,* ❽Ⓓ❺Ⓥ *to Broadway-Lafayette,* ❿Ⓜ *to Bowery,* ⓃⓇⓌ *to Prince. Pudding $4-8.*

Tribeca Treats *Dessert, Bakery*
Quality trumps quantity at this sparsely decorated bakery, which you may at first mistake for a stationery store—so conspicuously absent are the expected rows of tightly packed goodies. Rather, you will find a limited selection of meticulously executed desserts. The light, airy cupcake frosting and the single grain of salt adorning each chocolate bar evince a sensibility prone to both balance and adventure. With owner Rachel Thebault,

your taste buds are in good hands.
94 Reade St (near Church St). 212-571-0500. Mon-Sat 10am-7pm. ❶❷❸Ⓐ❻ *to Chambers.*

Zucker's Bagels & Smoked Fish *Deli*
With steel countertops and old-fashioned subway-style tiling, Zucker's looks like a relic from TriBeCa's industrial past. The aroma of fresh hand-rolled bagels wafts out the doorway, ensnaring customers with the promise of creamy spreads, such as the kalamata olive or bold Jalapeño, slathered atop the bagel of your choosing, from garlic to pumpernickel and beyond. The cool lox on the "Traditional" sandwich conjures visions of a seaside boardwalk on a fresh summer day, while the spicy mustard and hot corned beef on the "NYC Deli Classic" will end up all over your fingers. Before you leave, unchain your inner child and nab a handful of moist chocolate chip cookies from the baker's jar.

146 Chambers St (between W Broadway and Greenwich St) 212-608-5844. Daily 6:30am-8pm. ❶❷❸ *to Chambers. Sandwiches $6-10.*

NIGHTLIFE

Antarctica *Bar*
This far-west SoHo saloon is still a bit of a hike unless you happen to work or live nearby. The old wood bar and candle fixtures on the walls give Antarctica a nostalgic character—probably why Ed Burns used it as a location in several films. The friendly staff and eager-to-relax after-work crowd, along with $6 pint glasses full of your choice of mixed drink, make it easy for a sober man's thoughts to become a drunk man's words. First names are drawn out of a bucket each night: if it matches the name on your ID, drinks are on the house.

287 Hudson St (at Spring St) 212-352-1666. Mon-Wed 4:30pm-2am, Thurs-Friday 4:30pm-4am, Sat 7pm-4am, closed Sun. ❶Ⓐ❻Ⓔ *to Canal. Average drink $6.*

B-Flat *Restaurant, Bar*
B-Flat is fixated on the art of the cocktail—there aren't any plastic cups or coffee-stirrer straws here. Perfectly blended cocktails are served in tall glasses with suitably sized ice cubes. You may find it difficult to pick your

poison, as the menu is dominated by high-end selections of every variety of liquor, along with original fruit-infused house cocktails. Instead of greasy bar food you'll find a pristine selection of Asian-inspired small plates to go with your drink. Despite the name, B-Flat is far from an authentic jazz bar, but the dark leather upholstery and wood-paneled walls are authentically chic. Drinks are served only to patrons seated at bar or booth so the bartender can focus on his craft.
277 Church Street (between Franklin St and White St). 212-219-2970. Mon-Sat 5:00pm-4:00am. ❶ *to Franklin,* Ⓐ Ⓒ Ⓔ Ⓝ Ⓡ Ⓠ Ⓦ ❺ *to Canal. Average entree $12. Average drink $10.*

Bubble Lounge *Champagne bar*
Hundreds of bottles of lavishly priced champagne line the dimly lit walls of this extravagant champagne bar. A full bar serves up cocktails like the Green Fairy, a popular absinthe based drink, but there's no question that it plays second fiddle to the champagne menu. Here, it's all about the bubbly: tied for first with its sister location in San Francisco, Bubble Lounge has the largest selection of champagne in the U.S., and a markup to match. Its a popular destination for investment bankers and big spenders looking to impress their dates or business partners, so come looking sharp and be ready to burn a hole straight through your wallet.
228 W Broadway (between Franklin St & White St) 212-431-3433. Mon–Thurs 5pm–2am, Fri, Sat 5pm–4am. ❶ *to Franklin. Average drink $12.*

Circa Tabac *Smoking lounge*
Tobacco enthusiasts on the run from New York's draconian smoking ban find sanctuary at this Art Deco shrine to the cigarette—one of only six locations in the city where indoor smoking is still legal. You can bring your own pack, but many take advantage of the impressive selection of boutique cigarettes and knowledgeable servers, who can direct you to exactly the smoke you're looking for. Non-smokers will find what they need at the exceptional bar that provide a selection of classic New York house drinks and champagne cocktails that perfectly suits the dim, speakeasy vibe. In the early evening a quiet crowd and tranquil street view make this a soothing oasis. Around midnight, expect to hear a feel-good playlist as the room fills with smoke and smartly dressed patrons. N.B.: the bartender makes a perfect Manhattan.
32 Watts St (between 6th Ave and Thompson St) 212-941-1781. Sun-Mon 5pm-2am, Tues-Sat 5pm-4am. ❶ Ⓐ Ⓒ Ⓔ *to Canal. Average Drink $12.*

Patriot Saloon *Bar*
"Save a horse, ride a barmaid," slurs a slogan scrawled on a chalkboard sign outside this saloon. Country music blares, bras hang from the ceiling, and scantily clad bartenders encourage dancing on the bar and dish out free shots to a mixed crowd of locals, southerners, frat boys, and the occasional female. The Patriot has pool tables, dartboards, full bars on two floors, and ridiculously cheap drink specials, such as $5.50 pitchers of PBR. Waitresses dressed as schoolgirls serve greasy snacks for around $2. Beware slow weekday evenings, when the festive turns feeble.
110 Chambers St (between W Broadway and Church St). 212-748-1162. 11am-4am. ❶ ❷ ❸ Ⓐ Ⓒ Ⓔ *to Chambers. Average drink $4.*

EDITOR'S PICK

Santos' Party House *Dance club*
Owned by musician Andrew W.K., this bi-level dance space has all the hardcore partying of his previous success, Studio B. Because of its predecessor's rep, Santos' draws some of the hottest DJ's for weekend sets. The interior is painted in carnival funhouse colors, with signs posting club rules, the most important being 'NO PHOTOGRAPHS'. The vast top floor, showcasing big name DJs and bands, is the place to be, while the bottom bar level has typical dance music (and spots to sit if you punk out). With plenty of space to move and 3 bar areas with quick service, this is a venue for people who love music, love to dance, and love to get shitfaced.
100 Lafayette St (at Walker St). 212-714-4646. See website for showtimes/hours. Ⓙ Ⓜ ❷ Ⓝ Ⓡ Ⓠ Ⓦ ❻ *to Canal. $5 Cover, Average Drink $10.*

Thom Bar *Bar*
This is the place to see and be seen. Girls with twiggy legs, minidresses, and stilettos, cuddle up with their yuppie guys in the plush, but not very private, booth areas where PDA becomes rampant after a few martinis. Almost non-

existent lighting and a DJ generate the self-conscious "cool" atmosphere. Whether this be your scene or sociology project, the menu will keep you from smirking. Cocktails are made with fresh ingredients like huge chunks of strawberries, pineapple, and coconut that make straws impossible and forks desirable. The Thom, a martini spin on a classic mojito, tastes like mint fresh out of the garden from the first to the last sip.
60 Thompson St (between Spring St and Broome St). 212-219-2000. Mon-Sun 5pm-2am. ❻❼ to Spring. Average cocktail $12.

Tribeca Tavern *Bar*
An extensive beer menu and good food make this popped-collar bar stand out amongst the deadly dull chic of the surrounding area. Though the bar itself does little to differentiate itself from other pubs, taverns, or sports bars in Manhattan, the atmosphere makes for a guaranteed good time. The jukebox is full of road trip favorites (Journey, Stray Cats, etc.) and the crowd never overwhelms the space, even at peak drinking hours. The staff is friendly and knowledgeable, which is crucial considering the vast assortment of exotic beers. They have killer pizza, plenty of seating, and a pool table. For those seeking unpretentious fun, an anomaly in the area, this bar has it down to a T.
247 W Broadway (at Walker St). 212-941-7671. 11am-4am. ❶ to Franklin, ❹❻❼ to Canal. Average Drink $5.

SHOPPING

Agent Provocateur
This vampy boutique is more than a little kitschy. Chandeliers in the dressing rooms and uninterested salesgirls clad in fishnet stockings add to the boudoir-like atmosphere. The style is classic pin-up with a sexy, modern twist, and with sizes running from 32A to 36F, you won't have trouble finding the perfect fit. Downsides? Some may find $60 a bit steep for a pair of underwear, but the shop's prices are on par with its SoHo neighbors.
133 Mercer St (between Prince St and Spring St). 212-965-0229. Mon-Sat 11am-7pm, Sun 12pm-6pm. ❶❻❼ to Prince.

Built by Wendy
Started in 1991 by Chicago native Wendy Mullin, who began her business by selling guitar straps, Built by Wendy now has a full line of men and women's clothing in chic and innovative prints and cuts. The clothing sells for standard prices for the trendy neighborhood (jeans go for $135 and T-shirts for $35), but steep price tags are worth it for smart specialty pieces which will become closet staples and won't go out of style anytime soon. The store also carries Wendy's signature guitar straps, in plaid, striped, suede, tweed, and canvas varieties, as well as Sew U, a sewing guide series created by the designer.
7 Centre Market Pl (near Broome St). 212-925-6538. ❶❻ to Prince, ❻ to Spring. Mon-Sat 12pm-7pm, Sun 12pm-6pm.

Daily 2.3.5.
This colorful gift store is home to gag gifts, stationery, rare toys, candy, and collectibles spanning countries and decades. Among the items you can find in this store are talking alarm clocks from Japan, Buddha statuettes, and Danish housewares. Don't come looking for a specific object, but you're certain to find the perfect knick-knack amidst the store's tastefully arranged selection. Reasonable prices have kept this shop popular for years.
235 Elizabeth St (near Prince St). 212-334-9728. Mon-Sat 12pm-8pm, Sun 12pm-7pm. ❻❼❽❾ to Broadway-Lafayette, ❹❺❻ to Bleecker.

Dö Kham
Should you step inside Dö Kham to escape the trendy streets of Soho, you'll find racks full of beautifully embroidered, brightly colored silk kaftans as well as Tibetan rugs both new and antique—the commercial treasures of the Himalayas. Pick out a unique gift for a friend or grab a Himalayan painting for your own walls. This small shop is especially well-known for its range of silk and fur hats, as well as for the vast selection of pashminas that are available in an overwhelming array of rich colors.
51 Prince St (near Mulberry St). 212-966-2404. Mon-Sun 10am-8pm. ❶❻ to Prince.

Gotham Bikes
This bike shop is jam packed with all the gear any cyclist, be they leg-shaving racer

or casual peddler, could ever need. Racks of bikes include everything from $4,000 carbon-fiber feathers to $200 cruisers. Regardless of how much you spend, the store's lifetime tune-up policy will keep you in the saddle. The knowledgeable staff members are all cyclists themselves, and they're always happy to come to the aid of the weary. Visitors looking for weekend wheels should drop by as well; daily rental rates are extremely reasonable.
112 W Broadway (at Reade St). 212-732-2453. Mon-Sat 10am-6:30pm, Sun 10am-5pm. ❶❷❸Ⓐ Ⓒ to Chambers. Rentals $10/hr, $30/day.

MarieBelle
Filled with chandeliers, bright blue packages, and dark-paneled wooden and glass shelves and tables, the interior of this unique chocolate shop is almost as enchanting as the sweets it holds. The chocolates come in a large variety of flavors, including lavender, dulce de leche, and dark meyer lemon. The colorful designs that identify the flavors turn each chocolate into a small work of art. Welcoming salespeople will help you choose a combination of flavors for a box of chocolates, or you can create your own mixture. Boxes run between $15 and $260.
484 Broome St (near Wooster St). 212-925-6999. Mon-Sat 11am-7pm, Sun 12pm-7pm. Ⓝ Ⓡ Ⓦ to Prince, Ⓒ Ⓔ to Spring.

Opening Ceremony
While this ultra-hip clothing store may be intimidating, its attitude comes with a selection of trendsetting, edgy clothing and accessories for men and women. The apparel here is not for the timid or bashful; the clothing racks are full of innovative shapes and surprising materials, often designed by big names and celebrities such as Chloe Sevigny and Kate Moss. Prices are as high as you'd expect, but many of the items here merit a splurge when just looking becomes impossible.
35 Howard St (near Crosby St) 212-219-2688. Mon-Sat 11am-8pm, Sun 12pm-7pm. Ⓝ Ⓡ Ⓠ Ⓦ ❻ to Canal.

Pinky Otto
Take a break from mainstream apparel and duck into this minuscule boutique, where playful, feminine dresses and tops in interesting cuts hang from the racks, all under

DAY TO DAY

Community Board 2: *3 Washington Square Village Suite 1A. 212-979-2272.*

Local Media: SoHo Politics, *sohopolitics.blogspot.com.* The SoHo Journal's Blog, *sohojournal.com.*

Groceries: Dean & Deluca, *560 Broadway (at Prince St). 212-226-6800.* Grand Food Market Inc, *133 Grand St (near Crosby St). 212-966-2020.*

Gyms: New York Sports Club, *503 Broadway (between Broome St & Spring St). 212-925-6600.* Equinox Fitness SoHo, *69 Prince St (at Crosby St).* Kevin Heaphy Fitness Studio, *30 Vandam St (near 6th Ave). 212-337-9913.*

Hostels and Hotels: Holiday Inn Downtown, *138 Lafayette St (near Howard St) 212-966-8898.* SoHo Grand Hotel, *310 W Broadway (between Canal & Grand). 212-965-3000.*

Movie Theater: Film Forum, *209 W Houston (between 6th and Bedford). 212-627-2035.* Angelika Film Center, *18 W Houston (between Broadway and Crosby). 212-995-2000.*

Best Happy Hour: Yard, *310 W Broadway (between Canal & Grand St). 212-965-3271.*

the boutique's own label. Girls will find plenty to choose from, with multiple items featuring floral patterns and lace details. Many of the pieces have a vintage feel, while others are thoroughly modern and on-trend. Prices are reasonable, considering the store's location and the quality of the clothing, at around $150-$200 for a dress. A small selection of accessories, including flashy, beaded necklaces and peep toe heels are also for sale.
49 Prince St (near Mulberry St). 212-226-3580. Mon-Sat 11am-8pm, 11am-7pm. Ⓝ Ⓡ Ⓦ to Prince, ❻ to Spring St.

杏福西餐廳
咖啡 糕餅 西蛋 月餅 甜品

皇上皇酒家

HON CAFE
杏福西餐廳

HON CAFE
杏福西餐廳

CHINATOWN & LITTLE ITALY

Over 130 years ago, the first Chinese immigrants began moving eastward to escape discrimination in the western states. Today, what was once a tiny community of 200 Cantonese has become one of the largest Chinese communities in the western hemisphere, with almost 300,000 people representing every region of China.

Its borders have grown along with its population. Old Chinatown, the space bound by Canal St, Bowery, Worth St, and Baxter St, is now but a fraction of a sprawling neighborhood that overlaps with Little Italy, SoHo, Tribeca, and the Lower East Side.

Though its borders are permeable, there is a flavor to its streets that can be found in few other Manhattan neighborhoods. Tourists will be familiar with the open-air market vibe of the most frequented parts of Chinatown. This form of commerce takes on a less gaudy feel as one penetrates past the vulgar facade that is Canal St. Produce vendors and fish mongers replace counterfeit purse and perfume hawkers. Take note of these merchants; they offer some of the freshest fish and produce in New York, and they stock many ingredients you will be hard-pressed to find elsewhere in the city. Prepared food is similarly unbeatable; while in much of America General Tso's Chicken threatens to annihilate authentic Chinese regional cuisine, here restaurant owners specialize in the best dishes of their home provinces.

But rapidly rising rents have slowed Chinatown's expansion and threaten to send it the way of its neighbor, Little Italy. There, market forces brought tourists in and gradually drove immigrants out, leaving Little Italy a Disneyland-like simulacrum of its former self. For the intrepid, there do remain a few outposts of authentic Italian food and culture, you just have to know where to look.

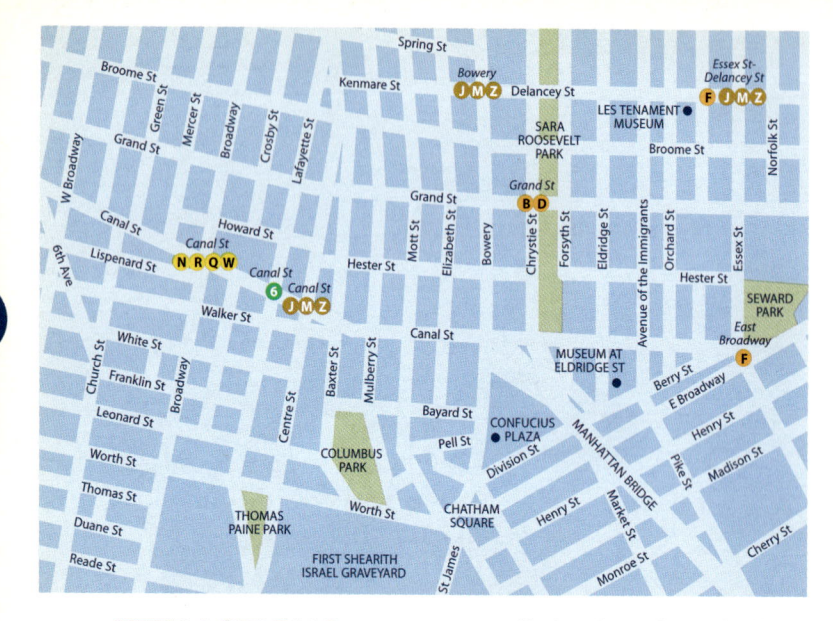

ATTRACTIONS

Columbus Park
Located at the heart of Chinatown, Columbus Park is both a green space and a community center. On weekends, it can be loud—a soccer field brings teams of every age, and across the way, the Community Pavilion hosts Chinese operas. You might not be able to break into a circle of bridge or xiangqi (Chinese chess) players, but the pavilion offers tours and art lessons, in addition to salsa, bachata, and merengue classes throughout the week. Seating abounds, so consider bringing lunch from Mott or Mulberry St or buying fresh fruit from one of the many vendors on nearby Canal Street.
Between Mulberry & Baxter St (at Bayard & Worth St). B D *to Grand,* J M Z N R W Q *to Canal.*

Chatham Square
This landmark and popular neighborhood rendezvous point lies at the intersection of seven primary Chinatown streets: Bowery, East Broadway, St. James Place, Mott Street, Oliver Street, Worth Street and Park Row. Once home to seedy saloons and tattoo parlors during the Five Points era, now Chatham Square houses the Kimlau Memorial Arch, which honors Chinese Americans who "lost their lives in defense of freedom and democracy." While the more famous Confucius statue stands across the street to the north, a statue of Lin Zexu, a Qing era Chinese official known for his vigorous opposition to the opium trade, is prominently featured in the square. Because of its central location, Chatham Square is the site of numerous community events and parades throughout the year, particularly during the Lunar New Year.
F *to East Broadway*

Manhattan Bridge
Built in 1909, this suspension bridge isn't as famous as its older cousin to the south, but it offers one of the loveliest ambles in the neighborhood. A stroll across the pedestrian walkway offers an aerial view of Chinatown, and the vertiginous section above the East River provides a stunning vista of the Financial District, the Brooklyn Bridge, and the Statue of Liberty. For the less pedestrian, the N, Q, B, and D trains pass over the bridge as well and provide the same view without the walk.
Bowery Ave at Canal St. F *to East Broadway.*

110 CHINATOWN & LITTLE ITALY

CULTURE & ARTS

Asian American Arts Center
For over thirty years, this museum and cultural center has been devoted to promoting Asian American artistic and creative expression. Exhibitions range from traditional folk art to post-modern sculpture, and the museum also hosts Asian American dance performances. One of the largest historical archives of Asian American artists is stored here, with records dating to 1945. Don't miss the Lunar New Year Folk Arts Festival, which features performances and hands-on arts and crafts demonstrations.
26 Bowery Ave (at Bayard St). 212-233-2154. Mon-Wed 12:30pm-6:30pm, Thu 12:30pm-7:30pm, Fri 12:30pm-6:30pm. ⓑⒹ to Grand or ⓙⓜⓏ to Canal.

EDITOR'S PICK
Barometer
In a part of town infamous for replications, forgeries, and tchotchkes, something else has sprung up. Jenna Wainwright and Anna Studebaker, colleagues at the Metropolitan Museum's Objects Conservation Department, set up shop in 2006 to bring authentic, "deathless bric-a-brac" back: Anna scrounges up curiosities like a 1950s steel mechanical juicer and tin wind-up toys, and Jenna designs jewelry around (and with) her finds. Their growing collection and likeminded friends have inspired a slate of recent exhibitions, themed, respectively, Ice Cream, Dinosaurs, and Upstate, and featuring found objects alongside art made to order.
89 Walker St (near Lafayette St). 917-796-7367. Sat-Sun 12pm-7pm. ⓖⓙⓜⓏⓝⓇⓞⓌ to Canal. Public openings.

Miguel Abreu Gallery
More cerebral than many local galleries, perhaps less willing to surrender to bourgeoisie sensibilities, it is no surprise that this gallery names Alain Badiou as its patron saint. Innovative projects like the Sequence exhibition, which organized its display temporally rather than spatially, and agapé, an exhibition of experimental music concerts, set the tone for this engaging, unusual art space.
36 Orchard St (between Canal St and Hester St). 212-995-1774. Wed-Sun 11am-6:30pm. Ⓕ to East Broadway, ⒷⒹ to Grand, or ⓙⓜⓏ to Essex.

DINING

MID-RANGE
Nice Green Bo *Shanghainese*
The constantly jam-packed dining room has all the charm of a hospital waiting room, and half of the time you'll be asked to sit at a table with strangers, but this eatery also offers some of the best Shanghainese food around. The pork and crab "tiny buns" are among the best in Chinatown, made to order and full of rich, steaming broth and topped with delicate morsels of crab. The Peking duck, with crispy, tea-smoked skin and moist, rich flesh, is fantastic and more than enough for two. Try to branch out from beef-and-broccoli and order from the dim sum menu, which includes surprising treats like cold aromatic beef and wined chicken feet.
66 Bayard St (between Mott St and Elizabeth St) 212-625-2359. Open daily 11am-12am. ⓝⓡⓞⓌⓖⓙⓜⓏ to Canal. Average entrée $8.

Oriental Garden *Chinese*
Dim-sum for the white tablecloth set, Oriental Garden competes with the best Elizabeth Street eateries on weekend mornings. Service is courteous and efficient, and the exotic fish that line the walls in clear blue tanks have arrived recently enough to still have some pep in their step. Cart pushers offer a variety of bite-sized treats from shumai to sticky rice, many of them mixing surf and turf for different effects, sweet to savory, in each different dish. Oriental Garden stakes its reputation on the fish and shellfish though, from hearty oversized oysters to famously tender lobster in appropriately paired sauces. Those who pay a visit at dinnertime are advised to make reservations, if only to beat the crowds that have brought star chefs like David Bouley into this restaurant's dining room.
14 Elizabeth St (at Bayard St). 212-619-0085. Mon-Fri 10am-11pm, Sat-Sun 9am-11pm. ⒷⒹ to Grand, ⓙⓜⓏ to Canal. Average entrée $14-25.

Wild Ginger *Asian, Vegan*
Vegan with no regrets is an unusual concept in Chinatown, but it turns out that Asian food without a scrap of chicken, pork, or egg can be delicious – a few items on the menu at Wild Ginger substitute seitan for poultry, including a soft, barely charred vegan skewer with green pepper and onion, marinated in a light peanut

sauce. Most draw inspiration from sauces and spices instead, as with a dish of crispy, chewy jade mushrooms fried in orange sauce, with a side of organic brown rice. Careful attention to ingredients makes something special even out of the humble miso soup. Delivery is available, though Wild Ginger's dining room, done up in dark woods and burnt shades of green and yellow, is as pleasing to the eye as the kitchen's food is to the palate.

380 Broome St (between Mott & Mulberry St). 212-966-1883. Sun-Tue 12pm-11pm, Fri-Sat 12pm-12am. ❻❿ to Bowery; ❻ to Spring; ❻❿ to Grand. Average entrée $10.

EDITOR'S PICK

Yeah Shanghai Deluxe *Shanghainese*
Yeah Shanghai is not the best known of Chinatown restaurants, but it's certainly one the best for soup dumplings. Here, they're made fresh and called "juicy pork buns." Bite off the top of each morsel and slurp up the broth inside so you don't scald your tongue – they come out of the kitchen piping hot. Likewise, a casserole of eggplant and pork came to the table boiling, cooked to the perfect consistency, and seasoned with just the right amount of spice and sugar. Yeah Shanghai's waiters serve dishes swiftly to keep them warm, but service is otherwise inattentive. Listening to Chinese pop oldies, sipping complimentary tea, and admiring the restaurant's absurd concrete pond, garden, and bridge, you won't mind.

65 Bayard St (near Mott St). 212-566-4884. Sun-Thu 11am-11pm, Fri-Sat 11am-12am. ❻❿❿❿❻❿ ❿ to Canal, ❻❿ to Grand. Average entrée $10. BYOB.

CHEAP
Banh Mi Saigon Bakery *Vietnamese*
Woe to those who come to Chinatown seeking the city's finest banh mi sandwich, only to lose their way, confused by the jewelry store façade that conceals this sandwich stand. Ignore the cheap trinkets up front and proceed directly to the back, where the true gems are kept: warm crusty baguettes bursting with pickled vegetables and your choice from a wide selection of meats, like roast pork and pâté, all garnished with cilantro, cucumbers, and spicy chili sauce. These sandwiches are big enough for two, but at $3.75 each, most prefer to save their leftovers for later.

138 Mott St (between Grand St and Hester St). 212-941-1541. Tues-Sun 10am-7pm. ❻❿❿❿❻❿❿ to Canal. Sandwiches $3.75.

Doyer's Vietnamese *Vietnamese*
Tucked under an alleyway, this unassuming restaurant serves a variety of classic dishes and more traditional treats in a wood paneled, incomprehensibly partitioned dining room. Servers are brisk if uncomprehending, and the dishes they bring are solid picks: the pho is cinnamony and not as greasy as others. An entrée of pork in caramel with black pepper was delicious at dinner and as takeout, and don't think you'll be leaving without a doggie bag. An appetizer of shrimp paste grilled on sticks of sugarcane was an unwieldy but winning mix of seafood and sweets that justifies a visit on its own. Stop in for a relaxed meal full of reliably pleasant surprises, or order for delivery.

11 Doyers St (between Bowery and Pell Sts). 212-513-1527. Sun-Thurs 11am-10pm, Fri-Sat 11am-11pm. ❻❿❿❿❻❿❿ to Canal, ❻❿ to Grand. Average entrée $8.

Eastern Noodle *Fujianese*
This humble noodle shack serves delicious bowls of soup for dirt-cheap. Hand-pulled noodles, carefully stretched by hand and cooked to order, are the specialty of the house. The house special soup is a standout; the light beef broth is mildly flavored with cinnamon, leek, and star anise and filled with duck, beef, and fried egg in addition to the flavorful and hearty noodles. Locals who frequent this joint, far from the touristy bustle of Canal Street, know not to be shy with their soup—guzzling the flavor-packed broth straight from the bowl is customary, and a bit of gnawing and nibbling is always necessary for the oxtail soup.

27 Eldridge St (near Canal St). 646-613-1023. 9am-8pm. ❻❿❿❿❻❿❿ to Canal, ❻ to East Broadway. Soups $4.50-$6. Cash only.

Grand Sichuan *Sichuan*
Despite the cool service and retirement home décor, the original outpost of New York's Sichuanese food empire still serves the best Sichuan cuisine around. Avoid American Chinese dishes like Moo Soo Pork and head straight for the Sichuan classics. Dishes like sautéed pork with Szechuan bean sauce, which is served atop a bed of fresh hot peppers, are blazing hot. It's worth the burn: these meals are packed with flavor and dirt cheap. With crisp brown skin and moist, fatty flesh, the

smoked tea duck is a less spicy but equally flavorful option.
125 Canal St (at Bowery Ave). 212-625-9212. Mon-Sun 11:30am-11pm. 6JMZNROW *to Canal St. Average entrée $10.*

Jing Fong *Dim Sum*
This is the real dim sum deal: walkie-talkies blaring from the downstairs host-stand to the upstairs seating area, enormous crystal chandeliers hanging above tables where strangers are made to sit together, women pushing carts, frantically spraying sauce on anything and everything and convincing you that the little pot in their hands is absolutely what you want to be eating for brunch. Dishes—plenty large enough to share—cost about $3 each. It's hectic, it's loud—but also delicious and cheap. The innumerable dishes contain ingredients both classic and surprising—always in a good way. Dumpling carts, dessert carts, and seafood carts have something for everyone. Don't leave without trying something that is a complete mystery. Dinner is a little more of a regular dining experience, but still delicious and brilliantly cheap.
20 Elizabeth St (near Canal St) 212-964-5256. 6JMZNROW *to Canal. 9:30am-10pm. Dim sum 10am-3:30pm. Average entrée $10. Dim sum $2-6.*

Paris Sandwich Corp. *Vietnamese*
Post-colonial guilt aside, this place offers some of the best bahn mi in Chinatown, which is really saying something. Fresh, warm baguettes (baked daily on premises) can barely contain all the juicy grilled pork, daikon radish, pickled carrot, and cilantro that is stuffed into them. If you're not one for pork, bahn mi are also offered with a variety of other meats, as well as in a vegetarian option. Green tea waffles are sweet, hot, and floral—they're especially delicious when smeared with coconut jam. Try to shrug off the McDonalds-like décor and focus on your fantastic, dirt-cheap meal.
113 Mott St (between Hester St and Canal St) 212-226-7221. Mon-Thurs 8am-8pm, Fri-Sun 8am-9pm. 6JMZNROW *to Canal,* BD *to Grand. Sandwiches $3.50.*

Prosperity Dumpling *Chinese*
It's $1 for five of the best dumplings you'll ever eat, and that's all you really need to know about this closet-sized hole in the wall. The chive and pork fried dumplings and Chinese vegetable and pork boiled dumplings are handmade and cooked to order. It makes a steaming hot snack, or get two orders and make it a meal. The sesame and chive pancakes are like Chinese foccacia—soft, hearty, hot, and, more importantly, 75 cents. Seating is limited to

CHINATOWN & LITTLE ITALY 113

six bar stools.
46 Eldridge St (between Canal St and Hester St) 212-343-0683. Open daily 7:30am-9pm. BD to Grand St, F to East Broadway, JM to Bowery. Average entrée $1.

EDITOR'S PICK

Super Taste *Fujianese*
Super Taste Restaurant packs its narrow space with quiet Chinatown locals intent on slurping noodles out of plastic bowls while waiters scream out orders over their heads. This contrast can be jarring, but after you've ordered your own bowl of noodles, you'll understand. They are made fresh on the premises by a chef who whips them through flour before yanking them into hundreds of individual strands and boiling them in a dark transparent broth made from cattle bones and beef. This is street food with a pedigree of several hundred years, originating on the Silk Road in Lanzhou, and it has universal appeal.
26N Eldridge St (near Canal St). 212-625-1198. Mon-Sun 10am-10:30pm. BD to Grand, F to E Broadway. Average entrée $5.

NIGHTLIFE

EDITOR'S PICK

Café Katja *Bar, Café*
Surprised newcomers stumble into this café when they look through the sheet glass window and see customers swilling beer from massive glass boots. They keep coming back after they've tasted what's inside: ice cold, hard-to-find German and Austrian imports like Hofbrau and Gosser, all at domestic prices, and all filled well past the menacing 2-liter mark on the side of the glass. An incredibly friendly wait-staff bustles around the cozy nook all night, setting plates of delicious Teutonic pub food next to the towering beers. Hot sandwiches like the toasted emmentaler and smoked ham are cut into strips and served with sauce, making them perfect for sharing, as are the hot sausages and the meat and cheese platters. An excellent, affordable regional wine selection and a group of well-conceived Alpine cocktails round out the menu. Just remember: drink with the toe down. You'll understand.
79 Orchard St (at Grand St). 212-219-9545. 4pm-1am. BD to Grand, FJMZ to Essex. Average beer $5.

Good World *Bar, Grill*
An undeniably cool spot in the otherwise blighted borderlands between Chinatown and the Lower East Side, Good World draws a sharp looking crowd that is hip but not hipster. Local artists and designers newly transplanted to the area frequent this rough wood and wrought iron watering hole, as do the occasional grizzled (but well-dressed) old-timers. Regulars love the burgers and Swedish meatballs, offered well into the morning, as well as the stylish cocktails that mercifully top out at $12. Squeeze through the crowded bar to the courtyard in back, where smokers take refuge from the high-volume, little known tracks spun by the excellent DJ. The beer selection is noteworthy.
3 Orchard St (near Canal St). 212-925-9975. Daily, noon-4am, Brunch Sat-Sun 11am-5pm. F to East Broadway. Average beer $6.

Home Sweet Home *Bar*
Some hate it, some love it, all agree that the taxidermy theme is kind of weird. Either way, there's no question this sign-less basement bar is a cool place to grab a drink. Ceramic jackalopes and stuffed animals adorn the bar, illuminated by rusty chandeliers hanging

from a pipe-cluttered ceiling. Ignore the late night prowlers and sink into their broken-in velveteen couches with a beer. DJs spin well chosen tracks on weekends to the delight of the dancing hipster crowds.

*131 Chrystie St (between Broome & Delancey St). 212-226-5708. Tues-Sun 3pm-4am, Mon 8pm-4am. **J M Z** to Bowery; **B D** to Grand. Average drink $6.*

Katra *Lounge*
Without velvet ropes, long lines, or cover charges, this Moroccan-inspired hideaway has all the fun but none of the pretension of a typical New York City club. On the weekends big crowds come to drink and dance to to hip hop, pop, and house music. On the weeknights the place eases into a lounge vibe and features performances of everything from Burlesque to belly dancing. The Moroccan-Indian-French fusion appetizer list offers notable items like crab cakes and almond crusted chicken wings for early patrons looking for light fare. The food is hot and spicy, but the creative drinks are equally refreshing; the lychee martini and the Moroccan mojito (which comes in a variety of flavors) are perfect compliments to the flavorful dishes.

*217 Bowery (between Rivington St and Prince St). 212 473 3113. Tues-Sat 5pm- 4am. **N R** to Prince, **F** to 2nd Ave, **J M Z** to Delancey. Average drink $11.*

Oro *Wine Bar*
At 6 pm each evening, the owner of this little cafe begins wiping coffee off the bronze counter, putting out low stools in the back, and lighting candles along serving mats and over the comfy couches by the window. The lights go down, the music changes from oldies to electronica, and within an hour, a coffee shop becomes a comfortable wine and beer bar. Taking its Parisian model seriously, Oro serves shots of espresso alongside sparkling sake to the after dinner set. A simple wine rack of rebar sunk into its exposed brick walls holds mostly organic, small-batch wines. The menu also draws on regional ingredients, with cheese selections that change every season. Hearty foods like deviled eggs, a berry and white chocolate mousse, and cupcakes highlight the benefits of doing your nighttime drinking in a daytime cafe.

*375 Broome St (near Mott St). 212-941-6368. Mon-Wed 7pm-12am, Thurs-Sat 7pm-2am, Sun 8pm-12am. **6** to Spring; **J M Z** to Bowery. Glasses $8-12.*

The Randolph at Broome
Cocktail Bar
The latest bar to join the speakeasy revival that's sweeping the city , this bar differs in its attempt to be the great equalizer— there is no nefariously hard door policy, no shifting phone number, no hidden location or celebrities with which to vie for attention. The Randolph, still a neophyte compared to surrounding Nolita bars, draws an interesting, diverse, but not always cohesive crowd. While a laid back lounge soundtrack (sometimes R&B, sometimes House, sometimes dance tunes) plays in the background, sip on painstakingly concocted beverages under pressed tin ceilings while you sink into luxurious leather booths. Sample the refreshing Strawberry Cucumber fizz or The Eskimo Kiss built for two to share, or one to pound. There are several drinks inspired by the city itself (Eastside, Westside, etc.) that are truly unique. Sometimes the crowd is dancing, sometimes not, but every patron is always drinking well. Sunday nights feature a Prince dance party: enough said.

*349 Broome St (between Bowery & Elizabeth St). 212-274-0667. Mon-Sun 9pm-4am. **J M Z** to Bowery. Average drink $13.*

Sweet Paradise *Dive, Bar*
It's hard to put a finger on Sweet Paradise. It's narrow space, filled with banks of seats. It's filled with loud drum rock, but nobody is dancing. The patrons range from vaguely hip people to more casual Lower East Siders, but there's an ebony cougar prowling above the bar. Spend no time trying to make sense of it: this isn't the singles scene, but hot bartenders, Hot Tamales, and a happy hour between 6 and 9 p.m. (with $2 well drinks!) will keep all but the most particular patrons coming back for more.

*14 Orchard St (between Canal & Hester St). 4pm-4am. **F** to East Broadway. Average drink $4. Cash Only.*

CHINATOWN & LITTLE ITALY 115

SHOPPING

EDITOR'S PICK

Di Palo Fine Foods

The tragedy of Little Italy is economic; there's no value in starting an authentic restaurant to serve tourists. Italians who still live in the neighborhood appreciate good food though, and that's where the Di Palo family comes in. Any given week, they will be visiting Tuscany to cut a deal with cheese suppliers, or Rome to arrange export licenses for a producer of porchetta – roast seasoned crackling pork– whose wares they know customers in New York will love. If it can't be brought back to America from Italy, then the Di Palos will make it here; if there's not enough demand to justify a regular shipment, just ask and they'll be happy to place a special order. The men behind the counter here are not just knowledgeable, friendly, and willing to give samples – they're loyal to their customers, too.

200 Grand St (between Mott and Mulberry Sts). 212-226-1033. Mon-Sat 9am-6:30pm; Sun 9am-4pm. B D *to Grand;* J M Z *to Bowery.*

Exquisite Costume

This boutique is full of hand-picked pieces which range from the exquisite to the bizarre. On this street, however, the shop takes special significance—it is a history lesson for the designers clustered down the block. Each piece of clothing in the shop has a known history and is each dated according to time period (some spanning three centuries) and designer. This place is as much for a woman who loves to play dress-up as it is for a woman looking for a special piece to add to her wardrobe. Many pieces will set you back more than $300, but a sharp eye can find a great purse or belt for around $60. Watch for designers visiting the shop to get inspiration and study unique fashions from the past.

377 Broome St (between Mott and Mulberry). 212-966-4142. 6 J M Z N R Q W *to Canal.*

Muji

The conservative size and minimalist aesthetic of this life-supplies superstore belies the treasures that lie in store for the fanatically organized and obsessively design conscious.

KITCHEN ROW

Clustered on Bowery Ave between Canal and Houston, an improbable number of restaurant supply stores compete for the title of cheapest kitchen equipment distributor in the city. Don't be turned off by the massive deep fryers and industrial sized ovens in the front of these stores; inside you will find everything you need to outfit your kitchen on the cheap. Williams-Sonoma this is not: tools and appliances are designed for daily use by line chefs. They're not pretty, but they're affordable, durable, and functional. **Hung Chang Imports Inc.** (14 Bowery Ave at Pell St. 212 349-3392) has an excellent selection of knives: take the helpful staff's advice and skip the $100 Wusthof for a $25 blade that is less flashy but equally functional. Many of these stores also offer plain cutlery, glasses, and utensils for dirt cheap, so come here before you head to Bed, Bath, and Beyond or Ikea.

On Allen St between Canal and Rivington is another cluster of restaurant supply stores worth visiting. **Fortuneline Kichen Supply** (52 Allen St between & Grand St) has a Japanese focus, with items like sushi boats, sake carafes, and soy sauce holders in additoin to standard kitchen supplies.

Bowery Ave (between Canal and Houston). 6 J M Z N R Q W *to Canal;* B D *to Grand.*

From stationery to futons, backpacks to soap dispensers, everything in this store is appealingly simple and brand-less. Prices are moderate, perhaps higher than their no-frills style would indicate, but newcomers looking to outfit their apartments or offices will not be disappointed. Clothes are sold as well, their style more hippie than hipster. Check out the pen bar, where you can mix and match interchangeable parts to create your ideal writing implement.

455 Broadway (between Grand St and Howard St). 212-334-2002. Mon-Sat 11am-9pm, Sun 11am-8pm. 6 J M Z N R Q W *to Canal.*

New Beef King

Chinese beef jerky isn't dehydrated and preserved like traditional American jerky. Rather, beef is cooked daily in a laborious four-oven process and then grilled with a variety of sauces, yielding moist, tender strips of richly fla-

vored meat. Owner Robert Yee flew to Hong Kong to bring back his grandmother's recipe, and the results are fantastic. Jerky is available in a variety of flavors, both wet and dry, but you really can't go wrong with any of them.
89 Bayard St (at Mulberry St). 212-233-6612. 10am-8pm. 6JMZNRQW to Canal, BD to Grand. Average price $13/lb.

Pearl Paint
This art supply superstore offers everything the serious or budding artist could ever need. Six floors are organized by medium: one floor is devoted to canvas frames and stretching, another is packed only with varieties of paper, others hold paint, stationary, and sculpture supplies. It's a maze of supplies that offers endless variety, so grab your map at the front door and check your bank account before you come: even with directions, you may find yourself spending hours here.
308 Canal St (at Mercer St). 212-431-7932. Mon-Fri 9am-7pm, Sat 10am-6:30pm, Sun 10am-6pm. 6JMZNRQW to Canal.

Project No. 8
The eighth collaborative project of Elizabeth Beer and Brian Janusiak, this high concept boutique is somewhere between store and museum. In addition to the four racks of elegant men's and women's clothing, primarily from European designers, the store displays a collection of sophisticated bric-a-brac, from German fountain pens to "non-verbal communication mittens." Charming in its irregularity, their selection is fun to browse, even if you have no intention of buying. Regular sales make the high prices on the clothes and shoes easier to stomach.
138 Division St (at Orchard St). 212-925-5599. Tues-Wed 1pm-8pm, Thurs-Sat 1pm-9pm, Sun 1pm-8pm, closed Mon. F to East Broadway.

Tai Pan Bakery
This frenetic bakery offers an overwhelming variety of sweets and savories to a crowd of Canal crawlers. Dealing in everything from hot dogs to cakes and sweet waffles, the store offers all their delicious selections at dirt cheap prices. A highlight is the sweet pork buns, tender sweet pastries stuffed with rich braised pork. Be sure to get a seat at the bar looking out on Canal Street and watch the street bustle from behind

DAY TO DAY

Community Board 3: *59 East 4th St. 212-553-5300.*

Local Media: Downtown Express. *downtownexpress.com.*

Groceries: Dynasty Supermarket. *68 Elizabeth St (at Hester). 212-966-4943.*

Average Rent: One-bedroom: $1800-2500. Two-bedroom: $2500-3500

Hospitals: Saint Vincent's Hospital Chinatown Clinic, *25 Elizabeth St (near Canal). 212-431-5501.* New York Downtown Hospital, *170 William St. 212-312-5000.* University Settlement: Psychiatric Consultation Center, *185 Eldridge St (at Rivington). 212-674-9121.*

Movie Theaters: Sunshine Cinema. *143 E Houston St. (212) 330-8182.*

Best Happy Hour: Sweet Paradise. *14 Orchard St (near Hester). 212-226-3612. Daily 6pm-9pm. Well drinks $2.*

the safety of sheet glass.
194 Canal St (at Mulberry St). 718-888-1111. 7:30am-8:30pm. 6JMZNRQW to Canal. Average pastry $1. Cash only.

Ten Ren Tea and Ginseng Co.
One of six branches in the city, this tea-lovers' mecca boasts a vast selection of loose leaf teas imported from China and Taiwan. Offering everything from bargain greens to $150/lb "King's Tea", Ten Ren appeals to both connoisseur and amateur. For those unfamiliar with tea preparation and etiquette, store managers are happy to answer questions and offer guidance to the best leaves. Teas are available by the ounce for easy sampling. Medicinal teas and varieties of ginseng are also offered at reasonable prices.
75 Mott St (at Canal St). 212-349-2286. Sun-Thurs 11am-11pm, Fri-Sat 11am-12am. 6JMZNRQW to Canal.

CHINATOWN & LITTLE ITALY 117

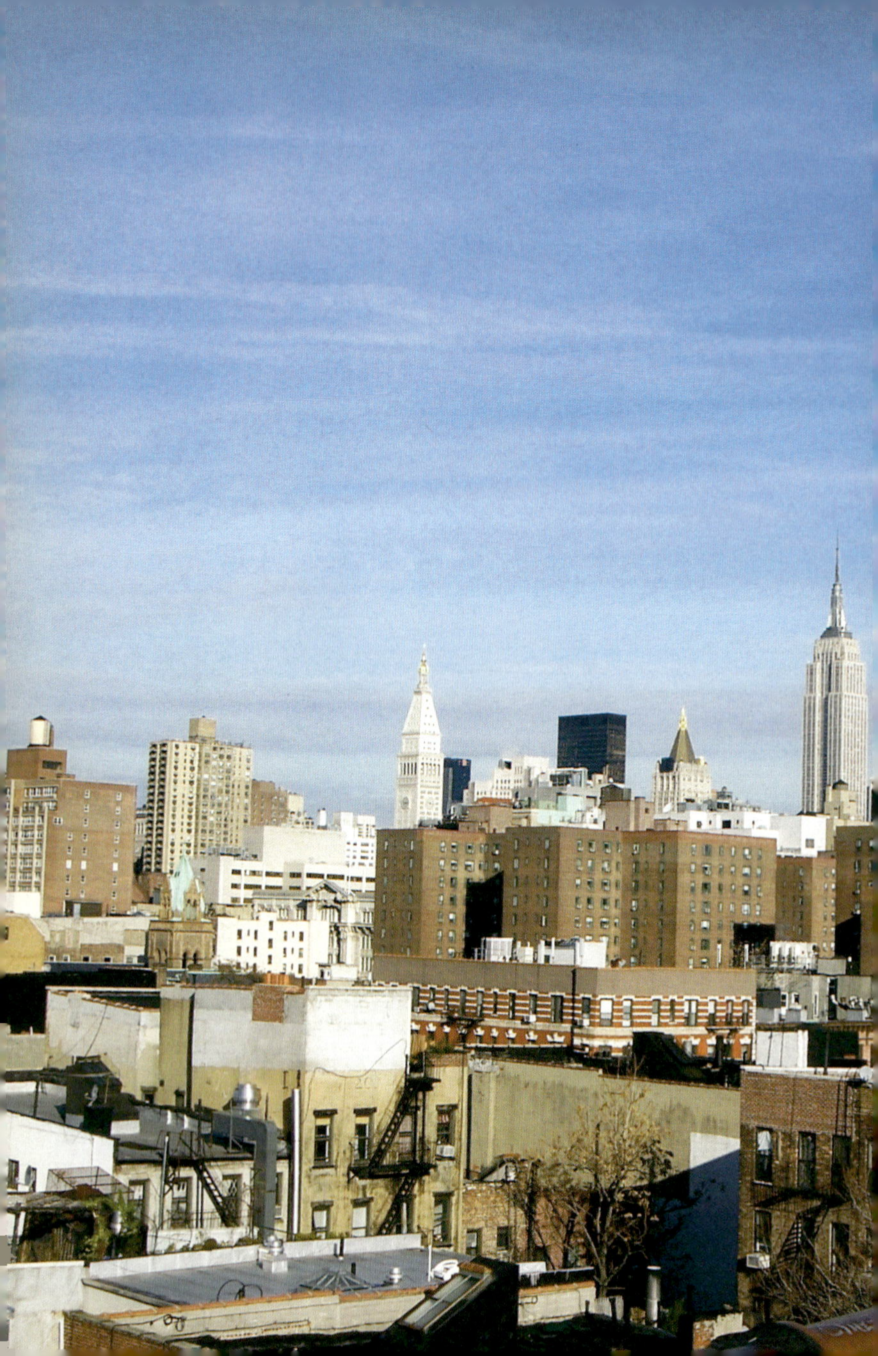

LOWER EAST SIDE

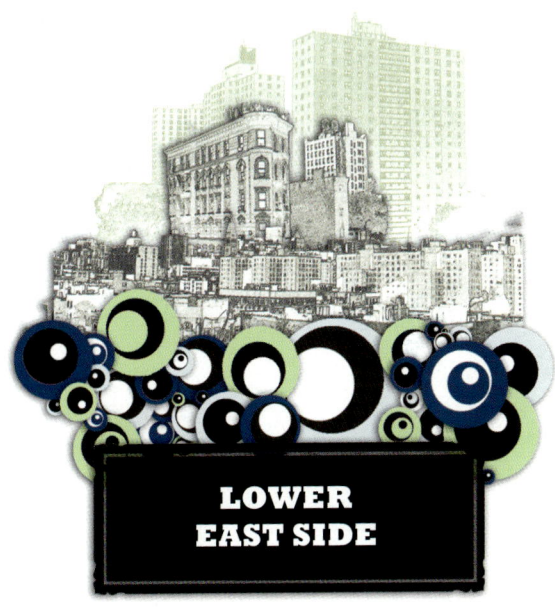

As journalists, real estate agents and community boards found various reasons to distinguish their turf, Little Italy, Chinatown and the East Village have all been carved from the Lower East Side, leaving behind a smaller area that still retains some of the city's richest history. A first stop for immigrants as long as the city has had them, it has been home to populations of Germans, Jews, Italians and Eastern Europeans, each group making way for the next as soon as it had the capital to move away.

The newest immigrants are refugees not from poverty or famine but from the gauche uptown club and restaurant scene. They have come in droves for the last decade to open bistros, bars, and clubs, making the neighborhood popular for the first time since the start of the last century, when it was a destination for prostitute enthusiasts. Although the party scene here is overhyped, a tolerance for high-minded (read: expensive) experimentation has drawn some of the city's best chefs.

Although the West Village tops it, the Lower East Side has a high concentration of Greenmarket fetishists, restauranteurs whose entire philosophy is based on fresh ingredients bought four times weekly in Union Square. Fresh doesn't have to mean boring, but those spooked by ideological dining take haven at the many inexpensive ethnic restaurants that have survived (for now) the onset of gentrification

If the Lower East Side's history is a case study of shifting neighborhoods, then it is fitting that Chinatown is leaking in from the West. The continuing influx of mainland Chinese, though a trickle compared to the statistics of the early 20th century, means the neighborhood's present, as well as its past, bears the stamp of another country. More practically, it means there are not one but two bargain dumpling houses on Eldridge. Multiculturalism is a delectable thing.

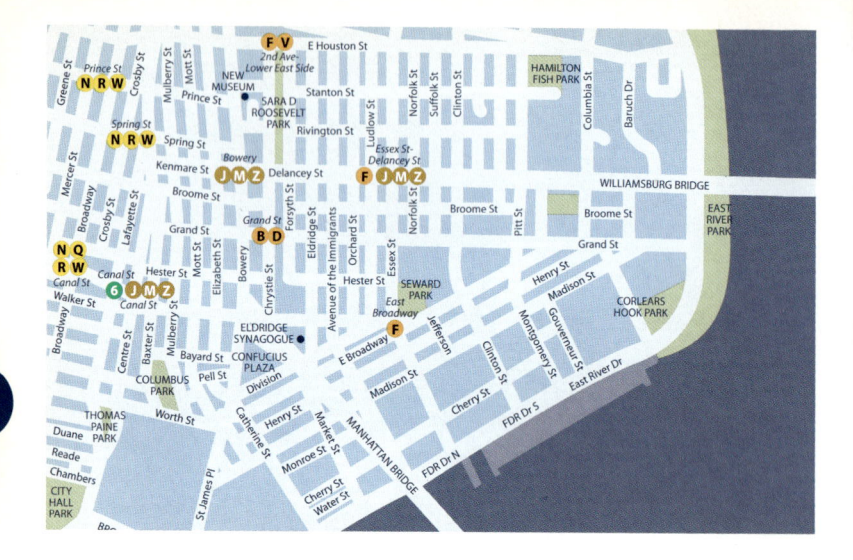

ATTRACTIONS

East River Park
Designed about 80-years ago as a companion to FDR Drive, East River Park spans almost 60 acres. Boasting some of the best views of the East River, the park offers great recreational facilities for basketball, tennis, handball, softball, football, baseball, and track. Other visitors can fish, picnic, or bike alongside the river promenade. The recently restored 1,000-seat East River amphitheater, which overlooks the waterfront, is the site of a regular concert series and plays host to various performances throughout the year. Footbridges over the expressway offer easy access at 10th and Delancey streets.
East River (between Montgomery St and East 12th St). L to 1st Ave; F J M Z to Delancey. Daily 6am-1am.

Sara Delano Roosevelt Park
This recently renovated escape from Manhattan now has an entrance at Canal and Chrystie that opens onto a fresh turf field, complete with new benches, lighting, and walkways. The Houston St side features steps where Lower East Siders congregate to munch on Whole Foods sushi and watch basketball players go at it on the full length courts. Besides the many athletic pursuits available, the park includes the beautiful Wah-Mei bird garden, a senior citizens center, and a market. Public restrooms are available for the adventurous. Locals recommend taking leisurely walks away from the busier North or South ends of the park.
Chrystie St and Forsyth St (bound by E Houston and Canal St). B D to Grand St, F V to 2nd Ave, J M Z to Bowery.

Williamsburg Bridge
Constructed over 100 years ago, the Williamsburg Bridge was once the longest suspension bridge in the world. Although it will likely forever remain overshadowed by its older and more popular cousin – the Brooklyn Bridge – academics consider the Williamsburg Bridge to be the acme of practical engineering. Either way, crossing this Williamsburg-Lower Manhattan bridge offers a beautiful elevated view of the city, its waterways, and that other, prettier bridge. The bridge's full span is roughly a mile, which makes it ideal for joggers, bikers, and walkers. Those looking for a leisurely and scenic walk to Brooklyn will find a much less crowded journey here, especially on weekends.
Delancey St to S 5th St J M Z *to Marcy Ave or* F J M Z *to Delancey.*

CULTURE & ARTS

ABC No Rio
ABC No Rio started as a showcase for community art in an abandoned building. Now there are weekly poetry readings, and the sometimes notable "HardCore/Punk" Saturday Matinee. Sunday nights have experimental and improvisational performances followed by open stage time. They also offer an art gallery, a screenprinting studio, a darkroom, a radical zine library, and a computer lab. Use of their resources can be had with only a moderate fee, usually on the honor system. It's the ultimate counter-culture resource center catering to the starving artists of the Lower East Side.
156 Rivington Street (between Suffolk and Clinton St). 212-254-3697 Mostly evening hours. **F J M Z** *to Essex-Delancey St.*

Jen Bekman Gallery
This rising-star gallery tucked into a compact space near the Bowery exhibits photography, paintings, and mixed media, but it is best known for its special projects. "Het, Hot Shot!" allows emerging photographers to submit photographs for panel review; winners receive a cash prize, an exhibition, and the opportunity to be represented by Bekman. "20x200" is an affordable art project perfect for aspiring collectors short on cash: original prints by up and coming artists are offered for as low as $20.
6 Spring St (at Bowery Ave). 212-219-0166. Wed-Sat 12pm-6pm. **6** *to Spring,* **N R** *to Prince,* **F V** *to Second, or* **J M** *to Bowery.*

New Museum of Contemporary Art
The stack of white boxes that makes up the New Museum is an architectural destination in itself. The anti-monumental exterior of the museum recalls the Lower East Side's tenement past, while the inside of the museum exalts contemporary art. More contemporary than the MoMA (its mission statement is simply "New Art, New Ideas"), the New Museum offers a chance for the newest emerging artists to shine. The fifth floor houses a library where patrons can leisurely thumb through photos and art archives. The café, which offers fantastic rooftop views, is open on the weekends only. Free tours are offered every day at 2pm and Thursdays from 7pm til 10pm.
235 Bowery (at Prince Street). 212-219-1222. Closed Mon-Tue. Wed, Sat, Sun 12pm-6pm; Thurs – Friday 12pm-10pm. **F V** *to 2nd Avenue,* **J M Z** *to Bowery. General Admission $12, Students $6.*

Woodward Gallery
It's billed as a Lower East Side gallery, but Woodward started out in SoHo and landed in the northern reaches of Chinatown in 2007, taking over a beautiful space shaped around a central island, with a private viewing room downstairs. Famous artists exhibited by John and Kristine Woodward include Picasso, Warhol, Basquiat, and Johns. Exhibitions come and go every two months, showcasing a deeper collection of pop art, abstract painting, photography, and gritty urban prints from influential East Village artists, the latter group dating from the 1980s to the present.
133 Eldridge St (between Broome and Delancey). 212-966-3411. Tues-Sat 11am-6pm, other times by appointment. **B D** *to Grand,* **F** *to Essex,* **J M Z** *to Bowery.*

DINING

MID-RANGE
Eat-pisode *Thai*
The most enchanting thing about Eat-pisode is the bathroom: where a sink would normally stand, there is instead a tangle of faux bamboo shoots, one of which, riddled with holes, spouts water into a pit of smooth stones. The food holds up well to the high standards the lavatories set. Organic black sticky rice, minced chicken, turnips, onions, and roasted sesame in a coconut sauce make the Eat-pisode roll a standout starter. The diverse flavors of the eggplant salad—shrimp, chicken, a medley of fruits and veggies in a carrot-tossed lime dressing—hold together very well. Duck tamarind is tops: crispy, juicy, and meaty, smothered with the distinctive flavor of the tamarind fruit. For dessert, the mango sticky rice is sweet, savory, and wonderful. Beverage wise, the "coconut drink" and the matoom, or wood orange tea, are both sweet, crisp, and subtle. Concrete and dark wood-paneled create the charming atmosphere of a lavishly appointed monastery.

123 Ludlow St (between Rivington St and Delancey St) 212-677-7624. Mon-Thurs 12pm-11am, Fri-Sun 1pm-12am, Sun 2pm-11pm. **F** *to Delancey ,* **J M Z** *to Essex. Average entree $14. BYOB*

Grotto *Italian*
Keep your eyes open for the hidden staircase that leads to this former basement, which has been refurnished to resemble the interior of a submarine: black wood paneling, wooden tables, and portholes line the walls. For starters, the crostini are magical; the arugula-topped carpaccio is excellent as well. For a main course, the creamy ravioli, filled with ricotta and spinach, is delightful, as is the steak, which is given an unexpected kick from a garnish of grape tomatoes. The German chef paid homage to her motherland with dessert: the Kaiserschmarrn, a Teutonic dish composed of a thick crepe that is chopped into pieces and sprinkled with sugar, will make you weak in the knees.

100-b Forsyth St (between Grand St & Broome St) 212-625-3444. Mon-Wed 6pm-11pm, Thurs-Sat 6pm-12am, Closed Sun. **B D** *to Grand,* **J M Z** *to Bowery. Average entrée $17.*

Katz's Delicatessen *Deli*
Grab a ticket at the door and join the lines waiting to pile their plates with high-cholesterol favorites at this classic deli. Diners have the option of table or counter service—the latter is invariably more fun, with visitors straight off the tour bus and famously surly waiters. It's hard to go wrong with any of the deli classics on the menu (save the burgers and tuna sandwiches), but there's no question that the pastrami sandwich, sliced thick to order and piled onto pieces of rye bread, is the main attraction. The pungent salami sandwiches are equally filling and the matzo ball soup and chopped liver are similarly authentic appetizers. Be sure to order a plate of thick, hot fries and a Dr. Brown's black cherry soda to go with your meal, and good luck fitting through the doorway as you leave.

205 E Houston St (at Ludlow St) 212-254-2246. Mon-Tues 8am-9:45pm, Wed-Thurs 8am-10::45pm, Fri-Sat 8am-2:45pm, Sun 8am-10:45pm. **F V** *to Lower East Side. Sandwiches $5.95-$16.45.*

EDITOR'S PICK
Little Giant *New American*
Little Giant is exactly what its name insinuates: a tiny restaurant that boasts a menu with gargantuan flavor. With daily-purchased market produce, the food is super fresh and retains the integrity of each ingredient. Seasonal pickled vegetables and succotash highlight nature's bounty. Artichoke dip and chicken liver mousse are popular and wonderful appetizers, pairing well with drinks from the bar like a Pisco sour or strawberry-rhubarb margarita. Orecchiette is an indulgence filled with egg, bacon and mushroom; its soft, marshmallow-like texture is seductive, and a hint of creamy pesto adds explosive flavor. Presentation of dishes is home-style and nothing too impressive, but who cares when the food is so divine? Sticky toffee pudding is akin to ambrosia for the Greek gods. This is modern comfort food at its most comforting, and the casual, cool ambiance and music playlist (Dylan, Johnny Cash, Joni Mitchell) make it a destined favorite.

85 Orchard St (at Broome St) 212-226-5047. Mon 6pm-11pm, Tue-Thu 11:30am-3pm 6pm-11pm, Fri 11:30am-3pm 6pm-12am, Sat 11am-4pm 6pm-12-am, Sun 11am-4pm 6pm-10pm. **B D** *to Grand,* **F** *to Delancey. Average entrée $23.*

Mercat *Spanish*
This new addition to the quickly evolving Bowery neighborhood serves up aggressively seasoned Catalan tapas. Although it certainly isn't the best value in the neighborhood, Mercat provides beautiful dishes to both observe and devour. Enjoy the open kitchen and quiet dining room, complete with dark exposed brick walls and wine bottles peering down from the narrow catwalk above. When crowded, the room can get downright loud, making conversation a difficult proposition. For a full meal order at least 2 dishes per person. Must-orders include the baby octopus salad (Pop) and the mushroom croquetas (Croquetas De Pollastre).

45 Bond St between Lafayette and Bowery). 212-529-8600. Mon-Fri 6pm-12am, Sat 11am-4pm, 6pm-12am, Sun 11am-4pm, 6pm-11pm. **G** *to Bleecker,* **B D F V** *to Broadway. Average entrée $16.*

CHEAP
Bereket *Middle Eastern*
From hummus and doner to tabouleh and every other pita-stuffing under the Turkish

sun, this Houston St stalwart whips up quality Middle Eastern standards. The kebab window, which opens onto Orchard St, caters to the neighborhood's bar crowd by dishing out skewers into the wee hours of the morning. During the daytime, the small seating area is crammed with customers looking for an affordable way to fulfill their falafel fix. When they say "hot" sauce, they mean it, so don't be too liberal with self-seasoning.
187 E Houston St (at Orchard St). 212-475-7700. Open 24/7. F V to 2nd Avenue. Average entrée $6.

El Castillo de Jagua *Dominican*
An ugly restaurant with a mouth watering menu, El Castillo neither disappoints nor overcharges. It takes discipline to order something besides fried plantains, but the rest of the menu is worth exploring. There are steaks, fried chicken and sundry fish, all served with red beans and rice. The chuleta especial plate is an amalgam of fried pork and sides, essentially making three meals for eight dollars. There isn't much offered for vegetarians--even the vegetable soup has meat in it--but a plate of vegetables and rice and an avocado salad makes a pleasant, if simple meal. The ingredients are fresh and everything is intelligently spiced.
113 Rivington St (near Essex St) 212-982-6412. Mon-Sun 8am-12am. F to Delancey, J M Z to Essex St. Average entrée $9.

Sugar Sweet Sunshine *Bakery*
Less trafficked, less touristy, and less talked about than Magnolia cupcakes, NYC's original cupcake bakery whips up the definitive version. It also offers a cozy space for relaxing with a cup of coffee and a tasty treat. The "black and white" contains perfect semisweet dark chocolate cake that gives every other bakery in New York a run for its money. Other unusual and well executed flavors include "Bob" (yellow cake with chocolate almond butter cream), "Sexy Red Velvet", Pistachio, and Pumpkin. Cakes, puddings, and breakfast sweets are also available.
126 Rivington St (between Essex St and Norfolk St) 212-995-1960. Mon-Thurs 8am-10pm, Fri 8am-11pm, Sat 10am-11pm, Sun 10am-7pm. F J M Z to Delancey/Essex. Cupcakes $1.50.

Tiny's Giant Sandwich Shop
Sandwiches
This is Subway on steroids, with a soul. A vegetarian's dream of a sandwich joint, their Big Mack Daddy veggie burger topped with tofu bacon is tastier than many a beef burger. For those wedded to their carnivorous ways, caramelized onions, melted mozzarella, and Portobello mushrooms make the roast-beef sandwich so much more than mere meat on a roll. The creative menu provides numerous appetizing combinations, but feel free to assemble your own from the lengthy ingredient list.
129 Rivington St (between Essex & Norfolk Sts) 212-982-1690. F J M Z to Delancey-Essex, F V to 2nd Ave-Houson, B D to Grand. Sandwiches $4.50-$8.25.

NIGHTLIFE

205 *Club*
Tinfoil covered brick walls and a bar built on filing cabinets pay homage to Warhol's infamous Factory at this too-cool-for-school club. Club-goers play their parts, posing in cliques on the small plush love-seats, lazily enjoying the music—pretending to be somebodies. Those who prefer to be anonymous will be most comfortable downstairs where the walls are covered in Craigslist sex ads—yearnings for "butt injections" and "lesbian lovers" are everywhere you look. The DJ spins trance, electronica, and techno, and the people are either pretty serious about dancing or on pretty serious drugs. In terms of drinks, canned beer or Colt 45 are your best bets--anything too fancy will confuse and upset the bartenders.
205 Chrystie St. (at Stanton). 212-477-6688. Tue-Sat 10pm-4am, Sun-Mon closed. Beers $6+, Cocktails $10. J M Z to Bowery, F V to 2nd Ave.

Bluestockings *Cafe*
Activists and their allies find their niche at literary-themed and community building events run by this bookstore and cafe. Before the events, curl up in a window seat with a graphic novel or one of the many selections of texts on women's studies or queer theory and grab an organic, vegan, fair trade treat from the cafe. The budget-conscious need not fret about admission prices to these free or "suggested donation" events. A women and trans poetry slam on the third Tuesday of every month gives novice poets and published authors alike the opportunity to find their voices. Many poems address feminist,

LGBT and other subversive political themes, mirroring the mission of Bluestockings itself as both a "radical bookstore" and "activist center."
172 Allen St (between Stanton St & Rivington St) 212-777-6028. Mon-Sun 11am-11pm. 🅕 to 2nd Ave.

The Box *Club*
Mirrored walls, bejeweled chandeliers, and veiled mezzanine booths make this arena of sin feel like the love child of a prohibition-era speak easy and a Wild West brothel. The city's gilded lumpenyouth, brought to the brink by the DJ's jagged rhythms, order drinks beneath scantily-clad acrobats twirling from circus hoops, as beautiful women squeeze by wielding bottles of overpriced booze. This one of a kind performance space encourages it all. Performing five nights a week is a positively raw burlesque variety show, featuring a Cirque du Soleil inspired orgy, a strip teasing John Belushi, and a female Nixon duo clad only in gas masks and boxing gloves, waving American flags and dancing to techno beats.
189 Chrystie St (between Stanton St and Rivington St) 212-982-9301. Tues-Fir, 11pm-4am; Sat, 7:30pm-4am, Sun-Mon, closed. 🅕🆅 at Lower East Side-Second Ave, 🅙🅜🅩 at Bowery. Cover charge $45.

Darkroom *Bar*
Walk too fast down bar-laden Ludlow and you'll miss the subterranean Darkroom. You'll be worse off for the passing, as this barely-lit spot offers a thoroughly good time. Much larger than it's basement location belies, the space is full of dark corners and leather banquettes for clandestine activities, while the two bar spaces guarantee enough speedy social lubrication to make use of the dance floor. DJs spin typical LES tunes—80's New Wave, 90's Alt-Rock, and some indie hits—but they get the crowd moving. For bar patrons interested in after-hours companionship, Darkroom has a reputation as a hook-up hotspot. On the weekends, the underage B&T crowd and surly bouncers are detractors; go on Thursday nights when the older crowd brings a less desperate vibe with it.

165 Ludlow St (at Stanton St). 212-353-0536. Daily 7pm-4am. 🅕🆅 to 2nd Ave, 🅙🅜🅩 to Essex-Delancey. Average drink $7.

EDITOR'S PICK
epistrophy *Wine Bar*
By day epistrophy is a sidewalk café offering the best hot chocolate in the neighborhood alongside filling but unremarkable Italian antipasti. The relaxed daytime attitude carries over well into the evening. The seats are comfortable, the tables are well spaced, and the service is unassuming and friendly—bring a few close friends or a date and settle in. The Sardinian owners have picked a great selection of unique and affordable wines from every region of Italy. Pours are generous, so order by the glass and experiment. The staff is knowledgeable and able to help make selections, just don't expect them to hover.
200 Mott St (between Spring St & Kenmare St) 212-966-0904. Mon-Thurs, Sun 12pm-12:30am, Fri-Sat 12om-1:30am. 🅙🅜🅩 at Bowery, 🅖 at Spring St. Average drink $7. Cash Only.

Mason Dixon *Bar*
$15 gets you a lot at this western themed bar – a beer, a shot of whiskey, and a bullride, to be precise. Unlike Manhattan's other Rodeo themed bars, Mason Dixon is geared towards the heavy drinking, intellectual set. The kitschy barn-themed adornments—saloon doors, lots of wood and gas lamps at every table—provide a watering hole that draws in LES neighborhood types as well as young white-collar workers looking to indulge in a shot of one of 16 varieties of Bourbon. Though watching clueless patrons fall off the mechanical bull is the main source of entertainment, the bar also boasts live music from 8-11 pm on Tuesdays and Wednesdays.
133 Essex St (between Stanton St and Rivington St). 212-260-4100. Tues-Sun 6pm-4am. 🅙🅜🅩 to Essex, 🅕🆅 to 2nd Ave. Average drink $6.

Milk & Honey *Bar*
This hyper-exclusive speakeasy is a throwback to Prohibition-era, complete with an inconspicuous entrance, candlelight, and a strict code of conduct.

Don't even consider ordering a Sex on the Beach; drinks are freshly made, custom cocktails crafted by New York's finest mixologists. Snuggle up with an amour or a few close friends in one of the secluded booths and enjoy the absence of the typical nightlife din while sipping on a Pimm's Cup or a Dark and Stormy. The catch? Entry is by reservation only, and the unlisted phone number is a well-kept secret amongst patrons. Persistence and creativity will reward the most diligent Googlers with the prized digits. Remember: M&H dictates that Gentleman will not approach ladies uninvited, so enjoy the company with which you came.
134 Eldridge St (between Delancey St & Broome St). No phone number. Every day, 9pm-4am. Cash only. F J M Z to Essex St, B D to Grand St. Average drink $15

Nurse Bettie *Bar*
The candle-lit, brick-walled room gives the illusion of a cozy lounge spot, but the sleek black couches are rarely occupied. A mix of vintage clad beauties, Euro-preppies and cooler-than-thou neighborhood regulars balancing their drinks and cigarettes wander past walls subtly decorated with photos of pin-up girls. The music is a bit loud, but their fun high-energy playlist is perfect for the atmosphere. You may have to wait a while for the Bazooka Bettie, a favorite bubblegum flavored cocktail, or the more sophisticated Ginger Martini, but you'll still want to linger until the second happy hour at 3am.
106 Norfolk St (between Rivington St & Delancey St) 917 434 9072. Sun-Tues, 6pm-2am; Wed-Sat, 6pm-4am. F J M Z to Delancey. Average Drink $7.

Pianos *Bar*
Taking up space in an old piano shop, this bar maintains the relation with music one would expect. With live bands in the back, DJs and a dance party in the upstairs lounge, and a DJ spinning ambient tunes at a level just below distracting in the front bar, this is a place for musicians and musicphiles alike. And with Guitar Hero Tuesdays, even the most novice music appreciators have a chance to shred like rock gods. Though yuppies complain that it's overrun with hipsters and hipsters bemoan the invasion of the yuppies, the crowd is actually quite diverse and amicable—as long as you don't cut at the ever-crowded bar.
158 Ludlow St (at Stanton St). 212-505-3733. Daily 3pm-4am. F V at 2nd Ave. Average drink $7.

The SKINnY *Bar*
This long, narrow space stays packed day and night with locals in the know looking for an atmosphere that is cool with a capital C. Guests are greeted by banquettes in the low-lit space, with a bar leading to further seating in the rear. On weekends, DJs entertain the crowd with rock, funk, '80s and a little old-school hip-hop; the entire scene can be observed from a small balcony at the far end. For the most part, drinks are simple, with domestic and imported bottled beer and cocktails, all for relatively cheap prices. Twists on the classic Manhattan are

LOWER EAST SIDE 125

worth the price. Call ahead for party or special event planning.

174 Orchard St (at Stanton St). 212-228-3668. Mon-Sun 4pm-4am. 🟢🟣 *to 2nd Avenue,* 🟠🟤🟡 *to Essex-Delancey. Average drink $7.*

Stanton Public *Bar*

Boasting a wide and exotic selection of draught and bottled beers, this infectiously friendly pub offers thick, rich stouts, fruity pale ales, and tangy wheats from a variety of domestic and international breweries. On weekend nights, DJs descend from the nearby indie scene to spin until closing, but the local hipsters and young after-work crowd usually skip dancing and choose instead to dig into comfort-food appetizers and memorable pints. With a plush, candlelit downstairs lounge and a relatively spacious outdoor patio, the Stanton is the perfect place to go for a round or three with a large group of friends. Try the special cask-conditioned ale—a weekly rotating all-natural brew, fermented with live, unpasteurized yeast cultures and hand-pumped by "beer engine," yielding an unparalleled vivid flavor.

17 Stanton St (between Bowery & Chrystie St) 212-677-5555. Mon-Fri 4pm-4am, Sat 2pm-4am, Sun closed. Appetizers served until 12am. Happy hour Mon-Sat 4pm-8pm. 🟢🟣 *to 2nd Ave,* 🟠🟤🟡 *to Bowery,* 🟢 *to Spring St. Average entrée $8, Average drink $6.*

Welcome to the Johnson's *Bar*

The 1970s rec-room theme here harkens back to the days of drinking cheap booze in your parents' basement. From the VHS playing on an ancient TV in the corner, to the faux wood paneling, to the vintage family photos, this place reeks of nostalgia and comfort. Though patrons are friendly, most are neighborhood locals or groups of friends who keep to themselves—not the best place for a pick-up but good for a game of pool on the antiquated table. Drinks are cheap and strong—two dollars will get you a PBR, while six will get you a blackout-inducing pint of vodka iced tea.

123 Rivington St (between Essex St & Norfolk St). 212-420-9911. 🟢 *to Delancey St;* 🟠🟤🟡 *to Delancey-Essex. Mon-Fri 3pm-4am, Sat-Sun 1pm-4am. Average drink $4.*

SHOPPING

David Owen's Vintage Clothing

This basement level vintage shop offers both men's and women's vintage apparel spanning the 1940s to the 1990s. Men definitely have more selection here: slick ties, hats, blazers, and coats are all on display, but women have their share of dresses, jewelry, and men's cross-over items. The space offers a great selection of tasteful vintage garb without the pretentious shopkeepers that generally accompany such stores. Owen's is much better merchandised than similar shops and not overpriced like so many others in Manhattan.

154 Orchard St (between Stanton & Rivington St). 212-677-3301. Mon-Fri 1pm-10pm, Sat 12pm-10pm, Sun 11am-7pm. 🟢🟣 *to 2nd Ave,* 🟠🟤🟡 *to Essex.*

Donut Plant

Thanks to the plump, made-from-scratch desserts that leave Dunkin' Donuts and Krispy Kreme looking like posers, this donut shop has developed a true cult following. The owner, Mark Israel, creates banana crème-filled donuts glazed with peanut butter in honor of Elvis, pin-striped donuts for baseball season, jelly-filled square donuts because he can, and festive donuts for every holiday and event that visits New York. The Tres Leches cake donut and the seasonal creations offer something truly unique and delicious. Come early as the shop sells out by late afternoon.

379 Grand St (Between Essex St & Norfolk Sts) 212-505-3700. Tue-Sun 6:30am-6:30pm. 🟢 *to Delancey,* 🟠🟤🟡 *to Essex.*

Essex Street Market

This sprawling warehouse is home to over twenty food vendors ranging from tiny specialty booths to full sized grocery stands. In addition to gourmet foods, such as the locally crafted cheeses sold by Saxelby Cheesemongers, you can find excellent quality meat, fish, and produce here. Luis Meat Market has a wide variety of meat and offal that can be difficult to find in chain stores, and Essex Farm Fruits & Vegetables offers fresh produce that puts Whole Foods to shame. N.B.: don't come hungry or you're certain to break the bank.

120 Essex St (between Rivington St and Delancey St) Mon-Sat 8am-7pm. 🟢🟠🟤🟡 *to Essex.*

EDITOR'S PICK
Girls Love Shoes
The name says it all—this vintage shoe store on the border of Chinatown offers more than 250 pairs that change daily. In fact, the selection is so volatile that most patrons make scrounging the shelves a weekly habit rather than reserving GLS for pure reward shopping. A trip is not complete without upending boxes and scrounging for shoe steals on the floor. And because vintage brands vary in sizing, shoe dimensions are provided along with the instructions and means for measuring your own foot. Choose carefully though as there are no returns.
29 Ludlow St (at Hester St). 917-250-3268. Tues-Sun 12pm-7pm. Closed Mon. 🅱🅳 *to Grand;* 🅵🅹🅼🆉 *to Delancey.*

The Pickle Guys
Opened by a seasoned pickler from Guss' Pickles just down the block, The Pickle Guys serves the whole gamut of pickle varieties, with fresh pickling done each day on premises. Each pickle explodes with flavor, and you can expect a brilliant 'snap' with every bite. They have off-the-wall flavors like fresh horseradish and have been known to experiment with pickled watermelon; luckily the friendly staff will usually let patrons try the goods before deciding.
49 Essex Street (btwn Grand & Hester St). 212-656-9738. Sun-Thurs 9am-6pm, Fri 9am-4pm. 🅵🅹🅼🆉 *to Delancey. $6/quart.*

Pixie Market
The owner travels to Amsterdam, England, Japan, and beyond to bring clothing and accessories that stand out amongst the overly trendy boutiques in this area. Prices are steep, but affordable in comparison to those found in neighboring shops. Brands like Maria Bonita Ruiz and Rojas can only be found here and new merchandise is added every week. When exploring their unique collection, check out Maud, the store's own shoe line.
100 Stanton St (between Ludlow & Orchard Sts). 212-253-0953. 🅵🅹🅼🆉 *to Delancey-Essex,* 🅵🆅 *to 2nd Ave,* 🅱🅳 *to Grand.*

Whole Foods Bowery Beer Room
This one of a kind addition to Whole Foods promises beer enthusiasts an experience nearly beyond comprehension. Six beers are always on tap and offered in the Growler—a reusable ½ gallon glass jug which can be refilled for around $7. Hundreds of standard varieties and rarer beers are available, although brands like Natty Ice have been omitted. Prices are reasonable, but the main reason to visit is to find specialty beers nobody else sells, ranging from Captain Lawrence Porter to Six Point Craft Ales to even more esoteric imports and microbrews. The store's affiliation with Whole Foods casts a green shadow over the whole enterprise, and many of the stocked brews are organic, low-impact, or otherwise environmentally friendly.
95 E Houston St (between Bowery and Chrystie St). 212-420-1320. Open daily 8am-11pm. 🅶 *to Bleecker St,* 🅵🆅 *to 2nd Ave. $3 for your very own Growler, $7 for a fill-up.*

DAY TO DAY

Community Board 3: *59 E 4th St (near the Bowery). 212-533-5300.*

Local Media: savethelowereastside.blogspot.com

Groceries: Essex Street Market. *120 Essex St (between Delancey & Rivington). 212-388-0449.* Jeffrey's on Essex. *120 Essex St Unit C. 212-475-6521.* Whole Foods. *95 E Houston St (at Chrystie St). 212-420-1320.*

Gym: Ludlow Fitness. *100 Delancey St (between Essex St & Ludlow St). 212-260-9222*

Hotels and Hostels: The Hotel on Rivington, *107 Rivington (between Essex & Ludlow). 800-915-1537.* Off SoHo Suites New York, *11 Rivington St (near Chrystie St). 212-353-0860.*

Dog Run: Tompkins Square Park

Movie Theater: Sunshine Cinema, *143 E Houston (between 2nd Ave & Chrystie St). 212-358-7709.*

Best Happy Hour: Verlaine, *110 Rivington St (near Essex St). 212-614-2494.*

LOWER EAST SIDE

boucarou
LOWER EAST SIDE

RESTAURANT & COCKTAIL LOUNGE
64 East 1st Street (btw 1st & 2nd Ave) New York, NY 10003

128 LOWER EAST SIDE

boucarou
LOUNGE

Venue	:	Boucarou Lounge
Address	:	64 East 1st Street
Contact	:	Brice Moldovan
Phone	:	212-529-3262
Fax	:	212-529-3248
Website	:	www.boucaroulounge.com
Email	:	info@boucaroulounge.com

Boucarou is a gorgeous restaurant/ lounge and event space located in downtown Manhattan's trendy Lower East Side . Boucarou boasts tasteful décor such as chocolate brown walls, bamboo panels and gold accents, all courtesy of designer Breanna Carlson. It stands apart due to its versatility as a multi-use space: whether you are looking for a multimedia corporate event, a sit-down dinner, a cocktail reception, an exposition or even a fashion show, boucarou has the perfect environment and experienced staff to accommodate every need.

Boucarou is also noteworthy as a restaurant. Chef Malik Fall, former executive chef of Asia De Cuba, has developed a unique French-African/ Asian fusion menu featuring famous dishes such as Tuna Pica, Seafood Martini and an unsweetened peanut butter lamb stew. The cocktail list offers drinks comprised of homemade fresh organic purees. Boucarou's spirit is inspired by the West African tradition of friends sharing and coming together, combined with the french "savoir vivre", a tribute to owner Patrice Bihina-Parade's mixed origins.

Venue size	: 3,400 sq. ft.
Capacity	: 300
Number of ppl. cocktail	: 300
Number of ppl. seated	: 170
On-site Catering	: Yes
Live Music/DJ/Sound System	: Yes
Amenities : 20 ft. multimedia projection screen	

130 LOWER EAST SIDE

ALL THREE FLOORS AVAILABLE FOR PRIVATE PARTIES AND RESERVATIONS. CALL 212-254-9920.

the delancey
BAR AND NIGHTCLUB

168 DELANCEY (BTW CLINTON & ATTORNEY)

THREE FLOORS WITH DJS, LIVE MUSIC, AND MORE.
WWW.THEDELANCEY.COM

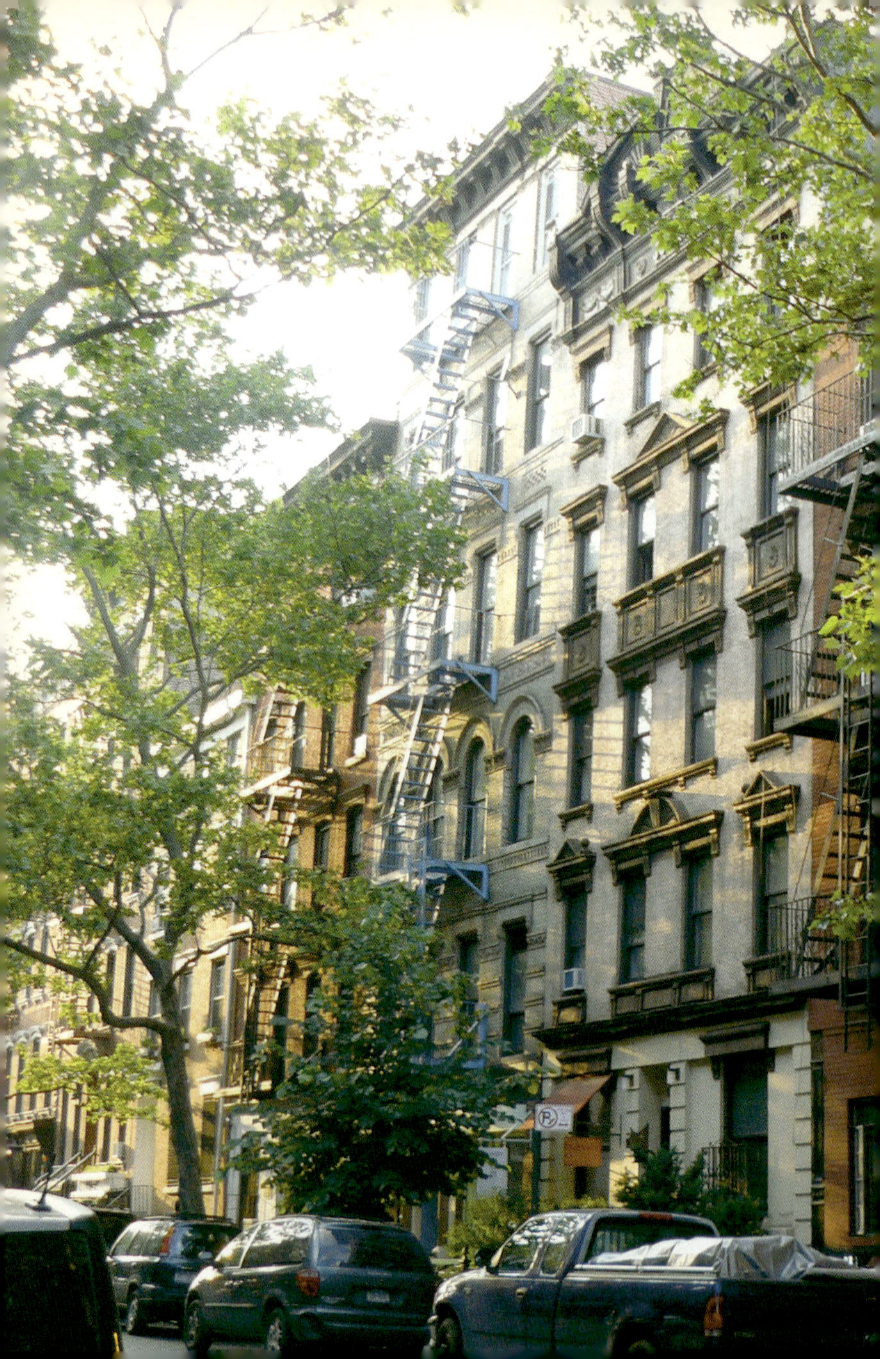

EAST VILLAGE

Unlike SoHo, real people actually live in the East Village, making it relaxing even though it is long past chic. The term "East Village" is, of course, a new one, coined by real estate developers as preferential to "Lower East Side," "Alphabet City," or the unabashedly ethnic "Loisaida." To look for cool in a neighborhood fabricated by ambitious builders is a mistake, but that doesn't mean it isn't a pleasant place to live, eat, or play.

The beauty of the neighborhood makes it understandable why the artists wrested it from the addicts, and why the yuppies drove out the artists. Tompkins Square, St. Mark's Church and the numerous community gardens of Alphabet City accent the landscape of picturesque townhouses and tenements, making this a sanitized version of the city that gave your parents nightmares before you were born. Boutiques dot the side streets but, indignant already about their rent, residents are miserly enough to keep more reasonable delis, bookshops specialty stores, and bars in business. The area boasts two of Manhattan's best tea retailers, a leather tannery and a Wiccan magic supplier, all testaments to a preference for individual shopping.

Largely inaccessible by subways, the East Village is a fickle destination neighborhood. There are only a few worthwhile music venues and no real gallery scene, but revelers from all over still make their way here to enjoy the constantly changing and relatively affordable bar and restaurant scene.

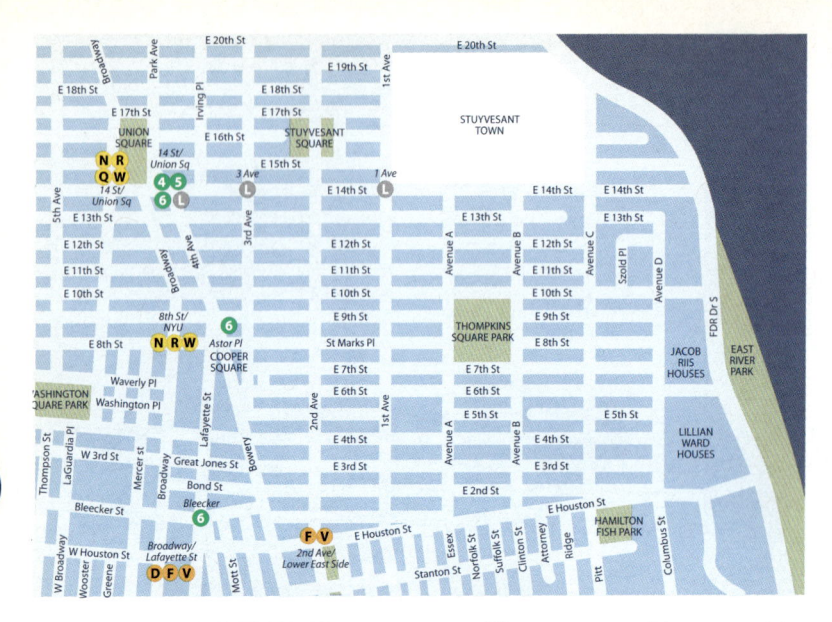

ATTRACTIONS

6th and B Community Garden
Until recently, this garden was defined by a thirty-seven foot structure of wood, scrap metal, and abandoned toys. Though enjoyed by locals, it was (probably accurately) condemned as a safety hazard, and torn down. The park is still lush, a warren of rock paths and overgrown gardening plots landscaped by someone's crazy aunt. The garden is open irregularly, mostly on weekends, and an outdoor concert series usually dominates the space when the gates are unlocked.
6th and B. www.6bgarden.org. **F V** *to 2nd-Lower East Side.*

Bowery Hotel
Originally intended to be an NYU dorm, and then a block of condos, this bizarrely shaped structure languished for months until it was deemed suitable for a hotel. The red-coated doormen, low lighting, and fireplaces dotting the library conjure up a stylized version of *fin de siècle* luxury, a time when good living and the Bowery didn't belong in the same sentence. The rooms are small but cozy and the location is unbeatable. If your parents have never been below 42nd St, send them here and they'll think they've come to a totally different city.
335 Bowery (at 4th St) 212-505-9100. **6** *to Bleecker St or* **B D F V** *to Broadway-Lafayette.*

Tompkins Square Park
Thronging with dog-walkers, strollers, and napping homeless men instead of noisy bands and students, this greener, more serene park is Washington Square's lesser known sister. Despite its punk and riot associated past, this park has now become quite the opposite, with the lawns opening on warm days to groups of sunbathers, yoga gurus, and retro crowds of crust punks. However, annual events such as the Wigstock drag festival and "Riot Reunion" summer concert attempt to recall the area's former days. Tompkins Square Park also boasts one of the city's best dog runs, as well as some of the most beautiful American elm trees anywhere.
10th St (between Ave A and Ave B) **L** *to 1st Ave,* **F V** *to 2nd.*

134 EAST VILLAGE

CULTURE & ARTS

Bowery Poetry Club
The music venue in back of this small café hosts a wide variety of acts, not just the whistling anti-folk one expects from the neighborhood. Offering a range of coffee drinks as well as hippiefied tea, salads, yogurts and soups, the café is noisy but more comfortable than the street outside. They host regular readings and seminars, such as last year's series on New York poets that included Whitman and Dorothy Parker. If all that sounds too pretentious to be amusing, they have lighter pleasures too, like comedy open mics and evenings of bingo.
308 Bowery (between Bleecker & 1st St). 212-614-0505. Mon 5pm-2:30am, Tue-Sat 5pm-2:30am, Sun 5pm-12am. **F V** *to 2nd Ave or* **6** *to Bleecker.*

EDITOR'S PICK
Forbes Magazine Gallery
Located in the Forbes Magazine building, this free museum displays an intriguing assortment of goodies that the late Malcolm S. Forbes, Sr., a notorious packrat, accumulated over his lifetime. The extensive collection showcases more than 12,000 toy soldiers, 500 toy boats, 12 Fabergé Imperial Easter Eggs (only Queen Elizabeth has more), Presidential papers, and historical documents—all as permanent exhibits. The gallery also displays other memorabilia including antique trophies and several original editions of the game Monopoly. Thursdays are reserved for group tours.
62 Fifth Ave (at 12th St) 212-206-5548. Tues-Wed, Fri-Sat 10am-4pm. Free. **L N R Q W 4 5 6** *to 14th.*

Giant Robot
While it may seem more like a store than a serious venue for art, the idea behind this famous magazine's gallery is to stake out mainstream turf for Asian American pop-culture. Featuring the newest in strange-looking dolls and paraphernalia, the store also aims to bring the newest art from Japan into American society. Some may think that they're just cartoons or kids' drawings, but for others they represent the pinnacle of contemporary aesthetics.
437 E 9th St (between Ave A and 1st St). 212-674-4769. Mon-Thu 1pm-8:30pm, Fri-Sat 12pm-9pm, Sun 12pm-7pm. **F V** *to 2nd,* **L** *to 1st Ave.*

La Mama La Galleria
While many have heard of La Mama's experimental theatre, few know about its small experimental art gallery, which aims to help artists at early stages in their careers further develop their ideas. Piquing discussion is their aim and, as with their theatre, you may exit the gallery bewildered but nevertheless hungry for dialogue and debate.
6 E 1st St (between Bowery and 2nd Ave) 212-505-2476. Wed-Sun 1-6pm, Closed Mon-Tue. **6** *to Lexington,* **N R** *to Broadway,* **F** *to 6th.*

The Public Theatre
For new, exciting theatre, the Public is hard to beat. Housed in a gorgeous, historic building on Astor Place, it contains five theatres as well as Joe's Pub, a well-known venue for emerging voices in live-music and performance. In keeping with their mission to produce new works, the Public holds the annual Under the Radar Festival (January) and the Summer Playwrights Festival (July) both of which showcase the newest voices in writing and performing at incredibly student-friendly prices (usually $10). The Public also produces Shakespeare in the Park, which entails a free nightly show of a Shakespeare original at Central Park's gorgeous Delacorte Theatre. Regular season shows bring the most exciting names in writing, directing, and acting to the Public. Student and rush tickets are available to almost every show, making the Public the perfect place to get a taste of the next act in theatre.
425 Lafayette Street (between 4th St and Astor Pl). 212-539-8500. **N R Q W** *to 8th St,* **4 5 6** *to Astor Place.*

New York Theatre Workshop
The NYTW is a creative factory that works with artists at every step of production and has produced works by Tony Kushner, Caryl Churchill, and dozens of other notable playwrights. They were also the original producers of Rent (which is a big deal, whether you like it or not). The Workshop turns 25 this year and remains committed to trying new things—a

recent production of Moliere's *Misanthrope* saw actors running onto Fourth Street to scream and pelt garbage at each other, while cameras relayed the scene to the audience inside. Not every show is as avant-garde (or as messy), but any project they embark on is sure to push theater to limits and offer a new look on the world—a definite place to check out.
79 East 4th St (near 2nd Ave). 212-780-9037. Box office open Tues-Sat 11am-5pm, Sun 1pm-7pm. F to 2nd, 6 to Astor, NR to 8th, BD to Broadway-Lafayette. Studentz $20, call 212-460-5475.

Theater for the New City
The place for Off-Off-Broadway in NYC, this four theater space is known for edgy political commentary. Founded in 1971, the theater is committed to the local community with their many programs including their Annual Summer Street Theater and the Lower East Side Festival of the Arts. The theater offers more than 30 performances a year. Its accolades include a Pulizer Prize for drama and more than 40 Obies for excellence in varying theatrical disciplines.
155 1st Ave (between 9th & 10th St). 212-254-1109. L to 1st Ave, 6 to Astor, RW to 8th St. $15-20.

DINING

UPSCALE
Knife & Fork *New American*
The dark treated wood and brick interior illuminated by flickering candles sets the tone for this culinary destination, whose rustic impulses have been carefully refined. For the best culinary experience, try the daily-changing 6-course chef's tasting menu. The evening starts with a rich and meaty homemade bread and the chef proceeds to dazzle the palate with intricate compositions. Dishes are always paired with sauces and garnishes that are both unexpected and, once tasted, utterly unforgettable—tangy red onion marmalades, chive and wasabi oils, fresh ginger and apricot purées. A sea scallop and octopus appetizer is served with a fresh pour of "white gazpacho," a delicate cold soup composed of almonds, grapes, and milk that nicely soaks up the briny seafood flavors. And everything clicks on an entrée of smoked lamb, dressed in sun-dried tomatoes, goat cheese puree, and a pistachio and black bean reduction.
108 E 4th St (between 1st & 2nd Ave). 212-228-4885. Tues-Sat 5:30pm-11pm. FV to 2nd. Average entrée $27, 6-course prix fixe $45.

MID-RANGE
Matilda *TuscMex*
This family establishment offers a fusion of Tuscan and Mexican flavors and dishes. The TuscMex decor combines sleek, Italian trattoria styles with the bright colors of a standard Mexican restaurant. The delicious house-made sangria and the basil, pepperoncini guacamole served with both rosemary foccaccia and salty tortilla chips are a perfect way to start any meal. The Taco Fiorentini is an exemplary TuscMex combination—soft tacos filled with tender Florentine bisteca. For seafood lovers, the salsiccine di pesce is an inventive combination of scallop and monkfish and while its casing is rugged, the flavor is well worth it. Though the entrées are satisfactory, sharing a variety of appetizers and sides with the table is economical, filling, and will give you the best taste of where the restaurant hits its stride.
647 E 11th St (between Ave B & C). 212-777-3355. Mon-Thurs 5:30pm-11pm, Fri 5:30pm-11:30pm, Sat 11:30am-4pm, 5:30pm-11:30pm, Sun 11:30am-11pm. L to 1st, 6 to Astor. Average entrée $16. Cash only.

Mercadito *Mexican*
From the worn yellow walls, to the loud Latin music, to the rough clay plates, Mercadito's dining area is all old Mexico. The menu is far from diminutive and offers Mexican dishes with a special flair. Light, spicy, and fresh choices like guacamole, ceviche, and tacos are all prepared with an innovative style, as are the seafood-heavy main dishes. Diners should take advantage of the guacamole and ceviche tastings and order several servings of tacos to sample and share with a group. Beverages include a selection of margaritas and mojitos alongside over fifty choices of aged tequila.
179 Ave B (between 11th & 12th St). 212-647-0830. Sun-Thurs 4pm-11pm, Fri-Sat, 4pm-12am. Brunch Fri-Sun 2pm-4pm. 6 to Astor, L to 1st, FV to 2nd. Average entrée $21.

136 EAST VILLAGE

UNION SQUARE

Fourteenth Street has been called a river, and if that's true it must be like the one to our east: fast flowing and dangerous. Union Square isn't much quieter than the crowd of vendors across the street, but at least there are places to sit down. The north side of the park is given over four days a week to the island's biggest green market, which sells restaurant-quality fruit and vegetables as well as, when seasonal, killer hot cider. Though stately, Union Square is too busy to relax in. Picknickers or out-door readers are better served by the underused **Stuyvesant Square**, at Second Avenue between Fifteenth and Seventeenth, a beautiful park that never seems to have more then ten or fifteen people inside.

But Union Square is pleasant for a fifteen minute cup of coffee, and the neighborhood offers some options. Visitors of taste will disregard the ubiquitous Starbucks for **Joe** on Thirteenth Street. A three store chain that started in the West Village, Joe's cappuccino—rich and never bitter—is probably the best in lower Manhattan. The big orange Mud trucks sell the best drip coffee around, and at Union Square and Broadway there is one that defected but still serves a similar brew: an orange and purple vehicle called "The Love Truck." **71 Irving Place**, a cafe whose name is its address, offers more atmosphere but a worse coffee. One block east of the Square, it is a comfortable place to drink excellent hot chocolate and read a novel, work on a novel, or eavesdrop on aspiring novelists trying to impress their dates.

It is a literary neighborhood, or at least has its pretensions. The Barnes and Noble flagship store is at the top of Union Square but should be disregarded, for not far south are some of the city's best independent bookstores. The disorganized, lumbering **Strand** sits at 11th and Broadway, a block below **Forbidden Planet**, a comics destination for serious, upstanding nerds of all kinds. As a famous used bookstore the Strand is never quite as cheap as it should be, although its size makes the selection unbeatable. A block away, at 4th just above 12th, sits **Alabaster Books**, a cozier version of its giant neighbor. So small that one third of their stock is on the discount racks on the sidewalk, Alabaster's collection of literature, art books and nonfiction is scattershot, but they do not make you check your bag.

At the west side of the square is **Coffeeshop**, a noisy bar and cafe open late into the night, and the **Blue Water Grill**, a well respected sushi and seafood place. Twenty-four dollar tuna is fine, but the best meal in the area has to be from the **halal cart on the south side of Fourteenth**, just east of Irving Place. So greasy you'll need a shower, the cart is manned 24/7 in all weather, though the cook occasionally sits down for a nap.

Momofuku Ssäm Bar *Korean, Global*
Chef/owner David Chang had been receiving attention and awards galore for his innovative cuisine at Ssam Bar as well as his other restaurants, Momofuku Noodle Bar and Momofuku Ko. Occasionally, the spotlight is deserved and other times not as much. Korean "burritos", rice cake, and squid salad are made fancier with high-quality ingredients and gourmet presentation, but are in abundance on street corners in Korea. Nevertheless, Chang and his practice of worshipping pork has attracted foodie followers, and with good reason. Ingredient selection and cooking technique are always impeccable. Offal preparations like sweetbreads, head terrine, and beef tendons are unusual and delicious. Steamed pork buns are addictive, as is every other pork dish.
207 Second Ave (at 13th St). 212-254-3500. Daily 11am-2am. ❶❷❸❹❺❻ *to 14th,* ❶ *to 1st or 3rd. Average entrée $22.*

EDITOR'S PICK
Persimmon *Korean*
There is little use in praising specific dishes from Persimmon's menu since most of it changes biweekly. Trust in the creativity and go—soon, and often. The chefs here are downright magicians, making tofu as creamy as mayo, pickling strawberries for kimchi, and writing menus that follow both Korean seasonality and American produce availability. Refined touches set many dishes apart from the norm, but at heart the menu and spirit of the place is unabashedly traditional. The long communal table is not an attempt to be trendy, but an earnest way to evoke the feel of the in-home dinner table. Sure, spices might be tempered somewhat for untrained tastebuds, but even Korean expats will be impressed by both the old and the new. Befriend the chefs/servers, who are happy to explain the concept or history of the food.
277 E 10th St (near Ave A). 212-260-9080. Mon-Wed 5:30pm-11pm, Thurs-Sat 5:30pm-12am. ❻ *to Astor,* ❶ *to 1st Ave . Prix fixe $37.*

EAST VILLAGE

Tai Thai *Thai*
This tiny Thai eatery attracts a diverse crowd looking for a little fire in their food. To start extra spicy, try the duck salad. More timid palates will appreciate the delightfully crisp and delicious shrimp crabmeat net roll; order three and make an entrée out of it. The waitstaff is speedy and friendly, and dim lighting makes for an intimate setting in which to enjoy unique flavors at reasonable prices. If you're new to Thai food, watch out for the heat.
78 E 1st St (between 1st & Ave A) 212-777-2552. Mon-Thurs 11:30am-11pm, Fri-Sat 11:30am-12am, Sun 5pm-11pm. ⑤ to 2nd Ave. Average entrée $12. Cash only.

CHEAP

EDITOR'S PICK
Artichoke Basille's Pizza & Brewery *Pizza*
Judging from the never-ending queues, this new pizzeria is fast on its way to becoming a Village institution. The celebrity slice is the spinach and artichoke pie, a rich and heavy pizza with a cream sauce that recalls artichoke dip. It would be a mistake, however, to discount the other offerings. For purists, the margarita slice's crispy crust, topped with fresh tomato sauce, mozzarella, Parmesan and basil, will more than satisfy. A rotating cast of special pies are all also worth trying. Be advised that the store features nary a table or chair.
328 E 14th St (near 1st Ave) 212-226-8123. ⓛ to 1st, ⓃⓇⓆⓌ④⑤⑥ to Union Square. Mon-Sun 12pm-late. Average slice $3. Cash only.

Belgian Fries *Fries*
Cheaper and greasier than its more well-heeled cousin, Pommes Frites, and lacking any real artistry, Belgian Fries nevertheless turns out a satisfying snack. Though unseemly jars of ketchup, mayonnaise, and other mysterious condiments might horrify a person of sound and sober mind, after 2am on a Saturday night, it all begins to make sense. Of *course* you need a pint of chili to dip your quarter pound of fried potatoes in. After a few debauched hours, it's an absolute necessity for making Sunday morning a tad more tolerable. Belgian Fries isn't that good, except for the times when it's absolutely perfect.
113 Avenue A (near 7th St). Open late. ⑥ to Astor, ⓛ to 1st. Average slop plate $5.

Café Pick Me Up *Coffee Shop*
The two rooms of this wood-floored coffee shop are rarely full, and its convenient location and late hours make it an ideal spot for meeting up with friends. The coffee and espresso are on par, and the baked goods, particularly the brownies, are fresh and filling, although perhaps overly sweet. Tables outside look onto Tompkins Square, making this a low key vantage for people watching—alone or with company.
145 Avenue A (between 9th and 10th St). 212-673-7231. Sun-Thurs 7am-1:30am, Fri-Sat 7am-2am. ⓛ to 1st. Average item $7.

ST. MARK'S PLACE

Offering an endless variety of fingerless gloves, pink wigs, and shirts that say "fuck" on them, St. Mark's is *the* hip destination for badass thirteen year olds. While waiting for their abominable fake IDs, the little tykes can eat monstrous sausages at **Crif Dogs** (*112 St. Marks near Ave A, 212-614-2728*), bargain falafels at **Mamoun's** (*22 St. Marks near 2nd Ave, 212-387-7747*) and rewarmed sandwiches at **BAMN!** (*37 St. Marks near 2nd Ave, 212-358-7685*), a space age update on the traditional automat. Past 2nd Ave St. Marks is, thankfully, more quiet. **St. Mark's Books** is an East Village fixture, a tidy used bookstore with a sense of neighborhood history. Besides architecture and city history, they have sections on sex and drugs intended to capture the soul of the area. The **Porto Rico Importing Company** sells some of the best whole bean coffee in the city, supplying many cafes, while nearby **Cappuccino & Tattoo** (*94 St. Marks near 1st Ave*) offers a more daring caffeine fix. Just before Avenue A is **Sympathy for the Kettle** (*109 St. Marks near 1st Ave, 212-979-1650*), a low slung, low key tearoom with a commitment to a traditional cuppa that places it miles from the frenzy of a few blocks west.

Fresh Juice, Strong Coffee *Vegan*
This outhouse-sized juice stand delivers on its promise in spades. The coffee is hot, potent, and brewed with chicory for flavor—hands down the best quick cup of coffee in the area. Smoothies are made with fresh fruit and offered with apple juice instead of milk, an option even non-vegans should sample for the refreshing apple-cinnamon flavor it adds. Other health-conscious offerings include vegan baked goods, energy bars, and wheat grass.
NW corner of 1st St and 1st Ave. Morning-11ish. **F V** *to 2nd-Lower East Side . Coffee $1. Smoothies $4.*

Kenka *Japanese, Sushi*
Well-hidden Kenka often eludes tourists, so keep your eyes open for the lawn ornament helpfully placed outside. Inside, the restaurant is humble but raucous: bring friends, order an $8 pitcher of Kirin, and watch the chefs prepare food behind the bar. Kenka's menu is full of oddities, which the waitstaff will be happy to explain, and there are plenty of options for the less adventurous. Try the yakimeshi, Japanese style pork fried rice, hamachi no kamayaki, yellow tail neck, yaki morokoshi, grilled corn slathered with sweet sauce, or the takoyaki, grilled doughballs stuffed with octopus. The bill comes with small cups of pink sugar for the cotton candy machine outside; grab a chopstick and discover how hard it is to spin the perfect puff for your walk home.
25 St. Mark's Place (between 3rd & 2nd Ave). 212-254-6363. 6pm- 2am. **Q W** *to 8th,* **6** *to Astor. Average entrée $8.*

Max *Italian*
Max is a neighborhood staple, if only because a pasta place in "Loisaida" is automatically remarkable. A dark brown front room is connected by a narrow corridor to a back garden decorated with painted on clotheslines and windows, a stab at tenement chic that keeps the restaurant from feeling too slick. Putting aside such socioeconomic questions is easy once the massive pieces of bread arrive, and when the pasta comes it's hard to even pretend to care. The dishes are simple, filling and large, easily enough for a second meal the next day. A two dollar price break makes it tempting to come at lunch, when the restaurant is deserted, but eating among the dinner crowd is pleasant too. It's not the best pasta in the city, but the prices are good enough to make it crucial to those living in the delivery radius.
51 Avenue B (near 4th St). 212-539-0111. Mon-Sun 12pm-12am. **F V** *to 2nd. Average entrée $12.*

Mudspot *Café*
They call themselves an "anti-establishment" coffee shop, taking a shot at the many Starbucks locations nearby and alluding to their roving counterparts, the Mud Trucks. Their laid-back approach really does work: people are happier around the neon orange cups and amazing coffee that separate it from the rest. Tasty pastries, soups, salads and sandwiches go great with a mug, and can be eaten outside in the garden.
307 E 9th St (between 1st & 2nd Ave) 212-228-9074. **6** *to Astor Place,* **L** *to 3rd Ave-14th St,* **R W** *to 8th.*

NIGHTLIFE

Angel's Share *Lounge*
The lore surrounding Angel's Share is only heightened by its blink-and-you'll-miss-it location. A small and swanky lounge atop a dingy looking Japanese restaurant, Angel's Share is perfect for couples or small groups (four or less) seeking cocktails and a touch of class. While the food is unremarkable, the enormous drink menu more than makes up for it. Tasty and strong, if slightly overpriced, the boozy concoctions combine champagnes and liquors with exotic flavors like elderflower to unique effect. Angel's Share is a wonderful place for conversatin', but come with a large crowd and you could find yourself seat-less and disappointed. Bring a friend or two and you may be pleasantly surprised.
8 Stuyvesant St (at 9th St) 212-777-5415. Sun-Wed 6pm-2:30am, Thurs 6pm-2am, Fri-Sat 6pm-2:30am. **N R W** *to 8th,* **6** *to Astor,* **L** *to 3rd. Average drink $8.*

EAST VILLAGE 139

CURRY ROW

It's not easy to dispute the joke that every restaurant on Curry Row shares a kitchen. Most of them offer a particular type of good-but-not-great Indian that too often features limp naan or timid spicing. This would be ruinous if the competition hadn't forced the price of lunch specials to a shockingly low mean of $4.95, which will get rice, bread, curry, and an appetizer or two. **Brick Lane Curry** (306-308 E 6th St. 212-979-8787) is a standout, a London-style curry place whose prices reflect the step up in quality. Between the rest there is not much to choose from. The appropriately confusing Raj Mahal and Taj Mahal are the worst on the block, though Taj offers a delicious banana pakora and the ambience of a railway dining car. **Calcutta** (324 E 6th St. 212-982-8127) is larger than the others and underground, making it better for dinner than lunch. **Spice Cove** (326 E 6th St. 212-674-8884) is dark, cozy and well decorated, with food suggesting ambitions towards being more than another faceless curry joint.

6th St (between 1st Ave and 2nd Ave). 6 to Astor Pl, R W to 8th-NYU.

Arlo & Esme *Bar, Café*
Named after the owners' nephew and niece, this beautiful, new location has been blossoming of late. The upstairs is a sun-lit cafe, while the 4,000-square-foot basement is a nightlife playpen, complete with pool room, Ms. Pac-Man machine, and nightly DJs spinning sweet beat science. To put you in the proper dancing mood, knowledgeable bartenders concoct spot-on renditions of classic libations. Come back early the next morning for some great espresso and pretty decent people-watching. Free WiFi.
42 E 1st St (near 2nd Ave) 212-777-5617. Mon-Fri 8am-4am; Sat-Sun 10am-4am. F V to 2nd, 6 to Bleecker St. $10.

Burp Castle *Beer Bar*
This temple of beer provides a sanctuary to faithful disciples of good drinking. Bring a date or a few close friends, but never a boisterous posse: it's all about enjoying the brews here, and though the "whisper only" policy is only loosely enforced, bartenders have been known to shush distractingly loud revelers. The staff has an excellent knowledge of beer, and will help you decide which of the 12 drafts and dozens of bottles are right for you (tasting is allowed before committing to a full pint). Beer nerds will be glad to see that all beers are served in their proprietary glass. The selection is primarily Belgian, and the décor pays homage to the bar's Trappist taste. Bordering on camp, yet strangely charming, the walls are covered with monks in various stages of revelry and undress. Vaguely monastic music plays in the background, which could be annoying if the beer wasn't so good.
41 East 7th St (between 2nd Ave and Taras Shevchenko Pl). 212-982-4576. Mon-Thurs 5pm-12am, Fri 5pm-2am, Sat 4pm-2am, Sun 4pm-12am. 6 to Astor, R W to 8th St, F V to 2nd Ave. Average beer $8.

EDITOR'S PICK
Death & Co. *Bar*
At this chic speakeasy, cocktails are mixed with precision and careful attention is paid to individual tastes. The bartenders ask specific questions about flavor preferences to concoct artfully created drinks that satisfy both cocktail aficionados and less refined palates. Grab a date or a few friends for a classy night of libations consumed at the marble-topped bar or at small tables with black leather seats. The menu changes from time to time, but always showcases high-quality spirits and clever additions like chocolate bitters to round out strong alcohol flavors. In 1920s style, groups can order punches to share, which are ladled into teacups.
433 E. 6th St (between 1st Ave and Avenue A). 212-388-0882. Daily 6pm-12am. F V to 2nd Ave-Lower East Side, L to 1st Ave. Average drink $12.

Joe's Pub *Live Music*
This intimate candlelit cavern wildly varies its bookings, showcasing world music, jazz, blues, classical, folk, and whatever else the lips and fingers of man can devise, from beat boxing to burlesque to Cambodian psychedelic surf rock, so long as it's good. A hip, diverse crowd enjoys the

beautiful cabaret's impeccable acoustics, universally clear sightlines, elevated bar, and Italian dinner menu. Elegant matrons of the arts and academic parents with geometric glasses and kids in tow sit alongside old hippies, young couples, and dreadlocked musicians in fedoras and porkpies. Aside from the variety and pure spine-tingling quality of the artists, there's a touching sense of community when some West African drummer or Tibetan songstress rouses this disparate Noah's ark of music lovers to join as one in hand claps or oms.

425 Lafayette St (between Astor Pl & 4th St) 212-967-7555, 212-539-8778 (Reservation line). ❻❿ *to 8th,* ❻ *to Astor. Tickets $10-40.*

Lit Lounge *Bar*
Saturday nights are tops at this artsy, dirty, dive bar, when the wait for the dungeon-basement is outdone only by the wait for the bathroom. Grab a few drinks and admire the fresh artwork on the walls of the crowded upstairs bar, in which rascals and revelers populate skanky leather seats. Mingling and people-watching may be captivating enough for most bar-goers, but know that the real party is down the precarious staircase, where DJs and live bands keep a sweaty, jam-packed crowd dancing 'til the wee hours.

93 2nd Ave (between 5th St & 6th St) 212-777-7987. Mon-Sat 5pm-4am, Sun 9pm-4am. ❻❿ *to 2nd-Lower East Side,* ❻ *to Astor Pl. Average drink $5.*

The Marz Bar *Dive Bar*
Perhaps the skuzziest dive bar left on the island, this spectacular shit hole is a perfect place to get absolutely hammered. 6-foot tall trannies dance on (and fall off) the bar, junkies nap on their bar stools, and the batty regulars are known to take up broken bottles in defense of their comrades. The bartenders are spirited (often drunk themselves) and friendly; they keep the place running on generously poured drinks and bottles of iced beer (no refrigeration and certainly nothing on tap here). The jukebox, broken for years, no longer accepts money, but a few spirited kicks are known to set it playing random songs for brief spurts, which are always, miraculously, the perfect drunken-sing along ballad.

25 E 1st St (at 2nd Ave). 212-473-9842. Daily 11:30am-4am. ❻❿ *to Second Ave,* ❻❿ *to Broadway-Lafayette,* ❻ *to Bleecker. Average drink $4.*

Nuyorican Poets Café
Performance Space, Bar, Café
Nuyorican is the home and heart of slam poetry in NYC. Diehards line up over two hours in advance for prime seating, since late-comers are relegated to the floor. At Friday night slams, three poets perform in multiple audience-judged rounds of high-speed versifying, frequently weaving together personal experiences with opinions on social justice. A diverse and enthusiastic crowd hangs onto every syllable, snapping their fingers approvingly at worthy lines. After the slam, the mic is open to anyone brave enough to compete with the experts. In addition to poetry, the Café's roster of events offers offbeat theater, screenplay readings, and live music.

236 E 3rd St (at Ave B). 212-505-8183. ❻ *to Bleecker St,* ❻❿ *to 2nd,* ❶❷❸ *to Essex-Delancey. Cash Only. Average drink $7.*

EAST VILLAGE 141

EDITOR'S PICK
Planet Rose *Karaoke Bar*
This is far from your average karaoke bar. Less pretentious, cliquey, or creepy than most, Planet Rose offers both an inexplicably hopping singles scene and a forgiving crowd for those brave, tone-deaf souls daring enough to take the mic. Most of the bartenders sing, and sing well, as do a cadre of regular performer-patrons, meaning when Pat Benetar's "Love is a Battlefield" comes on, it probably won't suck. The song selection is huge, people's choices are generally creative, and the price is quite right: only two bucks a pop—if the bartender is matching you shot for shot, as they often do, a song is free. All of the drinks served are confidence inducing (read: dangerously potent). When you're feeling sufficiently self-assured—or simply trashed—ask the bartender Missy for her famed flaming shot, and watch out for your eyebrows.
219 Ave A (between 13thSt & 14thSt) 212-353-9500. L to First Ave, **N R Q W 4 5 6** *to 14th-Union Sq. Average drink $6.*

Sly Fox *Bar, Dive*
The closest NYU has to its own bar, Sly Fox used to be famous for freshman loutishness, the result of a lax ID policy. While it may have tightened up its ID standards, Sly Fox still offers cheap pitchers, while a good jukebox and friendly bartenders keep the customers coming back to dance—at least on weekends. Weeknights tend to be more low-key. The wooden panel decor gives the room the feel of an unusually ugly Wisconsin roadhouse.
140 2nd Ave (at 9th St). 212-614-3283. **Q W** *to 8th-NYU,* **6** *to Astor Pl. Average Drink $5.*

Snapshot at Bar 13 *LGBT*
This weekly dance party began in March 2004 in response to a perceived lack of representation of varied racial, sexual and gender identities at lesbian parties of that time. Now established as the most eclectic queer dance party, *Snapshot* attracts a crowd of all sexual orientations and races shaking it to current top 40s hits, late 90s hip hop, and 80s favorites. Black leather couches line the walls providing a comfortable place to catch your breath between songs or to scope the scene. The ambiance of the quieter rooftop patio compliments the louder party atmosphere downstairs. Check out their five large annual parties—Anniversary, Queer Prom, Pride, Fashion Show and Halloween, which further reflect the party's mission to represent an array of identities.
Hosted every Tuesday at Bar 13, 35 E 13th St (between University Place and Broadway). 212-979-6677. **L** *to 1st,* **N R Q W 4 5 6** *to Union Square. Doors at 9 pm, $5 cover begins at 10pm.*

Tom and Jerry's *Bar*
Tom and Jerry's is a grown-up kind of bar. There's no half-panel wood, there's no leather chair smoking lounge--but you definitely might find vomit on the bathroom floor. It's a bar for people who stopped those shenanigans years ago and are embarrassed to be reminded of them. Though packed on weeknights, full of young professionals bouncing up and down to Duran Duran songs they've heard 5,000 times, Tom and Jerry's is exquisite in late afternoons and early evenings when it is mostly empty, light pours in through the large window onto the street, and $6 beers are sometimes slightly discounted. The staff is pleasant but not friendly; the prices are reasonable only in that they're not insane. Overall, it's a consistently above average experience.
288 Elizabeth St (at Houston St). 212-260-5045. Daily 12pm-4am. **B D F V** *to Broadway-Lafayette,* **6** *to Bleecker. Average Drink $5. Cash only.*

SHOPPING

7A Farmer's Market
Just as Tompkins Square is more quiet and more beautiful than Union Square, its green market is much easier to navigate. Open only on Sundays, it takes up just the south-west corner of the Square. Fewer stalls mean fewer superfluous vendors—no art, herbal supplements, or wheat germ extract here, meaning shoppers can focus on produce, which is all local and mostly organic.
SW corner of Tompkins Square. **6** *to Astor,* **L** *to 1st,* **F V** *to 2nd.*

Enchantments, Inc.
Its shelves packed with powdered elderberry and skull-shaped candles, Enchantments, Inc carries all the dark materials you will need for your sorcery. All of it has, in theory, magical applications, and it's not hard to see that a tiny portable cauldron would be useful to a witch on the go. The shop is disorderly and musty, exactly as a magical shop should be, and it makes one wish that rents were low enough for more businesses to waste space so whimsically. In the back there is a small collection of old paperbacks, an excellent sampling of classic science fiction and adventure novels that suggests the store is maintained more carefully than it lets on.
341 E 9th St (near 2nd Ave). 212-228-4394. 6 *to Astor,* L *to 1st.*

Fourth Street Food Co-Op
The Fourth Street Co-Op is charming, but not an easy place to shop. Fruits and vegetables are not the gleaming specimens routinely found at Whole Foods; dry goods (flour, salt, nuts) are displayed in plastic bins–not cute, Earth-themed packets. The staff is made up completely of volunteers, which considerably slows down the checkout service. But, there is some charm in this utter lack of finesse. Not only is the fruit consistently delicious, everyone working, no matter how slowly, truly loves the store. No matter how hard he squints, the man behind the counter will never give you the grimace of the Whole Foods cashier. He'll just smile, apologize, and hand you the organically ugly pear as though every store is this ragged.
58 East 4th St (near the Bowery). 212-674-3623. 6 *to Bleecker.*

St. Mark's Bookshop
The success of St. Mark's Bookshop is a testament to the neighborhood's unapologetic intellectualism. They sell all-new books, emphasizing critical theory, new fiction, and serious social science. Unlike the charming mess of the other bookstores nearby, St. Mark's is carefully organized—a mark, perhaps, of its proximity to Cooper-Union.
31 3rd Ave (near 9th St). 212-260-7853. Mon-Sat 10am-12am, Sun 11am-12am. 6 *to Astor Place,* L *to 3rd Ave.*

DAY TO DAY

Community Board 3: *59 E 4th St. 212-533-5300.*

Local Media: eastvillageidiot.com

Groceries: Trader Joe's, *142 E 14th St, 212-529-4612.* Whole Foods, *4 Union Sq South, 212-673-5388.*

Gym: Gladiator's Gym. *503 E 6th St (at Avenue A). 212-674-9803.*

Hotel & Hostels: 60 Thompson. *60 Thompson St (between Broome & Spring St). 877-431-0400.* Jazz on the Town Hostel. *307 E 14 St. 212-228-2780.*

Dog Run: First Run Dog Run. *Tompkins Square Park. 212-979-5327.*

Movie Theater: Sunshine Cinema, *143 E Houston St (between 1st & 2nd Ave). 212-330-8182.*

Best Happy Hour: Lit Lounge, *93 2nd Ave (between 5th & 6th St). 212-777-7987. $3 beers and well drinks until 9pm.*

St. Mark's Comics
Dusty, jumbled, mad and messy, the back room of St. Mark's is brimming with older comics packed tightly in large boxes. What they have in selection they lack in space and cleanliness, so be prepared to crouch on your knees and do some exploring if you're looking for something in particular. Less corporate than the Midtown stores, St. Mark's has a hipper, punker customer base, one more likely to snatch up the latest Optic Nerve than the new Captain America.
11 St. Mark's Pl (near 3rd Ave). 212-598-9439. Mon 10am-11pm, Tues-Sat 10am-1am, Sun 11am-11pm. R W *to 8th,* 6 *to Astor.*

EAST VILLAGE 143

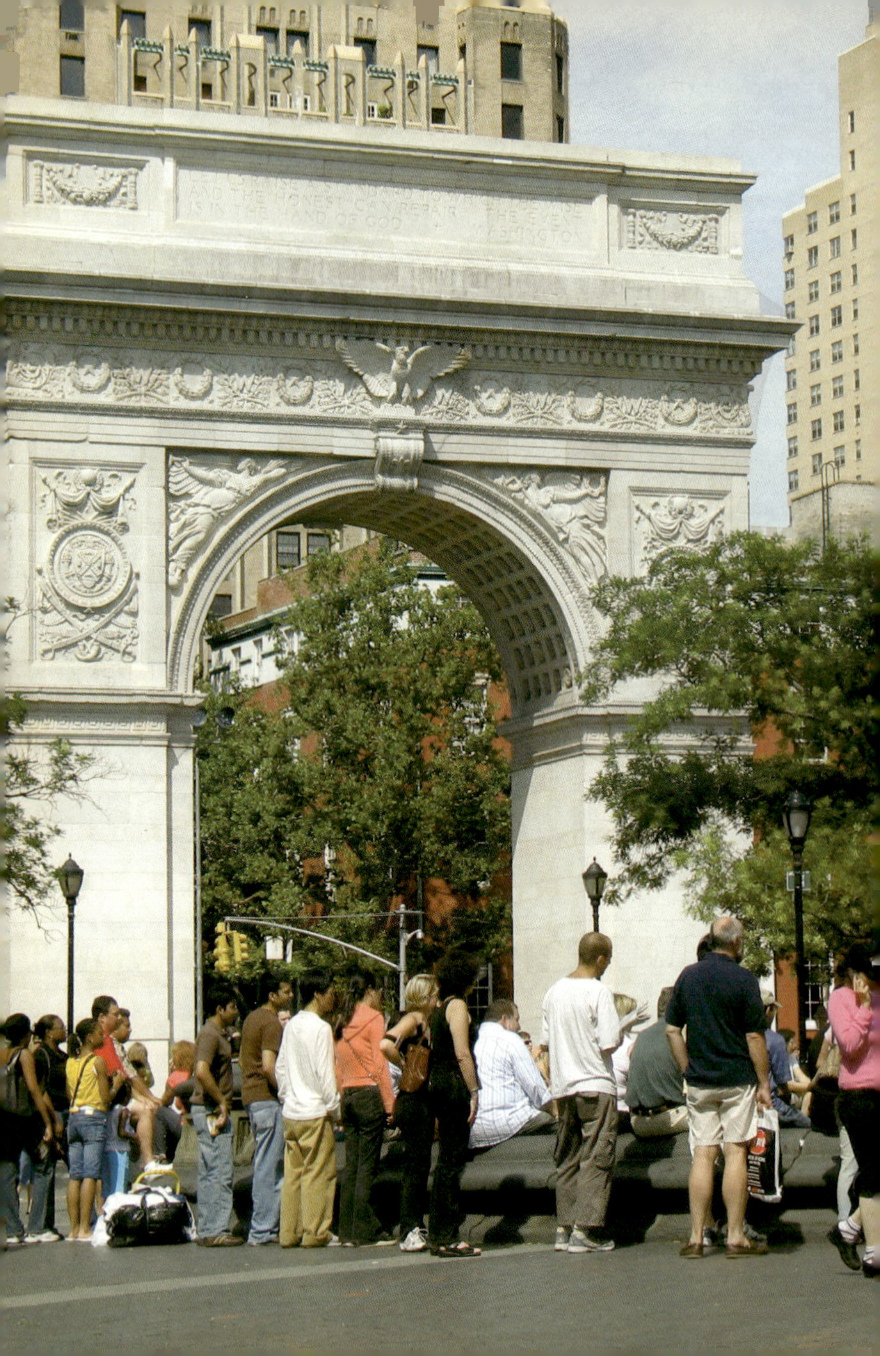

GREENWICH VILLAGE

Do not come to Greenwich expecting the village of lore. Though its brownstones once sheltered artists from O'Neill to Dylan, its radical landmarks are a waste of time, since nothing famously cool can stay that way very long. Encouraged by the continental style of its narrow, confusing streets, artists began migrating to the Village a century ago, founding a Bohemia that was self consciously avant garde. It was quickly overrun by curious slummers from uptown, so much so that by the end of World War I many had declared the Village "already over." That cycle repeated itself several times, and now where once lived playwrights and dancers are Hollywood celebrities with artistic mindsets.

It is easy to understand why they pay what they do to live here. Its shady, tree-lined streets will always be beautiful, and as long as they are adorned with restaurants, delis and shops run with creativity and honesty they should escape Disneyfication. Urban activist Jane Jacobs used the West Village as her chief example of a healthy neighborhood, holding it up as a counterargument to the dehumanizing towers of Midtown. The West Village is overrun by charm, and no matter how lost one gets, every wrong turn leads to something lovely: a restaurant or bookstore so perfect that it can never be found again.

East of Sixth Avenue the grid plan asserts itself and makes it much easier to navigate. Third and Bleecker Streets are a dull strip of bars and delis, but NYU's presence makes the side streets excellent for greasy, budget eating.

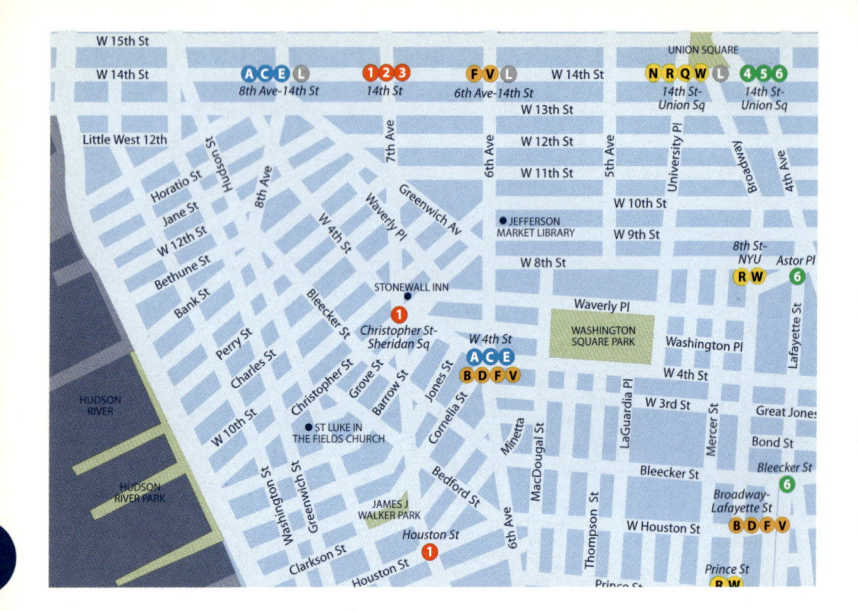

ATTRACTIONS

Washington Square Park
A grand arch rivaling Napoleon's marks this spot, home to chess players, street musicians and NYU students. Once a place for folk and beatnik gatherings with the likes of Bob Dylan and Allen Ginsberg, the park remains a meeting place for young people who prefer lounging in the shade to taking on a day job. This longing to loll does not exclude neighborhood regulars or anyone passing through the park on their way around the village. A sanctuary from the surrounding bustle, the trees provide shelter from the sun, and plenty of benches line the paths. Take note that the fountain area is currently fenced off for construction, but the park retains its charm as a neighborhood retreat.
W 4th and MacDougal. **A C E F V** *to W 4th.*

CULTURE & ARTS

Angelika Film Center
This famed indie art house offers the newest films on the independent circuit. Whether it's the latest Sundance hit or the next Oscar underdog, the Angelika will probably show it. For lesser known films, a forum with the director after the show is not uncommon. If you're not in the mood for a film, you can still sit in the café that doubles as their lobby, which dishes up typical, bland coffee-house fare—but be prepared to endure the pretentious droning of loud-mouthed film aficionados.
18 W Houston St (at Mercer St). 212-995-2000. **B D F V** *to Broadway-Lafayette. Adults $10.*

Film Forum
Among New York City's art house offerings, Film Forum stands out as a rugged individualist. On the scene since 1970, Film Forum is distinguished by its meticulous film selection process—be it independent premieres or overlooked classics, its movies are guaranteed to be of the highest caliber. Their proclaimed mission is "presenting an international array of films that treat diverse social, political, historical and cultural realities." Check its online calendar to catch the frequent filmmaker appearances and other creative programming—such as evenings of live piano accompaniment to silent

146 GREENWICH VILLAGE

classics—all part of Film Forum's mission to capture the power and relevance of cinema.
209 W Houston St (between Varick and Ave of the Americas). 212-727-8110. www.FilmForum.org. ❶ *to Houston and Varick.*

MCC

One of off-Broadway's most respected and well-known theatres, MCC makes its performers its foremost priority. This is evident in the innovative and ambitious shows they tackle with finesse. Education and community outreach also play an important role for this downtown theatre—in August, their FreshPlay Festival showcases the work of high-school writers in full-scale professional productions at theatres around the city. A $15 student rush is available twenty minutes before every mainstage show.
The Lucille Lortel Theatre at 121 Christopher St. 212-727-7722. ❶❷❸ *to Christopher.*

Pratt Gallery

The Pratt Manhattan Gallery, the official gallery of the Pratt School, exhibits artists from around the world. Guest curators, who come from as far away as the Museo Nacional in Madrid, bring fresh and exciting ideas to their exhibits, which are reliably innovative. Past exhibits have focused on video-art, interior design, and technology design tools.
144 W 14th Street, 2nd floor (near 6th Ave). 212-647-7778. Tues-Sat 11am-6pm. ❶❷❸ 🄵🅅 ❶ *to 14th.*

Village Vanguard

For seventy years, the Village Vanguard has been the venue of choice for jazz greats like Thelonious Monk and Miles Davis. Where other venues have expanded, moved or modernized with time, the Vanguard has remained true to its roots, right down to its intimate 123 seat size. Walls are crowded with pictures of the greatest performers to have graced the club in its seven decade existence. The smiles of these greats are mirrored on the faces of patrons. The semi-steep cover charge is well worth it, both for the huge names and the experience of an authentic piece of New York culture.
178 Seventh Ave (near 11th St). 212-255-4037. Sun-Thu 8pm-1am, Fri-Sat 8pm-2am. ❶❷❸ 🄵🅅 ❶ *to 14th. $25 cover Tues-Wed, $35 cover Thurs-Sat (both include 1 drink).*

DINING

UPSCALE

Antica Venezia Ristorante *Italian*

A night out at this hidden destination feels like a dining experience worlds removed from the city. Large groups and couples alike go to Antica for its exquisite service, lavishly prepared dishes, top-shelf bar, and exceptional wine list. The meal starts with complimentary fried zucchini and fresh bruschetta and ends with table-side dessert liqueurs, such as the tangy limoncello and rich coffee sambuca. The pastas are the standouts: homemade noodles, like the impeccably al dente penne, pappardelle, and gnocchi, come gorgeously dressed in mouth-watering pesto, truffle, and ragù sauces.
396 West St (at W 10th St) 212-229-0606. Sun 3pm-11pm, Mon-Thurs 5pm-11pm, Fri-Sat 5pm-12am. ❶ *to Christopher-Sheridan. Average entrée $28.*

Bistro Bagatelle *French*

Mirrored ceilings reflect candlelight glitz and a gorgeous clientele at this hip new bistro where traditional French cuisine meets Chelsea chic. The food is tasty but never as exceptional as you would expect from a place that costs about $100 a head, making Bagatelle feel like a spot to be seen rather than eat. The staff is both charming and beautiful. Dishes such as the foie gras appetizer, which comes dressed in strawberry sauce, are decadent and plated beautifully. Specialty cocktails, like the $14 gin and cucumber mojito, tend toward sweet rather than strong. On weekends, those with deep pockets keep the place lively with Dom Pérignon and Cristal flowing until closing. The best offerings come on the dessert menu, including the sublime Chibouste—a rich passion fruit custard with a caramelized top and strawberry crust—as well as a rotating selection of vivid sorbets.
409 W 13th St (at 9th Ave). 212-675-2400. Dinner Sun-Wed 5:30pm-12am, Thurs-Sat 5:30pm-1am. Brunch Sat-Sun 11:30am-5:30pm. 🄰🄲🄴 ❶ *to 14th and 8th. Average entrée $28.*

Centro Vinoteca *Italian*

In a manner befitting her mentor, Executive Chef Anne Burrell, protégé of Mario Batali, serves updated Italian fare in a chic, modern setting. The most attractive (and affordable) feature of Burrell's menu is the selection of small plates, or

GREENWICH VILLAGE 147

piccolini. The tastiest among them include garlic truffled deviled eggs, zucchini fritters, and grilled pizzetta with stracchino cheese, hot sausage, and arugula. Equally fetching are Centro's entrées—the wild boar ragù over gnocchi is top-notch. The dining experience is enhanced by the elegant black and white interior, where ornate chandeliers stand out against the white-washed exposed-brick walls.

74 Seventh Ave (at Bleeker St). 212-367-7470. Mon-Fri 9am-2pm, Sat-Sun 11am-2am. ❶ to Christopher St, ❹❻❸❺❻❼ to W 4th. Average entree $25.

Chinatown Brasserie *Chinese*
Meant to evoke the mythos of America's early Chinatowns, Chinatown Brasserie is decked out with everything from elaborate paper lanterns to an indoor coy pond. The cavernous interior is full of banquet tables for large parties, with more intimate nooks sprinkled here and there for couples. Be sure to sample widely from the justifiably famous Dim Sum list—it's hard to go wrong with the tempura lobster tail or the spicy pork and shrimp dumplings with savory ginger seasoning. The piquant Szechuan chicken shines amongst the traditional Chinese entrées. Surprisingly, the seared filet mignon is the highlight of the menu. Smooth as butter and served atop a raft of white asparagus, you can practically cut it with chopsticks.

380 Lafayette St (between Great Jones St and 4th St) 212-533-7000. Mon-Fri 11:30am-11:30pm, Sat 11am-12am, Sun 11am-10pm. ❻ to Bleecker or ❶❷❸ to 8th-NYU. Average entrée $18.

Strip House *Steakhouse*
This is the consummate steak house for the discerning carnivore. The sexy strip club decor is all red leather and dim light, making the atmosphere in this shrine to beef somewhere between temple and bordello. Knowledgeable waiters will guide you to the perfect selection of meat for the evening, whether it be a 22oz ribeye or a 10oz filet. Every steak is seared dark, simply seasoned with sea salt and cracked pepper, and served alone on white ceramic. No sauce is needed for these top-grade cuts, but ask for uni butter on your steak: the briny flavor of the urchin perfectly complements the meat's rich flavor. Creamed spinach with black truffles is a favorite with regulars and won't disappoint. Bring a date: the atmosphere is unexpectedly romantic despite the burlesque theme, and the 24-layer chocolate cake is a rich and buttery aphrodisiac to finish off your meal.

12 E 12th St (near 5th Ave). 212-328-0000. Mon-Sat 5pm-11:30pm, Sun 5pm-10:30pm. ❶ to 14th, ❶❷❸❹❺❻ to 14th. Average entrée $40.

Wallsé *Austrian*
Neighborhood locals and gourmands alike flock to dine on Austrian staples with a French twist in this modern yet comfortable space. The walls boast artwork from the private collection of Julian Schnabel while cherry branches decorate the sleek bar where conversation flows as freely as the wide variety of Austrian wines. Foods are paired with fresh seasonal vegetables, light sauces, and sharp herbs - even greasy, bar-hall staples like wiener schnitzel have a modern flair. Complemented with lingonberry sauce and a chilled potato cucumber salad, schnitzel becomes an elegant, composed dish in Chef Kurt Gutenbrunner's kitchen. A well-rounded cheese selection and wonderful desserts—like the apple strudel with chestnut ice cream—cap off a satisfying experience.

344 West 11th St (at Washington St). 212-352-2300. Mon-Sun 5:30pm-11:30pm, Brunch Sat-Sun 11am-2:30pm. ❶❷❸❹ to 14th and 8th, ❶ to Christopher. Average entrée $30.

MID-RANGE
BLT Burger *American*
Chef Laurent Tourondel may hail from France, but his casual burger joint taps into New Yorkers' craving for all-American diner grub. Juicy beef burgers, savory sides, and thick milkshakes are tasty enough to make you forget their high calorie content. Chili-cheese waffle fries with sour cream, tangy wings, and garlicky buttered green beans are especially worth the indulgence. The American Wagyu Kobe Burger and signature BLT Burger with smoked tomato aioli make BLT a name among New York's finest burger joints. The place is always loud and often packed—a testament to the food and the fun atmosphere—so be sure to reserve ahead for a large group.

470 6th Ave (near 12th St). 212-243-8226. Mon-Sun 11:30am-11pm. ❶❷❸❹❺❻ to 14th. Average entrée $10.

Good *American*
Though the classic American menu may not

initially impress, creative and subtle touches on every plate—like the textural contrasts of toasted pecans, bacon slivers, and kabocha squash alongside a grilled pork chop—reveal keen insight and gentle care. Gracious service, al fresco dining, and service for three meals a day provide an even better reason to dine here regularly. The room is simple and understated, but all for the better; it makes it equally amenable to dining in a large group or alone to enjoy straightforward salads or snuggle up with warm banana-chocolate-chip bread pudding. Patrons and waitstaff alike swear by the weekend pancakes.

89 Greenwich Ave (between W. 12th St and Bank St). 212-691-8080. Dinner Mon-Thurs 6pm-11pm, Fri-Sat 6pm-11:30pm, Sun 6pm-10pm. Lunch Tues-Fri 11:30am-3pm. Breakfast Tues-Fri 8am-11:30am. Brunch Sat 11am-3:30pm, Sun 10am-4pm. ❶❷❸Ⓐ Ⓒ Ⓔ Ⓛ to 14th St. Average entrée $21.

Gusto Ristorante e Bar Americano *Italian*

With Viennese chandeliers, chic furnishings, and an eat-in wine cellar, Gusto is a comfortable and refined escape from the tumultuous neighborhood in which it dwells. Priding itself in cooking elegant yet modestly priced Italian food, the restaurant offers an extensive list of unique dishes. The carpaccio di manzo with rocket and parmesan is an excellent starter. For meat lovers the Sicilian meatballs are a must; packed with pine nuts and raisins, they're crunchy, juicy, and hearty. Most impressive are the dishes that feature home made pasta. The malfatti, organic spinach and ricotta dumplings infused with sage butter, are creamy little bites of gold.

60 Greenwich Ave (at 7th Ave). 212-924-8000. Mon-Fri 12pm-3pm 5:30pm-12am, Sat-Sun 12pm-4pm 5:30pm-12am. ❶❷❸Ⓐ Ⓒ Ⓔ Ⓛ to 14th. Average entrée $20.

Jules *French*

This streetside bistro is set back slightly from St. Mark's Place, isolating the dining room and allowing for a fantasy recreation of the perfect French dive. The food is equally classic but less inspired. A mushy steak tartar and bland escargot taste of tourist traps, while the best part of the steak frites is hardly the salty, tough steak. A trio plays jazz classics nightly, not breaking ground but certainly improving the atmosphere. The fondant au chocolat is as gooey as the steak tartar, but goo is exactly what warm chocolate cake needs. That and a superb mousse, combined with the lighting and music, make this a great place to end a date. Just don't try to start here.

65 St. Marks Pl (near 1st Ave) 212-477-5560. Mon-Fri 11am-12am, Sat-Sun 10:30am-12am. ❻ to Astor. Average entrée $13

Lima's Taste *Peruvian*

The fuchsia-and-orange walls, gold-framed paintings, and Spanish colonial chairs are a vibrant and perfect match for the explosively flavorful food at this casual restaurant. The anticuchos, made of skewers of rare, tender grilled cow heart served with yucca sticks and sauce, is a must for adventurous diners. Heaps of cilantro garnish the excellent chicken escaveche, marinated in a bittersweet sauce of onions and peppers. Desserts lack the entrees' innovation, and the small staff can be inattentive. Still, the prospect of a postprandial stroll in nearby Hudson River Park makes indulging in the rich food more than worth it.

122 Christopher St (at Bedford St). 212-242-0010. Mon-Sun 12pm-12am. ❶ to Christopher St. Average entrée $23.

The Little Owl *New American*

With a kitchen that pumps out unfussy yet artful creations, this tiny restaurant's tables stay full every night of the week. The menu's seasonal focus takes full advantage of the Greenmarket's bounty, and inventive seasonings complement every ingredient. Every dish is a hit—tender slices of duck breast with truffled arugula and springtime soft-shell crab are excellent. A true standout, the broiled halibut with English peas and corn proves fish can be as flavorful and meaty as beef. To finish, share the pleasure of dipping raspberry-filled beignets in Nutella. The dining room gets noisy at peak hours, but the food is so satisfying that it all fades into the background.

90 Bedford St (between Grove St and Barrow St). 212-741-4695. Mon-Thurs 5pm-11pm, Fri-Sat 5pm-12am, Sun 5pm-10pm. Lunch Tues-Sun 11am-2pm. ❶ to Christopher St, Ⓐ Ⓒ Ⓔ Ⓑ Ⓓ Ⓕ Ⓥ to W 4th. Average entrée $25.

GREENWICH VILLAGE 149

EDITOR'S PICK
Market Table *New American*
Food and decor here are rustic yet elegant in their expert craftsmanship. The intimate dining area behind the retail country store out front is great for a date or small gathering and give Market Table personality—that and its short, meticulously crafted menu, which carries itself with confidence and perfection. The dishes are flavorful and visually rewarding, from the perfectly assembled light and tender gnocchi, served with short ribs and parmesan broth, to the braised lamb shank, a hearty repast that can suffice for two meals. After your entrée, try the house's take on pastry legend Maida Heatter's famous polka-dot cheesecake, an easy contender for the title of best cheesecake in the city. Don't forget to pick up some of the gourmet foodstuffs or heat-and-eat dishes from the store on your way out.
54 Carmine St (between Bedford St and Bleecker St) 212-255-2100. Mon-Fri 11:30am-2:30pm, 5:30pm-12:00am, Sat-Sun 5pm-10pm. ❶ to Houston, ❹❸❺❻❼❽❾ to W 4th. Average entrée at $26.

The Pink Teacup *Soul Food*
This soul food outpost has been drizzling syrup over fried pork-chops and pancakes for over thirty years and is the only place below 14th St boasting fried chicken on the breakfast menu. Diners without a sodium deficiency may find the menu slightly too authentic, but skipping the gravy on the smothered chicken should spare the arteries. The jukebox in the corner blares soul standards and mellow R&B at a slightly uncomfortable volume. The menu is classic meat and three sides, including squash, collared greens, and terrific apple fritters. At $7.50 for four courses—soup, salad, the main plate and bread pudding for dessert—lunch gets you one of the best deals in the neighborhood.
42 Grove St (near Bleecker St). 212-807-6755. 8am-12am. ❶ to Christopher-Sheridan, ❹❸❺❻❼❽❾ to W 4th Ave. Average entrée: $13.

CHEAP
A Salt & Battery *British*
Touted by some transplanted Brits as the most authentic fish 'n chips shack in town, this counter-service restaurant serves mainly locally grown sustainable produce: pollock replaces over-fished cod, and thick, crisp fillets top off heaps of chips made from Long Island potatoes. Regulars know to be generous with splashes of malt vinegar and dollops of ketchup and aioli. Wash hearty victuals down with Newcastle beer or British cider and muster up the courage to dive into their signature fried Mars bar - a batter-encased gooey mess, handily worth the coronary bypass it will cost you.
112 Greenwich Ave (between 12th St and 13th St). 212-691-2713. Mon-Sun 11:30am-10:30pm. ❹❸❺ to 14th and 8th, ❶❷❸ to 14th and 7th, ❻❼ to 14th and 6th. Average entrée $8.

Dessert Truck *Dessert*
This purveyor of sweets is out on a mission to make luxurious desserts an everyday occasion. The menu items are neatly packed in a to-go cup, and all the confections have a level of quality that far exceeds what one might expect from a mere truck. Silky, molten chocolate cake is topped with crunchy pistachios and sea salt, while chocolate bread pudding is lent a subtle flavor from bacon crème anglaise. Rotating specials, like the poached apple tart, warrant frequent visits.
At 8th St and University Place. Mon-Sun 6pm-closing. ❶ to Christopher, ❹❸❺❻❼❽❾ to W 4th St, ❸❼ to 8th St, ❻ to Astor. Desserts $5 each plus $5 tax on total bill.

Peanut Butter & Co. *American*
It's always peanut-butter-jelly time at this deli devoted to America's favorite pseudo-nut. The company whips up numerous peanut butters, like Smooth Operator, Crunch Time, and Mighty Maple, as well as fruit jams, to create yummy sammies for your inner child. Gourmet combinations are curiously good and include "The Heat is On"—spicy peanut butter with grilled chicken and pineapple jam—and "Dark Chocolate Dreams," chocolate peanut butter with cherry jam and coconut. But the classics hearken back to your lunchbox days with favorites like Ants on a Log and the Fluffernutter sandwich. The Elvis sandwich, grilled with bananas, honey, and bacon, is king of them all.
240 Sullivan St (near 3rd St). 212-677-395. Sun-Thurs 11am-9pm, Fri-Sat 11am-10pm. ❹❸❺❻❼❽❾ to W 4th-Washington Sq. Sandwiches $5-7.

EDITOR'S PICK

Taïm *Middle Eastern*
Competitors can't beat Taïm's falafel—it's among the best in the city. Falafel sandwiches come in three varieties: traditional, roasted red pepper, and harissa. All are served with hummus and tahini on a white or whole wheat pita. The meatball-sized filling is more flavorful and much less greasy than typical falafel. Order a side of tabouli or Israeli salad if you wish, but homemade French fries with saffron aioli boast a nutty flavor from the frying oil, perfect salting, and a dipping condiment that puts ketchup to shame.
222 Waverly Pl (near Perry St). 212-691-1287. 11:30am-10pm. ❶ *to Christopher St. Average entrée $5.*

NIGHTLIFE

Blind Tiger *Bar*
Certainly one of the top beer bars in the city, this paradise for beer lovers offers 28 microbrews on tap and over 60 bottled varieties. Don't even ask for a Corona; $3 4oz samples are available for the uninitiated who'd like to try their beer on for size before committing to pint-long happiness. On alternating Wednesdays, Alan, the owner and mastermind behind the brewtiful operation, hosts beer tastings that feature extensive offerings from select breweries. Now-popular brands like Lagunitas and Smuttynose were first premiered here, so expect to hoist some delightful new pints. There's no liquor available, but bartenders are happy to make beer cocktails on request, including their spin on the Bloody Mary and the Kir Royale. The rush starts around 6:30 with the after-work crowd and continues into the night, so expect to fight a crowd for your crack at the kegs.
281 Bleecker St (at Jones St). 212-462-4682. 11:30am-4am. Ⓐ Ⓒ Ⓔ Ⓑ Ⓓ Ⓕ Ⓥ *to W 4th,* ❶ *to Christopher. Average drink $6.*

The Blue Note *Jazz Club*
The Blue Note has been New York's premier jazz venue since 1981. Without the dingy, vintage charm of other New York jazz institutions like the Village Vanguard, the Blue Note is always good for a night of upscale dining, drinking, and listening. The club features two full sets each weeknight, plus a late night set on Friday and Saturday nights. You can either make a table reservation (about $35 per person) or take your chances getting a seat at the bar for a more reasonable $20. The choice of libations is top-shelf and the drinks are well mixed. The food menu consists of fairly common dishes like steaks, burgers, salads, and fried appetizers. As far as the music goes, the Blue Note plays host to the very best from every corner of the jazz universe, from John Scofield and B.B. King to Coleman Hawkins and Chick Corea.
131 W 3rd, St (Between 6th Ave & McDougal St) 212-475-8592. Sets Mon-Thurs 8pm and 10:30pm, Fri-Sat 8pm, 10:30pm and 12:30am. Ⓐ Ⓒ Ⓔ Ⓑ Ⓓ Ⓕ Ⓥ *to W 4th,* ❶ *to Christopher. Average Drink $10.*

Bowlmor Lanes *Bowling*
If you like bowling, Bowlmor with fulfill your needs. If you don't like bowling, Bowlmor will exceed your wildest expectations. So much more than throwing an overweight ball at stationary pins, this place is the future of disco bowling. With a velvet rope at the door and a drink list rivaling any bar in town, Bowlmor is more reminiscent of a club than a bowling alley. You can't take yourself seriously here – all you can do is go with the flow, dance to the music, drink (heavily), absorb the flashing disco

lights, and occasionally take your turn to bowl. On Mondays, Night Strike gets you unlimited bowling for $22.
110 University Pl (between 12th St and 13th St). 212-255-8188. Fri-Sat 11am-3:30am, Sun 11am-12am, Mon and Thu 11am-2am, Tue-Wed 11am-1am. ❶❷❸❹❺❻❼❽ *to Union Sq.*

Dove Parlor *Bar*
This welcome refuge from the plethora of beer halls in the area surrounding NYU offers flower and spice infused cocktails along with sophisticated alternatives to bar food. The intimate, fireplace warmed Victorian setting creates a perfect space for a first date or a relaxed meeting of friends. The signature cocktails are as carefully constructed as a fine perfume: the French Lavender, infused with gin, orange liqueur, and grapefruit offers a perfect balance of fruit and flowers and tart and sweet flavors. In addition to the cocktails, wines and various liquors, Dove offers two preparations of absinthe to the adventurous drinker, including the Green Fairy, served chilled and shaken with fresh mint leaves. The tasty tea sandwiches, toast with a tapenades of crimini mushrooms and mozzarella, and well-selected assortment of cheeses all nicely complement the drink offerings.
228 Thompson St (at 3rd St). 212-254-1435. Tues-Sat 4pm-4am, Sun-Mon 4pm-2am. Happy hour daily 4pm-8pm. ❶❷❸❹❺❻❼ *to W 4th.*

The Duplex Piano Bar & Cabaret
LGBT, Cabaret
The Duplex has an infectiously friendly scene where you can hum along to 60s pop without irony, get lost in the affable cross chatter between onstage acts and barroom antics, and catch your favorite Hollywood musical on the TV. The bar downstairs features open mic sessions every night at a piano dressed in a rainbow flag—you may find your bartender fixing a drink one moment and leaping onstage with a tambourine to belt The Ronettes the next. Things are calmer at the upstairs bar, where the mainstream pop-heavy jukebox and plush leather seating make for a more casual evening out. Even theatergoers can get their fix at the Duplex's intimate cabaret, a tiny redbrick venue that comes alive each night with a variety of innovative offbeat musical-comedy and acts from local talents. Every Friday night, the Cabaret hosts "Mostly Sondheim," an open mic party where the audience sings through the virtuoso composer's works until closing.
61 Christopher St (at 7th Ave). 212-255-5438. Mon-Sun 4pm-4am. Happy hour 4pm-9pm. ❶ *to Christopher-Sheridan. Average drink $8.*

EDITOR'S PICK
En Shochu *Japanese Bar*
Shochu, a Japanese vodka, is rumored to never give a hangover. Without the burden of a rough morning after, you'll want to sample almost all of the cocktails at this gorgeous specialty bar. Over 20 flavors of Shochu are housed in jars eerily illuminated behind the bar. Sample each one by glass or choose your favorite bottle of poison to share with others. The cocktails are amazing as well, each a tribute to Far East ingredients and flavors. The best of the best, the Seppun, combines shochu with yuzu citrus, fresh grapefruit juice and shiso. The ceilings are aristocratically lofty, while the heavy wood carvings on the wall are all antique Japanese works of art. Sit at a communal table closer to the bar or gather at one of the the smaller tables in the back to drink and sample some of the fantastic "bar food" offerings like the Ebi Shinjo—shrimp fritters deep-fried with salt. Stop in for a drink and a bite before going out to nearby spots, or make a night of it with a few friends or a date.
435 Hudson St (at Leroy St). 212-647-9196. Mon-Thurs, Sun 5:30pm-11pm, Fri-Sat 5:30pm–12am. ❶ *to Houston. Average drink $12.*

The Half Pint *Pub*
Just a block from Washington Square Park, there's a little slice of Dublin where everything—food, drink, atmosphere, location—clicks. The warm and welcoming redbrick interior is generously lit and a vast window façade opens the pub to the pulsating buzz of the West Village. With 24 draughts that run the gamut from familiar favorites to exotic Chocolate and Blueberry ales, a daily-special all-natural, richly flavored cask ale, and a treasure trove of international and little-known domestic bottles, you're sure to find what you want—and at reasonable prices. The menu offers spins on well-worn American comfort foods and pub fare—bacon pies, Reuben pizzas, bratwurst burgers. There's a lively, jocular crowd, and

you're likely to share a "table tap"—six pints at your fingertips—with a new best friend from NYU by night's end. The Half Pint feels like the pub all the other pubs try to be.
76 W 3rd St (at Thompson St) 212-260-1088. Mon-Sat 12pm-4am, Sun 12pm-2am. ⒶⒸⒺⒷⒹⒻⓋ to W 4th, ❶ to Christopher-Sheridan. Average drink $6. Average entrée $9.

Le Royale *Club*
This nightclub has its own cult following. Frequent live music acts haunt the spacious upstairs, which also doubles as a dance hall when DJs get their turn. The first floor shimmers in Art Deco beauty, lit up by the prominent bar. With a more relaxed door than most nearby hotspots, the party starts to jump around midnight. The scene is not to be missed for those who favor rock and electric, though the crowd has long graduated college. Robot Rock Friday nights are a must.
21 7th Ave South (at Leroy St) 212-463-0700. 7pm-4am. ❶ to Christopher, ⒶⒸⒺⒷⒹⒻⓋ to W 4th. Average drink $12.

Pop Burger *Lounge, Bar*
Waiters and bartenders in brightly colored jumpsuits serve up sliders in the front diner of this '80s throwback, while a bouncer lets the late night crowd into the back lounge. Smooth, creamy milkshakes go well with these bite-size burgers, which are topped with cheese, pickles, and special sauce. While munching on sliders, lobster nachos or steak with watercress may not exactly fit with the blaring '80s tunes, low couches, and dancing crowds, fighting the alcohol munchies while drinking more alcohol is actually a welcome experience. When the music gets too loud, the pool table in back offers a more relaxed atmosphere.
58-60 9th Ave (between 14th & 15th St) 212-414-8686. 5pm-4am. ❶❷❸ to 14th. Average Drink $12, Average entrée $12.

Rouge *Wine Bar*
This cozy and plush bar provides a great venue for a romantic evening or a private party. A throwback to Parisian café society, Rouge is decorated with Talouse-Lautrec-inspired murals and lit only by candles. The extensive wine list features traditional French vintages alongside South African wines and California vintner Bonny Doon's innovative blends. Rouge also serves dishes prepared by the restaurant Paris Commune, located upstairs. The menu compliments the wine well and features classic bistro fare with modern flourishes, such as garlicky escargot served atop baguette slices and three unique takes on filet mignon, including a version generously stuffed with crab and served atop mashed potatoes. If you still have room for dessert, share the indulgent Pot de Chocolate with your date.
99 Bank St (between Greenwich St and Hudson St). 212-929-0509. Sun-Thurs 6pm-11pm, Fri-Sat 6pm-12am. ❶ to Christopher, ⒶⒸⒺⒷⒹⒻⓋ to W 4th St. Average drink: $10. Average entrée $12.

Smalls *Jazz Club*
Practically impossible to see from street level if you're not looking for it, Smalls could be the last real jazz dive in a part of town that used to be packed with them. Subterranean and dimly-lit, the living-room sized club is a veritable film-noir set-piece repackaged as a West Village yuppie hang—which is perfectly fine, since the music might be the strongest of all the small jazz clubs in town. Smalls has built a well-deserved reputation as one of the best places in the city to see rising talent in the New York jazz scene, and with a $20 cover that includes a free drink (and no minimum), it's a much better deal than the nearby Village Vanguard. There's also no cover for sets that start after 1 AM, making Smalls a perfect last stop on a downtown bar hop.
183 W 10th St (at 7th Ave) 212-252-5091 Sets at 7:30, 9:00, 12am. After hour jam sessions 1:30am-4am. Cover charge $20 for entry, show, and a drink.

S.O.B.'s *Dance Club*
This diverse club boasts several different styles of dancing and fun to match, even on a weekday. With a multi-ethnic audience and multi-genre musical selection, one can feel the vibe of exotic dance upon entering the club. Bhangra Thursday features an interactive dance lessons, teaching even the most straight-laced patrons to shake their hips. Similar nights also take place with samba, salsa, and other genres. The room is decorated with lanterns, projectors, and a spacious dance floor. The service is somewhat impersonal—definitely not a bar where everybody knows your name—but the enthusiastic, somewhat older crowd makes up for it.
204 Varick Street (at West Houston). 212-243-4940.

GREENWICH VILLAGE

Mon 12am-2am, 6:30pm-2am, Tues-Thurs 6:30pm-2am, Fri 5pm-4am, Sat 7pm-4am, Sun 7pm-12am. ❶❷❸ to Houston. Average drink $11.

Socialista *Lounge*
Potted palm trees that scrape the ceiling, white shuttered windows, and lazily spinning fans transport patrons to 1940's Cuba by day. By night this hotspot turns into an uber-exclusive lounge where the DJ spins good-time tunes and crowd favorites like the Jackson 5. For those seeking a more authentic experience, a live Cuban band plays after 11pm on Tuesday nights, turning the spacious upstairs lounge into a place to mambo, salsa, or cha-cha. The hopping atmosphere and innovative, yet expensive, cocktails, such as "the Mojito Rojo"— a rum, blood orange, honey and mint concoction- make the club a favorite for socialites and celebs.
505 West St (at Jane St). 212-929-4303. Café open Mon-Wed 6pm-11pm, Thurs-Sat 6pm-12am. Lounge open 10pm-4am, live Cuban Band Tuesdays 11pm. Ⓐ Ⓒ Ⓔ *to 14th,* Ⓛ *to 8th. Average drink $12.*

Vol de Nuit *Bar*
Many have walked past the unmarked red door that leads to this beer garden, known to many NYU students simply as "The Belgian Beer Bar," never to know the frothy delights hidden inside. There are actually two bars connected by a courtyard—head to the larger one in the back, where you'll find 13 beers on tap, ranging from the comparatively low-brow Stella Artois to Trappist brews like Corsendonk and Delirium Tremens. Vol de Nuit is equally good for romantic dates and casual outings; dim red lighting casts a sexy glow over the bar and its patrons, and the spacious patio flickers with lamplight while a magenta sky and plaster walls evoking Casablanca cool. The moules frites are considered to be among the best in the city.
148 W 4th St (at 6th Ave). 212-982-3388. Sun-Thurs 4pm-1am, Fri-Sat 4pm-3am. Ⓐ Ⓒ Ⓔ Ⓑ Ⓓ Ⓕ Ⓥ *to W 4th. Average drink $6.*

SHOPPING

Geminola
Crystal chandeliers and voluminous tulle skirts adorn the ceiling of this unique vintage women's clothing boutique. The shop features one-of-a-kind pieces refashioned from vintage materials found around the world. The designer and store owner hand-sews and dyes all apparel, transforming each garment into a work of art. The dresses made of lace, tulle, and silk resemble creations from a fairytale. Few items sell for less than $200, but the dresses here are ideal for a special occasion. The boutique also carries a small selection of accessories and home items, including hand towels, bedding, and curtains.
41 Perry St (near Waverly Pl). 212-675-1994. Mon-Wed 12pm-7pm, Thurs-Sat 12pm-8pm, Sun 12pm-6pm. ❶❷ *to Christopher.*

House of Cards and Curiosities
Whether you are looking for a cicada whistle, a rubber ducky, or a voodoo doll, you've come to the right place. This wizard's den is best known for its wide selection of artful and quirky greeting cards, but it is packed floor to ceiling with other interesting and strange things that, while possibly useless, are at least fun and well worth browsing through. The tiny space contains tarot cards, fossils, notebooks, little plastic farm animals and anything necessary for your witch's brew: a perfect place to find a random present or a gag gift.
23 8th Ave (between Jane St & West 12th St). 212-675-6178. Mon-Fri 9am-10pm, Sat 10am-10pm, Sun 10am-7pm. Ⓐ Ⓒ Ⓔ Ⓛ *to 14th. $2-25.*

Partners and Crime Mystery Booksellers
Seasoned mystery lovers and amateur detectives will love the selection in this mystery bookstore. Dedicated solely to the mystery genre, Partners and Crime carries classic mysteries, new releases, and a number of out-of-print and signed novels and mysteries. Divided into multiple sections, including first-in-a-series, science-fiction mysteries, and historical mysteries, the store is easy to navigate. Handwritten notes taped to all of the shelves provide helpful recommendations of various books for customers browsing without anything specific in mind, so everyone who comes in will be sure to leave with a mystery, or two, perfectly suited to their tastes.
44 Greenwich Ave (at Charles St). 212-243-0440. Mon-Thurs 12pm-9pm, Fri-Sat 12pm-10pm, Sun 12pm-7pm. ❶❷ *to Christopher.*

Porto Rico Importing Company
A low cost retailer with a wholesale atmosphere, Porto Rico has been keeping the city caffeinated for over one hundred years. The coffee is displayed in burlap sacks, grouped by organic, shade grown, decaf and regular, and guarded by signs forbidding dipping one's hands into the shiny, inviting beans. Tea is on the back wall in drums, an unpretentious selection of classic, upstanding blends. The tea is not spectacular but it is a fantastic value, since unlike every other tea retailer in the city, Porto Rico does not gouge. Their coffee really is remarkable and priced for bulk purchase.
201 Bleecker St (near 6th Ave), 40 1/2 St. Mark's Pl (near 2nd Ave) or 107 Thompson St (near Prince). 212-979-2303. Hours vary by store. Main location Mon-Sat 8am-9pm. ❶❷❸ *to W 4th St,* ❻ *to Astor Pl or* ❶❷❸ *to Houston St.*

Roger's Time Machine
This tucked-away treasure is more organized than the better-known St. Mark's Comics, and though not as well stocked, Roger's wins out when it comes to oddball stuff. Get lost in the vortex of comics and memorabilia, some of them almost a hundred years old. They have a large selection of ancient underground comics, Disney and children's comics, monster magazines, lobby cards, sheet music, and vintage Playboys. Prices vary from the great bargain to the shocking outrage, though this is one of the few New York comic stores where it is possible to haggle.
207 W 14th St. 212-691-0380. ❶❷❸❹ *to 8th and 14th,* ❶❷❸ *to 14th.*

The Strand
A giant sprawled atop the downtown book scene, The Strand is impossible to ignore—and difficult to use, being so large, crowded, and poorly organized that hunting for specific titles is a chore. But the search pays off big: you'll find stuff you weren't looking for, which is way more fun anyway, and everything you find in the Strand's towering shelves will be dirt cheap. The sale tables in particular are a draw, offering dozens of volumes of contemporary and classic fiction—the stuff you're always meaning to read but haven't yet—at a nearly eighty percent discount.
828 Broadway (at 12th St). 212-473-1452. ❶❷❸❹❺❻❼ *to Union Square.*

DAY TO DAY

Community Board 2: *3 Washington Square Village, #1A. 212-979-2272.*

Local Media: Greenwich Village NYC

Groceries: Morton Williams, *255 W 14th St. 212-645-7260.*

Gym: Crunch, *152 Christopher Street. 212-366-3725.*

Average Rent: One-bedroom: $2300-3500, Two-bedroom: $3000-3700

Hotel: Washington Square Hotel, *103 Waverly Place. 212-777-9515*

Dog Run: West Village D.O.G, *Little W 12th St (between Washington St and 10th Ave).*

Movie Theater: Quad Cinema. *34 W 13th St (between 5th & 6th Ave). 212-255-8800.*

Best Happy Hour: Fiddlesticks, *56 Greenwich Avenue (at Perry St). 212-463-0516. Mon-Fri 4pm-8pm $3 beer, wine, and spirits.*

Tea and Sympathy
Stop by this quaint Greenwich Village shop for a taste of the English countryside in New York City. Situated in the midst of a block known locally as 'little Britain,' they carry a wide range of teas, including a selection exclusive to the store. A selection of decorated, white teapots adorns the shelves, and seated next to them are a number of foods not normally seen on this side of the Atlantic. You can find all of the ingredients that you would need to have your own tea party: English biscuit and scone mixes, lemon curd, jam, and clotted cream, and if you don't feel like cooking yourself, take afternoon tea at the restaurant next door.
108 Greenwich Ave (near Jane St). 212-989-9735. Mon-Fri 11:30am-10:30pm, Sat-Sun 9:30am-10:30pm. ❶❷❸ *to 14th.*

GREENWICH VILLAGE 155

156 GREENWICH VILLAGE

Against the lush green leaves of the West Village streets, a dozen can-can dancers cut quite a figure. Paris Commune, the legendary downtown bistro, is full of these beautiful creatures, painted into poses against scarlet walls and a tangled wreath of twinkling lights. Add in the city's handsomest waiters, rose petal strewn cocktails and beautifully plated food, and you'll see why Paris Commune has been home to New York's pretty young things (regardless of age) for almost thirty years.

This summer, Paris Commune is in the midst of its own little revolution, having brought in a new executive chef and a few culinary surprises to round out the traditional French bistro fare. An ever-changing Foie Gras de Jour leads the menu of new additions. Inventively seared and paired with Paris Commune's famous gingerbread one day, then served atop a poached egg and English muffin another (a la Eggs Benedict with some serious flair), the delicious amuse-bouche creations are as surprising as satisfying. New seasonal appetizers like the Ahi Tuna Ceviche join old favorites like Steak Tartar (served in the classic style and topped with a quail egg) and French Onion Soup (complete with the crispy, gooey indulgence of a crouton and melted Gruyere top) – and traditional bistro entrees like Coq au Vin, Steak Frites and Lobster Thermador now share equal billing with Ostrich, Pan Roasted Chilean Sea Bass, and Beef Wellington.

Famous throughout the city for its brunch, Paris Commune now offers its unparalleled French Toast and Frittatas seven days a week – along with its lengthy Bloody Mary menu and refreshing champagne cocktails. There's never been a better reason to drink before sundown...

But just in case you do wait until sunset to sip something sultry, the Paris Commune's Rouge Wine Bar has you covered. Recently voted one of the top five wine bars in New York City, Rouge offers an impressive array of French wines – then tops it off with an eye-opening (and taste-bud-tickling) variety of South African, Chilean, and American bottles. With a full cocktail menu, dinner service, and weekly live music acts, Rouge is the best surprise in the West Village. Located underneath the main dining room, the wine bar blooms into view beneath a side staircase, revealing a mirror-ceilinged room with full-wall murals and a bar scene so convivial, even a revolutionary would cozy up for a drink.

Paris Commune is the downtown bistro for the whole city – a destination for anyone in search of a lively environment, an unparalleled meal, a real New York City night, and a dozen can-can girls ready to call this place home.

For reservations, please call 212.929.0509.

★ PARIS COMMUNE ★

99 BANK STREET at GREENWICH STREET, NEW YORK

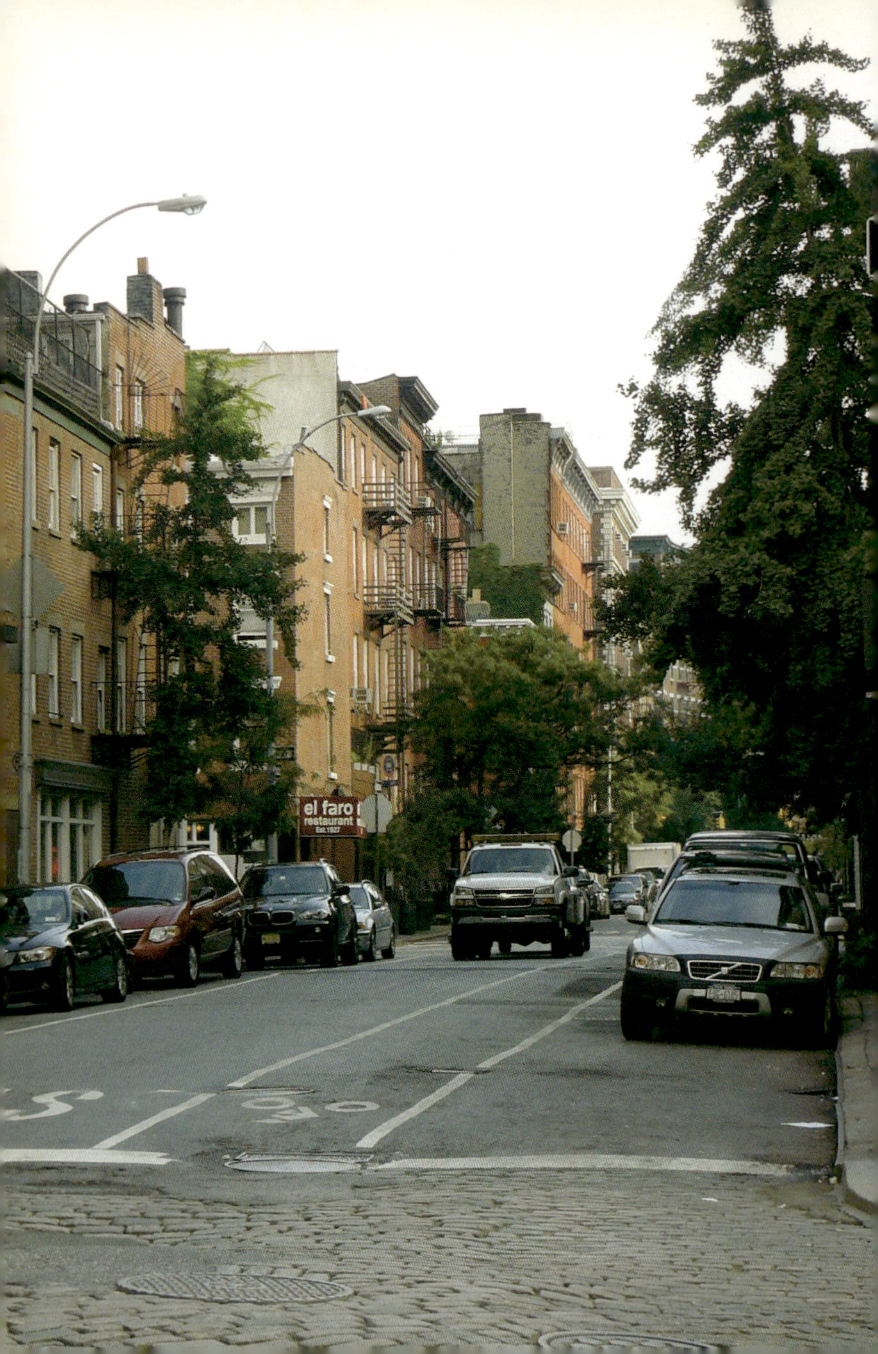
el faro
restaurant
Est.1927

CHELSEA

Gorgeous brownstones line one side of the street and towering projects occupy the other in this neighborhood where boutiques are nestled between untidy bodegas, and beautiful, bronzed gods descend to walk amongst men.

Although today, it is largely associated with the hard-bodied, gym-going, look-at-me-not-looking-at-you gay men who call it home, Chelsea was once one of the city's premier shipping ports. When Chelsea Piers opened in 1910, designed by the same team responsible for Grand Central Terminal, they soon becmae the prime docking space for both passenger and military ships. During the 1950s and 60s, the piers served as a cargo terminal, but soon thereafter fell into disrepair and decay. It wasn't until the 1990s that the pier was overhauled and rebuilt, saving it from joining the ranks of other forgotten New York relics.

Chelsea also boasts a rich history of artistic movements. As one of the stops on the Theater District's uptown crawl from SoHo to Times Square, the neighborhood enjoyed a brief tenure as the premier place to catch a live performance of classics new and old. In the first half of the 20th century, the Chelsea Hotel was home to some of the modern era's greatest writers, actors, and musicians. The 1990s art boom saw an influx of studios and galleries move into the neighborhood, as artists were priced out of more traditional visual art enclaves such as SoHo.

Today, residents and visitors alike wine, dine, and unwind in the area's many coffee shops, chic lounges and restaurants, or peruse the ultra-sleek, ultra-hip art galleries, all in the shadows of the neighborhood's history as a bustling center of the working class.

ATTRACTIONS

Chelsea Piers
Once a passenger terminal in the early 1900's, this multiplex is now a gigantic playground for New Yorkers of all ages. With a health club, day spa, two basketball courts, indoor field turf, batting cages, a rock climbing wall, dance studios, and even a multi-floor outdoor driving range where you can launch balls into the Hudson river, you'll be hard pressed to find a sad face. If you are of age, the AMF bowling center turns into an adult's only disco bowl at 9pm.
Pier 60 (23rd St & 12th Ave). 212-336-6666. Hours vary. ❶ to 23rd Street.

General Theological Seminary
Centered around a garden known as the Close, the entire block houses educational facilities dedicated to the study of the Anglican faith. This is a great vantage from which to take in the neighborhood's historic architecture, as well as observe the educational life of a small, hermetic institution. Saint Mark's Library houses a collection that includes rare Bibles and important religious texts from the last five centuries. Wander by yourself or with a little help from the free self-guided tour materials available every day from 9am to 5pm in English, German, French, Spanish, and Japanese.
175 9th Ave (from 20th to 21st Sts and 9th to 10th Aves). 212-243-5150. ❶ ⒸⒺ to 23rd.

EDITOR'S PICK
Trapeze School of New York
Situated atop Pier 40 and overlooking most of the Hudson River and downtown NYC, this is a place to let your inhibitions go, spread your arms, and fly. You can conquer your fear of heights, soar through the air, and get a great workout, all the while taking in some of best views in Manhattan. Although the classes are slightly pricey ($75 for a first timer), the experience is worth every penny. It's safe and exhilarating and the staff is encouraging and as professional as they come. You don't have to be an acrobat or fit to come here; with an open mind and some guts, you'll be hooked.
518 W 30th St (between 10th Ave and 11th Ave). 212-242-8769. ❶❷❸ or ⒶⒸⒺ to 34th St, ❶ to 28th St. Open all week. Average class $57.

CULTURE & ARTS

Chelsea Art Museum
This three story gem focuses on 20th and 21st century international artists who have received little exposure in the United States. A striking three-story space, CAM is also home to the Jean Miotte foundation, so much of the permanent collection focuses on this post-World War II abstract artist.
556 West 22nd St (at West Side Hwy). 212-255-0719. Tues-Sat 11am-6pm, Thurs 11am-8pm, closed Sun-Mon. 🅒🅔 *to 23rd and 8th. Adults $8, Students $4.*

The Irish Repertory Theatre
The Irish Rep has celebrated the pleasantries of Irish theatre for over twenty years, from the masters to the new generation of Irish and Irish-American writers who are transforming the stage. This is the city's most notable institution to enjoy an engaging perspective on the Irish and their unique contributions to the world of drama.
132 W 22nd St (between 6th & 7th Ave), 212-727-2737. 🅒🅔🅵🅵🅥 *to 23rd.*

Joyce Theater
Founded by dancers, the Joyce Theater offers an intimate performance space for local and international dance companies. Movement is celebrated in all its forms in this Art Deco building, welcoming styles ranging from the long-established and familiar to the ultramodern and avant-garde. The Joyce also offers opportunities to learn more about the form with a series of talks and educational programs.
175 8th Ave (at 19th St). 212-242-0800. 🅐🅒🅔 *to 14th,* 🅵 *to 18th. Tickets $34-$44.*

Museum at the Fashion Institute of Technology
New York's only fashion-focused museum displays designs both old and new. The central gallery provides a brief history of couture through the centuries, rotating in pieces from FIT's massive permanent collection. On the side, however, are the temporary special exhibitions that provide more detailed and intimate looks at particular facets of fashion. Many of these features are curated by the designers of tomorrow, as student work is often the focus. Call ahead to reserve a spot at one of the many lectures, tours, and book signings held throughout the year.
7th Ave (at 27th St). 212-217-4560. Tues-Fri 12pm-8pm, Sat 10am-5pm. Closed Sun-Mon. 🅵 *to 28th,* 🅒🅔 *to 23rd,* 🅵🅥 *to 23rd,* 🅝🅡 *to 28th-Broadway.*

Rubin Museum of Art
The Rubin Museum is dedicated to the artistic history of the Himalayas. Patrons can peruse books, artifacts, textiles and photographs, as well as many varied and interactive exhibits. Five-minute tours focus on explaining elements of Himalayan art via a single work and one-hour themed tours examine groups of works through specific focus questions. Fridays at 6, the lights dim, a DJ starts spinning Himalayan inspired music, and the museum transforms into the K2 Lounge. In addition to specialty drinks and a cool atmosphere, the lounge also sponsors events, such as movie screenings and group discussions. Mainly, it's a good place to grab a drink while avoiding the typical lounge crowd.
150 W 17th St (at 7th Ave). 212-620-5000. Mon 11am-5pm, Tues closed, Wed 11am-7pm, Thurs 11am-5pm, Fri 11am-10pm, Sat 11am-6pm, Sun 11am-6pm. $10 Adults, $7 Seniors/Students/Artists with id/Neighbors in zip codes 10011 & 10001; Free on Fridays 7-10pm. 🅒🅔🅵🅵🅵🅵🅛 *to 14th.*

DINING

UPSCALE
Buddakan *Asian*
Although the glitterati have migrated elsewhere since its 2006 opening, this is one of only a few big-box, Asian-themed restaurants in the city that has not lost its luster. Tourists, celebrities, and foodies still come to be part of the production; with mammoth-size, jaw-dropping décor, dinner is part theater—and good theater at that. Consider yourself lucky if you score a prime-time table in the "Chinoiserie" room, which is akin to a dramatic and gorgeous

set. Surprisingly, the food is on par with the décor. Stick with the more interesting flavor combinations and your meal might be a hit: taro puff lollipops (crispy, saucy, pork and ginger puffs), duck and foie gras spring rolls, and "Wok Hay Frog Legs"—all fried and all good. Lamb chops ordered medium-rare are exactly so, and have a delicious crystallized ginger crust. It may not be the most impressive culinary experience, but it's certainly novel, and a lot of fun.
75 9th Ave (near 16th St). 212-989-6699. Sun-Mon 5:30pm-11pm, Tues-Wed 5:30pm-12am, Thurs-Sat 5:30pm-1am. ❶❸❺❼ to 14th-8th. Average entrée $26.

Trestle on Tenth *French, Swiss*
Chef Ralf Kuettel has created a rich menu of traditional American meat and fish dishes with European refinement. Appetizers offer twists on common snacks and familiar comfort food: the crèpinette combines savory pork shoulder and spinach in a miniature crepe. For a more sophisticated take on the conventional bagel and lox, try the house-cured salmon with sour cream and toasted brioche. The decor is simple; exposed brick walls and soft lighting contribute to a cozy dining experience. The secluded outdoor dining room, situated underneath a cherry blossom tree and illuminated by candlelight, makes Trestle on Tenth perfect for an intimate summer gathering.
242 10th Ave (at 24th St) 212-645-5659. Mon 5:30pm-10pm, Tues-Thurs 12pm-10:30pm, Fri 12pm-11pm, Sat 11am-11pm, Sun 11am-10pm. ❶❸❺ to 23rd. Average entrée $21.

MID-RANGE
202 *British, American*
The severe tinted windows facing the street belie what's hidden inside this meatpacking pearl. Enter the high glass door and you will be enchanted to find Nicole Farhi's lovely boutique featuring men's and women's clothes, home furnishings, and a delightful café. Note that everything is for sale at this rustic, hodge podge store, so come to shop or relax in the homey café environment. Favored for its brunch (buttermilk pancakes with blackberry compote and crème fraiche are a must) it's also excellent at lunch and dinner—the tuna burger with house-made guacamole is stellar, as are its accompanying thick potato fries.
75 9th Ave (at 16th St) 646-638-1173. Breakfast Mon-Fri 8:30am-11am, Sat and Sun 10am-11:30am. Brunch Mon-Fri 11am-4pm, Sat and Sun 11:30am-4pm. Dinner Tues-Sat 5:30pm-11pm, Sun 5:30pm-9pm. Special Bar Night Mon 4pm-11pm. ❶❸❺❼ to 14th. Average entrée $20.

162 CHELSEA

El Cocotero *Venezuelan*
Images of Venezuela and a large Venezuelan flag adorning the walls make this a homey setting in which to consume delicious arepas and Venezuelan specialties. The beef of the pastelitos—pink, tender meat in a fried pastry—will melt in your mouth. Arepas offer a little something for every taste: vegetarians can try the Miss Venezuela (avocado and tomato), while adventurous types can sample the baby shark. No knife is required for the deliciously slow-cooked Asado negro, which mixes its juices with earthy black beans and rice as it falls apart on the plate. Finish with a creamy bien me sabe sponge cake, which drips with sweet, sugary coconut milk.
228 W 18th St (near 7th Ave) 212-206-8930. Mon, Wed 11am-10pm, Tues, Thurs, Fri 11am-11pm, Sat-Sun 11am-9pm. ❶ *to 18th. Average entrée $10.*

Izayaka Ten *Japanese*
This traditional Japanese restaurant stands out from neighboring skyscrapers with its diminutive size, all aswirl with ocean blue and green design. The charming and intimate atmosphere of rich mahogany, dim lighting, and welcoming waitstaff provides an escape from the chaos of 10th Avenue. The Nasu Hasami, or deep fried eggplant stuffed with pork and vegetables, is warm and crispy. The roast duck, served cold, explodes with teriyaki flavor. Sake, however, is the pride of Izayaka—their large collection is displayed all over the restaurant.
207 10th Avenue (between 22nd and 23rd St). 212-627-5168. Mon-Sat 12pm-12am, Sun 12pm-10pm. ❶ ❸ ❺ *to 23rd. Average entree $15.*

La Luncheonette *French*
Chef/owner Jean-Francois Fraysse and his wife Melva serve up bona fide Southwestern French fare in this tiny

---

EDITOR'S PICK

Hill Country *BBQ*
To call it the best barbecue joint in New York doesn't do Hill Country justice; the meat they serve here could easily go hoof-to-hoof with some of the best dry-rub, slow-cooked barbecue in Texas. Everything, from tender spare ribs to the jalapeño-cheddar sausage, is excellent, but the moist brisket is the true standout. The outside charred and salty, the inside moist and sweet, these long slices of meat fall apart under your fork, barely held together by succulent beef fat. Texans will appreciate the nods to idiosyncratic products from their home state. Big Red soda, Lone Star beer, and Blue Bell ice cream are all imported from Texas, as the menu proudly drawls. The attention to accuracy may frustrate some New Yorkers accustomed to cushy service: orders are placed separately at separate meat, side, and dessert stands, where they are priced by the pound and dished onto wax paper. The margaritas are fantastic.
30 W 26th St (near Broadway) 212-255-4544. Mon-Wed 12pm-10pm, Thurs-Sat 12pm-11pm, Sun 11am-10pm. ❶ ❽ ❻ ❻ *to 28th,* ❻ ❻ *to 23rd. Meat $8-$29/lb.*

CHELSEA 163

bistro. The restaurant is a family business, in the best sense of the term—an asset that shines through in the care that accompanies the preparation and service of every dish. Standout appetizers include marinated beet salad and puree soup of avocado and artichoke. Beef bourguignon and roast rack of New Zealand lamb au romarin are among the best of an excellent collection of entrées. Simple—if outdated—décor and homely charm make the restaurant a romantic place to bring a date, or just a comfortable spot to enjoy some superior French cooking.
130 10th Ave (at 18th St) 212-675-0342. Mon-Fri 12pm-3:30pm, 6pm-11:30pm, Sat-Sun, 11:30am-3:30pm, 6pm-11:30pm. ❶ *to 18th,* Ⓐ Ⓒ Ⓔ *to 14th. Average entrée $25.*

CHEAP
Billy's Bakery *Bakery*
The wonderful smell in this homey bakery builds with each fresh batch of cakes and cupcakes. There are a few tables inside this pastel-painted joint so customers can cram in for a sweet snack, but plan on ordering a dozen cupcakes and saving some for later. The banana, coconut, red velvet, and carrot cake varieties are especially tasty.
184 9th Ave (between 21st St and 22nd St). 212-647-9956. Mon-Thurs 9am-11pm, Fri-Sat 9am-12am, Sun 10am-10pm. ❶ *to 23rd-7th,* Ⓒ Ⓔ *to 23rd-8th. Average item $3.50.*

Kofoo *Korean*
Walk too fast and you might miss this nondescript Korean takeout joint. With barely any room to stand, it's a relief that the food arrives promptly, and freshly made. Stick to the kim bob—cheese, jalapeño, or chicken fillings—or the generously portioned bi bim bob, a mix of vegetables, egg, and your choice of meat over rice; both make for a healthy and filling lunch. Avoid the noodle soups like Bu Dae Ji Gae, where the dearth of noodles and heavy broth-drenched meat are less than appetizing.
334 Eighth Ave (near 27th St). 212-675-5277. Mon-Sat 10:30am-10pm. ❶ *to 28th-7th,* Ⓒ Ⓔ *to 23rd-8th. Average entrée $6.*

Tebaya *Japanese*
Though the fried chicken market is cornered by Korean counters in Flushing and soul food joints uptown, Tebaya's debut brings flavorful fries to the former warehouse district. Their recipe for chicken wings originated in Japan and calls for fatless, skinless wings fried twice in soy oil—less burdensome on the arteries than most other variations. Perfectly crisped, they are tossed in sesame seeds and a special garlicky sauce for the final touch. Counterbalance the oil with fresh salad or soba noodle, and iced green tea for a clean finish.
144 W 19th St (near 7th Ave) 212-924-3335. Daily 11am-11pm. ❶ *at 18th. Average meal $9.*

NIGHTLIFE

Comix *Comedy Club, Club*
This spacious venue aspires to be more than a mere comedy club. The muscle-bound bouncers, sleek décor, and showy décor all signal a desire for upward mobility, for the creation of a new category: the comedy nightclub. The space is aesthetically pleasing, but the dinner menu is not particularly inspiring-- the highlight being "slow baked Atlantic salmon." The rest of the menu is equally low-fare, small pizzas list among the cheaper options, while a standard bar serves standard cocktails. Ultimately though, it's the jokes that count, and Comix's upscale trappings (and 320-seat showroom) attract major comedic talent.
353 W 14th St (near 9th Ave) 212-524-2500. Sun-Thurs shows start at 8; Fri-Sat times vary. ❶❷❸ⒶⒸⒺ *to 14th St,* Ⓛ *to 8th Ave. Two drink minimum. Average drink $7.*

The Highline Ballroom
Music Venue
Though Highline is an enormous, state of the art performance space, it feels just as intimate as some smaller venues. With a huge stage, multiple bar areas, and cozy seating areas with good views, the space draws in

GALLERY HOPPING

With over 200 galleries in a ten-block stretch, one will not have time patronize most of Chelsea's world-renowned galleries, and as such must be appropriately choosey. Start by heading to 24th St, where many of the best and most well-known galleries are located. Start with the cavernous **Barabara Gladstone Gallery** (515 W 24th St, 212-206-9300). Over 25 years in the business, she knows everything there is to know and attracts some of the most prominent international contemporary artists, such as Matthew Barney and Sarah Lucas.

Matthew Marks (523 W 24th St, 212-243-0200) is another must-see. Attracting the likes of Willem de Kooning, this gallery always exhibits an artist worth knowing and the space is larger than most, giving room for you to take in the works. Further along the street is the **Zach Feuer Gallery** (530 W 24th St, 212-989-7700) that deals with the most unpredictable, bleeding-edge painters.

Don't forget to include the **Gagosian Gallery** (555 W 24th St, 212-741-1111), whose prestige carries with it the power to make names overnight. At the larger space on **522 W 21st St** (212-741-1717) huge installations like Richard Serra's sculptures are displayed.

Notable galleries such as these host attractive openings; the clientele that show up demand nothing less. If you're around the first week of September, follow limos and pretties and you will undoubtedly find the best openings. While it may get crowded and you may feel a bit out of place, the hors d'œuvres and drinks are well worth it. Openings happen year round, but the beginning of fall season is usually the busiest and most exciting so don't miss out.

the crowds and a diverse array of acts—from burlesque to big name musicians to tribute shows. Whether standing or sitting, concert goers can enjoy a menu of bar food of mini Kobe burgers or salmon tartar served in a martini glass. Table seating, though tempting, is overly expensive and tends to detract from the concert experience; opt for standing room only and really get into the show.
431 W 16th St (between 9th Ave & 10th Ave). ⒶⒸⒺⓁ *to 14th. 212-414-5994. Average drink $10.*

CHELSEA 165

Mansion *Club*

The interior of this swank club, lavishly adorned with crystal chandeliers, is divided into themed rooms like the Ballroom, Study, and Library that recreate the splendid haunts of the rich and famous. Beautiful servers dressed like French maids add to the theatrics and give the club a needed playful feel. At the center of the action is the Ballroom, where the DJ spins house music flawlessly all night. Don't waste time looking for a dance floor—there isn't one. Instead, the young and wealthy mingle over bottle-serviced tables until dawn.

530 W 28th St (at 10th Ave) 212-629-9000. Tues, Thurs-Sat 9pm-4am. ❶ to 28th. Average drink $13.

Marquee *Club*

One of the kings of the club scene, this 'hotspot' wrote the book on the velvet rope. Though the door policy is a pain in the ass for civilians and the drinks are pricey, the eternally beautiful and hip (sometimes star-studded) crowd writhing to every song you want to hear is an experience often worth the hassle. The bottom level, with pulsating house, top-40 and hip-hop beats, acts as a bit of a meat-market while the top floor draws in a more low-key crowd of people with totally different music tastes—leaning towards indie, alt-rock and obscure 80's. Paul Sevigny hosts an unbeatable dance party on Wednesday nights, so if you're only clubbing one night a week, make it hump day.

289 10th Ave (between 26th St & 27th St). 646-473-0202. Tues-Sat 10pm-4am. ❻❸ to 23rd St. Average drink $12.

Rebel NYC *Club*

Despite an impressive space split into four inviting dance floors, Rebel NYC struggles to make an impact on the competitive Chelsea club scene. However, this lack of identity is not a problem for the unpretentious twenty-something crowd that dances here. Bouncers are efficient and reasonable unlike the strict doorkeepers of "superclub" neighbors. The crowd is diverse and laidback, the drinks come strong, and the bartenders are friendly, but be prepared to fight your way up to the bar, which gets crowded and slow. The club regularly hosts live music private events and parties, including the exclusive "Skin Party"—a monthly erotic dance party.

251 W 30th St (btwn 7th & 8th Ave) 212-695-2747. Thurs-Fri 10pm-4am, Sat 11pm-4am. ❶ to 28th St, ❹❻❸ to 34th. Average drink $8.

Taj *Lounge*

Dramatically upholstered, plushly pillowed booths lit by dim candles and huge fabric lamps create an exotic atmosphere for dining, drinking, and dancing at this Indian themed nightclub. Wednesday "salsa" nights are the highlight of the theme nights—they feature a saucy salsa band and dance lessons. The democratic VIP lounge is open to all and provides respite from the overly loud dance floor. Cocktails are where Taj really shines—the Budina, which infuses vodka with cucumber, lime, and mint, and the Elderflower, a tasty mix of vodka, elderflower cordial, lemon, and champagne, are tops.

48 W 21st St (between 5th Ave & 6th Ave) 212-620-3033. Mon 5pm-1am, Tues-Thurs 5:30pm-11pm, Fri-Sat 5:30pm-4am, Sun closed. ❶❻❾ to 23rd. Average drink $10.

Upright Citizens' Brigade Theatre *Comedy Club*

The "buddy's basement" feeling to this theater packs at best around 200 people, many of whom end up sitting on the floor. The back-at-high-school ambience plays right into the intimate setting that the improv comedians cultivate. Initially you may walk inside skeptical, but you're guaranteed to leave with a headache from laughing so hard. At $8 a seat for a one hour show, you'll leave wishing the show was just a little longer. Make sure to reserve space ahead of time and come early: seats are assigned on a first come first serve basis.

307 W 26th St (at 8th Ave). 212-366-9176. Sun-Sat 8:00 pm-2am. Call ahead for tickets. ❶ to 28th. Average drink $4.

SHOPPING

The Family Jewels
It's easy to see why this Chelsea store has earned a reputation as one of the best vintage shops in the city. The long racks and shelves along the walls are stocked with everything from fur coats to sequined tank tops, all of it from any time between the turn of the century and the 1980s and organized according to type, material, and color. True to its name, Family Jewels also has an impressive selection of jewelry, displayed in glittering heaps in glass cabinets.
130 23rd St (near 7th Ave). 212-633-6020. Mon-Sun 11am-7pm. ❶❷ *to 23rd,* ❻❸ *to 23rd.*

Jim Henley's Universe
The largest competitor of the NYC comics behemoth that is Midtown Comics, Jim Henley's Universe outdoes its rival by focusing a bit more on alternative, independent, and underground comics. Their stock includes a sizable selection of zines, mini-comics, back issues, and a t-shirt collection in addition to the usual statues and action figures.
4 W 33rd St (at 5th Ave). 212-268-7088. Mon-Tues 9am-11pm, Wed 8:30am-11pm, Thurs-Sat 9am-11pm, Sun 10am-9pm. ❽❿❻❼❽❹❺❻❼ *to 34th St-Herald Sq,* ❻ *to 33rd.*

Pippin Vintage Jewelry
If you're looking for jewelry but can't afford to spend much, Pippin Vintage is a pretty safe bet. Prices vary with age and quality, but most items go for less than $50, with drawers full of bracelets, pins, earrings, and rings for $5-$15. Customers will find a frequently updated selection of cameo pins from the '60s, silver bangles from the '70s, and long chain necklaces from the '30s. Pippin also sells handbags, silk scarves, and vintage hats—the discarded vestments of someone's stylish great-aunt. A narrow alleyway next to the store leads to a smaller store—Pippin Home—containing furniture and wall decorations, silverware and glasses, obscure books filled with musty pages, and a variety of other knickknacks, all at very reasonable prices.
112 17th St (near 6th Ave) 212-505-5159. Mon-Sat 11am-7pm, Sun 12pm-6pm. ❶ *to 18th St,* ❻❼❽ *to 14th.*

DAY TO DAY

Community Board 4. *330 West 42nd Street 26th Fl. 212-736-4536.*

Local Media: *Chelsea-Clinton News, chelseanow.com*

Groceries: *Whole Foods Market. 250 7th Ave (btwn 24th and 25th St). 212-924-5969*

Average Rent: *One-bedroom: $3,705.*

Hospital: *New York Presbyterian Hospital 119 W 24th St (between 6th & 7th Ave) 212-746-7200.*

Hotel: *Chelsea Star Hotel, 302 W 30th St (between 8th & 9th Ave) 212-465-8664.*

Dog Run: *Chelsea Waterside Park, 11th Ave & 22nd St.*

Movie Theater: *AMC Loews 34th St 14, 312 W 34th St (between 8th & 9th Ave). 212-244-8850.*

Best Happy Hour: *Peter McManus, 152 7th Ave (between 19th & 20th Ave). 212-929-6196.*

THE IRISH REPERTORY THEATRE

Visit our website at
www.irishrep.org
for information on upcoming productions, student discounts, internship opportunities, and other ways to get involved.

Call **212.727.2737** for tickets

132 West 22nd Street (between 6th & 7th Avenues)

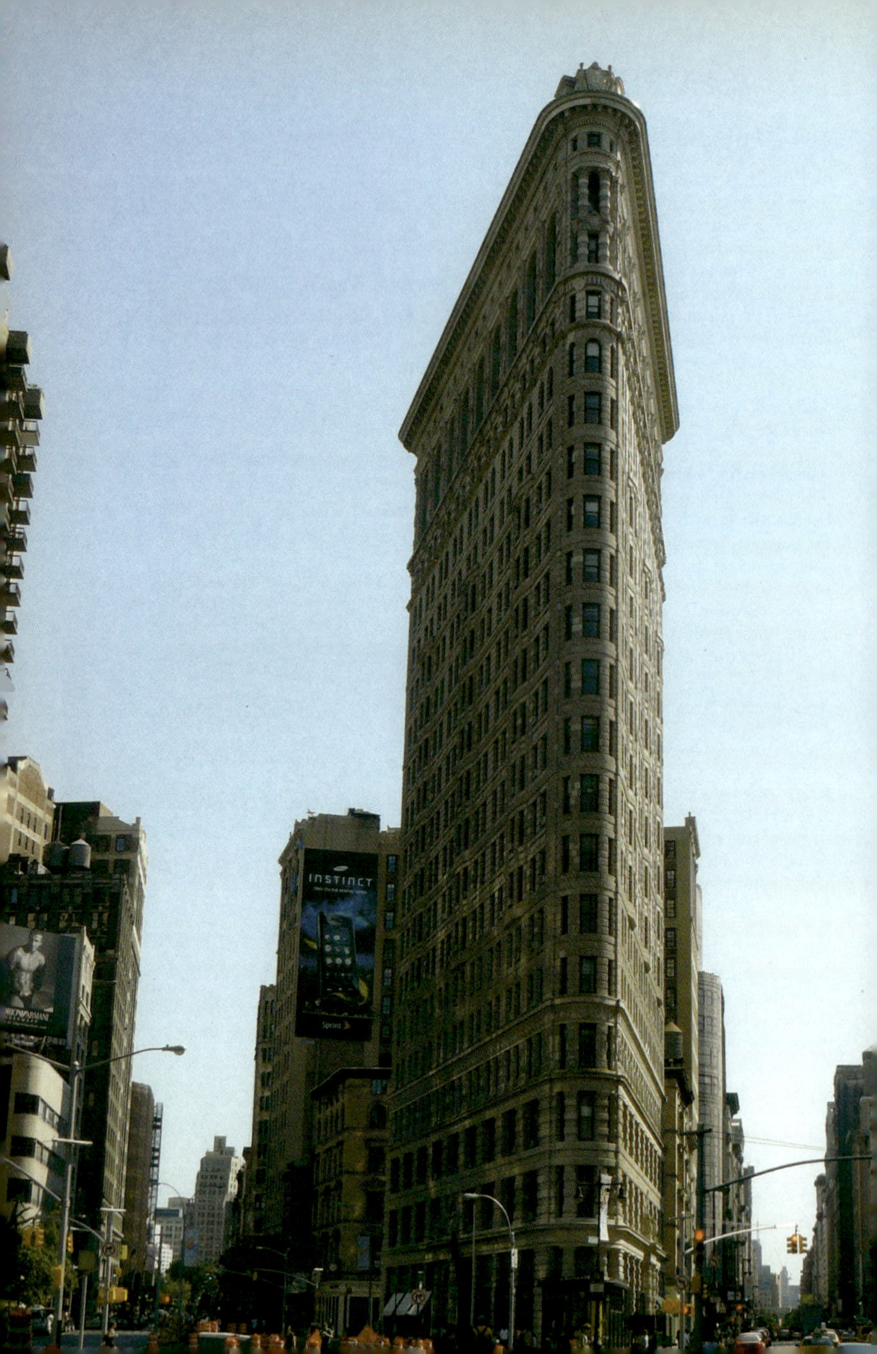
INSTINCT
Sprint

GRAMERCY

Always pretty quiet, never very fashionable, the Gramercy area is an anchor of calm in the middle of cooler, more hyperactive neighborhoods. Exclusive residential streets lined with multi-million dollar townhouses branch off avenues of office buildings, many of which house publishers, ad agencies, and the occasional web start up.

The boundaries of this largely residential area are vague, largely because it lacks a distinct character to differentiate it from the other upscale, mixed-zoning neighborhoods on the east side of Manhattan. Sectioned off into Kips Bay, Murray Hill, and the Flatiron District, one would be hard pressed to parse the different breeds of Rich and White that you will find here.

Still, there is much to be enjoyed in this neighborhood, if only because of the lack of frenetic energy which draws so many to Manhattan. Tree lined streets offer pristine strolls along architectural masterpieces. The epitome of these well-groomed streets surround Gramercy Park, one of the largest and most elegant private parks in the country. Unfortunately, you will need a key to get in, but feel free to stroll around the surrounding (public) sidewalk to get a glimpse of some excellent landscaping.

Southwards, a more diverse community keeps things interesting. Curry Row, on 28th St, has what is perhaps the greatest density of Indian restaurants this side of Mumbai.

At the southern border of Gramercy, the density of colleges, some NYU affililated, some not, keeps things more interesting. Though few students can afford to live in this area, class attendance demands their presence, and their youthful attempts at urban dissipation keep things from getting too stuffy.

ATTRACTIONS

The Empire State Building
Seventy-eight years after its completion, this 103-story building remains the tallest and most recognizable skyscraper in the city. The top tower is no longer used as a mooring mast for blimps, but the unrivaled panoramic views it offers attracts over 3.5 million visitors each year. With elevators that travel at seventeen feet per second, you'll find yourself in the climate controlled, glass-enclosed 86th floor observatory in less than a minute, though the spacious outdoor promenades offer a better view.
350 Fifth Avenue (at 34th St). Open 365 days/year 8am-2am, last elevator ascends at 1:15am. ❶❷❸ⒶⒸⒺⒷⒹⒻⓃⓇⓆ *to 34th. Adults $19.*

Flatiron Building
One of New York's most iconic buildings, the Flatiron building is also one of the city's first skyscrapers. At 22 stories and 285 feet its size may no longer impress, but its intricate Beaux-Arts design will captivate eyes weary of sheet-glass and steel. Because of the dramatic triangular shape, strong, unpredictable bursts of wind blow through the area; in the 20s men used to hang out around the building to grab a peek at women's ankles being scandalously exposed by the gusts.
156 5th Ave (at 23rd St). ⓃⓇⒻⓋ❻ *to 23rd.*

Gramercy Park
Enclosed by a tall metal fence and gates, the park is one of only two remaining private parks in the city and is said to be the oldest in the country. Jointly owned by nearby residents, its neatly pruned hedges and colorful flowerbeds can only be truly enjoyed by the holders of the exclusive park key, changed annually. Apart from the locals, some of whom reside in the renowned Greek revival, Italianate, Gothic

revival, and Victorian Gothic structures that surround the park, only members of the Players Club, National Arts Club, and guests of the Gramercy Park Hotel have access. But even shut-out visitors can enjoy the tranquility and shade of the park grounds. Lofted, oversized Victorian bird houses dot the east and west ends of the perimeter, guarding the park centerpiece, a statue of Edwin Booth—the great 19th century American actor whose dramatic achievements have been overshadowed by the notoriety of his brother, John Wilkes Booth. Get a closer look by sneaking in with a resident, but be careful—you'll need the key to escape.
Between 20th and 21st streets on Lexington Ave. ❹❻ to 23rd St; ❶ Ⓐ Ⓒ Ⓔ Ⓝ Ⓡ Ⓠ Ⓦ ❹❺❻ to 14th.

Madison Square Park
A welcome spot of green in the center of the Flatiron District, this park has recently been transformed into over six acres of prime turf devoted to communal relaxation. Lie on the grass amidst modern sculptures and watch the working hordes flock to the area at lunch. Though one frequently finds families attending the many cultural programs, on weekdays the park is mobbed by young professionals, often in line at the ever popular Shake Shack.
Between 23rd St, 26th St, 5th Ave, and Madison Ave. ❻ Ⓡ Ⓦ to 23rd St.

CULTURE & ARTS

Museum of Sex
A sign above the black leather divans in the lobby instructs visitors: "Please do not touch, lick, stroke, or mount the exhibits." The rest of the museum is less tongue-in-cheek and more tongue-on-nipple. If the gigantic phallus made of roses that looms behind the ticket-takers makes you uncomfortable, it would behoove you to turn back. With temporary exhibits on subjects like kink and sex in movies, the museum takes an intellectual approach to racy subjects, but succeeds mostly at titillating the young couples who stroll through the exhibits grinning goofily. The permanent collection includes innovative homemade sex machines, explanations of "basic BDSM terminology," footage from early double-penetration porn movies, and old sex-ed teaching materials.
233 5th Ave (at 27th St) 212-689-6337. Sun-Fri 11am-6:30pm, Sat 11am-8pm. Ⓡ Ⓦ to 28th. Adults $14.50, students $13.50.

National Arts Club
Located in the historic Tilden Mansion, the exclusive National Arts Club (membership is by invitation only) supports both established and emerging artists. The Victorian sandstone façade and stained glass dome ceiling are impressive in their own right, while high quality exhibitions signify the club's position in the art world. The five galleries are open weekdays to the public, but check ahead as events often close the galleries to visitors. The website lists upcoming book signings, lectures, and concerts.
15 Gramercy Park South (near Irving Pl). 212-674-8824. www.NationalArtsClub.com. Mon-Fri 10am-5pm. ❻ Ⓡ Ⓦ to 23rd St.

SVA Museum
Take advantage of the exhibitions and lectures orchestrated for the benefit of SVA students at this welcoming two-room museum. The gallery is best known for its Master's Series, an annual awards exhibition honoring prominent visual artists. Programs and exhibitions are cohesive, pedagogical, and quite manageable, representing about an afternoon's worth of information.
209 E 23rd St (near 3rd Ave). 212-592-2145. Mon-Fri 9am-7pm, Sat 10am-6pm. ❻ Ⓡ Ⓦ Ⓕ Ⓥ ❶ Ⓒ Ⓔ to 23rd.

DINING

UPSCALE

EDITOR'S PICK

15 East *Japanese*
The room has a tranquility otherwise unheard of on the downtown dining scene. The waitstaff is keen and informative—an unmistakable set-up for high epicurean expectations. Deep, savory dashi broth provides the base for many dishes, including octopus, massaged and poached in broth, tender from coddle and care. Though

GRAMERCY 171

the menu changes seasonally, it maintains consistence with super-silken house-made tofu and delicate seasonings of ginger, sesame oil, and scallion. Order ten-piece sushi or sashimi omakase; the selection of fish depends on availability and the chef's whim, but freshness and quality are on par with preparations found on far Eastern shores. A reprieve from inauthentic restaurants tarting up frozen filets for higher prices, this piscine temple has a devoted expat and knife at the helm, serving dishes that would be equally adored in the mother country—a special dining destination worth breaking the piggy bank.

15 E 15th St (near Union Square West) 212-647-0015. Mon-Fri 12pm-2pm, 6pm-10:30pm; Sat 6:00pm-10:30pm. ❹❺❻❻❶❶❶❶❶ to 14th St-Union Square. Average entrée $55.

Asia de Cuba *Fusion*

Hefty family-style plates match the prices at this hotel restaurant that blurs the line between restaurant and chi-chi bar scene. A bi-level dining room outfitted with white leather and curtains, dramatic lighting, and an alabaster communal table provides a glamorous setting that would be formulaic further downtown, but is unexpected in the milieu of the residential block. The extensive cocktail menu and newfangled cuisine cater to hordes of foreign tourists and power suits who nosh on the Asian-meets-Latin calamari salad and expertly-seared scallops. Plantains have a place in many dishes—a boon to some, monotony to others. Nothing on the menu bows to the trend of fussy dolls' portions, including a buttery carrot cake with black currant ice cream, so grab a group of friends and go Dutch to make it an affordable night out.

237 Madison Ave (between 37th St & 38th St) 212-726-7755. Lunch Mon-Fri 12pm-3pm. Dinner Sun-Thurs 5:30pm-11pm, Fri-Sat 5:30pm-12am. ❹❺❻❼❽ to Grand Central, ❻❻ to 33rd St. Entrées $22-80.

Devi *Indian*

A colorful crowd of couples and mixed professionals fills Devi's dining room, a hidden balcony, and private nooks lit with candles and lanterns. Many are here for chefs Hemant Mathur and Suvir Saran, who bought the place from their manager to focus on what could be the best Indian food in New York City. A slate of tasting menus evolves over time, but a diner might find the warmth of an expertly grilled scallop balanced against bitter orange chutney, the sweetness of pear placed in juxtaposition with a spicy tandoor lamb chop, or buttery and light poached halibut set next to a garnish of sour peanut slaw as noteworthy as the main dish. The chefs' attention to taste showed as well in uncanny wine pairings, and in the bread pudding, which is based on nothing more secret than a slice of white and his inimitable mastery of traditional spices.

8 E 18th St (at 5th Ave). 212-691-1300. Dinner Mon-Sat 5:30pm-11pm, Sunday 5pm-10pm. Lunch Mon-Fri 12pm-2:30pm. ❶❻❻❻❻❹❺❻ to Union Square. Average entrée $27, tasting menus $25-$110 (with wine).

Japonais *French, Japanese*

Start with the trademark "Sakitini," sit back, and allow Japonais to overwhelm you with sensory delight. A blend of Japanese and French cuisine, Japonais lets loose on every front. The décor is extravagantly done, dimly lit with glass-blown installations sporadically intertwined with large bonsai trees. The sushi and sashimi menu is exquisite: be sure to sample the chutoro and unagi. Prepared by the cold foods chef, they are absolutely transporting. Hot entrées are more adventurous. "The Rock," a sampling of ginger infused raw meats, allows you to cook your meal atop a steaming hot stone. The akaushi ribeye, a 12 ounce steak served with uni butter, is more classic but perfectly done steak. A superb specialty drink menu featuring multiple champagne based concoctions blends quite fittingly with the modern and chic interior.

111 E. 18th St. (near Park Ave. S) 212-260-2020. Mon-Thurs 5pm-11pm, Fri-Sat 5pm-11pm. ❶❻❻❻❻❹❺❻ to Union Square. Average entrée $29.

Tocqueville *New American*

Tocqueville is, simply and spectacularly, fine dining done right. Executive Chef Marco A. Moreira prepares an extensive menu of revelations in presentation and taste, reflecting a variety of culinary influences. A

KOREATOWN

There is more activity packed into these few blocks than exists in some entire neighborhoods. For those literate in Korean, the heavily-trafficked streets offer resources like travel agents, acupuncturists, saunas, commercial banks, a church, grocery store, bookstores, and even two galleries—the **Lee Young Hee Museum** (*2 W 32nd St, 3rd fl, 212-560-0722*), displaying traditional Korean dress, and the **Hun Gallery** (*12 W 32nd St, 3rd fl, 212-594-1312*), exhibiting contemporary works by Korean artists.

But for the happy hour, Saturday night, and foodie crowds, the area has become a true dining and nightlife destination. Young twenty and thirty-somethings cavort from restaurant to bar to karaoke room, slurping down boiling, clay-pot stews, and quaffing soju, the Korean compatriot of vodka and sake.

For the night owls, the sexy lounge **Maru** (*11 W 32nd St, 3rd fl. 212-273-3413*) mixes solid cocktails, offers bottle service, and has posh karaoke rooms upstairs. **Kunjip** (*9 W 32nd St, 212-216-9487*) serves up hearty Korean mainstays until the wee hours of the morning, while **Gahm Mi Oak** (*43 W 32nd St. 212-695-4113*) specializes in oxtail bone stew, a comforting and sobering broth with noodles that beats out chicken noodle soup any day. Bars with unbeatable snacks include **Bon Chon** (*314 Fifth Ave, 2nd fl, 212-221-2222*) and **Forte Baden Baden NY** (*28 W 32nd St, 2nd fl. 212-714-2266*)—wings are fried to a crisp twice at the former, and perfumed with buttery roasted garlic cloves at the latter.

For toothsome fare during the day or for dinner, some restaurants, like **Kang Suh** (*1250 Broadway, 212-564-6845*) and **Choong Mu Ro** (*10 W 32nd St. 212-594-4963*), offer a wealth of traditional menu items—all high-quality and well-prepared. Others specialize in particular dishes. **New York Komtang Sootbul Kalbi** (*32 W 32nd St, 212-947-8482*) boasts wood-charcoal grills for tasty barbecue, and on 35th street, **Cho Dang Gol** (*55 W 35th St, 212-695-8222*) makes tofu in-house. For a lesser-known traditional dish, **Hyo Dong Gak** (*51 W 35th St,212-695-7167*) offers noodles in black bean sauce (jja jjang myun), created in Korea by Chinese immigrants hundreds of years ago.

W 32nd St to 35th St between Broadway and 5th Ave.

---

tuna tartare served with peppered sashimi, wasabi dressing, and a cilantro and tangerine sauce has an Asian flair while an aged and salted beef dish is pure bistro bliss. The confit meatball of dark hen meat dressed in rich jus may be evidence of a kitchen just showing off, but the taste lives up to the culinary showmanship. The main dining area is a windowless, soundproof retreat from nearby Union Square, bathed in candlelight. Service is friendly but deliberately paced such that an evening out at Tocqueville moves to its own stately tempo.
1 E 15th St (at 5th Ave) 212-647-1515. Lunch Mon-Sat 11:45am-2pm, Dinner Mon-Sat 5:30pm-10:30pm. ❶❷❸❹❺❻ *to Union Square/14th St,* ❼❽❾ *to 6th Ave & 14th St. Average entrée $29.*

MID-RANGE
Bao Noodles *Vietnamese*
When Chinatown is not an option, check out Bao Noodles in Gramercy, a fancified Vietnamese place in the guise of a French cafe. Prices are only slightly higher than a Baxter Street dive, a small premium to pay for consistency. A long sake list and excellently greasy spring rolls complement the undeniably good soups, which have as much flavor as their downtown cousins but none of the questionable meats. Desserts are over-sweet, but the soup portions are big enough to guarantee lunch for tomorrow.
391 2nd Ave (between 22nd & 23rd St) 212-725-7770. Sun-Wed 11:30am-11pm, Thurs-Sat 11am-12am. ❻❼❽ *to 23rd,* ❶ *to 3rd. Average entrée $12.*

Novita *Italian*
The antipasti at this local gem are the very definition of delicacy and freshness. Especially of note are the Kobe beef carpaccio, the sharply flavored artichoke salad, and the melt-in-your-mouth eggplant parmesan. For entrées, avoid the meat dishes, which are nothing special; instead, stick

with pasta and fish, the excellence of which have built Novita a devoted neighborhood following. The menu is accompanied by a massive wine list, which the knowledgeable waiters are more than happy to walk you through. Reservations are recommended, and even then, come prepared for a wait. A cozy, dimly-lit interior offers a casual yet sophisticated ambiance, though poor acoustic design amplifies the gabbing of the crowd—for a quieter setting, try the outdoor seating.

102 E 22nd St (near Park Ave South). 212-677-2222. Mon-Fri 12pm-3pm, 5:45pm-11pm, Sat 5:30pm-11pm, Sun 5pm-10pm. ❹❺❻ⓛⓝⓡⓞⓦ to Union Square. Average entrée $22.

Penelope *American*

Serving down-home food with a light and creative twist, Penelope is sure to charm first-time visitors. The candlelit tables, cozy interior, and accommodating menu make this café/bakery/bar an ideal date spot. Chicken meatballs with pesto dipping sauce are a house signature and shouldn't be missed; they can be ordered as an appetizer, in a salad, or on a sandwich. The deliciously gooey mac & cheese tastes just as good as it did when you were a kid, and is a filling main course. Be sure to leave room for dessert; the carrot and red velvet cakes are the most popular options, but, as the enchanting display of sweets at the counter shows, it would be difficult to make a wrong decision.

159 Lexington Ave (at 30th St). 212-481-3800. Breakfast Mon-Fri 8am-11:45pm. Lunch and dinner Mon-Fri 11:45am-11:45pm, Sat-Sun 4pm-11pm. Brunch Sat-Sun 8am-4pm. ❻ⓝⓡⓦ to 28th. Average entrée $9.

Rosa Mexicano *Mexican*

The elegant table settings, festive lighting, and sexy décor would make even mediocre grub taste perfectly acceptable; however, this popular restaurant delivers plates of tasty fare. This place attracts a young crowd, but all ages can be seen watching in delight as the guacamole station wheels from table to table, creating dip tailored to their spice tolerance. Ask your server to help you in choosing the perfect tequila for your margarita; the selection is impressive, as is the servers' expertise. Main courses are substantial and hold few surprises, yet nuts and fruit delicately integrated into many dishes elevate the food.

9 E 18th St (between 5th Ave & Broadway) 212-533-3350. Lunch Mon-Fri 12pm-5pm. Dinner Mon-Sat 5pm-closing, Sun 4pm-closing. Brunch Sat 11am-5pm, Sun 11am-4pm. ❶❷❸❹❺❻❹❺❻ to 14th St-Union Square. Average entrée $24.

Saravana Bhavan Dosa Hut *Indian*
Savarana's authentic Indian cuisine is no well-kept secret: families journey here from around the island to enjoy dishes like Kaima Idli—a starter with tender sautéed idli (tofu-like chunks made from a rice and black lentil paste) and a full-flavored spicy sauce, complimented by cool cucumber raita. Many dishes lend themselves to sharing with the table, like South Indian Thali, with an array of accompanying sauces, from spicy citrus to sweet rice pudding to lentil curry. Show up later in the evening or make a reservation to beat the crowds.
81 Lexington Ave (at 26th St). 212-679-0204. Mon-Fri 8:30am-3pm, 5pm-10pm, Sat-Sun 8:30am-4pm, 6pm-10pm. ❻ *to 28th St. Average entrée $26.*

Wildwood *BBQ*
Wildwood is not a brawler of a barbecue joint. Instead, the restaurant pulls its punches, preferring a 'fun' attitude to a boisterous one. The dining room is like a ski lodge: cavernous with exposed beams and iron. The din of rock and country on exposed walls stays a notch below loud and doesn't tangle with the civilized conversation of curious young locals and amorous couples. Likewise, sauces here are a notch less than potent. The brisket chili is watery, as are a side of beans, the potato salad, and a plethora of barbecue and hot sauces. The outstanding pulled pork conspicuously lacks its promised vinegar mop sauce. However, pit-master Lou Elrose's dry-rubbed pork spare ribs, procured upstate and smoked in-house, are unbeatable with or without sauce, as is his barbecue chicken. Both are firm and tender at once. This is barbecue for New Yorkers, and it does have finer points.
225 Park Ave South (at 18th St). 212-533-2500. Mon 11:30am-11pm, Tues-Thurs 11:30am-12am, Fri 11:30am-1am, Sat 12pm-1am, Sun 12pm-11pm. ❶❷❸❹❺❻ *to 14th St-Union Square. Average entrée $20.*

CHEAP
2nd Avenue Deli *Deli*
Have no fear: the new location of this former East Village landmark still serves up hugely satisfying sandwiches and other old favorites. Be careful not to fill up on the delicious matzoh ball soup or the hearty mushroom barley, or else you'll have no room for the enormous sandwiches. These famous sandwiches can be as big as your head (depending on your cranial girth) and feature well-marbled meat. If any room remains in your stomach, the warm chocolate babka is a perfect finale to this comforting meal.
62 E 33rd St (between Lexington & 3rd Ave). 212-689-9000. Open 24 Hours. ❻ *to 33rd St,* ❶❷❸❹❺❻❹❺ *to 34th St-Herald Sq. Average entrée: $16.*

Crêpe Mania
This small Midtown creperie is refreshingly simple. The friendly staffers fill the restaurant with a homey ambience that attracts diverse crowds—students and businessmen alike watch the smiling chefs as they batter, fill, and roll fresh crepes. The cooks prepare each dish with a fine attention to detail; the "chip-chip" crêpe is decorated with whip cream, covered sliced strawberries, and topped with dark chocolate chips. Their savory crêpes are presented with the same flair, and the perfectly proportioned combination of light cheeses in the fresh turkey and wild mushroom crêpe makes for just the right lunch or midday snack. Their smoothies are also enjoyable, and the Mango Mania makes for a good morning pick me up.
533 3rd Ave (between 35th & 36th St). 212-684-6733. Daily 9am-9:30pm. ❹❺❻ *to 33rd. Crêpes $5-$10, Smoothies $5-$7.*

Indo Munch *Indian, Chinese Fusion*
The Indian tapestries and Chinese paper lanterns adorning the walls mirror this restaurant's ambitious fusion cuisine. Though at times a bizarre combination, like in the heavy-handed Manchurian sauce, the results often exhibit the best of both worlds. Indian chili accompanies Chinese staples like spring rolls and rice, providing a refreshing kick, while Indian vegetables like cauliflower and okra benefit from Chinese ginger. The spicy hakka noodles stand out as

GRAMERCY 175

the marriage of flavors perfected.
182 Lexington Ave (between 31st and 32nd St). 212-545-0010. Lunch Mon-Fri 12pm-3pm, Sat-Sun 12:30pm-3:30pm, Dinner Sun-Thurs 5:30pm-10:30pm, Fri-Sat 5:30pm-11pm. ❹❺❻ *to 33rd St. Average entrée $10.*

Republic *Asian*
Communal tables set the mood for loud conversation and happy eating in this Union Square landmark. Southeast and East Asian cuisine blend harmoniously into a menu famous for pad thai and coconut chicken dishes that locals worship. Come summertime, the diverse crowd of patrons spills onto sidewalk tables to chow on glass noodles, wontons, green papaya mango salad and other vegetarian-friendly dishes.
37 Union Square West (between 16th & 17th St) Sun-Wed 11:30am-10:30pm, Thurs-Sat 11:30am-11:30pm. ❶❽❻❿❽ ❹❺❻ *to 14th St-Union Square. Average entrée $10.*

NIGHTLIFE

Copper Door Tavern *Bar*
On first sight, the copper door may be the only thing to distinguish this bar from the strip of generic sports bars in this area; however, the lack of a frat bar mentality makes it remarkably different. Though the beer offerings are standard, the specials (Twofer Burgers and Bud) are enticing. A friendly bar packs in college-aged bar patrons Thursday through Saturday, when the wood paneled booths are crowded and loud. The game is always on, but nobody is watching, opting instead to yell conversations and sing along to tunes blaring from the jukebox.
272 3rd Ave (between 21st St & 22nd St). 212-254-3870. Mon-Wed 2pm-2am, Thurs-Sat 11am-4am, Sun 11am-4am, Sun 11am-10pm. ❻ *to 23rd St. Average drink $7.*

The Ginger Man *Beer bar*
Stop by after work or on a weekend night to sample one of the finest brews offered in the city. With seventy beers on tap and well over 100 bottled varieties available, the choice of what to drink can be overwhelming, but the staff will help find your way. When supplementing your tall cask-drawn brew with food, the Ginger Man hot dog and tater tots is hard to beat. Everything in the bar, from the scarcity of televisions to the wonderfully comfortable couches in the back, points to a beer drinking experience— and a wonderful one at that.
11 East 36th St (between 5th Ave and Madison). 212-532-3740. Mon-Thurs 11:30-2am, Fri 11:30-4am, Sat 12:30pm-4am, Sun 3pm-12am. ❶❷❸ *to Penn Station,* ❽❿❺❻❹❽❻❿❽ *to Herald Sq,* ❻ *to 33rd. Average drink $12.*

Jazz Standard *Jazz Club*
Big band, Brazilian piano, Colombian harp, Afrobeat, the Jazz Standard has it all, and an audience that sits down and listens politely when it's time to. It would be tempting to say that's because their mouths are full of delicious barbecue from Blue Smoke, which sends down orders from its kitchen upstairs, but then you would expect to hear utensils in use. Maybe it's because the waiters are well trained—they are—but more likely, it's because the caliber of musician attracted to Jazz Standard will put a spell on you. He'll have help from the only stage for jazz musicians in New York (excepting Dizzy's Club Coca-Cola) that can be seen from every seat in the house.
116 E 27th St. (at Park Ave South). 212-576-2232. Sun-Thurs 6:30pm-11pm, Fri-Sat 6:30pm-1am. ❻❿❽❻ *to 28th St. Cover $15-30. Average drink $8.*

Rare View *Rooftop Bar*
The elevator ride to this rooftop bar is cramped and sweaty, but those brave enough to make the trip up are rewarded with dizzying views of midtown. An enormous, airy space, the bar covers the entire 16th floor of the Shelbourne Hotel. Being Murray Hill, the crowd is mostly horny, frenzied finance types looking to blow off steam and have a rocking good time. Some perch on the wooden beds that act as chairs, some dance to Top 40 tunes, while others try to infiltrate the private parties that are often thrown in the space—most make overly friendly conversations with other bar patrons. Though wine and beer are offered, the minuscule selection is dwarfed by an extensive cocktail list. Sample with caution. The Sexy Sexy, a pink tinted, sickeningly sweet blend is an odd favorite amongst the men at the bar; opt for the more successful mojitos and flavored

margaritas. Thanks to its residential location, the outdoor bar closes up relatively early, so be prepared to party hard in a short time span.
303 Lexington Ave (at 37th St, 16th floor) 212-481-8439. ❹❺❻❼Ⓢ to 42nd St–Grand Central. Mon-Sat 3:30-11pm. Average drink $11.

Tonic East *Bar*
This three-story bar transforms from popular after-work hangout for college-grads and young professionals (with excellent happy-hour specials) to medium-energy weekend nightclub. The canopied rooftop is starkly different from the rest of the club—quiet and friendly— while the two floors below pump out late-80s and 90s pop and hip-hop hits until late into the night. The service is better than average, but actually reaching the bar can prove difficult, since all three floors are often packed. Though the food is fairly humdrum, every drink on the menu is worth a fight to the bar.
411 3rd Ave (at 29th St) 212-683-7090. Mon-Sun 11:30am-11pm. ❻ to 28th St & Lexington Av. Average entrée $14.

SHOPPING

City Opera Thrift Shop
With nary a costume in sight, this vintage shop carries clothing fit for a night at the opera. All proceeds go to City Opera and donations are tax-deductible, which may explain why Valentino and Dior are no strangers to the clothing racks. Beautiful clothing is complemented by furniture, prints, and paintings from various decades, all in great condition. A stop here will leave you drooling over numerous items, but cursing the price-tags.
222 E 23rd St (near 3rd Ave). 212-684-5344. Mon-Fri 10am-7pm; Sat 10am-6pm; Sun 12pm-5pm. ❹❻ to 23rd St, Ⓛ to 3rd Ave.

Reminiscence, Inc.
When stumped for a gift or with a spare hour to stroll down memory lane, stop by this pricey shop and let your eight-year-old self go wild. Action figures, whoopie cushions, retro lunch boxes, and rubber ducks wearing every conceivable expression are just amusing enough that you may be able to overlook the

DAY TO DAY

Community Board 5: *450 7th Ave Suite 2109. 212-465-0907.*

Groceries: Morton Williams. *278 Park Ave S (between 21st St & 22nd St). 212-982-7326.*

Gym: Equinox. *897 Broadway (between19th St & 20th St). 212-780-9300.*

Rent: One-bedroom: $1700-2300. Two-bedroom: $3000-4000.

Hospital: Beth Israel Medical Center. *307 1st Ave. 212-420-2000.*

Hotel: Hotel 17. *225 E 17th St. 212-475-2845.*

Dog Run: East 15th St (between 1st & 2nd Ave).

Movie Theater: AMC Loews. *890 Broadway. 212-260-8173.*

Best Happy Hour: Black Bear Lodge. *274 Third Ave (near 22nd St). 212-253-2178. Happy hour: Daily, 2pm-7pm; $2 off drafts, $4 well drinks, $10 six-packs of PBR, Rolling Rock and Natural Light.*

inflated prices. Check out their selection of vintage clothing in the back of the store as well as the quality selection of anti-Hallmark birthday cards.
50 W 23rd St (between 5th Ave and Ave of the Americas) 212-243-2292. ❺❻Ⓡ❿ to 23rd St.

Vintage Thrift Shop
When you tire of vintage shops charging you an arm and a leg or thrift shops devoid of any quality goods, try this goldmine of interesting bargains. Romantic slips, wildly patterned tops with sequins galore, and piles of accessories from the 50s, 60s, and 70s are organized to prevent frustration but maintain a haphazard appearance, like the closet of an eccentric aunt. The goodies extend to pictures, kitchenware, books, and more. Nothing lacks character nor breaks the bank; if money is truly tight, however, then wait for their sales, when many items can be got for under ten bucks.
286 3rd Ave (between 22nd St and 23rd St). 212-871-0777. Mon-Thurs 10:30am-8pm, Fri 10:30am-4pm, Sun 11am-7pm. ❻Ⓡ❿ to 23rd.

GRAMERCY 177

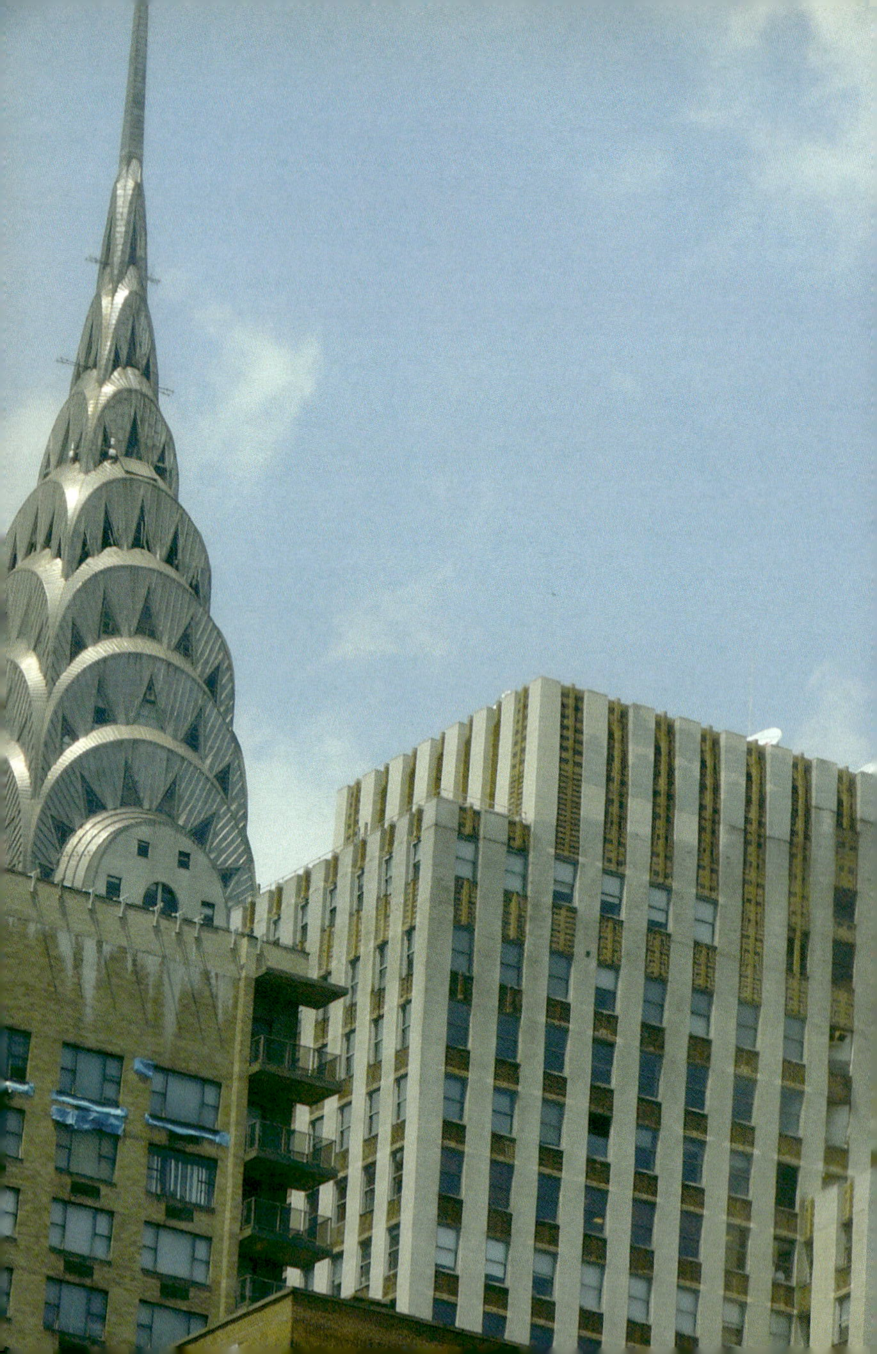

MIDTOWN EAST

While its neighbor to the West has more familiar, engaging environs, Midtown East is a strange amalgamation of landmarks, buildings, and businesses that stresses wealth as the lowest common denominator. During the day, streets are strangely segregated with power suits walking to work on Lexington and Park Aves, well-heeled ladies who lunch using their plastic on Madison Ave, and a jumbled mix of tourists on Fifth Ave. Further uptown is a quiet bubble—home to the United Nations and the elite residential addresses at Sutton Place—while further downtown grows busier near the Murray Hill border.

With Fifth Ave as the western boundary, the far northern and southern corners best represent the polarity and stratification of the district. The area above 42nd St boasts remnants of New York's Gilded Age past, today translated into old-money haunts: the Plaza hotel, Waldorf-Astoria hotel, and Bergdorf Goodman department store. Going downtown along Fifth, you'll run into attractions like the original Saks Fifth Avenue, the classic F.A.O. Schwartz, New York Public Library, Grand Central Terminal, the Chrysler Building, the Empire State Building, and Macy's. But the other avenues that make up the flesh of Midtown East are quiet and near-barren after working hours.

After market-closing and happy hour, the area becomes distinctly silent as offices close shop, commercial districts shut down, and residents come home to brownstones and converted high-rises in areas like Tudor City and Turtle Bay. It goes without saying that there isn't much to see at night. Day visits are well worth it to a few attractions, upscale restaurants, and happy hour watering holes; be prepared, however, to travel with a full pocketbook since most things worth purchasing come at an inflated price.

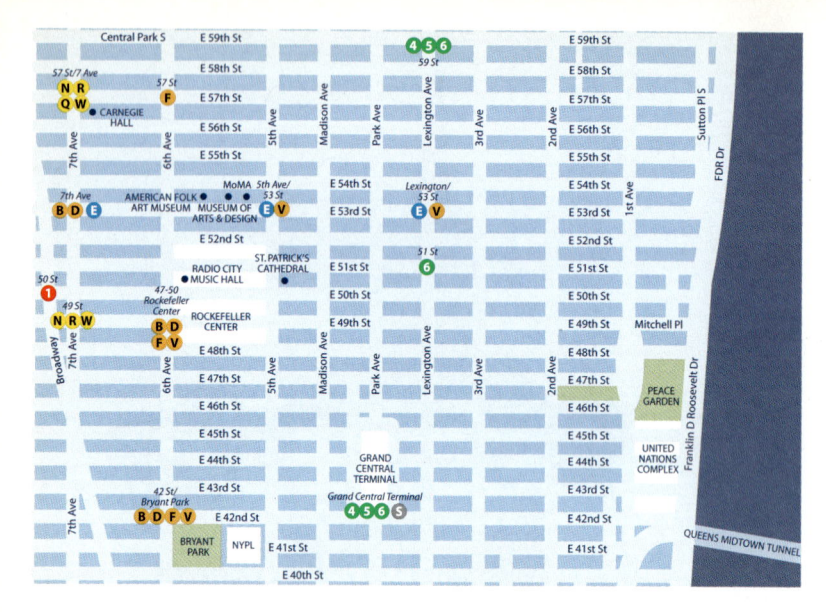

ATTRACTIONS

Bryant Park
Just one block east of Times Square, Bryant Park is the backyard of the monolithic and ornate New York Public Library. It boasts a well manicured central lawn, wide open gravel pathways, and a sea of forest-green tables and chairs. Visitors will discover a carousel, gravel pétanque courts (sort of like bocce ball), chess tables, and the "open air library"—an outdoors area for borrowing books, newspapers, and magazines. Free wireless access attracts local employees who come for a working lunch, while seasonal events like the New York Yankees' "Pinstripes in the Park," HBO's Summer Film Festival, and Fashion Week all draw thousands.
Between 40th St and 42nd St, and 5th Ave and 6th Ave. **B D F V** *to 42nd St-Bryant Park,* **7** *to 5th Ave.*

Grand Central Terminal
With 660 trains, 125,000 commuters, and 500,000 visitors passing through each day, this station may seem daunting. The numbers, however, do not diminish the sweeping elegance of the Beaux Arts Main Concourse—the elaborate night sky ceiling, the marble staircases, and of course, the iconic information booth topped with a four-sided clock in the center. The lower concourse houses the food court and the famous Oyster Bar (be sure to make a stop at the whispering arches outside the restaurant), while shops tending towards the pricier end line the various corridors. The exterior is just as majestic, with a landmark clock on the south facade surrounded by mythological deities. Free tours are offered every Wednesday at 12:30pm starting from the information booth.
42nd Street and Park Ave. 212-935-3960. **4 5 6 7 S** *to Grand Central.*

New York Public Library
The imposing main branch of the New York Public Library seems better suited to housing works of arts than books. Two stone lions, nicknamed Patience and Fortitude, guard its gates. Natural light streams through the many windows of the main reading room, which is adorned with two rows of small chandeliers, lined with shelves of reference books, and

topped with an ornate gold ceiling. Candelabras and classical murals appear throughout the rooms and corridors, creating quite the scholarly environment. In addition to its regular circulation collection, the library is also home to various historical documents including a copy of the Gutenberg Bible, first folio editions of some of Shakespeare's works, and the original Winnie the Pooh (the stuffed bear, not the book).

476 Fifth Ave (at 41st St). 212-930-0830. Oct-May: Mon and Thu-Sat 10am-6pm, Tue-Wed, 11am-7:30pm, Sun, 1pm-5pm, Jun-Sep: Mon and Thu-Sat 10am-6pm, Tue-Wed, 11am-7:30pm, Sun closed. B D F V at 42nd, 1 2 3 7 N R Q W S to Times Square, 4 5 6 7 S to Grand Central.

St. Patrick's Cathedral

The intricately decorated Neo-Gothic white marble edifice and twin spires that rise 330 feet from street level seem out of place in the midst of the department stores and law firms of midtown Manhattan, but once inside this quiet sanctuary all the bustle dies away. Since its completion in 1879, St. Patrick's Cathedral has served as the seat of New York's Roman Catholic Archdiocese while maintaining the functions of a parish church with regular mass and confession.

14 E 51st St (at 5th Ave). 212-753-2261. 7am-8-:30pm. B D F V to 47th-50th.

United Nations

Technically located on international territory, the United Nations Headquarters is an homage to the ideals of global community. Outside, the flags of all 192 member nations trace the entire complex, including the 38-story glass Secretariat Building. A sculpture of a gun with a knotted barrel stands at the visitor's entrance, while the surrounding UN garden contains similarly themed sculptures donated from various member nations. The highlights of the hour-long tour, led by highly knowledgeable multilingual guides, are the Security Council Chamber and the General Assembly Hall. Access to the rotating UN exhibits are free to the public, as is the UN postal office, where visitors can send postcards with specialized UN stamps.

46th St and 1st Ave. 212-963-8687. Mon-Fri 9:45am-4:45pm. 4 5 6 7 S to Grand Central Station. Students $9.00, Adults $13.50.

CULTURE & ARTS

Carnegie Hall

Though the venue hosts two smaller stages, the Judy and Arthur Zankel Hall and the Joan and Sanford I. Weill Recital Hall, the Stern Auditorium & Perelman Stage plays host to the world's most renowned classical performers and is the main attraction. The sheer grandeur and history of the place are immediately felt in the main hall. The setting—red velvet, gilded crown molding, ushers in red jackets with coattails and gold buttons—is breathtaking. Regular ticket prices can soar to hundreds of dollars, but students can take advantage of $10 student tickets released the week of show and $45 subscriptions that guarantee seats for three pre-determined concerts. Shows are available year round, but the orchestral season runs from late September to mid-March.

154 W 57th St (at 7th Ave). 212-247-7800. Box office Mon-Sat 11am-6pm, Sun 12pm-6pm. 1 A C B D to 59th, N R Q W to 57th, E to 7th.

City Center

New York City Center is one of Manhattan's oldest and most prestigious theaters, yet it still features some of the freshest performances around. For theater lovers, the spring brings Encores!, and dance lovers get the Paul Taylor Dance Company and the Flamenco Festival. Late fall brings the technical precision and grace of the American Ballet Theater and winter brings the soul and passion of the Alvin Ailey Dance Company. The Fall for Dance Festival is a must-see. For ten straight nights the City Center brings together the best dance troupes in the world from a myriad from dance styles, all for just $10 a ticket.

130 W. 56th St (between 5th Ave and 6th Ave). 212.581.1212. A C B D 1 to 59th, N R Q to 57th.

Museum of Modern Art

Undoubtedly one of the most influential museums in the world, MoMA was founded in 1929 as the first museum to focus exclusively on modern art. Today, masterpieces from the likes of Picasso, van Gogh, Warhol, Monet, and Pollock are on display in the permanent collection, while special exhibitions feature work from more contemporary artists. Don't miss the

MIDTOWN EAST 181

architecture and design collection; MoMA was the first museum to feature such works in its permanent collection. In addition to the gallery space, MoMA offers regular screenings of films both classic and cutting edge, as well as a library of over 300,000 primary source documents about contemporary art and artists.

11 West 53rd St (between 5th & 6th Ave). 212-708-9400. Sat-Mon 10:30am-5:30pm, Tues closed, Wed-Thurs 10:30am-5:30pm, Fri 10:30am-8pm. ❸ ❼ to 5th Avenue-53rd Street, ❸ ❹ ❻ to Rockefeller Center. Adults $20, Students $12.

Paley Center for Media

Formerly known as the Museum of Television and Radio, the Paley Center was founded in 1975 by CBS tycoon William S. Paley for serious academic research on television, radio, and new media. Equipped with multiple screening rooms and two full-sized theaters, as well as over 120,000 television shows, commercials, and radio programs in their vaults, the center's greatest attraction is allowing visitors to select programs from their library to watch (or listen to) at individual consoles. The Paley Center also offers frequent seminars, panels, and interviews with influential people in media, including creators and cast members of shows such as The Simpsons, Seinfeld, and South Park as well as luminaries like Al Franken, Lucille Ball, and Bob Hope.

25 W 52nd St (between 5th & 6th Ave). 212-621-6800. www.PaleyCenter.org. Mon Closed, Tue-Wed, Fri-Sun 12pm-6pm, Thu 12pm-8pm. ❸ ❼ to Lexington Ave, ❶ ❷ ❸ to 49th, ❶ to 50th, ❸ ❹ ❻ to Rockefeller Center. Adults $10, Students $8.

DINING

UPSCALE

EDITOR'S PICK

Artisanal Bistro & Fromagerie
French

Expect this Midtown bistro and wine bar to be packed every day of the week. Wonderful French-inspired cuisine and a menu of over 250 cheeses from around the world make this a popular destination for the post-work crowd and large parties sharing vats of fondue, cheese and charcuterie, and raw seafood platters. Duck and foie gras rillettes, a rich, fatty spread for country bread, pairs well with a dry wine, which can be ordered by the bottle, glass, or taste from a list of 160. Grilled lamb chops served atop an orzo salad and parsley pistou is exceptional and cooked perfectly, as is the filet mignon. Of course, no experience is complete without partaking in a cheese course. Listed on the menu by animal variety, selections are shuttled to you from the in-house cheese cave, where cheeses are aged and stored under optimal conditions. Finish up with a classic tarte tatin or pavlova.

2 Park Ave (between 33rd St and 32nd St) 212-725-8585. Mon-Thu 5pm-11pm, Fri-Sat 5pm-12am, Sun 5pm-10pm. Brunch Sat-Sun 11am-5pm. ❻ to 33rd, ❸ ❹ ❻ ❼ ❶ ❷ ❸ to 34th. Average entrée $25.

Brasserie *French*

The atmosphere at Brasserie is just as enticing as the food; a set of glass steps leads patrons down into the spacious, cavernous room, furnished with chic décor by Diller and Scofidio. Though corporate diners comprise a visible segment of their clientele, Brasserie also caters to families and couples. As for the food, the highlights are appetizers and desserts—the entrées, while satisfying, sound better on paper

than they actually taste. Of note is the French onion soup, a savory melt-in-your-mouth cheesy treat. The appetizer meats, too, tend to be juicy and finely flavored. For dessert, don't miss the chocolate beignets—cut one in half, fill it with praline ice cream, and dip it in rich chocolate sauce for the ultimate indulgence.
100 E 53rd St (between Lexington & Park Ave) 212-751-4840. Mon-Thurs 4:30pm-12am, Fri-Sat 4:30pm-1am, Sun 4:30pm-10pm. **E V** *to Lexington,* **6** *to 51st St. Average entrée $30.*

Metrazur *New American*
Having enviably scored one of the most dramatic and well-trafficked spaces in town, Metrazur's kitchen juxtaposes the concourse's historic sensibility with contemporary American cuisine. Dishes are refined, yet unfussy—making full use of nature's bounty. The Summer menu takes advantage of heirloom tomatoes, fresh greens, and even fresher seafood. Entrées like risotto and ravioli are more suited to Winter, but available year-long, as is "Ten-Hour-Veal" pappardelle—a pasta dish graced with a sauce of caramelized porcinis, parmesan foam, and a fine veal stock—that is buttery yet clean, rich in flavor yet light. Known for its wine selection, which is on full display near the entrance, the restaurant also accommodates lunchers, the after-work scene, and special events, thanks to free WiFi, a wraparound bar, and a semi-private dining area. Glasses of wine are marked down to $5 per glass on Wine Wednesdays and pair well with the day's selection of fresh oysters.
Grand Central Terminal, East Balcony (42nd St at Park Ave) 212-687-4600. Mon-Fri 11:30am-11:00pm, Sat 5pm-10pm, Sun 2pm-8pm. **4 5 6 7 S** *at Grand Central Station. Average entrée $26.*

MID-RANGE
Chola *Indian*
Chola offers one of the most authentic Indian culinary experiences this side of Jackson Heights. Located on the so-called "upscale curry row," the restaurant is modestly decorated and pleasantly unassuming. Traditional tapestries depicting pastoral bliss grace the walls, while the menu features short lessons in Indian history and culture. Try selections hailing from both North India, such as any of the thick curries, and South India, such as the dosas, enormous lentil crepes. The Bhindi Masala and Chicken Tika stand out as its true winners. Avoid the appetizers, which tend to be greasy and bland compared to the typically flavorful main courses.
232 E 58th St (between 2nd & 3rd Ave) 212-688-4619. Daily 12pm-3pm, 5pm-11pm. **4 5 6** *to 59th. Average entrée $14.*

Islero *Spanish*
While the bar maintains a social vibe, the dining room has high leather chairs along communal, marble tabletops and is more subdued—great for a first date. The menu offers a number of playful tapas plates such as cochinitas, a twist on traditional crispy pork belly that contrasts the salty pork with sweet peaches. The paella for two is filling and packed with fruit de mare. Leave room for the exquisite Galician cheesecake and specialty cocktails like the Pisco Sour, which combines fresh lime juice, egg white, ginger cognac, agave nectar, and grape brandy. Make reservations, the tight quarters are packed by 7pm.
247 E 50th St (between 2nd & 3rd Ave) 212-752-1414. Mon-Sat 5pm-2am. **E V** *to Lexington,* **6** *to 51st. Average entrée $20.*

Rodeo Bar & Grill *Tex-Mex, Bar*
Depending on your point of view, this 20-year-old southwest-themed location, with its vintage neon signs, in-house water tower, and barn door décor, is either sublimely kitschy or wholeheartedly earnest. Either way, homesick Texans and burnt out Midtowners agree that it's a comfortable, welcoming place to go for thick margaritas and generous portions of tex-mex and BBQ fare—all served with a rich smattering of all-American sides. Herbivores can find relief from the smoked ribs and hefty steaks in the (relatively) wide selection of vegetarian quesadillas. Every night offers live alt-country/bluegrass music at the adjacent bar, which is built into an old, broken down bus. Thrill seekers should check out the Rodeo's moan-inducing signature dessert: the Fat Elvis, a deep fried tortilla with banana stuffing, topped with caramel and chocolate sauces and two heaping scoops of vanilla ice cream.
375 3rd Ave (at 27th St) 212-683-6500. Sun-Thurs 11:30am-3am, Fri-Sat 11:30am-4am. Happy Hour: Mon-Sat 4pm-8pm, Sun 6pm-9pm. **6** *to 28th. Average entrée $18.*

MIDTOWN EAST 183

CHEAP

EDITOR'S PICK

Tea Box Café *Teahouse*
This tiny, hushed café, with brushed metal walls, angular furniture, and serene lighting, creates a modern Zen environment in which to unwind. While items from the lunch menu delight—the Jasmine tea-flavored sautéed shrimp salad is perfectly executed—opt for the tea service instead. The East/West Afternoon Tea plays on traditional tea services with salmon and cucumber sandwiches on pressed rice, and chicken and wasabi mayonnaise sandwiches on Japanese bread. A fusion of traditional Asian flavors and French pastry techniques, the dessert selections—including the Green Tea Crème Brulee—are the best part of the experience. Visit the accompanying store for Japanese sweets, teas, and stunning tea sets.
Lower level of Takashimaya, 639 5th Ave (at 54th St) 212-350-0180. Mon-Sat 11:45am-2:45 pm, 3pm-5:30pm. **B D F V** *to 47th-50th St,* **E V** *to 53rd St. Tea Service $7.50-$18.*

Treats Truck *Dessert*
Though many food trucks in the city hold permits for permanent parking, Kim Ima drives her mobile bakery, a truck named Sugar, around the city to different locations daily to serve up her treats in as many neighborhoods as she can. The menu has both standards and rotating specials that all hearken back to retro standbys, like oatmeal jammys and rice crispy squares. The brownies are chewy and satisfying, and Kim will even ask if you prefer the middle or the edge. And for pure, bite-size joy, the caramel crème sandwich and sugar dot seal the deal. Keep a lookout for the silver truck, and if it stops on your block, know that sweet, sweet deliverance awaits.
Most often at 38th St & 5th St (location changes; weekly schedule online at TreatsTruck.com). 212-691-5226. Mon-Sat 12pm-5pm.

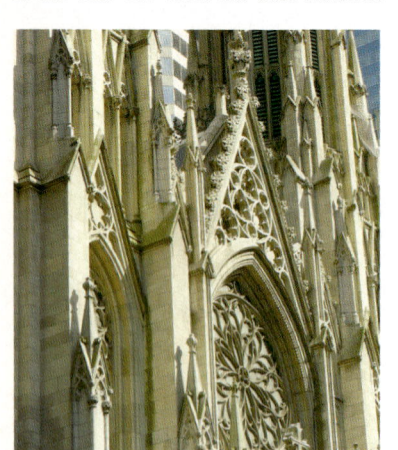

NIGHTLIFE

Beer Bar *Bar*
Located under the Metlife building, this casual watering hole attracts Midtown workers in droves during happy hour. Though there is seating indoors in the space next to Café Centro, most patrons choose to park at one of the high tables outside. The eponymous beverage is of course what everyone is drinking—especially with a good regular selection of draughts, and rotating "guest-taps" as well. Ideal for groups of friends or coworkers still in their corporate get-up, the outdoor area is crowded and deafeningly loud, but a favorite place to unwind or network with fellow corporate types.
200 Park Ave (at 45th St) 212-818-1222. Mon-Fri 11:30am-10:30pm. **4 5 6 7 S** *to Grand Central-42nd St.*

Rink Bar *Bar*
Situated on the grounds of Rockefeller Center's winter ice rink, this chic outdoor bar/restaurant attracts an unpredictable crowd that ranges from tourists to cubicle types. A canopy covers the bar and after a few piña coladas you'll get that familiar rush—it's summertime, and the living is easy. Should you happen to get the munchies, the bar serves food from the Rock Center Café. The drinks, though a tad expensive, are no more over-priced than anywhere else in the area.
5th Ave (between 49th & 50th St) 212-332-7620. Mon-Fri 11:30am-10pm, Sat 11am-11pm, Sun 10am-9pm. **1** *to 50th. Average drink $9.*

Snafu *Bar*
This no-frills fun-house feels like three bars in one. First, there's your purposefully dingy dive,

184 MIDTOWN EAST

with familiar favorites on tap and a cinema-style kettle filling bottomless bowls of salty popcorn. The mezzanine level offers a more subdued lounge vibe, with plush chairs, candlelight, a faux fireplace, and red curtains—an ideal spot if the party downstairs is too much to handle. Finally, there's the subterranean den of retro arcade games like Golden Tee and an ever-active pool table where young professionals blow off steam over 8-ball. On weekend nights, DJs spin top 40 tunes and management breaks out a disco ball and fog machine to stir things up.
127 E 47th St (between Lexington & 3rd Ave) 212-317-9100. Mon-Fri 12pm-4am, Sun-Sat 4pm-4am. ❻ to 51st. Average drink $8.

Turtle Bay Grill and Lounge *Bar*

Turtle Bay is the perfect hybrid of the quintessential laid-back college bar and the swanky Midtown lounge. Although the feasting begins at noon and the festivities continue until the wee hours, this bar/lounge was made for after-work drinks with co-workers and friends. With incredibly reasonably priced drink specials (e.g. Trailer Park Tuesdays featuring $2 PBR and $3 Buds) and three semi-sturdy Beirut tables, Solo cups aplenty, Turtle Bay will get your jobless, couch-hopping friends out of your apartment and your over-ambitious, workaholic co-workers out of the office. The warm, sultry décor (including a functional fire place) keeps this watering hole from feeling too much like a frat house basement while fostering that sense of camaraderie and brotherly love that is inevitable in a room full of twenty-somethings filled to the brim with cheap booze.
987 Second Avenue (Between 52nd and 53rd Streets) 212-223-4224. Mon-Sun 12pm-4am. Average drink $6.

The Volstead *Bar, Lounge*

Named for the sponsor of the Prohibition Act, this spot sees a changing of the guard in the early evening as business diners disperse and the off-work crowd comes to drink and capitalize on the ample lounge space. A number of unusual specialty cocktails are enjoyed by those with a variety of tastes. Try the Eastsider, or, if you are daring, the Jalapeno margarita. The array of mirrors scattered across the walls reflects the sparkling chandeliers, creating a stately and unique décor. Come sunset, the lights dim and the DJ takes control. If you come on a lucky Thursday night you might get to see Babyblu spinning some sweet, sweet vinyl.
125 E 54 St (near Park) 212-583-0411 Mon-Wed 11am - 2am, Thu-Fri 11am-4am, Sat 5pm-4am. ❻ to 51st. Drinks $12.

DAY TO DAY

Community Board 4. *330 West 42nd St. 26th Floor. 212-736-4536*

Local Media: East Midtown Association. *eastmidtown.org.*

Groceries: Food Emporium, *969 2nd Ave. 212-593-2224.* Delmonico Gourmet Food Market, *55 E 59th St, 212-751-5559.* Katagiri, *224 E 59th St. 212-838-5453.*

Gyms: Crunch Fitness, *1109 2nd Ave. 212-758-3434.*

Average Rent: One-bedroom: $3527

Hospital: New York Presbyterian Hospital, *16 E 60th St (between Madison and 5th), 877-697-9355.*

Hostels and Hotels: Pod Hotel, *230 E 51st St (between 2nd and 3rd). 212-355-0300.*

Dog Run: Peter Detmold Park, *E 49th St, at FDR Drive.*

Movie Theater: AMC Loews Kips Bay 15, *570 2nd Ave. 212-447-0638.*

Best Happy Hour: O'Neill's Irish Bar, *729 3rd Ave (between 45th and 46th St), 212-661-3530.*

SHOPPING

Bookoff

Split into three levels, this wonderfully cheap shop has Japanese books in the basement, CDs/DVDs, magazines, and English language books on the first floor, and Manga on the second floor. Charging only $1 a book and $3-7 for CDs, the store has developed something of a cult following. The store offers great prices and a great selection of new music and classics alike that are all in near mint condition. Sell them your old stuff and leave in the black.
12 E 41st St (between 5th & Madison Ave) 212-685-1410. ❼ ❽ ❾ ❿ ⓫ *to 42nd St,* ❹ ❺ ❻ ❼ Ⓢ *to Grand Central,* ❶ ❷ ❸ ❼ Ⓢ ⓃⓇⓆⓌ ⓐⒸⒺ *to Times Square.*

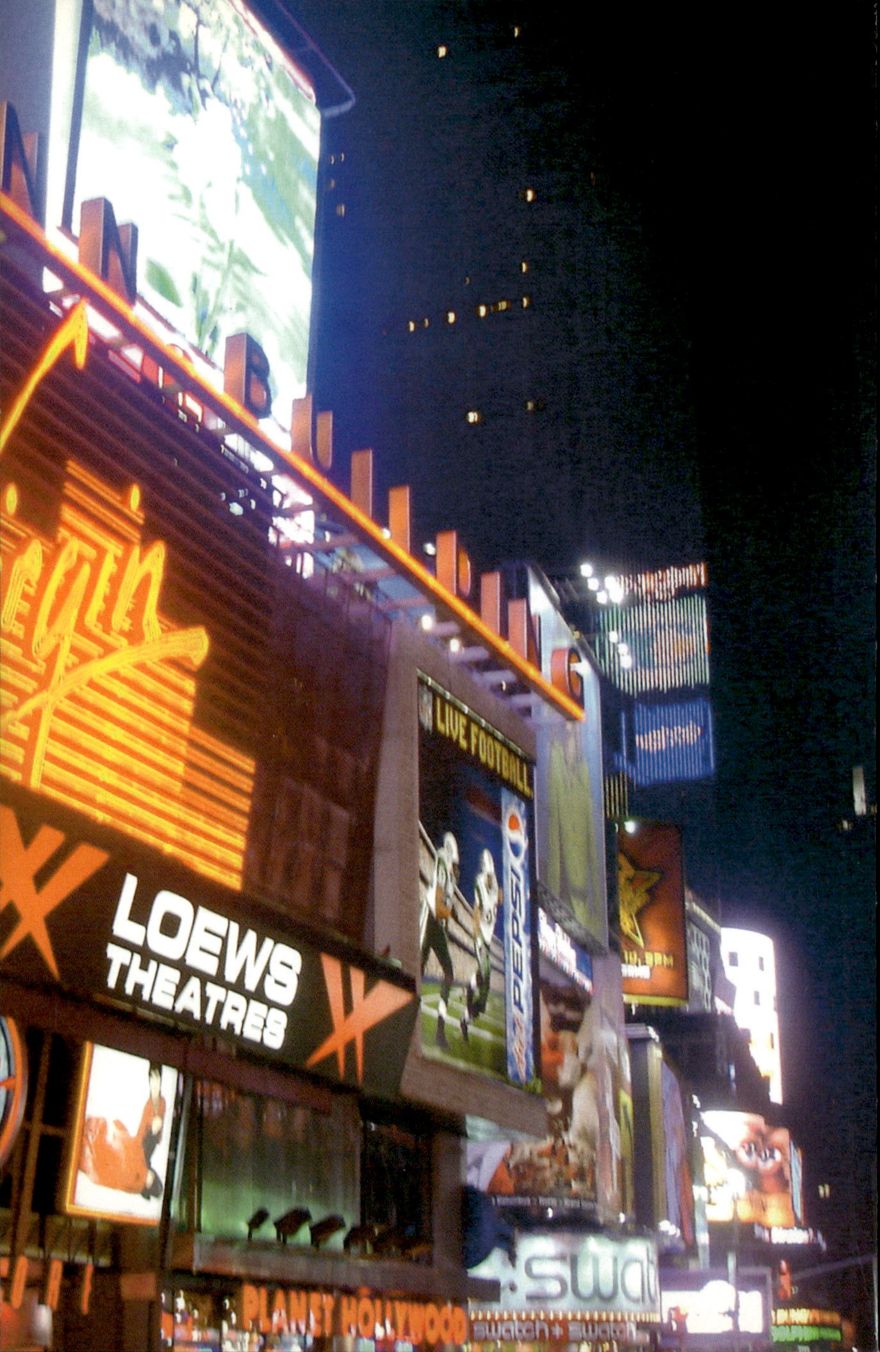
LOEWS
THEATRES
LIVE FOOTBALL
PEPSI
PLANET HOLLYWOOD

MIDTOWN WEST

Midtown West is the glittering intersection of New York's media, commerce, and theater worlds. Laden with the most familiar Big Apple icons, such as landmark skyscrapers, Times Square, Broadway, and Rockefeller Center, the area's appearance today—a teeming field of tourists, corporate workers, and yuppies—belies its seedy past.

The Great White Way was once plagued with drug-trafficking and sordid adult businesses, but a massive cleanup effort polished it anew and transformed it into a family-friendly attraction. Likewise, 8th Ave provides the western boundary for Hell's Kitchen, the historic neighborhood made famous in West Side Story that was once home to immigrant strongholds, machine bloc votes, and organized crime. Following extensive redevelopment and gentrification beginning in the 1990s, real estate agents now pimp the neighborhood as "Clinton" to a moneyed creative class that has brought with it pricey boutiques and 9th Ave's newly abundant dining and nightlife options. Other changes are afoot in Hudson Yards, the far Western portion of the area, which is the current hotbed of development. Proposals include replacing much of its working-class housing and warehouse infrastructure with an extension of the 7 train, a new Penn Station and Madison Square Garden, tax-abated high-rises, a convention center, and a rezoned business district.

There is a dual landscape here—one both magnetic and repellent. It is home to some of the most satisfying and exciting food and theater in the world, but also to garish commercialization perpetuating a snow globe image of the city.

188 MIDTOWN WEST

ATTRACTIONS

Herald Square
If honking horns and the flapping of pigeon wings is music to your ears, forget the Philharmonic and head straight to Herald Square–an hourglass-shaped oasis of greenery divided into two triangular sections (Herald Square to the north and Greeley Square to the south) by the crossing of Broadway and 6th Avenue at 34th street. Once the location of the New York Herald, Herald Square is now home to a 19th century clock with mechanical figures that "strike" a massive bell on the hour. Greeley Square, in turn, celebrates the legacy of the New York Tribune, a past rival of the New York Herald, with a statue of its renowned publisher, Horace Greeley. Join in with the locals by taking advantage of one of the neighborhood delis or pizza places and finding shade in the Square, offered by rows of tall branching trees and bushes that insulate park-goers from the traffic.
B D F V N R Q W to 34th.

Ice Skating at Rockefeller
Couples on dates, playful friends, and young families approximate idyllic wintertime bliss at this classic skating rink guarded by Rockefeller's Prometheus statue. The lengthy wait to get on the ice and fifteen-dollar admission make this strictly a destination spot at night, but during the day beginner skaters dot the rink and give it a friendlier atmosphere.
600 5th Ave (between 48th & 49th St). 212-332-7654. Oct-Apr 8:30am-12:00am. **B D F V** to *Rockefeller Center.*

Madison Square Garden
Affectionately known as simply "The Garden," this arena welcomes slight variations of the same mid-twenties to thirty year old enthusiasts literally everyday. With 20,000 spectators breathing the same air, it often gets sweaty and muggy, but it is this atmosphere, rich with the excitement of so many like-minded, crazed fans, that makes the Garden a powerhouse of straight-up excitement whether it is hosting a regular Rangers game or a sold-out Rolling Stones gig.
Between 31st & 33rd St, 7th & 8th Ave. 212-465-6741. **1 2 3 A C E** to *Penn Station.*

NASDAQ Market Site
It is neither ads nor streetlights that give Times Square its glow, but this blazing tower of information parading the heartrate of the world's economy for all to see. Walk into the base of this glimmering seven-story cylinder of information and see the MarketSite itself, a wall 44 feet tall and 14 feet wide with constantly updated information on market conditions. A robotic studio, with more than twenty remote-operated cameras, shoots footage of news broadcasters for a slew of syndicated television broadcast networks. Public groups are now invited to attend market opening and closing ceremonies, but you must be there before 9am for opening and 3:30pm for closing.
4 Times Square (between 42nd & 43rd St). **1 2 3 7 N R Q W S** to *Times Square.*

CULTURE & ARTS

The Juilliard School
Juilliard is a world-renowned conservatory for actors, musicians, dancers, and playwrights. The School sponsors many free or reduced-price concerts to the public in its famed Alice Tully Hall as well as plays in its several theaters and studios. Tickets are usually free, but because their student performers are so talented, they often get snatched up quickly.
60 Lincoln Plaza. 212-799-5000. **A C B D** to *59th,* **1** to *66th.*

Manhattan Theatre Club
The Manhattan Theatre Club is among the most glitzy and well-known theatre in New York. Since purchasing Broadway's Biltmore Theatre in 2001, they have produced several highly renowned shows (including the Pulitzer prize-winning *Rabbit Hole* and Caryl Churchill's *Top Girls*) and have become known as a leader in bridging the gap between new works and older audiences. MTC's shows are also performed at the New York City Center, an off-Broadway venue. Between the two locations, the company produces seven shows each year. Student subscriptions, which allow you to see shows at both the off-Broadway and

Broadway theatres, are available at highly discounted rates.
Office: 311 W 43rd St, 8th fl. 212-399-3000.
Biltmore Theatre: 261 W 47th St (between 8th & Broadway). ❶❷❸ *to 48th,* ❶❷❹❺❻ *to 50th.*
New York City Center: 131 W 55th St (between 6th & 7th Ave). ❻❼❽❾❿ *to 57th,* ❶❷❸ *to 7th.*

New Dramatists
New Dramatists is a theatre company that provides core infrastructural and artistic support for playwrights. Though ND does not produce any full performances, they hold about 100 readings each year of new works, which are free and usually open to the public. ND has a library which houses all the plays of current and alumni writers. It is open to anyone and is often used by other writers and actors looking for a comfy spot to read in search of inspiration or monologues.
424 W 44th St (near 9th Ave). 212-757-6960. Mon-Fri 10am-6pm. ❶❷❸❹❺❻❼❽❾❿ *to 42nd.*

Playwrights Horizons
Playwrights Horizons is a 37-year-old theatre company which is now one of Off-Broadway's most influential theatres. Each year, Playwrights produces five new plays and one new musical. Past premier productions have included *Sunday in the Park With George*, *I Am My Own Wife*, and *Driving Miss Daisy*. The brightest writing stars choose to have their shows produced at Playwrights, and the biggest acting stars come along for the ride. A student flex pass costs just $60 and gives you 6 tickets to use however you please for an entire season.
416 W 42nd St. 212-564-1235. ❶❷❸❹❺❻❼❽❾❿ *to Times Square. Student rush tickets $15.*

Radio City Music Hall
Radio City is, in many ways, a throwback. The neon lights of the exterior are reminiscent of the 50s, while the interior is classic Art Deco; orange-tinged curtains and the sun-like arc of the stage are suggestive of a refined European style. With seating for just under 6,000, the theater has hosted everything from lectures by the Dalai Lama to the annual Christmas Spectacular featuring the Rockettes. Three mezzanines and no support pillars in the auditorium ensure that every view is a memorable one.
1260 6th Ave (between 50th & 51st St) 212-247-4777. ❶❷❸ *to 50th St.*

DINING

UPSCALE
China Grill *Chinese*
Midtown steakhouse opulence meets Chinese cuisine at this impressively decorated and lamentably overpriced restaurant. Preparation is top quality, but many dishes are Chinese only in name. Szechuan beef is little more than a New York strip sliced thin and drizzled with a spicy sauce—delicious steak, but hardly Szechuan. Shanghai lobster is a standout; the 2.5 pounds

of sweet female lobster basted in butter, curry, and ginger sauce evince the potential of this unlikely culinary fusion. Other dishes seem a bit awkward; high quality wasabi-crusted tuna sashimi is combined with a delicious but overwhelming butter and soy sauce, and the moo shu duck confit with scallion crèpes tastes little different (or better) than its take-out cousin. But for the regulars, mostly bankrolled midtown execs and their clients, the point is not the food, it's the image of success that the 50-foot ceilings and granite floors reflect so well. The bar serves well-made, nothing-new cocktails with fancy names.

60 W 53rd St (between 5th & 6th Ave). 212-333-7788. Dinner Mon-Wed 5:30pm-11pm, Thurs-Sat 5:30pm-12am, Sun 5:30pm-10pm, Lunch Mon-Fri 11:45-5pm. ❺ ❼ *to 53rd,* ❽❾❿ *to 7th,* ❶ *to 50th. Entrées $28-$79.*

DB Bistro Moderne *French*

Daniel Boulud's modern take on the French bistro may be more casual than the other destinations in his New York restaurant archipelago, but the food it serves is far from slouchy. The DB Burger is deservedly the most lauded item on the menu: a warm parmesan bun ensconcing a ground prime rib patty stuffed with braised short rib, foie gras, and black truffle and served with a side of perfectly cooked pomme frites. If you're ever going to spend $32 on a burger, this is the one. Like the burger, other entrées add decadent flourishes to classic bistro fare that, despite the tony clientele and slick dining room, remain true to their hearty pasts. Desserts are equally splendid. The rhubarb tart, when in season, is not to be missed. The noise in the main dining room is deafening, so request a table towards the rear.

55 W 44th St (between 5th & 6th Ave). 212-391-2400. Breakfast Mon-Fri 7am-10am, Sat-Sun 7am-10am. Lunch Mon-Sat 12pm-2:30pm. Dinner Mon 5pm-10pm, Tues-Thurs 5pm-11pm, Fri-Sat 5pm-11:30pm, Sun 5pm-10pm. ❶❷❸❹❺❻❼❽❾❿⓫⓬ *to 42nd. Average entrée $37.*

Kellari Taverna *Greek*

Kellari Taverna serves up authentic, unadulterated Greek cuisine. For starters, don't pass up the katsikisio, a sumptuous dish of warm goat cheese baked with honey, apricot, and almond. The restaurant has an impressive display of fresh fish; it's hard to go wrong with the perfectly grilled and seasoned Fagri, a Mediterranean snapper that drips with flavor. The bustling interior can get loud during the pre-theater dinner rush, but it calms down to a romantic murmur towards the end of the evening. The wine list is extensive and features many Greek varietals.

19 W 44th St (between 5th & 6th Ave). 212-221-0144. Mon-Sun 11:30am-11:30pm. ❶❷❸❹❺❻❼ *to 42nd. Average entrée $27.*

Kobe Club *Japanese*

From the exorbitantly priced imported beef to the 2,000 samurai swords that dangle ominously from the ceiling, Kobe Club is a study in NYC extravagance and excess. Its finest dishes are prepared with beef from Wagyu, Japan. There, cattle are kept docile with a diet of sake and beer and given daily massages, producing "Kobe-style" beef, famed for its unparalleled tenderness and rich flavor. Nowhere in Manhattan will you find a steak as meticulously and professionally prepared, even if that perfection comes at an unreasonably high price. Stick with the Wagyu; the second-tier American and Australian beef dishes do not merit their high costs.

68 W 58th St (between 5th & 6th Ave). 212-644-5623. Mon-Wed 5:30-10:30pm, Thurs-Sat 5:30-11:30pm. ❻ *to 57th. Entrées $34-$240.*

The Sea Grill *Seafood*

A steady flow of tourist dinners and business lunches may provide the backbone of this restaurant, but the unbelievably fresh, locally sourced fish make this a worthy splurge for anyone. The menu changes daily to reflect the day's catch but usually spans an impressive variety of fish and nationalities. A few constants include crabcakes, perfectly crispy and paired with a grainy mustard sauce, oysters on the half shell, and a sushi tuna roll that's well-textured and admirably balances mouth-melting fish with just enough wasabi mayo. Thick, lightly fried portobello fries are served with a ponzu sauce and complement the seafood dishes, and the rich, innovative desserts, such as a crème brulee parfait, are not to be missed.

19 W 49th St (at Rockefeller Center). 212-332-7610. Lunch Mon-Fri 11:30am-2:30pm, Dinner Mon-Sat 5-10pm. ❽❾❿⓫ *to Rockefeller Center-47th St. Average entrée $36.*

MIDTOWN WEST

MID-RANGE
Casellula Cheese & Wine Café
American Nouveau

Cheese connoisseurs rejoice: this laid back location has what you crave and more—gourmet food and a hip, casual vibe. The daily-changing, mind-boggling list of international and exotic cheeses is hand picked by an in-house fromagier who will match that lavender-and-coffee-rubbed Gouda or rose-and-juniper sheep's milk cheese with the perfect garnish. Cheese amateurs need not fear—friendly and knowledgeable servers can steer you to the plate of your dreams. Familiar treats like the Reuben sandwich, made anew with goose breast, and mac 'n' cheese—complete with three cheeses, caramelized onions, and bacon—are made with fresh, locally grown ingredients and gourmet meats. Save room for the plate-licking-good chocolate cake, drenched in rich cream, which goes great with a glass of dark and sweet Bellum Monastrell.

401 W 52nd St (near 9th Ave). 212-247-8137. Mon-Sun 5pm-2am. ❶❷❸ *to 50th,* ❻❼ *to 50th,* ❽❾ *to 49th & 7th. Cheeses $6 each, average entrée $12.*

EDITOR'S PICK

Empanada Mama *Latin American*

At Empanada Mama, traditional fried wheat flour empanadas are packed with a huge variety of non-traditional ingredients. Two standouts are The Viagra, a flavorful stew of shrimp, scallop, and crab meat, and The Polish, an oversized pig-in-a-blanket stuffed with kielbasa and sauerkraut. It is the classic Brasil, though, with its mouth watering mix of ground beef, sautéed onions, olives, and potatoes, that steals the show. In a list of 40 surprising and tasty choices there is hardly a misstep; even the questionable Cheeseburger empanada is a complete success. Sweet sangria makes for a nice counterbalance to the heavy, fried textures. Finish with a rich dessert empanada of fig, caramel, and cheese. Just be prepared to wait in line.

763 9th Ave (between 51st & 52nd St). 212-698-9008. Mon-Sun 11am-12am. ❶❻❼ *to 50th,* ❽❾❿ *to 49th. Empanadas $3, Average entrée $11.*

Kyotofu *Japanese*

This restaurant's specialty is tofu, and even soybean skeptics will be impressed by the dishes that integrate tofu in unique and satisfying ways. The green tea soba noodles have the savory saltiness of soy sauce with an herbal aftertaste and the standout dish, the tofu chicken sliders made with a teriyaki grilled tofu chicken, is exquisite. Kyotofu is also known for its dessert; the best choice is the Kaiseki, a three-course dessert sampler. The first is the signature sweet tofu, a simply phenomenal dish, which tastes like the world's best flan. As for drinks, the sake selection is somewhat intimidating but the extremely helpful staff can suggest the right pairings for your meal. The restaurant interior, which is divided into a bar and seating area, is somewhat cramped, but aesthetically pleasing and exceptionally comfortable.

705 9th Ave (between 48th & 49th St). 212-974-6012. Lunch Tue- Sun 12pm-5:30 pm. Dinner and Dessert Bar Sun, Tues, Wed 5:30pm-12:30am Thurs-Sat 5:30pm-1:30am. ❶ *to 50th. Average entrée $10.*

EDITOR'S PICK

Norma's *American*

It's worth the trouble to wake up early for breakfast if it's going to be at Norma's. Located in a bright, lofty space in the lobby of Le Parker Meridien hotel, the restaurant turns the most important meal of the day into the best one, and the most interesting. The selection is a trove of innovative dishes, like sunny-side-up eggs with duck confit hash, or the Waz-Za, a waffle with fruit in the batter, fruit piled on top, and a thick bruléed raspberry hollandaise topping. Service is gracious and quick to refresh your carafes of French press coffee while you peruse the morning paper. Other niceties include a complimentary shot of the day's smoothie before the meal and palate-cleansing dried orange chips after. Hotel prices mean a hefty bill, but terrific food and cheery environs will ensure you start the day on the right foot.

Le Parker Meridien, 118 W 56th St (near 6th Ave). 212-708-7460. Mon-Fri 6:30am-4:00pm, Sat-Sun 7:00am-3:00pm. ❶❷❸❹ *to 57th St,* ❺❻❼ *to 7th Ave. Average entrée $21.*

Queen of Sheba *Ethiopian*

Diners happily trek to the far West side for the best Ethiopian food in the city. Framed textiles, traditional tables, and depictions of the Queen of Sheba fable set the scene for the classic Ethiopian menu. Kategna, an

amber toast covered in a specialty butter, is a delicious start that rivals the best bread-and-spread baskets. Most entrees include a stew which is eaten by using a piece of injera, a spongy bread made of a grain called teff. The selection of vegetarian and meat sampler dishes are the perfect way to taste a variety of the exotic and flavorful stews. The tibs wot packs a surprisingly spicy punch and stands out among the beef dishes. If you're looking for something a little less messy than the stews, try the lega tibs—sauteed leg of lamb cubes—which offers a milder, though still hearty, option.
650 10th Ave (at 46th St). 212-397-0610. Sun-Thurs 11:30am-11:30pm, Fri-Sat 11:30am-12am. Ⓐ Ⓒ Ⓔ
Ⓝ Ⓡ Ⓠ Ⓦ Ⓢ ❶ ❷ ❸ *to 42nd. Average entrée $12.*

CHEAP
Bread & Olive *Middle Eastern*
A favorite with the lunch crowd, the chicken and beef shawarma are the star of this show, though they sell out quickly. The next best option is the baba ghannouj, a delightfully luscious mash of cool, smoky eggplant and tahini sauce. The simple cracked wheat with tomato is an impressive dish that doesn't appear on the menu, but is usually available by special request. The samboussek jibneh, a crusty pastry stuffed with feta, onion, & parsley, makes a great snack, and surprisingly outperforms its meatier cousin, the beef and pine nut filled samboussek lahme. The sweets, like an overly dry baklava, may not make an impression, but the savories undoubtedly will.
24 W 45th St (near 5th Ave). 212-764-1588. Mon-Thurs 11am-9pm, Fri 11am-7pm. Ⓑ Ⓓ Ⓕ Ⓥ *to 42nd St-Bryant Park,* ❶ *to 42nd-Times Square,* ❼ *to 5th. Average entrée $6.25.*

Burger Joint *American*
Arguably the home of New York's best hamburger, the Burger Joint is hidden at the end of a short corridor in the Parker Meridien hotel's lobby, in a room that conjures up fancy bistros and frathouse basements at the same time. At dinnertime, you will have to stand in line for your food, and fight for one of the few booths. Still, once you're seated at a softly-lit wooden table with French fries in a paper bag, a burger topped with swiss cheese, and a pitcher of beer, you'll be happy you made it.
Le Parker Meridien, 119 W 56th St (near 6th Ave) 212-708-7414. Sun-Thurs 11am-11:30pm, Fri-Sat 11am-12am. Ⓕ Ⓝ Ⓡ Ⓠ Ⓦ *to 57th. Burgers $7.50. Cash only.*

Go!Go! Curry *Japanese*
If the lines are any indication, this fast food joint receives more than its fair share of attention. Two stars share the show: Japanese curry and Hideki Matsui. The latter may not be there in the flesh, but the entire restaurant pays homage to, if not idolizes, the Yankee outfielder. As for the food, the curry is available in five sizes with any of four breaded meat toppings (the pork katsu is best). Skeptics might initially be put off by the strange brown goop ladled over rice, but will indubitably be silenced after savoring just one bite. With ineffable flavor that hints at a mix of vegetables and spices, the curry is a reminder of home for Japanese expats and a new darling for first-timers. Go on the 5th, 15th, or 25th of every month for special coupons.
273 W 38 St (near 8th Ave). 212-730-5555. 10:55am-9:55pm. ❶ ❷ ❸ ❼ Ⓝ Ⓡ Ⓠ Ⓦ Ⓢ *to 42nd,* Ⓐ Ⓒ Ⓔ *to 34th or 42nd. Plates $5.50-9.50.*

MIDTOWN WEST 193

Halal Chicken & Gyro *Halal*
There was once a time when only one chicken and rice stand occupied the 53rd and 6th intersection. The resulting line became so long that a second stand opened up across the street to accommodate the demand, but zealots maintain that the second stand is no substitute. One taste of what the original offers, and you'll understand why. Their chicken and rice is not only cheap and filling ($6 for a generous platter, which includes lettuce and pita bread), but probably one of the best anywhere. The white sauce, a carefully guarded recipe, is heavenly, and the hot sauce is no joke. Although the chicken and rice platter is the most popular dish, the lamb and combination platters are equally tasty, as are the wraps and sandwiches. Beware the imitation carts that clutter the area—look for the trademark yellow uniforms bearing the slogan "We are Different." Indeed!
Southwest corner of 53rd and 6th. 7:30pm-4:30am. **E V** *to 53rd,* **B D E** *to 7th,* **1** *to 50th,* **N R W** *to 49th. Average entrée $6.*

Lucky's Famous *American*
The bright mustard-yellow and ketchup-red walls may at first make this hidden burger joint seem a bit cramped, but the food will win over even the most discerning burger-lover. The classic Cheddar Burger is substantial, basic, and delicious, while the BBQ Bacon Cheddar Burger is sloppy and explosively flavorful. For those who steer clear of steer, the menu includes fully satisfying veggie and turkey burger selections. Fries, thick milkshakes, and Boylan's sodas are perfect burger accompaniments.
370 W 52nd St (near 9th Ave). 212-247-6717. Mon-Sat 11am-1am, Sun 11am-12am. **1** *to 50th,* **C E** *to 50th. Average entrée $6.*

NIGHTLIFE

BB King Blues Bar & Grill
Music Venue, Bar, Restaurant
For B.B. King, nothing goes better with a night of rocking out than a plate of grilled meat. At this dinner club middle-aged music fans and a smattering of youth bond over beers, steaks, and a shared appreciation of good music. The Showcase Room downstairs serves up the booze, and Lucille's Grill upstairs provides the meat. In addition to the price of any concert ticket, the $10 minimum per person per table is excessive, but cushy leather booth seats are well worth the cost. Within walking distance of Penn Station and Port Authority, the music venue attracts tourists and native New Yorkers alike. If the late night Times Square crowd is too much to handle, check out the Sunday Gospel Brunch for performances by the Harlem Gospel Choir and an "all you can eat" southern buffet for some cornmeal crusted fried catfish.
237 W 42nd St (between 7th & 8th Ave). 212-997-4144. Open daily 11am-1am for lunch, dinner, & drinks. Most shows begin at 8pm and 10:30pm. Contact the box office for specific show times. Gospel Brunch every Sunday from 12:30pm-2:30 pm. **1 2 3 7 N R Q W S** *to 42nd St. Average entrée $17. Average drink $11.*

Caroline's on Broadway
Comedy Club
As the premier comedy club in New York, Caroline's is a great night out for locals and tourists alike. With headliners like Janeane Garofalo and Dave Chappelle, the comedians are the real draw, but the club provides an

194 MIDTOWN WEST

ideal setting. Before the show begins, visitors are given a number and wait in the Supper Lounge where they can enjoy a meal—mostly bar food—or drink at the bar. Near show time guests are escorted into the showroom and seated according to number and group size. There is a two drink minimum but the long martini list will loosen up the crowd and satisfy any taste. After the show, visitors can stick around and meet the talent.
1626 Broadway (near 50th St). 212-757-4100. Call for showtimes. ❶ *to 50th,* ❷❸ *to 50th,* ❹❺❻ *to 49th. Average ticket $15-40. Average drink $10.*

Eden and Opera *Nightclub*
What once was the legendary China club is now a three-level club giant. Each level has it's own theme and feel but all are equally decadent. The bottom floor, Crest, is billed as Euro-lounge, with booming techno music and private seating areas. The dramatic second floor, Opera, is painted bordello red and hosts huge seating areas, dance floors, two bars and an area for live music. Eden, the rooftop bar, is missable but offers a reprieve from the sweaty interior. From the bottom up, this club is a study in the ornate, luxurious, and borderline gaudy. Its convenient midtown location and easy door policy lends itself to out of town visitors and those sick of the strict velvet ropes further downtown.
268 W 47th St (between Broadway and 8th Ave). ❷❸ *to 50th. Average drink $11.*

Holland Bar *Bar, Dive*
About twenty people can squeeze into this hole-in-the-wall dive bar. Budweiser and McSorley's ale are always on tap, and pints will run you just four dollars. If you're looking for something harder, the place offers just a small handful of lower shelf whiskeys. But what the Holland lacks in selection, it makes up for in character. The brick walls are covered in newspaper clippings, photos, flags, neon signs, and beer pint Christmas lights dating back to the bar's opening in 1927. If you stop by on Mondays, Wednesdays, and Fridays, you'll get to meet the Holland's "mascot," Doctor Bill, B.S.M.D., who's been tending bar with no-nonsense, easygoing New York charm for the last twenty years. The Holland's most expensive drink is five dollars, and if the Doc is in, that will take you pretty far.
532 9th Ave (between 39th & 40th St). 212-502-4609. Mon-Sat 8am-4am, Sun 12pm-4am. ❶❷❸ *to 42nd. Average drink $4.*

Jimmy's Corner *Dive, Bar*
Former boxing legend Jimmy Glenn is ever-present at this narrow bar, visiting each table to either knock someone's feet off a barstool or regale others with stories of his days in the ring. Aside from the entertainment Glenn offers up, this is your basic dive: offering cheap drinks, a mix of questionable clientele and hip tightwads in dingy yet comfortable quarters. The beer is always cold, the jukebox is usually piping a decent selection of jazz and motown and the crowd is always affable and heavily inebriated.
140 W 44th St (between 6th Ave & Broadway). 212-221-9510. Mon-Fri 11am-4am, Sat 11:30am-4am, Sun 12pm-4am. ❶❷❸❹ *to 42nd,* ❺ *to 5th Ave. Average drink $4.*

Mé Bar *Rooftop Bar*
On the fourteenth floor of La Quinta Inn, Me Bar puts the Empire State Building at your fingertips. Happy hour socializing goes down on the large rooftop, which is modestly decorated with a quaint white picket fence, Christmas lights, and pillow adorned benches to accommodate a crowd that is ready to relax. Young urban professionals drink, swap industry gossip, and try out their best pickup lines while sipping on pomegranate martinis. Between possible business contacts and the hotel's middle-aged guests who have shyly wandered onto the fourteenth floor, an evening of laid-back conversation is a guarantee. Insider's tip: make use of the affordable Korean food that awaits you across the street, this budget friendly bar is B.Y.O.S (Bring Your Own Snacks).
17 W 32nd St (between 5th& 6th Ave). 212-290-2460. Sun-Thurs 5:30pm-12am, Fri 'il 1am, Sat 'til 3am. Happy hour 'til 8. ❶❷❸❹❺❻❼❽❾❿ *at 34th. Average drink $8.*

Rudy's Bar & Grill *Bar, Dive*
With duct-taped booths, dirty floors and some somewhat seedy patrons, nothing

MIDTOWN WEST 195

in this place is polished, but free hot dogs, ridiculously cheap pitchers, and outdoor patio space produce all around dive bar greatness. Though Rudy's teeters precariously between kitschy cool and just plain shady, the friendly neighborhood feel welcomes all types. The booze is dirt-cheap: a bucket—yes, a bucket—of the house beer will set you back a mere $2. The place becomes extremely crowded on the weekends, when even the spacious outdoor patio gets packed with thirsty, cheap, twenty-somethings.
627 9th Ave (near 44th St). 212-974-9169. 8am-4am. ❶❷❸❼ⒷⒹⒻⓋⓃⓇⓄⓌⓈⒶⒸⒺ *to 42nd. Beer $3, $8 for a pitcher. Average cocktail $5. Cash Only.*

Russian Vodka Room *Vodka Bar*
Serving 50 kinds of vodka and 10 homemade infused vodkas, this bar is not for lightweights. The decor is unremarkable, but let's face it, patrons aren't here for the ambiance. Focus on the the flavor of infused vodkas, from the delicious peach or cranberry to the odd, yet still appetizing, horseradish or coriander. Avoid the Garlic, Pepper, and Dill at all costs. The clientele is quirky, to say the least, true slavs mingle with tourists, post-theater patrons and adventurous drinkers, all pounding shots while listening to the live jazz band that plays nightly. Food choices are odd, fish, bread, and cream heavy, but three shots in, they're a godsend. The bar manager is tougher than the KGB, so try your best to stay in line in the face of copious amounts of vodka.
265 W 52nd St (between Broadway & 8th Ave). 212-307-5835. 4pm-4am. ❶ⒸⒺ *to 50th. Shots $5.*

Terminal 5 *Music Venue*
It's big enough to accommodate every last fan (3,000 of them to be exact), but there are enough balconies and floor space to ensure clear sightlines and top-notch acoustics from all three levels. Oddly enough, this huge venue has a cozy feel with vintage furniture dotting the lounges and 4 bars that are usually uncrowded and speedy. For those who get the munchies before, during, or after the show, the third floor has an Empanada Mama outpost. The billings are largely indie and the opening acts are usually the "next big thing," so arrive early to beat the crowds.
610 W 56th St (at 11th Ave). 212-260-4700. Terminal5.NYC.com. ⒶⒸⒷⒹ❶ *to 59th.*

SHOPPING

Midtown Comics
Clean and extremely well organized, Midtown offers a vast selection of graphic novels both mainstream and alternative. Their back issue prices are fair and their stock regularly changes. Midtown gets extremely crowded on new-comic book day, but they offer a subscription service to avoid the rush. The Grand Central store is similar but smaller. Keep an eye out for semi-regular sales on back issues.
200 W 40th St (at 7th Ave). 212-302-8192. Mon-Sat 11am-9pm, Sun 12pm-7pm. ❶❷❸❼Ⓝ🅁Ⓠ🆆Ⓢ *to Times Sq. Grand Central location: 459 Lexington Ave (at 45th St). Mon-Sat 11am-9pm, Sun 12pm-7pm.* ❹❺❻❼ *to Grand Central.*

Minamoto Kitchoan
This confectionary would like to broaden your geo-culinary outlook. The education comes at a price. A box of the pastries can run to three figures; however, sample one or two at $3-5 a pop to experience what many consider the most authentic Japanese pastry in the city. The helpful ladies behind the counter are crucial in reassuring newcomers wary of desserts containing ingredients such as red beans. Their fukuwatshi senbei, a vanilla filled cookie, is delicious. Be sure to check for seasonal treats.
608 5th Ave (at 49th St). 212-489-3747. ❽Ⓓ🅕Ⓥ *to 47th-50th.*

Redbag
For discounted jeans and drool-worthy garb with top designer labels, this friendly shop is the place to come. The owner sells his own line alongside Nicole Farhi, J Brand, Joe's, and Missoni, to name a few. He is happy to adjust clothes to give them a perfect fit and will fix you a coffee as you shop. Although new merchandise comes in regularly, check the website for sample sale dates to get a jump on the shop's growing base of loyal clients.
250 W 39th St (between 7th & 8th Ave). 212-719-0001. Mon-Fri 9:30am-7:30pm, Sat 10am-6pm. ❶❷❸❼ⒶⒸⒺ Ⓝ🅁Ⓠ🆆Ⓢ *to 42nd.*

DAY TO DAY

Community Board 4 : *330 W 42nd St # 26 212-736-4536.*

Local Blog: midtownlunch.com

Groceries: Whole Foods, *10 Columbus Circle, 212-823-9600.* Food Emporium, *810 8th Ave, 212-977-1710.*

Gyms: Physique 57. *24 West 57th St. 212-399-0570.*

Rent: One-bedroom: $1500-3000, Two-bedroom: $2000-4000.

Hospital: Saint Vincent's Midtown Hospital, *415 W 51st St. 212-459-8277.* St. Luke's Roosevelt Hospital, *425 W 59th St. 212-523-6003.*

Hotels: Holiday Inn, *440 West 57th St. 212-581-8100.* Herald Square Hotel, *19 West 31st St. 212-279-4017.*

Dog Runs: Hudson River Park, *Pier 84 at W 44th St.* DeWitt Clinton Park, *W 52nd St & W 54th St.*

Movie Theaters: AMC Empire 25, *234 W 42nd St. 212-398-3939.* AMC Loews 14, *312 W 34th St. 212-244-8850.*

Best Happy Hour: O'Reilly's Pub, *54 W 31st St. 212-684-4244. Mon-Sat 11:30am-4am, Sun 11:30am-12am.*

Ruby et Violette
This boutique devoted to that least pretentious of desserts is a must-visit. A dozen may set you back $18, but the cookies are substantial enough and come in such interesting flavors that the occasional cookie upgrade is worth it. They claim to bake the best chocolate chip cookies around, but bypass that simple creation for the espresso bean or the kitchen sink. Pretty packaging makes for a yummy gift.
457 W 50th St (at 10th Ave). 877-353-9099. Mon-Sat 10am-10pm. ⒸⒺ *to 50th.*

198 MIDTOWN WEST

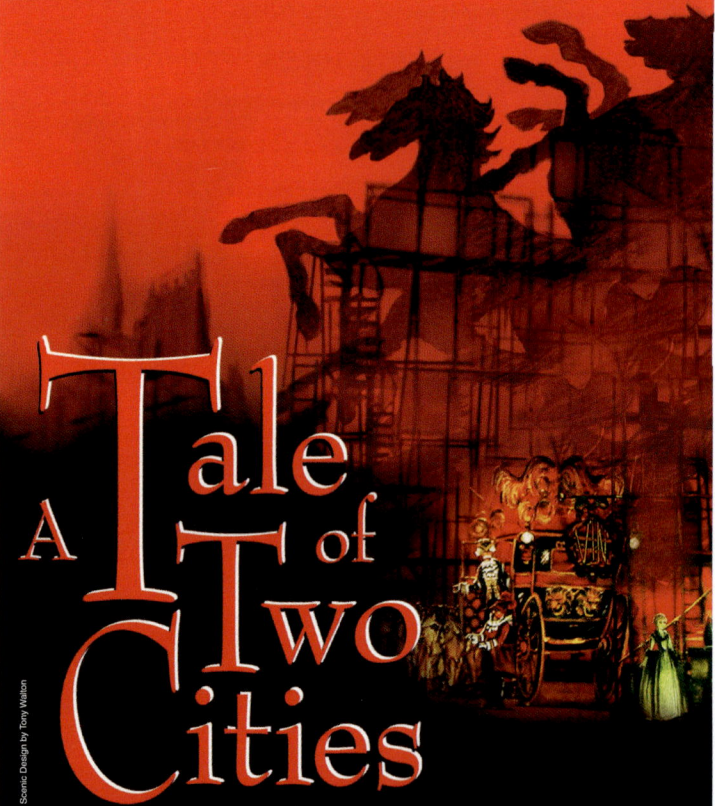

"NO MATTER HOW LONG YOU LIVE, YOU'LL NEVER SEE A MORE EXCITING PRODUCTION!"
–Terry Teachout, The Wall Street Journal
PATTI LuPONE
GYPSY
TONY AWARD® WINNERS!
PATTI LuPONE BEST ACTRESS
BOYD GAINES BEST FEATURED ACTOR
LAURA BENANTI BEST FEATURED ACTRESS
GOLD CARD EVENTS PREFERRED SEATING
800-292-9465
RESTRICTIONS APPLY
Telecharge.com or 212-239-6200 • Groups (10+) 1-800-BROADWAY
St. James Theatre, 246 West 44th Street • GypsyBroadway.com
Photo: Joan Marcus

200 MIDTOWN WEST

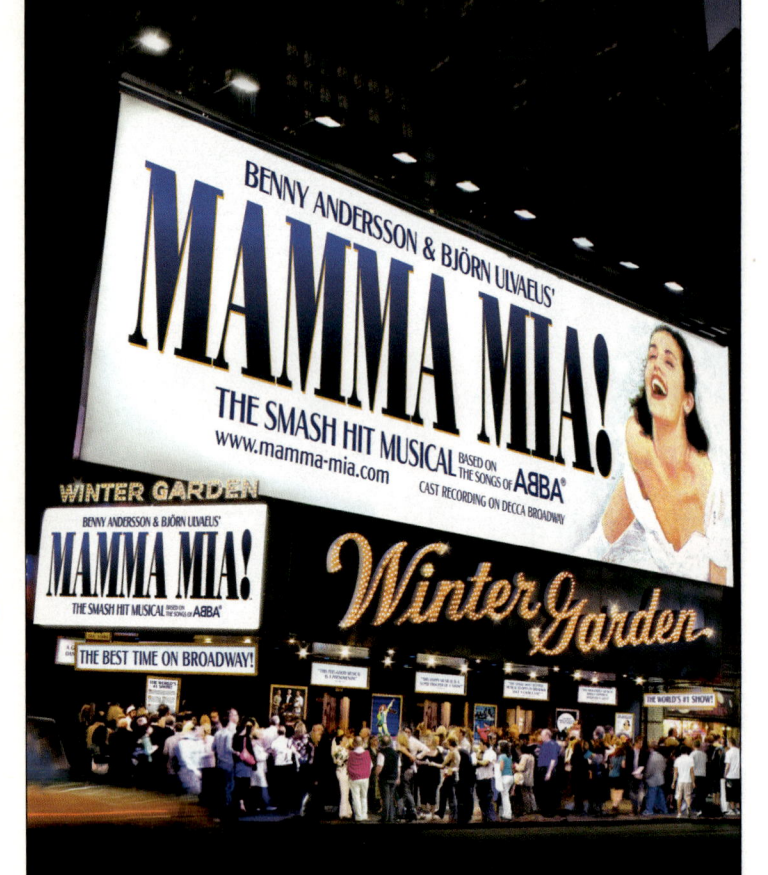

Tonight belongs to...

PHANTOM

TICKETS AVAILABLE FROM $26.50 TO $111.50*
TELECHARGE.COM or (212)239-6200 MAJESTIC THEATRE, 247 W. 44th St.
*Higher prices may apply to holiday performances.

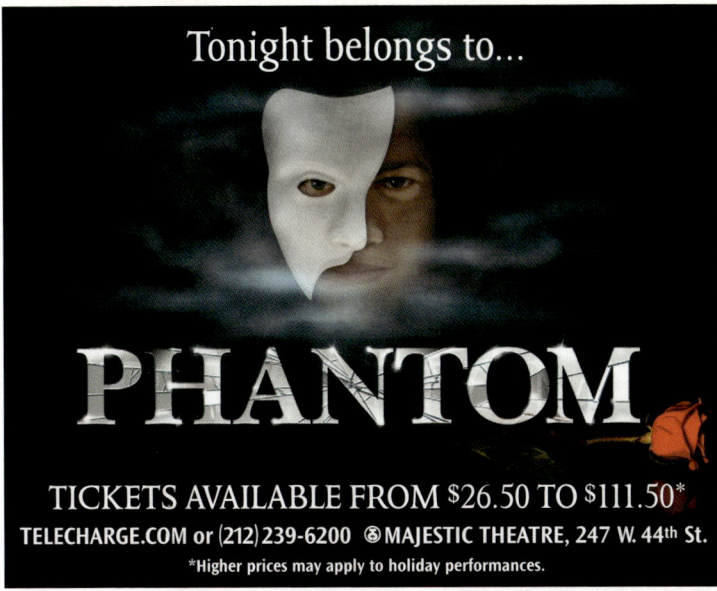

Before Stephen Schwartz wrote "Wicked," he wrote...

GODSPELL

BACK ON BROADWAY!

Telecharge.com
(212)239-6200
Groups (15+):
1-800-BROADWAY

Barrymore Theatre
243 West 47th St.

GodspellOnBroadway.com

MIDTOWN WEST 201

"STOMP DOES FOR RHYTHM WHAT FREUD DID FOR SEX!"
—TIME OUT, LONDON

STOMP

$40 Sundays @ 7PM

Tue-Fri @ 8
Sat @ 3&8
Sun @ 3&7

ORPHEUM THEATRE

Second Avenue @ 8th Street www.stomponline.com
Box Office (212) 477-2477 *ticketmaster* (212) 307-4100

202 MIDTOWN WEST

MIDTOWN WEST 203

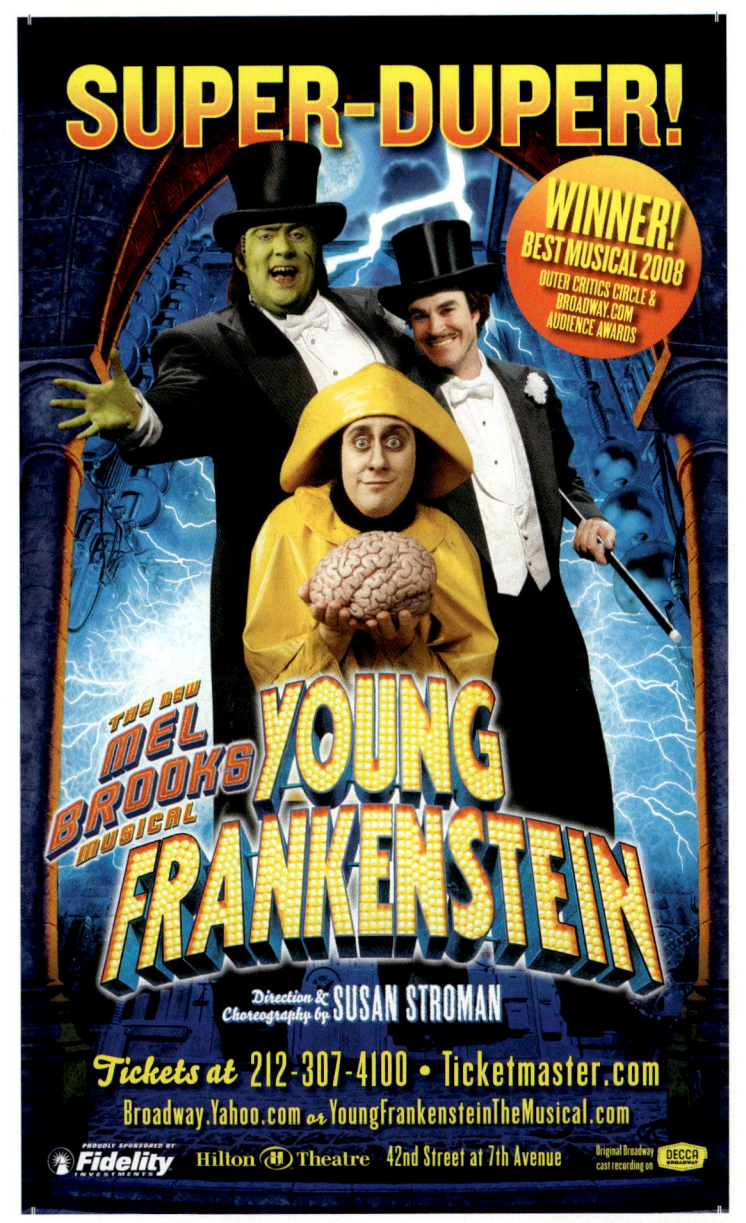

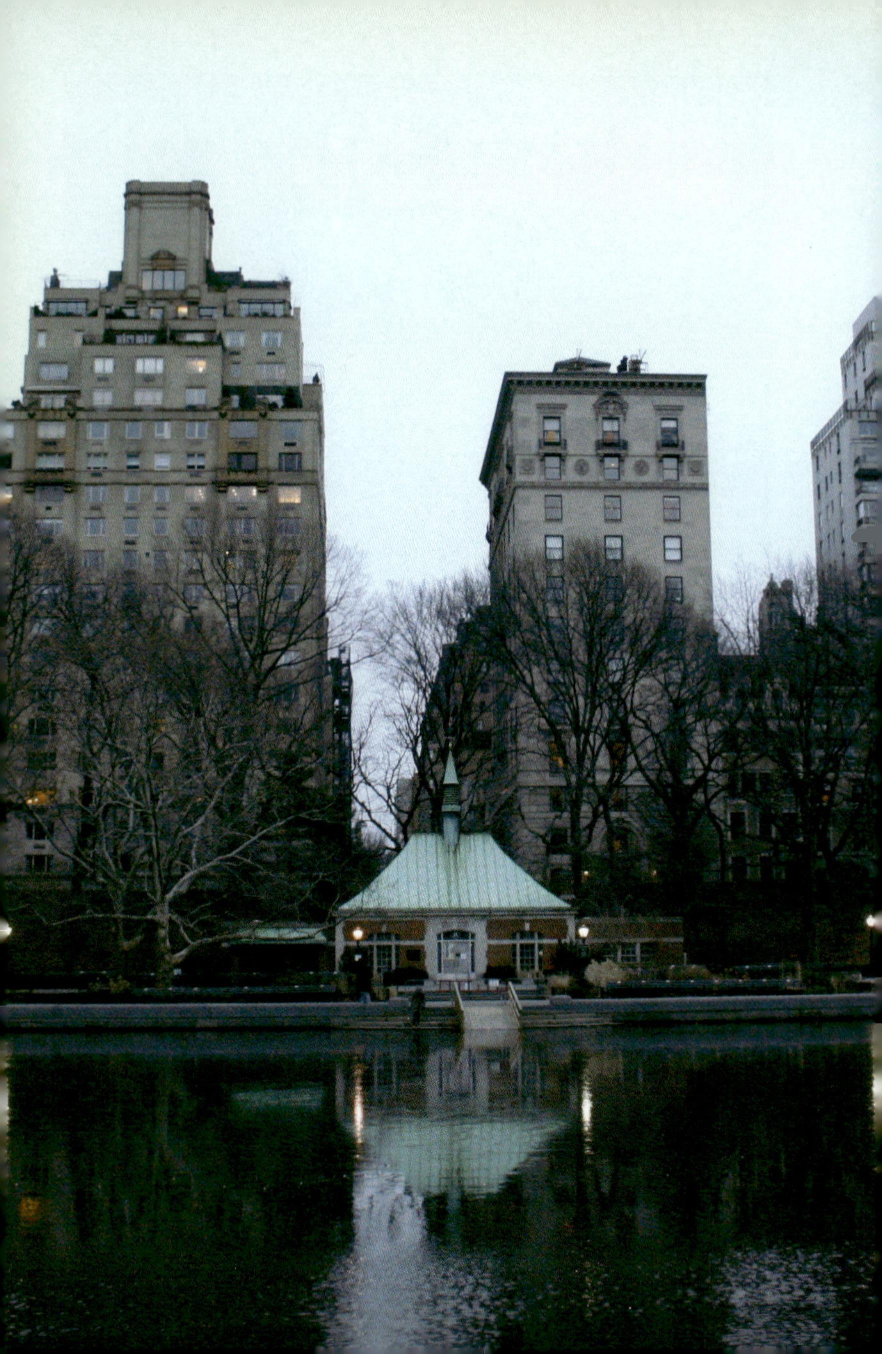

UPPER EAST SIDE

Woody Allen immortalized it, Tom Wolfe parodied it, Sex and the City reveled in it, and the tell-all book The Nanny Diaries scandalized it. The Upper East Side is the first and last word in old money, style and aristocracy.

Of course, an area as large as the Upper East Side could not be so homogeneous; sprawling over nine avenues and almost 40 blocks, the neighborhood includes both palatial luxury townhouses as well as cramped studios. A few blocks from the Fifth Avenue duplexes with views of Central Park lie the bars, burrito-joints, and high-rises that line Second, Third, and Lexington Avenues.

As with most of upper Manhattan, there wasn't much to see here until Central Park opened to the public in the 1860s. The eastern section of the region developed quickly as the Second and Third Avenue elevated lines, completed in 1879, eased transportation between the urban center and the outlying regions. The development that would earn the Upper East Side its elite reputation, however, was construction to the west along what would become the luxurious Fifth, Madison, and Park Avenues. From Astor to Tiffany, New York's wealthiest barons erected mansion after mansion facing the new park.

The Upper East Side today is a top cultural destination. Museum Mile, a section of Fifth Avenue home to nine museums, is here, in addition to the prestigious Frick Collection and Whitney Museum of American Art. The neighborhood's galleries are among the city's most esteemed, offering Picassos, Braques, and Chagalls to a public that can actually afford them. But don't let the gated community feeling intimidate you; the only thing you need to appreciate the artistic splendor of the Upper East Side is a pair of eyes.

206 UPPER EAST SIDE

ATTRACTIONS

Carl Schurz Park
Picturesque Carl Schurz Park offers unobstructed views of the East River, Randall's and Roosevelt Islands, and the Triborough and Queensboro bridges along its promenade—perfect for an early morning jog. A popular community hangout for Yorkville residents, the park schedules a variety of events year-round, including a summer concert series, art shows, and the holiday tree-lighting. For those with pets or small children, the park's amenities include two dog runs and a playground. With plenty of benches, Carl Schurz Park is a great place to have lunch or to take a breather, especially during the springtime bloom. The park is also the home of the beautifully restored Gracie Mansion, the mayor's official residence, which offers free tours every Wednesday.
East End Ave to East River, 84th-90th Sts. 212-459-4455. ❹❺❻ *to 86th.*

The Seventh Regiment Armory
Dedicated in 1880 to Colonel Lefferts' Seventh Regiment of the State Militia, this building is still used as an Army National Guard command post. Despite the soldiers in fatigues and Gothic crenellations, an interior built under the direction of the wealthy members of the "Silk Stocking Regiment" boasts a more luxurious aesthetic: coffered ceilings, carved wood panels, marble fireplaces, and Tiffany windows. The Armory is now a venue for the fine arts, exhibiting everything from operas hosted by Lincoln Center to Asia Week's International Asian Art Fair. A list of upcoming events can be found on the Armory website, and tours can be scheduled over the phone.
643 Park Ave (between 66th & 67th St). 212-616-3930. ❻ *to 68th St.*

Temple Emanu-El
Since its founding in 1845 as the first Reform Jewish congregation in New York City, Temple Emanu-El has become one of the most prominent and visible symbols of Judaism in New York City. Built in the Romanesque Revival style, Temple Emanu-El is the largest Jewish house of worship in the world. Its façade showcases a circular stained glass window which has a six-pointed star in the center. Symbols representing the twelve tribes of Israel are displayed in an arch framing the window as well as on the three bronze doors at the entrance. Famous members of the Temple Emanu-El congregation include Joan Rivers, Louis Marshall, Eliot Spitzer, and Mayor Michael Bloomberg.
1 E 65th St (at 5th Ave). 212-744-1400. Thurs-Sun 10am-4:30pm. ❻ *to 68th.*

CULTURE & ARTS

Asia Society and Museum
The Asia Society headquarters in New York houses the Rockefeller Collection of Asian Art, which displays artifacts dating from the eleventh century BCE to the nineteenth century CE in addition to a contemporary Asian art collection. Particular pieces of note include the Song and Ming Dynasty Chinese ceramics, Chola-period Indian bronzes, and Southeast Asian sculptures. Also, visit the Society for educational programs and events, which include films, lectures, and performing arts shows. For a bit of tranquility amidst the bustling city, go to the glassed-in Garden Court, complete with skylights, flowering trees, and a café that serves seasonal, pan-Asian cuisine.
725 Park Ave (at 70th St). 212-288-6400. Tue-Sun, 11am-6pm, Fri 11am-9pm. Adults $10, Students $5. ❻ *to 68th.*

Cooper-Hewitt National Design Museum, Smithsonian Institution
This museum includes over 250,000 objects and an extensive library showcasing both the history of design and contemporary projects. Situated in the old Carnegie Mansion, it is the only museum in the country dedicated entirely to design. Cooper-Hewitt is also committed to education, offering programs for all levels and ages from youth programs to a Masters of Arts. They offer free daily tours of the museum and special design events.
2 East 91st St (at 5th Ave). 212-849-8400. Mon–Thur 10 am–5 pm, Fri 10 am–9 pm, Sat 10 am-6 pm, Sun 12pm-6 pm. Adults $15, Students with ID $10. ❹❺❻ *trains to 96th.*

French Institute Alliance Française
The French Institute Alliance Française is a non-profit organization dedicated to French language and culture. Housed in a beautiful Beaux Arts building, their Language Center has over 6,000 students, holds classes and workshops for all ages, and claims the lowest price per hour with the smallest class size in the city. The Haskell Library has the most complete collection of works of any private French library in the country with 35,000 volumes. FIAF also offers live performing arts events and the year-round French cinema series, CinémaTuesdays.
22 East 60th St (between Park & Madison Ave). 212-355-6100. Mon-Thurs 9am-8pm, Fri 9am-6pm, Sat 9am-5pm (closed Sat July 7–September 2). N R W *to 5th Ave.*

Goethe-Institut
The Goethe-Institut is committed to presenting German culture to an audience of Americans and ex-pats. Their language department mainly focuses on teaching workshops and seminars for German language educators and offers a range of marketing and teaching materials designed to encourage the study of the German language. The Goethe-Institut library collection is comprised of books, audio-visual materials, newspapers, and journals in addition to displays of new German literature. The institute is also committed to promoting German arts; they have film series, exhibitions, and a variety of performing arts presentations, all of which are open to the public.
1014 5th Ave (at 83rd St). 212-439-8700. Tues 12pm-7pm, Wed 12pm-5pm, Thurs 12pm-7pm, Fri-Sat 12pm-5pm. 4 5 6 *to 86th.*

The Frick Collection
Formerly the home of steel tycoon Henry Clay Frick, the Frick Collection is one of the best small art museums in the country. The collection, which is made up of over 1,100 works of art from the Renaissance to the late nineteenth century, contains painting, sculpture, furniture, porcelain, textiles, enamels, silver, and gilt bronzes from mostly European origin. Just a few of the artists represented at the Frick: Giovanni Bellini, El Greco, Frans Hals, Rembrandt van Rijn, Johannes Vermeer, and James McNeill Whistler.
1 E 70th St (between 5th & Madison Ave). 212-288-0700. Thur-Sat 10am-6pm, Sun 11am-5pm. 6 *to 68th.*

Solomon R. Guggenheim Museum

Hailed as one of the most iconic achievements of architect Frank Lloyd Wright, the simple, circular exterior of the Solomon R. Guggenheim Museum is a stark contrast to the rest of rigid and ornate Fifth Avenue. Inside, the permanent collection flows organically around the spiraling hallways and boasts the largest collection of works by famed Russian abstract painter Vasily Kandinsky. Go on Fridays, when Pay What You Wish admission begins at 5:45pm. For something a little different, on the first Friday of every month the Guggenheim hosts First Fridays where, for $25, you can get a drink, dance to a live DJ, and enjoy the world-class art from 9pm to 1am.

1071 5th Ave (at 89th St). 212-423-3500. Sat-Wed 10am-5:45pm, Fri 10am-7:45pm. ❹❺❻ *to 86th. Adults $18, students $15.*

Jewish Museum

Housed in the remarkable French Gothic chateau-style Walburg mansion, the Jewish Museum is committed to investigating the wide range of achievements in Jewish culture. The permanent collection is home to over 28,000 objects ranging from paintings, sculpture, and photographs, to ethnographic and archaeological artifacts, to ceremonial objects and mass-media materials. The museum is also famous for its interdisciplinary exhibitions and its exhibitions that highlight the arts in terms of social history.

1109 5th Ave (at 92nd St). 212-423-3200. Sat-Wed 11am-5:45pm, Thurs 11am-8pm, Adults $12, Students $7.50, Saturday free. ❻ *to 96th.*

Metropolitan Museum of Art

This world famous museum stretches almost four New York City blocks, nearly a quarter of a mile long. The more than two million works of art found in the museum's permanent collection are taken from around the globe and date from ancient to contemporary times. From Hokusai's *The Great Wave off Kanagawa*, to Velázquez's *Juan de Pareja*, to Jasper Johns' *White Flag* to the oldest existing piano, some of the world's greatest treasures are housed here. The Met can get very busy on the weekends; to avoid crowds try going on a Friday or Saturday evening when the museum is open until 9pm.

1000 5th Ave (at 81st St). 212-535-7710. Closed Mon, Tues-Thurs 9:30am-5:30pm, Fri and Sat 9:30 am-9:00 pm, Sunday 9:30 am-5:30 pm. ❹❺❻ *trains to 86th. Admission free with student ID. Suggested donation $20.*

The Neue Galerie

Situated on the famed Muesum Mile in an ornate Louis XIII building designed by the architects of the New York Public Library, the Neue Galerie is a museum exclusively devoted to German and Austrian artistic movements. Covering works made from 1890-1940, the collection is comprised of a wide range of mediums including painting, sculpture, works on paper, decorative arts, and photographs. Austrian fine and decorative arts, including paintings by Gustav Klimt, are located on the second floor of the building, while German works by artists such as Paul Klee and Otto Dix are featured on the third floor. For some of the best Linzertorte and other Viennese delicacies, take a trip to one of the museum's two cafés, both of which are outfitted with designs by Josef Hoffmann.

1048 5th Avenue (between 85th & 86th St). 212-628-6200. Sat, Sun, Mon, and Thurs 11am-6pm, Fri 11am-9pm. ❻ *to 86th.*

Whitney Museum of American Art

Founded in 1931, the Whitney Museum of American Art houses one of the preeminent collections of twentieth-century American art. Drawings, paintings, prints, photographs, sculptures, and multimedia installations are all included in the the museum's 12,000 work permanent collection. It is also distinguished by its thorough representation of several renowned artists. The museum's Edward Hopper and Alexander Calder collections are the largest in the world, and their concentration of Reginald Marsh's works is also incomparable. Their biennial exhibition, which presents work by young, up-and-coming artists is widely considered to be gold standard amongst trend-setting expositions of contemporary art.

945 Madison Ave (at 75th St). 212-570-3600. Closed Mon-Tues, Wed-Thurs 11am-6 pm, Fri 1pm-9pm, Sat-Sun 11am-6 pm. Adults $15, students $10. ❻ *to 77th.*

UPPER EAST SIDE 209

DINING

UPSCALE

EDITOR'S PICK
Café Boulud *French*
Daniel Boulud's first, eponymous restaurant was founded in Café Boulud's current location, just off Central Park. The restaurateur still supervises his talented executive chef, Gavin Keysen, and a waitstaff among the city's most skilled. An order of ravioli is garnished with chanterelles, delicate fiddlehead ferns, and mild garlic foam; seared arctic char melts away like a much lighter fish; braised duck in Moroccan spices are both peppery and subtle. The menu is centered on four culinary themes—tradition, season, garden, and world. Though it changes from month to month, some things never will. The kitchen's silverware bears the reassuring marks of regular use, and a section of cushion in one booth has been worn in—like a favorite armchair—by a single loyal patron. Settle in and save room for the desserts, crafted with as much care and attention to detail as Café Boulud's main courses.
20 E 76th St (at Madison Ave). 212-772-2600. Mon 5:45pm-11pm, Tues-Sat 12pm-2:30pm and 5:45pm-11pm, Sun 11:30am-2:30pm and 5:45pm-10pm. ⑥ *to 77th. Average entrée $36. Jacket recommended.*

Daniel *French*
The Renaissance dining room is regally appointed and hosts an upper-crust clientele; but service is so remarkably genial and attentive, catering to and anticipating every need, that every patron dines in comfortable splendor. A three course prix-fixe menu is overrun with exquisite preparations from the renowned chef and his first-rate kitchen lineup. As top restaurants do, the menu swaps out dishes and experiments with new ones frequently, but typically French preparations of foie gras, confits, beef cheek or short ribs can always be found, and are superlative indulgences. Discerning diners will appreciate touches like a spinach subric (croquette with bechamel sauce) accompanying seared ribeye, a dish mined from the French culinary bible of Escoffier. But global cuisine is also given a nod on the menu; za'taar, a Middle Eastern herb blend, kataifi phyllo pastry, and Indian vadouvan spices have all made cameos. No matter the influence, every dish is a lesson in careful crafting and winning flavor. In all respects, Daniel stands alone.
60 E 65th St (at Park Ave) 212-288-0033. Mon-Thu 5:45-11pm, Fri-Sat 5:30-11pm. ⑥ *to 68th. Prix fixe $105. Jacket mandatory.*

Payard Patisserie *French*
From the mahogany doors to the bi-level dining room, Payard captures the spirit of an age-old Parisian bistro. Dark lacquered wood and ivory marble are reminiscent of chocolate and cream, both of which are trophy ingredients in Payard's gorgeous confections—eye candy displayed in the café that is enough to distract any diner bound for dinner. A proper meal should not be skipped, but used as a prelude to a sweet finale. Twice-baked upside-down cheese soufflé is velvety and drowned in a decadent parmesan cream sauce and white truffle oil. And steamed sea bass is tender and light, in a broth with fennel, lemon, and thyme. But dessert is the unequivocal main attraction; the bistro's composed desserts include dark chocolate soufflé and a hazelnut candy bar—a gourmet take on a Snicker's. Or feel free to order a feast from the glass cases out front: tarts dolled up with fresh fruit, marzipan, and meringue, neat slices of Opera cake, glossy chocolate éclairs, mousse cakes in a number of colors, mini cookies, champagne truffles…
1032 Lexington Ave (near 74th St). 212-717-5252. Mon-Thurs 5:45pm-10:30pm, Fri-Sat 5:45pm-11:00pm. Lunch Mon-Sat 12pm-3pm. Tea Mon-Sat 3:30pm-5pm. ⑥ *to 77th. Average entrée $30.*

Savarona *Turkish*
This polished restaurant serves modern Turkish dishes influenced by royal Ottoman cuisine. The spacious, minimalist dining room provides a soothing background for a fantastic, if sometimes overwhelmingly complex, meal. Their preparation of fish is nothing less than genius. The smoked salmon roll—cooked with feta, spring onion, and caviar—is an elegant study in Mediterranean seafood, while the roasted umbrina, served in a parchment paper bowl with pumpkin, mushrooms, and champagne foam, is an unusual treat. Meat and poultry are equally excellent; chicken and beef kebabs will satisfy the strongest primal cravings

for meat on a stick, while the grilled lamb chops & loin is a more restrained and subtle dish. Cocktails complement the food without being gimmicky. Gin and tonics infused with basil and lime and blood orange margaritas are but a few of the tasty concoctions offered at the bar. Service is professional, but sometimes uninformative, a frustrating flaw when sampling the unfamiliar flavors of the chef's tasting menu.
420 E 59th St (between 1st Ave & Sutton Pl). 212-371-6300. Dinner Mon-Sun 5pm-12am. Brunch Sat-Sun 11am-4pm. N R W 4 5 6 to 59th, F to 63rd. Average entrée $26.

MID-RANGE

Alice's Tea Cup *American*
Sparkly butterflies dot the ceiling above Alice in Wonderland mural-covered walls, providing a whimsical backdrop for teatime. The 11-section tea menu caters to every tea lover's tastes, from sweet Chocolate Chai to exotic Red Bush Phoenix. Classic smoked salmon or black forest ham with Gruyere tea sandwiches abandon their dainty English progenitors and make for a satisfying meal. Combination meals such as The Mad Hatter allow patrons to sample tea, sandwiches, dessert, and the daily selection of fresh scones. Don't miss Jean's Not-Yet-But-Soon-To-Be-Famous Mocha Chocolate Chip Cake—it's the perfect indulgent end to any meal or cup of tea.
220 East 81st St (between 2nd & 3rd Ave). 212-734-4832. Mon-Sun 8am to 8pm. 4 5 6 to 86th. Average entrée $7.

Felice Wine Bar *Italian*
With glass jugs hanging from the ceiling, exposed brick walls, and wine barrels incorporated into its décor, Felice Wine Bar exudes rustic comfort and provides an ideal venue for a romantic evening or an oenophilic adventure. More of a full-service restaurant than many of the city's ubiquitous wine bars, Felice offers an impressive array of Tuscan wines and Milanese food. The generously portioned tri-colored salad with avocado and diced mozzarella makes a nice starter, as does the sharable plate of crostini. The pan-seared Mediterranean sea bass marinated in a lemony silmoriglio sauce with fresh vegetables is a light yet satisfying main course that perfectly compliments the Felice house wine, a blend of Chardonnay and Vermentino. The four cake desserts are simple, but well-executed.
1116 1st Ave (at 64th St) 212-593-2223. Sun-Wed 11:30am-11pm. Thurs-Sat 11:30am-12am. 6 to 69th. Average entrée $20.

EDITOR'S PICK

Fig and Olive *Mediterranean*
Priding itself in its namesake ingredients, every dish is infused with figs, olive oil, or both. With a vast selection of olives, an even broader offering of foreign olive oils, and wonderfully tasty figs, the restaurant provides a gimmick that is pleasantly satiating. For lighter dishes, a varied choice of Mediterranean pastas, salads, and soups all exceed expectations. Go with the Fig and Olive Mediterranean tasting: a mix of rosemary chicken, grilled skewered lamb, and grilled shrimp. But with so much to try on the menu, the possibilities are endless – and it's hard to go wrong.
808 Lexington Ave (between 62nd & 63rd St) 212-207-4555. 11am-11pm daily. F to 63rd, 4 5 6 N R W to 59th. Average entrée $25.

Hacienda de Argentina *Argentinian*
Plush cow-hide booths, Spanish brick walls,

and hanging candle chandeliers create a fabulously romantic atmosphere. Meats are Hacienda's real specialty and while no steak is a bad choice, the filet mignon rises above and beyond, as do the juicy, tender chicken skewers. All meats are enhanced with Argentinean Chimichurri sauce—a unique blend of parsley, garlic, and olive oil. The best meat accompaniment is the bizarre and incredible grilled provolone dish, consisting of a plate covered in melted, grilled, seasoned provolone. No meal is complete without the banana crepe dessert, drizzled with rich chocolate and divine dulce de leche.

339 E 75th St (between 1st & 2nd Ave) 212-472-5300. Sun-Tues 5pm-12am, Wed-Sat 5pm-3am. ❹❺❻ *to 77th. Average entrée $25.*

Peri Ela *Turkish*
With a warm, comfortable interior, this small casual restaurant resembles a modern-day Turkish eatery. Try the simply prepared, traditional starter dishes that come alive with fresh ingredients and vivid flavor. The patlican salatasi, an eggplant dip mashed with garlic and olive oil, is perfectly textured and packs a powerful, smoky flavor. The peynir tabagi—feta cheese served with tomatoes, onions, and cucumbers—benefits from very fresh cheese and a strong, refreshing taste. These tapas-like plates are meant for sharing, and provide a more appealing alternative to main course options. Save room for dessert, though—it would be criminal to go home without trying the stellar baklava.

1361 Lexington Ave (between 90th & 91st St). 212-410-4300. Lunch 12pm-4pm Dinner 5pm-11pm. ❹❺❻ *to 86th. Average entrée $21.*

Pig Heaven *Chinese*
Having owned and managed Pig Heaven since 1984, Nancy Lee knows how to bring authentic and delicious Chinese cuisine to the Upper 80s. Her success is hardly a secret: from the spicy homemade dressing on the complimentary starter salad to the cinnamon-sweet glaze atop the heavenly BBQ spare pig ribs, every bite is flavorful. Don't neglect the Szechuan Dumplings, served with a hot peanut sauce that leaves you craving seconds. Favorite dishes include the Three Glass Chicken, Singapore Noodles, and the Scallop and Shrimp Sizzle.

1540 2nd Ave (at 80th St) 212-744-4333. Sun-Thurs 12pm-11:30pm, Fri-Sat 12pm-12:30am. ❹❺❻ *to 87th St. Average entrée $15.*

Sel et Poivre *French*
While the white tablecloths and hardwood floor create an elegant dining ambiance at this classy and simple bistro, nothing is overdone. The

music and lights are properly understated and keep the delicate balance between comfort and mood. The dishes are rich, French classics done right. Start with the buttery escargot and move on to the nicely crisped duck with haricots verts or apple-roasted pork chop accompanied by rosemary potatoes. The staff is knowledgeable without a shred of the infamous French haughtiness. Sel et Poivre takes their dessert as seriously as any other course, an attention to detail which makes it stand out among the many small French establishments of the city.
853 Lexington Ave (between 64th & 65th St). 212-517-5780. Sun-Thurs 12:00pm-10:30pm, Fri-Sat 12pm-11pm. ❼ to 63rd. Average entree $18.

CHEAP
Effy's Café *Café*
With a wide variety of gourmet salads, sandwiches, and beverages, Effy's homey atmosphere makes it a neighborhood favorite. Whether you go with a laptop or book while sipping on a cup o' joe, or share a full meal with friends, the staff is always friendly and accommodating. Overall, it is a welcome change from the Starbucks feed 'em and street 'em mentality. If you need further encouragement, nothing on the menu is over $10.
1638 3rd Ave (near 91st St). 212-427-8900. Open daily 6am-10pm. ❻ to 96th. Average entrée $6.

Java Girl Inc. *Café*
For funky, downtown chic in an uptown location, Java Girl Inc. is the place to go. Star-shaped lampshades and hand-painted tables give this local haunt a bohemian feel where the patrons order simply "the usual." Go for a hot or cold beverage or quick bite—the mochas are quite delicious and the grilled sandwiches are a great hot snack. With the incredibly diverse selection of coffee beans and loose tea by the pound, it's nearly impossible to leave Java Girl empty-handed.
348 E 66th Street (between 2nd & 1st Ave). 212-737-3490. Mon-Fri 6:30am-7pm, Sat-Sun 8:30am-7pm. ❻ to 68th

William Greenberg Jr. Desserts *Dessert*
Since 1946, this attraction has developed into a New York institution. Famous for having the world's best black and white cookies (a classic Gotham treat), Greenberg's is also known for using high-quality, kosher ingredients. In addition to the cookies, other favorites include rugelach, brownies, and all types of yummy custom cakes.
1100 Madison Ave (near 83rd St). 212-861-1340. Mon-Fri 8am-6:30pm, Sat 8:30am-6pm, Sun 10am-4pm. ❹❺❻ to 86th. Average yummy $3.

NIGHTLIFE

EDITOR'S PICK
The Auction House *Lounge*
Tucked away on an inconspicuous corner, the dingy doors of Auction House feel a bit like the entrance to some clandestine sex club. Inside, the bordello red wallpaper, heavy red velvet drapes and Victorian nudie paintings on the wall do little to prove otherwise, but once your eyes adjust to the candle lit room, the intimate corners and sexy indie rock piping softly through hidden speakers provide the perfect setting for a date. Couples, safe from prying eyes, lose all inhibition while snuggling on comfortable couches. There are no official specialty drinks, but the bartenders are adept—and flirtatious. While a poor choice for groups of friends—the suggestive atmosphere might be a tad awkward— Auction House offers up a mature, sultry ambience in which to impress a paramour.
300 E 89th St (between 1st & 2nd Ave). 212-427-4458. Mon-Thurs 7:30pm-2am, Fri-Sat 7:30pm-4am. ❹❺❻ to 86th. Average drink $7.

Biddy's Pub *Dive Bar*
When pushing off for an evening on the Upper East Side, a boozy dive the size of your grandmother's cedar closet is probably not what you had in mind—but then, you've never been to Biddy's. Biddy's offers neighborhood residents a cheap and mellow alternative to the raucous, collar-popping shenanigans permeating UES nightlife. Owned and operated by a group of Irish transplants, Biddy's successfully weds unpretentious drinking with a fun and cozy atmosphere. The bartenders take an active interest in their patrons' drinking habits—once a regular you'll never have to remind the staff of your beer of choice. A pint will usually run you $4,

but that price can fluctuate at the bartender's discretion. Hard liquor is generally limited to scotch and whiskey. Mixed drinks are not an option. Try the Biddy's ale—it's unclear whether or not it's brewed in the alley out back, but it's delicious either way.
301 E 91st St (between 1st & 2nd Ave). 212-534-4785. Daily 5pm-4am. ❹❺❻ *to 86th. Average drink $5.*

Dorrian's Red Hand
Restaurant, Sports Bar
This popular bar is usually filled with financially-minded Ivy Leaguers and their acolytes. Strong cocktails and a happy, hard-partying crowd remedy a generally unimpressive drink selection. Those fluent in frat will find a home in the jam-packed front room with wood-paneled walls and nightly "Sweet Caroline" sing-alongs. Avoid the back bar, where Top 40 tunes and nonexistent lighting make for too-close encounters with the opposite sex. Sparse on conversation, generous with the Jager-bombs, Dorrian's is a place to blow off steam and enjoy a night of no frills, frat boy fun.
1616 2nd Ave (between 83rd & 84th St) 212-772-6660. Mon-Sat 11am-3:45am, Sun 12pm-3:45am. ❹❺❻ *to 86th. Average drink $8.*

Iggy's *Bar, Karaoke*
Iggy's has mastered the recipe for a good time: copious amounts of cheap booze, a loyal following of fun-loving twenty-somethings, and a small karaoke stage on which drunken revelers can play out their dreams of stardom. The front of the bar is beyond cramped, so grab a drink and choose a song as fast as you can and make a beeline for the back where the real entertainment is. Whether you sing well, love to sing poorly, or enjoy mocking those who do, Iggy's will tickle your fancy. In between sets, Iggy's jukebox plays actual good music and the chummy, young bartenders make genuine conversation with everyone, creating a friendly, supportive vibe—until you mess up the lyrics.
1452 2nd Ave (between 75th and 76th St). 212-327-3043. Daily 1pm-4am. ❻ *to 77th. Average drink $5.*

Martini Bar, Roof Garden of Metropolitan Museum of Art *Bar*
Seats are scarce at the Met's swanky outdoor martini bar for good reason—the roof boasts some of the best views of the city, not to mention rotating sculpture exhibits. The bar features cocktails named after the rooftop artwork currently on display, such as the refreshing "balloon dog," made with vodka, elderflower cordial, and sparkling pear nectar, or the "coloring book," which is distilled in a glass with colorful cubes of jello. On Friday nights, the martini bar draws an after-work crowd, while Saturday's crowd is generally a mix of tourists and natives soaking up the sun, the views, and the art.
1000 5th Ave (at 82nd St). 212-879-5500. Fri-Sat 5:30-8:15 pm. ❹❺❻ *to 86th. Average drink $12.*

Session 73 *Bar, Music Venue*
This late-night music hotspot is unassuming from the outside, but step into the lounge and this live music bar will keep you dancing with the young, hip crowd all night long. The tapas menu favorites are the Trio Burgers, perfectly prepared "From France Fries," and a hefty portion of artfully presented Runaway Nachos. Signature drinks are a bit pricey, but well worth it for the out of the ordinary mixtures including the Transfusion, a mix of five different alcohols and tasty fruit juices, and the Fruit Stripe, featuring melon liqueur, vodka, and pineapple juice. Most scrumptious is the one-of-a-kind Oatmeal Cookie Highball. The bands are talented, and theme nights like Tango Sunday, Salsa Monday, Open Mic Tuesday, and Karaoke Wednesday guarantee a good time.
1359 1st Ave (at 73rd St). 212-517-4445. Mon-Wed, Sun 5pm-2am, Thurs-Sat 5pm-4am. ❹❺❻ *to 68th. Average drink $10.*

SHOPPING

Billy Martin's Western Wear
Want a pair of stingray boots? Can't live without a pair of alligator wingtips? A trip to Billy Martin's Western Wear is a necessity for every urban cowboy, even if it is only to look–after all, hippopotamus hide is awfully pricey these days. Since 1978, country-western fans have flocked to Billy Martin's, which sells everything from boots, belts, and buckles to home furnishings, all constructed with the highest quality materials and workmanship. Wild West enthusiasts outfitted by the store include: George H.W. Bush, Madonna, Bono, Bob Dylan, MC Hammer, Johnny Cash, Eric

Clapton, and even Mikhail Gorbachev.
1034 3rd Ave (between 61st & 62nd St). 212-308-7272. Mon-Fri 11am-6:30pm, Sat 11am-6pm, Sun 12pm-5pm. ❹❺❻ⓃⓇⓌ *to 59th.*

Dylan's Candy Bar
With over 5,000 kinds of candy, a trip to this sweet store is sure to raise the insulin levels of even the strictest dietician. Everything from forgotten childhood favorites to the latest gourmet confection is housed within this two-story (soon-to-be three) candy wonderland. There's also a café that serves ice cream and a party room on the basement level that's available to rent for private functions.
1011 3rd Ave (between 60th & 61st St). 646-735-0078. Mon-Thu 10am-9pm, Fri-Sat 10am-11pm, Sun 11am-8pm. ❹❺❻ⓃⓇⓌ *to 59th.*

French Sole
If you want a pair of ballet flats, this petite boutique is the place to go. Don't be fooled by the size, they carry a large inventory of styles (with over 300 treatments for ballet flats alone) and sizes ranging from 4 to 12. Though the shop has catered to the likes of Elizabeth Taylor, Cindy Crawford, and The Duchess of York, these shoes won't break the bank. The majority of styles retail around $160, but French Sole has frequent sales that make it possible to get a pair of these unique shoes for less than half that price.
985 Lexington Ave #2 (between 72nd & 73rd St). 212-737-2859. Mon-Fri 10am-7pm, Sat 11 am-6 pm, Sunday 12pm-5pm in Oct, Nov, and Dec. ❹❺❻ *to 68th.*

Housing Works Thrift Stores
Two of these seven popular thrift stores are stationed in the Upper East Side. Specializing in high-end, gently used items, these stores have everything from a brand-new pair of Marc Jacobs flats for $15 to a funky vintage lamp for $40. Nice mid-level instruments can often be found among these stores' stocks, although scoring one might take repeat trips. Like shopping at any thrift store, a bit of digging around is required, but that's part of the fun.
202 E 77th St (between 2nd & 3rd Ave). 212-772-8461. 1730 2nd Ave (at 90th St). 212-722-8306. Mon-Fri 11am-7pm, Sat 10am-6pm, Sun 12pm-5pm. ❻ *to 77th*

DAY TO DAY

Community Board 19. *153 E 67th St. 212-452-0600.*

Local Media: *uppereast.com*

Groceries: Grace's Marketplace. *1237 3rd Ave. 212-737-2902. Mon-Sat 7am-8:30pm, Sun 8am-7pm.*

Dean and Deluca. *1150 Madison Ave (at 85th St). 212-717-0800. Daily 8am-8pm.*

Classes/Sports/Gyms/Fitness: 92nd St YMCA. *1395 Lexington Ave. 212-415-5500.*

Hospital: Lenox Hill Hospital. *100 East 77th St (between Lexington & Park). 212-434-2424.*

Hotel: Marmara Manhattan. *301 E 94th St. 212-427-3100.*

Dog Run: Carl Schurz Park. *85th St & York Ave. 212-675-4380.*

Movie Theater: United Artists. *1210 2nd Ave (at 64th St).*

Best Happy Hour: Lollipop. *27 East 61st St. 212-752-8900.*

Memorial Sloan-Kettering Thrift Shop
This thrift shop can make buying new and nearly-new designer duds possible at a fraction of the original cost. In addition to designer and vintage clothing, the shop also sells jewelry, accessories, books, artwork, and home furnishings. Their repertoire is entirely dependent on donations, so designers vary, but past featured donators have included Chanel and Carolina Herrera. Vintage shop dealers line up around the block to get their hands on some of the stuff that comes out for the openings and showcases, so be sure to get there early.
1440 3rd Ave (between 81st St and 82nd St). 212-535-1250. Mon-Fri 10am-5:30pm, Sat 11am-5pm. Donations accepted Mon-Fri 10am-3pm, Sat 11am-1pm. ❹❺❻ *to 86th.*

UPPER EAST SIDE 215

CENTRAL PARK WEST DRIVE

HOV 2+ ONLY
8AM - 10AM
MON - FRI

CENTRAL PARK WEST

W 72 ST

Central Park West

30

Central Park West

UPPER WEST SIDE

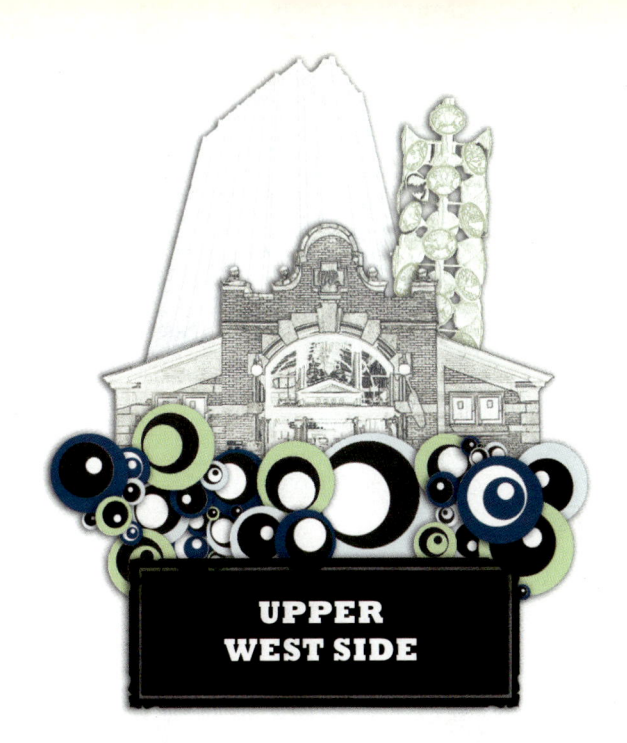

Originally called the Bloomingdale District, the Upper West Side was mostly farmland until the turn of the 20th century, and was considered a suburb of the more developed downtown Manhattan. The pastoral neighborhood quickly changed with the construction of Central Park and the completion of the 9th Ave elevated train in the late 1800s. That led to a building boom in the neighborhood and the construction of grand residences, many of which, like The Dakota, are still standing.

Playing the quirky socialist uncle to the Upper East Side's rich Republican grandpa, the Upper West Side is home to the most notable center for performing arts in the city, Lincoln Center, and has traditionally been home to New York's artistic and cultural elite. It is no accident that it is has been called the psychiatrist capital of the world. These days it is a magnet for young families and yuppies alike. The former appreciate the neighborhood's proximity to both Riverside and Central Parks, while the latter regularly pass their nights on Beer Row between 80th and 86th street on Amsterdam.

The Upper West Side frequently serves as a starter neighborhood for recent transplants, providing convenient transportation to most of Manhattan (six subway lines run along Broadway and Central Park West), as well as a quieter introduction to city living—not to mention moderately less exorbitant prices for rambling pre-War apartments.

UPPER WEST SIDE 217

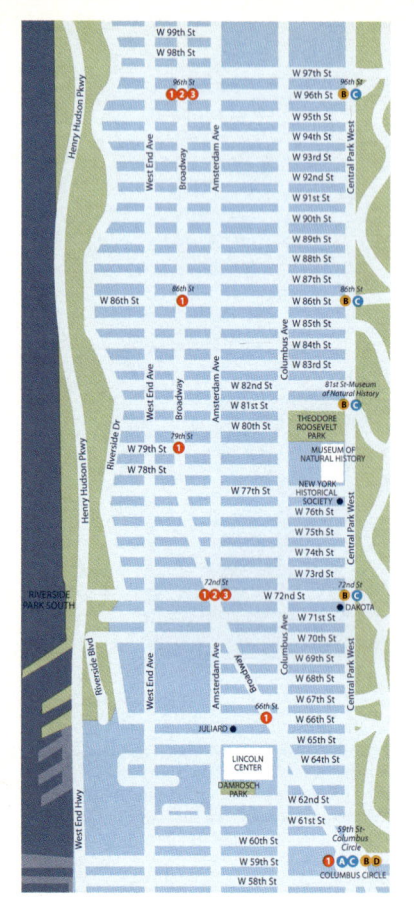

ATTRACTIONS

The Dakota
Commissioned by Edward Clark, one of the founders of the Singer Sewing Machine Company, and built by the same architectural firm that designed the Plaza Hotel, The Dakota's sixty-five apartments (ranging from four to twenty rooms) were completed in 1884. The German Renaissance-style building, with apartments organized around a courtyard, have ornate interior details and originally featured croquet and tennis courts in the lot behind the building.

It is prominently featured in the film *Rosemary's Baby*, as well as in the novel *Time and Again*. It has been called home by famous New Yorkers such as Andrew Carnegie, Lauren Bacall, Judy Garland, Gilda Radner, Leonard Bernstein, and, most famously, Yoko Ono and John Lennon, who was tragically shot outside the building's entrance in 1980.
1 West 72nd St (at Central Park West). 212-362-1448. B C to 72nd St.

Museum of Natural History
With exhibits on topics both animal and anthropological, this museum will captivate anyone who is interested in living things—that is, everyone. The hall of human origins is worth a special trip and has been recently renovated, and much of the museum is organized geographically into various habitat groups. A visit to the Rose Center and Planetarium, an 87 foot sphere where you can see shows voiced over by celebrity actors like Tom Hanks and Robert Redford, is well worth the extra cost. No trip to the museum is complete however, until you see the dino skeletons on the 4th floor. Visiting at non-peak hours during the week will make your time much more enjoyable
200 Central Park W (at 79th St) 212-769-5100. Sun-Sat 10am- 5:45pm. B C to 81st St. Adults $15, Students $11.

New York Historical Society
Attracting mostly students, professors and history buffs, the New York Historical society is primarily a research center intended to present exhibitions related to the history of New York. Filled with various artifacts both famous and ordinary dating back to the 17th Century, NYHS is very informative, and features one of the world's greatest collections of American historical paintings. On Fridays admission is free from 6pm to 8pm.
170 Central Park West (between 76th & 77th St). 212-873-3400. Tue-Thu, Sat 10am-6pm; Fri 10am-8pm; Sun 11am-5:45pm. B C to 81st. Adults $10, Students $6.

CULTURE & ARTS

Symphony Space
The Upper West Side may not be known for its

LINCOLN CENTER

Lincoln Center was developed in the 1960s by John D. Rockefeller III during the era of Robert Moses and features buildings designed by such notable architects as Phillip Johnson, Eero Saarinen, Gordon Bunshaft, and Wallace Harrison. Today the 12 cultural facilities and 16.3-acre campus are home to all things performance-art in New York City including the **Metropolitan Opera** (which broadcasts live Saturday matinees on the radio for those unable to shell out $25-$320 for the real thing) and the **American Ballet Theater**. These two beacons of New York art are both housed in the Metropolitan Opera House which also features murals by Marc Chagall and the 3,800 seat proscenium theater with its must-see rising crystal chandeliers.

Opera buffs unable to afford the Metropolitan Opera should check out the **New York City Opera**, also at Lincoln Center, which has student tickets starting at $16. The archive of **New York Public Library for the Performing Arts** is open to the public by appointment and shelves more than 70,000 scores, autographed manuscripts, and videos of virtually every show and musical produced on Broadway in the last 50 years. For classical music, the **New York Philharmonic** is housed in Avery Fisher Hall, though the **Julliard School**, the nation's foremost school of performing arts, offers less bank-breaking, and sometimes even free, concerts and plays. The **Chamber Music Society of Lincoln Center**, located in Alice Tully Hall, is the nations premier repertory of chamber music, and **Jazz at Lincoln Center** is located in a spectacular new space, off-site in the Time Warner Center, with a breathtaking view of Central Park South

The **New York City Ballet**, famed for its annual performance of The Nutcracker, was formed by George Balanchine and Lincoln Kirstein, and still regularly performs Balanchine's works. The **Lincoln Center Theater** produces Broadway musicals and plays in the Vivian Beaumont Theater and the Mitzi E. Newhouse Theater, and the **Film Society of Lincoln Center** has hosted the New York Film Festival every fall for the last 45 years. Even the **Big Apple Circus** finds a home at Lincoln Center in Damrosch Park every October.

The complex is currently under construction– expanding the Julliard School, re-landscaping the plaza (which comes alive in summer as home to Lincoln Center Out of Doors), and gussying itself up for its 50th anniversary in 2009. For those who can't get enough Lincoln Center, consider taking the one-hour docent-led tour of the complex ($15 for adults, $12 for students and seniors), where you'll view the theaters and peek in on a rehearsal in progress.

Lincoln Center for the Performing Arts. 62nd-65th Sts (between Amsterdam Ave and Columbus Ave). 212-875-5456. ❶ *to 66th.*

---

art scene, but music, dance, readings, and film can all be found at the same venue on Broadway and 95th. Symphony Space's thoughtfully orchestrated film series features everything from the classics to the cutting edge, a lovely option when current Hollywood blockbusters fail to entice, and double features make $11 tickets well worth the price. Book readings attract such names as Salman Rushdie, and dance acts come from across the globe.
2537 Broadway (at 95th St). 212-864-5400. ❶❷❸ *to 96th.*

Walter Reade Theater
Serving as the base of operations for the renowned Film Society of Lincoln Center, Walter Reade is the place to go for beloved classics, international film series, director's retrospectives, and talks and forums about film. World cinema features and big name guests make this the ultimate stop for anybody who wants to learn more about the art and the medium. The intimate theater of 270 seats is always packed with film lovers
165 W 65th St (between Broadway and Amsterdam) 212-875-5600. ❶ *to 66th. Adult $11, Students $7.*

DINING

UPSCALE
Bar Boulud *French*
Daniel Boulud salutes his hometown with a modern version of a bouchon, a type of restaurant in that specializes in roasts, pâté, and other hearty victuals. The menu includes classics like

UPPER WEST SIDE 219

coq au vin, but the sausage and charcuteries, like head cheese terrine, are rare finds this side of the Atlantic so make sure to have your fill. Boudin blanc, a white version of the sanguine boudin noir, is a perfect link of juicy, porky meat with a silken texture. A basic chicken terrine, pâté de Bourgogne, has a subtle, acidic aftertaste lent from Meyer lemon while pâté de grand-mère's combination of cognac, chicken liver, and pork is reminiscent of the Gallic countryside. For dessert, the "floating island" is chic and light—a fluffy, steamed meringue swimming in crème anglaise with pink pralines. With a menu amenable to lunch, pre-theater, and late-night wine and nibbles, Bar Boulud provides an easy way to experience Lyon without ever stepping on a plane.

1900 Broadway (near 64th St) 212-595-0303. 5:00pm-11:00pm. Lunch Mon-Fri 12pm-3pm, brunch Sat-Sun 11am-3:30pm. ❶ *to 66th. Average entrée $25.*

EDITOR'S PICK

Eighty One *New American*
Although knowledgeable wait-staff and posh digs are employed at the Excelsior Hotel, the creative approach to seafood is the reason to go. The crowd is noticeably older, but diners of any age will appreciate Chef Ed Brown's thoughtful, often stunning, dishes. Balanced flavors and textures are his culinary leitmotifs; in the crudo appetizer, yuzu's tart acidity and wasabi's bite is tempered with basil and white soy, Kona kampachi's fatty flesh with cucumber. Grapefruit and cold Israeli couscous with red onion play accompaniment to savory, crisp softshell crabs—a Spring entrée worth waiting all year for. Brown also favors specialty ingredients like milk-fed veal for a duo of rack and cheek with pepato cheese-wrapped asparagus. Unlike the savory plates, desserts are less balanced and very rich, but both the bourbon banana bread pudding and chocolate-hazelnut millefeuille are worth the sugar overdose. The complimentary petit-fours and individual Kenyan coffee are a perfect coda, leaving you not only well-fed but pampered too.

45 W 81st St (between Columbus Ave & Central Park West). 212-873-8181. Sun-Thurs 5:15pm-10:30pm, Fri-Sat 5:15pm-11:30pm. ❽❻ *to 81st,* ❶ *to 79th. Average entrée $35.*

Ouest *New American*
Do yourself a favor and eat here. Revered chef Tom Valenti has created a restaurant whose excellence is singularly sufficient to put the Upper West Side on the culinary map. Divided into three categories, the menu offers selections of fish, poultry and game, and braised meats. Indulge in the squab-topped duck liver risotto if you're feeling adventurous; if not, stick with the specialty braised and roasted beef selections—the gnocchi special with braised beef side is particularly divine. For dessert, lemon cheesecake with a mint twist is a unique take on the conventional. You cannot go wrong at Ouest. The service is all smiles, the food is celestial, and the experience is priceless.

2315 Broadway (near 84th St). 212-580-8700. Mon-Thurs 5pm-10:30pm, Fri-Sat 5pm-11:30pm, Sun 5pm-9pm; Serves brunch Sunday 11am-2pm. ❶ *to 86th. Average entrée $31.*

Picholine *French*
Chef Terrance Brennan provides a menu that ensures your dinner hours are well spent. Salty, rich flavors are favored, but rarely overdone. Ingredients begin their journey to the plate by undergoing atypical preparations, and finish in the highly interpretative dishes. Tuna cru "Napoleon" pairs olive oil ice cream with layered fatty tuna and crunchy tapioca crisp, while foie gras shabu-shabu means dipping perfectly seared foie gras into sweet and sour marmalades. But the award for innovation goes to the Heirloom Chicken "Kiev"—juicy flash-fried chicken breast rolled around a molten foie and black truffle center. There remain more traditional French flourishes like table-side ladling of soups, a complimentary cheese course, and genial service. The fromagier will guide you through the day's choices and provide you with an aperitif tasting to pair with your rare-find cheese. Desserts, like liquid chocolate tart, are so divine you'll fight your fullness to finish them.

35 W 64th St (near Central Park West). 212-724-8585. Mon-Thurs 5:00-10:00pm, Fri-Sat 5pm-11:45pm, Sun 5pm-9pm. ❶ *to 66th. Four course prix-fixe $98.*

MID-RANGE
Celeste *Italian*
Simple, well-prepared Neapolitan classics take center stage at this pastoral neighborhood favorite. Portions are generous, prices are low, and ingredients are high quality. Eggplant rolls come stuffed with prosciutto and pecorino imported from Italy—rumor says the owner smuggles it into the States in his suitcase—and make for a standout appetizer. Pasta is handmade daily and cooked *al dente*; the tagliatelle with shrimp and pecorino is creamy and rich yet not heavy. Meat dishes are also impressive, though their accompaniments sometimes underwhelm: beautifully prepared veal with lemon and capers is served with uninspiring spinach and potatoes. Rustic wood tables are packed together under a gently lit sky-blue ceiling—a relaxing or romantic scene, depending on your intentions. If possible, grab a seat on the glass-enclosed patio. Reservations are not accepted and the restaurant stays busy, so expect a wait if you come at peak dinner hours.
502 Amsterdam Ave (between 84th & 85th St). 212-874-4559. ❶❽❻ *to 86th. Average entrée $12. Cash only.*

Firehouse *American*
Like off-Broadway shows, uptown off-Broadway restaurants are personable rather than glitzy. At Firehouse, the friendly staff serves a local crowd including many regulars. The bar room is capacious, and there is sidewalk seating year-round. Some indoor tables are communal, but you'll enjoy rubbing elbows with neighbors while you watch the Yankees, Mets, or Rangers on one of the bar's many televisions. To start, tuck into Firehouse's fresh, lemony guacamole or a plate of perfectly cooked, spicier than average wings. Don't expect anything daring from the menu: its focus is American comfort food, from burgers, chili, and ribs drenched in Dinosaur Barbecue sauce, to pizza. The standout is an unusually tender turkey burger, which can be done up in one of the restaurant's six custom sauce combinations.
522 Columbus Ave (at 85th St). 212-787-3473. Mon-Thu 11:30am-2am, Fri-Sat 11:30am-3am, Sun 11:30am-1am. ❶❽❻ *to 86th. Average entrée $10.*

Luzia's *Portugeuse, Mediterranean*

This Portuguese oasis mixes the charm of a cozy, family run eatery with the class and sophistication of an upscale metropolitan restaurant. The house bartender ladles out sangria from a candy jar for a perfect accompaniment to the excellent tapas. Everything that includes seafood is delicious—the light mix of crabmeat, butter, shallots, mushrooms, and pineapple makes for a pot of heaven in the "Costa del Sol". For a land-fare option, the campesinas, artichokes stuffed with cheese and roasted peppers, are a great choice. Classic entrées, like the paella brimming with savory sausage and fresh seafood, are kicked up to a new level.

429 Amsterdam Ave (between 80th & 81st St). 212-595-2000. Daily 11:30am to 12:30am. ❶ *to 79th. Average entrée $22.*

Madaleine Mae *Southern*

Texas-born Andrew Curren dug deep into his grandmother's family recipe book when crafting the menu for this southern delight, which specializes in down home cooking that makes no concessions to delicate uptown tastes. Entrées like the gumbo—spicy and thick with the flavors of andouille, shrimp, and chicken—are traditionally and competently prepared. Collard greens, heavy on the bacon, and hush puppies, deep fried and studded with nuggets of fresh corn, are excellent side dishes, if not easy on the heart. The bar specializes in rum concoctions and features an extensive list of aged Caribbean rums. "Rhum cures," shots of rum infused with a variety of spices and fruit flavors which tout health benefits sexual and otherwise, are hit and miss—stick to the fruity varieties.

461 Columbus Ave (at 82nd St). 212-496-3000. Mon-Thurs 8am-11pm, Fri 8am-12am Sat 10am-12am Sun 10am-10pm. ❶ *to 79th,* ❽ ❾ *to 81st. Acerage entrée $20.*

Nonna *Italian*

Rich and hearty without being leaden, the comfort food at Nonna tastes like a tribute to the culinary heritage of Italian grandmothers. The antipasti are simple and pleasing—the silky prosciutto is particularly delicious. The creamy, delicately fried arancini (rice balls) are the standout starter, but the baked eggplant and fried calamari are also satisfying. For a main course, the strozzapretti in a wild boar bolognese is an enticing option—though there may be a little less boar than you'd like. Or try the pork bracciole, a cutlet with sausage stuffing served over blissfully creamy mascarpone polenta. Save room for dessert: the panna cotta with a hint of citrus is cool and lush, and the almond zeppoles with amaretto honey are little puffs of heaven. Come any

day but Sunday for the six-course prix-fixe feast at an unbeatable price.
520 Columbus Ave (between 85th & 86th St). 212-579-3194. Mon-Thurs 5pm-11pm, Fri-Sat 5pm-12am, Sun 4pm-10pm. Lunch served Mon-Fri 10:30am-2:30pm, Sat/Sun Brunch 10am-3pm. ❶ to 86th. Average entrée $15.

Penang *Malaysian*
Warm wood and exposed brick accentuate the staid elegance of this neighborhood favorite. The beautiful modern bar at the front offers great deals on wine, while the dining room in back seduces with relaxing green walls and a comely skylight. For dinner, regulars usually begin with either the roti canai—chicken and potatoes in a rich curry—or the sotong goreng, a dish of perfectly cooked calamari that easily trumps its banal Italian cousins. The rich, slow-cooked beef rendang is traditional Malaysian comfort food, while the Masak Lemak is a tangier, even barbecue-like dish. For dessert, the banana pancake is surprisingly light, reminiscent of a crèpe. Generous servings make the lunch specials among the best deals in the area.
127 W 72nd St (near Columbus Ave) 212-769-3988. Sun-Thurs 12pm- 10:45pm, Fri-Sat 12pm-11:45pm. ❶❷❸ to 72nd. Average entrée $18.

Sido *Middle Eastern*
This take-out counter, with a few tables for dining, boasts delicious schwarma and falafel. The owner, one of the friendliest hosts in the neighborhood, is known to dole out free samples while you wait for your order. You won't be waiting long—the service is speedy—but don't skip over the appetizers. They are well worth indulging in before moving to the main course.
403 Amsterdam Ave (at 79th St.). 212-874-2075. Mon-Sat 11am-11pm. ❶ to 79th. Average entrée $12.

CHEAP
Big Nick's *Pizza, Diner*
Though riddled with tourists from the nearby Belleclaire Hotel, Big Nick's still has that cranky, gritty, I-wonder-if-they-wash-their-dishes, Upper West Side charm. A diner on one side, a pizza place on the other, Big Nick's is open 24 hours a day and 365 days a year, giving you plenty of time to stop in and sample the joint's delicious burgers (they have 53 different kinds on the encyclopedic menu) or pizza (which comes with more toppings than imaginable).
2175 Broadway (near 77th St). 212-362-9238. Daily 24 hours. ❶ to 79th. Average entrée $9. Cash only.

Juice Generation *Juice Bar*
One of the original healthy juice bars, Juice Generation utilizes a variety of exotic fruits like mangosteen and açai in their delicious smoothies. Less tropical blends like "I Love Watermelon" and "Peaches and Dreams" are mixed simply, refreshing, and made with fresh fruit. The juices, including the bright green "Mr. Greengenes," is given a kick in the form of spirulina shots. The mostly vegan, all organic soups and salads are also popular with the lunch crowd.
104th and Broadway. ❶ to 103rd.
117 West 72nd St. ❶❷❸Ⓐⓒ to 72nd. 8:00am-9:00pm except W 4th, which is open until 10 on Sundays. Most items $4-$10.

Nanoosh *Middle Eastern*
This specialty restaurant has one thing they do exactly right– hummus. The menu features nine varieties of the Middle Eastern favorite, ranging from the mild hummus tahini to the zesty hummus with spicy sun-dried tomato pesto. Each order of hummus comes with two warm pitas, salty olives, and tangy pickles. The quinoa salad, a sweet and crunchy blend of organic quinoa, walnuts, and cranberries, goes well with your dip, and the apple cake with cinnamon sauce is a great way to round out any meal. Seats fill up quickly on weekday nights, so be sure to arrive early or make a reservation.
2012 Broadway (between 68th and 69th St). 212-362-7922. Mon-Sun 11am-11pm. ❶ to 66th. Average entrée $9.

Super Tacos *Mexican*
Though they may not compare to better and beefier tacos in Brooklyn or East Harlem, the taco truck serves tacos, tostadas, and tortas all day long and into the late night for Upper West Siders in search of fiery flavor on the cheap. Al pastor or carnitas are the best taco fillings—both variations on roast pork—and are even better with a splash of spicy red and

green sauces and a squeeze of lime. Neither benches nor stoops are nearby for sitting and noshing, but the railing bordering Gristedes will do. Chances are you'll be on your way, or back in the line, in a matter of minutes.
SW corner of 96th St at Broadway, 917-837-0866. Mon-Thu 6:00pm-2:00am, Fri 6:00pm-3:00am, Sun 12:00pm-2:00am. Menu $1-6. Cash only.

NIGHTLIFE

EDITOR'S PICK

Barcibo Enoteca *Wine Bar*
Shoved between a shoe store and a standard diner, this charming enoteca is easily missed. For those who spot it, a real treasure is waiting. Warm and unpretentious, this 2-level wine bar attracts neighborhood locals of all ages. Specializing in Italian wines and tapas, patrons munch on standard panini and crostini loaded with meats and cheeses. The bar is petite, and the high bar chairs are squashed together, so sit on the 1st level and escape boiling temperatures of the 2nd level bar located near the kitchen. Though usually the perfect spot for a drink and a conversation, the crowd at Barcibo can sometimes get a little boisterous as the night progresses.
2020 Broadway (between 69th St and 70th St) 212-595-2805. Tues–Fri 5pm–12:30am, Sat-Sun 11am–12:30am. ❶ ❷ ❸ *to 72nd. Average drink $11.*

Bourbon Street *College Bar*
Bourbon Street claims to hold a year round Mardi Gras; as regulars know, this is not far from the truth. Wednesday through Saturday the bar is packed with young people looking to party 'Nawlins style, with loud music and plentiful drink specials. Gents be warned, on happening nights you can expect a minimal cover. Other days of the week the bar has special events—like karaoke Tuesdays and ladies night Wednesdays—that draw a substantial regular crowd, though nothing like the end-of-the-week pandemonium. Knock back some $2 shots, pound a Hurricane, and party-hardy.
405 Amsterdam Ave (between 79th & 80th St). 212-721-1332. Sun-Wed 4pm-2am, Thurs-Sat 4pm-4am. ❶ *to 79th Average drink $5.*

The Dead Poet *Irish Bar*
Poetry adorns the walls at what may just become your new favorite neighborhood bar. The well-worked pool table takes up what little space there is in its cozy interior, but it only adds to the charm of the place. Be prepared to scoot by your neighbor to reach the lively bartenders, who just may take some shots with you. The top-notch beers on tap are moderately priced and signature drinks like The Dead Poet Cocktail, a combination of seven liquors, are strong enough to kill.
450 Amsterdam Avenue (between 81st & 82nd St). 212-595-5670. Mon-Sat 10am-4am, Sun 12pm-4am. ❶ *to 79th. Average drink $7.*

Jake's Dilemma *Bar*
Great music, great atmosphere, a vibrant & young crowd and amazing happy hour prices are the draw here. The perfect place to start a night out, the bar offers a happy hour with everything half off from 12-8pm. The clean, spacious front area includes a long bar, while pool, beer pong, and foosball dominate the back area.
430 Amsterdam Ave (near 81st St). 212-580-0556. Mon-Thurs 4pm-4am, Fri 3pm-4am, Sat, Sun 12pm-4am. ❶ *to 79th. Average drink $2.50.*

Yogi's *Bar*
Bar top dancing, bra throwing, and drunken brawls inspired are not unusual at this country western watering hall, inspired as they are by cheap drinks and pitchers of beer starting at $6. Yogi's attracts all types of patrons, from hipsters to doormen, yuppies to local mail carriers, and even some mean darts players at all hours of the day. Velvet paintings, undergarments, and a blown up photo of the owner with Elvis during his bloated years, hang above the bar as signs of the establishment's pride in being trashy.
2156 Broadway (at 76th St) 212-873-9852. Daily 11-4 am. ❶ *to 79th. Average drink $3.*

SHOPPING

Master Bike
Master Bike owner and sole employee Imbert Jimenez is reputed to be the best bike mechanic in the city. Cyclists pedal from all

over to this 400 square foot hole-in-the-wall for speedy and reliable service, as well as hand-picked bike accessories. Conveniently located between Riverside and Central Park, it's also the perfect place for the amateur to rent a bike: just $30 for a 24-hour rental. Tune-ups start at $75 and with same day service, Jiminez will have you back on two wheels in no time.
225 W 77th St (between Broadway & Amsterdam Ave). 212-580-2355. Mon-Fri 10:30am-7pm, Sat-Sun 10am-6pm. ❶ *to 79th.*

Maxilla & Mandible

An oddity among oddities, this small shop, dedicated to Osteology (the study of bones), is the perfect detour after a visit to the Natural History Museum. Where else in New York City can you buy genuine woolly mammoth hair for $380, or cricket lollipops for $4? Take a peek inside this "world renowned natural history and science emporium" to marvel at the collection of shells, whale jawbones, taxidermy animals, and fossils, or to pick up an eccentric gift for the person who has everything.
51 Columbus Ave (between 81st & 82nd St) 212-724-6173. ❽ ❼ *to 81st..*

Steven Alan Outpost

This uptown discount store caters to a downtown sensibility. Carrying men's and women's labels like Rag & Bone, Shipley, A.P.C, Philip Lim, and Repetto, the stores (there are three more, in Tribeca, Nolita, and the West Village) also stock men's and women's button-downs and dresses sure to make you look cool. With floor-to-ceiling shelves, library ladders, and antique glass display cases, the store resembles a haberdashery right out of Paris; its hip, attentive clerks and a store soundtrack featuring Serge Gainsbourg may make you feel like you're shopping in the Marais. What's more to love? Threads here run 30-70% less than at retail stores, though the duds are still pricey at that rate.
465 Amsterdam Ave (between 82nd & 83rd St). 212-595-8451. Mon-Sat 11am-7pm, Sun 11am-6pm. ❶ *to 86th.*

Zabar's

It's easy to see why this specialty foods store, packed with carefully picked cheeses,

DAY TO DAY

Community Board 7: *250 W 87th St, 2nd Fl. 212-362-4008.*

Groceries: Citarella, *2135 Broadway (between 74th & 75th St). 631-324-9190.*

Gyms: Equinox, *344 Amsterdam Ave (between 76th & 77th St). 212-721-4200.*

Average Rent: $1,968/Studio.

Hospital: New York Presbyterian Hospital, *21 W 86th St (btwn Columbus and Central Park Wwest). 877-697-9355.*

Hostels and Hotels: Milburn Hotel, *242 W 76th St (between Broadway and West End Ave), 212-362-1006.*

Dog Run: Riverside Park *(Riverside Dr. at West 72nd).*

Movie Theater: AMC Loews Lincoln Square 13, *1998 Broadway (between 68th & 69th St), 212-336-5000.*

Best Happy Hour: Jake's Dilemma, *430 Amsterdam Ave (between 80th & 81st). 212-580-0556.*

olives, smoked fish, and prepared foods, is visited by New Yorkers from all over the city. Founded as a small deli 74 years ago, this grocer is now a Manhattan institution. A self proclaimed "epicurean emporium," Zabar's sells everything from caviar and ruggulah to Cuisanarts and vacuums; the second floor is famous for its bargain-priced house wares. Those on a tight budget should check out Zabar's an hour before closing, when sandwiches go for half price. If you choose to brave Zabar's on weekends or holidays, come ready for a battlefield—the crowd can be brutal as customers fight over the last challah and checkout lines run deep into the store. For the survivors, however, the spoils of war are delicious.
2245 Broadway (at 80th St). 212-496-1234. Mon-Fri 8am-7:30pm, Sat 8am-8pm, Sun 9am-6pm. ❶ *to 79th.*

UPPER WEST SIDE 225

NEW YORK CITY BALLET

Symphony in Three Movements Abi Stafford

George Balanchine's
THE NUTCRACKER™
November 28 – January 3
Tickets start at $20

2009 SEASONS
Winter: January 6 – March 1
Spring: April 28 – June 21
Student Rush Tickets – $12

nycballet.com or CenterCharge 212-721-6500
New York State Theater at Lincoln Center

New York Philharmonic
Lorin Maazel Music Director

CREDIT SUISSE
Global Sponsor

AN AMAZING ORCHESTRA AT AN AMAZING PRICE.

WHAT A RUSH! Students can purchase $12 rush tickets for select concerts up to 10 days before the concert at nyphil.org/studentrush.

ORDER ONLINE NYPHIL.ORG/STUDENT RUSH
AVERY FISHER HALL BOX OFFICE BROADWAY AT 65TH STREET

226 UPPER WEST SIDE

Bambú®

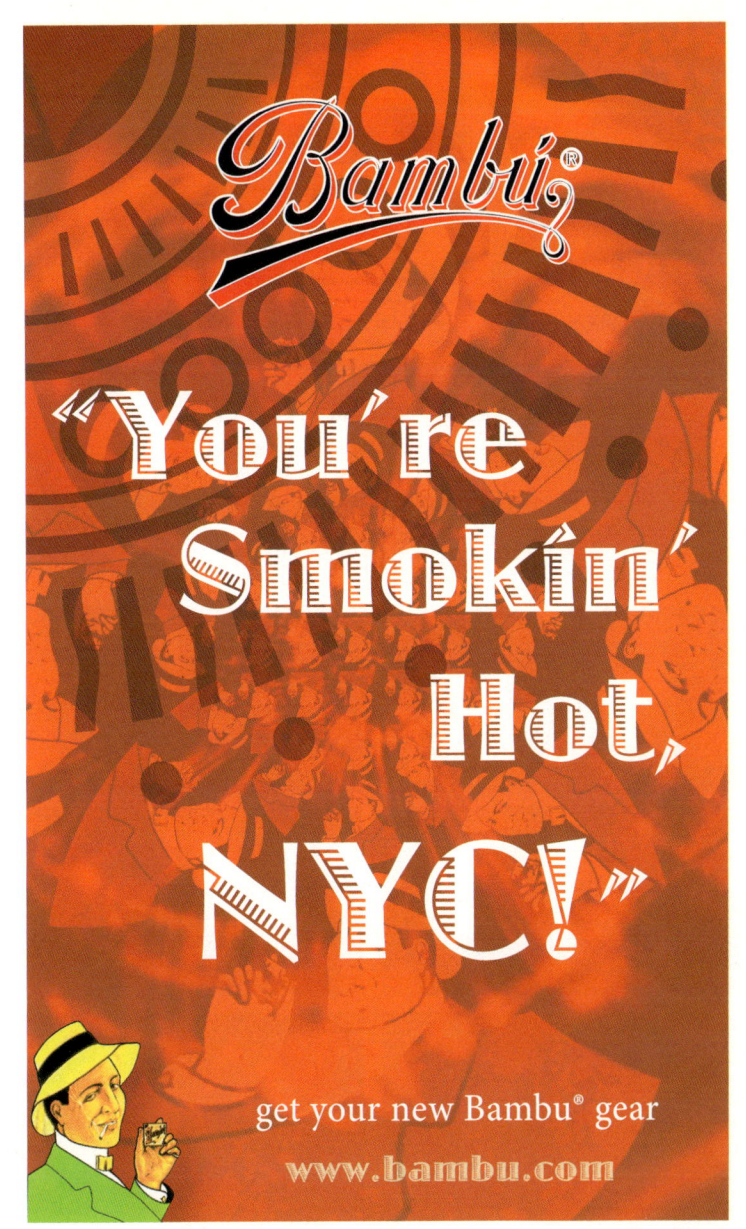

"You're Smokin' Hot, NYC!"

get your new Bambu® gear

www.bambu.com

UPPER WEST SIDE 227

HB
HOTEL BELLECLAIRE

Hotel Belleclaire welcomes Columbia University's Students, Family, Friends & Faculty.
Set in the heart of the romantic Upper West Side, the Belleclaire is within walking distance to Central Park, Beacon Theatre, Central Park and Lincoln Center.

Up to date amenities include: 32 inch Flat Screen TV's; iPod Docking Stations, wireless high speed internet access and complimentary, state of the art, fitness center.

Special 10% Discount to all Columbia Affiliates on 3 or more consecutive nights stays

250 West 77th Street, New York, NY 10024
www.hotelbelleclaire.com
phone: 212.362.7700 fax: 212.362.1004

TwoDo Salon Day Spa
Upper West Side

210 West 82nd Street
New York, NY 10024
212-787-1277

www.twodo.com

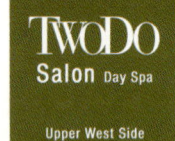

10% off with student I.D.
Tues, Wed, Thurs
9am to 4pm

call For Appointment

228 UPPER WEST SIDE

OTA
ON THE AVE
NEW YORK

2178 Broadway @ 77th St.   212 362-1100
www.ontheave-nyc.com

THE EXCELSIOR
HOTEL

45 West 81st Street NY, NY 10024
Tel: (212) 362-9200
e-mail: hotelexcel@aol.com

The Excelsior Hotel is a beautiful luxury four-star landmark in Manhattan's Upper West Side. Our Manhattan Hotel is located in a fashionable neighborhood between Central Park and Columbus Avenue where you can overlook many of the West Side's attractions from Central Park, American Museum of Natural History and the Rose Center for Earth and Space.

UPPER WEST SIDE 229

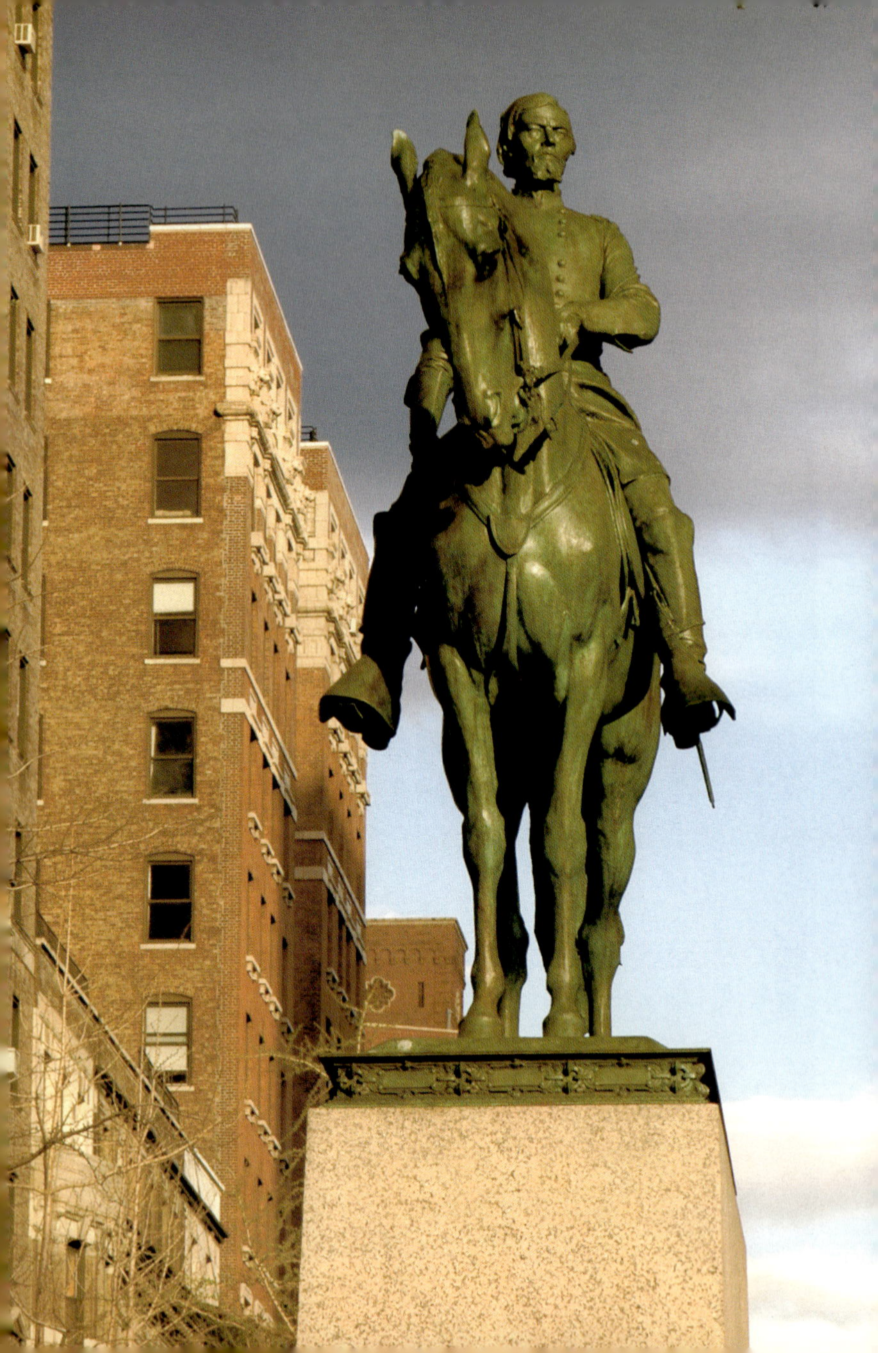

MORNINGSIDE HEIGHTS

A neighborhood that has always been defined by its local institutions, the history of Morningside Heights could be told in its many names. Throughout the 19th century the Bloomingdale Insane Asylum lent its namesake to the neighborhood and its unpleasant presence kept wary developers away. However, with the relocation of Columbia University and the construction of St. Luke's hospital, the neighborhood soon underwent a development explosion. Middle class families flocked to the area, and ever since it has been a place of residential and collegiate calm. Into the 20th century there was a competition between the names Morningside Heights, preferred by the students and families, and Cathedral Heights, preferred by the St. John the Divine Cathedral and St. Luke's Hospital. Home to five renowned academic institutions, Morningside is also sometimes referred to as the Acropolis of New York.

With an abundant population of students and young families come the many restaurants, cafes and small bars that line Broadway and Amsterdam. The quaint look and beautiful campus buildings at almost every street have made the neighborhood a site of many movies, books and plays. With Broadway becoming the main track of the gentrification express, much of the charm of the neighborhood, as chronicled by Jack Kerouac and Federico Garcia Lorca when they were Columbia students, is fast disappearing. In its place are the chain stores and suave restaurants with hip yet meaningless names. With a low crime rate and high rent prices, this one time middle class haven is being taken over by the wealthy. However, the students still make their presence known. Rows of used book tables on Broadway continue to testify to the neighborhood's academic pedigree, and most bars and restaurants in the area cater to collegiate budgets and tastes.

MORNINGSIDE HEIGHTS 231

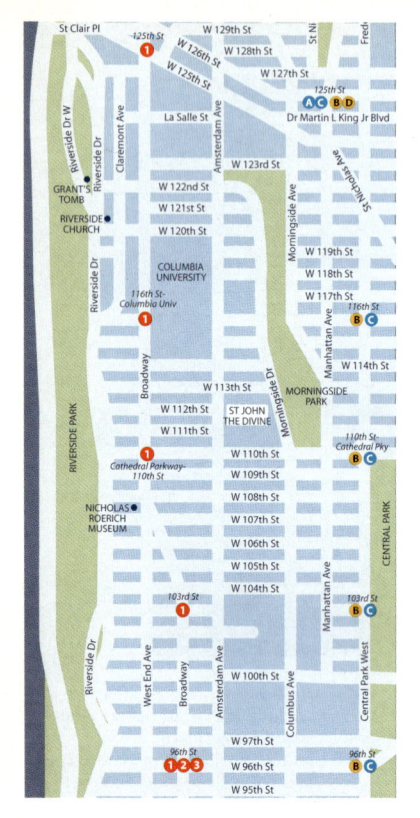

ATTRACTIONS

Cathedral Church of St John the Divine

As long as two football fields and as tall as the Statue of Liberty, Saint John is, by some measures, the largest cathedral in the world. It has also had one of the most difficult paths to completion. Begun in 1892 and still unfinished, St. John has seen generations of contractors and architects come and go during construction; as a result, in some ways its architecture reflects the city's diverse composition. Though designed primarily in Gothic Revival style, examples of numerous other architectural movements are on display, including Romanesque and Byzantine. Each of the seven chapels represent one of the primary ethnic groups that came into New York City via Ellis Island, which opened the same year construction of the cathedral began. Outside, well-groomed gardens attract locals on sunny days; linger long enough and you may get a glimpse of the resident white peacock.
1047 Amsterdam Ave (between 113th & 110th St). 212-316-7490. Mon-Sat 7am-6pm, Sun 7am-7pm. ❶❽❿ to 110th. Nave restoration tours 12pm and 2pm Saturdays. Adults $15, students $10.

Grant's Tomb

Styled after the Mausoleum of Mausolus, one of the Seven Wonders of the Ancient World, the resting place of Ulysses S. Grant is also the largest tomb in North America. Though when it opened in 1897 a procession of almost 1 million people showed up in remembrance, during the 1970s and '80s the building fell into disrepair and was covered in graffiti. Recent renovations have restored its original luster, and the white granite and marble structure now presides over Morningside Heights from its hilltop perch in stately elegance. The well-kept grounds surrounding the tomb offer a lovely view of the Hudson River.
Riverside Dr (at 122nd St). 212 666-1640. 9am-5pm. ❶ to 125th.

Morningside Park

Because of the steep and rocky cliff that runs from 113th St to 121st St, city planners in the 19th century decided to avoid the cost of extending the street grid and built a park there instead. Initially designed by Frederick Law Olmstead, the park features octagonal pavilions along its west side which provide sweeping vistas of central Harlem. The views are particularly gorgeous at sunrise and are the namesake of the park and the neighborhood it borders. Secluded narrow paths and sweeping stairways wind down the side of the cliff and through the verdant park to baseball fields, playgrounds, and a picnic area. The park was extremely dangerous during the crack epidemic of the 80s and 90s and, though it has cleaned up significantly in the past years, it is still unwise to linger alone long after sunset.
Morningside Dr (between 110th & 123rd). ❶❽❿ to 116th.

Riverside Church

Built in 1930, largely under the guidance of John D. Rockefeller Jr., Riverside Church promotes a more liberal, interdenominational interpretation of Christian scripture and also runs numerous social outreach programs. Inspired by the Gothic cathedral at Chartres, the 23 story tower contains a 74-bell carillon, the biggest in the world, with bells ranging from 10 pounds to 20 tons. On Sundays, relax in the park across the street and enjoy the sounds of one of the world's largest instruments.

490 Riverside Dr (between 119th St and 122nd St). 212-870-6700. ❶ *to 125th. 7am-10pm. Free tours Mon-Fri 9am-4pm, Sunday 12:15pm.*

Riverside Park

A lush green ribbon running four miles down the west side of Manhattan, Riverside offers something for everyone. Frederick Law Olmstead's elegant boulevard, lined by benches and mature elm trees, dominates the middle of the park. The views of the Hudson it provides are breathtaking, and it is one of New York's most attractive pedestrian spaces. The park offers a kayak launch at 148th St, a skate park at 108th St, and a marina at 79th St, as well as tennis, volleyball, soccer, and basketball facilities. The park covers an AmTrak railway; abandoned for decades until it was revived in 1991, the tunnel housing the tracks was once a haven for the homeless and graffiti artists. The adventurous can view this relic of a past era by entering the tunnels through the hidden entrances at 86th St and 125th St, but should beware of the trains which now speed through there. The less daring can check out the Eleanor Roosevelt Monument at 72nd St, the Soldiers and Sailors Monument at 89th St, or the Joan of Arc statue at 93rd St.
❶❷❸ *to stops between 72nd and 125th.*

CULTURE & ARTS

Miller Theater

This performance space on the campus of Columbia University hosts a variety of jazz, dance, and opera performances. Don't miss the composer spotlight concerts, which highlight a range of international masters from the old (Edgard Varese) to the new (Frank Zappa). While ticket prices can be steep, those under 25 get 40% discounts and Columbia students can get seats at any event for $7.
2960 Broadway (at 116th St) 212-854-7799. Call for schedule. ❶ *to 116th.*

Nicholas Roerich Museum

Philosopher, theologian, aspiring statesman, three-time Nobel Peace Prize nominee, Nicholas Roerich was a man of many talents and goals. When not attempting to found a new Buddhist nation from parts of Russia, Tibet, Mongolia, and China, he painted gorgeous images about his personal journey for spiritual peace. Over 200 of these impressionist oils are on display at the NRM, which is dedicated to celebrating his philosophical and artistic legacy. The museum also sponsors concerts and poetry readings, part of Roerich's dream of peace through cultural exchange.
319 W 107th St (at West End). 212-864-7752. Tue-Sun 2pm-5pm. ❶ *to 110th. Suggested donation.*

DINING

MID-RANGE

EDITOR'S PICK

A Café and Wine Room
French-Carribean

All the dishes on this adorable nook's minimal menu are prepared with eco-certified, all-natural ingredients. Sandwiched between a much larger café and a laundromat, you might unknowingly breeze by the petite restaurant, but make it inside and the food will ensure that you won't miss it again. Try the baked d'Anjou pear, smothered in raw honey and coated with Roquefort cheese, or the escargot with cilantro-chili butter for a burst of French and Caribbean flavors. The café is quiet in late afternoon, but when eight o'clock rolls around an 80s playlist clicks on and a varied crowd of collegians and older patrons arrive. The place is BYOB with no corkage fee, so take advantage of the conveniently-located liquor store down the street.
973 Columbus Ave (at 108th St). 212-222-2033. Tues-Sat 6:00-11:00pm. ❶❸❷ *to 110th. Average entrée $16.*

Alouette *French*
Alouette replicates the feeling of a casual bistro,

MORNINGSIDE HEIGHTS 233

forgoing the pageantry of bigger brasseries downtown—effortlessly fashioning the place as the European equivalent of your favorite diner. The menu is traditional and far from inventive, but provides a wide variety of well-executed, comforting Gallic dishes. Appetizers bear a rustic slant; warm goat cheese tart, escargot, foie gras pâté, and mussels are all familiar, in a welcome way. Steak frites and duck breast with Vichy carrots and orange sauce are the best choices for main dishes, neither overly rich nor skimping on portion size. Bathed in a soft crimson glow with the velvety sound of a French chanteuse in the background, the duplex space is laid back enough for family and friends, but certainly romantic enough to cozy up with an amour.

2588 Broadway (near 98th St). 212-222-6808. Mon-Thu 5:30-11pm, Fri-Sat 5:30-11:30pm, Sun 5:30-10pm. ❶❷❸ *at 96th. Average entrée $22.*

Camille's *Italian*

This underground mom-and-pop spot is often overlooked by visitors, but it's frequented by Columbia University employees and students looking to enjoy a quiet, unfussy meal at a reasonable price. Over the past 15 years the restaurant has grown a small following of regulars who return day after day for the classic, well-made dishes and on-the-go breakfast pastries. The menu sticks to simple Italian fare. The chicken pasta, a perfect comfort food, comes with the choice of creamy pesto or sun dried tomato sauce and comes in leftover-guaranteeing portions. Stop by Tuesday or Friday for all you can eat pasta dinners.

1135 Amsterdam Ave (at 116th St) 212-749-2428. Mon-Fri 7:30am-10pm, Sat 8:30am-5:30pm. ❶ *to 116th. Average entrée $10.*

Campo *Italian*

Candle-lit, rustic decor provides the backdrop for innovative antipasti like eggplant caponata and truffle-infused egg yolk ravioli, at this casual neighborhood trattoria. The arancini (savory saffron rice and cheese balls) and fried green tomato caprese are great starters, as well as the thin and crispy grilled pizzas that support hearty topping combinations like forest mushroom and ricotta. Pasta dishes and main courses consist of both Italian mainstays like linguini and clams as well as less common choices like wild boar bolognese and duck risotto. The bar, manned by expert mixologists from downtown speakeasy PDT, serves up excellent drinks and late-night bites until 2am.

2888 Broadway (between 112th St and 113th St) 212-864-1143. Daily 10:30am-4pm, 5-11pm (Bar until 2am); Sat-Sun Brunch 10am-3pm. ❶ *to 116th. Average entrée $14.*

Community Food & Juice *American*

Families, friends, and strangers share communal banquet tables at this minimalist restaurant. Everything on the menu—from the veggie egg white scramble, to the muenster and beefsteak tomato sandwich—is made from organic or local ingredients. The kitchen is liberal with portions; the buttery stacks of their famed pancakes are packed with blueberries. Those with a sweet tooth will particularly enjoy the brioche French toast, which is loaded with a banana-nut topping. The fresh-squeezed juices are on par with the food, and combinations like apple-carrot-ginger will surprise and refresh while complimenting any meal. The restaurant doesn't take reservations, so be prepared to wait; college students and locals alike fill this restaurant during peak hours.

2893 Broadway (between 112th and 113th St) 212-665-2800. Mon-Fri breakfast 8am-11:30am, lunch 11:30am-3:30pm, dinner 6pm-11pm; Sat-Sun Brunch 9am-4pm; Sunday Dinner 6pm-11pm. ❶ *to 116th. Average entrée $15.*

Miss Mamie's Spoonbread Too *Southern*

Everything about Miss Mamie's screams "home," from the white walls adorned with comforting domestic images, to the stray watermelon cutout, to, most decisively, the menu: homemade lemonade & iced tea (both deliciously sugary), fluffy cornbread, and ancestral recipes for all the soul classics. Chicken can be ordered fried, roast, jerk, smothered, or, best of all, barbecued. Juicy spare ribs fall off the bone, while tender, melt-in-your-mouth oxtails are too good for words. And let's not forget the sides; mac & cheese and mashed potatoes both meet Miss Mamie's high standards, while candied yams absolutely exceed them. For dessert, the red velvet cake is divine. Everything Miss Mamie's serves is sophisticated at heart; nuances in the flavors peek through and successfully meld with the bold tastes

required of Southern cooking.
366 W 110th St (near Manhattan Ave) 212-856-6744. Mon-Thurs 11:30am-10pm, Fri-Sat 11:30am-11pm, Sun 11am-9:30pm. 1 B C to 110th. Average entrée $15.

Pisticci *Italian*
This chummy restaurant provides Columbia students and locals with a reliable dinner of steadfast fare like crisp salads and hearty pastas, enlivened by a commitment to fresh ingredients. Occasionally, though, the food surpasses the modesty expected of it. House-made fettuccine, so perfectly soft that chewing is superfluous, gains an earthy taste from wild mushroom sauce, and a drizzle of truffle oil—an oft-overused condiment for fussy dishes—makes for a superb and welcome addition here. Daily fish specials promise fresh and flavorful preparations—get the black pepper-crusted tuna if you can. The tucked-away library room, filled with tchotchkes, Victorian touches, and regulars chatting with friends at the bar, is a cozy retreat from the dining area. Snuggle into a worn, plush chair with your bowl of pistachio gelato and you'll be seduced into returning to this welcoming den.
125 LaSalle St (near Broadway) 212-932-3500. Everyday 11:00am-11:00pm. 1 to 125th. Average entrée $16.

Rack and Soul *Southern*
Good fried chicken is hard to find above the Mason Dixon line, but this relaxed, barbecue joint fries up an exceptional bird, among other things. The meal starts off with biscuits sent straight from heaven; brushed with the slightest bit of honey, they are fluffy and delicious. While a pleasing mix of Motown and Bluegrass plays, the neighborhood crowd gets down to some serious grubbing over succulent, slow-cooked ribs that are bursting with flavor. Pulled pork, saturated in a sweet, tangy sauce, is so tender you don't even have to chew it. Most sides do just fine, the collard greens are a little tough but the yams, mashed potatoes and mac 'n cheese make up for it. If at all possible, save room for dessert: a hulking piece of moist red velvet cake.
2818 Broadway (at 109th St) 212-222-4800. Mon-Thurs 11am-10pm, Fri, Sat 11am-11:30pm, Sun 11am-9:30pm. 1 to 110th. Average entree $15.

MORNINGSIDE HEIGHTS 235

Symposium *Greek*
With white-washed walls, boarded floors, and a friendly wait staff, the Greek themed restaurant offers an escape from impersonal eateries nearby. The menu features dishes that combine exotic and simple flavors to produce multilayered entrees. The saganaki is a cheesy starter that is the restaurant's best appetizer. The pastitsio, a macaroni dish baked with ground meat, is a customer favorite, while the red snapper filet, coated with an egg-lemon sauce, is a favorite among seafood lovers. For dessert, the traditional Greek baklava is excellent, as is the kataifi (shredded wheat and nuts flavored with honey).
544 W 113th St (between Broadway and Amsterdam Ave). 212-865-1011. Daily 12pm-10pm. ❶ to 110th. Average entrée $12.

Toast *American*
The menu at Toast boasts classic diner grub as well as interesting variations on staples such as the feta-stuffed lamb burger. Their namesake appetizers, various meats served on toast, are complemented by cheese and spices. The house favorite is the grilled skirt steak, served with garlic toast and chipotle mayo. And if after your appetizer you haven't had your fill of the crunchy toast, it is also served with every dish along with delicious homemade mayonnaises. Reservations are not accepted and seats fill up fast.
3157 Broadway (near 125th St) 212-662-1144. Mon-Wed 11am-11pm, Thurs-Fri 11am-12am, Sat 10am-12am, Sun 10am-11pm. ❶ to 125th. Average entrée $12.

CHEAP
Columbia Cottage *Chinese*
Columbia students flock to this neighborhood staple to get their Chinese food fix and quaff free carafes of wine, served on request with unlimited refills. Standard dishes such as a light wonton soup, chicken with broccoli, and moo shu pork are consistently well executed, but the overly greasy lo mein and sesame noodles should be avoided. Specialty dishes of note are the chicken with young ginger roots, which packs a punch with its spicy pepper sauce, and the tangy mango shrimp. Take-out is inconsistent, so stake out a spot before the room fills up and enjoy the Cottage in person.
1034 Amsterdam Ave (at 111th St) 212-662-1800. Mon-Fri 11:30am-11pm, Sat-Sun 11:30am-12am, Lunch served daily 11:30am-4pm. ❶ to 110th. Average entrée $9.

The Hungarian Pastry Shop *Café*
This local mainstay is the perfect spot to indulge your sweet tooth and have an extended conversation with close friends. Feel free to take a seat and stay for hours while enjoying the brainy atmosphere and eavesdropping on your chatty neighbors. While the service is somewhat lacking, treats like the enormous slabs of honey-drenched baklava and carrot cake, washed down with bottomless cups of coffee, keep the shadowy interior packed with neighborhood intellectuals and Columbia students late into the evening. Before heading out, stop by the bathroom to view what is perhaps the most pretentious graffiti in the city.
1030 Amsterdam Ave (between 110th St and 111th St). 212-866-4230. Mon-Fri 8am-11:30pm, Sat-Sun 8:30am-11:30pm. ❶ to 110th. Average pastry $3.

Koronet *Pizza*
In the endless, intractable debate about the best pizza in New York City, Koronet holds uncontested right to at least one pizza superlative:

the largest slice in New York. They really are giant—floppy slabs around which whole disciplines of eating techniques have evolved, dripping with near-liquid grease and melted cheese. And at $3 a slice, they're a deal that's hard to beat. The store is open late; on weekends expect to see lines out the door at 4am, shortly after last call has driven Columbia students stumbling dorm-ward.
2838 Broadway (between 111th St and 112th St) 212-222-1566. Open 9am-2am Sun-Wed, 9am-4am Thu-Sat. ❶ *to 116th. Slices $3.*

Max SoHa *Italian*
A dark, cozy nook to warm up in on cold winter nights, this rustic Italian joint is dearly loved by students and locals for its high-quality meals at dive prices. Massive bowls of perfectly cooked pasta are served in bowls rather than plates, a homey touch that also ensures perfect sauce distribution. The sauce! Hearty and rich lamb ragus, pancetta cream sauces, and plain marinaras alike are heart wrenching remembrances of imaginary Tuscan childhoods past, not carefully prepared but lovingly. No reservations are taken so expect a bit of a wait at any reasonable dinner hour, but if waits are longer than ten minutes you will be directed to Max Caffé next door, where you can ease into velveteen armchairs with a class of wine as you await the call for your table. The killer atmosphere makes it a classic Columbia first date spot, but it's no less perfect for the ubiquity.
1274 Amsterdam Ave (at 123rd St) 212-531-2221. 12pm-12am. ❶ *to 125th. Average entrée $12.*

EDITOR'S PICK
Panino Sportivo *Sandwiches*
This sandwich shop's theme is soccer, but its specialty is the classic Italian panini. No soggy flatbread deli nightmares here—Sportivo grills crusty rolls to warm perfection in the traditional way. Inside the roll are fresh ingredients, many of which are imported from Italy, like real mozzarella di Buffala, prosciutto di Parma, and fresh plum tomatoes. Every sandwich is simply excellent. Vegetarian options like the Giovanni, with sliced bartlett pears, brie, arugula, and honey, offer the heft and flavor that many other vegetarian sandwiches cannot. The $9.50 soup/sandwich/drink lunch special is a bargain for the quality.
1231 Amsterdam Ave (between 120th & 121st St). 212-662-2066. Mon-Fri 8am-11pm, Sat-Sun 10am-10pm. ❶ *to 116th. Sandwiches $6-$9.*

Roti Roll *Indian*
This neon-illuminated, closet-sized snack joint specializes in 'frankies,' heavily-spiced Indian wraps, served late. Both vegetarians and their carnivorous friends are satisfied with wrap options ranging from marinated lamb to tofu and mushroom. Adding goat cheese to the roll is well worth the extra $1. Indian-spiced french fries, spicy chicken wings, and deep-fried calamari are great as greasy bar food, and can be ordered next door at Suite, a gay bar operated by the same owners. On weekends, Roti Roll remains crowded until its 4am closing with locals craving post-barhopping munchies.
994 Amsterdam Ave (between 109th & 110th St). 212-666-1500. Sun-Mon 11am-2am, Tues-Wed 11am-3am, Thurs-Sat 11am-4am. ❶ *to 110th. Frankies $3-6.*

Silver Moon Bakery *Bakery*
Butter, eggs, sugar, and flour work their magic in the cramped corner space where the unending line snakes out the door, even if it moves quickly. Freshly baked, American-style breads and European-style pastries line the display cases—so many sinful temptations to choose from you're bound to walk out with an armful. Sourdough is tangy and wonderfully crusty, and apricot-hazelnut parisienne makes for an indulgent breakfast if smeared with Nutella. Whole wheat challah braids, only available on Fridays, give you a reason to wake up early and snatch one up. The house coffee, one of the better finds in the neighborhood, serves as the perfect foil to chocolate croissants—buttery and flaky bliss—or chewy, gooey, unbeatable cookies.
2740 Broadway (at 105th St) 212-866-4717. Mon-Fri 7:30am-8pm, Sat-Sun 8:30am-7pm. ❶ *at 103rd.*

Taqueria y Fonda la Mexicana
Mexican
With only 10 tables, this tiny taco joint is almost always packed to the door with starving Columbians and locals waiting for pickup or a seat. Almost everything is cooked on two flattop grills by the door, where the moist, spicy chicken, beef, and pork that form the basis of many dishes are constantly sizzling. The chicken tortas are enormous rolls stuffed with refried beans, avocado, onion, tomato, lettuce, cheese, and hot sauce, as well as the ubiquitous (but delicious) lettuce. The massive burritos

MORNINGSIDE HEIGHTS 237

aren't the daintily wrapped snacks you'll see at other joints, but sprawling meat packed messes. Mexican purists gripe about the strange cheese used in almost every dish here, but most still acknowledge that this is as good as it gets for miles.
968 Amsterdam Ave (at 108th St). 212-531-0383. 11am-1am. ❶ ❽ ❼ *to 110th. Average entrée $8.*

NIGHTLIFE

1020 *College Bar, Dive*
From fledgling English majors to grizzled grad students, nearly every Columbia student will knock back a $3 pint at this dimly lit corner bar at some point in their university career. When class is in session, weekend nights here are sweaty, crowded, and horny—it's not to be missed. Though it looks like a sports bar, the music is good, the crowd is brainy, and trashy movies are projected on the back wall instead of the big game. On busy nights the line of thirsty undergraduates can extend down the block; locals looking for a quieter scene know to come on weekdays (Sunday to Tuesday for Columbia types) or clear out before midnight, when the rush really starts.
1020 Amsterdam Ave (between 110th & 111th St). 212-531-3468. Daily 4pm-4am. ❶ *to 110th. Average drink $4.*

The Ding-Dong Lounge *Bar*
This spacious, barely lit dive was built in the remains of a vacated crack den and has defiantly retained some of that old-time seedy character in the face of neighborhood evolution. The beer taps are actual guitar handles, and the mahogany bar was—according to lore—bankrolled by selling pornography left behind by the former owners. DJs are on hand every night and aside from old punk-rock concert posters and carefully cultivated grafitti on the bathroom doors, the décor is rigidly Spartan. Ultimately more of a place to hang out than get a groove on, the perennially available plush chairs and candlelit tables offer a welcome retreat. Feel free to test your skills with the hula-hoops hanging from a hook on the wall or the vintage Galaga/ Ms. Pac Man.
929 Columbus Ave (at 106th St). 212-663-2600. Mon-Sun 4pm-4am. Happy hour 4pm-8pm. ❶ ❽ ❼ *to 103rd. Average drink $5*

The Heights *Bar, Grill*
Boasting an upstairs deck with a retractable roof, The Heights is a pleasant and affordable place to grab a decent lunch or dinner with friends. It can be loud and boisterous, but that's its appeal as a Columbia hangout. Come nighttime it turns into a full-throttle University bar. The elevated bar and retractable roof deck are favorites with Columbia sports teams, frats, and their hangers on, but the margaritas are famous throughout the neighborhood. Strong and cheap, at $3 a piece during their happy hours (5pm-7pm and 11pm-1am), they're reason enough to brave the crowds.
2867 Broadway (at 111th St). 212-866-7035. Daily 11am-2:30am. Average drink $5. ❶ *to 110th.*

La Negrita *Coffeehouse, Bar*
By day, this artsy Uptown hangout is a coffee and tea shop, serving up sandwiches and soups to young professionals and bookworms taking advantage of the free wi-fi, comfy seating, and perpetual calm. But when night falls, loyal regulars and local students arrive en masse for the bar's rotating schedule of karaoke nights, trivia contests, live music, and poetry readings. Things slow down again after midnight, making La Negrita the ideal spot for a casual late-night get-together with friends, where amicable bartenders serve beer buckets and stiff drinks long into the night.
999 Columbus Ave (between 109th & 110th St) 212 961 1676. Open daily 7am-4am. Happy hour Mon-Fri 3:30-7:30pm. Drinks $3-9. ❶ ❷ ❸ ❽ ❼ *to 110th. Average drink $5.*

O'Connells Pub *College Bar, Dive*
After midnight on weekends, cheap beer and 80's music attract swarms of Columbia University frat boys and sorority girls to this classic Irish Pub. It's a tough place to sit and have a quiet drink with friends, but with pitchers of draft Bud running just $8, braving the crowds can be worth it for the boozer on a budget. The bar empties out and becomes more relaxed on weekdays and during summer months, when colorful locals and sports zealots replace sex-crazed undergrads. A cheap student crowd makes for

bitter bartenders: tip the first time if you expect to receive a second drink before last call.
2794 Broadway (between 107th St & 108th St) 212-678-9738. 10:30 am- 4am. 🌀 *to 110th. Average drink $6.*

Sip *Bar, Coffee*
This strangely decorated nook attracts a more mature Morningside Heights crowd, both day and night. Into the early evening locals and grad students clatter on laptops, drawn by the good coffee and free wireless, but when night falls they satchel their work and replace it with beer. A high perch overlooks the tiny bar, manned most evenings by an eager DJ—to the annoyance of some of the more studious patrons. A 2am-4am happy hour offering $2 off beer and wine brings patrons in late, while the $3 "Sipwich," a delicious egg and chorizo sandwich on an English muffin, has them crawling back the next morning.
998 Amsterdam Ave (between 110th & 109th St) 212-316-2747. 10am-4am. 🌀🅑🅒 *to 110th.*

Smoke *Jazz Club*
This inconspicuous uptown haunt is a hidden gem for all, no matter their level of jazz education. A different style of live jazz is performed every night, ensuring a packed house and a diverse clientele. The club's brick walls and rustic ambiance give off a warm, friendly vibe, making it a great place for a casual drink or a hot date. Make reservations, especially on the weekends, or you'll be waiting in line to pay a $30 cover charge (and then the minimum food & beverage charge of $20/person at the table). But it's worth the dough when you finally get to sit back and enjoy the music. If you're feeling adventurous, try the "Better than Jazz" cocktail for a sweet surprise.
2751 Broadway (at 105th St). 212-864-6662. Mon-Sun 5pm-2am. 🌀 *to 103rd. Average drink $6.*

SHOPPING

Book Culture
This is New York's premier academic bookstore, so don't come looking for fancy stationary or a latte. Instead, expect to find a fantastic selection of texts by any number of authors from Beckett to Bakhtin. Many Columbia University professor order their class books from here, a hearty endorsement of their selection; head to the back stacks on the top floor to browse books from the profs' reading lists. The foreign language literature selection is particularly impressive, as is their assortment of scholarly journals.
536 W 112th St (between Amsterdam Ave and Broadway) 212-865-1588. Mon-Fri 9am-10pm, Sat 10am-8pm, Sun11am-7pm. 🌀 *to 110th.*

Yarntopia
This shop carries everything a knitter could need, from imported yarns of all colors and textures to glow in the dark needles and how-to books. Downstairs, a 70s-themed room with bright purple walls and a neon orange couch serves as a lounge for knitting and crocheting classes. Courses such as "Circular Knitting for Socks" and "Sweater Construction" are available for around $20 per session. Custom-made clothing, hand-knit by the store's owner, is for sale as well, though many pieces run upwards of $300.
974 Amsterdam Ave (at 108th St). 212-316-9276. Tue, Thurs 12pm-9pm, Wed, Fri-Sun 12pm-7pm, closed Mon. 🌀 *to 110th.*

DAY TO DAY

Community Board 9. *16-18 Old Broadway. 212-864-6200.*

Local Media: Columbia Daily Spectator *columbiaspectator.com;* Bwog *bwog.net*

Groceries: West Side Market. *2840 Broadway. 212-222-3367.*

Gym: Body Strength Fitness. *250 W 106th St. 212-316-3338.*

Rent: One-bedroom: $1200-1400; Two-bedroom:$2400-2600.

Hospital: St. Luke's Hospital. *1111 Amsterdam Ave. 212-523-3335.*

Hotels/Hostel: West Side Inn. *237 W 107th St. 212-866-0061*; Central Park Hostel. *19 W 103rd St. 212-678-0491.*

Dog Run: Morningside Park. *Morningside Ave and 116th St.*

Best Happy Hour: The Heights Bar and Grill. *2867 Broadway (between 111th & 112th St). 212-866-7035. Happy hour nightly 5pm-6pm and 11pm-12am, $3 frozen margaritas.*

MORNINGSIDE HEIGHTS

Haakon's Hall

If you still think there's no place like home, you haven't stepped into Haakon's Hall, the newest addition to the booming restaurant scene around Columbia University. Designed lovingly to evoke "rooms" of a house, this neighborhood hangout instills comfort from the eclectic cuisine to the cozy décor. Kick back on the living room couch with a glass of boutique wine or a root beer float. Or pull up to the communal table for former Café Des Artistes chef James Lenzi's take on mom's home cooking. Enjoy everything from meatloaf or rotisserie chicken to vegetarian paella, monster salads and gluten-free fare—all without draining your bank account. Don't want a full meal? The pantry menu offers homey touches like eggs all day long, PB&J sandwiches and milk and cookies.

During mid-terms and finals, you can caffeinate and cram for exams twenty-four hours a day (you've got to love free WiFi), and during the year hang out for our nightly events to play Jeopardy, watch old movies and listen to poetry readings. **Like home, only better.**

OPENING FALL OF 2008

1187 Amsterdam Avenue (between 118th and 119th) 212-932-0707
www.haakonshall.com
Eclectic homestyle comfort cuisine
7 a.m. to 4 a.m. daily.
1 TRAIN TO 116TH STREET

Haakon's Hall

a taste of home in the heart of the city

240 MORNINGSIDE HEIGHTS

★★Voted Best of NYC 2004★★

"PRESSING SOME OF THE BEST SANDWICHES IN TOWN, A BOON TO HOMESICK ITALIANS."
– Robert Sietsema, THE VILLAGE VOICE

The New York Times
Florence Fabricant

"58 FIRST-RATE SANDWICH COMBINATIONS WITH IMPORTED CHEESES AND MEATS ...EXCELLENT ESPRESSO."

DAILY ● NEWS
Irene Sax

"SURPRISING...IT MAKES YOU WONDER WHAT THIS NEIGHBORHOOD DID BEFORE PANINO SPORTIVO ROMA."

PANINO SPORTIVO

- Soups
- Desserts
- Beer + Wine
- Fresh Baked Pastries
- Salads
- Grilled Toasts
- Sorbet + Gelato
- Delicious Espresso

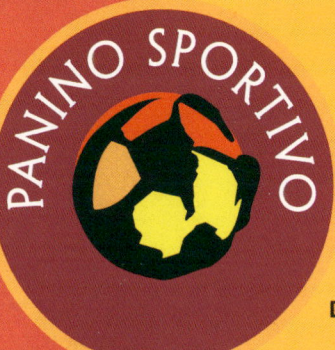

...And New York's Most Authentic Italian Sandwiches

1231 AMSTERDAM AVE
-BETWEEN 120TH AND 121ST-
212 662-2066
WWW.PANINOSPORTIVO.COM

BREAKFAST, LUNCH & DINNER
CATERING/DELIVERY

2 FOR 1 BEER SPECIAL EVERY NIGHT. NIGHTLY DINNER SPECIALS
10% OFF W/ STUDENT ID. DON'T FORGET TO PICK UP YOUR VIP CARD!

Bring This Ad In To Be Entered Into A Drawing For A $20 Gift Certificate At Panino Sportivo And Receive A Free Canned Soda With A Panino Or Salad Purchase.

NAME:_____ EMAIL_____

242 MORNINGSIDE HEIGHTS

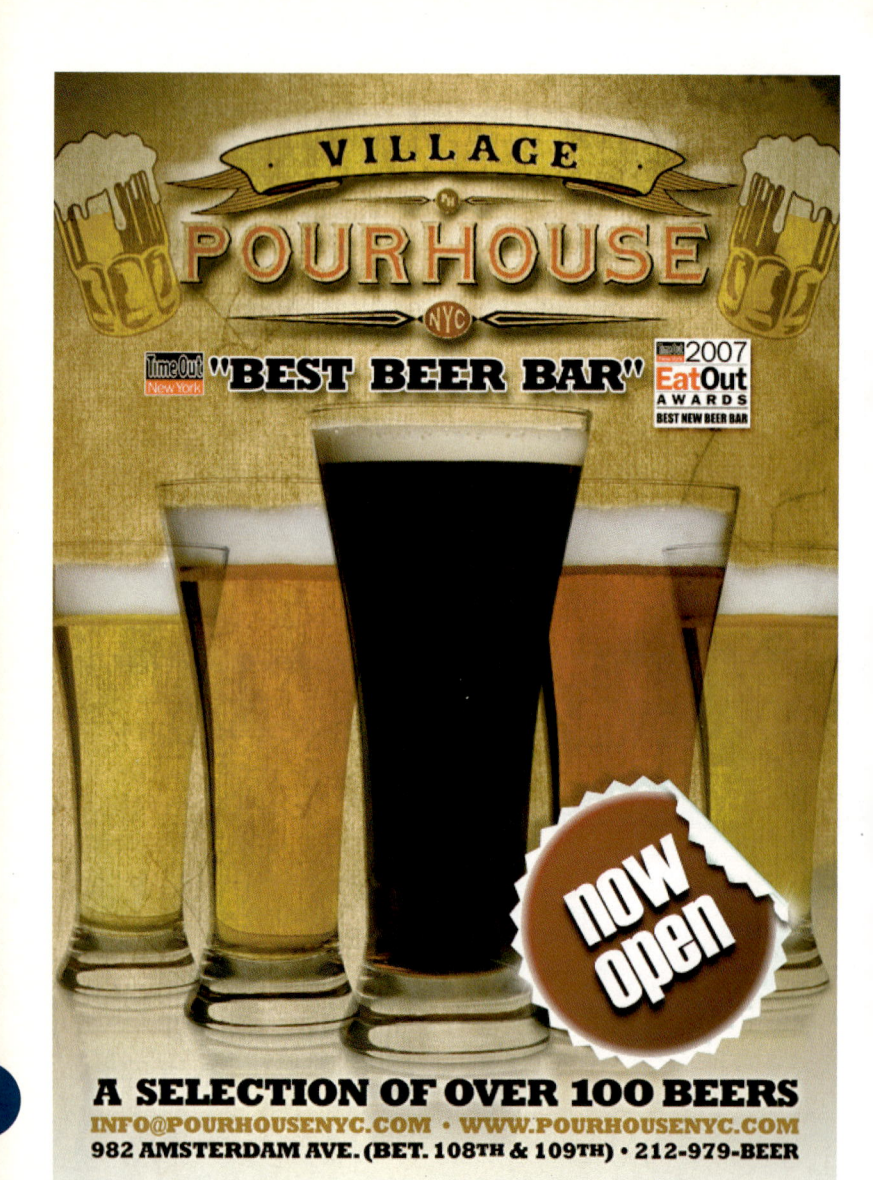

VILLAGE POURHOUSE

212-979-BEER
982 AMSTERDAM AVE.
(BET. 108TH & 109TH ST.)
NEW YORK, NY 10025
INFO@POURHOUSENYC.COM
WWW.POURHOUSENYC.COM

CALL NOW & BE ONE OF THE FIRST TO HAVE A PARTY AT THE NEW POURHOUSE

SUN. NFL GAME WATCH SUNDAYS
2 for 1 bloody mary's, mimosas

MON. WING IT MONDAYS
25¢ Wings
$8 Bud Light Pitchers

TUE. ALMOST FAMOUS TUESDAYS w/ ROCK BAND, GUITAR HERO, & KARAOKE
2 for 1 Drinks & 1/2 price appetizers all night (9pm-close) Game Night

WED. TRIVIA WEDNESDAYS
$5 bombs starting at 10pm & Free drink prizes during trivia

THU. BEER PONG THURSDAYS
$8 Bud/Bud Light Pitchers

FRI. LADIES' NIGHT FRIDAYS
Ladies drink half price 10pm-close

SAT. DAYTIME: COLLEGE FOOTBALL GAME WATCH

SAT. NIGHT: DJ PLAYING GREAT MUSIC ALL NIGHT

VILLAGE POWER HOUR
10pm-11pm Every Night
$2 Bud & Bud Light Draft
$2 Well Drinks

OPENS 11AM DAILY 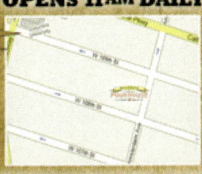
POURHOUSENYC.COM

Daily Lunch HAPPY HOUR 12PM TO 7PM
$1 Bud & Budlight Drafts
2 for 1 Sauza Margaritas
2 for 1 Absolut drinks

20% OFF ENTIRE DINNER WITH STUDENT I.D.
coupon expires July 31, 2009

ONE FREE DRINK 21 I.D. REQUIRED
coupon expires July 31, 2009

10% OFF ENTIRE BILL
coupon expires July 31, 2009

CU IT

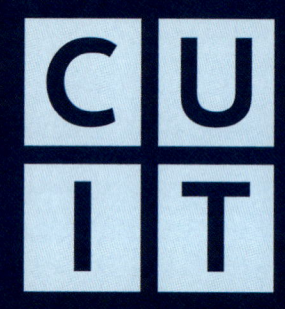

COLUMBIA UNIVERSITY INFORMATION TECHNOLOGY

http://askcuit.columbia.edu

» email
askcuit@columbia.edu

» by phone
212.854.1919

» in person
102 Philosphy Hall

PRINT SERVICES

THE SERVICES YOU NEED... FAST!

DESIGN
Graphic design
Consultation
Scanning
Typesetting

OFFSET PRINTING
Prepress expertise
1 and full color printing

PRODUCTION
Full and self-service copying
Color and black & white copies
Poster and banner printing
Sheet-fed scanning

BINDERY
Binding
Foam-core mounting
Laminating

BULK MAIL
Addressing
Postage metering
Fulfillment

OFFICE COPIERS
Copier leasing and purchasing
Maintenance contracts

Ask About Our Wide Format Posters and Banners

Morningside Locations
SCHOOL OF JOURNALISM BUILDING
2950 Broadway, Room 106
Tel: 212-854-3233
Fax: 212-854-4421

INTERNATIONAL AFFAIRS BUILDING
420 West 118th Street, Room 401
Tel: 212-854-4300
Fax: 212-864-2728

Medical Center Location
PHYSICIANS & SURGEONS BUILDING
630 West 168th Street, Room 2-466
Tel: 212-305-3614
Fax: 212-342-2925

COLUMBIA UNIVERSITY

WELCOME CLASS OF 2012!

For all your student needs, please contact the following offices:

Dean of the College
212.854.3075

Dean of Studies
212.854.2024

ASAP*
212.854.2128

Career Development
212.854.2033

College Activities
212.854.2096

Disability Services
212.854.4634

Financial Aid
212.854.2154

Health Service
212.854.2091

HEOP Scholars
212.854.3583

Furman Counseling Center
212.854.2092

Multicultural Affairs
212.854.9130

Registrar
212.854.2011

Residential Life
212.854.5561

Well-Woman**
212.854.3063

*Alcohol & Substance Awareness Program
**Health Promotion

BARNARD
THE LIBERAL ARTS COLLEGE
FOR WOMEN
IN NEW YORK CITY

THE EARLY BIRD GETS THE JOB.

It's never too early to start planning your career!

Visit the Center for Career Education at Columbia University to attend workshops and events, meet with a counselor, receive job and internship postings and more.

- Meet with a Career Counselor for walk-in hours, from 1 – 4 p.m. during the semester or call us to make an appointment.

- Register with LionSHARE to gain access to full-time job listings, internships and part-time jobs on and off campus.

East Campus, Lower Level
116th Street between Morningside and Amsterdam
(Enter through Wien Courtyard)

212-854-5609
www.careereducation.columbia.edu

COLUMBIA UNIVERSITY CENTER FOR
Career Education

Serving Columbia University for 20 years!

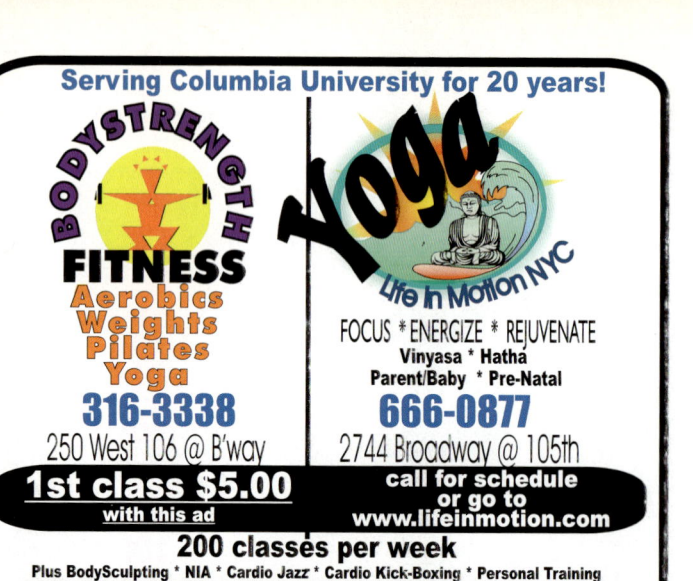

BODYSTRENGTH FITNESS
Aerobics
Weights
Pilates
Yoga
316-3338
250 West 106 @ B'way

1st class $5.00
with this ad

Yoga — Life In Motion NYC
FOCUS * ENERGIZE * REJUVENATE
Vinyasa * Hatha
Parent/Baby * Pre-Natal
666-0877
2744 Broadway @ 105th

call for schedule
or go to
www.lifeinmotion.com

200 classes per week
Plus BodySculpting * NIA * Cardio Jazz * Cardio Kick-Boxing * Personal Training

*Anyone who purchases a class card or Life In Motion membership after their first class receives a 20 % savings. Class cards are good at Life In Motion (105 & Broadway), BodyStrength Fitness (106th & B'way), Namaste Yoga (77th & Amsterdam), Park Slope Yoga and Devi (Brooklyn).

THE BEST RENTAL AGENT IN NYC IS HERE TO HELP YOU FIND YOUR NEW HOME!

Work with an agent with the most residential rental listings in Manhattan.
No pressure agent. Listening to all your housing needs is key. It's not just about finding apartments, it's about finding your next home!

*Call for details and FREE consultation

Brian McEnany Licensed Real Estate Salesperson
Phone: 646-342-6536 **Email:** bmcenany@citi-habitats.com
Proud member of REBNY

$100 Visa giftcard with every lease signed!*

248 MORNINGSIDE HEIGHTS

Days Hotel

215 W. 94th St. (Broadway & 94th)
New York, NY, US, 10025
Phone: (212) 866-6400 or (800) 834-2972
Fax: (212) 866-1357

DAYS HOTEL
Broadway

10% Discount to Columbia students, faculty, families, and friends

---

Welcome CC & SEAS

Class of
2012

from the
Center for Student Advising

212.854.6378
http://www.studentaffairs.columbia.edu/csa/

DIVISION OF STUDENT AFFAIRS
AT COLUMBIA UNIVERSITY

Landmark Guest Rooms
at Union Theological Seminary

Comfortable guest rooms within the Seminary's walls blend the best of old and new.

Our peaceful garden is an ideal spot for strolling, reading, and meditation. But it is just a short bus or cab ride away from all the excitement that New York City has to offer.

UNION 3041 Broadway
at 121st Street
New York, NY 10027

Telephone: 212-280-1313 • Fax: 212-280-1488
Visit the Seminary at www.uts.columbia.edu

MORNINGSIDE HEIGHTS 249

WEST WAY Café

Prompt Delivery

**Breakfast - Lunch
Dinner - Smoothies
Fresh Juice Bar**

**2800 BROADWAY
(corner of 108th)**

(212) 932-9059

Mill
Korean Restaurant

2895 Broadway
New York, New York 10025
tel: (212) 666-7653

LUNCH SPECIAL

250 MORNINGSIDE HEIGHTS

FOTORUSH/DIGITAL

One Hour Processing • CD/Digital Media • Passport Photo

Either CONVENTIONAL or DIGITAL PHOTOGRAPHY come to FOTORUSH

We will SERVE your IMAGING NEEDS

PASSPORT + IMMI-GRATION PHOTOS

2878 Broadway @112th St, New York, New York 10025
TEL 212 749-0065

Breakfast, Lunch, Dinner, Brunch, Catering

Fresh Baked Pastries & Breads
Daily Recipes

Camille's

1135 Amsterdam Ave.
(Under the awning at 116th St.)
New York City, New York 10025
212.749.2428

Beer & Wine

Take Out & Delivery

COLUMBIA UNIVERSITY DERMATOLOGY ASSOCIATES

The Dermatology Associates of Columbia University Medical Center understand the importance of maintaining proper care of your skin in order to protect it against skin cancer and infections and to retain its radiance and beauty. Our board certified dermatologists provide the latest state-of-the-art treatment for conditions of the skin, hair and nails for patients of all ages.

The Dermatology Associates of Columbia University Medical Center provide clinical expertise in the following subspecialty areas:

- Contact Dermatitis and Occupational Dermatology
- Cosmetic Dermatology
- Dermatologic Surgery
- Hair and Nail Disorders
- Laser Surgery
- Mohs Micrographic Surgery
- Skin Cancer Prevention and Early Detection
- Pediatric Dermatology
- Psoriasis and Phototherapy

To schedule an appointment or consultation please contact our office at 212.305.5293. For more information about our services please visit our website at www.dermatology.columbia.edu.

We are conveniently located at two Manhattan locations

Herbert Irving Center for
Dermatology and Skin Cancer
161 Fort Washington Avenue
12th FL
New York, NY 10032

Columbia University
Dermatology Associates
16 East 60th Street, Suite 300
New York, NY 10022

COLUMBIA UNIVERSITY
Department of Dermatology

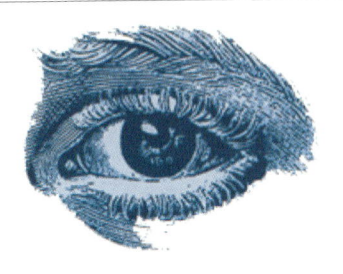

Columbia Ophthalmology Consultants, Inc.

The full-time faculty practice of the Department of Ophthalmology at Columbia University Medical Center. We are a group of consulting ophthalmologists trained and board certified in all subspecialties including:

General Ophthalmology, LASIK, Adult & Pediatric Glaucoma, Vitreoretinal and Macular Diseases, Cataract Surgery, and Pediatric Ophthalmology.

All are dedicated to offering outstanding clinical care.

We participate in many insurance plans and have several practice locations for your convenience.

212-305-9535
www.columbiaeye.org

COLUMBIA SCHOOL OF MIXOLOGY

where bartenders are made

MASTER YOUR DRINKS WITH A FULLY STOCKED BAR

LOWEST FEE IN THE CITY
CLASSES OFFERED YEAR ROUND

COLUMBIA BARTENDING AGENCY
www.ColumbiaBartending.com

We don't just make drinks,

We make experiences

HIRE A BARTENDER TODAY

*Private Events
*Office Parties
*Baby Showers
*Wedding Receptions
*Birthday Parties

Able to Accomodate Your Every Need

bartenders -- servers -- waiters
SERVING YOU SINCE 1965

COLUMBIA BOOKSTORE

General reading Selection of Over 50,000 Titles
Legal Outlines & Study Aids
Huge Selection of Columbia Apparel
Dorm Accessories & School Supplies
Online Textbook Reservations

Friendly Customer Service • Open 7 Days

Located in Lerner Hall • www.columbiabookstore.com
2922 Broadway @ 115th St. • 212-854-4131

TAP-A-KEG

2731 BROADWAY
BET. 104th & 105th STS
INTERNET JUKEBOX
FREE WIFI
POOL TABLE   DARTS
12 BEERS ON TAP

*WE HAVE NO KITCHEN SO BRING YOUR OWN
OR HAVE IT DELIVERED
HAPPY HOUR EVERDAY 12 NOON UNTIL 7PM
OPEN 7 DAYS FROM 12 NOON TO 4AM
212-749-1734*

Columbia Hardware
Has expanded after years to...

University Hardware
2905 Broadway
(212) 662-2150
113th Street

and

University Houseware
2901 Broadway
(212) 882-2798
113th Street

*For All your Hardware and Houseware Needs
Mention Inside New York and Get a 10% Discount*

Gl🌐bal COPY

"THE COPY SHOP THAT CAN'T BE DUPLICATED"

2578 BROADWAY (BET. 97TH & 98TH ST.)
PHONE: 212-222-COPY (2679) ▪ FAX: 212-222-3269

STORE HOURS
MONDAY - FRIDAY
8:00AM - 9:00PM
SATURDAY
9:00AM - 7:00PM
SUNDAY
11:00AM - 7:00PM

Xerox Copies ▪ Canon Color Laser Copies ▪ Fax Service
High Speed Internet Access ▪ Computer Rentals
Binding ▪ Cutting ▪ Folding ▪ Laminating
Video to DVD Conversion ▪ Mailbox Rentals ▪ Keys Cut
Customized Photo T-Shirts and Calendars
Same Day Business Card, Letterhead and Envelope Service

Mention This Ad For A 10% Discount

Mailbox Rentals Available

FedEx & UPS
Shipping Services Available

A Professional, Caring, Comfortable Environment
Established Practice For Over 20 Years

Help When You Need It Most
Same Day Appointments Available Mon. Thru Sat.

ABORTION SERVICES

- 5-24 Weeks ▪ Awake or Asleep ▪
- Abortion By Pill ▪
- RU486 ▪ Morning After Pill ▪
- Birth Control/STD Testing ▪
- Complete Obstetrical/Gyn Care ▪
- Gentle Examinations ▪
- Personalized Attention ▪

Free Pregnancy Testing
Safe & Confidential

WE'RE AFFORDABLE!
Most HMO's, Insurance & Medicaid Plans Accepted

Walk-Ins Welcome

Eastside Gynecology
A COMPLETE WOMEN'S CARE FACILITY

212-308-4988

Medical Care By Board Certified Obstetricians & Gynecologists

Hablamos Espanol   225 E. 64th St. ▪ Manhattan (Midtown, Bet 2nd & 3rd Aves.)

See Why We Are Different From The Rest

ARCHITECTS, ENGINEERS & BUSINESS FREINDS WORKING FOR THE FUTURE OF COLUMBIA

- Construction Management
- Consulting
- General Contracting
- WBE Certified

Construction Contractors of NY Corp.
YOUR SINGLE SOURCE BUILDER

Visit Our Website • www.ccnycorp.com

Monica Mastrapasqua
President

208 Russell Place
Hackensack, NJ 07601

Tel: 201-996-1115
Fax: 201-996-1116

Ammann & Whitney provides architectural and engineering services for new buildings, expansion or renovation at universities nationwide

AMMANN & WHITNEY

96 Morton Street, New York, NY 10014 ▪ (212) 462-8500
www.ammann-whitney.com

Serving the entire New York Metropolitan Area for over 65 years

Visit our website to review our services:
- Residential
- Commercial (O & I)
- Library
- Hotel Installation

CLANCY-CULLEN
MOVING & STORAGE CO. INC.

www.clancy-cullen.com

"Moving you in the right direction since 1934"

800-223-8340

2339 Cross Bronx Expressway
Bronx, NY 10462

TRANE

TRANE NEW YORK
45-18 COURT SQUARE
LONG ISLAND CITY, NY 11101
PHONE: **718-269-3600**

Your Partner for Products Applications to Comprehensive System Solutions

Equipment
System and Control Service
HVAC Parts and Supplies
Building Automation System
Turnkey Installations
Temporary Cooling
24-Emergency Service

www.tranenynj.com

JB&B

Jaros Baum & Bolles
Consulting Engineers

80 Pine Street
New York, NY 10005

WEIDLINGER
ASSOCIATES

Structural Engineering • Civil Engineering • Applied Sciences

Weidlinger Associates Consulting Engineers, P.C.
375 Hudson Street New York, NY 10014
(212) 367-3000 Fax: (212) 367-3030
http://www.wai.com

MORNINGSIDE HEIGHTS 259

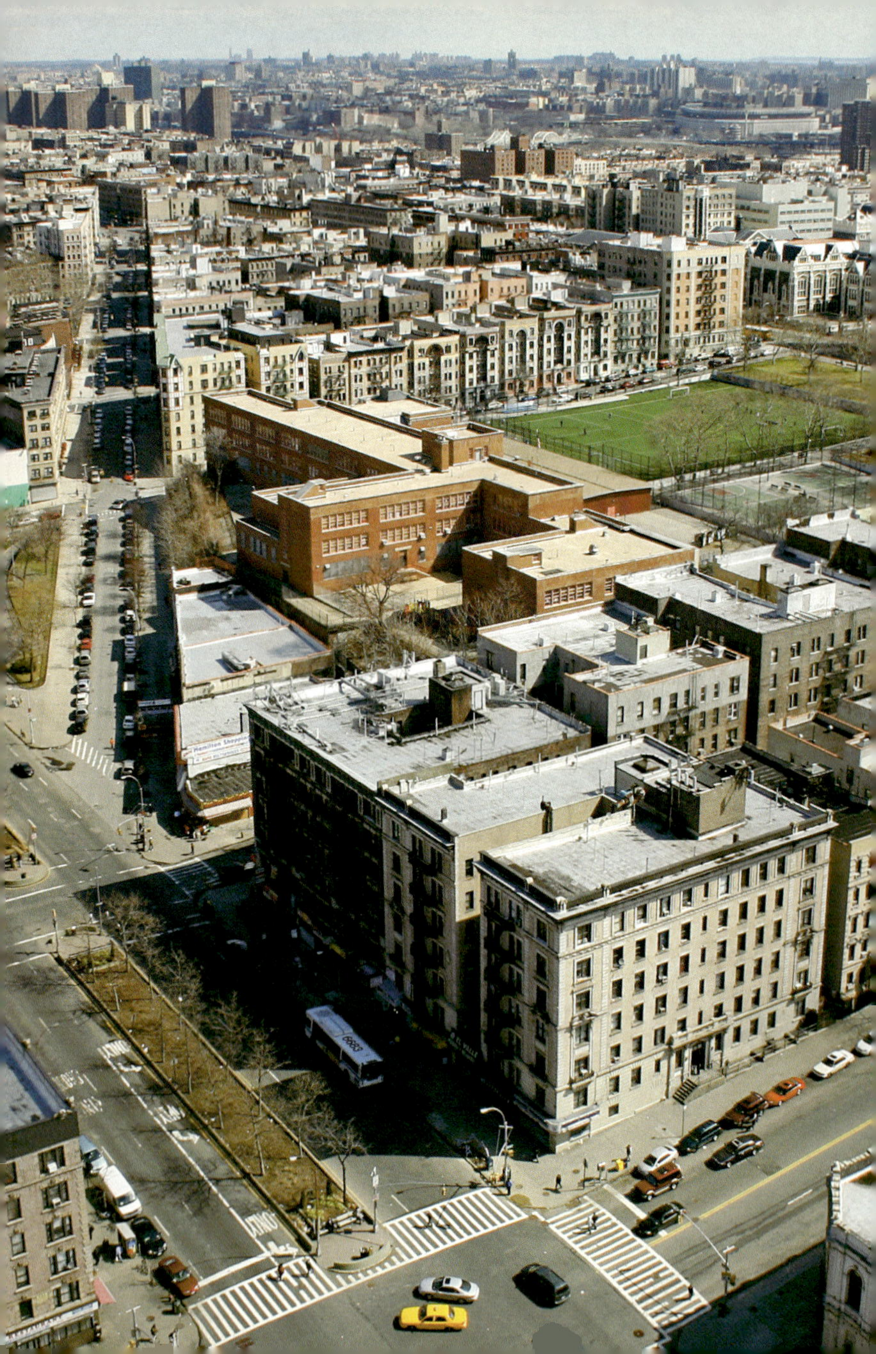

CENTRAL HARLEM

Once the home for wealthy black professionals and their families half a century ago, the streets of Central Harlem still bear connections to a culturally rich past, as well as to an uncertain future of poor health, continued impoverishment, and inadequate public education.

Around the late 1800s, a boom of prosperity brought in an influx of young families to construct gleaming townhouses and opulent brownstones along Saint Nicholas Avenue and the surrounding areas, such as Striver's Row, the Saint Nicholas Historic District, and Astor Row. However, in the period between 1940 and 1990, as the general region of Harlem fell into an economic slump, many of these houses became ramshackle husks of their former majestic selves. Then, roughly in 1980, the rows of townhouses were converted into historic landmarks, allowing both locals and tourists to enjoy the renovated façades.

As the Harlem Renaissance exploded in the early 1920s, Central Harlem, along with West Harlem and East Harlem, enjoyed the fruits of local writers, artists, and musicians. W.E.B. DuBois, Langston Hughes, and Nora Zeale Hurston spun out literary masterpieces, while audiences of the Apollo Theatre and the Lenox Lounge reveled in Amateur Nights and jazz acts. Yet, those artistic achievements during the years of the Renaissance were eclipsed by the heroin and then crack epidemics, which brought with them poverty and nightmarish crime rates.

Steps have been taken to remedy some of Central Harlem's problems—former Mayor Rudolph Giuliani, using highly controversial tactics, ensured that many of the crime-infested housing projects were systematically cleaned up during his term, and today Central Harlem is among the safest neighborhoods in Manhattan. As in most other neighborhoods, gentrification is in the minds of all Harlem residents, but today the cultural heart of this thriving community is once again beating strong.

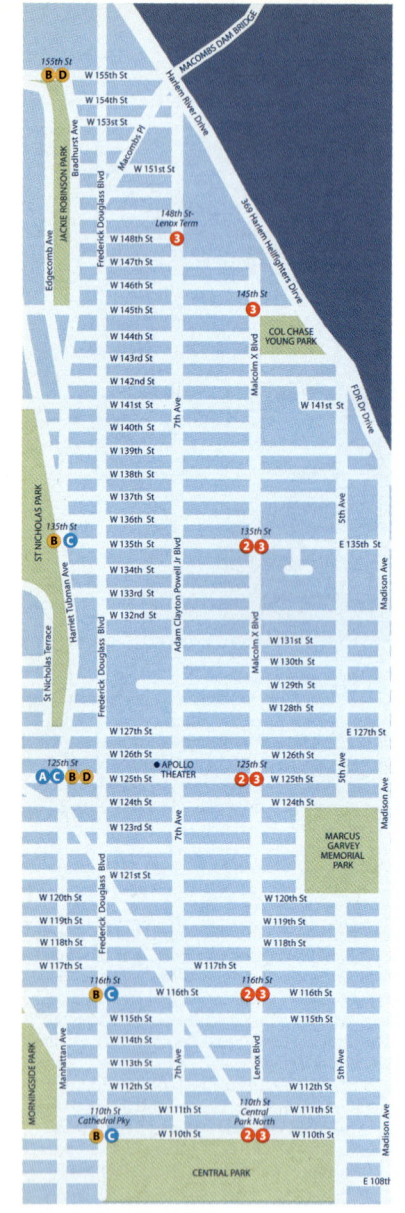

ATTRACTIONS

Marcus Garvey Park
In 1973, what was once Mount Morris Park became Marcus Garvey Park, in honor of the publisher, journalist, and founder of the black nationalist organization, Universal Negro Improvement Association. Now, for locals looking to gather with friends and take a break from hectic city life, this is the place to come. Grab a picnic on top of the Acropolis, an artificial plateau in the middle of the park with views of Yankee Stadium and The Empire State Building, or swim in the public pool located at the north side of the park.
Madison Ave (from 120th to 124th St). ❷ ❸ ❹ ❺ ❻ *to 125th.*

Rucker Park
Upon first glance, this may look just like any other park, but look closer and you may see a famous basketball player dancing down the court. This is perhaps the most filmed basketball court in the country, partially because of the baffling number of NBA stars who got their start here. During the summer the court hosts the All-Pro Summer Basketball League. The season kicks off during mid-June, so kick back, relax and catch a game Monday through Thursday, or a higher pressure tournament on Friday night. Just don't be surprised to see a few contenders playing well out of their league.
155th and Frederick Douglass Blvd. ❽ ❶ *to 155th.*

Schomburg Center
This branch of the New York Public Library includes over five million texts, photographs, paintings and other items describing and documenting experiences of people of African descent from around the world. It was named after Arturo Alfonso Schomburg, who added his personal collection to the Division of Negro Literature, History and Prints at this branch and later served as the curator of the division. Don't miss the impressive collection of art from Africa, the African diaspora, and the Harlem Renaissance. Check out some of the free or cheap concerts hosted here as well.
515 Malcolm X Blvd (at 136th St). 212-491-2200. Mon-Wed 12pm-8pm, Thurs-Fri 11am-6pm, Sat 10am-5pm, Closed Sun. ❷ ❸ *to 135th.*

262 CENTRAL HARLEM

CULTURE & ARTS

Apollo Theater
This famed Harlem venue shows no sign of slowing. The Apollo offers a variety of ongoing programs, like the famous weekly open-mic Amateur Night, where hopeful talents work their acts in front of an enthusiastic (and enthusiastically critical) crowd. Well-known and emerging musicians, comedians, and dancers continue to take the stage at this community mainstay as well. Group tours exploring the theater's rich past are available by appointment.
253 W 125th St (between 7th Ave & Frederick Douglass Blvd). 212-531-5300. Hours vary. Ⓐ Ⓒ Ⓑ Ⓓ ❷ ❸ *to 125th.*

Canvas Paper and Stone Gallery
This contemporary gallery/art supply store hybrid is perfect for those looking to decorate dreary dorm rooms on a budget. Much of the selection is rooted in African American, Latin American, and Hellenic cultures; however, the collection also encompasses bold Art Deco designs, Pop Art figures and objects, vintage patterns, and Native American drawings—a home for all types of eccentric art. The supply store complements the gallery nicely: you pick the piece, you pick a frame, and you leave a satisfied customer.
2611 8th Ave, Studio 2N (near W 139th St). 212-694-1747. Tues-Sat 12pm-6pm. Ⓐ Ⓒ Ⓑ *to 135th,* ❷ ❸ *to 137th.*

Harlem School of the Arts
Despite humble origins (only twelve kids showed up for the first day), the Harlem School of the Arts now serves almost three thousand children every year and offers fun courses for all ages, like Physical Acting, Camera Antics, and Pastel Techniques. With Birthday Parties in the Arts and a six-week summer arts camp called Artscape, the faculty seeks to promote and preserve an intensive knowledge of the arts for the residents of Harlem and beyond. Drop by the state-of-the-art theater and check out one of the monthly performances or exhibits, such as the amateur-friendly tap dance extravaganza "Hoofer's Night."
645 Saint Nicholas Ave (between 141st & 145th St). 212-926-4100. Mon-Fri 2:30pm-8pm, Sat 9am-8pm. ❶ *to 145th.*

National Black Theatre
The National Black Theatre showcases monthly events, ranging from somber recitals to boisterous musicals, which celebrate the work of local artists and honor African-American culture. Founded more than forty years ago by the late Dr. Barbara Ann Teer, the theatre consists of two cavernous compartments – the Theatre Performance Space and the Temple of Liberation. Check out the Performance Space, where talented thespians weave the stories of Dorothy Dandridge and Billie Holiday, or swing by the Temple and admire the prominent Yoruba Sacred Art.
2031-33 Fifth Ave (between 125th & 126th St). 212-722-3800. 9am-5pm daily. ❷ ❸ *to 125th.*

Studio Museum in Harlem
Founded in 1968, this was the first American museum devoted to the art of African Americans; in addition to art made in the US, it now includes work from the Caribbean and Africa, making it an international hub for black artists. The exhibits often center on issues of African or African American identity. Some even address the immediate community, asking viewers questions about Harlem's place in black culture

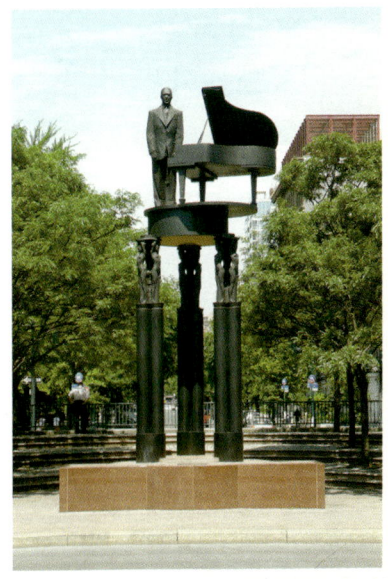

CENTRAL HARLEM 263

and history.
144 W 125th St (between 7th Ave and Lenox Ave). 212-864-4500. Wed-Fri 12pm-6pm, Sat 10am-6pm, Sun 12pm-6pm. Suggested donation adults $7, students $3. 🅐🅒🅑🅓❷❸❹❺❻ *to 125th.*

DINING

MID-RANGE
Amy Ruth's *Southern*
Amy Ruth's passes the true food-quality test—a quarter of an hour after dining, when the easy charm of fat and salt has faded, the home-style cooking induces a fully pleasing food coma. The fried chicken is crispy and moist, while the BBQ spare ribs are luscious, tender, and come doused in a magical barbecue sauce. More importantly, each entrée comes with two (2!) sides, options for which include heavenly mac 'n' cheese, fluffy and wonderful mashed potatoes, agonizingly sweet (in a good way) candied yams, and probably the best collard greens north of the Mason-Dixon. This glory of a meal is served in a friendly, old school dining room with an authentic sense of history. Service can be less than attentive, but you'll be too busy stuffing your face to mind.
113 W 116th St (near Lenox Ave). 212-280-8779. Sun-Thurs 7:30am-11pm, Fri-Sat 24 hours. ❷❸ *to 116th,* 🅑🅒 *to 116th. Average entree $13.*

Billie's Black *Soul Food*
Old meets new at this upscale soul food restaurant and lounge, where you can wash down a heaping pile of Grand Marnier BBQ ribs with a cup of new-agey "think tea". Red velvet drapery, mood lighting, and stylized collages of African women rule the décor. While waiters sway to R&B beats under an idly circling disco ball, the seriously formidable fireplug chef churns out hearty standbys, including the Billie's specialty—toothsome golden fillets of fried catfish. Appetizers and sides are solid but unremarkable, so try your best to save room for dessert, since the recommended red velvet cake is required eating—a thick, moist slab of solid scarlet anchoring swirls of sweet icing and whipped cream.
271 W 119th St (near St. Nicholas Ave). 212-280-2248. Tues-Thurs 12pm-12am, Fri-Sat 12pm-4am, Sun 12pm-8pm. Bar open til 4am every night. 🅑🅒 *to 116th. Average entrée $18.*

EDITOR'S PICK
Miss Maude's Spoonbread Too
Soul Food
The décor follows through on the menu's promise to take you back on home, with checkered tile floors, frayed floral curtains, and shelves of antique utensils hanging beside old sepia portraits of matriarchs in their Sunday best. Below the frames, uptown church ladies sip the tart, sweet-ish Spoonbread punch and chat over humming fans. For $17.95, only a few dollars more than most entrees, Miss Maude's Sampler offers several of them in alleged "sample" portions—in reality, a loaded tray of soul-food splendor that rewards those gluttonous enough to struggle through a smorgasbord of fried chicken, succulent beef ribs, catfish, and more, along with your choice of three large sides like toothsome cornbread stuffing. Beware: you'll probably have to endure a groaning walk home before you can unbutton your pants and collapse for a hard-earned nap.
547 Lenox Ave (near 138th St). 212-690-3100. Mon-Thurs 12pm-9:30pm, Fri-Sat 12pm-10:30pm, Sun 11am-9:30pm. ❷❸ *to 135th. Average entrée $15.*

264 CENTRAL HARLEM

Mobay *Caribbean*
With live jazz, R&B, and reggae music every Tuesday through Saturday, and a gospel music brunch on Sunday, Mobay's dining room is always festive. The swanky red-lit bar sets the mood for the rest of the restaurant, which retains the intimate feel of a neighborhood lounge. Venture out into exotic territory by sipping on house-made Sorrell, or try one of the inventive tropical cocktails; though pricey, the strawberry mango mojito will not disappoint, especially if ordered with a plate of tender grilled shrimp, served with rich and tangy barbecue sauce. With coconut curried salmon, Smokey Joe's St. Louis style barbecue ribs, and brown stewed veggie chicken, Mobay's menu has an entrée for every palate. Save room for the spicy, punch-packing famous rummy rum cake or the death by chocolate cake, which oozes with rich molten goo.
17 W 125th St (between Lenox Ave & 5th Ave) 212-876-9300. Mon-Wed 11am-11pm, Thurs-Sat 11am-12am, Sun 11am-10pm. ❹❺❻ *to 125th. Average entrée $18.*

Oklahoma Smoke BBQ *American*
A grandfather's time tested BBQ sauce recipe and a smoking process of eight hours combine to make one tasty rack of ribs with meat that falls right off the bone. Prepared in the unique dry-rub Oklahoma style, Midwest expats swear by its authenticity. It isn't just the meats here that will have your mouth watering. The collard greens are stewed to a salty perfection and the candied yams are a richly spiced treat. The best side, however, may be the creamy potato salad with just enough paprika and the perfect amount of mayonnaise.
231 West 145th St (near Adam Clayton Powell Jr Blvd). 212-862-5335. Tues-Sun 11am-11pm. ❹❶❷❸❸ *to 145th. Average entrée $10.*

Revival *New American*
In this handsome building, slide into a cozy booth and ready your stomach for hearty soul food with a dollop of sophistication. Many come to sit and chat at the bar, but the food is too comforting to pass up. In portions that stretch the definition of appetizer to its breaking point, neighborhood favorites like cornbread and shrimp are elevated by wonderfully flavorful mushrooms and creamy risotto. Save room for the well cooked entrées, liberally flavored with garlic and butter. If you wish to finish on a sweet note, the passion fruit mousse is light and tart after such substantial fare.
2367 Frederick Douglas Blvd (at 127th). 212-222-8338. Lunch Tues-Fri 12pm-3pm. Dinner Sun-Thurs 5pm-10:30pm, Fri-Sat 5pm-11pm. Brunch served Sat-Sun 11am-3:30pm. ❹❶❷❸ *to 125th. Average entrée $17.*

LITTLE SENEGAL

This is Le Petit Senegal—a three-block slice of Dakar in central Harlem, and the main social and shopping enclave for Harlem's many West African immigrants. Running along West 116th street, roughly from Frederick Douglass Boulevard to St. Nicholas Ave, its exact borders are ill-defined, in large part because the neighborhood is so new, having exploded from nonexistence in 1985 into a bustling community of around 6,500 today. The streets are packed and vibrant, twitchy with the chaotic energy of a cultural community packed into a few random blocks. Neighbors chatting and laughing in French and Wolof crowd front stoops and folding chairs as shrieking kids on scooters rocket past. Specialty stores sell everything from dashikis and dried herbs to Koran audiobooks and badly dubbed Nigerian movies about true love and corrupt politics. At 116th and Frederick Douglas, the large **Africa Kine Restaurant** (*256 W 116th St, 212-666-9400*) acts as unofficial embassy for the immigrant community – every day expats meet in its elegant second-story dining room to catch up, watch Senegal Lions soccer matches on flat-screen TVs, and enjoy a sizeable taste of home.

CHEAP
Make My Cake *Bakery*
Done up in bright pastel paint and tasseled with silk butterflies and flowers, the inside of this bakery has been made as lollipop-sweet as humanly possible. The baked goods more than hold their own, though, against the adorable interior decorating. A wide selection of cupcakes fills a glass display, routinely luring casual visitors into $3 of caloric indulgence;

the red velvet cake with buttercream icing alone is worth the trip. With ample seating next to large plate glass windows and coffee by the cup, those who can't wait for their sugar high often choose to eat up right in the store. Custom cakes are available, call 48 hours in advance.
121 St. Nicholas Ave (at 116th St) 212-932-0833. Sun 9am-7pm, Mon-Tues 7am-pm, Wed-Thurs 7am-8pm, Fri 7am-9pm, Sat 9am-9pm. **B C** *to 116th. Cupcakes $3.*

Manna's Soul Food *Southern*
A steaming four-aisle buffet of soul food and salad bar standbys allows even the most ravenous appetites to fill up on the cheap. At $5.49 per pound for home-style delicacies such as slow-cooked brisket, smothered barbeque ribs, crispy fried chicken, and collard greens, this is a restaurant that attracts large crowds all competing for the serving spoons. After the cashier has weighed your plastic container filled with a delicious dinner or lunch, it might be a good idea to pack it up for home and avoid the cacophony in the dining area.
2311 8th Ave (at 125th St) 212-749-9084. Mon-Sat 10am-9pm, Sun 10am-8pm. **A C B D** *to 125th. Food $5.49/lb.*

Settepani Bakery *Cafe, Italian*
This spacious café, with ample seating and a large outdoor patio, offers a huge selection of baked goods in all shapes and sizes: bite-sized cookies, fresh bread, thick and varied cakes, tarts and pastries—jelly-filled, almond-crusted, frosted, sugared, and dipped in chocolate. Settepani also serves up a small menu of steadfast Italian fare for lunch and dinner, served daily, as well as a Sunday brunch.
196 Lenox Ave (at 120th St) 917-492-4886. Sun-Thurs 7am-11pm, Fri-Sat 7am-12am. **2 3** *to 116th. Average panini $10, baked goods $10.50.*

Sokhna *Senegalese*
This homey diner ladles up delicious, no-frills, stewed-for-hours curries. Pony up your $10, which is the most anything on the menu costs, and have the server tell you which items are really being served—with so many of these stews slow-cooked, about half of the menu is only available once a week. It's always worth the wait, though; vegetable-laden entrées are packed with standards like carrot, tomato, and onion, then supplemented with exotic fare like cassava and spiced up with Scotch Bonnet peppers. Hard-to-find drinks like baobob juice are sweet and delicious accompaniments to your meal. The décor is simple but comfortable; multi-colored lightbulbs cast a warm glow over the dining room, dark draperies line the walls, and African league football matches play on a lone television.
225 W 116th St (near 7th Ave). 212-864-0081. Daily 9am-2am. **6 B C** *to 116th,* **A D** *to 125th. Entrées $10.*

NIGHTLIFE

The Den *Bar, Lounge*
The Den is the destination lounge of Harlem. The cocktail menu features 27 drinks all with fun and vaguely ominous names such as "Get drunk or die tryin'," "Wifey potentiale,"and "Sex in the Inner City." The menu features soul food standards as well as "Soul" sushi rolls cleverly combining soul food ingredients in sushi roll form (ie: fried chicken rolled into waffles and topped with strawberries). The huge menu, strong drinks (often served with

a shot), and nightly music mixed by great DJs attracts a blend of sophisticated singles and private parties.
2150 5th Ave (between 131st & 132nd St). 212-234-3045. Wed-Thurs 6pm-1am, Fri-Sat 6pm-6am. (Serving breakfast from 2am-6am). ❷❸ *to 135th. Average drink $13.*

Harlem Lanes *Bowling*
More than your friendly neighborhood bowling alley, Harlem Lanes maintains a local feel while providing a far from typical multi-media experience. Hip-hop music blasts, lights flash, and twenty four plasma screen TVs play everything from sitcoms (slightly distracting when trying to get that last pin) to sports games. For those not interested in bowling, a pool table, arcade games, a lounge, and a sports bar offer plenty of alternatives. This is a favorite hangout for everyone from families to twenty-somethings to middle aged professionals looking to unwind after work. Friday and Saturday nights after 8pm offer a repreive from the families that otherwise dominate, as do special event nights which include karaoke on Mondays and open-mic on Wednesdays.
2116 7th Ave (between 125th & 126th St), 3rd fl. 212-678-2695. Sun 11am-9pm, Mon-Thurs 11am-11pm, Fri-Sat 11am-3am. ❷❸Ⓐ🅒🅑🅓 *to 125th. Mon-Thurs $ 5.50 per person/per game Friday-Sunday $7.50/person/game. $4.50 shoe rental.*

SHOPPING

AtmosNY
As Harlem's main thoroughfare is increasingly blanketed with big-name clothing franchises, this Spartan "streetware boutique" manages to maintain some integrity and preserve some the neighborhood's character. Check out this fluorescent-lit chamber of concrete and glass, which boasts established brands as well as works from independent designers for a daily swarm of tourists and local shoppers.
*203 W 125th St. 212-666-2242. Mon-Sat 11am-8pm, Sun 12pm-7pm.*❷❸Ⓐ🅒🅑🅓 *to 125th.*

Harlem's Heaven Hat Boutique
Besides the staggering array of every sort of hat imaginable, this specialty shop also

DAY TO DAY

Community Board 10: *215 West 125th Street, 4th Fl. 212-749-3105*

Local Media: Harlem World. *harlemworldblog.wordpress.com.*

Groceries: C Town Supermarket. *2117 7th Ave, 212-368-5700.*

Gym: New York Sports Club. *2311 Frederick Douglass Blvd. 212-316-2500.*

Rent: One Bedroom: $1,757

Hospital: Harlem Hospital Center. *506 Lenox Ave. 212-939-5000.*

Hostels and Hotels: 102 Brownstone Hotel. *102 W 118th. 212-662-4223.*

Dog Runs: Marcus Garvey Park. *Madison Ave & E 120th St.*

Movie Theater: AMC Magic Johnson Harlem 9. *2309 Frederick Douglass Blvd. 212-665-6923.*

Best Happy Hour: Billie's Black. *271 W 119th St. 212-280-2248.*

offers quirky bags, iridescent hat pins, and eccentric vintage gear, including armadillo skin earrings and Indian head brooches. The store's extensive hat collection for women covers everything from demure church bonnets to practical "working girl" caps, while the men's hat line is equally impressive in breadth – dapper fedoras sit side-by-side with sturdy sun-hats. Prices start at around $35, though a regularly updated clearance rack and the wide selection should more than compensate.
2538 7th Ave (at W. 147th Street) 212-491-7706. Tues-Sat 12pm-6pm. ❷❸Ⓐ🅒🅑🅓 *to 148th.*

Malcolm Shabazz Harlem Market
The shops in this open-air market boast imported crafts, clothing, and jewelry from all across the African continent. Get past some of the kitschier items, and you'll find a wide variety of burning incense, exotic soaps, authentic robes, rugs, hats, earrings, statuettes, and other handmade treasures.
52 W 115th St (between 5th & 6th Ave). 212-987-8131. Mon-Sun 10am-8pm. ❷❸ *to 116th.*

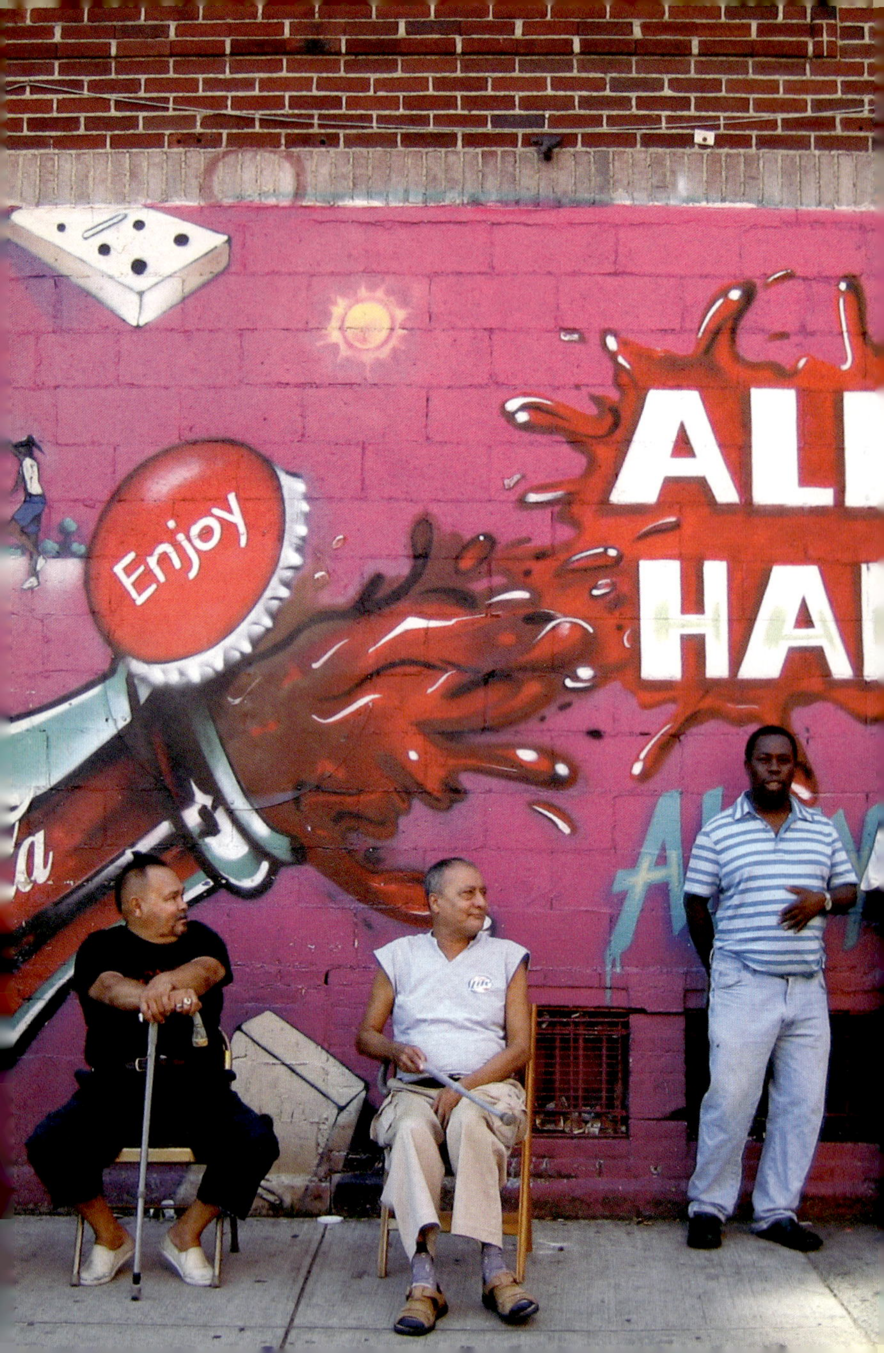
Enjoy

SPANISH HARLEM

Although contractors are poised to invade on every side, and hungry realtors, having eaten up every other neighborhood, are turning their eyes to East Harlem, this is one neighborhood that still remains just that: a neighborhood. From morning to the wee hours of night, residents sit on their stoops or in the many community gardens chatting, cat calling, and swaying to the salsa music on the radio. On the main strip of East 116th St, the same vendors come every day to sell cheap goods, corn-on-the-cob, shaved ice, fresh fruit, and bags of Mexican corn snacks.

Historically one of the poorest areas in New York, East Harlem was a site of widespread drug addiction, public health problems, poor living conditions, and poverty throughout the 60s and 70s. While it struggles with these problems today, this is a neighborhood that has never been lacking in culture. Musicians Tito Puente (whose name now graces 110th St) and Ray Barretto both began their careers in Spanish Harlem, crafting their music from the traditions of the neighborhood. The visual art of Spanish Harlem is on the walls of the neighborhood itself; for many years murals and graffiti art have been the expression of disenchanted youth and guerrilla artists such as James de la Vegas.

And while some see East Harlem as the hot new destination itching for a make-over, to the locals this area will never be SpaHa, it will always be El Barrio.

270 SPANISH HARLEM

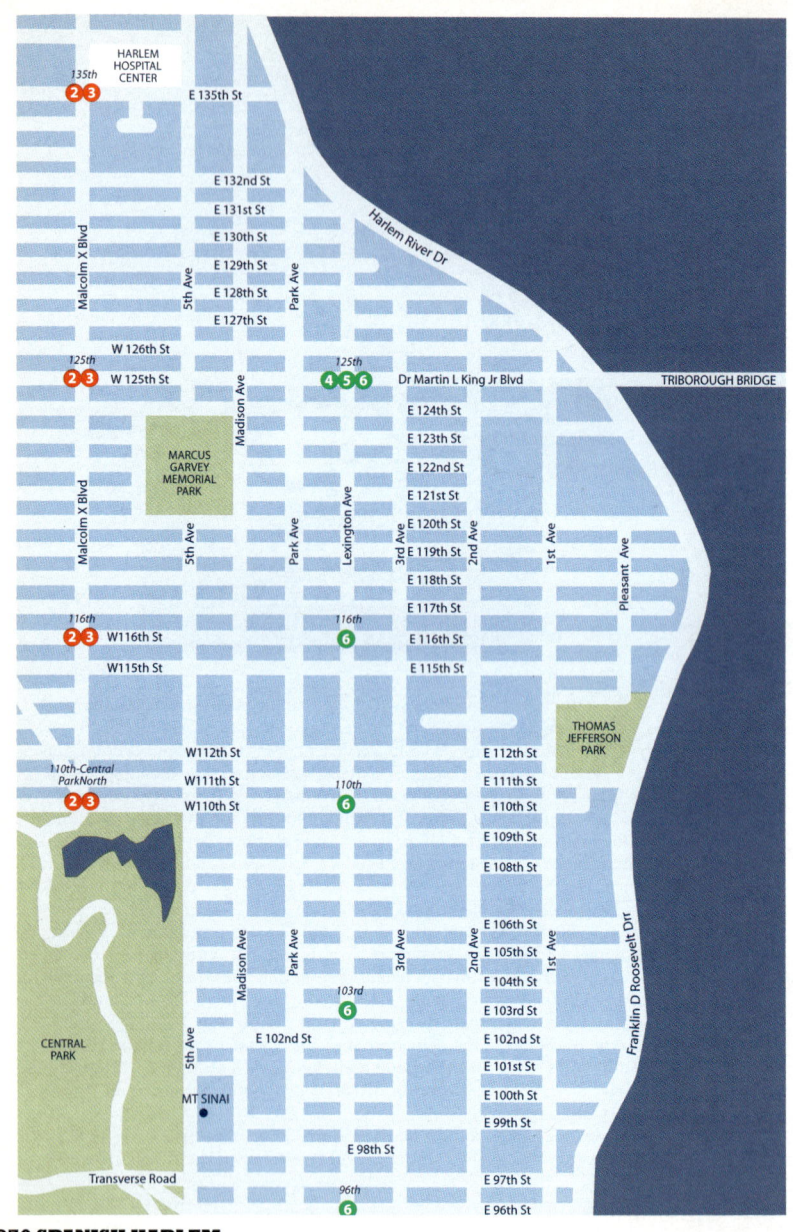

ATTRACTIONS

Conservatory Gardens
These European-style gardens, tended to by the Central Park Conservancy, consist of the northern French Garden, the central Italian Garden, and the southern English Garden. At the entrance of the park, just past a beautiful wrought-iron gate that once adorned the Vanderbilt Mansion, is a wonderful fountain where young kids gather in the summer. Explore the many paths that twist and wander throughout, past flowers that bloom from Spring through Autumn, past elegantly sculptured fountains, and along the banks of pools and ponds. The gardens are a designated quiet space, ideal to sit down with a book or to take a date for a stroll.
105th St (at 5th Ave) 212-360-2766. 8am to dusk. Free Tours: Sat 11am April-October. ❻ *to 103rd.*

El Museo Del Barrio
The only museum in NY dedicated solely to the cultures of Latin America and the Caribbean, El Museo del Barrio has fascinating collections and well-curated exhibits. Not only are there paintings, sculptures, and photographs by talented Latin American and Caribbean artists, there are also two collections, the Pre-Columbian and Traditional Arts, that display ceremonial objects, musical instruments, masks, dolls, and a collection of 360 Santos, carved wooden saints used for household devotion in Puerto Rico. The museum events are also worth a trip: concerts happen often, and free walking tours of the Barrio meet every Saturday at 3pm to take visitors on an excursion of arts, food and culture.
1230 5th Ave (at 104th St). 212-831-7272. Wed-Sun 11am-5pm. Suggested admission $6. ❻ *to 103rd,* ❷❸ *to 110th.*

La Marqueta
Once the pride of the Puerto Rican immigrants who made it thrive, this bazaar and community meeting place is currently in renovation limbo. During the 40's pushcart vendors drew in huge crowds of neighborhood residents looking for herbs, spices, produce, and a good haggle. The ever shifting plans and proposals for this city owned public market space have included building three modern "green" centers to house produce and other goods. So far the only change has been the installment of a red metal picket fence padlocked and closed to the public except during special events. If the city and surrounding community can get the money and support they need, La Marqueta could once again be a site of pride and booming commerce. For now it is a silent memorial to a time that has passed.
Park Ave from 111th to 116th. ❻ *to 116th.*

Museum of the City of New York
Housed in a grand and beautiful neo-Georgian building from the 1920s, this museum holds a huge collection of paintings, photographs, costumes, furniture and other artifacts from New York City's long and colored past. Notable ongoing exhibits include "Perform," a history of theater in New York, and "New York Interiors," a look at New York homes from the 17th to 20th century. The museum admission is suggested donation, so the crowd ranges from tourists looking for cheap sight seeing to New Yorkers who come to fall in love with their city all over again. Stop by the shop to pick up some high quality prints of the museum's amazing photographs.
1220 5th Ave (at 103rd St) 212-534-1672. Tues-Sun 10am-5pm. ❻ *to 103rd.*

New York Mosque
On the southern border of Spanish Harlem rises the largest center of worship for Islam practitioners in the city. Built through a joint effort by the governments of Libya, Saudi Arabia and Kuwait, the mosque took almost thirty years to complete. The mosque's architecture is distinctive for its incorporation of modern features into medieval elements traditional to mosque design; in order to point toward Mecca, the building is set in a jutting diagonal direction. Even those who do not practice Islam will find it a remarkable experience to enter this building, where over 4,000 people come to worship on Fridays.
1711 3rd Ave (at 96th St). 212-722-5234. ❻ *to 96th.*

CULTURE & ARTS

Graffiti Hall of Fame
Not for just any teenager with a can of spray paint, this run-down school yard wall is a canvas for some of New York's most talented graffiti artists. The murals change from year to year but are always impressive. Currently the wall is home to a mural by a group who call themselves The Ghost Writers, who have sprayed their own individual tags as well as a stunningly detailed, larger than life image of a chain-wielding skeleton riding a motorcycle. The Hall of Fame is not as large as its title would imply, extending only half a block. Even on this modest canvas, though, the talent and intricacy of design that marks each tag may take hours to fully appreciate.
106th St (at Park Ave). 6 *to 116th.*

Julia de Burgos Cultural Center
Established in the memory of Puerto Rico's famed poetess and national hero, this cultural center is a space for art, music, and community bonding located in an old elementary school. The Taller Boricua galleries/Puerto Rican workshop located on the first floor may not be the hottest art gallery in the city, but it does provide a quiet place to view works by up and coming Latin artists. The gallery halls are usually empty, but the staff, consisting of one man at an information table, is helpful and willing to converse freely about the art. For more exciting times, stop by for the special events such as Uptown Salsa Wednesdays, which draw in the crowds and allow this center to shine as a cultural hub of the neighborhood.
1680 Lexington Ave (between 105th & 106th St). 212-831-4333. 6 *to 104th.*

DINING

MID-RANGE
Camaradas El Barrio *Puerto Rican*
This neighborhood hangout is more than just a restaurant, it's also a venue for music, comedy, and open-mic performances. The food is pretty good, too. There is an extensive selection of fried Caribbean snacks, cuchifritos, which are crispy on the outside and filled with warm, mouthwatering beef plus your choice of yuca, plantain, shrimp, chicken, or steak. The mofongo, a traditional Puerto Rican dish of mashed plantains mixed with gooey cheese and shrimp, chicken, pork, or vegetables, is absolutely delicious and very filling. If you have room left for dessert, flan is rich and creamy, and chocolate empanadas served with ice cream are a swell melt-in-your-mouth treat.
2241 1st Ave (at 115th St) 212-348-2703. Sun-Wed 4pm-1am, Thurs-Sat 4pm-3:30am. 6 *to 116th. Average entrée $10.*

WALKING TOUR: MURAL ART

The history, the people, the pulse of Spanish Harlem comes alive through the paint on its very walls. What some lawmakers call graffiti is known in this neighborhood as street art and since the 70s has been a way for the disenchanted, the disenfranchised, the impoverished, and the rebellious to express the emotions of the neighborhood. To explore these murals—some cracked and peeling, some freshly gleaming—is to look into the heart of Spanish Harlem.

104th St is known as **Mural Row**—it doesn't take long to understand why. As soon as you exit the 6 train at Lexington, the smiling face of famed salsa singer Cecilia Cruz is there to greet you. The "Queen of Salsa" is known for rising from humble beginnings in Havana to major international success. Next to Cecilia is Pedro Pietri, a long time Spanish Harlem resident known for founding the Nuyorican Poets Café.

Across from these two portraits is the crown jewel of Spanish Harlem's street murals. Titled *The Spirit of East Harlem* this four-story depiction of neighborhood characters, many of whom lived in the building it covers, is a collaboration between Hank Prussing, who first created the mural in 1973, and his apprentice Manny Vega, who restored it to its original grandeur in 1997.

Fans of hip hop should take a detour at 103rd St and 3rd Ave to see the mural of **Big Pun**, the Puerto Rican rapper, which is located underneath a massive animal rights mural (hence the chihuahua floating above Big Pun's head).

At 105th St is one of many politically minded murals. This one calls back to a time of Cuban and Puerto Rican unity with a **portrait of Che Guevara and Albuiza** side by side over the flag of their respective nations.

At 106th and Lexington is a mural of **Julia de Burgos**, a Puerto Rican poet and national hero whose verse inspired generations of immigrants, which combines her portrait with excerpts from her poetry.

Some murals are more personal and, for that, more poignant. At 116th and Lexington is a mural in memory of **Papote**, a young man whose life was cut short, a symbol of a neighborhood torn by violence.

There are murals which stress the importance of community, declare Puerto Rican pride, and even a unique homage to Pablo Picasso. The most concentrated stretch of street art ends at 116th. Here, at the corner of Park Ave, you can see one of the greatest displays of graffiti craftsmanship in the city, the **Graffiti Hall of Fame**. The technical skill and visual intensity of this ever changing canvas for the best spray paint artists in the city is absolutely astonishing.

Creole Restaurant *Cajun*
Creole tries to do it all by claiming to be a one-stop shop for jazz, art, food, and culture. Live musicians play regularly and there is a constant rotation of over-priced art prints on the walls. As for the food, there is a lot of variety, with everything from Italian-inspired mussels bruschetta to the Louisiana delicacy, Gator étouffé, and a multitude of gumbo variations. The menu boasts exquisite sounding offerings, but occasionally the food falls a little short. Dishes such as the Haitian Creole Chicken stew are good but lack the oomph to make them truly special. One standout dish is a side, the four cheese baked macaroni, which is crusty on the outside and full of gooey flavor on the inside.
2167 3rd Ave (at 118th St). 212-876-8838. Daily 12pm-4pm, 5pm-10pm. ❹❺❻ *to 116th St. Average entrée $23.*

La Fonda Boricua *Puerto Rican*
Diners will find a warm sense of community in this neighborhood restaurant and lounge. Savory appetizers, such as the tasty shredded beef quesadillas or shrimp with passion fruit, make for perfect nibbles while enjoying a Latin jazz performance every Thursday, Friday, Saturday, or Sunday night. The music is so captivating that it almost makes diners forget about the authentic cuisine in front of them, but not quite. And while the jazz and the food are of the best quality, the atmosphere is laid-back and unpretentious. Those with a larger appetite should try the broiled chicken, which comes stuffed and wrapped in bacon with a side of vegetables and mashed potatoes, or the excellent paella.
169 E 106th St (near Lexington Ave) 212-410-7292. Daily 11am-10pm. ❷❸ *to 110th,* ❻ *to 103rd. Average entrée $20.*

CHEAP
El Barrio Juice Bar *Smoothie*
Stop by the window of this small juice bar and watch the servers chop fresh fruit before throwing them into the blender as they concoct 100 percent natural smoothies. There are 25 flavors ranging from the quotidian banana, blueberry, or strawberry to the more exotic pineapple and ginger and the over-packed beet, carrot, celery, orange, ginger, and lemon. If you sit at the lone table inside, you're entitled to a par-

tial refill with the leftovers; the servers here don't like to waste.
308 E 116th St (at 2nd Ave) 212-828-0403. Mon-Sun 9am-7pm. ⑥ *to 116th. Smoothies $3.50.*

Island Spice Kitchen *Caribbean*
This friendly restaurant serves authentic Caribbean food with an American twist. The tasty entrées provide a feast for one and include tasty curry dishes of goat or chicken, oxtails, and of course jerk chicken, accompanied by Caribbean choices like banana and dumplings or all-American macaroni and cheese. Vegetarians can sample the calaloo, a leafy soup with tomatoes, onions, and herbs. The restaurant also carries an array of tropical drinks like sugar cane juice, which is about as sweet as it gets. Slow service goes hand in hand with the slow rhythms of Caribbean and Jamaican tunes playing in the dining room.
172 E 118th (between 3rd Ave & Lexington Ave). 212-831-5354. Daily 9am-9pm. ⑥ *to 116th. Average entrée $7.*

Taco Mix *Mexican*
It's easy to pass by this tiny taco place when walking past the many storefronts of 116th street. Those who do miss out on some of the neighborhood's best tacos, tortas, and quesadillas. There are only three chairs, so the locals crowd the bar and eat their food while standing. Although the menu is fairly standard as far as taquerias go, Taco Mix's servings are more liberal and its meat more flavorful than most. The quesadillas, crispy tortillas loaded with gooey cheese and topped with black beans, lettuce, and enchilada sauce, exceed all expectations for a small-time shop.
234 E 116th St (between 2nd & 3rd Ave). 212-369-7757. ⑥ *to 116th. Average entrée $4.*

SHOPPING

Casa Latina Music Shop
For over 40 years, this veritable museum of Latin music has brightened the neighborhood. It offers every genre from reggaeton to meringue, available in CD

DAY TO DAY

Community Board 11. *1664 Park Ave. 212-831-8929.*

Local Media: eharlem.blogspot.com

Rent: One-bedroom: $1400-1600; Two bedroom: $1700-2000.

Hospital: Mt. Sinai Hospital. *One Gustave L, Levy Place. 212-241-6500.*

Hotel: Bubba and Bean Lodges. *1598 Lexington Ave. 917-345-7941.*

Dog Run: Tom's Dog Run. *Jefferson Park. 1st Ave to FDR Drive from 111th to 114th St.*

Best Happy Hour: Camaradas El Barrio. *2241 1st Ave. 212-348-2703. $15 pitchers of sangría, Thursday ladies' night.*

or old school cassette. The staff of this family-operated store is very friendly and extremely knowledgeable, making this a great place to become acquainted with latin music.
151 E 116th St (at Lexington Ave) 212-427-6062. Mon-Thurs 10am-6:30pm. Fri-Sat 10am-7pm, closed Sundays. ⑥ *to 116th.*

Justo Botanica
Established in 1930, this is one of the oldest and best-known Botanicas in East Harlem. A botanica carries religious, spiritual, and herbal products for practitioners of Afro-Cuban Santeria, a mix of Catholicism and Yoruba religious traditions. Even if you aren't a believer, Justo is a great place to learn more about an aspect of Hispanic culture and to pick up a unique gift. There are candles for nearly every occasion and purpose: marriages, court cases, luck in love, or success in business; and there is also a wide range of incense, herbs, good luck necklaces, religious statues, and books for sale.
134 East 104th St (at Lexington Ave). 212-534-9140. Fri-Wed 10:30am-7:30pm, Thurs 10:30pm-5:30pm. ⑥ *to 103rd.*

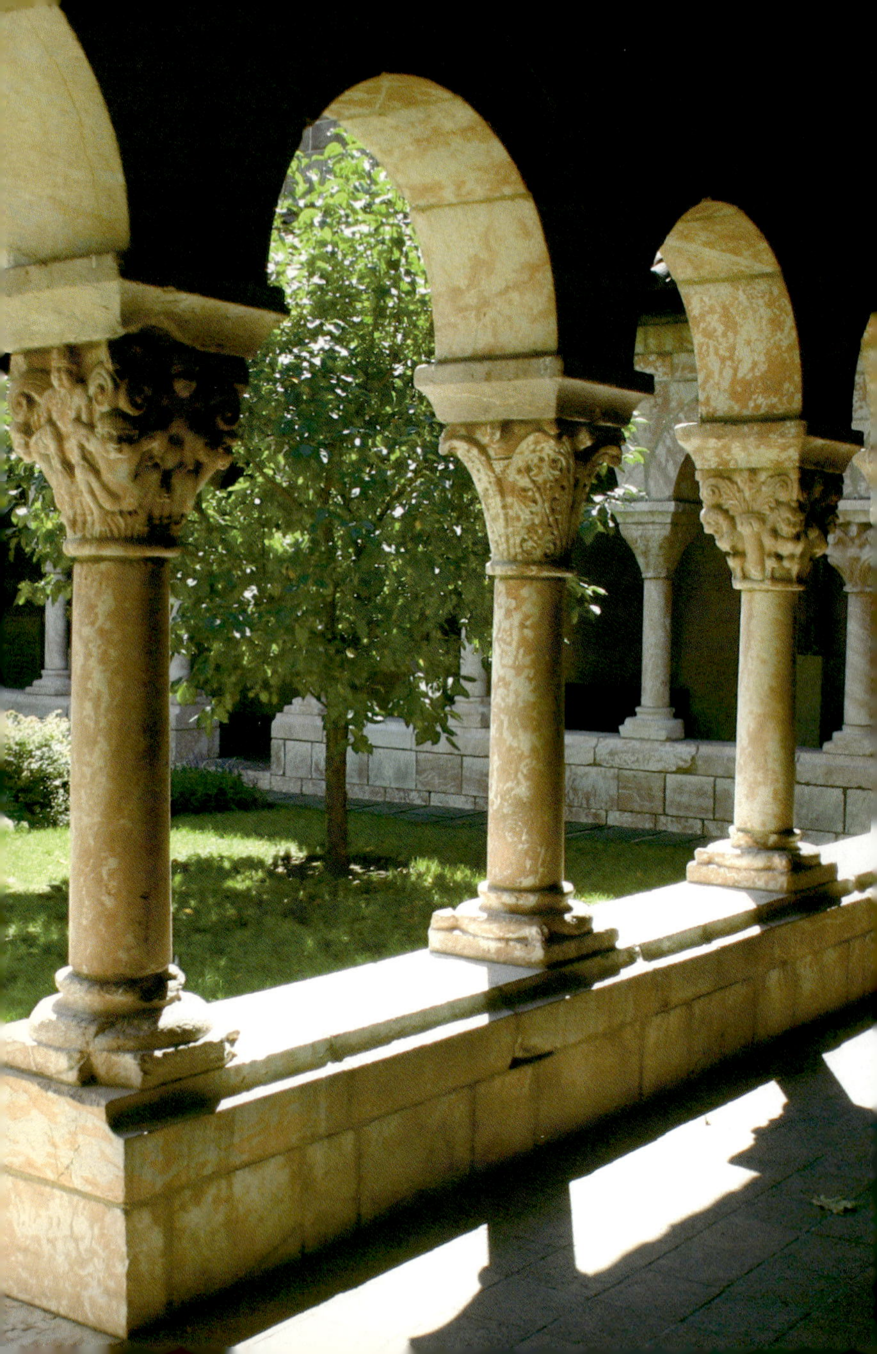

UPPER MANHATTAN

Snatches of reggaeton and hip-hop beats boom from the window ledges of tightly packed brownstones along Saint Nicholas Avenue, as students make their way to the nearby City College of New York and the Dance Theatre of Harlem. Several blocks further, families looking for a recreational sanctuary march towards Riverbank State Park, past colorful boutiques selling even brighter ensembles, restaurants boasting the best soul food in the city, international bakeries, and a second Museum Row.

Once a small farm where Alexander Hamilton spent the last years of his life, Hamilton Heights developed into a center of trade and manufacture with the construction of subway lines in the early 1900s. A changing of the guard took place around 1940 when white residents started looking elsewhere for dwellings and black professionals began moving in. Sugar Hill, once referred to as "the sweet life" of Harlem because of its affluent residents, was home to Duke Ellington, Thurgood Marshall, and W.E.B. DuBois, whose presence fueled the Harlem Renaissance in the mid-1950s.

To the north lies Washington Heights, named after Fort Washington, a fortification constructed by George Washington's army that the British troops barely managed to capture in 1776. Two centuries later it was the onslaught of cocaine, crime, and poverty that overtook the neighborhood. Once home to perhaps the most vicious drug gang in New York, the Wild Cowboys, Washington Heights acquired the title of "Crack City" and a stigma of crime and poverty that it has been unable to shed even today, despite massive community efforts to clean up the area. As a solid middle class redevelops, residents begin to prepare to withstand waves of gentrification, perhaps the neighborhood's next major battle.

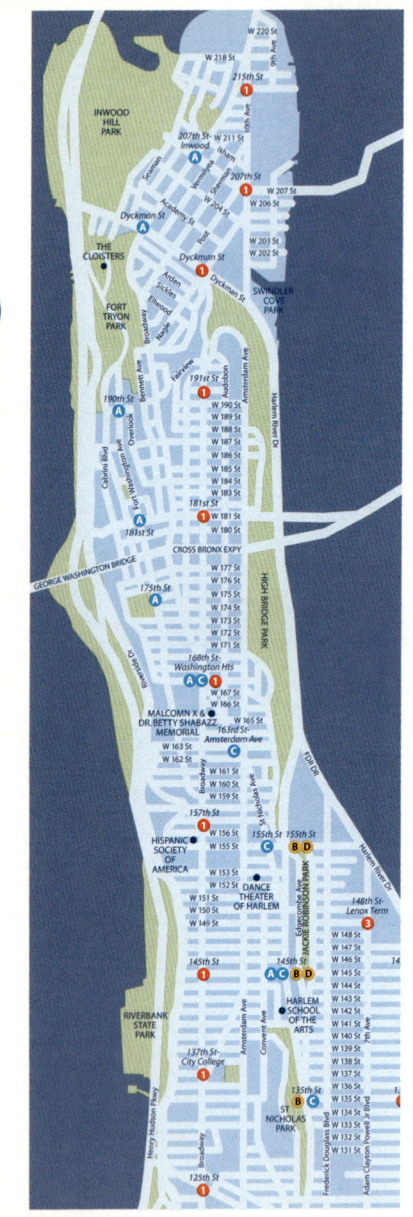

ATTRACTIONS & ARTS

The Cloisters
Hidden in the depths of verdant Fort Tryon Park, the Cloisters lives up to its reputation for secluded grandeur. A discrete cobblestone road leading uphill to the entrance can make for some serious huffing and puffing, but the toil is worth it for a taste of the Middle Ages in Post-Modern Manhattan. Ornate tapestries, including those depicting the famous unicorn hunt, are hung in dimly lit rooms with stone floors and walls the color of clay. Tourists from around the world marvel at Byzantine-influenced religious art in a elaborately constructed arcades, supported by intricately decorated pillars. Join a group tour given by top Medievalists, or lounge in the herb garden and enjoy a breathtaking view of the Hudson.
99 Margaret Corbin Dr. 212-923-3700. Mar-Oct, Tues-Sun 9:30am-5:15pm, Mon closed, Nov-Feb, Tues-Sun 9:30am-4:45pm, Mon closed. Adults $20, Students $10. Ⓐ *to 190th, M4 bus to Cloisters.*

Fort Tryon Park
Home to the Cloisters, Inwood's Fort Tryon Park is frequented by local families and the occasional adventurous tourist. The landscape is rocky, carved out by the glaciers that shaped Manhattan. Hiking trails twist throughout the park, leading visitors under stone pedestrian overpasses and hills with stunning views—especially in Autumn—of the Palisades. Another Autumn attraction is the local Medieval Festival, which typically takes place on the last Sunday of September or on the first of October and hosts minstrels, craftsmen, and musicians; stay until dusk to see jousting knights and one of the most beautiful sunset views in the city.
Open daily. Closes after dark. Ⓐ *to 190th, M4 to Cloisters.*

Hispanic Society of America
The last museum standing at Audobon Terrace, the Hispanic Society of America has been looking for an opportunity to follow its erstwhile neighbors – the Museum of the American Indian and the American Numismatic Society – ever since their moves downtown several years ago. Regardless, this museum merits a visit to see its collection of pristine 17th century wooden sculptures and master portraits by artists including Goya and El Greco. Numerous artifacts, from

278 UPPER MANHATTAN

Moorish tapestries and ancient cabinetry to miniatures and marble caskets that depict their owners, illustrate centuries of Hispanic culture. Outside, the conqueror El Cid astride his steed stands guard over the compound.
Audobon Terrace. 212-926-2234. Sun 1pm-4pm, Tues-Sat 10:30am-4:30pm. Tours at 2pm on Saturdays. ❶ *to 157th St. Donation suggested.*

Malcolm X and Dr. Betty Shabazz Memorial and Educational Center

Located in the notorious Audubon Ballroom, the site of Malcolm X's assassination on February 21st, 1965, the Malcolm X and Dr. Betty Shabazz Memorial both celebrates and reflects upon the achievements of one of the foremost leaders of the Black Nationalist movement. With three multimedia kiosks, created by the Columbia University Digital Knowledge Ventures, featuring a running loop of videos and photos dealing with Malcolm X's private life, this memorial provides a valuable look at the man behind the fiery demagogue.
3940 Broadway (between 165th & 166th St). 212-568-1341. Mon-Fri 9am-4pm. ❶ *to 168th.*

Riverbank State Park

Seventy feet above the Hudson, the 28-acre Riverbank State Park hosts a view of the George Washington Bridge that is stunning enough to allay even dedicated acrophobes. The park also boasts a 2,500-seat athletic complex, four basketball courts, four paddleball courts, four tennis courts, and an Olympic-sized pool. Let out your shrieking inner child at the Totally Kid Carousel, or at one of the two playgrounds. An occasional stench of sewage may linger from the North River Wastewater Treatment Plant situated right below the park, but the constant stream of holiday music festivals, free jazz concerts, and lunchtime dancing more than compensates.
679 Riverside Dr (at 145th St). 212-694-3600. 6am-11pm. ❶ *to 145th.*

Swindler Cove Park

Once a wasteland brimming with the skeletons of discarded ships and construction projects, Swindler Cove Park now occupies five lush, serene acres of the Harlem River waterfront. Thanks to the laborious efforts of the New York Restoration Project in the late 1990s, the former landfill has now become a treasure of the neighborhood. On sunny weekends, families partake in rowing races at the Peter Jay Sharp Boathouse, where enthusiastic members of the New York Rowing Association show novices the ropes. From the Scenic Overlook, enjoy a view of the city you won't see anywhere else, or take up a pair of binoculars and scope out the wildlife from the Wetlands Bridge.
Harlem River Drive and Dyckman St (10th Ave). Daily 8:30am-6pm. ❶ *to Dyckman.*

DINING

UPSCALE

EDITOR'S PICK

Hudson River Café *New American*
The few pieces of edible fish left in the Hudson seem to have jumped straight from the river onto the plates at this sleek spot with a killer waterfront location. Attracting a young, local crowd, the restaurant's seafood offerings shine brightest. Both the seafood linguine, tossed in a light, spicy tomato sauce, and Hamlet's Paella, which combines shellfish, chicken, and chorizo on top of perfectly cooked saffron rice, are loaded with fresh fish. For poultry, the buffalo chicken, made of juicy pieces of chicken soaked in a tangy sauce, is flavorful and healthy, but lacks the satisfying crunch of fried wings. The passion-fruit crème brulée ends the meal with a sly wink, while the flourless chocolate cake with dulce de leche ice cream is a masterwork of textural balance.
697 W 133rd St (at West St) 212-491-9177. Mon-Tues 5pm-11pm, Wed-Sat 5pm-12am, Sun 11am-3pm, 5pm-10pm. ❶ *to 125th. Average entrée $25.*

MID-RANGE

107 West Eclectic *Southern*

Not only is traditional southern cuisine done right at this laid back location, dishes from other locales have its exciting flare too. Jalapeño dipping sauce adds a subtle spice to the satisfying crunch of the coconut shrimp, though the shrimp could benefit from more seasoning. The smoky tuna and vegetable roll comes served in a delicious grilled tortilla and drizzled in a mild wasabi and miso puree. The smoky theme continues with surprising success in the rigatoni—adding a twist to a basic pasta favorite. Their specialty is fried chicken, which is made

exactly as it should be with a crisp exterior and juicy chicken underneath.
811 W 187th St (between Pinehurst Ave & Fort Washington Ave). 212-923-3311. Mon-Sat 11:15am-10:45pm, Sun 11:15am-10:15pm. Ⓐ *to 190th.*
2787 Broadway (at W 107th St). 212-864-1555. ❶ *to 110th St. Mon-Sun 11:30am-11pm. Average entrée $12.*

809 Sangria *Latin*
A diamond in the rough, this lush Dominican spot is a welcome retreat for locals and foodies alike. The local, seasonal menu includes shellfish-infused black rice, several fish dishes, and a perfectly cooked filet mignon. Butternut squash tamale and crab cakes with a vanilla-guanabana coulis are an excellent choice. Six different types of sangria, both white and red, compete with an extensive wine list; many diners stop by just for a pitcher of the fruity sangria and pineapple guacamole. The staff is friendly, attentive, and contributes to the dining area's warm and inviting environs.
112 Dyckman St (near Nagle Ave). 212-304-3800. Mon-Thurs 11am-12am, Fri-Sat 11am-2am, Sun 3pm-11pm. ❶ Ⓐ *to Dyckman. Average entrée $22.*

Dinosaur Bar-B-Que *BBQ*
Fast, friendly service and delicious pork distinguish this must-visit Harlem treasure. Most nights of the week you'll find it packed with families, dates, and large groups of friends, all justifiably enthused about the grub. Go for the Bar-B-Que combination meals and you'll walk home fat and happy. If you can stomach the extra cholesterol, try the highly regarded Syracuse-style salt potatoes. If the mouth-watering pulled pork and mac 'n' cheese aren't enough to keep you entertained, check out the full bar and live blues every Friday and Saturday.
646 W 131st St (near 12th Ave) 212-694-1777. Tues-Thurs 11:30am-11pm, Fri-Sat 11:30am-12am (bar until 1), Sun 12pm-10pm. ❶ *to 125th St. Average entrée $16.*

The River Room *Cajun*
Located on a lookout over the Hudson River, the comfy patio offers an unbeatable view of the George Washington Bridge ablaze with electric lights against the night sky—the perfect place to enjoy dinner or drinks with friends at sunset. The place is hardly packed, but devotees come for blaring live jazz, cocktails, and Southern flair. But a dining destination it isn't. The pork chop has all the texture and nuance of a hockey puck and what the jerk chicken wings lack in tangy flavor they make up for in rivers of tongue-numbing hot sauce. However, the macaroni and cheese croquettes, seafood gumbo, and a vodka tonic can set you right. Though the food is a bit overpriced, the bill is a small pittance to pay for the marvelous view.
Riverbank State Park (Riverside Dr at 145th St). 212-491-1500. Wed-Thurs 5:30pm-10pm, Fri-Sat 5:30-11pm, Sun 11:30am-3pm. ❶ *to 145th. Average entrée $19.*

CHEAP
El Presidente Restaurant *Dominican*
Like more than a few area restaurants, El Presidente serves lunch at the bar in front, with specials displayed on illuminated panels above stacks of takeout containers, a stocked shelf of liquors, and a coffee machine. In the back, however, there's a nicely appointed dining room done up in bright crimsons and yellows. Dominican radio imparts a lively atmosphere, and a projector in the back is used in regular Saturday and Sunday dance parties thrown by the friendly, courteous staff. If you're just here for lunch or dinner, it will be hard to go wrong with any dish, but it would be a mistake to order more than one. Try the mofongo con pernil – lightly salted, buttery roast pork with fried plantain – on your first visit, and then come back for more.
3938 Broadway (at 165th St) 212-927-7011. Mon-Sun, 24 hours. ❶ Ⓐ Ⓒ *to 168th. Average entrée $9.*

The Trie Café *Café*
After plodding past unicorn tapestries and medieval architecture, refuel at this quaint café, named for a cross-adorned fountain in the Cloisters. Tucked under the lower level of the museum, the café relies more on the mesmerizing view than the menu to attract the hordes of exhausted tourists milling around. The fare is conventional and errs on the safe side, though the crackly roasted pear and spicy cranberry mustard atop the turkey sandwich are delicious exceptions. Skip the soggy pastries and the chalky ice cream and go for a handful of wasabi peas instead.
799 Fort Washington Ave (at Margaret Corbin Drive) 212-923-3700. Tues-Sun 10am-4:15pm. Ⓐ *to 190th. Sandwiches $8.25.*

NIGHTLIFE

EDITOR'S PICK

St. Nick's Jazz Pub *Live Music*
This historic jazz club in the heart of Harlem is a great place to grab a drink, kick back, and let the music take over. With live shows every night, including Monday night jam sessions and West African music nights every Saturday at midnight, the music at St. Nick's will get your toes tapping, your hips shaking and your heart throbbing. Jazz lovers from all walks of life gather here nightly, some nostalgically reliving the golden years, others discovering new musicians. The bar serves a variety of reasonably priced drinks including the locally brewed Sugar Hill Golden Ale, and ten dollars will get you a plate full of home-cooked soul food until 3AM.
773 St. Nicholas Ave (at 149th St). 212-283-9728. Mon-Sun 1pm-4am. ❶❹❸❽❾ *to 145th,* ❸ *to 148th. Average drink $8. Cash only.*

DAY TO DAY

Community Board 9. *16-18 Old Broadway. 212-864-2600.*

Local Media: *HarlemOneStop.com*

Grocers: Blashy Deli Grocery. *500 W 170th St. 212-543-1851.*

Gym: Harlem Armory Track and Field Center. *216 Fort Washington Ave. 212-923-2068.*

Rent: One-Bedroom: $1,600-2,800, Two-Bedroom- $2,000-3,500.

Hospital: New York Presbyterian Hospital. *622 West 168th Street. 212-305-2500.*

Hotel: Hamilton Heights Casablanca Hotel. *511 W 145th St (between Amsterdam & Broadway). 212-491-0488.*

Dog Runs: Fort Tryon Park. *Margaret Corbin Drive. 212-942-0009.*

Movie Theaters: Coliseum Theatre. *703 W 181st St. 212-740-1545.*

SHOPPING

Moscow on the Hudson
Stock up for an Imperial banquet at this specialty store, which carries only Russian delicacies. Standouts include the peppery, smoky Cherkizovskaya salami that puts all other lunchmeats to shame, and the crunchy "Slodych" cookies embedded with chewy raisons. The store also features bear and badger oils, Happy Hippo candies, a range of caviar, yogurt drinks, and even a line of greeting cards sporting colorful platitudes. Unless you happen to be fluent in Russian, you'll have to rely on a combination of pointing, nodding, and grunting to nab the abundant samples.
801 West 181st Street (at Fort Washington Avenue). 212-740-7397. Mon-Sat 9am-10pm, Sun 9am-9pm. ❶ *to 181st.*

Probus
Sleek ensembles with a tinge of hip-hop exemplify this boutique's mission of fashion, art, and music. Exposed brick walls and a flashing disco ball set the scene for neon-colored T-shirts emblazoned with cheeky prints. The shop stocks Mod accessories galore, like the unique monochromatic, geometrically-shaped Nooka Zub Zot watches. Stock up on sneakers with outrageous attitude and stylish retro sunglasses with large lenses to complete any funky wardrobe.
714 West 181st St (at Bennett Ave). 212-923-9153. Mon-Sat 10:30am-7pm, Sun 12pm-7pm. ❶ *to 181st.*

Straight out of Harlem
Step inside this boutique bursting with neighborhood pride and you'll find every household item and knick-knack you could ever need. Straight out of Harlem has everything from the usual (stationary sets and floor mats) to the downright bizarre ("Dammit Dolls" and rainsticks). Make sure to check out the extensive jewelry line, much of which is designed and created by local artists, as well as the array of quilts sporting bold prints and vibrant designs. The store's art gallery, which boasts a range of cultural influences as diverse as the surrounding community – Puerto Rican, Brazilian, African, Cuban, and more – is worth a browse.
704 St. Nicholas Ave (at 145th St). 212-234-5944. Tues-Sat 12pm-6pm. ❶ *to 145th.*

UPPER MANHATTAN 281

THE SLICE IS RIGHT @

Vinnie's Pizzeria

148 BEDFORD AVE.
(Bet. N.8th and N.9th)
718.782.7078
WE DELIVER • OPEN LATE

BROOKLYN ALE HOUSE

14 Beers on Tap • Drink Specials
Pool Table • Darts • WiFi

NORTH 8TH & BERRY
718.302.9811 • www.brooklynalehouse.com

4:27

MARKET   OPEN 24 HRS   N7 MARKET   OPEN 24 HRS

Pete's

BUY • SELL • TRADE
RECORDS
25,000+ LPS
96 N. 6TH BTWN
718.218.8200

ATM

199 North 7th St.
(718) 599-9399

N 5 ST

GREENPOINT

Originally farmland, Greenpoint did not begin to grow until regular ferry service to Manhattan was established in 1850. After that, it exploded, rapidly becoming a center of maritime commerce. With massive docks lining the East River, some of that century's greatest feats of shipbuilding took place here, including the construction of one of the first ironclad warships, the Monitor. Large numbers of German, Irish, and Polish immigrants formed the backbone of this industrial community, which also housed rope factories and lumber yards.

Today, Greenpoint is still home to the city's largest Polish community, and it still clings to its middle class identity.

However, massive gentrification in the 80s made parts of it amongst the most expensive in the five boroughs. Today it manages to juggle its simultaneous white and blue collar identities. The ultracheap dive bars, underground hangouts, and hidden gastronomic gems appeal to locals and visitors, as do the old-world stores selling blintzes, and kielbasa. Just down the street, though, are rather expensive boutiques and restaurants peddling designer clothes and haute cuisine. Ultimately, the panoramic views of Manhattan and proximity to ultra-hip Williamsburg may be its downfall, though inconveniences such as the unsteady G-line prevent it from being immediately overrun.

284 GREENPOINT

ATTRACTIONS

American Playground
When searching for this park, look up to locate the water tower emblazoned with the Polish flag. The watertower, though not on park grounds, oversees these minimally used basketball and handball courts. In the hotter months the slides, swings and benches are frequented, but the real draw are the spray showers, cleverly disguised as a cactus and a swan.
Franklin Ave (between Noble St & Milton St). **G** *to Greenpoint Ave.*

Barge Park
At the northernmost tip of Greenpoint, Barge Park is little more than a rundown playground with a couple benches; however, the views of the Manhatten skyline from this spot are beautiful. Come at dusk but bring a couple friends, the spot is too secluded to frequent solo.
Franklin St & Dupont St. **G** *to Greenpoint Ave.*

Brooklyn Brewery
This New York favorite not only churns out one of the top 40 most popular beers in America, it has become a destination for beer, food, and music lovers alike. Come for Friday Happy Hour when $4 beer and live music encourages lingering or tour the brewery on the weekend. Tours of the facilities conclude with an obligatory beer-tasting in which one of the eight beers on tap will convert even beer-wary visitors into believers.
1 Brewers Row, 79 N 11th St (at Wythe Ave). 718-486-7422. Brewery Tours Sat-Sun 12pm-6pm. **L** *to Bedford,* **G** *to Nassau.*

McCarren Park
When first wandering around Greenpoint, the lack of benches and trees may feel oppressive, but a short walk downtown brings you to McCarren Park, a thirty-five acre oasis of athletic fields and greenery to lounge in. Perhaps its greatest attribute is the pool, one of the eleven opened by Robert Moses in 1936, which is now a venue for arts fairs, concerts, and film screenings. Tuesday nights at sunset, Summer Screenings presents free screenings of modern coming-of-age classics. Make sure you get there early and bring a blanket to sit on as no chairs are allowed. No outside food or drink is allowed either, so bring cash for the snack bar.
Nassau Ave, Bayard St, Leonard St & N 12th St. **7** *to Courthouse Square,* **G** *to Nassau ave.*

Metropolitan Pool & Fitness Center
As far as public fitness centers go, this is one of the few whose facilities won't make you cringe. The surprisingly clean swimming pool on the first floor is open for adult swim in the mornings and evenings. The fitness center upstairs provides the necessities, but not necessarily a pleasant atmosphere. While not luxurious, the price is ideal, an affordable $75 dollars a year or $40 for six months, and membership gives you access to all New York City recreational centers.
261 Bedford Ave (between Bedford Ave & Metropolitan Ave). 718-599-5707, Mon-Fri 7am-10pm, Sat 7am-6pm, Sun 10am-6pm, **L** *to Bedford Ave or* **G** *to Metropolitan.*

Monsignor McGolrick Park
If leafy seclusion is what you require, head east from crowded McCarren Park to McGolrick Park, where visitors are quieter and fewer by far. An older crowd frequents the WWI war memorials as well as Shelter Pavilion, a romantic structure modeled after the Grand Trianon of Versailles. Rest on one of the many shaded benches and watch the trickle of baby carriages and dog walkers. The dog run on the southern side of the park receives plenty of use, especially in the late afternoon.
Btwn Driggs Ave, Russell St, Nassau Ave & Monitor St. **G** *to Nassau.*

Waterfront: Huron and Java St.
Locals use these parking lots on the western ends of Huron and Java streets as a key social spot. High schoolers and fishermen alike ignore the signs prohibiting water access. Stop by to catch a breeze and check out the debris in the water as it floats by.
Huron St and Java St (by Watt St). **G** *to Greenpoint Ave.*

GREENPOINT 285

CULTURE & ARTS

Black & White Project Space
The Black & White Gallery may have altered its name, but it still maintains its dedication to promoting up-and-coming artists. High ceilings cap off a space housing site-specific contemporary art installations. Exhibitions focus on socially conscious art, maintaining a traditional artistic integrity that results in impressive visuals that give you something to think about.
483 Driggs Ave (at 10th St). 718-599-8775. Fri-Mon 12pm-6pm. ◐ *to Bedford.*

Slate Gallery
This North Side gallery provides a solid selection of contemporary artists. The atmosphere is borderline stuffy and tends towards the high-concept mindfuck, but the curators are happy to answer any questions you might have or provide often fascinating background information on the artists featured.
136 Wythe Ave (between 8th & 9th St). 718-387-3921. Fri-Mon 1pm-6pm. ◐ *to Bedford,* Ⓖ *to Nassau.*

DINING

MID-RANGE
68 Restaurant and Bar
Mediterranean
The modern interior suits the trendy neighborhood, but the menu features worthwhile innovative flavor combinations and classic appeal. The goat cheese brûlée served with beets and blueberries is a unique and tasty way to start your meal, while oysters or escargot in garlic provide more traditional indulgences. For entrées, the classic steak au poivre with fries and the wild mushroom risotto with spinach and pecorino cheese are hearty and enjoyable. A relaxed atmosphere and delicious food at affordable prices sums up this welcoming neighborhood joint.
68 Greenpoint Ave (near Franklin St). 718-389-6868. Brunch Sat-Sun 10am-5pm, Dinner Sun-Thu 5:30pm-12am, Sat 5:30pm-1:30am. ◐ *to Bedford Ave,* Ⓖ *to Greenpoint Ave. Average entrée $12.*

Paloma *New American*
The restaurant seems to have little aspiration to be anything more than an inviting neigh-

borhood hangout where good times are to be had. Rotating artwork, video projection of cartoons and clips, and guest DJs keep the vibe quirky and friendly. But dinnertime promises good food, with dishes occasionally reaching a lofty level of sophistication. Seafood items, like scallop and wild striped bass, are cooked perfectly, sumptuous, fleshy textures preserved. Octopus is super-tender with the right amount of charred flavor—even better slattered with aioli and tapenade. More interesting items like seared kangaroo, mussels in Thai coconut broth, and red lentil croquettes are an inventive dalliance on the specials menu. Liberally garnished with coarse sea salt, chocolate caramel tart is like a luxurious pudding, an ideal dessert to tuck into before heading home.
60 Greenpoint Ave (near Franklin St) 718-349-2400. Tue-Sun 6pm-11pm. Brunch Sat-Sun 11am-3pm. ❻ to Greenpoint Ave. Average entrée $18.

CHEAP
Brooklyn Label *Coffee*
This coffee haven has long been a notorious hangout for Brooklyn scruffles and has the lines to prove it. The baristas are all trained in latte art, pouring foamed milk into frivolous designs. The elaborate patterns found in your morning caffeine infusion may make you think twice before sipping, almost too pretty to ruin as they are. They serve food too, but it falls far short of their artful java.
180 Franklin St (near Java St). 718-389-2806. Mon-Wed 7am-10pm, Thu-Fri 7am-11pm, Sat 8am-11pm, Sun 9 am-4pm. ❼ to Courthouse Square, ❻ to Greenpoint Ave. Average coffee $3.

Café Grumpy *Coffee*
Unlike most of the coffee shops in New York, this bare-bones coffeehouse has plenty of space, a friendly personality, and phenomenal coffee to boot. Bring a book, a laptop and make yourself comfortable, there is no rush to clear out and no hoard of impatient customers. A low-key place to get some work done, it lacks frills but provides greatly appreciated breathing room.
193 Meserole Ave (near Diamond St). 718-349-7623. Mon-Wed 7am-7pm, Thu-Fri 7am-9pm, Sat-Sun 9am-8pm. ❼ to Courthouse Square, ❻ to Greenpoint Ave. Average coffee $3.

Urban Rustic *Organic, Grocery*
Fitting in nicely with the rampant organic, earth-friendly craze, this grocery store offers goods from local farms. The salad bar and produce section vary daily since they slavishly uphold the principle of never selling produce more than two days old. They also have prepared sandwiches and soups for dining in the back of the store or on the patio. Ciabatta sandwiches are hefty for the price. For vegetarians there are interesting and delicious combinations that are more substantial than other shops', such as the fig, goat cheese, arugula and balsamic sandwich.
236 N 12th St (near Driggs Ave). 718-388-9444. Daily 7am-10pm. Brunch Sat-Sun 10am-4pm. ❶ to Bedford, ❻ to Nassau. Sandwiches $4.50-$9.

NIGHTLIFE

Pencil Factory *Bar*
Brick, tin and aged wood lend this Greenpoint mainstay a legitimacy that attracts a young crowd to this old-timers' haunt. Rather than cater to Greenpoint's hipster population, the bar has maintained an allegiance to draught beer and single malt scotch. Cocktails have been added and are in no way stingy, but come for happy hour weekdays 3pm-8pm when the beer is $3 and the atmosphere is relaxed and friendly. In nice weather, sit outside for a drink and a sandwich with a view. The clientèle grows increasingly male dominated as the evening progresses, so move to Greenpoint's edgier clubs if you prefer a coed scene.
142 Franklin St (at Greenpoint Ave). 718-609-5858. Mon-Fri 3pm-4am, Sat-Sun 1pm-4am. ❼ to Courthouse Square, ❻ to Greenpoint. Average drink $5.

Studio B Music *Venue, Club*
Buried in a deserted warehouse district 15 minutes from the nearest subway, Studio B may not look like much from the outside, but it books some of the finest dance bands in the city. Most of the crowd arrives after midnight, but getting there early ensures you will miss the lines and get to see the

usually strong opening acts. In between sets, the skilled DJ keeps the sweaty crowd hot for more, but it's after the musicians go off that the club really shines—hipsters, sexed up by their favorite bands, stick around to dance until their legs give out. The three bars are perpetually crowded and have notoriously snotty service. Stick to beer: no one should have to pay $10 for a cocktail served in a Dixie cup. A maze of lounge chairs in the back and the new rooftop seating area provides comfortable seating, but languid loungers are missing the real party on the dance floor.
259 Banker St (near Meserole Ave). 719-389-1880. ❻ to Greenpoint Ave. Average drink $6.

SHOPPING

Alter
The fashion-conscious can find unique, high quality pieces from all over the world at this boutique featuring distinct regional fashions. Collared shirts undergo identity crises, re-cut in funky fabrics. Grandpa sandals from Tel Aviv take on an air of high fashion placed alongside vintage suits and ties. The shop also features local artists like Greenpoint native Erin Considini, who draws inspiration from the natural world for her sterling silver jewelry. Almost everything remains below $100, though the shop features creativity first with affordability as a bonus.
109 Franklin St (at Greenpoint Ave) 718-784-8818. Tues-Fri 1am-9pm, Sat 12pm-9pm, Sun 12pm-8pm. ❼ to Courthouse Square, ❻ to Greenpoint Ave.

Dalaga
This shop is what every girl wishes her bedroom could look like. Chandeliers are suspended over romantic Victorian furniture with just enough exposed brick to bring one back to the modern age. The clothes range from dressy to casual but all are reasonably priced and all are a step away from what is common. Men's clothing and a healthy collection of accessories round out the store nicely. The owner Michelle is likely to be ready and eager to help you find which rack of clothing suits your own particular style. Make sure you try something on to experience the oh-so-pretty dressing rooms.
150 Franklin St (between Greenpoint Ave & Kent St) 718-389-4049. Tue-Sun 12pm-9pm. ❼ to Courthouse Square, ❻ to Greenpoint Ave.

Kill Devil Hill
A visit to this two-room interpretation of a 1890s general store should be treated as a trip to a museum, but one in which everything is for sale. Antiques and modern made tributes to the past mingle in 'Cowboy Mark' and Mary's playful collection. They carry vintage denim and old army uniforms by way of clothing, but check out the bones for a real thrill. Prices are

both reasonable and quirky: antlers sold by the pound, penny candy raised to ten cents on account of inflation. Before saying goodbye, snag a peanut chew and leave smiling.
170 Franklin Ave (between Myrtle & Willoughby Ave). ❼ to Courthouse Square, Ⓖ to Greenpoint Ave.

Permanent Records
This store may seem to have a high concentration of rock albums, but there is also a large range of genres, although it may take a bit of searching. When in doubt, the lady behind the cash register has an encyclopedic knowledge of music and can answer all your questions without any condescension. Her attitude is the same as the entire staff, but your fellow customers, arch hipsters all, may make you want to shield your purchases from judgmental eyes. Check out the used bins and the occasional freebies before heading for the door.
181 Franklin St (at Green St) 718-383-4083. Mon-Sat 11am-9pm, Sun 11am-8pm. ❼ to Courthouse Square, Ⓖ to Greenpoint Ave.

The Thing
The garage sale from hell, The Thing is a junk heap with hidden treasures for those with plenty of time and patience. Empty coffee cups mingle amongst cassettes, books, clothing and odds and ends scraped from far-off attics. Their basement of vinyl piled floor to ceiling is what keeps people coming back for more. No matter what record, it will set you back a cool two dollars. If you are strapped for cash or have an afternoon free, take your time to comb through the stacks of clutter. Your perseverance could be well rewarded.
1001 Manhattan Ave (between George Apen St and Huron St) 718-349-8234. ❼ to Courthouse Square, Ⓖ to Greenpoint Ave.

Word
This local business offers much more than an intriguing book browsing experience. A bibliophile's dream, they offer ten percent off their book of the month and hold both in store and online discussions well-attended by literati of all ages. Game nights, author signings, and live music make this a community hub to peruse a thoughtfully chosen selection of texts and purchase beautifully crafted greeting gards. The helpful staff can order any title desired or direct readers towards new titles and staff picks.
126 Franklin St (between Greenpoint Ave & Kent St) 718-383-0096. Mon-Thu 11am-7pm, Fri-Sat 11am-8pm, Sun 12pm-8pm. ❼ to Courthouse Square, Ⓖ to Greenpoint ave.

Zoe's Beauty Products
Although a sign across the street offers to slaughter your live poultry, the ladies at Zoe's are glamorous without an ounce of snobbery. Eager to suggest their favorite products while evaluating your complexion, they are equally happy to divulge the previous night's gossip and the area's best night-spots. While it is no Sephora, Zoe's carries many of the same brands, as well as beauty basics one might buy in Duane Reade. The salon and spa attached make this truly a one stop gem of a store.
119 Greenpoint Ave (between Greenpoint Ave & Franklin Ave) 718-383-7400. Mon, Tue, Wed & Sat 10am-7pm, Thu & Fri 10am-8pm. ❼ to Courthouse Square, Ⓖ to Greenpoint Ave.

DAY TO DAY

Brooklyn Community Board 1. *435 Graham Avenue. 718-389-0009.*

Local Media: greenpunkt.com

Groceries: Met Food. *131 Driggs Ave (at Russell St). 718-389-6429*; The Garden. *921 Manhattan Ave (at Kent St). 718-389-6448.*

Gym: Maxim Health & Fitness. *500 Driggs Ave (between 10th & 9th St). 718-486-0630.*

Hospital: Woodhull Medical & Mental Health Center. *760 Broadway (at Marcus Garvey Blvd). 718-963-8000.*

Hostel: Greenpoint YMCA, *99 Meserole Ave (at Lorimer St). 718-389-3700.*

Dog Run: Monsignor McGolrick Park. *Between Driggs Ave, Russell St, Nassau Ave & Monitor St.*

Movie Theater: UA Court Street Stadium 12. *108 Court St (between State & Schermerhorn St). 718-246-8170.*

Best Happy Hour: The Pencil Factory. *142 Franklin St (at Greenpoint Ave). 718-609-5858. Happy Hour: Mon-Fri 3pm-8pm*

SHIPYARD

WELCOME
BROO
NAVY

"WE USED TO LAUNCH SHIPS...

BROOKLYN NAVY YARD DEVE
ALAN H. FIS
ANDREW H. KIMBALL

HON. MICHAEL R. BL

WILLIAMSBURG

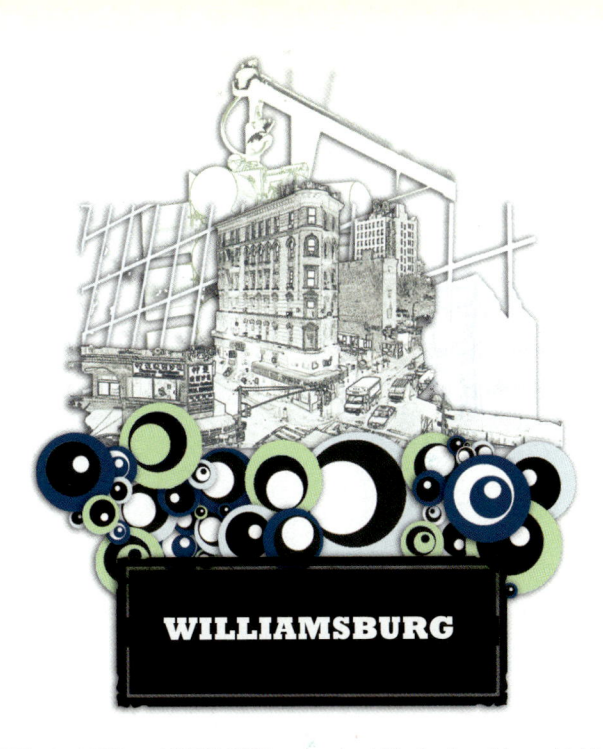

In the 1800's and 1900's Williamsburg quickly developed into a highly industrial neighborhood. Factory jobs attracted large numbers of Hasidic Jews, Italians, and Hispanic immigrants who populated the neighborhood until the late 20th century, when factories underwent rampant closures. As huge unused factory-buildings were converted to lofts in the 1990's, New York's artistic crowd, pushed out of Manhattan by increasing prices in the LES and SoHo, took over Williamsburg and made it the young, artsy neighborhood it is today.

Low buildings, tree lined streets, and row house filled side roads make Williamsburg feel more like a quaint little city of its own rather than the first stop off the L train from Manhattan. Scruffles dominate the scene—men wear nothing but plaid shirts and very-skinny-jeans and women go for anything that looks like it was made in 1970 and costs $2 at a vintage store (when in reality, favorite neighborhood vintage store Beacon's Closet probably charged at least $30 for it).

Unfortunately, the last few years have seen a drastic increase in prices in Williamsburg. Today housing prices creep ever closer to those of Manhattan. Locals from the 90's complain that the neighborhood has lost its authenticity and become too much of a faux-hipster haven. But the thousands of twenty-something residents who subsist on low-wage art jobs still find a unique and wonderful community filled with like-minded peers in the neighborhood. There's no question that beneath the façade of coolness, Williamsburg exudes charm and friendliness.

292 WILLIAMSBURG

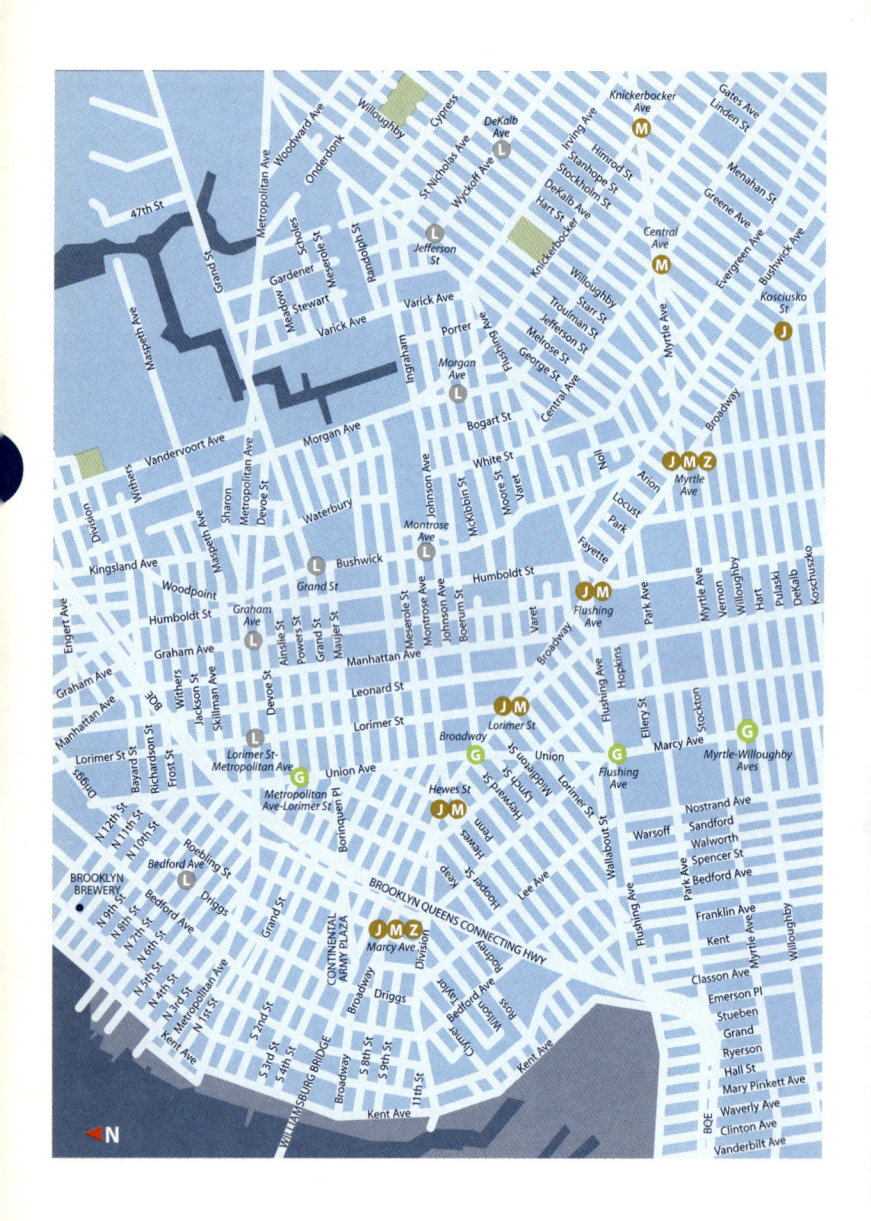

ATTRACTIONS & ARTS

City Reliquary Museum and Historic Center
Unlike the average museum, the City Reliquary is an intimate space filled with memorabilia from all the boroughs, some of it as old as the city itself. Pieces of the city's oldest buildings, Statue of Liberty trinkets, and a 1939 World's Fair exhibit are on permanent display, while the "Community Collections" store-front window displays circulating exhibits of found New York treasures. The Reliquary also prides itself on being a community center and offers several annual events, like Bike Fetish Day, during which people exhibit their bikes on the sidewalk and come together for an old-fashioned neighborhood barbeque and party.
370 Metropolitan Ave (at Havemeyer St). 718-782-4842. Sat-Sun 12pm-6pm or by appt. ● to Lorimer.

Glasslands
The owner of this space hopes that it is seen as an art gallery that sometimes doubles as a concert hall, but even that can't define what this place is. The space is constantly changing; the owners even encourage you to pick up a marker or paintbrush and express yourself on the walls. Although this place seems to try too hard to be that alternative spot, it emerges as a truly creative space that attracts the likes of Thurston Moore to perform and a crowd that matches its enthusiasm for an out-of-body experience.
289 Kent Ave (near S 1st St). 718-599-1450. Tue-Sun 5pm-12am, Mon closed. Hours may vary with performances. ● to Bedford Ave.

Pierogi 2000
Housed in an abandoned warehouse but with a polished new age interior, this artist-run show room is one of the oldest and most respected galleries in Williamsburg. It features works by both emerging and mid-career artists and hosts monthly solo shows highlighting an individual artist. It is most noted for the "Flat Files," a traveling exhibition featuring 700 portfolios that has been shown in Vienna, London, San Francisco, and LA, among other cities.
177 N 9th St (at Bedford Ave) 718-599-2144. Thurs-Mon 11am-6pm. ● to Bedford Ave.

DINING

MID-RANGE

Baci and Abbracci *Italian*
This destination transforms everyday pizzas into gourmet treats. Crusts are baked to perfection in a wood-burning oven imported from Naples and smothered with mozzarella and fresh toppings. Avoid the meat selections, which can be overcooked and under-seasoned. Pasta is a better bet, enjoyed with either a creamy cheese sauce or meat ragu. In warmer months, diners can savor their meal al fresco on the wood-paneled patio. Service is relaxed, and occasionally, painfully slow. The large wine list includes a selection of mostly Italian varietals. Dessert is prepared competently, if not adventurously.
204 Grand St (between Bedford & Driggs Ave). 718-599-6599. 4pm-12am. ● to Bedford Ave. Average entrée $16.

Dressler *New American*
This airy eatery boasts an imposing bar, which would suffice for a relaxed Sunday afternoon drink or a nightcap, but obviously the real draw is for gastronomes willing to splurge on an elegant meal in a friendly, laid-back setting. The French-influenced menu is laden with well-executed, familiar gourmet items like diver scallops, duck, short ribs, and Berkshire pork chop and belly, as well as elegant, more out of the ordinary appetizers—not to mention a thick, damn good burger. Of note is the friendly yet unobtrusive service, as well as an outstanding wine list with lesser known bottles from Portugal and South Africa.
149 Broadway (near Bedford Ave). 718-384-6343. Mon-Thurs 6pm-11pm, Fri-Sat 6pm-12am, Sun 5:30pm-10:30pm. Brunch Sat-Sun 11am-3:30pm. Mid-day Sat 3pm-6pm, Sun 3:30pm-5:30pm. ● to Bedford Ave.

WILLIAMSBURG 293

Fanny *French*
This cozy neighborhood joint presents traditional French fare, as well a smatter of Spanish and Mexican dishes, with a cheeky flair. The emphasis on fresh ingredients and bold flavor shows; carrot soup strikes the perfect balance between hearty and refreshing, and skirt steak is as beautifully prepared as one found in a far stuffier restaurant, except here it's for half the price. The real standout, however, is the classic croque monsieur, a mouth-watering triumvirate of buttery bread, smoky Swiss cheese, and tender slices of ham. Sip a few cocktails in the lovely backyard garden and try the fluffy lavender blanc manger or the creamy espresso flan for dessert. Remember to make a reservation on weekends – the space is small and tables are few.
425 Graham Ave (near Frost St). 718-389-2060. Sun-Thu 10am-11pm, Fri-Sat 11am-11pm. ⓛ *to Graham Ave. Average entrée $14.*

Miranda *Italian, Latin*
Miranda is no-nonsense, no-gimmick, good food. Innovative chefs combine Latin American and Italian flavors to create dishes that are as stunning to the eye as they are to the palate. The Orata a la Plancha exemplifies the restaurant's multicultural mission, fusing Mexican molé sauce with Mediterranean-style bass to create a wonderful entrée. The pasta dishes, made with fresh in-house noodles, are conveniently available in either small or large portions. Fettuccine in particular is a perfect balance of buttery pasta and richly flavored mushrooms. Step out of your comfort zone and order something unfamiliar—it's guaranteed to be good. The cozy atmosphere, wide-open windows, and delicious food make it a perfect place for a romantic outing or a quiet dinner.
80 Berry St (near N 9th St). 718-387-0711. Mon-Wed 5:30pm-10:30pm, Thurs-Sat 5:30pm-11pm, Sun 12pm-3:30pm, 5:30pm-10:30pm. ⓛ *to Bedford Ave. Average entrée $19.*

EDITOR'S PICK

Peter Luger *Steak*
Sometimes a restaurant's owners understand that they have made their mark, and this is when they dispense with all pretension and begin to do things their own way. Peter Luger is such a restaurant. Rated the city's best steakhouse for more than two decades, it offers wooden tables and wisecracking waiters, and asks that its patrons bring wads of cash to cover their bills. The menu must (and should not) be asked for. At lunch, it is the burger. At dinner, order your table a porterhouse for every two people. If you see steak sauce on your table, this is not for your steak: it is for the classic tomatoes and onions that should be ordered for starters. Those who pine for something green are arguably lost, except that Luger's has (but does not boast) the best creamed spinach in the five boroughs. In terms of what to wear, just know it's O.K. to wear something less expensive than your steak.
178 Broadway (at Driggs Ave). 718-387-7400. Mon-Thurs 11:45am-9:45pm, Fri-Sat 11:45am-10:45pm; Sun 12:45pm-9:45pm. ⒿⓂⓏ *to Marcy. Average entrée $40. Reserve far in advance.*

Relish *American, Brunch*
Inside this unassuming and lovably tattered restaurant, you'll find a classic 50's diner

gone slightly upscale, complete with leather booths, egg-cream walls, and a garden patio. The food matches the décor with a small, unpretentious menu offering classic combinations, proving that bold and delicious food doesn't always require adventure. The chef lets the ingredients speak for themselves, adding a light touch that makes each "classic" dish his own.
225 Wythe Ave (near N 3rd St). 718-963-4546. Mon-Thurs, Sun 11am-12am, Fri-Sat 11am-1am. Ⓐ Ⓒ to Broadway-Nassau, Ⓛ to Bedford Ave. Average entrée $10.

CHEEKS
/eks/ *Frozen Yogurt*
Eks is a standard addition to the ever-increasing list of trendy fro-yo spots like Pinkberry and Yolato. But it attempts to spice up the appeal by having more than just the traditional tart yogurt and green-tea flavors, such as "Dr. Coconut" and "Dr. Coffee". The "Dr." reference seems arbitrary, but the flavors are a refreshing change to the norm. Fruit and other toppings are available as well, and at a lower price than their cousins' in Manhattan.
488 Driggs Ave (at N 9th St) 718-599-1706. Ⓛ to Bedford. Cones $3-8.

Anna Maria's Pizza *Pizza*
Locals come to get the best slice of pizza this side of the East River. Slices piled with several inches of toppings in delicious combinations like veggie, ricotta, and broccoli make Anna Maria's a crowded hotspot at lunch, dinner, and in the wee hours of the morning when people stumble in from bars to satisfy their munchies.
179 Bedford Ave (between 7th & 8th St). 718-599-4550. 11am-5am. Ⓛ to Bedford Ave. Slices $2-4.

L.A. Burrito *Mexican*
$2.50 for 3 delicious, filling, fresh tacos is a pittance, and the obvious reason to go to this Cali-style Mexican taco shack. For just a bit more, you can score specialties like tofu-sour-cream, brown rice, and a plethora of vegetable options. Seating is cramped and the music is loud, but the food is ever delicious. The street-front ordering window is a great option for a cheap takeout meal.
287 Bedford Avenue (near S 1st St). 718-782-7728. Sun-Thurs 11am-10pm, Fri-Sat 11am-12am. Ⓛ to Bedford Ave. $2.50 for 3 tacos.

Penny Licks *Dessert, Vegan*
The name points to the prize item at this old-fashioned sweets shoppe—the $1 ice-cream scoop. The size of the scoop matches the price, but the mini-cones are so petite and adorable that they add to

---

SATMAR HASIDIC NEIGHBORHOOD

Walking down Bedford Avenue in Williamsburg feels like being sucked through a kabbalistic wormhole to the old Jewish quarter of some unpronounceable city east of Hungary and short of the twenty-first century, where the signs are all unreadable and no one meets your eyes. This is the world capital of the Satmar sect of Hasidic Judaism, a theocratic denomination with communities from Buenos Aires to Jerusalem. It's a de facto homeland – the Eastern European Hasidic communities the Satmars came from were obliterated by the Holocaust, and the sect is famous for believing that the state of Israel is a secular folly. Thus, until Messiah comes and restores the temple, Williamsburg must suffice to shelter them from the storms and corruptions of the outside world.

Here they have grown and prospered greatly since the 5th Satmar Grand Rebbe landed in 1946 with the tattered remnant of his court – there are now over 50,000 Satmars in Williamsburg alone, peopling a whole world complete with its own kosher ambulance service, rabbinical courts, Byzantine internal politics, and a yeshiva school system which, if public, would be the fourth largest district in the state, after only NYC, Buffalo and Rochester. At about noon every Friday the entire neighborhood shuts down for the Sabbath, and remains universally shuttered through to Sunday morning – with sundown, the ghost-town streets flood with dark streams of turbaned women and men in enormous fur shtreimel hats filing down to Shabbos prayers, while high above, flocks of diapered kids play in caged tenement windows.

WILLIAMSBURG 295

the charm. Penny Licks also specializes in vegan baked goods, which many swear far surpass the norm. Moon-pies, cupcakes, and Peanut Butter Moose Bombs are among the best of their selection.
158 Bedford Ave (near N 8th St). 718-384-0158. Sun-Thu 10am-10pm, Fri-Sat 10am-12am. ⓛ *to Bedford Ave. $1 per scoop.*

NIGHTLIFE

Charleston *Bar*
Locals might look down on this right-off-the-subway bar, but free pizza and short travels make it, by default, a hip spot. The biggest draw is the free pizza that comes with any drink—no strings attached. They're small and not exactly gourmet, but considering the price tag (or lack thereof), they are a delicious deal indeed. The crowd is made up of every type of twenty-somethings: hipsters, students, professionals. Bands play sporadically in the basement and large groups of friends gather around the pool table in the back.
174 Bedford Ave (between N 7th & N 8th St). 718-782-8717. Mon-Sat 3:30pm-2am. ⓛ *to Bedford St. Average drink $6.*

K&M *Bar*
This Art Deco bar was a former pierogi factory back in its day, but now serves better than average beer to a slightly older Williamsburg set. Gone is the ubiquitous PBR that plagues all bars, instead artsy types knock back more obscure German beers and rarely seen domestics. Though spacious, the Saturday night crowd fills the bar so quickly it's impossible to engage in any kind of dancing, which is a shame as the music (indie rock and New Wave) is superb. The bourbon selection is also noteworthy, while the rest of the liquor offerings are nothing to write home about. The artsy crowd and bartenders are a little surly, so perfect your non-smiling face and don't try to make friends.
225 North 8th St (at Roebling St) 718-388-3088. Daily 4pm-4am. ⓛ *to Bedford Ave. Average drink $8. Cash Only.*

The Levee *Bar*
This bar's simple, low-key atmosphere is what sets it apart from Manhattan bars. The laid back bar and pool table areas provide the perfect space to spend a night out with good friends or to mingle with strangers. Bartenders are friendly and drinks are well priced. For a small sports bar, the Levee boasts a top-notch beer selection and a few odd-ball mixed drinks, like the Gatorita (Lemon-Lime Gatorade and Tequila) or the Beam and Cream, a strange mix of cream soda and Jim Beam. While there is nothing outwardly special about this spot, its old-fashioned familiarity is a comforting and pleasant retreat from the modern bars that plague the city.
212 Berry Street (at N 3rd St) 718-218-8787. Daily 12pm-4am. ⓛ *to Bedford St. Average Drink $5.*

Metropolitan *LGBT, Dive*
Gay men and women sip drinks together here in one of New York's few "mixed" gay bars. Patrons sporting ubiquitous hipster ensembles meander in around 11pm on weekends and fill the spot a few hours later. Red rope lights snake across the top of the bar and just below the ceiling, providing the majority of the light for the dim bar. Tattooed, pierced bartenders serve up drinks, while the DJ blasts gay and lesbian music standards like Madonna and Peaches. During colder months, friends and lovers cozy up next to the fireplace, while the foliage-covered patio attracts groups to plastic tables or wooden picnic benches when the weather gets warm. The crowd tends to be made up of groups of friends relaxing together, making it an awkward place to come solo.
559 Lorimer St (between Metropolitan Ave and Devoe St) 718-599-4444. Daily 3pm-4am. ⓖⓛ *to Metropolitan Ave.-Lorimer St. Average drink $4. Cash Only.*

Music Hall of Williamsburg
Live Music
Ironically, the cavernous Williamsburg branch of Bowery Presents lacks the Bohemian intimacy of its Manhattan digs. Bowery Ballroom it ain't (the acoustics aren't nearly as fantastic, for starters), and

it's pretty unfortunate that the Music Hall has replaced Warsaw as the Brooklyn go-to for top-flight indie acts. But the Music Hall still gives much-needed consistency to a neighborhood that sees its rock clubs open and close at a dizzying pace. In a year when local fixtures like Galapagos and Luna Lounge shut their doors, the Music Hall quickly established itself as Brooklyn's top musical venue. Sadly, the place just feels too damn big: deep-set walls and ceilings make the action onstage seem oddly distant, and the venue seems half-empty even when it's sold out. And while the Ballroom's basement bar is one of its best features, it is soundly beaten by the dozens of other hangouts in the area.
66 N 6th St (between Wythe St & Kent Ave). 718-586-5400. ⓛ to Bedford Ave.

Pete's Candy Store *Bar*
Adorned with pinup girl posters, paper birds, Chinese newspapers, and a back room fashioned out of an old cable car, Pete's Candy Store is a treasure chest well worth unearthing. Game nights, such as trivia every Wednesday, take over the bar and allow the geek-chic crowd sitting atop school chairs to replenish the brain cells they lose from imbibing a variety of beers on tap and unique if unremarkable cocktails. The best cocktail is the St. Germain, made with Sauvignon Blanc, elder flower liquor, and lemon twist; others, such as the Vanilla Shanti and the Agave Margarita, remind patrons of Pete's saccharine treats past. Pete's also offers live music nightly, which runs the sonic gamut, as well as stand-up comedy and poetry readings.
709 Lorimer St (between Richardson St & Frost St). 718-302-3770. Sun-Wed 5pm-2am, Thurs-Sat 5pm-4am. Free live music 8 pm-12-am. Adult Spelling Bee every other Mon 7:30 pm. Bingo every Tues 7:30pm-9pm. Quizz Off every Wed 7:30pm-9:30pm. ⓛ to Metropolitan or ⓛ to Lorimer. Average drink $5.

Radegast *Beer Hall*
Radegast Hall & Biergarten is a place of solace for those seeking refuge from Williamsburg dens overrun with Pabst Blue Ribbon. With upwards of 50 types of premium German & Eastern European beer, you can level up from hipster to connoisseur. Come in groups of three or more in order to stake out your own segment of the communal benches in the outdoor section; otherwise be prepared to be social whether you want to or not. The clientele can be a tad obnoxious (think drunken Brits, arrogant yuppies, and the ultra trendy), but the Hefeweizens are superb. If you just want something to sop up your Hacker Schorr Weisse, there are multiple sausage/sauerkraut/French fry or rye bread packages at the grill that will do nicely (along with Angus burgers) from $7-12. Surprisingly, the wine list is good, too.
113 N 3rd St (at Berry St) 718-963-3973. Mon-Thurs 5pm-3am, Fri-Sat 3pm-4am, Sun 3pm-3am. ⓛ to Bedford. Average beer $8.

Sweet Ups *Bar*
Sweet-ups serves up informal and borderline rowdy fun, alongside fantastic cocktails. Located on a mercifully deserted

WILLIAMSBURG 297

street in Williamsburg, this barely lit bar is crowded enough to ensure even the smallest groups of people will have room to mingle. Though the cocktail menu is merely a notebook (to be made official later this year), the drinks are well-thought out. A Whiskey sour is made with real egg-whites, just like they used to do it. The house speciality, the Blackberry bramble, is a fruity and biting concoction of gin and muddled blackberries. There is a special beer on tap, "Sweet-Ups", usually only $3, but it changes nightly so don't get too attached to one brew. The DJ—a scruffly guy with a MacBook–is highly accessible and plays a truly schizophrenic mix of music that will delight any ear. The bartenders are full of snarky, good-natured banter and have one mission and one mission only: to get you drunk enough that they can mock you for the rest of the night.
277 Graham Ave (between Powers & Grand St). 718-384-3886. 5pm-4am. ⓛ to Graham Ave. Average drink $10. Cash Only.

Zebulon Bar *Cafe, Live Music*
If you're in the mood for some live jazz or blues music by a local artist, you'll love this French-themed bar. With a different local musician or band performing every evening, there's always something new to check out. The staff members are warm and friendly, though they can get swamped when it gets crowded for a performance. While they have a number of beers, check out their fairly priced extensive list of French wines. You never know what new talent you may discover on any given night, so drop in and enjoy the music.
258 Wythe Ave (between Metropolitan & N 3rd St). 718-218-6934. Sun-Thurs 4pm-3am, Fri-Sat 4pm-4am. ⓛ to Bedford, ⓙⓜⓩ to Marcy.

SHOPPING

Amarcord Vintage Fashion
If you're looking for something to spice up your wardrobe, something splashy, gorgeous, and well made, then this is the place to come. Amarcord does not carry run of the mill, so-called "vintage" fashions—these are real designer pieces, imported directly from Italy where they are hand selected for the three New York City stores. Each piece is individual and spectacular—nothing is too used, everything is made with the care and completeness of old-world couture. Which comes at a price—a high one. Nothing at Amarcord is cheap. Still, for browsing or choosing one or two special pieces to complete a closet, it can't be beat.
223 Bedford Ave (between N 4th & N 5th St). 718-963-4001. 1pm-8pm. ⓛ to Bedford.

Beacon's Closet
Possibly the city's most notorious vintage clothing vendor, Beacon's rewards frugal shoppers with an eye for style. The mammoth 5,500 square-foot Williamsburg branch (there is also a Park Slope location) sells bags and shoes of every color, racks upon racks of coats and jackets, and clothes from every decade and designer. Be prepared for a hunt: racks are packed tightly and sizes are jumbled together. Beacon's buys clothes too, paying 35% in cash or 55% in store credit of the item's resale value. Pricing is haphazard, with unexpected bargains alongside gouging rip-offs.
88 N 11th St (between Berry & Whyte St). 718-486-0816. Mon-Fri 12pm-9pm, Sat-Sun 11am-8 pm. ⓛ to Bedford.

Buffalo Exchange
This is a great alternative to its more crowded Williamsburg cousin, Beacon's Closet. Clothes, shoes, and accessories are neatly hung and displayed on easy to peruse racks where they are categorized, not by color like at so many vintage stores, but by size. Everything is easy to find and wonderfully cheap. The store has bright lighting and is rarely crowded, making shopping a pleasant experience.
504 Driggs Ave (at 9th St). 718-384-6901. Mon-Sat 11am-8pm, Sun 12pm-7pm. ⓛ to Bedford.

Commune Salon and Gift
This serene salon and gift oasis lies tucked away on the residential Grand Street. Commune's mood is all white light, almost

a passing mood. Quiet music plays, hair is snipped, and sporadic shoppers drift through the racks of unique spa-related clothing items, such as the gorgeous silk robes, and one-of-a-kind accessories including leather belts and purses. Jewelry cases showcase stunning pieces that browsers are encouraged to try on. The salon offers standard cuts and colors as well as more exotic treats like an aromatherapeutic hair wash.
191 Grand St (between Bedford & Driggs Ave). 718-384-7412. Tues-Sun 11am-8pm. Ⓛ to Bedford.

Junk

From antique trunks, sofas, and mirrors, to shot-glasses, vinyl, and costume jewelry, Junk has everything and anything you may be looking for. Though most of the items are much more than "junk," they are thrown together in this basement store as if they were—it can take some time to find the real treasures. When you do, however, expect to be rewarded with an amazing price. Beautiful sofas run as little as $99 and many of the clothes (the most difficult to search through) are priced at $1. There's almost nothing you can't find here, and every piece is exciting and unique. If you're moving into a new apartment, Junk is a must-see.
197 North 9th St (between Bedford Ave & Driggs Ave). Mon-Fri 9am-11pm, Sat-Sun 9am-9pm. Ⓛ to Bedford Ave.

Spoonbill and Sugartown Bookstore

Come to this cozy bookstore prepared to rummage through a varied selection and surprise yourself with what you find. Spoonbill and Sugartown specializes in new and used books on art, architecture, and design, but they also carry carefully-selected works of literature and non-fiction, as well as a large number of unusual magazines. You're sure to find something to spark your interest in this atypical collection, with books ranging from volumes of photos of Finnish summer houses to guides to making high-tech paper airplanes.. The store also sells rare children's books and a few quirky home items, such

DAY TO DAY

Community Board 1. 35 Graham Avenue Brooklyn. 718-389-0009.

Local Media: freewilliamsburg.com

Groceries: *Matamoros Puebla Grocery. 3193 Bedford Ave. 718-782-5044*

Gyms: *Maxim Health and Fitness. 500 Driggs Ave. 718-486-0630.*

Average Rent: One-bedroom: $900-1300, Two-bedroom: $1200-1700/month

Hospital: *The Brooklyn Hospital Center. 121 DeKalb Avenue. 718-250-8000.*

Hostels and Hotels: *Glenwood Hostel. 339 Broadway. 718-387-7858. Hotel Le Jolie. 235 Meeker Ave. 718-625-2100.*

Best Happy Hour: *Brooklyn Brewery. 79 North 11th St. 718-486-7422. Happy Hour Fri 6pm-11pm, $3 beers.*

as an inflatable moose head to stick above your fireplace.
218 Bedford Ave (near N 5th St). 718-387-7322. Mon-Sun 10am-10pm. Ⓛ to Bedford.

Ugly Luggage

Affordable antiques fill this quaint home shop, which derives its name from the many old-fashioned and brightly-colored suitcases scattered throughout the store. Unique goods, including a large selection of lamps and tableware, pack the space. The furniture and home accessories for sale can be charming or kitschy, but they all have character and a hint of nostalgia. An antique armoire sells for around $300, and faded, undeniably charming prints in an ornate, vintage frames can purchased for less than $20.
214 Bedford Ave (near N 5th St). 718-384-0724. Mon-Fri 1pm-8pm, Sat-Sun 12pm-7pm. Ⓛ to Bedford.

WILLIAMSBURG 299

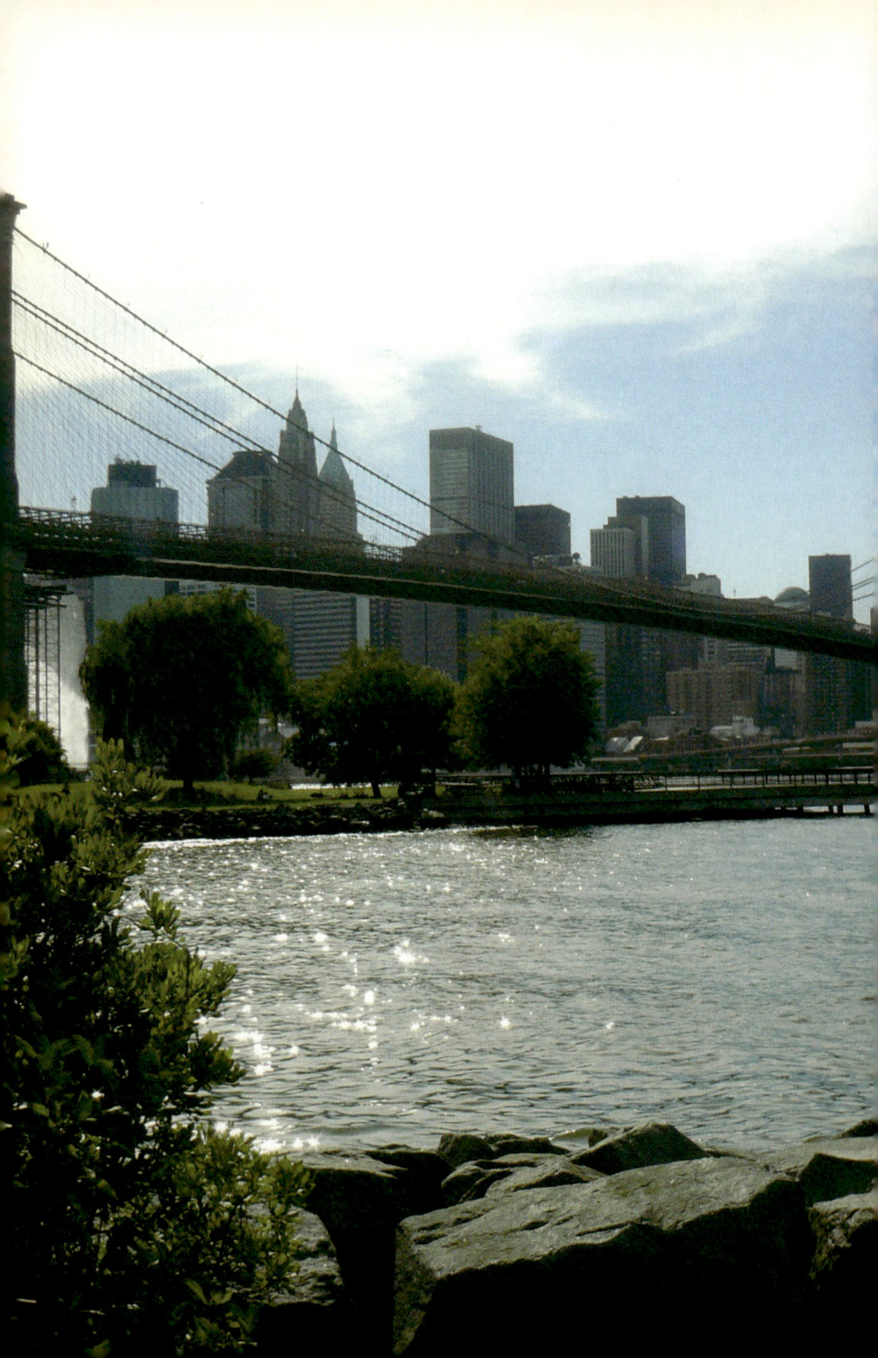

BROOKLYN HEIGHTS & DUMBO

What was once a blighted landscape of factories and parking lots is now home to the gentrified apartment buildings of resident families and the trendy studios of up and coming artists. DUMBO, for Down Under the Manhattan Bridge Overpass, encompasses both the fast-paced excitement of Manhattan and the pleasant comfort of the classic Brooklyn atmosphere. Artists, families, and tourists alike come to enjoy the diverse art, cuisines, and retail opportunities, as well as events that are frequently hosted by the neighborhood. The parks in DUMBO, bordered by old factories and warehouses that have achieved New York City landmark status, lie adjacent to the river and overlook what are arguably the best views in the city.

Further uptown from DUMBO lies Brooklyn Heights, a largely residential neighborhood with beautiful architecture and significant history. Known for its brownstones (and, more importantly, their stoops), its friendly eateries, its Borough Hall (New York City's original City Hall), and its Promenade, the atmosphere of Brooklyn Heights is lovely and peaceful—a refreshing get-away from the overwhelming energy of Manhattan. Local students, parents, nannies, and children can be found among the many playgrounds, parks, and schools in the neighborhood. The beautiful streets are conducive to a pleasant stroll through the neighborhood and make the perfect continuation to a walk across the Brooklyn Bridge.

ATTRACTIONS

Bargemusic
Bargemusic, DUMBO's floating concert hall, presents live chamber music five days a week, every week of the year. Located on Brooklyn's Fulton Ferry Landing below the Brooklyn Bridge, Bargemusic offers not only entertaining musical performances, but an unbeatable view and a romantic setting. Reservations are needed and can be made via telephone or e-mail; seats are assigned in the order that reservations are received.
2 Old Fulton St. 718-624-2083. BargeMusic.org. F *to York,* AC *to High,* 23 *to Clark. $20-$45.*

Brooklyn Borough Hall
New York City's original City Hall is also Brooklyn's oldest public building. The building is large and white with steps that stretch the width of the building and multiple tall columns at the entrance. There is a fountain and a spacious courtyard in front of the building and, if you go between 8am and 6pm on Tuesdays, Thursdays, and Saturdays, the courtyard hosts the Borough Hall Greenmarket, a local farmer's market that sells flowers, produce, baked goods, and seafood.
209 Joralemon St (at Court St). ACF *to Jay,* 2345 *to Borough Hall,* R *to Court.*

Brooklyn Bridge Park
The Brooklyn Bridge Park lies on the downtown shore of Brooklyn, overlooking Manhattan and the East River. The park contains a large grassy area, a dog-run, a playground (built to resemble a ship), and a small beach (not for swimming, unfortunately, though you'll see the occasional kayaker and fisherman). Surrounded by dozens of apartment buildings, retail attractions, and beautiful views, the park serves as a communal setting for both local residents and visitors.
Main St and Plymouth St. F *to York,* AC *to High.*

Brooklyn Heights Promenade
The view from the Brooklyn Heights Promenade, which stretches eight blocks on the coast of downtown Brooklyn, is unbeatable. It overlooks downtown Manhattan, the Brooklyn Bridge, the South Street Seaport, Ellis Island, New Jersey, and the Statue of Liberty. While the pathway is thin and crowded with bikers,

skaters, and strollers, there are plenty of benches to sit and admire the view.
Columbia Heights at Middagh St. ❹❻ to High, ❼ to Court, ❷❸❹❺ to Borough Hall.

Fulton Ferry Park
This nine acre grassland with a flanking boardwalk is the oldest of the downtown Brooklyn parks. Overlooking Manhattan and the East River, it is surrounded by the remains of landmarks Empire Stores and Tobacco Warehouse, two large brick buildings that bring a historic air to the area. In the summer, the area is also employed as a venue for a number of events, including concerts, film screenings, weddings and parties. The majority of the events are open to the public and many are free of charge.
Main St and Plymouth St. ❼ to York, ❹❻ to High.

CULTURE & ARTS

Dumbo Arts Center
The Dumbo Arts Center is a contemporary arts organization whose mission is to bring art to the masses through "experimentation, innovation, presentation, and advancement." The center is most known for its annual Art Under the Bridge Festival, though it also presents year-round exhibitions in its gallery, a spacious 3,000 square foot space sprinkled with wooden columns. It's never too crowded, and the artists it features are always worth checking out.
30 Washington St (at Plymouth St). 718-694-0831. Wed-Sun 12pm-6pm, or by appointment. ❼ to York, ❹❻ to High.

Art Under the Bridge Festival
A weekend-long event in Autumn, the Art Under the Bridge Festival is a showcase for local artists and galleries who display a diverse array of work that is frequently neighborhood inspired. From performance art to installations and interactive art, the festival is integrated into the parks, lobbies, elevators, streets, waters, and studios of DUMBO. Expect crowded streets brimming with music, food vendors, and exhibitions. There is no specific location for the festival; rather, it spans the entire neighborhood and most of the waking day, from 12pm to 2am and beyond. Let the crowds be your guide and you will have no trouble finding art.
DumboArtsCenter.org/Festival.html. ❼ to York, ❹❻ to High.

St. Ann's Warehouse
Appropriately located in a remodeled warehouse, the St. Ann's Warehouse, a performance-art organization that originated 28 years ago, came to DUMBO in 2001. With its self-proclaimed eclectic body of innovative productions that meet at the intersection of theater and rock-and-roll, the Warehouse has become one of New York City's most innovative live performance venues. Featured performances run each month, with occasional one-night events—check their website for listings. Tickets to performances are moderately priced and can be purchased on-line, by telephone, or at the Warehouse.
38 Water St (at Main St). 718-254-8779. StannsWarehouse.org. ❼ to York, ❹❻ to High. $25-$250.

DINING

MID-RANGE
Tazza *Café*
Tazza perfects the Brooklynite's image of the ideal café. Whether you're in the mood for a classic PB&J on whole grain or a Robiola, Arugula & Truffle Oil on Pizza Bianco, or simply a wonderful panini, Tazza doesn't disappoint. On the dessert side of the menu, Tazza's bakery offers cakes, cupcakes, bars, pies, cookies, and breakfast pastries—all of which are on display, making it impossible to leave the café without indulging yourself. Tazza also offers a variety of juices (including their well-known Watermelon Lemonade), and has both coffee and wine bars. Cell phones aren't allowed in Tazza, which makes it a rare and ideal spot to pull up a chair and relax.
311 Henry St (at Atlantic Ave). 718-243-0487. Mon-Fri 7am-10pm, Sat-Sun 8am-10pm. ❷❸❹❺ to Borough Hall, ❼ to Court. Average entrée $9.

CHEAP
Almondine *Bakery*
A small French bakery with the feel of a

BROOKLYN HEIGHTS & DUMBO 303

Parisian café, Almondine offers an assortment of croissants—plain, chocolate, chocolate-almond-raspberry, chocolate-almond, almond, and almond-raspberry—and each is authentic, crusty, and delicious. Every pastry can be enlarged to the size of a cake upon request. If you're in the mood for something salty, doughy pretzels or sandwiches on a perfectly baked baguette, Almondine will easily satisfy. Local residents can request "Almondine Room Service," a Sunday-morning croissant, baguette, and coffee delivery service. Those choosing to stay in the cafe, however, can enjoy the fragrance of freshly-baked bread and pastries while getting a clear view of the baking in the kitchen.

85 Water St (at Main St). 718-797-5026. Mon-Thurs 7am-7pm, Fri 7am-9pm, Sat 7am-7pm, Sun 10am-6pm. A C to High, F to York.

EDITOR'S PICK

Fascati's Pizza *Pizza*

A neighborhood favorite, the Fascati slice is close to perfect: delicious, filling, and cheap. Service in the pizzeria is fast; the staff, nearly all of whom have worked there since it opened in the seventies, have a special rapport with the locals, some of whom have been dining there daily for decades. Go for lunch and order the special: two slices and a drink for $4.50.

80 Henry St (between Pineapple & Orange St). 718-237-1278. A C to High, 2 3 to Clark. Average entrée $5. Cash only.

Lassen & Hennigs *Deli*

A jazzed-up version of your average deli, Lassen and Hennigs offers an extensive selection of sandwiches, salads, pastries, soups, and drinks, all moderately priced. Sandwiches are made to order, or can be selected from the Lassen and Hennigs specialties menu—many of which are named for streets around the neighborhood. More appealing than the food of Lassen & Hennigs, however, is the location. Right in the heart of Brooklyn Heights, L&H is a convenient spot to grab a sandwich before enjoying a relaxing lunch on the nearby Brooklyn Promenade.

114 Montague St (between Henry & Hicks St) 718-875-6272. Mon-Sun 7am-10:30pm. R to Court, 2 3 4 5 to Borough Hall. Average sandwich $7.

NIGHTLIFE

68 Jay Street *Bar*

Brimming over with camaraderie and local flavor, 68 Jay Street is as authentic and straightforward as Brooklyn bars come. In the heart of DUMBO, just a stone's throw from the East River, 68 is full of artsy-fartsy types looking to relax and have a little fun. Enjoy the totally decent wine selection, high quality beers, and fully stocked liquor shelf in an atmosphere devoid of vacuous frivolity. Located in the Grand Union Tea Company warehouse (the ceiling sports some lovely terra cotta arches), be sure to catch the quality blues-rock on Whiskey Wednesdays, or live jazz on Sundays.

68 Jay Street (at Water St). 718-260-8207. Sun-Mon 3:30pm-1am, Tues-Thurs 3:30pm-2am, Fri-Sat 3:30pm-4am. F to York. Average drink $5.

reBar *Bar*
Sharing its location with a plethora of local creative businesses, DUMBO's reBar is a high-quality watering hole thick with attitude and atmosphere. The elegant space lends itself well to a clientele of artists, self-proclaimed philosophers, and those just looking for a secluded date spot. The menu features some delicious, inexpensive food, including a variety of memorably hearty sandwiches and tapas. An exceptional beer and wine selection boasts organic, European, and rare brands, as well as 15 beers on tap. Wax poetic with the regulars, or cuddle up with your sweetie in the far corners of the warmly lit bar. Spacious digs, a separate room with a pool table, and kindhearted staff make reBar worth repeat visits.
147 Front St (between Pearl St & Jay St) 718-797-2322. Sun-Tues 4pm-2am, Wed-Sat 4pm-4am. F to York. Average drink $10.

SHOPPING

Jacques Torres
Don't let the long line at Jacques Torres turn you away—its beautiful and innovative chocolate truffles, treats, baked goods, and beverages are well worth the wait. Shelves are stocked with everything sweet: chocolate bars, chocolate lollipops, hot chocolate mix, chocolate covered nuts, cereal, popcorn, and dried fruit. Brownies dunked into their famous spicy hot chocolate provide a perfect double treat for any sugar high seeker, and French Kiss cookies are the holy grail of chocolate chip cookies. Anyone choosing to sit and indulge can watch the neighboring chocolate factory in action.
66 Water St (at Main St) 212-414-2462. Mon-Sat 9am-7pm, Sun 10am-6pm. A C to High, F to York.

Rowf
Resident dogs sitting excitedly at the door make it nearly impossible to walk by Rowf without taking a look inside. This doggie boutique carries fashionable outfits, toys, and leashes, as well as organic, pre-packaged, and home-baked snacks. Bring your dog and get a free sample of the treat of the day.
43 Hicks St (at Middagh St) 718-858-7506. Tues-Fri 11am-7pm, Sat-Sun 11am-5pm. A C to High, 2 3 to Clark.

DAY TO DAY

Brooklyn Community Board 2: *350 Jay Street, 8th Fl. 718-596-5410.*

Local Media: Downtown Brooklyn Star, *www.downtownbrooklynstar.com*

Groceries: Perelandra Natural Food Center, *175 Remsen St (between Clinton and Court). 718-855-6068.*

Gym: Gleason Gym, *75 Front St (btwn Main and Washington). 718-797-1050*

Rent: One-bedroom: $1750.

Hospital: New York Methodist Hospital. *210 Flatbush Ave (btwn Dean and Bergen). 718-783-0070.*

Hostels and Hotels: Awesome B and B, *136 Lawrence St (btwn Willoughby and Myrtle), 718-858-4859.*

Dog Runs: Palmetto Playground, *Atlantic Ave, Furman, Columbia, State Streets.*

Movie Theater: UA Court Street Stadium 12, *108 Court St (btwn State and Schermerhorn). 718-246-7459.*

Best Happy Hour: Waterfront Ale House, *155 Atlantic Ave (between Henry and Clinton). 718-522-3794. Sun-Thurs 11:30am-11:30pm Fri-Sat 11:30am-12am.*

Zoe
Zoe carries the designer clothes of a department store while maintaining the friendly ambiance of a neighborhood boutique. The staff is welcoming and laid-back, making the shopping experience anxiety free– unlike at large department stores or any one of the gilded temples where designer clothes would normally be found. Zoe carries clothing, jeans, shoes, and accessories including brands like Splendid, Marc by Marc Jacobs, Diane Von Fuerstenberg, Miu Miu, JBrand, and Jimmy Choo.
68 Washington St (between Front & York St). 718-237-4002. Mon 11am-7pm, Tues-Sat 11am-8pm, Sun 12pm-6pm. F to York, A C to High.

BROOKLYN HEIGHTS & DUMBO 305

HOLYLAND
AUTO REPAIR
FOREIGN
DOMESTIC
BRAKES
EXHAUST
N.Y.S. INSPECTION
A.C. RECHARGE
246-9695
MOTOR VEHICLE REPAIR SHOP

FORT GREENE

Literary luminary and social progressive Walt Whitman once called this area home, and his legacy lives on in the neighborhood to this day. Once an energetic community activist who had the first African American school in New York built on his property, Whitman was instrumental in the creation of Fort Greene Park, and even after his death the neighborhood continued to blossom as a cultural destination.

During the early to mid-19th century the neighborhood was popular with wealthy professionals tired of overcrowded Manhattan who were attracted by the short commute. Many mansions over a century and a half old still stand on Clinton Ave, including those of Charles Pratt, the founder of the prominent art and design school that bears his name. Today, the twenty-five acre campus of the Pratt Institute remains a center of activity in Clinton Hill, serving as a magnet for bohemian culture and artistic talent.

As more young professionals move in from Prospect Heights and Park Slope (where rent continues to skyrocket), gentrification is continually on the mind of the area's poorer residents, many of whom live in the industrialized area near the 19th century Navy Shipyard. Whitman's ghost seems to speak from the very streets, though, as his old romping grounds are well known for their unusually amicable economic and racial integration. Although Clinton Hill continues to evolve, the neighborhood is said to lack some of the amenities that are enjoyed by residents of nearby, more affluent neighborhoods (reliable train service, for one thing). Everything in life is a tradeoff, though: it is these very annoyances that keep the area affordable.

308 FORT GREENE

ATTRACTIONS

Commodore John Barry Park
Not far from the decrepit waterfront warehouses and old Navy Shipyard that border the East River lies Commodore John Barry Park, a recreational space named after the "father of the U.S. navy." Though only ten acres, Commodore Barry offers amenities like a public swimming pool, numerous handball walls, and paved blacktop with a kickball court and basketball hoops. It also hosts a number of seasonal events like the International African Arts Festival and Summer Children's Festival. The park also offers a large grass field with two baseball diamonds and plenty of space for soccer and football. The bustling Brooklyn Queens Expressway is overheard, giving pastoral athleticism a rugged inner-city feel.
Flushing Ave and Navy St. ⓜⓝⓡⓦ to Lawrence, ❷❸ to Hoyt.

Fort Greene Park
Fort Greene Park marks the spot of a revolutionary battleground once dominated by Fort Putnam, later renamed for General Nathanael Greene. In 1896 it became known as Fort Greene park when the masterminds behind Central Park in Manhattan were commissioned to design Brooklyn's first recreational park space. From the hill that forms the apex of the park's numerous rolling grassy knolls, you can't miss the Prison Ship Martyrs Monument, a massive column that sits on a plaza atop the park commemorating the bravery of the thousands of captives that died after the Battle of Brooklyn in 1776. Beyond its compelling history, Fort Greene park offers visitors a series of pathways perfect for a stroll, jog or bike ride, in addition to two playgrounds and six tennis courts. The fields on the southeast side of the park are perfect for ball sports.
Between Dekalb Ave and Myrtle Ave. ❸ⓓⓜⓝ, ⓡⓦ to Dekalb.

CULTURE & ARTS

BRICStudio
BRIC's performing arts space features a number of productions throughout the year. While sometimes simply used as rented rehearsal space, it also brings workshops, premieres, and international tours to the stage. It also provides brief residencies that culminate in a presentation followed by a discussion between performers and audience. The intimate setting provides a great contrast to the large theatre at BAM and is ideal for theater-lovers.
647 Fulton St (at Rockwell Pl) 718-855-7882 ext 53. ❷❸❹❺ to Nevins, ❸ⓜⓠⓡ to DeKalb.

Brooklyn Academy of Music
Known as BAM to New Yorkers, this venerable institution is perhaps the most popular performing arts destination outside of Manhattan. Featuring programs with respected acting troupes such as the Royal Shakespeare Company as well as many National troupes, a film series that focuses on new international cinema, and their own orchestra, this organization has done a great deal to create a racially and economically diverse neighborhood. They have presented a wide variety of artists over the years, such as Sufjan Stevens, Steve Reich, and Ingmar Bergman—a testament to their desire to bring progressive and avant-garde art to the community. Facilities include an Opera House, a theater, a cinema, and a studio that serves as rehearsal space. Tickets usually sell out early, so book ahead of time.
30 Lafayette Ave (between Ashland & St. Felix St) 718-636-4100. ❷❸❹❺❸ⓓⓜⓝⓠ to Atlantic.

Museum of Contemporary African Diaspora Art
Another relatively new arts center in the BAM cultural district, this museum focuses on contemporary African art. The center seeks to accurately depict the artistic and cultural contributions of people of African descent as well as to use the visual arts to discuss contemporary social and political issues relevant to the community. Featuring rotating exhibitions and a number of programs that include both films and fine art shows, MoCADA attracts both educational institutions as well as acclaimed international artists.
80 Hanson St (at South Portland St) 718-230-0492. Wed-Sun 11am-6pm. Suggested Donation: Adults $4, Students $3. ❷❸❹❺❸ⓠ to Atlantic.

DINING

MID-RANGE
iCi *New American*
The spirit of Alice Waters, famed food revolutionary, is fully present at this neighborhood restaurant located on the first floor and patio level of an old brownstone. With a menu bearing the mantra, "fresh, seasonal, local," iCi combines ingredients in light and innovative ways. Some days might bring a French-inspired menu, while others bring a bevy of market-driven items. The best choices are daily specials, or items with creative ingredient combinations. Tender octopus swimming in a pool of olive oil made vermilion from Spanish paprika, and watermelon salad with peppers, olives, and feta cheese are previous hits. An ample selection of seafood, vegetarian, and meat choices caters to multiple diets, with all of it guaranteed to be exceedingly fresh. In the same vein, desserts allow the ingredients to keep their integrity; Shaker lemon tart is hardly a reconstituted, saccharine curd, but bright, sour flavor with a slightly bitter aftertaste—just like a real lemon.

246 DeKalb Ave (near Vanderbilt Ave) 718-789-2778. Sun, Tue-Thu 9am-10pm; Fri-Sat 9am-11pm. **A C** *to Hoyt-Schermerhorn,* **D** *to DeKalb,* **G** *to Clinton-Washington. Average entrée $20.*

Maggie Brown *American*
Amidst Victorian, flocked velvet wallpaper, an oversized bison skull, and numerous antique decorations, visitors are transported to another era. Soothing background music and a wireless network offer customers the amenities of a local café or lounge, while extensive seating on the backyard patio is a colorful and lively alternative to the tranquil indoors. The portabello burger or thyme-encrusted tuna are adequate mains, while the "Mary Campbell," with Alchemia ginger infused vodka, ginger ale and fresh lemon juice, is an exquisite cocktail not to be missed. For dessert, rich chocolate almond cake is a must, the hot molten chocolate complemented nicely by vanilla ice cream and almond praline.

455 Myrtle Ave (between Washington & Waverly Ave). 718-643-7001. Mon-Thurs 11am-10pm, Fri 11am-11pm, Sat 10am-11pm, Sun 10am-10pm. Bar Sun-Thurs 11am-12am, Fri-Sat 11am-1am. **G** *to Clinton-Washington. Average entrée $14.*

CHEAP
Green Apple Café *Café*
The light and airy atmosphere provides the backdrop for a casual meal with friends or a good book. Their forte is the experimental approach to traditional ingredients—the Turkey Burger with gouda and honey mustard or the Chicken Mango Salad are delicious innovations. For smoothies, try the Chunky Green Monkey with peanut butter, banana, and chocolate sauce with regular or soy milk. If you don't mind eating dessert for breakfast, the ultra sweet Caramelized Banana Pancakes with roasted walnuts are a treat that will make your visit worthwhile.

110 DeKalb Ave (at Ashland Pl). 718-625-1248. Mon-Fri 8am-9pm, Sat 10am-9pm, Sun 10am-6pm. **B D M N R W** *to DeKalb Ave Station,* **2 3 4 5** *to Nevins. Prices $4-7.*

Urban Spring *Organic, Vegan*
Although Brooklyn offers no shortage of fresh, organic food, this quaint little juice bar serves up some of the more notable trendy vegetarian food. Portions are small and the waiters can be petulant, but the crisp crunch of the salads will make you forget all that. The menu is prone to green-minded pretense, like explanations of how different smoothies and juices will help your body. Ignore it, and order the Chick Pea Lemon Paté. Served with walnuts, cucumbers, carrots, and spinach, it should not be missed.

185 DeKalb Ave (between Cumberland & Carlton Ave). 718-237-0797. Mon-Wed 8am-7::30pm, Thurs-Sat 8am-8pm, Sun 9am-6pm. **C** *to Lafayette,* **G** *to Fulton. Average entrée $7.*

Zaytoons *Middle Eastern*
Serving delicious, succulent kebabs and fresh, crunchy salads at unbeatable prices, this is a great place to bring the family. Despite the seeming simplicity, the food is both complexly layered and perfectly prepared. Desserts are a wonderful end to an adventurous night out; muhalabia (milk pudding with orange blossom water and pistachio rice pudding with rose water) and Arabic coffee are both superb, exploding in a medley of tastes. Whether you're out with a group or a date, the dining experience

will be both delightful and delicious.
472 Myrtle Ave (between Mary Pinkett Ave & Hall St) 718-623-5522. Mon-Thurs 11am-11pm, Fri-Sat 11am-12am, Sun 12am-10pm. G to Clinton. Average entrée $9.

NIGHTLIFE

The Hideout *Bar*
Despite being a bit more sleek and modern than other neighborhood bars, The Hideout's exposed brick walls and affable patrons and employees lend it an authentic Brooklyn feel. The cozy, intimate space is reminiscent of a familiar living room, and the personable owner is an excellent host. A knowledgeable bartender mixes extremely sophisticated drinks, and will expand your horizons if you let him: the fusion of smooth bourbon with sweet fresh fruit make the American Beauty a novel treat.
266 Adelphi St (between DeKalb Ave and Willoughby Ave) 718-855-3010. Closed Mon, Tues-Sun 7pm-2am. C to Lafayette, G to Clinton. Average drink $13.

Moe's *Dive, Bar*
This vibrant spot is extremely popular with locals, who defend it against all detractors. Despite typical Brooklyn trappings (vintage furniture and whatnot), the clientele is rather diverse. Whether it's local guys who have never left Fort Greene or theater-goers stopping in for a pre or post- show drink, the casual and comfortable atmosphere keeps everybody coming back. The pitch perfect mojito, sweet and refreshing, is a delicious taste of Cuba. The underlying Simpsons theme adds a healthy dose of character.
80 Lafayette Ave (at S Portland Ave) 718-797-9536. Mon-Fri-3pm-4am, Sat-Sun 12pm-4am. Happy Hour 3pm-7:30pm. C to Lafayette, G to Fulton. Average drink $6. Cash only.

SHOPPING

Brooklyn Flea
One of Brooklyn's most popular attractions since it opened in April 2008, this outdoor market brings together nearly 200 top sellers of vintage antiques, clothing, and jewelry weekly. They also sponsor local artists and have their newest designs available for sale. With an extensive waiting list for the vendors, every week brings something new—whether you're searching for that one perfect dresser or a prop from a film set, this flea market is the place to find it.
Lafayette Ave (between Clermont and Vanderbilt Ave). Sun 10am-5pm. A C to Lafayette, 2 3 4 5 B D M N R W to Atlantic.

Little Piggy Market
Owned by the two friendly, local guys who also own the popular barbecue restaurant next door, this country market and café serve up good ol' Southern homecookin' such as cheesy grits and warm, homemade biscuits. They also sell $6 sandwiches, penny candy (for more than a penny), ham, and local produce. Their small but delicious desserts are perfect for an afternoon snack and the employees are always friendly.
64 Lafayette Ave (at South Elliot Pl) 718-797-1011. Closed Mondays, Tue-Thu, Sun 12pm-10pm, Fri-Sat 12pm-11pm. C to Lafayette, G to Fulton. Cash only.

DAY TO DAY

Community Board 2. 350 Jay Street, 8th Floor. 718-596-5410.

Local Media: Fort Greenster *ftgreenebk.blogspot.com*

Groceries: The Greene Grape. 765 Fulton St. 718-233-2700. 8am-9pm daily. Upscale.

Fitness: Crunch. 691 Fulton St. 718-797-9464.

Average Rent: One bedroom- $1200-1500. Two bedroom- $1700-2000.

Hospital: The Brooklyn Hospital Center. 121 DeKalb Ave. 718-250-8000.

Best Happy Hour: Moe's. 80 Lafayette Ave. 718-797-9536. Happy hour: Daily 3pm-7:30pm; two-for-one draft beers except Guiness; $6 frozen drinks; $1 off well drinks.

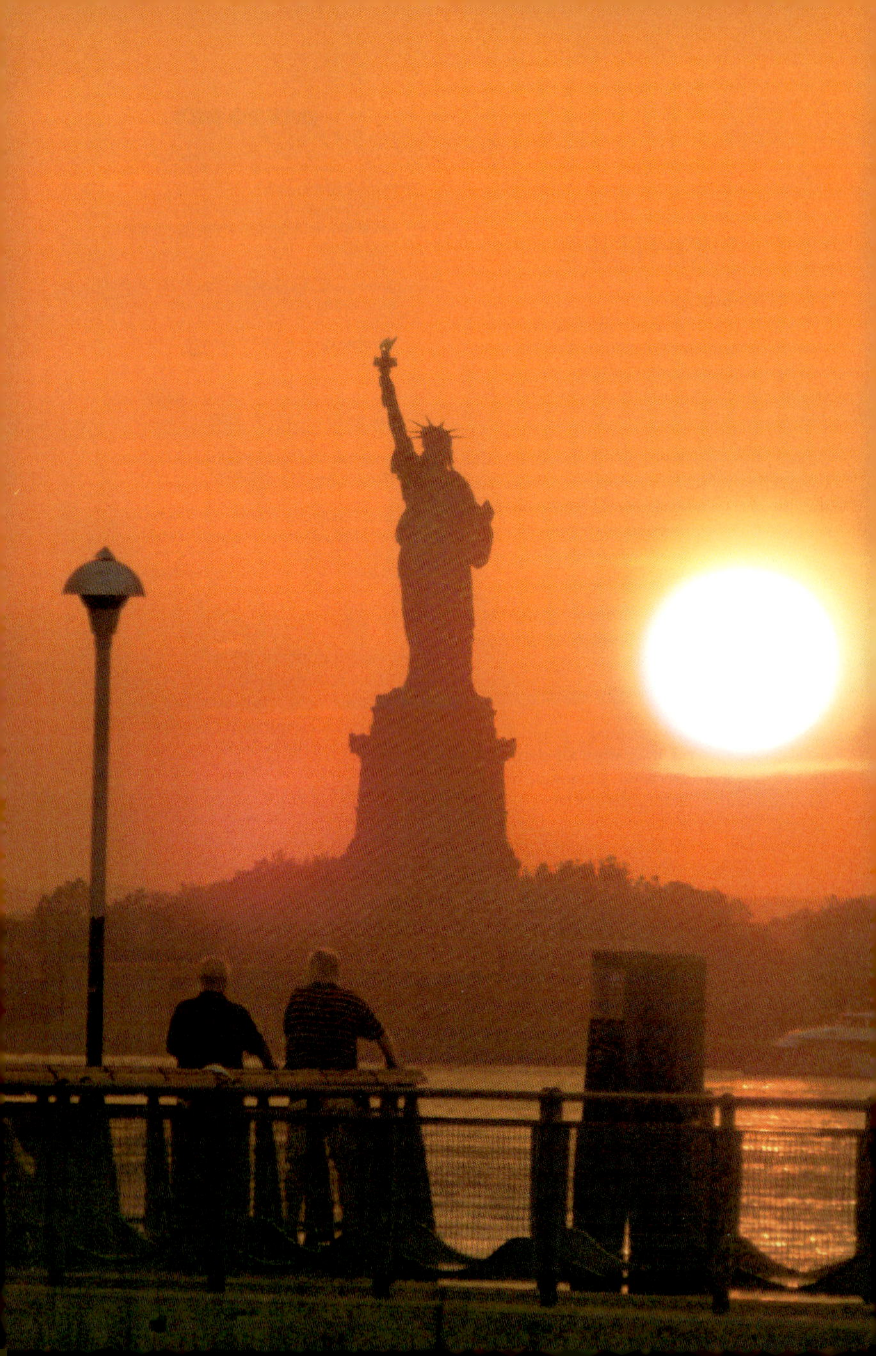

CARROLL GARDENS

Historically filled with working class Italian immigrants, the areas of Carroll Gardens, Cobble Hill, and Red Hook were once all known simply as Red Hook. In the mid 20th century, the construction of the Brooklyn-Queens Expressway cut off the lower portion of the region; the northern area, now Cobble Hill and Carroll Gardens, developed a more middle-class character, attracting young professionals and families tired of the noise and clamor of Manhattan. The lower area, now considered Red Hook proper, retained its working class character and is still considered one of the roughest parts of Brooklyn.

Regardless of class distinctions, the three neighborhoods all have vibrant personalities. Carroll Gardens, home to many young professionals, is filled with high-class boutiques and quirky, locally-owned stores. Large streets lined with oak trees offer pedestrians the feeling of comfort and security. The architecture and layout are masterful—stylish brownstones with long concrete stoops, abundant parks, and colorful gardens as far as the eye can see. Cobble Hill, too, is filled with creative shops and elaborate brownstones; most locals admit that the two neighborhoods run together seamlessly. Red Hook, on the other hand, is a concrete jungle—large brick apartment buildings, metal fences, grungy, creative graffiti, and a handful of corner stores and bodegas comprise the neighborhood. A few local artists seek to draw inspiration from Red Hook, but the population still consists mainly of minority working-class families.

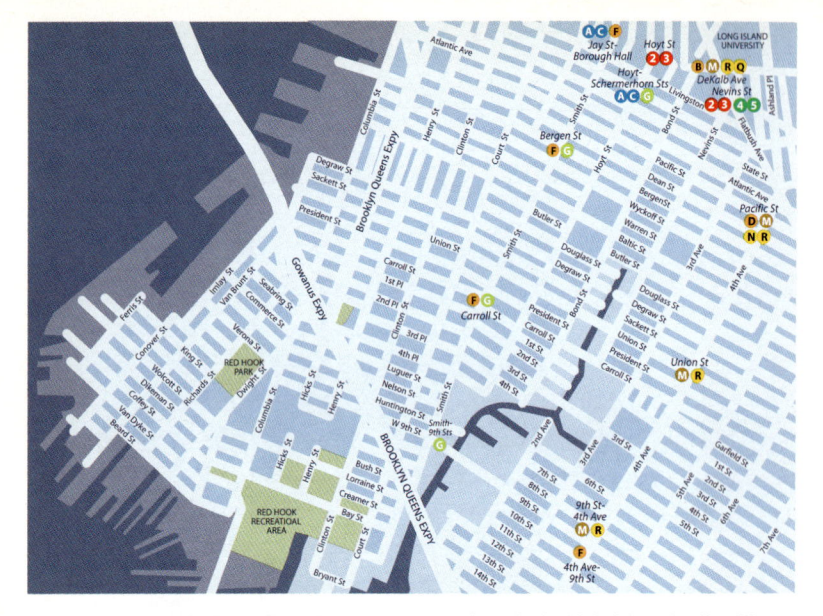

ATTRACTIONS

Carroll Park
Majestic oak trees, colorful tulips, and rich green shrubbery line the edges of this historic park. The Mr. Softee tune—familiar to all within New York's five boroughs—pervades the park during the summer months. Pressed in between brownstones and a large elementary school, Carroll Park attracts neighborhood children who meet up on the park's basketball courts, baseball diamond, and playground, or skip through sprinklers on sweltering summer days. Visitors seeking a moment of relaxation can take a seat in the park's shady picnic and bench areas.
President & Court St. Closes after dark. 🟠🟢 *to Carroll.*

Cobble Hill Park
Lush dogwood trees, bright yellow and cream-colored daffodils, and a wrought-iron fence provide an atmosphere of privacy and seclusion to the Brooklyn park-goer. All stony-cement paths lead to a clover-shaped monument in the middle of the park that doubles as a flowerbed with bright red tulips. Vacant grassy areas are hard to come by here, as Cobble Hill Park's visitors will never pass up the opportunity to sprawl out on its emerald lawns.
Bergen St (at Clinton St). 212-639-9675. Closes at sunset. 🟠🟢 *to Carroll.*

St. Paul's Episcopal Church
Hidden on an elegant, leafy, brownstone-lined block in Carroll Gardens, this landmark is notable for its architecture, a hybrid of European cathedral styles conceived during the American Industrial Revolution. Though its locked wrought-iron doors keep curious passerbys away for most of the week, its interior is breathtaking. The altar is adorned with dark oak, marble, and gold, and pews are substituted with individual wooden chairs strictly aligned in perfect rows facing the front of the cathedral. The dim lighting—St. Paul's few stained glass windows let little sun filter through—makes for an intimate setting.
199 Carroll St (at Clinton St). 718-625-4126. Prayer: Sunday 10am, Tues-Thurs 7:30am, Friday 9am. 🟠🟢 *to Carroll.*

Red Hook Park
Red Hook's residents fully appreciate this green space which is used as a recreational haven for youth. Basketball courts, a playground, sprinklers, and a swimming pool are usually crowded and noisy with the playful shouts of neighborhood children. Large oak trees and grassy meadows provide relief on scorching summer days.
155 Bay St (at Clinton St). 718-722-3211. F G to Smith-9th St.

CULTURE & ARTS

Bond Street Gallery
Housed in a renovated century-old townhouse in Gowanus, Bond Street Gallery encloses a wide selection of vintage and contemporary photographic art. It is a small building, seemingly squeezed into an alleyway, but the founders, two photographer agents say that it reflects their desire to expose artists who have fallen through the cracks. The space itself is gorgeous; smooth plaster covers old brick, dark-wood covers the floors, and bright lights point to the ceiling, creating the perfect atmosphere for enjoying the underappreciated.
297 Bond St (between Union & Sackett St). 718-858-2297. Tues-Sat 11am-6pm. R to Union.

Brooklyn Collective Artisan Gallery
The enthusiastic owners of this gallery have one goal in mind–to spark the interest and curiosity of their clientele. Anything goes in the waterfront showroom—photographs of personified coins, forks, and toothbrushes hang on fuschia-colored walls; yellow and brown butterflies flutter around a young girl's delicate face on a light wooden surface, and a robin nestles her fragile baby-blue eggs inside the same girl's skull. Jewelry made by local artists dangles from display areas along the walls, and clothing hangs from racks with vintage-style hats placed on top.
198 Columbia St (at E Houston St). 718-596-6231. Thurs-Sun 1pm-9pm. F G to Carroll.

Brooklyn Waterfront Artist's Coalition
Housed in a former warehouse, all wooden floors and low ceilings, this rough space leaves visitors free to focus on rotating exhibitions of local artists' work. Canvasses, photographs, and installations share space on green painted plaster and bare stone walls, recalling the cluttered salons that used to be at the art world's heart. Accordingly, artists' works are on sale for anywhere between $35 and $5,000. It's not just visual artists who lead exhibitions here to make their names—free music and dance performances, held regularly on weekends, are a draw and have helped to make the BWAC a focal point for the Brooklyn artistic community at large.
499 Van Brunt St (near Beard St). 718-596-2507. Weekends 1pm-6pm, Free Admission. Free Performances at 3pm. A C F to Jay, B61 to Van Brunt and Beard.

DINING

MID-RANGE
Jill's Café *Vegan*
Raw vegan food can actually taste delicious, and Jill's Cafe will prove it. With a helpful staff, local ingredients, and even a few cooked entrees on the menu, everyone can find something tasty. When it's nice out, guests can sit at a private table in the shady garden in the back. Otherwise, you'll be seated at a communal dining table, not a bad option if you enjoy the company of health food zealots. Raw pizza with sun-dried tomato-basil pesto and olives stands out as the most flavorful and inviting dish on the menu. It's easily filling enough for an entrée, and also approved by many a carnivore. Try some fresh pear, lemon, or ginger juice to complement the strong flavors of the raw vegetables. The menu changes depending on what's in season, but the commitment to healthy and satisfying dishes remains.
231 Court St (at Baltic St). 718-797-0330. Mon-Sat 11am-9pm, Sun 11am-8pm. F G to Bergen. Average entrée $13.

EDITOR'S PICK

Quercy *French Bistro*
This modest neighborhood mainstay proves you don't need the fuss and pretension of pretentious Manhattan bistros. Quercy turns out hearty and immensely satisfying dishes with laid back, easygoing charm and a welcoming, homey vibe. Skip the nothing-special soups and salads; go right for the robust meat options, prepared with fresh ingredients and juicy gusto—you won't be disappointed. Venison medallions are perfectly textured, served with generous portions of

roasted rosemary potatoes and a sublime quince sauce, which is as thick and boldly flavored as only the best French chefs can pull off. A small selection of reasonably priced French wines, candlelight, and a nicely assembled jazz playlist are all nice touches—proof that a place can have class without attitude.
242 Court St. (at Baltic St) 718-243-2151. Mon-Thu 5pm-10:30pm, Fri-Sun 11am-10:30pm. ❶❻ to Bergen. Average entrée $18.

PJ Hanley's *American*
This Carroll Gardens standby has been around for over a century, and with good reason. The tavern portion serves hearty Italian pastas and pizzas, but the outdoor bar area is home to the better scene. Bounded by a picket fence, the wooden benches and umbrellas are familiar and the atmosphere is comparable to a neighbor's backyard party. The menu is comprised of standard bar fare like calamari, burgers, and fish 'n chips, but not worth making a meal out of. Eat elsewhere and end the night at PJ's with a beer, chips, and salsa outside. It's hard to go wrong on a Saturday evening with live music, cheese fries, and a draft Shock Top.
449 Court St (at 4th Pl). 718-834-8223. Daily 11am-4am. ❶❻ ro Carroll. Average entrée $14.

CHEAP
Baked *Bakery*
This bright shop specializes in all things baked, from quiche to cake. The glass case features classic American goodies: scones, cakes, cupcakes, tarts, pies, cookies, brownies, bars, and homemade marshmallows in three flavors. Chocolate chip and oatmeal-cranberry cookies are gorgeous and tawny brown, with great crisp-to-chewy ratio. Cupcakes far outshine those found in popular Manhattan bakeries; moist cakes topped with a dollop of feather-light buttercream come in a variety of flavors including Malted, Sweet and Salty, and Red Hook Red Hot. It is worth outsourcing your next birthday cake to this lesser-known diamond in the rough.
359 Van Brunt St (at Dikeman St) 718-222-0345. Mon-Fri 8am-7pm, Sat-Sun 9am-7pm. ❶❻ to Smith.

Court Street Bagel *Bagels*
Glass jars filled with pink sugar cookies, sesame bagels stacked neatly in metallic crates, and cold cuts on display behind the glass of a typical, deli-styled counter are all visible from the door. With tight seating, customers are more likely to enjoy their cream-cheese-filled everything bagels and hot, green teas outside. The shop's fast-paced environment has a quintessential New York feel to it; regulars mill in throughout the day, and on the weekends it isn't unusual to see the line extend outside. Thick and creamy jelly and Boston Cream doughnuts are favorites among customers.
181 Court St (near Congress St) 718-624-3972. Mon-Fri 6am-10pm, Sat-Sun 6am-8pm. ❶❻ to Bergen St. Average meal $5. Cash only.

NIGHTLIFE

The Jake Walk *Bar*
The Jake Walk, the latest business from the owners of Brooklyn wine shop Smith & Vine and cheese shop Stinky Bklyn, offers a perfect location for enjoying these age-old companions. The cheese offerings are eclectic and extensive, ranging from cheddar to chevre, and the very reasonably-priced wines are grouped in cleverly-named categories such as "Roasty Toasty" on the white side and "Spice Rack" on the red. The impressive array of wines by the glass nicely compliment the cheese and charcuterie offerings alongside 50 whiskey labels. The fondue may be the best in the city and is perfect for sharing with a date in such an intimate candle-lit setting.
282 Smith St (at Sackett St). 347-599-0294. Mon-Thurs 4pm-2am, Fri 4pm-4am, Sat 2pm-4am, Sun 2pm-2am. ❶❻ to Carroll. Average drink $7.

SHOPPING

Artez'n
A charming gift shop and gallery located on a shady section of Atlantic Ave, Artez'n is known for its quirks. Alarm clocks made out of recycled pop-tart boxes, neon green martini shakers, and a complete combination

of scents called "cocktail party to go" sit on colorful shelves throughout the store. Though seemingly bizarre when compared to most other gift shops, it is normal at Artez'n to find a bottle of hot sauce and a Nine Inch Nails record of lullaby renditions within arms reach of each other. A bundle of Metrocards folded and fashioned into an elaborate star, and an attractive, crimson necklace created from shards of glass hang humbly under the "recycled items" section of the store. The environment is laid-back and friendly, and the staff waits patiently for you to find something that catches your eye.
444 Atlantic Ave (between Bond St & Nevins St). 718-596-2649. Open daily 11am-7pm. ❷ *to Nevins St.*

Astroturf
Vintage furniture spills onto the sidewalk from this attractive antique furniture store, offering a sample of the nostalgic assortment inside. Bright yellow office chairs and couches recalling the Brady Bunch living room fill the shop. 1950s style reading lamps light the walls, illuminating the store's scattered collection of old black and white newspaper clippings. The staff knows a great deal about antiques and helps direct enthusiasts and newcomers alike to great finds.
290 Smith St (between Union St & Sackett St). 718-522-6182. Tue-Sun by appointment only. ❻❼ *to Carroll.*

Freebird Books and Goods
The building itself might be a hole-in-the-wall, but this locally-owned used bookstore has an eccentric personality and more organization than its appearance may let on. The nostalgic aroma of vintage paper permeates throughout the store where free-spirited, intellectual, twenty-something bookkeepers share their literary expertise with well-dressed young customers. The newly refurbished back yard, complete with a two-tiered deck, hosts different events and parties for the devoted intelligentsia, while weekly book club discussions and the occasional book reading by local authors brings in literary connoisseurs from beyond Carroll Gardens' borders.
123 Columbia St (between Williamsburg Bridge & E Houston St). 718-643-8484. Thurs-Fri 6am-10pm, Sat-Sun 10am-10pm. ❻❼ *to Carroll.*

DAY TO DAY

Brooklyn Community Board 6. *250 Baltic Street. 718-643-3027.*

Local Media: Carroll Gardens-Cobble Hill Courier; Only the Blog Knows Brooklyn. *onlytheblogknowsbrooklyn.typepad.com.*

Gym: Body Elite. *348 Court St (between President St & Union St). 718-935-0088.*

Rent: One-bedroom: $1200-1600; Two-bedroom: $1800-2400.

Groceries: Good Food Store. *431 Court St (between 2nd Pl & 3rd Pl). 718-624-3788.*

Hotel: Baisley House. *294 Hoyt St. 718-935-1959.*

LeNell's
This tiny boutique in Red Hook has city's largest bourbon selection served with a healthy side of Southern hospitality. It feels as though the shop has been there forever—filled to the roof with knick-knacks like an old bathtub, orange blossom water, crystal decanters, well-worn books, and pewter flasks. LeNell, the shop's owner, knows her stuff and especially chooses to showcase lesser-known distilleries and small family-owned vineyards. The sales crew knows their booze, and can help guide you to the best selection in your price range.
416 Van Brunt St (near Coffey St). 877-667-6627 or 718-360-0838. Mon-Sat 12pm-12am, Sun 12pm-9pm. ❻❼ *to Smith.*

Rocketship Comics
This hipster comic store is the place to go for those who don't want X-Men snowglobes and Superman bookends mixed in with their "sequential art." Rocketship is dedicated to pure cartooning. They also frequently host signings and talks by prominent alternative cartoonists along with exhibitions of original artwork.
208 Smith St (between Baltic & Butler St). 718-797-1348. Sun-Mon 11am-7pm, Tues, Thurs 11am-8pm, Wed, Fri-Sat 11am-9pm. ❻❼ *to Bergen.*

CARROLL GARDENS 317

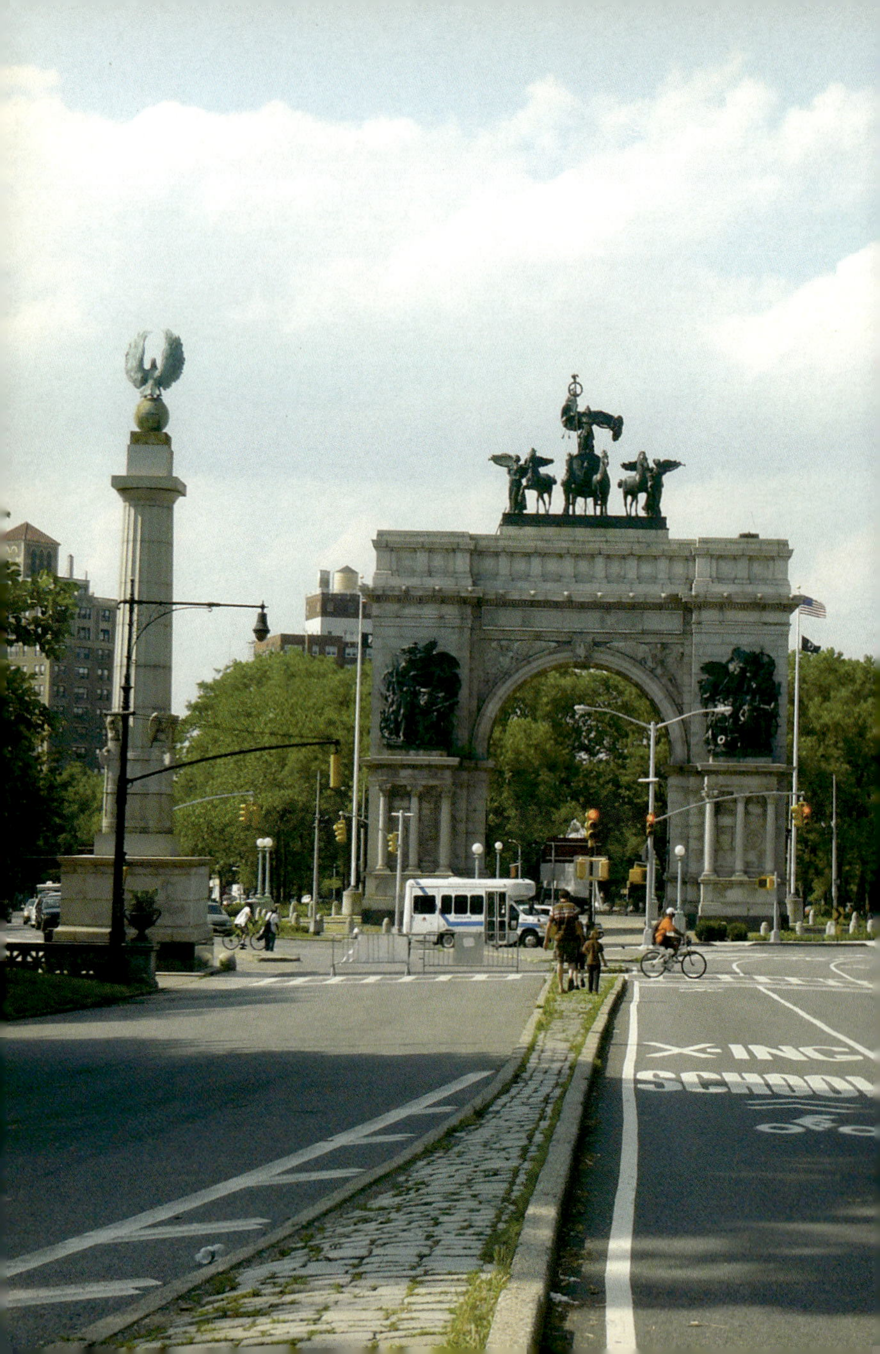
X-ING

PARK SLOPE

Like many New York neighborhoods, Park Slope has come full circle since its 19th century boom. In those days it was a thriving business center and home to New York's monied class who wanted to avoid the poverty of crowded Manhattan–it was briefly listed as the wealthiest community in the country. The late half of the century saw an influx of the middle-class, also seeking refuge from the same squalor, and a once gilded neighborhood became très gauche. From here Park Slope's story is like so many others: drugs, crime, and poverty in the 60s and 70s, followed by a gradual process of urban renewal and gentrification.

Today, Park Slope is home to the more family oriented cousins of the Williamsburg hipster elite. They still wear skinny jeans and American Apparel, but they push baby strollers instead of single speed bikes and they sport diaper bags over their strollers instead of satchels. Tree-lined streets and elegant turn of the century brownstones make this one of the most desirable residential neighborhoods in the five boroughs, not least because of its proximity to the beautiful Prospect Park.

This is Brooklyn's West Village, and it has a bar and restaurant scene to match (prices included). The bar scene is all indie bands and micro-brewed beer, but there is also a LGBT nightlife scene because of the many lesbians who call this area home. Weekends bring organic foodies to the weekly farmers' market, and bargain hunters from all over raid both the kitschy boutiques and the weekly fleamarket. Rents reach Manhattan prices, but the occasional bargain and rent stabilization have kept remnants of the former working class community in the area.

320 PARK SLOPE

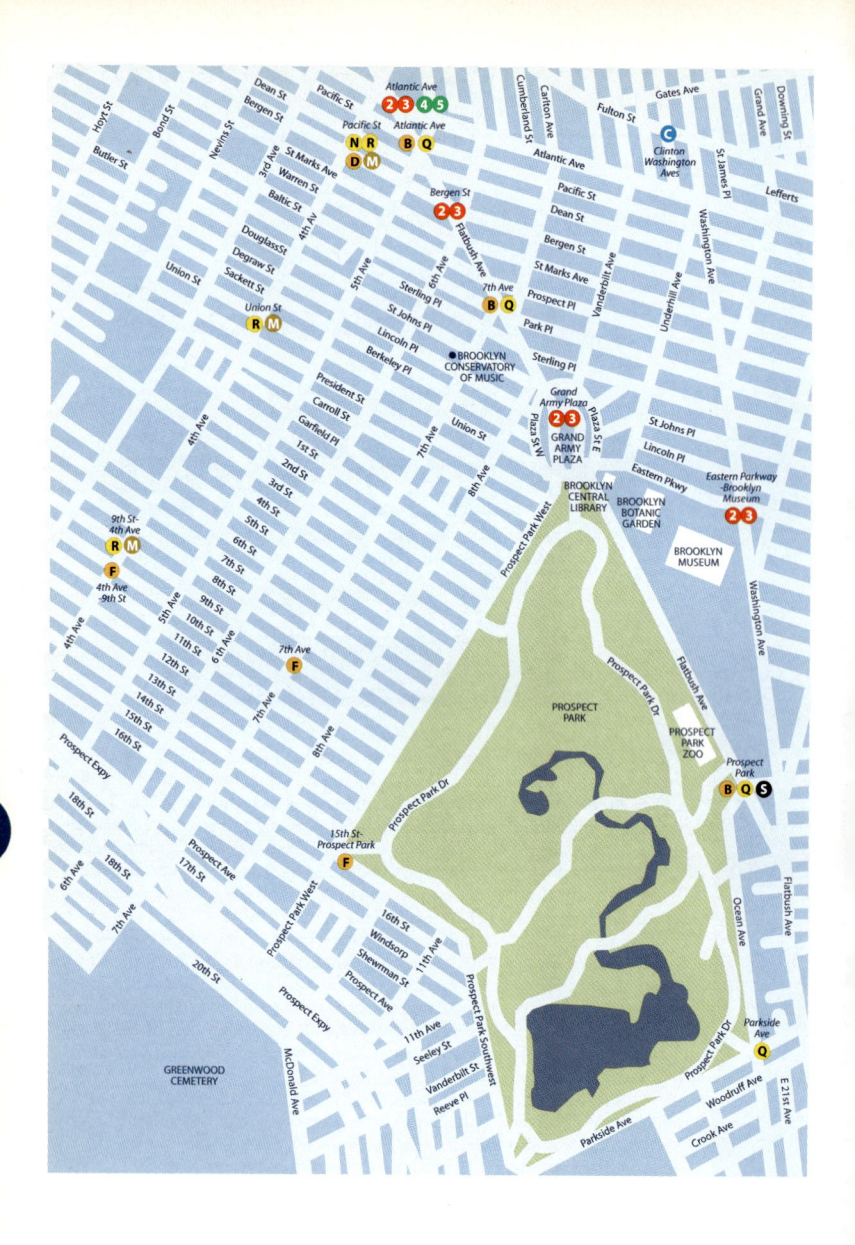

ATTRACTIONS

Brooklyn Botanic Garden

Each month, a new plant blooms at this green space designed nearly a century ago by the Olmstead Brothers and McKim, Mead, and White. The award-winning design for the lily pool terrace, featuring two rectangular pools surrounding a central fountain, is the perfect place to seek peace. Vaulted wooden bridges over the large pond, a bright reddish orange gate placed in the pond and a shrine to Inari, the Shinto deity of rice, are highlights of the Japanese Garden. Seasonal destinations include the Cherry Esplanade, which draws lines several blocks long in the early spring, and the Cranford Rose Garden, an attraction through early summer.
1000 Washington Ave. 718-623-7200. General Grounds: Mar 9-Oct 31—Tues-Fri 8am-6pm, weekends and holidays 10am-6pm, closed Mon; Nov 1-Mar 8—Tues-Fri 8am-4:30pm, weekends and holidays 10am-4:30pm, closed Mon. Steinhardt Conservatory: Nov-Mid-March—10am-4pm; Mid-March-Oct—10am-5:30pm. ❷❸ to Eastern Parkway. ❸❶❺ to Prospect Park, ❹ to Franklin Avenue.

Brooklyn Museum

Temporary exhibits at this well-known Brooklyn spot often include jaw-dropping, controversial pieces with nontraditional subjects scatological to topological. The permanent collection contains relatively tamer pieces, including a classical Egyptian exhibit. Politically-minded feminist work is displayed at the Elizabeth A. Sackler Center for Feminist Art. The museum features work from all over the world, from times ancient to modern, as well as twenty-eight American period rooms.
200 Eastern Pkwy (at Washington Ave). 718-638-5000. Sun 11am-6pm, Closed Mon and Tues, Wed-Fri 10am-5pm, Sat 11am-6pm—First Sat of each month 11am-11pm. ❷❸❹ to Eastern Parkway-Brooklyn Museum. Suggested donation $8, Students $4.

Central Library

The curved architecture of this bibliotheca mirrors an opening book, its spine resting on Grand Army Plaza and its covers opening on to Eastern Pkwy and Flatbush Ave. This major reference center of the Brooklyn Public Library system, it houses about 1.5 million books, magazines, and multimedia materials and offers free wireless within the building.
Grand Army Plaza 718-230-2100. Mon 9am-6pm, Tue-Thurs 9:00am-9:00pm, Fri-Sat 9am-6pm, closed Sun. ❷❸ to Grand Army Plaza, ❶ to 7th Ave.

Grand Army Plaza Greenmarket

This popular year-round farmers' market features a huge selection of vendors. Fresh fish, milk, meat, and cheese are perfect ingredients for a delicious meal, and a plethora of flowers provides endless opportunities for a beautiful centerpiece. Fresh veggies make salads extra crisp, while pre-made pizzas provide easy dinners that can be quickly popped into the oven.
Grand Army Plaza. Sat 8am-4pm. ❷❸ to Grand Army Plaza.

Prospect Park

Among the bustle of the city, this peaceful, 585-acre oasis gives the urbanite a chance to take a stroll among long and winding tree-lined paths. Designed by Frederick Law Olmstead and Calvert Vaux shortly after they completed Central Park, it contains Brooklyn's only lake as well as the Long Meadow, at 90 acres thought to be the largest meadow in any park in the U.S. The park hosts daytime and twilight tours, as well as numerous free concerts and cultural events in the park bandshell. On a Sunday morning, all drummers are welcome to join the Drummer's Grove drumming circle, in existence for more than 30 years. The park offers two locations with free wi-fi, the Audubon Center at the Boathouse and the Picnic House, perfect locations to get a little work done in the midst of a beautiful natural landscape.
Mon-Sun 5am-1am. ❶ to 7th Ave. ❷❸ to Grand Army Plaza, ❶❺❸ to Prospect Park.

Prospect Park Zoo

Originally an 1800's menagerie, this zoo later expanded to include more animals after opening to the public in 1935. These days, the 12-acre zoo is home to kangaroos, seals, reptiles, farm animals and more. Combine

it with a walk in Prospect Park, or make a day trip out of it.
450 Flatbush Avenue, 718-399-7339. November-March 21: daily 10am-4:30pm; March 22-November: Mon-Fri 10am-5pm, Weekends and Holidays 10am-5:30pm. Adults $6. Q S B to Prospect Park.

CULTURE & ARTS

Brooklyn Conservatory of Music
Music lovers can develop their talents or view concerts and special events here, one of the oldest and largest music institutions in the country. Classes are hosted in a restored five-story Victorian Mansion and are offered for students of all ages and skill levels. Whether looking for classical training or coaching in contemporary rock, all musicians are welcome.
58 7th Ave (near Lincoln Pl). 718-622-3300. B Q to 7th Ave, ❸ to Grand Army Plaza.

Brooklyn Lyceum
Music, movies, theatre and…baseball? This cultural center not only has nightly comedy shows, theatre festivals, and dance performances in their theatre spaces, they also offer batting cages and basketball courts. Local singer-songwriters as well as bigger names share the stage, friends settle in to watch classics and campy favorites, and athletes shoot hoops or take their place in the batting cage on the weekend.
227 4th Ave (near President St). 718-398-7301. M R to Union.

The Dance Studio of Park Slope
Whether you've been dancing since childhood or never stepped foot inside a studio, everybody is welcome in these dance classes that are offered in a fun, non-professional setting. Beyond ballet and tap classes, the studio also offers exercise classes to tone up, special workshops, and dance series. Evening and weekend class times make it easy for busy adults to hone their dancing skills on the side.
630 Sackett St (between 3rd & 4th Ave). 718-789-4419. M R to Union. Semester tuition $378 and up.

DINING

UPSCALE

Rose Water *New American*
The warm cabin-in-the-woods atmosphere provides the setting for a refined yet relaxed dinner which draws on the strength of seasonal ingredients. A starter of striped marlin crudo is thoughtful, served sashimi style with cilantro and a touch of sesame oil. Seasonal risottos, like spring pea and prosciutto, are carefully prepared and take full advantage of the freshest produce. When it comes to meat, the duck breast is tops, its chewy meat excreting bursts of juicy flavor. Careful, precise waiters exhibit their knowledge of the menu and function as de facto sommeliers, competently choosing wines to complement the meal. Light desserts, such as apricot steam cake and yuzu custard, have excellent balance and provide relief from heavier, guilt-laden treats..
787 Union St (between 5th & 6th Ave). 718-783-3800. Mon-Sun 5:30pm-close, Brunch Sat-Sun 10am-3pm. M R to Union, Q to 7th, ❷❸ to Grand Army. Average entrée $25.

EDITOR'S PICK

Stone Park Café *American*

This restaurant succeeds in combining great food with the casual and laidback vibe of a café. Desipite the cool attitude, the dining room has been gussied up enough to impress a date or business partner, as has the cuisine. Lacking an obivous theme to unite the menu, Stone Park settles on just preparing everything really well. The chilled corn bisque with lump crab and avocado, a New England classic with a Bay Area touch, will have you licking the bowl. Dishes are carefully composed and their layered flavors reveal thoughtful preparation. Seared scallops with homemade tagliatelle, pan-roasted tilefish, and strip steak are finished with delicate sauces with great mouth-feel and a sophisticated finish. End the meal nostalgically with a root beer float with homemade ice cream; some dishes don't need rethinking.

324 5th Ave (at 3rd St). 718-369-0082. Mon-Thu 6pm-10pm, Fri 6pm-11pm, Sat 5:30pm-11pm, Sun 5:30pm-9pm. Brunch Sat-Sun 10:30am-3pm. Ⓜ Ⓡ to Union, Ⓕ to 4th. Average entrée $26.

MID-RANGE

Café Steinhof *Austrian*

"Going to the Steinhof" for the Viennese means "going crazy;" appropriately, eccentricity is celebrated here and translated into creative culinary creations. Smoked salmon gives a peculiar twist to the celery and potato soup, but actually works well. The average sandwich gets bombarded by wiener schnitzel, and cod salad or sardine salad sandwiches provide a nice alternative to ubiquitous tuna. Some sausage or cheese spaetzle brings the meal to a pleasant end. The late night menu is served until 1am to satisfy those mid-barhopping munchies.

422 7th Ave (at 14th St) 718-369-7776. Mon-Thurs, Sun 5pm-11pm, Fri-Sat 5pm-1am. Ⓕ to 7th Ave. Average entrée $11.

Kiku *Japanese*

Generous sushi portions make this tiny Japanese fusion restaurant a great choice for the sushi-lover on a budget. Duck spring rolls offer a satisfying crunch complemented by sweet, syrupy, homemade hoisin sauce and shoestring sweet potato fries. Onion adds a surprising kick to the Volcano Roll, one of

many special rolls which balances creative ingredients with fresh fish to produce inventively delicious dishes. Aside from sushi, the menu also features many a la carte options, vegetarian rolls, and desserts, making it a place that pleases all.
177 5th Ave (between Berkeley & Lincoln Pl). 718-638-3366. Mon-Thurs 11am-11pm, Fri 11am-11pm, Sat-Sun 12pm-11pm. D M N R W *to Union. Average entrée $13.*

CHEAP

Beet Park Slope *Thai*
Affordable Thai food standards are prepared with a special flair at this hip eatery bedecked with earth-tone tiles and criss-crossed metal bars against red walls. The spectacular chicken satay skewers are served stuck into a half cucumber and lit on fire tableside. Spicy lemongrass soup, a mere $3, can be filling enough for a hot lunch on a winter day. French-influenced Cognac ginger beef exemplifies this restaurant's "Try Me" portion of the menu that features dishes incorporating both Thai and French flavors. Meanwhile, classic favorites like Pad Thai are solid for lower-than-Manhattan prices.
344 7th Ave (at 10th St). 718-832-2338. Mon-Thurs 12pm-11pm, Fri-Sat 12pm-12am, Sun 12:30pm-10:30pm. F *to 7th Ave. Average entrée $10.*

The Chip Shop *British*
This is a place to forget about dieting and shovel down some delicious, deep-fried eats. Comfort-food seekers can choose from crispy fish and chips options like cod or haddock or stranger options like deep fried pizza. The interesting English beer choices pair well with the greasy food. Complete the descent into a food coma with one of the ever-popular fried Twinkies. If you're crazy (or Scottish), they batter and fry pizza as well.
383 5th Ave (at 6th St) 718-832-7701. Mon-Thu 12pm-10 pm, Fri 12pm-10:30pm, Sat 11am-11pm Sun 11am-10pm. F M R *to 9th. Average entrée $10.*

Maria's Mexican Bistro *Mexican*
If the guacamole made table-side isn't enough of a draw, maybe the cheap all-you-can-drink brunch will convince you. Service here isn't great; you may rarely see your waiter as the place is often packed with plenty of needy customers, but the affordable, spicy options are worth it. The wooden chairs and tables and the Mexican art

adorning red walls imbue this spot with a homey ambiance. Try to grab a seat outside on the quiet residential street.

669 Union St (between 4th Ave & 5th Ave) 718-638-2344. Mon-Fri 11:30am-12am, Sat-Sun 11am-12am. Average entrée $7.

Naidre's Coffeeshop *Coffee*

Naidre's freshly-made pastries go perfectly with a refreshing cup of coffee. Each day a different comfort food, like creamy mac-and-cheese or brisket, is offered. Herb tuna sandwiches make a nice light summer sandwich alongside a glass of iced coffee. Free wi-fi draws in the college students and others trying to get a little work done.

384 7th Ave (between 11th & 12th St) 718-965-7585. Mon-Sun 7am-9pm. F to 7th Ave. Prices $6-9.

Willie's Dawgs *Hot Dogs*

Hot dogs at Willie's are elevated to near gourmet status. Blue cheese covers the appropriately named Blue; the strange Squigi douses the dog in peanut butter and honey (bacon, banana or marshmallow fluff can also be added). Beyond the normal beef, turkey, and tofu dogs, Willie's also offers chicken and even grilled, marinated carrot dogs. Make sure to save room for fries and a decadent, perfectly cheap cookie dough pie for only $2.

351 5th Ave (between 4th St and 5th St). 718-832-2941. Mon-Thu 11:30am-9pm, Fri-Sat 11:30am-12am, Sun 11:30am-6pm. F G D M N R W to 9th. Average entrée: $4.

NIGHTLIFE

EDITOR'S PICK

Beer Table *Beer Hall*

This closet-size brew house boasts one of the most impressive beer selections around. Locals and beer lovers from around the city sit shoulder to shoulder at three long tables sipping on any of hundreds of import beers. Owner and operator Justin Phillips is happy to share some of his encyclopedic knowledge of import beers: you'll want to tap him for advice, since the vast majority of beers available here are obscure European microbrews. The mood is less boisterous than most beer halls, think quiet coffee shop, but a hip soundtrack keeps the mood from darkening. Sausages, made on premises with imported campfire-smoked malts, are delicious: sultry, and dark, yet bright and never greasy. Served with olives, bread, and pickled onions, they are the perfect complement to the palate-expanding beers offered here. Grab a bowl of the surprisingly delightful malt gelato before you leave.

427 B 7th Ave (between 14th St & 15th St). 718-965-1196. Daily 5pm-1am. F to 7th Ave. Beers $7-$95. Average beer $8.

Buttermilk Bar *Bar*

This friendly place makes the perfect neighborhood bar. Bartenders chat with patrons and locals sit around together enjoying the cheap weekday drink specials and the free pizza on Wednesday nights. A selection of board games are kept behind the bar for that competitive round of drunken Monopoly. The last Thursday of the month brings out cowboy boot-clad country lovers for the CasHank Hootenanny Jamboree, an acoustic country open mic in memory of Hank Williams and Johnny Cash.

577 5th Ave (at 16th St). 718-788-6297. Daily 6pm-4am. M R to Prospect Ave. Average drink $5

Cattyshack *LGBT*

Queer women dance until the late hours at this popular bi-level lesbian club owned by the former owner of Meow Mix. Formerly an auto repair shop, Faux-hawked, cornrowed, baseball-cap-sporting lesbians have since taken over what used to be an auto repair shop and made it into a hip, modern club. Whether it's shooting pool downstairs, hip-shaking to hip hop in the back, strutting to Boy George upstairs, or cuddling up to that special girl under the stars on the rooftop deck, the place offers a little something for everyone.

249 4th Ave (at Union St) 718-230-5740. Mon-Fri, 2pm-4am, Sat-Sun, 12pm-4am. M R to Union.

The Gate *Bar*

A laid back bar near the park, The Gate at-

PARK SLOPE 325

tracts a casual crowd looking to relax, not revel. The bar features an excellent variety of draught beer, with a focus on strong, dark beers, such as Dogfish Head and Captain Lawrence Double IPA. An outdoor patio, complete with cushioned seats, picnic tables, and a large awning to beat back the sun, is excellent on warm summer evenings. Inside, rough hewn wood stools and booths make this a perfect place to take a load off and have a conversation over a potent microbrew. Dogs are welcome both in the bar and on the patio.

321 5th Ave (at 3rd St) 718-768-4329. Mon-Thurs 3pm-4am, Fri-Sun 1pm-4am. M R F to 9th. Average drink $6

Ginger's *LGBT, Bar*
Ginger's is the closest thing to the lesbian version of Cheers you'll ever get. The welcoming bartenders are happy to get to know you as are the neighborhood regulars who favor the bar seats. While other lesbian bars or parties can feel clique-y, this bar maintains an easy-going atmosphere. The bar offers tables in the front where you can sip drinks, pool tables in the back, and an outdoor deck where groups of friends hang out during the summer months— all to the sound of top 40's hits. But whatever you do, stay away from the watery, disgusting Ginger Brew.

363 5th Ave (at 5th St) 718-788-0924. F M R to 9th St-4th Ave. Average drink $6. Cash Only.

Southpaw *Live Music*
Featuring local talent and international favorites, this laid-back concert space hosts everyone from guitar-strumming folk singers to indie rock icons. The occasional dance party packs the place with skinny kids in tight jeans or more niche crowds during Pride month. Prices tend to be cheaper than Manhattan equivalents and offer a fun place for the 18-20 crowd to hang out, as most shows are 18+.

125 5th Ave (near Sterling Pl). 718-230-0236. 2 3 to Bergen St, B Q to 7th Ave, M R to Union. Average drink $6.

Union Hall *Bar, Live Music*
This bar, restaurant, and live music venue is covered in books, making it a social bookworm's dream come true. The drink and food menus are standard—sliders and a solid beer selection mostly, creating a low-key, fun driven night. The cozy library, two indoor bocce courts, and nightly live music draw in consistent crowds. Lately, Union Hall has been overrun with yuppies, but hold your ground—the completely unique nights offered here are worth braving the mob.

702 Union St (at 5th Ave). 718-638-4400. Mon-Fri 4pm-4am, Sat-Sun 12pm-4am. M R to Union St, Q 2 3 4 5 to Atlantic Ave, F to 4th Ave. Average drink $6.

SHOPPING

3R Living
Want to help out the environment and look stylish doing it? This store offers everything the eco-conscious shopper could need, from organic beauty products to solar-powered chargers. Reduce, reuse, and recycle by purchasing earrings made from the insides of wrist watches, bike chain bracelets, or necklaces made from old bottles. Prices can be steep, but the well-made offerings are well

worth it. The store also hosts a Recycling Center, so bring along your old batteries, cell phones, ink cartridges, CDs and cases, hand-held electronics, and crayons to offer up to reuse.

276L 5th Ave (between Garfield Pl and 1st St) 718-832-0951. Sun-Wed 11am- 7pm, Thurs-Sat 11am to 8pm. **M R** *to Union St.*

Brooklyn Superhero Supply Co.

Transform yourself into a crime-fighting superhero saving the city from your evil nemesis. The store offers a selection of capes to billow behind you as you soar through the air and grappling hooks to more effectively rappel down the sides of buildings. But the real reason this store exists is to directly support their nonprofit organization, 826NYC, helping kids aged 6-18 learn to write. 826NYC offers drop-in tutoring services, free workshops, and projects hosted in New York City schools. They're always looking for new volunteers with writing, editing or computer skills or who can act as a tutor—a smart way to really act as a superhero to these children.

372 5th Ave (near 5th Ave). 718-499-9884. Mon-Sun 11am-5:30pm. **F M R** *to 9th St.*

Cog and Pearl

This store carries every hand-crafted belt buckle, vintage camera, and painted dinosaur wallet you could ever want or need. Every item in the store exhibits some distinctive quality elevating it above run-of-the-mill gift shop bric-a-brac. Particularly cool are the Ex Libris Anonymous journals, made from recycled books. Independent designers from all over the world are featured, and anyone looking to break into the handicraft market can talk to the owners about putting their own creations on sale.

190 5th Ave (at Sackett St). 718-623-8200. Wed-Sat 12-8pm, Sun 12-6pm. **M R** *to Union,* **2 3** *to Bergen St.*

Loom

This store sells perfect idiosyncratic gifts for your hard-to-buy-for friend or lover. Pick up a silk-screened tote bag to carry that new leather wallet or hand-made beauty product you just had to have. This store stocks everything you could have never guessed you would want—quirky items destined to become your signature accessories.

115 7th Ave (near President St). 718-789-0061. Mon-Fri 11am-7pm, Sat 11am-6pm, Sun 12pm-6pm. **2 3** *to Grand Army Plaza,* **Q R** *to 7th Ave.*

Park Slope Flea Market (PS 321)

While it may not be as big as some of the other flea markets in the city, this one offers some of the most affordable quirky finds. Grab some cheap-yet-chic antique furniture to complete your living room set, or nab some hard-to-find records. Try on a letterman jacket and an old pair of pumps, or grab a kitschy lunchbox featuring some nostalgic '80s icon. Items are draped all over playground equipment, imbuing the scene with playful eccentricity.

7th Ave (at 1st St). 718-421-6763. Sat-Sun 8am-6pm. **2 3** *to Grand Army Plaza.*

DAY TO DAY

Community Board 6. *250 Baltic Street. 718-643-3027.*

Local Media: *parkslopeshops.com, onparkslope.com, dailyslope.com, psreader.com*

Groceries: Park Slope Food Co-Op. *782 Union St. 718-622-0560.* Back to the Lands Natural Food. *142 7th Ave. 718-768-5654.*

Gyms: Prospect Park YMCA. *357 9th Street. 718-768-7100.* New York Sports Club. *324 9th St. 718-768-0880.*

Rent: Two-bedroom: $3,900.

Hospital: New York Methodist Hospital. *506 6th St. 718-780-5500.*

Hotels and Hostel: Brooklyn Backpackers. *65 4th Ave. 212-966-9034.* Hotel le Bleu. *370 4th Ave. 718-625-1500.*

Dog Run: JJ Byrne Park. *Between 4th & 5th Ave (near 4th St).*

Movie Theater: Pavilion Park Slope. *188 Park Slope West. 718-369-0838.*

WELCOME TO 5POINTZ
PAINTING WITH A PERMIT ONLY!
NO PHOTOSHOOTS OR VIDEOS WITHOUT PERMISSION
EMAIL: MERESONE@AOL.COM FOR INFO
← OFFICE LOCATED UNDER STAIRS

LONG ISLAND CITY & ASTORIA

Long known for having one of the largest concentrations of Greeks outside of Greece, Astoria remains a stronghold for all things Peloponnesian—tavernas and Orthodox churches dot the landscape, while specialty supermarkets do big business stocking octopus and baklava. That said, immigration from Greece has dropped off dramatically since the last major wave in the 1960s. The 70s brought an influx of Arab immigrants from Tunisia, Yemen, Morocco, and especially Egypt, so much so that Steinway St, between 28th Ave and Astoria Blvd, is known as Little Cairo, where you can't walk a block without seeing a hookah parlor. Since the early 90s, both the Arab and Greek populations have been outstripped by a huge growth in the Latino population, including a sizable influx of Brazilians who have made the area around 36th Ave their home.

Despite the constant flux underlying this great ethnic mishmash, Astoria is an extremely harmonious neighborhood. Long, peaceful blocks of low brick buildings and shady trees suggest a transcendent stasis, as though things will never really change, no matter who happens to live there.

If Astoria is in the midst of a demographic transition, then Long Island City is undergoing a full-blown cultural renaissance. Once an industrial nether region covered with warehouses, it is now easily the most important neighborhood for the arts in the outer boroughs, a title it undoubtedly owes to the influence of the P.S.1 Center for Contemporary Art. However, the burgeoning art scene may soon be no more. The neighborhood is becoming increasingly popular with commuters; a half dozen luxury condos have sprung up in Hunters Point alone and it may not be long before creative types are chased away, again, by yuppies.

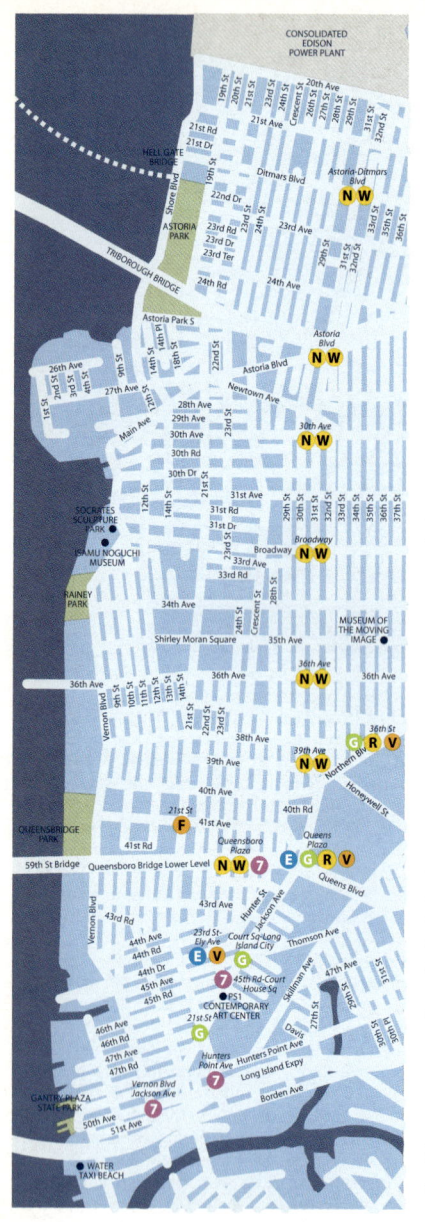

ATTRACTIONS

Astoria Park
Spanning the East River from Hell Gate to the Triborough, Astoria Park is one of the largest open spaces in Queens and boasts the best river views. The park is a perfect destination to escape the bustle of the city– or to swim: Astoria Pool, planned by Robert Moses, is the largest in the city and home to Olympic-sized diving and lap-swimming facilities, as well as a wading pool and an Art Deco bathing pavilion. Other recreational facilities include six tennis courts, bocce ball courts, two playgrounds, and a track. The northern end of the park is punctuated by massive Hell Gate Bridge supports, creating a ruinous feel to the place.
Astoria Park South, 21st St, Hoyt Ave North, Ditmars Blvd. 311 (Parks & Recreation info). Pool hours 11am-7pm, late June-Labor Day. N W to Astoria Blvd or Astoria-Ditmars, Q19A to Hoyt Ave.

Gantry Plaza State Park
Lolling in the shadows of several brand new Hunter's Point luxury apartment buildings, this 4 acre former dock facility has been revamped and refurbished, landscaped and prettified. People fish (and crab!) off the four piers, chase their children around a shiny new playground, walk their dogs on a small gravel pathway, cool off in the somewhat bizarre mist fountain, and otherwise lounge around enjoying the environs' unique aesthetic. Built around two restored gantries (a sort of stationary crane used to unload barges and rail cars), the park turns its commercial past into public art. Summer Tuesdays the plaza hosts Live at the Gantries, a music series featuring a wide array of regional folk musics. And the view is incredible.
Center Blvd between 48th & 50th Aves. 7 to Vernon Blvd-Jackson Ave.

CULTURE & ARTS

5 Pointz
This "graffiti mecca" is a run-down industrial warehouse, the inside of which has

been converted into artist space—a pretty common phenomenon in Long Island City. The outside has transformed into a giant canvas almost entirely covered with "aerosol art," as the site's proprietor Meres calls it. Larger than life cartoon figures and elaborate, bright colored tags blend in and pop out. Despite their stylized dimensions, some of the images appear unbelievably lifelike. Meres runs a tight ship: new work is allowed only with a permit, and placement depends on a review process. None of the work is permanent; old work is constantly sprayed over. A vibrant community has grown up around the building, transforming it into a collective creative endeavor of serious artistry and high craftsmanship.

Jackson Ave & 23rd St, across from P.S.1. 🅔🅥 *to 23rd St-Ely Ave,* 🟣 *to 45th Rd-Courthouse Square,* 🅖 *to 21st St-Van Alst.*

Isamu Noguchi Museum

This first American museum dedicated exclusively to the work of its namesake offers a comprehensive overview of Isamu Noguchi's oeuvre, featuring a permanent collection of works in stone, wood, metal, and clay: a placid outdoor garden and rotating exhibitions. Spare walls of white brick and cinderblock, coupled with floors of simple granite and speckled cement, lend austerity and elegance to the eerily organic shapes dotting the halls like the discarded playthings of giants. The museum and the neighboring Socrates Sculpture Park have turned this remote area of Queens, half a mile from the nearest subway, into a destination for the plastic arts.

9-01 33rd Rd (at Vernon Blvd) 718-204-7088. Wed-Fri 10am-5pm, Sat-Sun 11am-6pm, Mon-Tue closed. $10 admission, $5 for students. 🅝🅦 *to Broadway.*

EDITOR'S PICK

P.S.1

For over thirty years, P.S.1 has been a vital part of the contemporary art scene in New York. Because they have no permanent collection, the museum can dedicate most of its resources to up-and-coming artists through more than 30 exhibitions a year. Quite a few careers have been made through exhibitions at P.S.1—the young Basquiat garnered the attention of Andy Warhol while participating in a New Wave exhibition here in the '80s. The building itself is tall and stately, an old fashioned red brick schoolhouse. The behemoth granite walls in front enclose a gravel courtyard, the setting for the Young Architects Program, an annual competition of emerging architects who design and submit plans for an installation. That installation serves as the backdrop for Warm Up, a beloved summer music series running every Saturday from July to early September and featuring live bands, DJs, dancing, and beer.

22-25 Jackson Ave (near 46th Ave). 718-784-2084. Thurs-Mon 12pm-6pm. 🅔🅥 *to 23rd St-Ely Ave;* 🟣 *to 45th Rd-Courthouse Square,* 🅖 *to 21st St-Van Alst. $5 admission, $2 for students, free for MoMa members/ticket holders.*

SculptureCenter

Having P.S.1 so near can rather dwarf whatever presence this converted trolley repair shop might command on its own. It doesn't help that where P.S.1 is friendly and snappy,

SculptureCenter is austere, academic, a little drab, and even a bit antisocial—which is a shame, because despite these shortcomings the place has ample character. The upstairs is your standard high-ceilinged, granite-floored former garage, home to a rotating series of deconstructive pomo artjive exhibitions. The downstairs, though, is really something: the guts and bowels of the building have been transformed into a space with the potential to be seriously unsettling. Bring a flashlight if you spook easy.
44-19 Purves St (near Jackson Ave) 718-361-1750. Thurs-Mon 11am-6pm. **E V** *to 23rd St-Ely Ave;* **7** *to 45th Rd-Courthouse Square;* **G** *to Long Island City-Court Square. Suggested $5 admission.*

Socrates Sculpture Park
This grassy junkyard utopia was built out of an illegal industrial dump in the 1980s, at the initiative of local artists and community groups led by famed sculptor Mark de Suvero. As much a park as an art venue, the former brownfield attracts serious sculpture buffs as well as sunbathers, fishermen, and kids hanging out after school. Yet it remains a tranquil space of reclamation and bricolage, and of respite from the urban clutter beyond its gates. Two major exhibitions each year keep the park, which has no permanent collection, on the cutting edge of urban art. Public programs are offered free of charge year round, including workshops, fitness classes, and a summer film series.
32-01 Vernon Blvd (at Broadway) 718-956-1819. Open daily 10am-sunset. **N W** *to Broadway.*

DINING

MID-RANGE
La Vuelta *Latin Nouveau*
The dearth of quality eats in Long Island City is mitigated somewhat by this Latin-inspired bistro. Large, flavorful, and affordable sandwiches are popular with the lunch crowd—the massive BBQ pulled pork is particularly excellent, though the accompanying Cajun fries are a little over-seasoned. The beef "torta" is not very torta-like; it tastes more like any ordinary (but tasty) steak sandwich, and the side of tortilla chips with pico de gallo is a tad bland. Other notable items include the grilled tuna salad and the selection of tiny empanadas, or "empanaditas." A glass of sangria, or the popular tamarind martini, can make a dreary office afternoon hum along with remarkable ease. The enclosed patio in back is very cozy, allowing smokers to commiserate in peace.
10-43 44th Dr (near 11th St) 718-361-1858. Mon 11am-10pm, Tues-Fri 11am-11pm, Sat-Sun 5pm-10pm. **E V** *to 23rd St-Ely Ave,* **7** *to 45th Road-Court House Square. Average entrée $17.*

EDITOR'S PICK
Mombar *Egyptian*
Named for an Egyptian sausage, this wonderful Little Cairo establishment is a wellspring of delicate, delicious flavors. Fresh, superior ingredients prepared by a skillful chef make every dish a winner. For starters there is the Sahara mix, a beautifully plated mix of hummus, baba ghanoush, goat cheese, and fava bean spread, each dolloped atop crackling homemade bread and complemented with a suitable garnish. Surprisingly dainty for a sausage, the eponymous mombar is stuffed with beef, lamb, rice, herbs and spices, then sautéed in a tomato sauce with garlic and chickpeas. For seafood types, the roasted eel is tender and subtle, and the shrimp Alexandria—in a pepper, onion, and garlic sauce—is splendid. Perhaps most impressive is the rich and flavorful lamb tajeen, braised and served with peas and carrots over a currant-studded couscous. The place is decorated like a Pharaoh's cafeteria—long rugs, comfy cushions, mosaic tiles, and a unique stonecutting in every table.
25-22 Steinway St (near 25th Ave) 718-726-2356. Tues-Sun 5pm-11pm, closed Mon. **N W** *to Astoria Blvd. Average entrée $18.*

Omonia Café *Café, Lounge*
This tarted-up corner diner subverts the reputation that inauthentic "Greek" cafés lining Broadway often receive, at least where java and pastries are concerned. The Greek coffee comes in four varieties, all of them the consistency of mud—watch out for

clumps at the bottom. A local favorite, the glykos vrastos, or "sweet and boiled," lives up to its name. The pastries are a bit bland, though some are successful. Fluffy yet heavy, the Omonia Special is a chocolate sponge cake with a rich, dark fudge. The more authentically Mediterranean ekmek kataifi consists of a honey-sweet wheat pastry topped with custard and topped again with Chantilly cream and almond slices, resulting in a multi-textured delight.
32-20 Broadway (near 33rd St) 718-274-6650. Mon-Fri 6:30am-3am, Sat-Sun 6:30am-6am. N W to Broadway. Average entrée $12.

Zenon Taverna *Greek*
Scenic Mediterranean locales painted on white stucco walls and a hushed, easy-going ambience lend this local treasure the aura of a rustic Bronze Age inn, but with a much better menu. They feature all the hits of Greek and Cypriot cuisine: tender souvlaki, cool and creamy tzatziki, amazing keftedes (Cypriot fried pork meatballs) and loukaniko spitisio (Cypriot pork sausage), and crisp, powerful ouzo. What really elevates this place beyond the standards are their prix-fixe meze (Greek for "meal") of cold and warm appetizers; trust them when they say to eat siga-siga ("slowly-slowly"). For under $20 a person, the Kypriaki Mezedes includes, in the cold course, Cyprus salad, tzatziki, melitzanosalada (a smoky eggplant dip), the mashed potato garlic dip known as scordalia, tahini, red caviar dip, a wonderful beet salad, and a seafood salad of calamari, crab meat, octopus, and shrimp. Save room for the even better hot course, containing luntza (smoked pork loin), grilled Halloumi (sheep's milk cheese), keftedes, loukaniko, spitisio, souvlaki, char-grilled quail and sheftalia (grilled pork meatballs). The usually obligatory fried calamari unfortunately disappoints.
34-10 31st Ave (near 34th St) 718-956-0133. Mon-Thu 11am-11pm, Fri-Sun 11am-12am. N W to Broadway. Average entrée $12. Cash only.

CHEAP
5 Star Banquet & Restaurant *Indian*
Tucked away in the industrial nether-regions of Long Island City is this diamond-in-the-rough, slightly off-kilter restaurant/banquet hall duo. Unless you're planning the Punjabi social event of the year, you'll want to hit up the diner, in which the husk of an old-school American greasy spoon—bland mosaic tiling, worn leather uphol-

stery, creaky stools all present and accounted for—encases top-notch Indian cuisine. There's no menu to speak of. Rather, the big draw is an all-you-can-eat lunch buffet chock full of piping hot dishes (easy to identify if you're familiar with Indian food), all of them hearty and delicious. The dal makhani is particularly wonderful; the only weak spot is the assortment of pakoras and other fried fritters, which do not keep well and can become soggy and tepid. A nice touch, fresh, fluffy naan is served, compliments of the house, in an old fashioned red fry basket.

13-15 43rd Ave (near 21st St). 718-784-7444. Open daily, 11:30am-4am. Buffet Mon-Sat 12pm-4pm. E V to 23rd St-Ely Ave, 7 N W to Queensboro Plaza. Buffet $9.

Il Bambino *Soup & Sandwich*

This cozy panini parlor has a serious fixation with everything porcine. A huge pig silhouette wall-painting, with arrows indicating different cuts' points of origin stands out upon entering. Wooden pig cutouts adorn the dining area walls, interspersed with old-fashioned cooking equipment and mirrors. An educational glossary of the major pork varieties fills up the back of the menu. The front of the menu features a twenty-strong list of mouth-watering panini combinations, like the prosciutto with tomato fresca and chive oil, or the soppressata with hot peppers, asiago, and basil pesto. If the glossaries weren't evidence enough, one bite will convince you of the pride this restaurant takes in its ingredients. For a truly luxurious meal, pair your panini with a silky smooth Nutella hot chocolate.

34-08 31st Ave (near 34th St) 718-626-0081. Mon-Sat 8am-10:30pm, Sun 8am-9pm. N W to Broadway. Paninis $9.

La Espiguita *Mexican*

This neighborhood hole-in-the-wall serves authentic Mexican dishes with a modern flair. The standard panoply of tacos, burritos, quesadillas and so on are all available (and tasty, especially when stuffed with the pork), but the real treat is the Super Tortas, or as the menu puts it, the "Mexican Big Sandwich." The size of a small chicken, these monstrosities come loaded with avocado, mayo, beans, lettuce, tomato, onions, jalapeños, and a puissant combo of meats and cheese. Choices like the Albañil, with its tender chunks of steak, chorizo, and cheese, or the roast pork, egg, ham and cheese-topped Huerfana are a meat-lover's best friend. The mega-sandwiches taste best when complemented with a Mexican fruit soda or an old-fashioned glass-bottled Coke. Minimal ventilation and a loud television dedicated to the best of Spanish-language programming make delivery an attractive option.

32-44 31st St (near Broadway) 718-777-5648. Mon-Sun 9am-11pm. 🅝🅦 *to Broadway. Entrées $5-7.*

La Guli Pastry Shop *Bakery, Café*
Behind La Guli's unassuming exterior lies a charming old-time Italian bakery. There is nothing geriatric about this bakery's output though: a glass display counter brimming with an overwhelming variety of sugary sweets runs the length of the store, all the way down to a few gaunt tables at the end. The gelati is flavorful yet often soupy, but the Italian ices are natural and refreshing, lacking the chemical tang of their street-urchin cousins. However, the real stars are the pastries. Easily among the best in the city, the legendary cannolis alone are worth a trip.

29-15 Ditmars Blvd (near 29th St). 718-728-5612. Mon-Sat 7am-9pm, Sun 7am-8pm. 🅝🅦 *to Astoria-Ditmars. Average dessert $1-2.*

NIGHTLIFE

Canela *Club*
Outside of this Latino dominated club stands a long line of club hoppers and groups of young men smoking cigarettes and sizing each other up. The inside lounge area is complete with trendy, block-shaped leather seats, low oval tables, cream-colored walls, and wooden floors that reflect the posh lounges of Manhattan. Reggaeton, salsa, bachata, and merengue blast through the speakers and guests move quickly and seamlessly on the dance floor. The bartenders are quick and to the point, but the bouncers are more relaxed. Though cover charges and drinks are a bit pricy, Canela promises a good time without the hassle of Manhattan.

45-01 Northern Blvd (near 34th Ave) 718-786-5686. Tues-Sat 5pm-4am. 🅡🅥 *to 46th. Cover $10-15. Average drink $7.*

The Creek *Bar, Restaurant*
The Creek may look like a simple bar and restaurant to a passerby, but locals know better. Next to the high rise dining area is a theater where young bar-goers enjoy free comedy and music shows that would cost a pretty penny in Manhattan. Under the dining area and theater is a trendy lounge with comfy couches, a pool table, a DJ, and a bar. The famous mojitos—delicious and served in very large glasses—can be enjoyed on the relaxed and picturesque outdoor patio. The staff is friendly and laid back and draws in a young crowd with the same attitude. Whether you're looking to eat, watch a show, or just hang out, you will certainly find something at this unpretentious hotspot.

10-93 Jackson Ave (between 112th & 113th St). 718-706-8783. Mon-Thurs 3pm-2am, Fri 3pm-4am. Sat 5pm-4am, Sun 5pm-2am. 🅖 *to Vernon Blvd-Jackson Ave,* 🅔🅥 *to 23rd St-Ely Ave. Beer $4.*

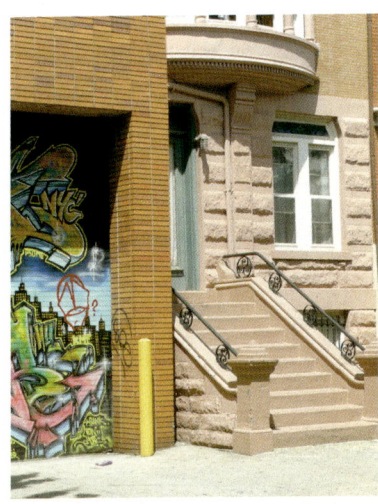

The Rapture *Lounge, Bar*
Rapture Lounge is a fun spot that boasts an unbeatably friendly staff, easy-going, loyal regulars, and one of the most generous happy hours in the city. There isn't an uncomfortable corner in this warm and welcoming lounge, sexily decked out with plush leather couches, mood lamps, red lanterns, vintage posters, and work from local artists. With a dazzling menu of specialty cocktails—such as margaritas with pineapple-infused tequila and a key lime pie martini as rich as the real thing, not to mention an astounding nine variations on the Long Island Ice Tea. The kitchen stays open every night until closing, and serves a wide variety of superior bar food, including homemade guac, crisp and flavorful coconut fried shrimp, and a house special hot dog with a secret recipe you won't want to miss.
34-27 28th Ave (at 34th St) 718-626-8044. Happy hour 5pm-8pm. Sun-Mon 5pm-4am. N W to 30th Ave. Average drink $8.

Harry's at Water Taxi Beach
Beach Bar
This ragged riverside outfit serves basic cocktails, a few draught beers, and a small assortment of grilled meat products (burgers, hot dogs, etc.), which are to be consumed while taking in the radiant view of midtown Manhattan. Its "beach" credentials are scanty: a modicum of sand, proximity to water, a few undersized volleyball courts, some park benches, a big tent, and a vaguely tiki-like atmosphere. The whole thing is a bit slapdash, but the drinks are tasty, the meat is meaty, and the view really is something. A friendly crowd begins to materialize before sundown to indulge in such wanton party-like activities as Guess Who, reading, and crossword puzzles. Things pick up later, especially on Saturdays, when the place fills up with the after-hours crowd from nearby P.S.1's Warm Up music series.
2-03 Borden Ave (at 2nd St) 212-742-1969 (New York Water Taxi agency). Hours vary; usually, closed Mon-Tues, Wed-Sun open 4pm-12am. Summer only. 7 to Vernon Blvd-Jackson Ave. Average drink $4.

SHOPPING

Cassinelli Food Products, Inc.
Behind a spare white showroom lies the heart of this family operation: a bustling factory that has been churning out some of the best pasta in the city for decades. Linguini, ravioli, tortellini, gnocchi, and other types of pasta are available in plain, egg, or spinach; fresh or frozen—at both wholesale and retail prices. In addition to the homemade pastas, the store sells a variety of imported gourmet treats, including delicious Balocco amaretto biscuits.
31-12 23rd Ave (near 31st St). 718-274-4881. Tues-Sat 7am-3:30pm, closed Sun-Mon. N W to Ditmars. Cash only.

Loveday 31
With the dignity of a couture shop, this vintage clothier provides a valuable service to Astoria's urbane poor and to the fashion-challenged. Flowery dresses share space with well-maintained leather jackets, a prismatic array of heels, and a tower of belts. High end accessories and locally-pro-

duced jewelry round out the selection, with not a spot of kitsch to be seen. Prices are moderate, with items like T-shirts at $24, dresses at $65, and jackets at $75.
33-06 31st Ave (near 33rd St) 718-728-4057. Tues-Sun 12pm-8:30pm; Mon by appointment. N W to Broadway.

Titan Foods

Titan Foods bills itself as "your source for fine Greek food." A slightly dilapidated appearance belies the wealth of gourmet treats inside: a bakery packed with phyllo-crusted, honey-sweet pastries (the soropiasta is amazing) and flaky spinach pies; a cheese bar with any variety of feta or olive you could ever want; a meat counter displaying buckets of octopus tentacles; and aisles full of honey, olive oil, preserved fruits, and beer, all from Greece. Prices are reasonable for the quality of the foods. Be prepared to weather the stink eye from employees and patrons alike if you don't look Greek enough.
25-56 31st St (near Astoria Blvd). 718-626-7771. Mon-Sat 8am-9pm, Sun 9am-8pm. N W to Astoria Blvd.

DAY TO DAY

Community Board 1. *36-01 35th Avenue (at 36th St). 718-786-3335.*

Local Media: *local718.wordpress.com*

Groceries: Titan Foods. *25-56 31st St (near Astoria Blvd). 718-626-7771.* Costco. *32-50 Vernon Blvd (near Broadway). 718-267-3680.*

Gyms: Astoria Sports Complex. *34-38 38th St (near Steinway St). 718-729-7163.* New York Sports Club. *38-11 30th Ave (near Steinway St). 718-932-1400.*

Average Rent: Two-bedroom: $1600

Hospital: Mount Sinai Hospital of Queens. *25-10 30th Ave (near 27th St). 718-932-1000.*

Hostels and Hotels: Fairfield Inn New York LaGuardia Airport/Astoria. *45-20 Astoria Blvd (near 45th St). 718-267-0008.*

Dog Run: Shore Blvd and Astoria Park South

Movie Theater: UA Kaufman Astoria Cinema 14. *35-30 38th St (near 36th Ave). 718-786-1722.*

Best Happy Hour: Rapture Lounge *(2-for-1s daily). 34-27 28th Ave (near 34th St). 718-626-8044. Daily, 5pm-4am.*

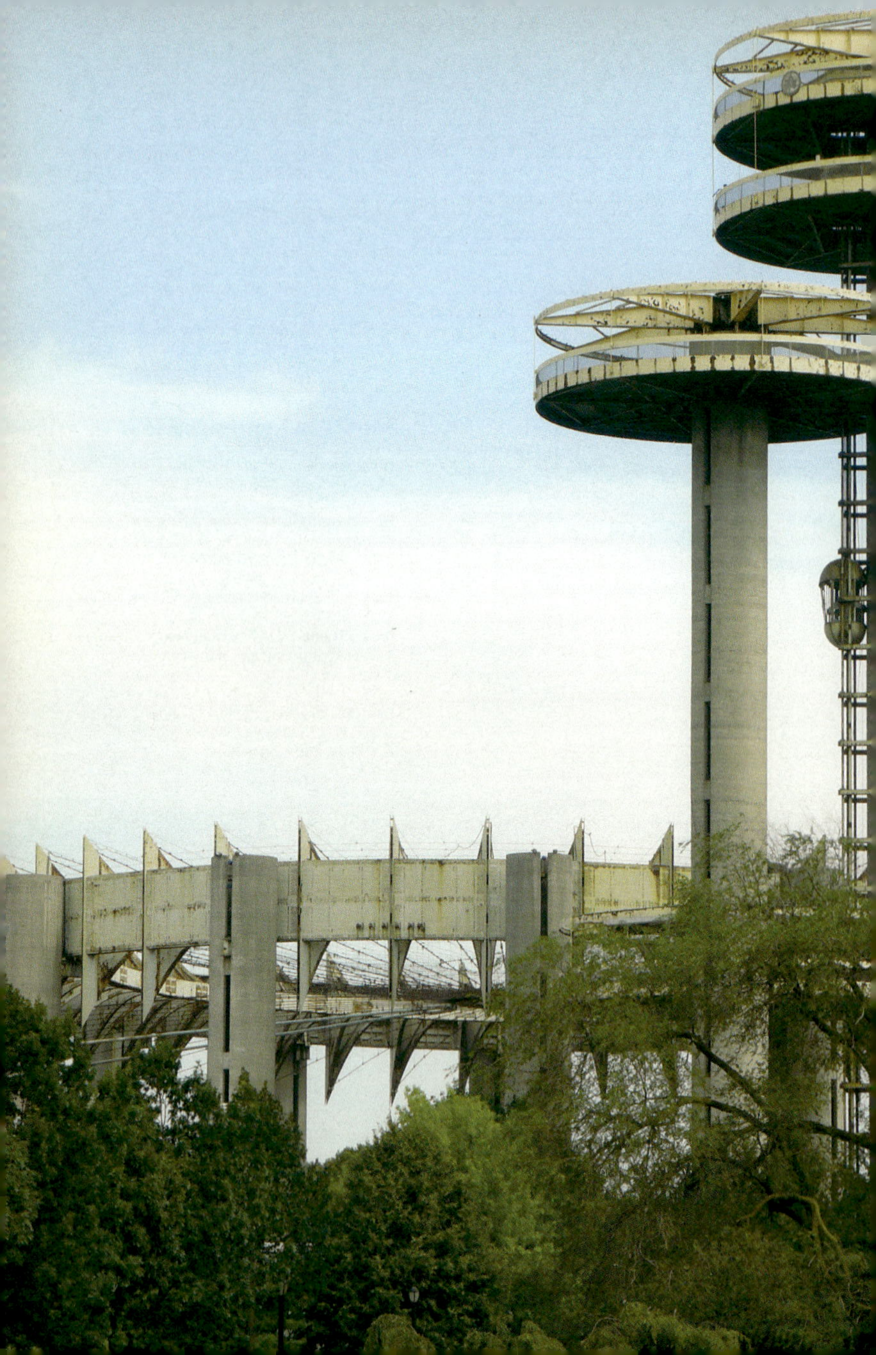

FLUSHING

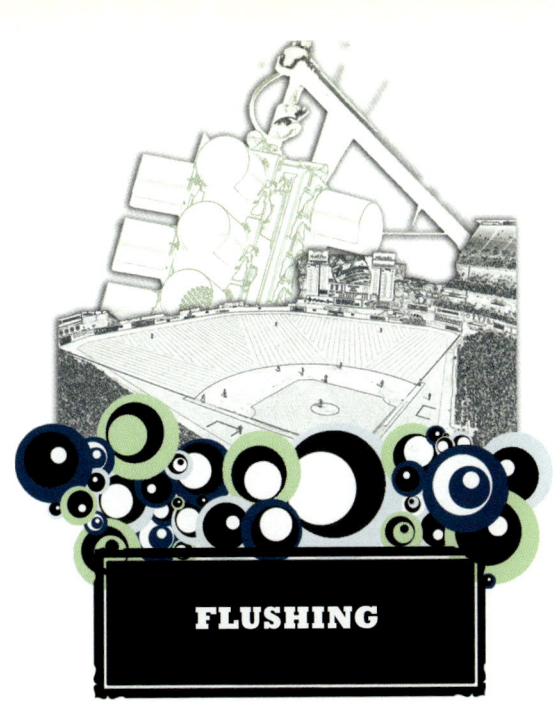

Founded as a Dutch colony in 1645 before it was captured by the British, Flushing is one of the oldest settlements in New York. Whereas many New York neighborhoods have undergone drastic fluctuations in fortune and wealth, Flushing has steadily grown in both size and affluence in its almost 400 year history. It was one of the earliest homes of the film industry, and it played host to two World's Fairs in the 20th century.

Today, downtown Flushing's central byway isn't your standard Main Street – it's more Guangzhou than Mayberry, the bustling heart of the second largest Chinatown in the U.S. East Asian culture, both old and new, dominates – Confucianism and Japanese bubble-gum pop are both chaotically grafted onto the rich historic backbone of this former village, where Quaker meeting houses still stand amidst neon characters and noodle shops. Downtown Flushing is a lesser-known and often cheaper culinary alternative to Manhattan's Chinatown, an affordable treasure-trove where superb Asian restaurants of every stripe sit cheek by jowl on cat-haunted back streets, offering authentic lesser-known delights from Szechuan to Taiwanese to Malaysian for anyone with a crumpled ten dollar bill and the patience to ride the 7 train out to the end. Up the street from downtown's Korean and Chinese core, a booming South Asian section supports sari shops and Hindu temples, while above gilded minarets testify to the area's exploding Muslim population.

Across the Van Wyck Expressway sprawls 1,255 acre Flushing Meadows-Corona Park, New York City's second largest – a huge green swath containing, among other things, a pitch-and-putt golf course, bike rentals, a zoo, seasonal dragon boat races, and a profusion of colliding soccer leagues, all overlaid on the recycled futuristic grid of two World's Fairs.

340 FLUSHING

ATTRACTIONS

Forest Hills Gardens
One of Queens' oldest and most exclusive communities, "the gardens" remains one of the most attractive areas of the borough. Founded in 1908 and designed by Frederick Law Olmstead Jr., the neighborhood's well preserved Tudor and Georgian homes stand on quiet, tree-lined streets with brick archways and the occasional stretch of cobblestone pavement. For a leisurely reprieve from city bustle, take a picturesque walk between the two main streets, Austin and Metropolitan.
Between Austin St and Metropolitan Ave (follow 71st Ave). E F V G R to 71st Continental Ave.

New York Hall of Science
Smashing exhibitions and a focus on hands-on discovery mean that fun and learning really do meet at this field-trip friendly palace of scientific wonders. You can drive a remote-controlled Mars rover, peer at the beautiful vapor trails of speeding electrons in a cloud chamber, and stomp around a distorted room that makes you appear to fluctuate wildly in height. Soap bubbles and incredible optical illusions teach crowds of schoolchildren about the properties of light and the quirks of human perception. Outside is a giant physics-themed playground and a rocket-garden sprouting decommissioned Atlas and Titan spacecraft. Get there early to fully enjoy the juxtaposition of seeing creative and elegant demonstrations of foundational truths about the physical world while enjoying simpler pleasures, like riding on a tilting surfboard simulator.
47-01 111th St (at 49th Ave) 718-699-0005. Sept-Mar: Tue-Thurs 9:30am-2pm, Fri 9:30am-5pm, Sat-Sun 10am-6pm, Apr-Jun: Mon-Thurs 9:30am-2pm, Fri 9:30am-5pm, Sat-Sun 10am-6pm, Jul-Aug: Mon-Fri 9:30am-5pm, Sat-Sun 10am-6pm. Holiday Weeks: Mon-Fri 9:30am-5pm, Sat-Sun 10am-6pm. 7 to 111th. $11, $8 with college ID.

The New York State Pavilion
The fantastical towers of this moldering monument to the 1960's future jut over the greenery at the far edge of Flushing Meadows-Corona Park. Originally constructed for the 1964-65 World's Fair, the "Tent of Tomorrow" and observation towers once sheltered the art and technological wonders of the age, as well as a magnificent 9,000 square foot terrazzo mosaic map of New York State. However, the pavilion found no lasting use after the fair – the roof was removed in 1976, exposing the interior to three decades of the ravages of weeds and weather. It is currently closed to the public—though visitors can walk right up to the external walls. The extraterrestrial character that inspired the producers of "Men in Black" to use it as a disguised spaceship endures—fallen into disrepair, it presently looms over the Grand Central Parkway like some rusting stargate abandoned by a race of alien astronauts long before the Dutch settled Flushing.
Flushing Meadows-Corona Park. Park closes at 9pm. 7 to Shea Stadium.

New York Table Tennis Club
This unassuming dynamo of ping pong excellence provides world-class instruction in the mysterious sport. Faded posters of table tennis greats decorate the front door while inside, intent middle-aged Chinese men in short shorts and high white socks play intense games, while a few Flushing youngsters learn from the club's coaches—some of them nationally ranked. If you're intimidated by the boxing-gym feel, come with a similarly incompetent friend and rent a table for yourselves—all skill levels are welcome.
35-26 Prince St (near Northern Blvd). 718-359-3272. Mon-Fri 2:30pm-11:30 pm, Sat-Sun 1pm-11pm. 7 to Flushing-Main St. $14/hr for private table rental, $1 paddle rental.

Queens Botanical Garden
In Queens but certainly not of it, the Botanical Garden provides a convenient respite from the teeming traffic and dusty heat of Flushing Main Street: a fresh rush of chlorophyll replaces the smell of noodles. Exhaust and asphalt give way to a lush patchwork of green including individual specialty gardens and extensive meadows and paths. Take one of the most

FLUSHING 341

idyllic naps Queens has to offer in the dappled sunlight of the orchard, as the whoosh of cars on College Point Boulevard blends with the hums and chirps of insects and birds, fading into a background lull.
43-50 Main St (by Elder Ave). 718-886-3800. Apr-Oct: Tues-Fri 8am-6pm, Sat-Sun 8am-7pm. Nov-Mar: Tues-Sun 8am-4:30 pm. ❼ to Flushing-Main St.

Queens Zoo

A walk along the long duck pond feels like a pleasant stroll in Central Park—until a passing glance from the garden bridge reveals a 6-foot alligator basking not 20 feet from the flocks of flapping waterfowl. This laid-back zoo replaces exhibit-to-exhibit hustle with the feel of a nature walk amongst a somewhat startling collection of animals peering out inconspicuously from behind the logs and bushes of Flushing Meadows-Corona park. All the animals are native to the western hemisphere, and most are from North America. The zoo's meandering circular trail replaces the large crowds and extensive concrete of conventional zoos with owls, trumpeter swans, and a geodesic aviary of songbirds. There are also bison, mountain lions, and Beagle-sized pudu, the world's smallest deer. A farm-style children's petting zoo is included in the price of admission, giving city kids a rare, close-up view of huge hogs and shaggy cows.
53-51 111th St in Flushing Meadows-Corona Park. 718-271-1500. Summer: Mon-Fri 10am-5pm, Sat-Sun (& Holidays) 10am-5:30pm. Winter Hours: Daily 10am-4:30 pm. $6 adult, $2 children. ❼ to 111th.

The Unisphere

At the heart of Flushing-Meadows Corona Park, this 12-story, 700,000 pound stainless steel globe is one of New York's most enduring and iconic images. Erected for the 1964-5 World's Fair, it was initially intended as a symbol of global interdependence and of mankind's great hopes and aspirations at the dawn of the space age. These days, it has become the unofficial symbol of Queens. It remains the crowded nexus of the park, and on any sunny afternoon it sits in Olympian grandeur—the external rings that once represented the orbits of John Glenn and Yuri Gagarin now trace those of a small galaxy of satellite skateboarders, rollerbladers, and BMX bikers circling in the drained fountain below.
Flushing Meadows-Corona Park. Park closes at 9pm. ❼ to Shea Stadium.

CULTURE & ARTS

Flushing Town Hall

For over a century, this stately brick edifice has followed Flushing through a number of transformations. From an actual town hall where Frederick Douglass spoke and Union volunteers mustered to the home of P.T. Barnum's sideshow, from a courthouse to a dilapidated eyesore, and now to a center for cultural events run by the Flushing Council on Culture and the Arts, Flushing Town Hall has played many

roles in the community. FCCA uses it to host everything from gallery openings to the Beijing Opera, and further celebrates Flushing's rich heritage via the Jazz Trail, whose red and gold trolleys tour the haunts of jazz greats and ghosts from the Queens scene's forgotten heydey. Among them are the neighboring Corona residences of Dizzie Gillespie and Louis Armstrong and Count Basie's block-wide Tudor estate. In the hall's balconied theater, the Jazz Live concert series continues to uphold Queens' bebop cred and promote awareness of a new generation of rising outer-borough jazzmen.
137-35 Northern Boulevard (at Linden Place). 718-463-7700. Box Office: Mon-Fri, 12pm-5pm. ❼ to Flushing Main St. Advance student tickets $10, Jazz Trail $35.

Kew Gardens Cinemas

This independent film house is a boon to Queens. It caters to the local Jewish community, heavily featuring Israeli cinema that might otherwise not be screened, but also hosts a fresh crop of films you might not even see on Manhattan. The screening rooms are small, but so are the crowds; check movie times online or on the phone, and don't worry about showing up too early. Tickets are still under $10, and refreshments include Edy's Dibs ice cream. Parking is scarce, so if you drive, leave time to find a spot.
81-05 Lefferts Blvd (near Austin St). 718-441-9835. ❸❻ to Union Turnpike. Tickets $9.50.

Queens Museum of Art

Residing in the only surviving building from the 1938 World's Fair, the Queens Museum of Art boasts as its unique crown jewel the Panorama of the City of New York, a massive 9,335 square-foot model of all five boroughs in precise topographic and architectural detail. Originally built for the 1965 World's fair, this vast toy Gotham is the largest such model in the world, and contains every single one of the city's 895,000 structures painstakingly recreated as they stood in 1992, when the model was last renovated – down to taxicab traffic and minute planes landing at JFK. Spend a strangely charming half hour picking out your apartment, office, and jogging route from a God's-eye view, until the room dims and the skyline winks on in a simulated dusk cycle. After a multimedia presentation, stick around and watch the miniature dawn, complete with bird calls, morning traffic noises, and a red spotlight sun rising over Queens.
Flushing Meadows-Corona Park. 718-592-9700. Sept. 4-Jul 3 Wed-Fri 10am-5pm, Sat-Sun 12pm-5pm. Jul 4-Sept 2 Wed-Sun 12pm-6pm, Fri 12pm-8pm. Suggested donation $5. ❼ to Willets St-Shea Stadium.

DINING

MID-RANGE
Bann Thai *Thai*

Guided by its "principles of harmony," Bann Thai serves up fresh, traditional Thai cuisine. Portions are fair, and though palm trees and yellow walls make the dining room more kitschy than authentic, it is nevertheless clean and homey. Exceptionally friendly waiters pepper suggestions with sharp witticisms and serve attentively. A satay dipping sauce made with fresh peanuts pairs well with a Singha beer.
69-12 Austin St (near 69th Road) 718-544-9999. Mon-Sun 11:30am-10:30pm. ❸❻❼❽❺ to 71st Continental Ave. Average Entree $15

Gala Manor *Dim Sum*

Though it is a conventional restaurant by night, this palatial banquet hall's crowning achievement is its high quality daytime dim sum. Heavily laden carts bump past tuxedoed hosts and huge families contentedly digging into steaming pyramids of steamed dumplings, vegetable pancakes, shu mai, and exotic specialities like chicken feet. Most of the servers don't speak English, but sight, smell, and a universal dim sum language of pointing and nodding can more than compensate for the average patron's flagging Mandarin. Make sure you come in numbers since as at most dim sum eateries, small parties are expected to share a table with other

guests.
37-02 Main St (at 37th Ave) 718-888-9232. Daily 11am-12am. Dim sum 9am-4pm. 🄻 *to Main. Dim sum $3 each. Average entrée $20.*

Sentosa
Shaded by carved ebony screens and frosted glass, the cool quiet of this elegant Malaysian restauraunt belies the sublime power of the spicy tastes it whips up, best exemplified by appetizers such as paper-thin roti canai—a fried crepe dipped in an molten orange curried chicken and potato sauce so savory that etiquette's barely enough to keep you from going at it with a lapping tongue. The hit-parade continues with main dishes like stick-to-your-ribs pad Thai and succulent beef rendang, simmered in chili powder and coconut milk curry. Though primed for fire, Sentosa's delights extend across the palate from spicy to sweet—with the honeyed, almost cake-like Grand Champion sesame ribs— and hot to cold, with shareable desserts like ice kanang ABC, a fantastical stalagmite of shaved-ice pitted with hidden cachés of red beans, nuts, and jelly.
39-07 Prince St (by 39th Ave) 718-886-6331. Daily 11am–11:30pm. 🄴🄵🅅🄴🄖 *to Jackson Heights-Roosevelt Ave,* 🄻 *to Flushing-Main St. Average entrée $13.*

CHEAP
A&J Pizza *Italian, Pizzeria*
While the food here is not the draw—it is authentic Italian, but with more Syosset than Sicily—the live music on pasta night would make you forget even the dullest penne. On Tuesdays, show up early to snag a prime seat for the night's entertainment. Skip out on the pasta and order a slice of pizza instead, with a crispy crust and heaping with cheese. An elderly Italian gentleman will begin to belt out old Italian folk classics with force and character; within minutes, the regulars are clapping in time and singing along to every word.
71-37 Austin St (at 71st Rd). 718-520-9018. Sun-Thurs 11am-9:45 pm, Fri-Sat 11am-10-:45pm. 🄴🄵🅅🄴🄖 *to 71st-Continental Ave.*

Eddie's Sweet Shop *Ice Cream*
There is nothing quite like Eddie's anymore—to walk into Eddie's is to turn the clock back fifty years and enjoy the sweets and treats of youthful Baby Boomers. Eddie's décor and inviting atmosphere is pure authentic kitsch and its family ownership and management is a further remnant of a bygone era. The sundaes are unmatched, built on homemade ice cream base and covered in rich, thick fudge, served up in a classic oversized egg cup. Have a seat on one of the ice cream bar's cast iron stools or, if you arrive with a larger party, settle into a booth where a friendly waiter will help you. If you are looking to bring something back home, small sweets can still be bought with pocket change.
105-29 Metropolitan Ave. 718-520-8514. Tue-Fri 1pm-11:30pm, Sat-Sun 12pm-11:30pm. **E F V B G** *to 71st- Continental Ave, Q23 bus to Metropolitan Ave*

Flushing Mall Food Court
Pan Asian
Not many suburban mall food courts offer takoyaki octopus meatballs or shabu-shabu hot pots built into the table. This pan-Asian food court's tables are often packed with a gaggle of teenagers or workers on break, chowing down on impressive quantities of sizzling black pepper steak, noodles, and fried eggs from Ay-Chung Steak House, or la mien, hand-pulled noodles, from the stand with a red sign and white characters. Though most stands here have bilingual menus, some don't and finding English-speaking employees can be difficult. Styrofoam bowls filled with shaved ice topped with fruits and beans are the perfect way to finish an authentic Sichuan meal and soothe a scorched tongue. Or, work off your meal with a few nostalgic rounds of Street-Fighter or DDR in the arcade in back.
Flushing Mall, 133-31 39th Ave (Prince St) 718-762-9000. Daily 10am-9pm. **7** *to Main St. Average dish $5.*

Gotta Getta Bagel *Bagels, Café*
In NYC the bagel still reigns as the carbohydrate king, and the bagels at this café are always fresh—baking goes on throughout the day. Crisp crusts, savory insides, and all the "shmear" you need, from traditional tuna and lox spreads to dozens of cream cheeses. The whitefish salad is excellent, too. Seating is no frills, but ample for a small bagel café.
10709 71st Ave (between Queens Blvd & Austin St.) 718-793-1640. Mon-Sat 6am-8pm, Sun 6am-7pm. **E F V B G** *to Continental Ave.*

Joe's Shanghai *Shanghainese*
Scores of awards, rave reviews, and magazine best-of lists hang arrayed like trophy heads of gold over the happy crowds of Flushing families and Manhattan pilgrims who pack Joe's Shanghai to the gills six nights a week. Though Joe's offers a full Shanghainese menu, the crowds usually opt for the famous soup dumplings, now a New York institution. Joe's is the acknowledged master of these plump doughy sacks, filled to bursting with tender crab and/or pork meat and an internal reservoir of hot soup. Dumplings come eight to a batch and require a certain element of respectful caution to enjoy. Gently

nibbling the top off and sucking out the soup is a must as they're exploding with scalding juices; an ill-advised chomp will temporarily make you a painful example of cross-cultural misunderstanding, and, worse, unable to enjoy the rest.
136-21 37th Ave (by Main St). 718-539-3838. Fri-Sat 11am-12am. ❼ *to Flushing-Main St. Dumplings $4.50-6.50.*

Tai Pan Bakery *Bakery*
Though it's priced like a dive—most buns are only $1—this crowded Chinese bakery is anything but. With a gleaming glass and metallic interior that would be spacious if it weren't always so packed. Tai Pan feels like it time-warped from some delicious, deflationary future. A huge selection of plump buns, from red bean to coconut cream to roasted pork pineapple, glisten in neat rows for customers' inspection and selection, while counter attendants help with larger cakes and sweets. The chaotic line requires some jockeying with sugar-crazed customers, but just grab a tray and a pair of tongs from the rack and plunge in—it's well-worth the wait and the madness. Ample shredded pork buns are enough for a big snack or a small meal, and a thick, heavenly scallion and egg roll bun is the best dollar you'll spend all week.
37-25 Main St (near 37th Ave) 718-888-1111. Daily 7:30am-8pm. ❼ *to Main St. Average entrée $1.*

NIGHTLIFE

5 Burro Café *Café, Bar*
This beacon of authentic Mexican food doubles as one of Forest Hills' most consistently packed bars just about every night of the week. Sitting down for an enchilada is worthwhile, but the bar is the real place to be. When the weather is nice, sit outside among the throngs of locals who push out onto the sidewalk. The music is lively, and the crowd is mixed, representing ages, fashions, and personalities of all kinds—a testament to Queens' diversity. The cocktails, with their unnatural colors and wild combinations, recall the joys of exotic spring breaks. Enjoy your flavored margarita and get comfortable, because this bar is the place to be until four in the morning, every night.
72-05 Austin St (between 72nd Ave & 72nd Rd) 718-544-2984. Dinner Sun–Thurs 3pm–12am, Fri-Sat 3pm-1am, Brunch Sat-Sun 12pm– 3am. ❺❻❼❽❾ *to 71st Ave-Forest Hills. Average drink $7.*

The Billiard Company
Bar, Pool Hall
The Billiard Company is the local pool hall. Recently redone, it now contains many more plasma screens and couches, giving it a yuppie-lounge vibe. Enjoy $5 drinks between 10pm and midnight as you work on your english. The music videos and young crowd can be distracting for the serious hustler, but make the place more hospitable for everyone else. The crowd skews super-slick, so bring your crew and party, or tune out the looping music videos and just play your game.
70-49 Austin Street (at 70th Rd). 718-520-7665. Daily 11am-4am. ❺❻❼❽❾ *to 71st Continental Ave.*

SHOPPING

Cheese of the World
The unassuming exterior of this little shop hides the neighborhood's best selection of world cheese, dry sausage, and handcrafted Belgian chocolates. The staff is friendly and welcoming, if not all-knowing, and they are glad to introduce you to their favorite cheeses. In addition to cheeses like Rochebaron and triple crème brie, their cracker section is as extensive as any in the best large chain supermarkets, making this an essential stop in preparation for a wine and cheese (and sausage) evening.
7148 Austin St (between 71st Rd & 72nd Ave) 718-263-1933. Mon-Sat 9am-8pm, Sun 10am-6pm. E F V R G to 71st-Continental Ave.

Magic Castle
This Korean pop stationery store is home to a menagerie of plump stuffed animals and school supplies decorated with cartoon characters like Hello Kitty, Blue Bear, and Pucca, all shouting ungrammatical English slogans. Magic Castle is the last word in Hello Kitty doll kimonos, giant bejeweled piggybanks, outlandish pens, and plush panda backpacks—all imported from distributors in Japan, Korea, and France on a biweekly basis. Different counters offer clothing, Asian pop music, bags, accessories, cosmetics, and cell phones. The other side of the store has a trove of eccentric imported costume jewelry, although not everything is cheap.
136-82 39th Ave (at Union St) 718-886-0695. 7 to Main St.

Toy Qube
This store/gallery is one of the major New York purveyors of designer vinyl toys, produced not by companies but in limited editions by artists with graffiti-tag monikers like MAD and SKET. Originating in Japan, these stylish toys are marked by cool design, serious artistry, subversive feel, and an urban, hip-hop aesthetic: Barbie hairbrushes and convertibles have been replaced with spray-paint cans and boom boxes. In the glass display cases wildly varied armies of B-boys and street people with Rubix-cube faces jockey for position with hard-eyed, gun-toting bears, huge-headed kids with giant smiles and jetpacks, and a rainbow of painstakingly detailed miniature sneakers. The small figures go for $5-7 dollars, while the larger ones start at about $65, and can get up to around $200 depending on the artist. Street resale value can be considerably higher.
Flushing Mall, 133-31 39th Ave (near College Point Blvd) 718-939-8605. Daily 1pm-8pm. 7 to Main.

DAY TO DAY

Community Board 7. *133-32 41st Rd, Suite 3B. 718-359-2800.*

Local Media: The Queens Tribune, The Queens Courier.

Groceries: Golden Market. *41-28 Main St. 718-359-5715.* Key Food. *79-15 Main St. 718-380-5159.*

Gyms: Flushing YMCA. *138-46 Northern Blvd. 718-961-6880.* Powerhouse Gym. *58-04 99th St. 718-592-4040.*

Rent: Studios $800 up. One-bedroom, $1,100-1,200. Two-bedroom, $1,400-1,500.

Hospital: Hospital Medical Center of Queens. *56-45 Main St. 718-670-1231.*

Hotel: Sheraton LaGuardia East. *135-20 39th Ave. 718-460-6666.*

Dog Run: Underbridge Dog Run. *64 Ave/64 Road on Grand Central Parkway service road.*

Movie Theater: National Amusements College Point Multiplex Cinemas. *28-55 Ulmer St. 718-886-4900.*

FLUSHING 347

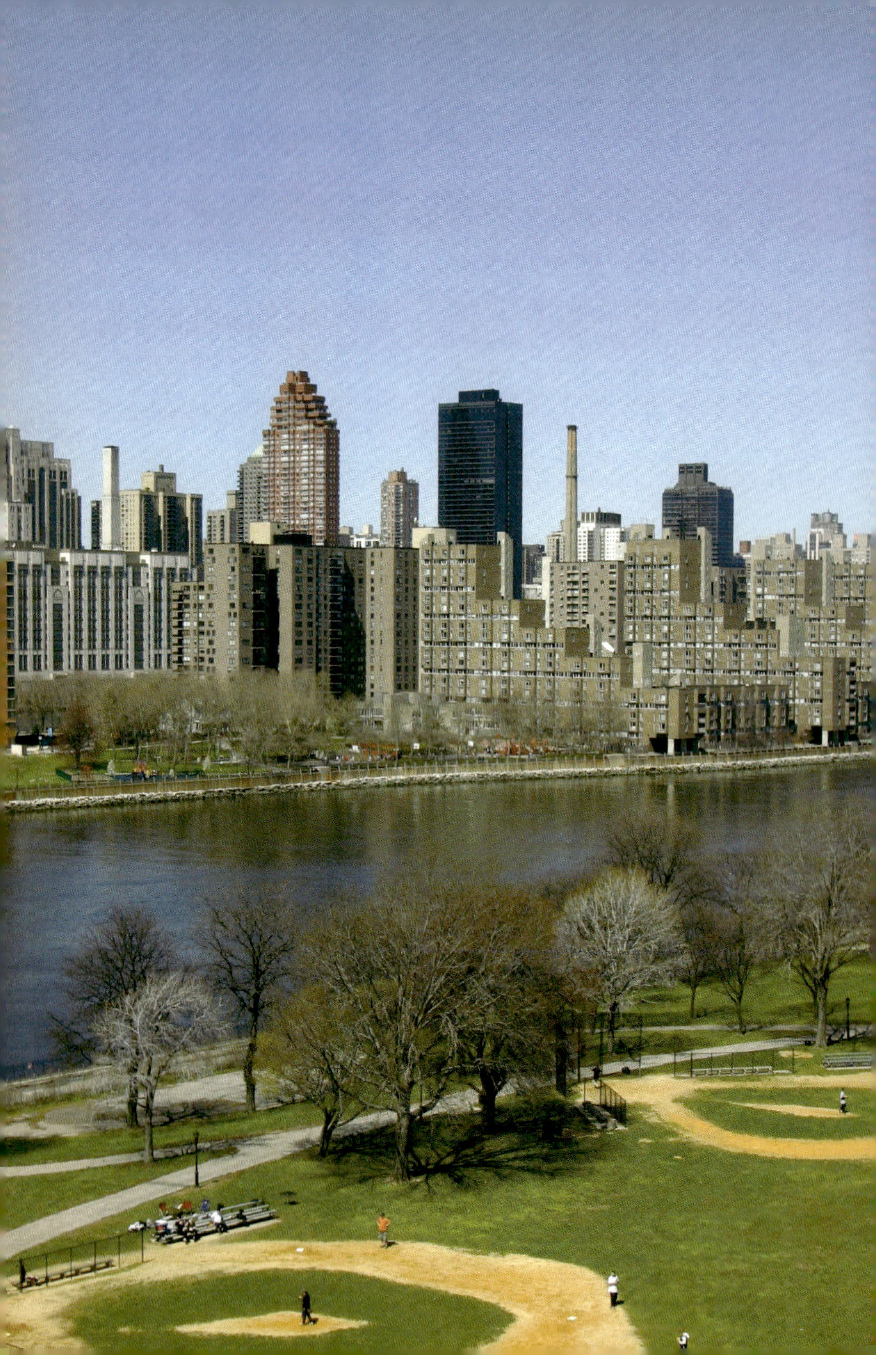

JACKSON HEIGHTS & WOODSIDE

Though it may be cliché to call New York a "melting pot," Jackson Heights is among the most diverse neighborhoods in the city; round a corner and the bustling, Spanish-speaking calle you've been cruising will become a Hindi-speaking sedaka. Despite being home to some of the best food in the city, Jackson Heights and Woodside are mostly locals-only, with run-down shops and an elevated train casting a constant shadow over Roosevelt Boulevard, the main thoroughfare.

While people are friendlier in far-away Queens, their amiability is in marked contrast to their sometimes inhospitable surroundings: the main drag has a distinctly industrial feel, though parks, gardens, and other green spaces dot the area. Besides the food, the major attraction for visitors is the ubiquity of cheap clothing stores, especially the unique ethnic shops in Little India. Family-run boutiques blare music over dirty sidewalks as street vendors busk to the masses. Rounding out the mix are jumping nightclubs—many of which are LGBT—with themes and décor inspired by the predominately Hispanic makeup of the neighborhood. After a sweaty night on the dance floor, cheap, delicious takeout is just around the corner.

350 JACKSON HEIGHTS & WOODSIDE

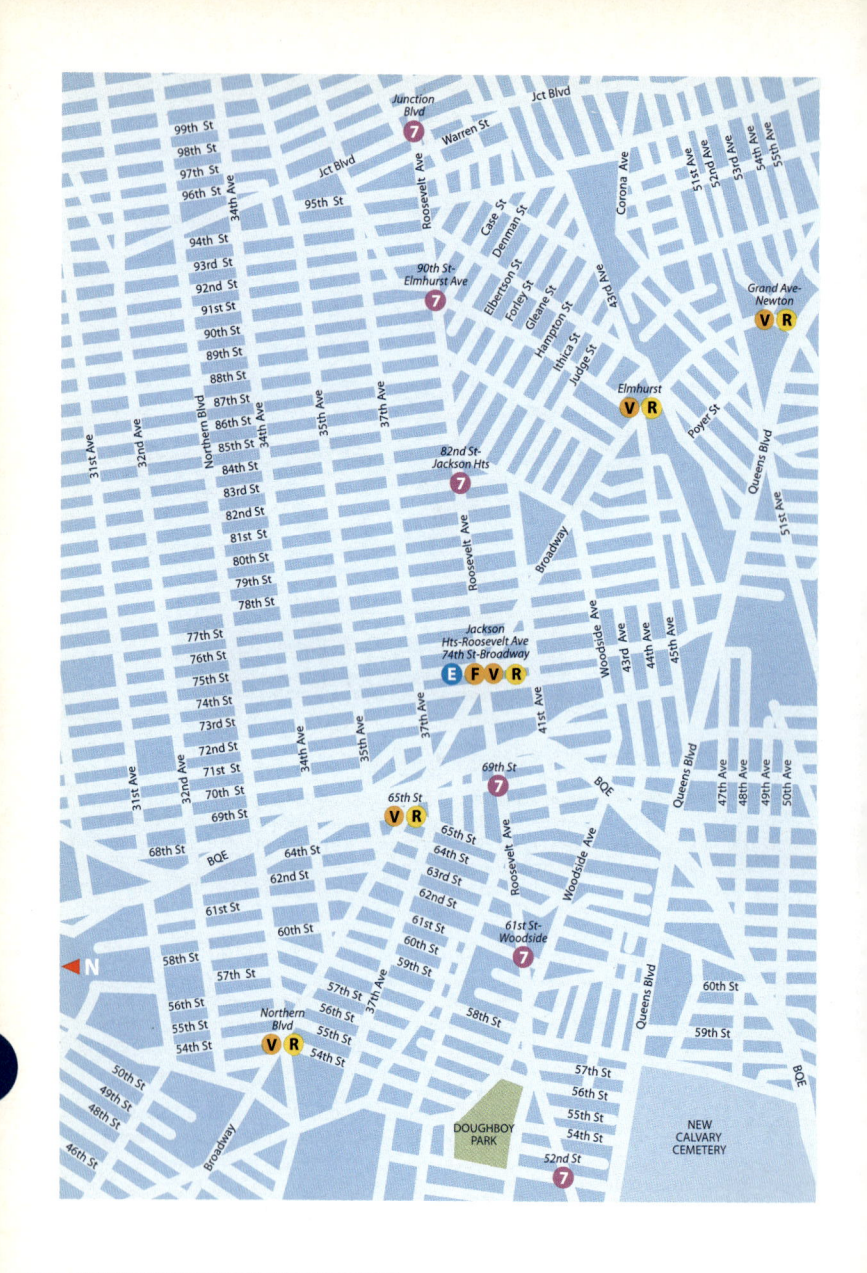

ATTRACTIONS

Doughboy Park
Sitting incongruously amid apartment buildings and in between two busy streets of urban sprawl, this park's grass and trees are an overgrown reminder of old New York. Locals sit at the cement surrounded benches, and children frolic on the large playground. Renovated several times, most recently in 1988, the playgrounds and paths are local haunts and serve as a rallying point for the diverse neighborhood. The park serves as a monument to Woodside war victims, including those of the September 11, 2001 attacks. The main attraction though is the delicately featured "Doughboy"-- a stunning reminder of the solitude of war.
Woodside Ave and Skillman Ave. 7 to 61st-Woodside Ave, R V to Northern Boulevard

New Calvary Cemetery
This sprawling set of graves (over three million) have stretched across Queens since 1847. While most of these graves are not of notables, there are several famous burials including mobsters (Joe Masseria, Peter Morello, Vito Boventre, to name a few) and several entertainers, including legend of the stage, Lionel Barrymore. While it may prove to be difficult to find these graves, time and diligence will find you in the presence of some great personalities.
49-02 Laurel Hill Blvd (between 48th St & 49th St). 7 to 46th.

CULTURE & ARTS

Eagle Theater
There is enough singing, dancing, and celluloid at the Eagle Theater to please even Broadway's Busby Berkeley. Built by architect John Eberson in 1936, this once grandiose art deco theater has seen better days, but its renaissance reflects the shifting values of a changing city. It moonlighted as a porn theater, and changed its name from the Earle to the Eagle before being boarded up for many years. But now, the Eagle is back and features the best of Bollywood. The theater has not been fully renovated, but is functional enough to screen pictures that give many locals a taste of home. The space is a bit worse-for-wear, and the narrow seats may give a modern audience incentive for a diet, but the tubs of samosas at the concession stand will shatter even the most iron-clad self-control.
73-07 37th Rd (at 73rd and Broadway). 718-205-2800. E R F V G 7 to Roosevelt Ave-74th St.

DINING

MID-RANGE
Arepa Lady *Latin*
A Jackson Heights fixture who also has an online fan page and cult following, the Arepa Lady is street food at its finest. While the arepa lady's comings and goings may be unpredictable, she generally sets up shop Friday and Saturday nights during the summer, grilling both sweet and savory corn cakes all night and sprinkling them with

JACKSON HEIGHTS & WOODSIDE 351

LITTLE INDIA

Though Jackson Heights is one of the most diverse neighborhoods in the city, it is also home the largest concentration of South Asian immigrants in the five boroughs. On 74th St between Roosevelt Ave and 37th Ave you will find a lively community of Pakistanis, Bangladeshis, and North and South Indians bustling about a congested area packed with people, stores, and restaurants.

The **Jackson Diner** (*37-47 74th St, 718-672-1232*) is the most legendary of these restaurants. Though it maintains the name of the greasy-spoon that preceded it, it now specializes in North Indian curries and tandooris. Dimple **Indian Vegetarian** (*35-68 73rd St, 718-458-8144*) is loved by vegans for its hearty meals that trounce hippie salads with rich, hearty flavor. **Shaheen Sweets & Cuisine** (*720 Broadway, 718-639-4791*) offers great naan and kebabs, but it specializes in Pakistani candies and desserts. Though odd looking to the untrained eye, these butter and sugar-based delights are jazzed up with nuts, fruits, and paneer, and they will only run you about $5 for a small assortment.

Patel Brothers Market (*3727 74th St, 718-898-3445*) offers a wide selection of the ingredients and spices you will need to make your own Indian cuisine, and are known for their selection of excellent curry blends. **Raaga Super Store** (*37-26 74th St*), offers an excellent selection of Bhangra music and other Indian hits, while **Melody Stop** (*3756 74th St, 718-429-7179*) stocks the best of Bollywood for sale or rent. There are, of course, numerous other noteworthy restaurants and stores to stop by, as well as the seemingly endless rows of sari tailors, jewelry stores, and beauty salons, you just need to be adventurous to try them out

E **R** **F** **V** **G** **7** to 74th St-Roosevelt Ave.

cheese. Choose from cheesy arepas, chorizo, or kebabs at a satisfying $3 per treat.
Roosevelt Ave (between 78th St and 79th St). Fri-Sat 10pm-5am. **E** **R** **F** **V** **G** **7** *to 74th-Roosevelt Ave. Arepas $3.*

Rajbhog Sweets *Dessert*
Bombay-style candies take center stage in this large family-owned restaurant, but vegetarian Indian food also sells for bargain prices in the tiled back of the shop. Rajbhog now distributes all over the country, but it is still worth tasting the sweets at their source. The Burfi melts like butter when eaten fresh, while the drier Halwa provides a saltier answer to the store's more sugar-laden options. The helpful staff will happily answer any questions you have about their products.
72-27 37th Ave (near 72nd St) 718-458-8512. Daily 10am-9pm. **E** **R** **F** **V** **G** **7** *to 74th-Roosevelt Ave.*

CHEAP
Frisby Fried Chicken *Colombian*
Ignore the tacky storefront. Once you get past the waving chicken on a bright yellow awning, you will find it hard to turn down Frisby's chicken, fried crispy in fat and drenched in honey. This spotless, spacious establishment is a fixture in its home country, Colombia, and local flavor can be found in sides like golden-brown yucca wedges, fluffy arepas, and slow cooked beans. In its new Jackson Heights home, Frisby is quickly gaining notice as one of the best cheap eats in New York for fast, delicious, and unhealthy food. They close early, however, which is bad news for club-goers with the munchies: take it out before 1AM.
83-17 Northern Blvd (near 34th Ave). 718-639-0500. Sun-Fri 11am-12am, Sat 11am-1am. **E** **R** **F** **V** **G** **7** *to 74th St-Roosevelt Ave. Average entrée $6.*

Rice Avenue *Thai*
The owner of Manhattan Thai chain Spice has started strong in the outer boroughs with Rice, which offers simple, delicious Thai food and isn't afraid to bring the heat. The almost electro-zen atmosphere lends a modernist edge, making the restaurant an unusual retreat on Roosevelt Avenue. In true Manhattan style, the space also provides free Wi-Fi. While the restaurant offers mostly generic American-

Thai offerings, the spicy dishes provide a welcome surprise. Cheap prices and large portions could make this a great date place, but a lack of privacy arises from the too-cool and closely situated high-backed chairs.
7219 Roosevelt Ave (at 72nd St). 718-803-9001. E R F V G 7 *to 74th St-Roosevelt Ave. Average entrée $10.*

Sammy's Halal *Middle Eastern*
Sammy's smiling face, peeking out from behind his halal cart, is a familiar one to his many patrons in Queens. His specialty is chicken and rice, served on a paper plate and covered with rivers of delicious green sauce. The key to tasty grub is his spice mixture; unknown to all but the man himself, it is a secret combination that makes for magical street cuisine.
73rd St (at Broadway). Daily 10am-12am. E R F V G 7 *to 74th St-Roosevelt Ave. Average entrée $7.*

Unidentified Flying Chicken *Korean*
People may initially be drawn to this Korean fast food joint for its curious logo, a Sanrio-style techno chicken, but the food will keep them returning. Fried chicken is new to Korea and UFC is new to Jackson Heights, but it is quickly becoming a neighborhood favorite. A variety of dipping sauces (the soy garlic is a favorite), daikon radish pickles, French fries, and macaroni salad go well beside a greasy plate. The chicken takes fifteen to twenty minutes to prepare, and choices are limited, so the best bet is to order ahead and carry out.
71-22 Roosevelt Ave (near 72nd Ave) 718-205-6662. Mon-Sat 11am-11pm, Sun 12pm-10pm. E R F V G 7 *to to 74th St-Roosevelt Ave. Average entrée $10.*

DAY TO DAY

Community Board 3. *82-11 37th Ave. 718-458-2707.*

Local Media: *jacksonheightsblog.com*

Groceries: Met. *81-02 Northern Boulevard. 718-458-9827.*

Rent: One-bedroom $900-1300; Two-bedroom, $1100-$2000.

Hospital: Elmhurst Hospital Center. *79-01 Broadway. 718-334-4000.*

Movie Theater: Eagle Theatre. *7307 37th Rd. 718-565-8783.*

Best Happy Hour: The Music Box. *40-08 74th St (at Roosevelt Ave). 718-429-9356.*

SHOPPING

India Sari Palace
This is the one-stop shop for all your sari needs. The 4,000 foot space, carpeted and clean, holds hundreds of feet of the light, airy, sari silk, which a local tailor can handcraft into a sari to order for around $50. Also offering ready-made saris for around $35, the place is a bargain. Right in the center of little India, the central location is a draw for many locals who swear by their service.
37-07 74th St (at 37th St) 718-426-2700. Daily 10:30am-7pm. E R F V G 7 *to 74th St-Roosevelt Ave.*

ENTRY

SOUTH BRONX

Once upon a time, the Bronx was a destination for Jewish and Italian families tired of the tenements of Manhattan. By 1930, the population was 49% Jewish, and the Bronx was known as the "Jewish Borough." It is from this period that Hollywood's most enduring conception of New York—all stickball and stoops—originates.

Then came the white flight of the post-war era; the area flipped from 2/3 white in 1950 to 2/3 African American and Hispanic by 1960. The Bronx had always been a working class borough, but with the 60s and 70s came a slew of disastrous policies and projects (the Cross Bronx Expressway, school busing, retrograde rent control policies and the subsequent abandonment by landlords of many buildings) which led to severe urban decay, particularly in the South Bronx. It is from this era that the modern image of the Bronx—an inner-city wasteland riddled with crime, poverty, and drugs—derives. "The Bronx is burning," said sports journalist Howard Cosell during the 1977 World Series at Yankee Stadium; landlords had taken to setting their buildings on fire to collect the insurance money, causing an epidemic of arson throughout the 1970s and contributing to the bombed-out war zone atmosphere. The 80s, of course, brought crack.

By the late 90s, there was nowhere to go but up. Citizens, tired of 30 years of near continuous neglect, began banding together to revitalize their community. Priced out of every other borough, artists have been trickling in slowly, attracted by rock-bottom rents. Mott Haven in particular is shaping up to be a vibrant cultural scene. The construction of New Yankee Stadium brings with it $1 billion for new athletic facilities, stores, restaurants, a Metro-North station, and, hopefully, a boom in residential redevelopment. For the first time in years, things are looking bright for the Bronx.

356 SOUTH BRONX

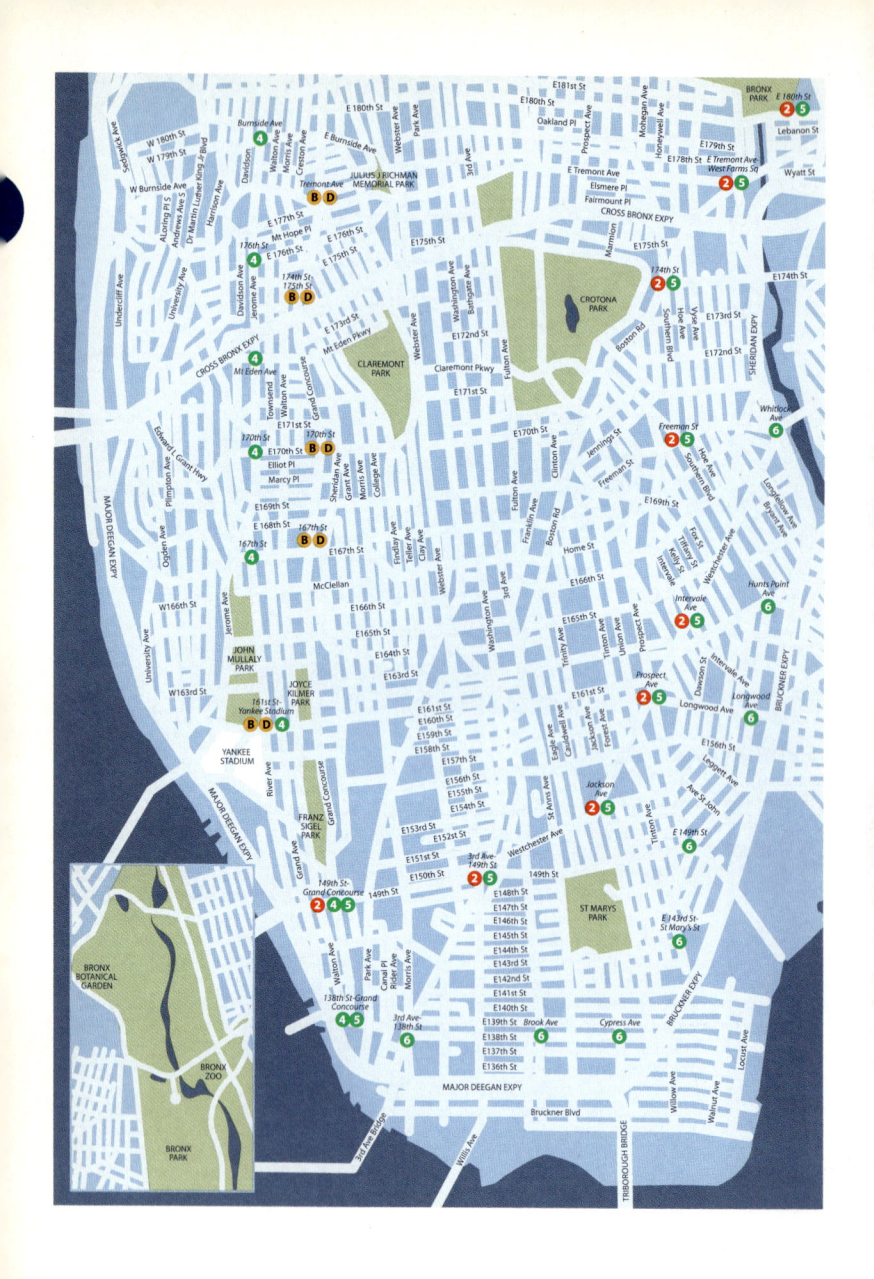

ATTRACTIONS

Alexander Avenue Antique District
Antique wise, this "district" consists of two blocks of dilapidated storefronts, housing poorly ventilated rooms full of old fashioned furniture and decor—velvety couches, ornate mirrors, idyllic paintings, imposing armoires, etc. If you have a fetish for the luxury goods of a bygone age and don't mind them being a little scuffed, it doesn't get much better than this. If, on the other hand, you're interested in emerging neighborhoods and want to know if the hype is true, you may be a tad disappointed. Certainly there are more artists and entrepreneurs in the area than there were ten years ago, but "a critical mass" of creative industry firms, as one municipal agency puts it? Hardly. The appearance of a few galleries does not a bohemia make. Nevertheless, seeds are being planted, and in a few years time this may be a neighborhood worth your attention.
3rd Ave to Willis Ave, Bruckner Blvd to 135th St. ❻ *to 138th.*

Bronx Culture Trolley
The Bronx Council of the Arts sponsors this trolley ride through the south Bronx cultural corridor. On the first Wednesday evening of every month, the ride stops at a variety of cultural events and destinations as well as dining establishments and entertainment venues. Poetry readings, arts exhibitions, and theatre performances are all featured and are all free, providing a great opportunity to explore the "Gateway to the New Bronx" without having to brave interminable walks or confusing bus service.
450 Grand Concourse (at 149th St, Hostos Community College). 718-401-9558. First Wed of each month, 5:30pm, 6:30pm, 7:30pm. ❷❹❺ *to Grand Concourse.*

Bronx Zoo
As aficionados know, even the best zoo visits end, inevitably, in disappointment. Hoping to connect with nature, one is reminded instead of the great gulf that divides us from our bestial brethren. Cages of glass are still cages, and still depressing, no matter how cozy they may appear. That said, the facilities at the Bronx Zoo are awfully cozy; 265 acres house over 4,000 animals, spirits only partially broken thanks to the valiant efforts of the Wildlife Conservation Society. The grounds are pleasant and well organized (taxonomically and geographically), and the usual zoo favorites all put in an appearance: lions, tigers, bears, monkeys, aquatic mammals, birds, reptiles, rodents, and so on. Special attractions (which cost a bit extra) include camel rides, a butterfly garden, an Asia-themed monorail ride, an excellent children's zoo, the Skyfari (a two-mile elevated cable car ride), and, best of all, the Congo Gorilla Forest, a 6.5 acre mini-rainforest housing two families of our not-so-distant cousins. Watch out for hordes of children during summer months, especially in the indoor facilities—the mouse house, reptile house, and new Madagascar exhibit all take on the imposing odor of baby farts and sweaty child stank.
2300 Southern Blvd. 718-367-1010. Hours vary seasonally; approximately 10am-5pm daily. ❷❺ *to West Farms Sq-East Tremont Ave. $15, seniors $13, children $11.*

New York Botanical Garden
Spanning over 250 acres (including 50 acres of uncut, native Forest), the exceedingly tranquil, immaculately manicured grounds of the NYBG are home to a staggering 1 million living plants, 7 million herbarium specimens, the world's most sophisticated botanical research center, and countless pairs of marauding middle-aged women who roam freely, chattering about brunch and taxes. Don't let them stop you from enjoying the garden's many floral pleasures: a 4000-strong rose garden (in bloom in June & November), a meditative rock garden, collections of lilies, orchids, daffodils, magnolias etc, greenhouses, a conservatory (featuring a winter holiday train show), a surprisingly interesting gift shop, and a totally decent tram ride; the Native Forest is the closest you're going to get to being alone with nature within the city limits. A constant stream of concerts, classes, and exhibits (a recent example being the monumental sculptures of Henry Moore) ensure there's more to do than just look at plants.

ARTHUR AVENUE
"NEW YORK'S REAL LITTLE ITALY"

Every day, droves of first and second generation Italians trek back to the old neighborhood's top-quality butcher shops, markets, and bakeries for fresh imported parmesan or the seven fish for Christmas Eve, a quiet cup of espresso, or Sunday dinners with waiters their fathers knew. But they don't stay – these days, Little Italy commutes. Except for the business owners, Fordham kids, and a few old-timers on park benches, the people who actually live and work here are now mostly Albanians, slowly making inroads on the neighborhood with two-headed eagle flags and specialty shops. However, Arthur Avenue's old-world soul hasn't vanished yet –it's just taken refuge inside the food and the storefronts, enduring in a legion of restaurants and gourmet shops like **Cosenza's Fish Market** (*2354 Arthur Ave, 718-364-8510*), with its outdoor oyster bar, and **Tino's Deli** (*2410 Arthur Ave, 718-733-9879*), where you can enjoy a sopressata sub and an imported Italian soda amongst bookshelves and majolica opera masks. Down the street, the venerable **Arthur Avenue Retail Market** (*2344 Arthur Ave*) hosts indoor stands where you can shop for fresh produce or espresso machine parts. Sample some olives or a sorbet-stuffed orange, and check out **La Casa Grande Tobacco Company** (*2344 Arthur Ave, 718-364-4657*), where you can sit alongside a life-size plaster Al Capone and watch a small factory of skilled men hypnotically twist, cut, and press smooth brown tobacco leaves into hand-rolled stogies, selling at 3 for $10. Afterwards, head next door to 90-year Arthur Avenue fixture **Mario's** (*2342 Arthur Ave, 718-584-1188*) for award-winning Neapolitan cuisine. The wonderful pizza, a secret of regulars, is often made personally by Joseph the owner, fifth in the bloodline from Mario himself.

2690 Dr Theodore Kazimiroff Blvd (near E Fordham Rd) 718-817-8700. Tues-Sun 10am-6pm. ❹❽Ⓓ to Bedford Park Blvd, Bx 26 to Mosholu Gate. All-garden pass $20, $18 students, grounds-only pass $6, students $3.

CULTURE & ARTS

Bronx Museum of the Arts
The Bronx Museum combines a taste for cutting-edge aesthetic endeavors with an emphasis on social justice (critiques of race, class, and gender are ubiquitous) and community interaction. The result is something of a rarity: a major municipal museum that spends more time looking forward than backward. Its most distinctive program, Artists in the Marketplace (AIM), now in its 28th year, provides practical career advice, critical evaluation, and professional guidance to 36 young artists every year, culminating in a group show. The artists write their own (surprisingly candid) plaques, occasionally shrill but always genuine; indeed, the language of every plaque in the museum is carefully calibrated to be direct and accessible, without sacrificing whatever depth there is in pseudo-philosophical art-speak. A $19 million renovation, completed in 2006, has provided a major new gallery and events space, an outdoor terrace, and an entire floor dedicated to classrooms and education programs. In the works is a plan to modernize the original structure and affix a residential co-op tower. More than any other museum in the city, BxMA is investing in its community.
1040 Grand Concourse (at 165th St) 718-681-6000. Mon, Thurs, Sun 12pm-6pm, Fri-Sat 12pm-8pm. ❹❽Ⓓ to 167th. $5 adults, $3 students.

DINING

MID-RANGE
Bruckner Bar & Grill *American*
A homey neighborhood eatery in an area largely devoid of consistent, friendly food, the Bruckner services the burgeoning creative community of the South Bronx. The menu is pretty standard low-brow American grub, with lots of fried starters—calamari, chicken fingers, jalapeno poppers, mozzarella sticks, etc—and sandwiches, salads, pastas, and grilled meats for dinner. Curious eyes may be drawn to the seemingly novel schnitzel, but it, too, is just an over-seasoned piece of fried meat (chicken, in this case). Your best bet is the burger, a 10oz hunk of juicy beef, char-grilled and served

GRAND CONCOURSE

Modeled after the Champs-Élysées in Paris, the Grand Concourse is easily the most famous street in the Bronx, a historically important thoroughfare that continues to abut some of the borough's most significant cultural landmarks. Take the ❷❹❺ up to 149th St-Grand Concourse and you'll find yourself at the base of a mile-long stretch full of architectural relics and tranquil green-space.

Right out of the subway is the **Bronx General Post Office** (*588 Grand Concourse at E 149th St*), the ground floor of which is covered with faded tempera murals by Ben Shahn. Produced during the Great Depression with New Deal art money, the murals, collectively entitled "Resources of America," glorify the nation's transformation into a modern industrial power and the laborers who made it so. The building itself is somewhat run down, but it makes a cool spot to rest on a hot summer day.

Just up the street, at 151st St, is **Franz Sigel Park**. Named for a German immigrant turned Union general in the Civil War, Franz Sigel Park has two baseball diamonds, a basketball court, a dog run, and some pretty steep hills (by city-dweller standards). Broad pathways wind around rocky outcroppings, rising into an open-air rotunda and a very pleasant clearing at the top.

Above the park is the **Mario Merola Building**, also known as the Bronx County Courthouse (*851 Grand Concourse at E 158th St*). Another New Deal project (cornerstone laid 1933), the courthouse is an imposing concrete structure with a sculptural frieze and two free-standing marble sculpture groups at each columned portico entrance. The perimeter smells like mustard: the building is across the street from Yankee Stadium, and kitty-corner to New Yankee Stadium.

The north end of the courthouse leads into **Joyce Kilmer Park** (*at 161st St*). Killed in action on the Western Front, Kilmer was a poet, journalist, and soldier, most famous today for that assault on literary good taste, "Trees" ("I think that I shall never see / A poem lovely as a tree"). Much flatter and more populous than Franz Sigel, Kilmer Park is perhaps notable only, and bizarrely, for a fountain honoring Heinrich Heine, a 19th century German Romantic who has little in common with Kilmer. A block north is the **Bronx Museum of the Arts** (*1040 Grand Concourse at 165th*).

If you're still not tired of the Bronx, hop on the ❽❹ at 167th and take it to Kingsbridge Road, where you'll find **Poe Park** and **Poe Cottage** (*2460 Grand Concourse*), the last home of Edgar Allan Poe. The cottage is open to the public on weekends, with group tours available during the week by appointment.

A few blocks south of Poe-ville is **Loew's Paradise Theater** (*2413 Grand Concourse*), now Utopia's Paradise Theater. Completed in 1929, the Paradise was one of the last 'Atmospheric' movie houses ever built, and remains, despite changes in ownership and renovations, a great example of the style.

SOUTH BRONX 359

WHOLESALE FOOD MARKETS

Stock markets may keep the city wealthy, but its food markets keep it healthy and well. Over the years, as space became tight, they moved north to Hunt's Point; the Fulton Fish Market, a downtown fixture, was the last to go, kicking and screaming, as the emergency crews at the World Trade Center Site demanded space to move their equipment. Buyers from restaurants and grocery stores swarm these markets before dawn breaks, and so can anyone with a healthy appetite and friends who don't mind splitting a crate of whatever they choose. Dealers at the **Terminal Produce Cooperative Market** offer good things like strawberries for little more than two dollars per pound, and raw peanuts for less than a dollar per pound. The **Fulton Fish Market** carries freshly caught delicacies like soft-shell crabs, red snapper, live scallops, and sushi-grade tuna. Less crunchy than it sounds, the **Hunt's Point Co-operative Market** sells only meat: its vendors stock suckling pigs, dry-aged prime beef, and trickier, gamier finds like mutton and goat. Every beautiful bit of food you've seen anywhere in New York came through Hunt's Point, and most of it is still in pristine condition. Come early, bring a handcart, and don't buy more than will fit your freezer.

Terminal Produce Cooperative Market: Halleck St (at Spofford Ave). 718-842-0143. Daily 10 p.m. to 3 p.m. Entry $3; parking $2. ❷ *to Prospect Ave;* ❻ *to Hunts Point Ave; 6bus to Spofford Ave.*

Fulton Fish Market: 800 Food Center Drive (near Halleck St). 718-378-2356. Daily 12am to 9am. ❷ *to Prospect;* ❻ *to Hunts Point, 6bus to Spofford Ave.*

Hunt's Point Cooperative Market: 355 Food Center Drive (near Farragut St). 718-842-7466. ❷ *to Prospect;* ❻ *to Hunts Point; 6bus to Spofford Ave.*

in an English muffin. Cutesy cocktails, a minimal wine list, and a rotating beer selection (usually including a Belgian import or two) make up the bar. A back room plays host to poetry slams, open-mike nights, and even the occasional live show.
1 Bruckner Blvd (near 3rd Ave) 718-665-2001. Sat-Thurs 11:30am-12am, Fri 11:30am-2am. ❻ *to 138th.*

CHEAP
Coals Pizzeria *Pizza*
This cozy pizza joint cum sports bar makes a non-traditional pizza to incredible effect. Instead of throwing them in the oven, the chef slaps each pizza onto a grill, yielding a flakey, thin, crunchy crust with a smoky taste like no other pizza in the city. In pies like the Pure Bliss, which combines fontinella, pecorino, and ricotta cheeses, tomato, and pesto, the toppings are creative and well balanced but neither overly exotic nor overwrought. You must end your meal with the Fluffernutter pizza, a thin buttery crust folded in half over Nutella and marzipan and sprinkled with powdered sugar.
1888 Eastchester Rd (at Morris Park). 718-823-7002. Mon-Thu 11:30am-10pm, Fri 11:30am-12am. Average entrée $10. ❹❺ *to Grand Concourse.*

SHOPPING

Casa Amadeo
Founded in 1927, the oldest Latin music store in New York has grown up to become a hub for cultural exchange in the South Bronx. Current owner Miguel Amadeo bought his first record in the store in 1947 before returning 22 years later to buy the whole shop. A musician himself, he promotes lesser known Latin musicians and local recording artists and stocks rare and hard to find albums. Today the store is frequented by notables like Ray Baretto, the famous conga player, and José Serrano, the Bronx congressman.
786 Prospect Ave (at Mary Place). 212-328-6896. Mon-Sat 11am-7pm. ❷❺ *to Prospect Ave.*

The Hub
Be wary of what others say—the Hub kind of sucks. There's a decent slice to be had at someone or other's "Famous Pizza," and the street ices are above average (Mmmm, mmmango), but vendors seem hell-bent on living up to their location's newly acquired epithet, "The Broadway of the Bronx," if by "Broadway" one means a shopping district dominated by big brand megastores and small time junk merchants. In addition to the recently opened Staples and Rite Aid, The Hub is home to retailers selling every imaginable variety of shoddily-made dreck: discount hats, discount shoes, discount belts, jeans, electronics, toys, and chachkas of every pointless size and shape. Supposedly, new hip-hop trends emerge here before spreading to the rest of the city, but good luck spotting them underneath all the clutter. Gentrification indeed.
The convergence of E 149th St, Willis Ave, Melrose Ave, and 3rd Ave. ❷ ❺ to Third Ave-149th St.

Mud/Bone Studio 889
This art gallery and theater aims to culturally revive Hunts Point, credited as the birthplace of hip hop, breakdancing, and salsa, by nurturing and supporting both urban artists of color and local neighborhood youth. The studio's print-making workshop gives artists free instruction, studio time, and exhibition space, theatrical performances employ only local artists, and exhibitions include artwork promoting positive social change.
889 Hunts Point Ave (at Garrison St). 718-620-2824. ❻ to Hunts Point Ave

NORTH BRONX ATTRACTIONS

Wave Hill
Wave Hill is a twenty-eight acre public garden and cultural center built along the Hudson River, with galleries, greenhouses, flower gardens, and woodlands. The space affords a serene oasis for quiet contemplation, reading, and enjoying art and nature. Free tours of the grounds by guides well versed in plant life and history are available, and special events include art and writing workshops, music, and cooking demonstrations. Secluded spots among the flowers or nestled in the hills, where the sounds of the city are absent, abound. The art gallery, housed in a 1927 Georgian Revival mansion exhibits contemporary art inspired by nature; past exhibits have included visual renderings of the works of Emily Dickinson and Henry David Thoreau. The next time you want a respite from crowds, congestion, and concrete, you need not leave the city to revel in greens, blues, purple stars, and yellow buds, just head to the Bronx.
675 W 252nd St (at Independence Ave) 714-549-3200. Tues-Sun 9am-5:30 pm. Free Tuesdays Nov-Apr, July and Aug, free Sat 9am-12pm, $6 adults, $3 students (free for Columbia students). ❶ to 242nd, Metro North to Riverdale. Free shuttle service to and from Metro-North Riverdale and ❶ at 242nd St.

Van Cortlandt House Museum
Located near the southern tip of Van Cortlandt Park, this museum is the perfect place to brush up on colonial history and catch your breath after strolling through the surrounding 1,146 acre park. Constructed around 1748, it served as headquarters for both George Washington and Sir William Howe during the Revolutionary War and is now the oldest surviving building in the Bronx. A stroll through the wood-paneled interior brings visitors past relics of the Van Cortlandt family: sleek china plates, wafer irons, pine dollhouses, ornate mantelpieces and the mysterious unfinished chamber on the third floor. Make sure to visit the herb garden showcasing intricate coils of sage and lavender, and the not-so-typical museum shop which stocks J.R. Liggett's shampoo soap and table top tenpins.
Broadway at W 246th St. 718-543-3344. Tues-Fri 10am-3pm, Sat-Sun 11am-4pm. ❶ to 242 St-Van Cortlandt Park

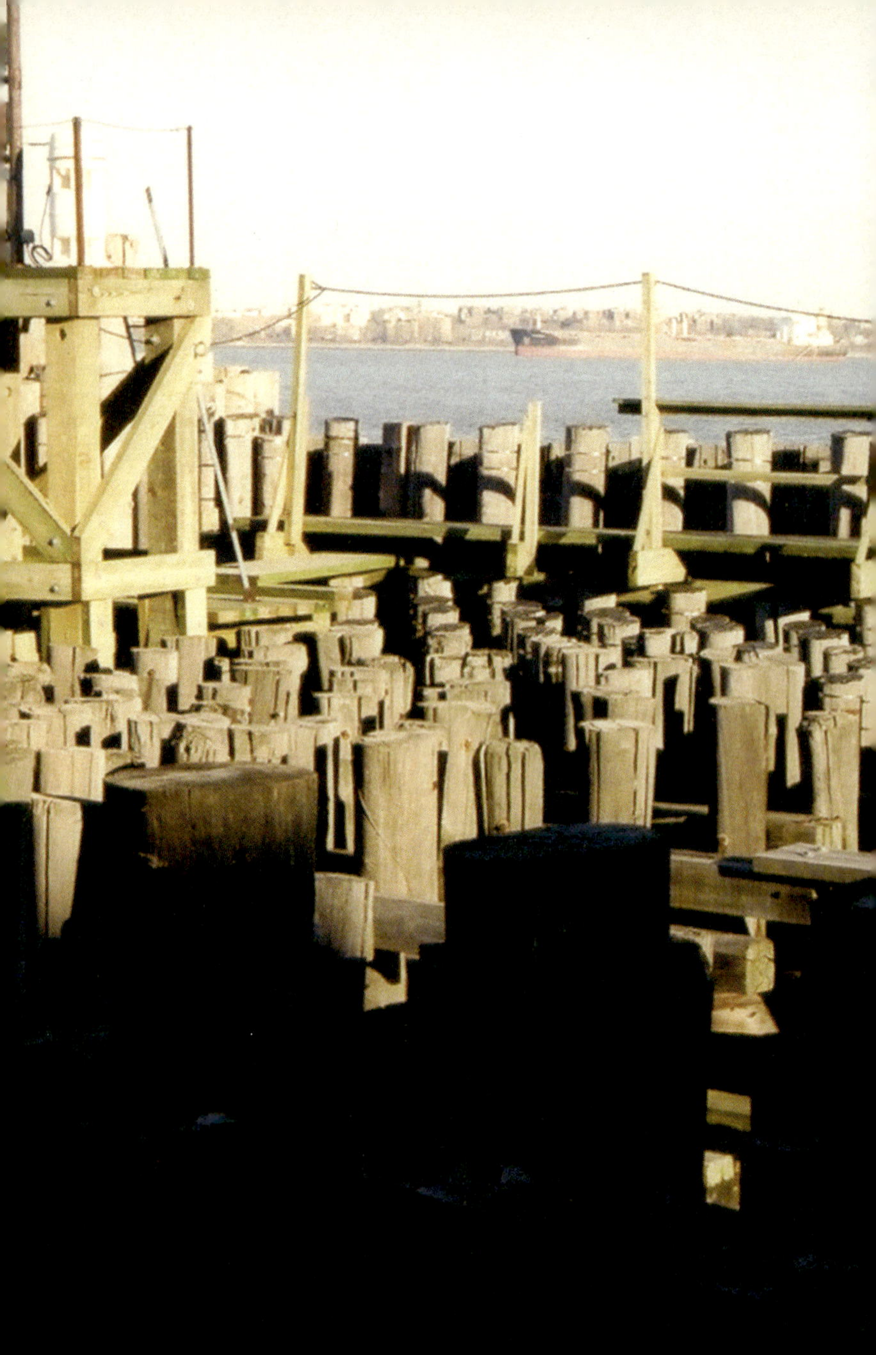

STATEN ISLAND

Although Henry Hudson gave Staaten Eylandt its original English name in 1609, the island remained largely isolated until 1713, when the now famous Staten Island ferry first started transporting passengers from Manhattan.

Officially incorporated into New York City in 1898, Staten Island is by far the least populous and most suburban of the boroughs. The island is now connected to Brooklyn via the Verrazano-Narrows Bridge, but it remains one of the greenest areas of the city, home to a large number of parks in addition to several large and well-preserved historic sites.

Although inhabitants of Staten Island sometimes call it "the forgotten borough" because of its relative lack of city council representatives, it is the dwelling place of some of the best Italian food in the city and the home of many fiercely independent New Yorkers (so independent, in fact, that there have been multiple attempts to secede from the rest of the city). The North Shore section of Staten Island, where both the Manhattan ferry and the Staten Island Museum are located, has consistently been the most urban part of the island. For most of the 20th century, the western edge of Staten Island was home to the largest landfill in the world, Fresh Kills, and although it was closed in 2002 many Manhattanites still think of the relatively undeveloped Staten Island skyline as part of a foreign land.

Luckily for all, many of the well-established and deeply loyal families here are happy to live spaciously suburban lives within the limits of what is a generally frenetic and crowded city. While their neighbors to the north and east deal with the high real estate prices and limited space, islanders kick back and enjoy a little breathing room.

364 STATEN ISLAND

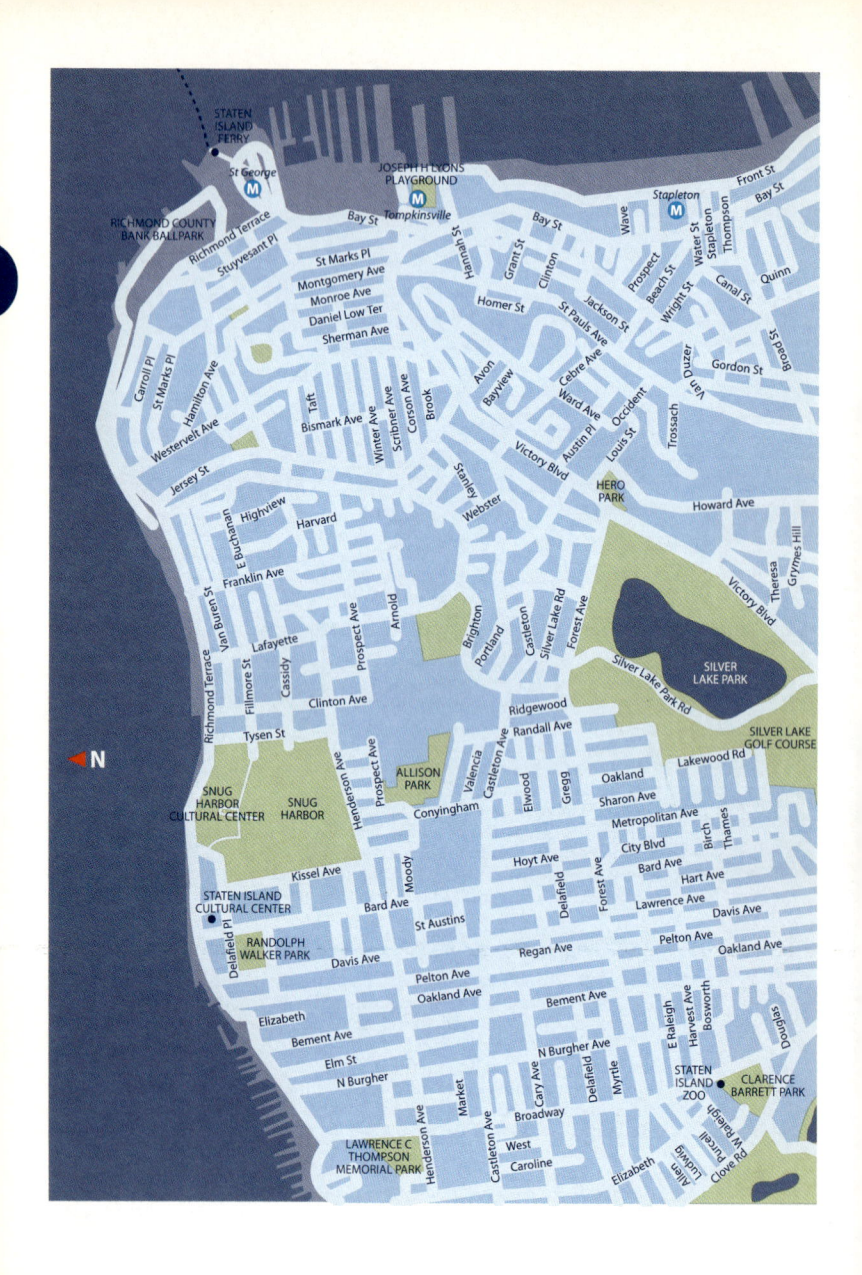

ATTRACTIONS

Historic Richmond Town
Located near the geographical center of the island, this was formerly the commercial center of an 18th century town. The historic town includes the one-time courthouse of Richmond County as well as 26 other commercial, governmental, farm, and residential buildings. The museum's village section occupies 25 acres (out of the 100 acre total) and boasts 15 restored edifices, many of which date back to the Dutch, English, and French Island residents of the 18th century. A visit to this historic town gives sightseers a chance to realistically and personally experience the domestic, commercial, and civic activities that supported many families over 300 years ago.
441 Clarke Ave (by Cedarview Ave). 718-351-1611. Sept-Jun Wed-Sun 1pm-5pm, July-Aug Wed-Fri 11am-5pm. Admission $3-$5.

St. George Theatre
Built in 1929, the newly restored not-for-profit St. George Theatre is a 2,800 seat venue and the home of a wide variety of national tours, musical concerts, dance performances, comedy shows, and children's productions. Centered in the historic St. George District close to the Staten Island Ferry, the beautifully ornate architecture is itself worth a visit. Some of the theatre's most unique features include a huge antique Wurlitzer organ, one of the largest cantilevered balconies ever built, velvet seats, gilded balconies, and grand staircases. The main architect was Eugene DeRosa, who is responsible for a number of classical buildings such as the Liberty and Victory theatres and the Ritz.
35 Hyatt St (at Central Ave). 718-442-2900. Box Office: Mon-Thur 9:30am-2:00pm, Sun 11:00am-2:00pm.

Staten Island Botanical Garden
Although this botanical garden was started with nothing more than some meager financial assistance from the nearby Staten Island Museum, the institution and its flowers have blossomed beautifully since it opened its doors to the public in 1977. Located close to the Staten Island Ferry terminal, this garden has evolved from a predominantly English-perennial planting ground to the home of Chinese scholars' gardens, a "secret garden", and other well-manicured varieties of flora. Because of its comparatively suburban location, this Botanical Garden has enjoyed the space needed to be a truly beautiful getaway.
1000 Richmond Terrace (across from Snug Harbor Rd) 718-273-8200. Dawn to dusk.

Staten Island Ferry
This ferry runs 24 hours a days, 7 days a week, is always free and provides the 75,000 passengers who use the ferry's services each day with a gorgeous view of the downtown Manhattan skyline, the Statue of liberty, and sections of Brooklyn. Both the ❶ and the Ⓝ Ⓡ Ⓦ subway lines have stops that let passengers off directly

in front of the ferry and, because of the ferry's size, no one has to fight for a seat. The ferry's 4-balconied sections provide excellent water-gazing space. Without taking a cumbersome drive, the 5 mile boat ride is the only way to get to Staten Island and well worth it, even if only for a day trip.
White Hall St. in Manhattan, 1 Bay St. in Staten Island. Staten Island Railway to St. George.

Staten Island Zoo
The smallest of New York area zoos, the Staten Island Zoo nonetheless features an internationally acclaimed reptile collection and several other exhibits which make it well-worth a visit. The zoo houses a tropical forest exhibit, an aquarium, and an African Savannah exhibit that feeatures a number of exotic animals native to the vast grasslands of central and southern Africa. If leopards, mandrills, lizards, and antelope don't peak your interest, the zoo's recent addition of a farm-themed Children's Center (complete with farm animals and educational programs) and an otter exhibit give the zoo something to interest everyone.
614 Broadway (between Clove Rd and Forest Ave). 718-442-3100. Daily 10am-4:45pm. Admission: $4-7.

CULTURE & ARTS

Jacques Marchais Museum of Tibetan Art
Opened upon the death of the mysterious American art lover Jacques Marchais in 1948, this museum is the holding place of a huge private Tibetan art collection. Home to an impressive array of sculpture, artistic relics, books, educational materials, and a gallery which hosts rotating special exhibits, this museum also hosts events such as poetry readings, guided meditations, Buddhist lectures, and Tibetan festivals.
338 Lighthouse Ave (close to St. George Rd). 718-987-3500. Wed-Sun 1pm-5pm. Adults $5, students $3.

Staten Island Museum
Founded in 1881 by four Staten Island residents concerned with the effects of rapid New York urbanization, the Staten Island Museum's official mission is to preserve, collect, and exhibit significant historical objects. Located a mere two blocks from the Staten Island ferry, the museum is now home to over a million natural science specimens, art pieces, historical objects, archival documents, photographs, and books. The founders' environmental activism has led to an especially interesting Hall of Natural Sciences and an impressive collection of relics of the Lenape, Native Americans who originally inhabited all of Staten Island.
75 Stuyvesant Pl (at Wall St). 718-727-1135. Mon-Fri 12pm-5pm, Sat 10am-5pm, Sun 12pm-5pm.

DINING

UPSCALE
Aesop's Tables *New American*
A rare and somewhat hard-to-find gem on Staten Island, this tiny Mediterranean and

New American bistro serves a sophisticated array of food. The beautiful garden in the back is a romantic place to eat either lunch or dinner. In spite of the fact that the restaurant is a bit off the beaten path the menu is ambitious, the staff is unendingly attentive, and the food is quite delicious—this a lovely spot for a long and quiet summer meal. Space is limited so make reservations ahead of time.

1233 Bay St (between Highland & Maryland Ave). 718-720-2005. Tues-Sat 5:30pm-10:30pm, Sun 10:30am-8pm. Average entrée $24.

Lake Club *American*
Located in the heart of Clove Lakes Park, the Lake Club is the oldest and possible the most romantic restaurant in Staten Island. Diners can sit fireside in the quaint stone cottage dining room or toss back some drinks at the patio bar, which overlooks a beautifully landscaped lake. Although the recent arrival of a new head chef and the addition of Italian cuisine to the menu has led some to doubt the continued excellence of the restaurant's cuisine, the Lake Club is undoubtedly a great place for a few drinks or a first date.

1150 Clove Rd (at Victory Blvd). 718-442-3600. Mon-Thurs 12pm-9pm, Fri 12pm-10pm, Sat 5pm-11pm, Sun 11am-2pm. Average entrée $20.

MID-RANGE

Trattoria Romana *Italian*
Opened in 1994 by two Italians dedicated to maintaining a traditional family-oriented Italian restaurant, today, Trattoria combines Northern and Southern Italian cooking to offer up a menu as extensive as it is delicious. What makes Trattoria Romana unique is the special one-on-one treatment their customers have come to expect from the management and staff.

1476 Hylan Blvd (between Benton Ave and Cooper Ave). 718-980-3113. Mon-Sun 12pm-10pm. Average entrée $18.

CHEAP

Denino's Pizzeria *Italian*
Denino's serves great pizza, perhaps the best, at a good price, and the service is always friendly. Although parking in the crowded Denino's lot can be a bit annoying and a Denino's pie has a slightly chewier crust than brick-oven places in other boroughs, Denino's pizza still has a famous crunch and it's topped off with a delicious homemade tomato sauce. The service is generally fast despite the constant crowds.

524 Port Richmond Ave (at Hooker St) 718-442-9401. Mon-Thu 11:30am-11pm, Sat-Sun 11:30am-midnight. Average entrée $10. Cash only.

DAY TO DAY

Community Board 1. *1 Edgewater Plaza, Room 217. 718-981-6900.*

Blog: *SILive.com*

Gym: *YMCA. 651 Broadway. 718-981-4933.*

Groceries: *AA Food Market. 62 Richmond Ter. 718-816-6733.*

Hotels: *Hotel Richmond. 71 Central Ave. 718-447-8445. Victory Hotel. 535 N Gannon Ave. 718-447-8445.*

Dog Runs: *Silver Lake Park. 700 Victory Blvd. Wolfe's Pond Park Dog Run. End of Huguenot Ave & Chester Ave.*

Movie Theater: *United Artists Theatre Inc. 2474 Forest Ave. 718-273-4200.*

SHOPPING

Everything Goes
This tiny thrift and vintage store is easy to miss; it's located inside of a small, mid-20th century home set back from the street. But once you've entered you will find a surprisingly large collection of 50s, 60s, 70s, and 80s clothing. The store is meticulously organized by style of clothing as well as by color, so it's always easy to locate whatever you are you looking for. The staff is exceptionally friendly, and the five showrooms contain a wide variety of casual, formal, and vintage clothing appropriate for men, women, and children. If you venture down to the basement you will find an impressive collection of theatrical costume wear.

140 Bay St (at Central Ave). 718-273-7139. Tues-Sat 10:30am-6:30pm.

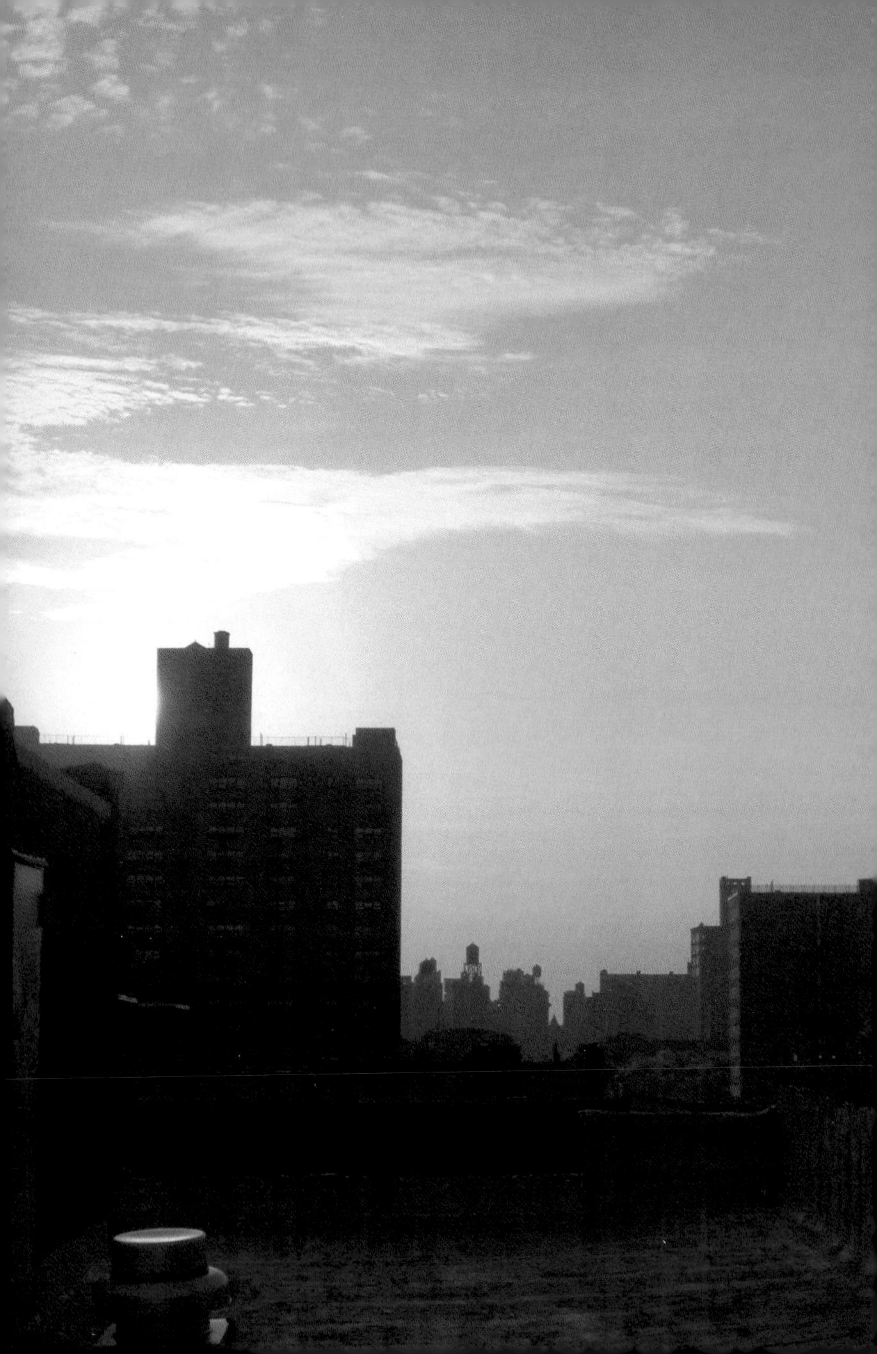

INDEX

#

202	162
1020	238
/eks/	295
107 West	279
15 East	171
205 Club	123
2nd Avenue Deli	175
3R Living	326
4th Street Food Co-op	143
5 Burro Cafe	346
5 Star Banquet	332
5Pointz	330
68 Jay Street Bar	303
68 Restaurant	286
6th & B Community Garden	134
7A Farmer's Market	142
7th Regiment Armory	207
809 Sangria Bar/Grill	280

A

A Café/Wine Room	233
A Salt & Battery	150
ABC No Rio	121
Adrienne's Pizza Bar	96
Aesop's Tables	366
Agent Provocateur	106
AJ Pizza	344
Alfanoose	96
Alice's Tea Cup	211
Almondine	303
Alouette	233
Alter	288
American Playground	285
Amy Ruth's	264
Angel Share	139
Angelika	146
Anna Maria	295
Antarctica	104
Antica Venezia	147
Antique District	357
Apollo Theatre	263
Aquagrill	101
Arepa Lady	351
Arlo And Esme	140
Armacord Fashion	298
Art Gallery Hopping	165
Artez'n	316
Arthur Avenue	358
Artichoke Basille's	138
Artisanal	182
Asia de Cuba	172

Asia Society	207
Asian American Arts Centre	111
Astoria Park	330
Astroturf	317
AtmosNY	267
Auction House	213

B

B.B. Kings	194
Baci and Abbracci	293
Bagatelle	147
Baked	316
BAM	309
Bann Thai	343
Bao Noodles	173
Bar 13 - Snapshot	142
Bar Boulud	219
Barcibo	224
Barge Park	285
BargeMusic	302
Barometer	111
Battery Park	91
Beacon's Closet	298
Beer Bar	184
Beer Table	325
Beet	324
Belgian Fries	138
Bereket	122
B-Flat	104
Biddy's	213
Big Nick's	223
Billiard Company	346
Billie's Black	264
Billy Martin's	214
Billy's Bakery	164
Bin 220	96
Black & White Project Space	286
Blind Tiger	151
BLT Burger	148
Blue Note	151
Bluestockings	123
Bonbon Chicken	104
Bond Street Gallery	315
Book Culture	239
Bookoff	185
Bourbon Street	224
Bowery Hotel	134
Bowery Poetry Club	135
Bowling Green	91
Bowlmor	151
Box	124
Brasserie	182

Bread & Olive	193
BRICstudio	309
Bridge Café	95
Bronx Culture Trolley	357
Bronx Museum	358
Bronx Zoo	357
Brooklyn Borough Hall	302
Brooklyn Botanic Gardens	321
Brooklyn Brewery	285
Brooklyn Bridge	91
Brooklyn Bridge Park	302
Brooklyn Collective Artisan Gallery	315
Brooklyn Conservatory of Music	322
Brooklyn Flea	310
Brooklyn Heights Promenade	302
Brooklyn Label	287
Brooklyn Lyceum	322
Brooklyn Museum	321
Brooklyn Superhero Supply	327
Brooklyn Waterfront Artist's Coalition	315
Bruckner Bar & Grill	359
Bryant Park	180
Bubble Lounge	105
Buddakan	161
Buffalo Exchange	298
Built by Wendy	106
Burger Joint	193
Burp Castle	140
Buttermilk Bar	325

C

Café Boulud	210
Cafe Grumpy	287
Cafe Katja	114
Cafe Pick Me Up	138
Cafe Steinhof	323
Camaradas El Barrio	271
Camille's	234
Campo	234
Canela	335
Canvas Paper & Stone Gallery	263
Canyon of Heroes	91
Carl Schurz Park	207
Carnegie Hall	181
Caroline's on Broadway	194

Carroll Park	314
Casa Amadeo	360
Casa Latina Music Shop	275
Casellula Cheese & Wine	192
Cassinelli Food Products	336
Cattyshack	325
Celeste	221
Central Library	321
Centro Vinoteca	147
Century 21	97
Charleston	296
Chatham Square	110
Cheese of the World	346
Chelsea Art Museum	161
Chelsea Piers	160
China Grill	190
Chinatown Brasserie	148
Chip Shop	324
Chola	183
Circa Tabac	105
City Center	181
City Hall	91
City Opera Thrift	177
City Reliquary Museum	293
Cloisters	278
Coals	360
Cobble Hill Park	314
Cog and Pearl	327
Columbia Cottage	236
Columbus Park	110
Comix	165
Commodore Barry Park	309
Commune	298
Community Food & Juice	234
Conservatory Gardens	271
Cooper Hewitt Design Museum	207
Copper Door Tavern	176
Court Street Bagels	316
Creek	335
Creole	274
Crepe Mania	175
Curry Row	140

D

Daily 2.3.5	106
Dakota	218
Dalaga	288

INSIDE NEW YORK 369

Dance Studio of Park Slope	322	**F**		Gotta Get a Bagel	345	India Sari Palace	353
Daniel	210			Graffiti Hall of Fame	271	Indo Munch	175
Dark Room	124	Family Jewels	167	Gramercy Park	170	Irish Repertory Theatre	161
David Owen's	126	Fanny	294	Grand Army Plaza Greenmarket	321	Island Lake Club	367
DB Bistro Moderne	191	Fascati	303	Grand Central	180	Island Spice Kitchen	275
Dead Poet	224	Fashion Institute	161	Grand Concourse	359	Islero	183
Death and Co.	140	Federal Hall National Memorial	92	Grand Sichuan	112	Izayaka Ten	163
Den	266	Federal Reserve Bank	92	Grant's Tomb	232		
Denino's	367	Felice Wine Bar	211	Green Apple Café	310	**J**	
Dessert Truck	150	Fiamma	102	Greenberg's	213		
Devi	172	Fig and Olive	211	Grotto	122	Jacque Marchais Museum of Tibetan Art	366
Di Palo	116	Film Forum	146	Guggenheim	209	Jacques Torres	303
Ding Dong Lounge	238	Firehouse	221	Gusto	149	Jake Walk	316
Dinosaur BBQ	280	Flatiron Building	170			Jake's Dilemma	224
Do Kham	106	Flushing Mall Food Court	345	**H**		Japonais	172
Donut Plant	126	Flushing Town Hall	342			Java Girl, Inc.	213
Dorrian's	214	Foley Square	92	Hacienda de Argentina	211	Jazz Standard	176
Doughboy Park	351	Forbes Magazine Gallery	135	Halal Chicken & Gyro	194	Jen Bekman Gallery	121
Dove Parlor	152	Forest Hills Gardens	341	Half Pint	152	Jeremy's Ale House	97
Doyer's Vietnamese	112	Fort Greene Park	309	Harlem Lanes	267	Jewish Museum	209
Dressler	293	Fort Tryon Park	278	Harlem School of the Arts	263	Jill's	315
Duane Park Cafe	102	Freebird Books and Goods	317	Harlem's Heaven Hat Boutique	267	Jim Henly's Universe	167
DUMBO Arts Center	303	French Institute	208	Harry's at Water Taxi Beach	336	Jimmys Corner	195
DUMBO Arts Festival	303	French Sole	215	Hasidic Williamsburg	295	Jing Fong	113
Duplex Piano Bar & Cabaret	152	Fresh Juice Strong Coffee	139	Heights	238	Joe's Pub	140
Dylan's Candy Bar	215	Frick Collection	208	Herald Square	189	Joe's Shanghai	345
		Frisby Fried Chicken	352	Hideout	310	Joyce Theater	161
E		Fulton Ferry Park	303	Highline Ballroom	165	Juice Generation	223
				Hill Country	163	Juilliard School	189
Eagle Theater	351	**G**		Hispanic Society of America	278	Jules Bistro	149
East River Park	120			Historical Richmond Town	365	Julia de Burgos Latino Cultural Center	271
Eastern Noodles	112	Gala Manor	343	Holland Bar	195	Junk	299
Eat-pisode	121	Gantry State Plaza Park	330	Home Sweet Home	114	Justo Fonda Botanica	275
Eddie's Sweet Shop	344	Gate	325	House of Cards and Curiosities	154		
Eden and Opera	195	Geminola	154	Housing	215	**K**	
Effy's Cafe	213	General Theological Seminary	160	Hub	361		
Eighty One	220	Giant Robot New York	135	Hudson River Café	279	K&M	296
El Barrio Juice	274	Gingerman	176	Hungarian Pastry Shop	236	Katra	115
El Castillo de Jagua	123	Ginger's	326	Huron St and Java St Waterfront	285	Katz' Delicatessen	122
El Cocotero	163	Giorgione 307	102			Kellari Taverna	191
El Presidente	280	Girls Love Shoes	127	**I**		Kenka	139
Ellis Island	91	GlassLands	293			Kew Gardens Cinema	343
Empanada Mama	192	Go!Go! Curry	193	iCi	310	Kiku	323
Empire State Building	170	Goethe-Institut	208	Iggy's	214	Kill Devil Hill	288
En Shocu Bar	152	Good	148	Il Bambino	334	Kitchen Row	116
Enchantments, Inc.	143	Good World	114			Kittichai	102
Epistrophy	124	Gotham Bikes	106			Knife and Fork	136
Epistrophy	124					Kobe Club	191
Essex Street Market	126					Koreatown	173
Everything Goes	367					Koronet	236
Exquisite Costume	116					Kyotofu	192

L

L&L Hawaiian BBQ	96
L.A. Burrito	295
La Espiguita	334
La Fonda Boricua	274
La Guli	335
La Luncheonette	163
La Mama La Galleria	135
La Marqueta	271
La Negrita	238
La Vuelta	332
Landmarc	103
Lassen and Hennigs	303
Le Royale	153
L'Ecole	103
LeNell's	317
Levee	296
Lima's Taste	149
Lincoln Center Box	219
Lit Lounge	141
Little Giant	122
Little India	352
Little Owl	149
Little Piggy	310
Little Senegal	264
Loom	327
Loveday 31	336
Luckys Famous	194
Luzia's	222

M

Madaleine Mae	222
Madison Square Garden	189
Madison Square Park	171
Maggie Brown	310
Magic Castle	347
Make My Cake	264
Malcolm Shabazz Harlem Market	267
Malcolm X Memorial	279
Manhattan Bridge	110
Manhattan Theatre Club	189
Manna's	266
Mansion	165
Marcus Garvey Park	262
Maria's Mexican Bistro	324
Marie Belle	107
Mariposa	97
Market Table	150
Marquee	166
Marz Bar	141
Mason Dixon	124
Master Bike	224
Matilda	136
Max	139
Max Soha	237
Maxilla and Mandible	225
MCC	147
McCarren Park	285
Me Bar	195
Mercadito	136
Mercat	122
Met Martini Bar	214
Metrazur	183
Metropolitan	296
Metropolitan Museum of Art	209
Metropolitan Pool & Fitness Center	285
Midtown Comics	197
Miguel Abreu	111
Milk and Honey	124
Miller Theater	233
Minamoto Kitchoan	197
Miranda	294
Miss Mamie's	234
Miss Maude's	264
MoBay	264
Moe's	310
MoMA	181
Mombar	332
Momofuku Noodle Bar	137
Monsignor McGolrick Park	285
Morningside Park	232
Moscow on the Hudson	281
MSKCC	215
Mud/Bone Studio 889	361
Mudspot	139
Muji	116
Mural Art	271
Museo del Barrio	271
Museum of Contemporary African Art	309
Museum of Natural History	218
Museum of Sex	171
Museum of the American Indian	94
Museum of the City of NY	271
Music Hall of Williamsburg	296

N

Naidre's	325
Nanoosh	223
NASDAQ MarketSite	189
National Arts Club	171
National Black Theatre	263
Neue Gallery	209
New Beef King	116
New Calvary Cemetary	351
New Dramatists	190
New Museum	121
New York Hall of Science	341
New York Table Tennis Club	341
New York Theatre Workshop	135
Nice Green Bo	111
Nicholas Roerich Museum	233
Noguchi Museum	331
Nonna	222
Norma's	192
Novita	173
Nurse Bettie	125
NuYorican	141
NY Botanical Garden	357
NY Historical Society	218
NY Mosque	271
NY Public Library	180
NY State Pavillion	341
NYC Fire Museum	101

O

O'Connell's	238
Oklahoma Smoke BBQ	264
Omonia Cafe	332
Opening Ceremony	107
Oriental Garden	111
Oro	115
Ouest	220

P

Paley Center for Media	182
Paloma	286
Panino Sportivo	237
Paris Sandwich Corp.	113
Park Slope Flea Market	327
Partners & Crime Mystery Booksellers	154
Patriot Saloon	105
Payard Patisserie	210
Peanut Butter & Co	150
Pearl Paint	117
Penang	223
Pencil Factory	287
Penelope	174
Penny Licks	295
Peri Ela	212
Permanent Records	289
Persimmon	137
Peter Luger Steakhouse	294
Pete's Candy Store	297
Piano's	125
Picholine	220
Pickle Guys	127
Pierogi 2000	293
Pig Heaven	212
Pink Teacup	150
Pinky Otto	107
Pippin Vintage Jewelry	167
Pisticci	235
Pixie Market	127
PJ Hanley's	316
Planet Rose	142
Playwrights Horizons	190
Pop Burger	153
Porto Rico Importing Company	155
Pratt Galleries	147
Probus	281
Project #8	117
Prospect Park	321
Prospect Park Zoo	321
Prosperity Dumpling	113
PS 1	331
Public Theater	135

Q

Queen of Sheba	192
Queens Botanical Gardens	341
Queens Museum of Art	343
Queens Zoo	342
Quercy	315

R

Rack and Soul	235

Radegast Hall & Biergarten	297	Silver Moon	237	Contemporary Art	101	Urban Rustic	287
Radio City Music Hall	190	Sip	239	Symphony Space	218	Urban Spring	310
Rajbhog Sweets	352	Skinny Bar	125	Symposium	236		
Randolph at Broome	115	Slate Gallery	286			**V**	
Rapture Lounge	336	Sly Fox	142	**T**			
Rare View	176	Smalls	153			Van Cortlandt House Museum	361
reBar	303	Smoke	239	Taco Mix	275	Village Vanguard	147
Rebel	166	Snafu	184	Tai Pan Bakery	346	Vintage Thrift Shop	177
Red Hook Park	315	Socialista	154	Tai Thai	138	Vol de Nuit	154
Redbag	197	Socrates Sculpture Park	332	Taim	151	Volstead	185
Relish	294	SOH	281	Taipan Bakery	117		
Reminiscence Inc.	177	Sokhna	266	Taj	166	**W**	
Republic	176	South Paw	326	Taqueria y Fonda la Mexicana	237		
Revival	264	South Street Seaport	93	Tazza	303	Wallse	148
Rice Avenue	352	Spoonbill/Sugartown Bookstore	299	Tea and Sympathy	155	Walter Reade Theater	219
Rice to Riches	104	Sports Museum of America	94	Tea Box Cafe	184	Washington Square Park	146
Rink Bar	184	St. Anns Warehouse	303	Tebaya	164	Waterstone Grill	95
River Room	280	St. George Theatre	365	Temple Emanu-El	207	Wave Hill	361
Riverbank State Park	279	St. John the Divine	232	Ten Ren Tea and Ginseng Co.	117	Welcome to the Johnson's	126
Riverside Church	233	St. Mark's Bookshop	143	Terminal 5	196	Whitney Museum	209
Riverside Park	233	St. Mark's Comics	143	Theater New City	136	Whole Foods Beer	127
Rockefeller Skating	189	St. Mark's Place	138	Thing	289	Wholesale Food Markets	360
Rocketship Comics	317	St. Nick's Pub	281	Thom Bar	105	Wild Ginger	111
Rodeo Bar and Grill	183	St. Patrick's Cathedral	181	Tiny's Giant Sandwich Shop	123	Wildwood	175
Roger's Time Machine	155	St. Patrick's Old Cathedral	101	Titan Foods	336	Williamsburg Bridge	120
Rosa Mexicano	174	St. Paul's	93	Toast	236	Willie's Dawgs	325
Rose Water	322	St. Paul's Episcopal Church	314	Tocqueville	172	Woodward Gallery	121
Roti Roll	237	Stanton Public	126	Tom and Jerry's	142	Wooster Projects	101
Rouge	153	Staten Island Botanical Garden	365	Tompkins Square Park	134	Word	289
Rowf	303	Staten Island Ferry	365	Tonic East	177	WTC Site	94
Rubin Museum of Art	161	Staten Island Museum	366	Toy Qube	347		
Ruby et Violette	197	Staten Island Zoo	366	Trapeze School of NY	160	**Y**	
Rucker Park	262	Statue of Liberty	93	Tratoria Romana	367		
Rudy's Bar & Grill	195	Steven Alan Outpost	225	Treats Truck	184	Yarntopia	239
Russian Vodka Room	196	Stone Park Cafe	323	Trestle on Tenth	162	Yeah Shanghai	112
		Storefront for Art and Architecture	101	Tribeca Tavern	106	Yogi's	224
S		Strand	155	Tribeca Treats	104		
		Strip House	148	Trie Cafe	280	**Z**	
S.O.B.'s	153	Studio B	287	Trinity Church	93		
Saigon Bahn Mi	112	Studio Museum of Harlem	263	Turks and Frogs	103	Zabar's	225
Sammy's Halal	353	Sugar Sweet Sunshine	123	Turtle Bay Lounge	185	Zaytoons	310
Santos' Party House	105	Super Tacos	223			Zebulon	298
Sara Roosevelt Park	120	Super Taste	114	**U**		Zenon Taverna	332
Saravanaas	175	SVA Museum	171			Zoe	303
Savarona	210	Sweet Paradise	115	UCB	167	Zoe's Beauty Products	289
Schomburg Center	262	Sweet Ups	297	Ugly Luggage	299	Zucker's	104
Sculpture Center	331	Swindler Cove Park	279	Unidentified Flying Chicken	353		
Sea Grill	191	Swiss Institue of		Union Hall	326		
Sel et Poivre	212			Union Square	137		
Sentosa	344			Unisphere	342		
Sequoia	95			United Nations	181		
Session 73	214						
Settepani Bakery	266						
Sido	223						

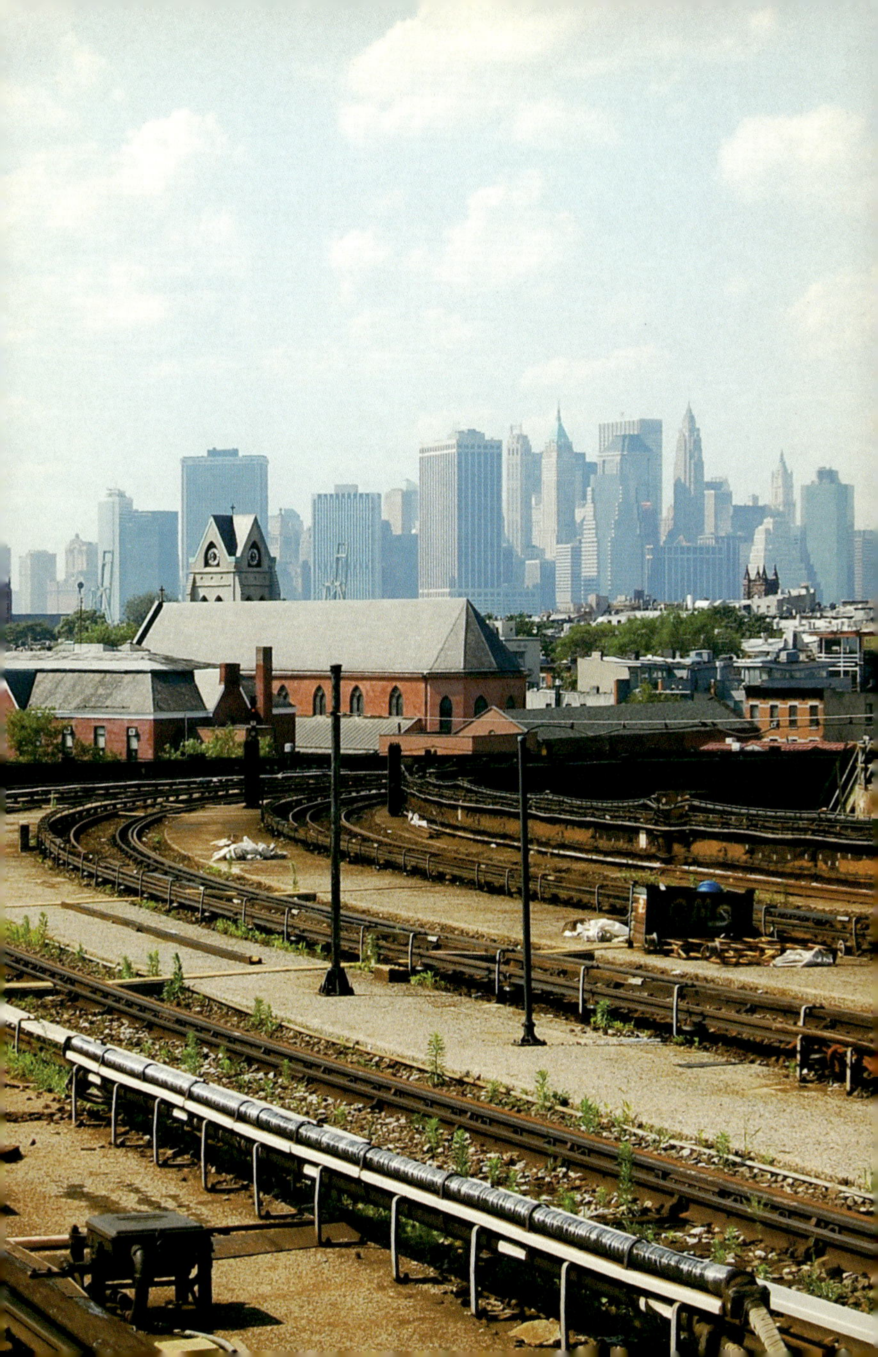

NOTES

NOTES

NOTES

HERE ARE ENSHRINED
THE LONGING OF GREAT HEARTS AND
NOBLE THINGS
THAT TOWER ABOVE
THE TIDE THE MAGIC
WORD THAT
WINGED WONDER STARTS THE GARNERED
WISDOM THAT HAS NEVER DIED

COLORSWIRL.COM
SHUTTERSWIRL.COM

JED DORE

IS FOR CHAPEAU CLASSIC CHAPLIN
FRAGRANCE FOR MEN

Jacob & Wilhelm Grimm's fairy tales

Jed Dore

An artist with a preference for illustration, a skilled photographer who loves to draw, and an experienced musician who pursued becoming a writer. These unique interests crafted Jed into an effective communicator with a sophisticated visual style driven by his diverse background and pursuit of knowledge. Much of his inspiration is pulled through personal experience, extensive research and a well-worn library card. A seasoned traveler, he has lived in the Pacific islands, amongst the Redwoods of Northern California and currently resides in Brooklyn, where he works as a freelance artist and designer. A recipient of numerous Merit and Scholarship awards, he graduated from Pratt Institute with a B.F.A. in Illustration. His work has been shown in Norman Schaffler Gallery, Tritón Museum of Art, Hammerstein Ballroom- Pratt Best of Senior Show, The Society of Illustrators Museum "Prevailing Human Spirit" A Memorial Exhibition.

DESIGN IMPACT

INSIDE NEW YORK 377

WEAR YOUR MUSIC

The Guitar String Bracelet Charity Project

Authentic Guitar String Bracelets custom crafted from strings donated by over 100 of the world's best guitarists.

Artists include Les Paul, John Mayer, Jack Johnson, Ben Harper, Peter Frampton and many more! 100% of profits are donated to charities of the artists' choice.

Or, get a funky fashion, one-size-fits-all guitar string bracelet. Available in 7 vibrant colors for only $9.99! A portion of all profits benefit MusiCares.

www.wearyourmusic.org

ARCHITECTS, ENGINEERS & BUSINESS FREINDS WORKING FOR THE FUTURE OF COLUMBIA

Best of Luck!

OMEGA
ENVIRONMENTAL
SERVICES, INC.

Gary J. Mellor, CIH

280 Huyler St. South
Hackensack, NJ 07606
Tel: (201) 489-8700 • Fax: (201) 342-5412
e-mail: mellorg@omega-environmental.net

GOOD LUCK
COLUMBIA LIONS

COSTAS KONDYLIS AND **PARTNERS**

AND

KONDYLIS DESIGN

31 West 27th Street, New York, NY 10001 Telephone 212 725 4655 Facsimile 212 725 3441

Galil Moving & Storage, Inc.

- MOVING
- STORAGE
- SHREDDING
- DISTRIBUTION
- DEBRIS REMOVAL

Corporate Headquarters:
111 Linnet Street
Bayonne, NJ 07002

Local Office:
103 East 125th Street
New York, NY 10035

Tel. (800) 464-6683
Fax: (201) 823-4988
www.galil.com
e-mail: info@galil.com

TEL. (212) 989-9293
FAX (212) 675-1782

M & J MECHANICAL CORP.

JEFFREY M. WEISS   Suite 416   1123 BROADWAY
                    NEW YORK, N.Y. 10010

PSEC

Plumbing & Heating Corp.
622-24 W 125th St.
New York, NY 10027

24 Hr Service
TEL: (212) 316-6406
FAX: (212) 316-0013
CELL: (914) 906-6254

PETE SKYLLAS

---

(718) 805-0554   Licensed Plumber # 412
(718) 441-5518 Fax

Total Service Ltd.
Plumbing, Heating & Cooling Contractors

Thomas Maniuszko   116-04 Atlantic Avenue
President   Richmond Hill, NY 11419

---

(212) 941-1120   Fax (212) 343-9928

Florin Painting, Inc.

JOE ALTUS

74 VARICK STREET
NEW YORK, N.Y.
10013

INSIDE NEW YORK 379

CONTRACTORS BUILDING FOR THE FUTURE OF COLUMBIA

FAX (718) 937-8418   PHONE (718) 784-1300

POWER COOLING, INC.
HEATING, COOLING, & VENTILATION SPECIALISTS

LAUREN LARSEN   43-43 VERNON BOULEVARD
PRESIDENT   LONG ISLAND CITY, NY 11101

JR Construction Corp.

Ramon Mayo

1727 Newman Ct.   Office (516) 486-3725
East Meadow, NY 11554   Cell. (917) 440-8380

DEGMOR, INC.

511 Canal Street, 3rd Floor, New York, NY 10013

T (212) 431-0696   F (212) 431-5764

"A complete remedial company"

Asbestos & Lead Abatement - Mold Remediation
Structural Drying & Humidity Control - Fire Damage Recovery
Document Restoration - Deodorization - Air Scrubbing
Duct Cleaning - Interior Demolition

Claridan Contracting, Inc.

PAINTING-WALLCOVERING-MBE & SCA CERTIFIED-DC 9 AFFILIATED

Ed Ramos

658-B Grand Street
Brooklyn, NY 11211

Cell 917.217.3601   Tel - 718.599.9189
eramos@claridaninc.com   Fax - 718.599.9740

Izzo Construction

Good Luck Columbia!

Tel: (212) 662-5695
Fax: (212) 749-8224

Jean Esposito
President

jean@izzoconstruction.com   80 Morningside Drive
www.izzoconstruction.com   New York, NY 10027

FK GENERAL CONTRACTORS, INC.

**CARMELO EMILIO
JOHN F. EMILIO**

1262 66th Street
Brooklyn, New York 11219
1-888-972-4488
1-917-578-2335 / 2336

380 INSIDE NEW YORK

Ray Beauty Supply Inc, a Hell's Kitchen Landmark, is approaching its 60th year in business. Located at 721st 8th Ave (Between 45th and 46th), this antiquated yet successful establishment is the only true barber and beauty supply left on the island of Manhattan.

We carry a full line of professional flat irons, hair dryers, and clippers. Our staff is friendly and knowledgeable.

We are highly acclaimed for excellent service and our wide range of professional products. We are Zagat rated and have been featured in Allure, The Daily News, Cosmopolitan, Elle, In Style, The New Yorker and the Village Voice.

BRING IN THIS AD FOR A FULL 20% DISCOUNT!

(212) 757-0175
Email Raybeauty.com

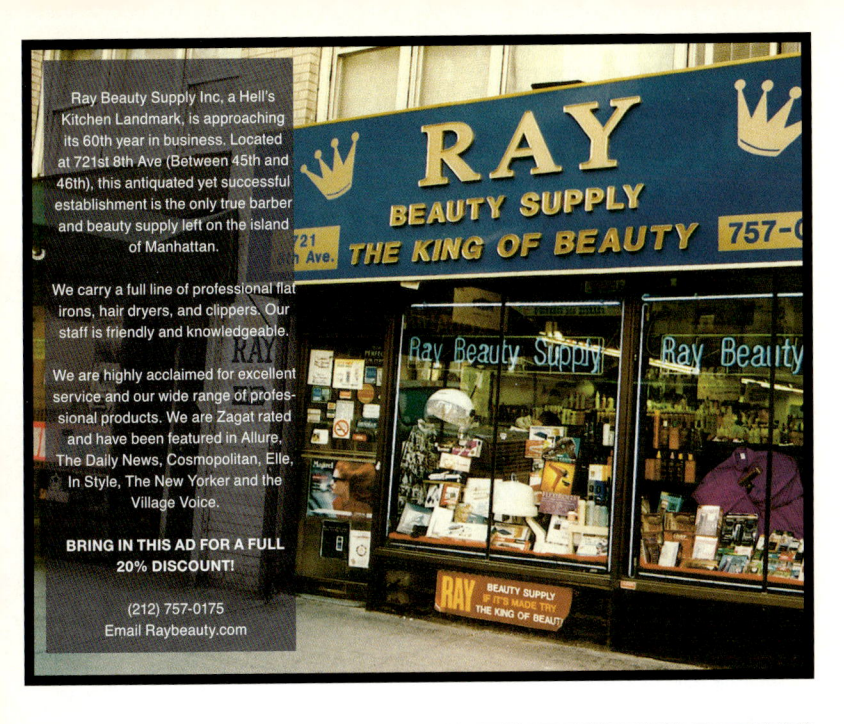

SIVIN & MILLER, LLP

ATTORNEYS AT LAW

170 BROADWAY
SUITE 600
NY, NY 10038
(212) 349-0300
FAX (212) 406-9462
www.sivinandmiller.com

Specializing in Civil Rights and Police Brutality Cases

Days Hotel

DAYS HOTEL BROADWAY
(Formerly Quality Hotel)

215 West 94th Street (at Broadway)

800-834-2972 • 212-866-6400 • 212-866-1357 (fax)

COLUMBIA UNIVERSITY SPECIAL
10% Discount to Columbia students, faculty, families, and friends

- Spacious Renovated Rooms
- Cable Television
- Free Wi-Fi
- Individual Climate Control
- In-Room Coffee Makers
- In-Room Safes + Hair Dryers

Greater Baltimore Neurosurgical Associates

Providing Comprehensive care of the spine and Specializing in minimally invasive surgery of the spine

Using Advanced technology solutions for pain and spinal conditions

PHYSICIANS PAVILION NORTH
SUITE 600
6535 N. CHARLES STREET
BALTIMORE, MARYLAND 21204

PHONE: (443) 849-4270

Haakon's Hall

Kick back on the living room couch or pull up to the communal table for our take on mom's comfort food. Enjoy everything from meatloaf or rotisserie chicken to PB&J sandwiches or milk and cookies. Come for the home cooking, stay for the home feeling.

OPENING FALL OF 2008
7 am - 4 am everyday
1187 Amsterdam Avenue
New York City 10027
212.932.0707 phone
212.932.1122 fax
haakonshall.com

Haakon's Hall
a taste of home in the heart of the city